CW00351039

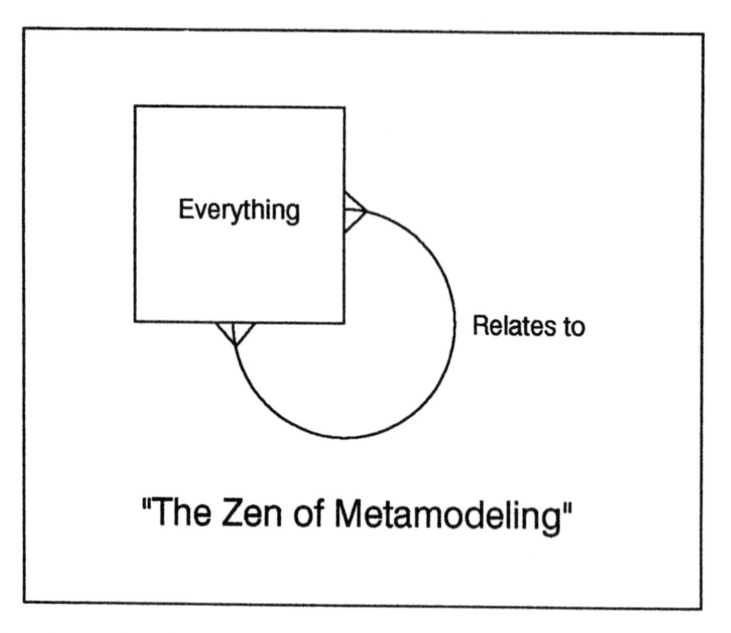

The far side of repository (reprinted with permission from *CASE Outlook* Vol. 6, No. 3 © CASE Consulting Group, Inc., Lake Oswego, OR. 503-245-6880)

IMPLEMENTING A CORPORATE REPOSITORY

The Models Meet Reality

Adrienne Tannenbaum

John Wiley & Sons, Inc.
New York • Chichester • Brisbane • Toronto • Singapore

Publisher: Katherine Schowalter
Editor: Theresa Hudson
Associate Managing Editor: Jacqueline A. Martin
Editorial Production: Science Typographers

This text is printed on acid-free paper.

Library of Congress Cataloging-in-Publication Data

Tannenbaum, Adrienne
Implementing a corporate repository: the models meet reality/ Adrienne Tannenbaum.
p. cm.
Includes bibliographical references and index.
ISBN 0-471-58537-8 (cloth)
1. Database management. 2. Management information systems. 3. Computer-aided software engineering. 4. Repositories I. Title.
QA76.9.D3T36 1994
658.4′038′011—dc20 93-28215
CIP

Printed in the United States of America

10 9 8 7 6 5 4 3 2 1

To Jim, who always believes in me, but often cannot keep up with me

CONTENTS

PART THREE
INTEGRATING TODAY'S MODELS: THE NEED FOR A BRIDGE 141

ABOUT THE AUTHOR

Adrienne Tannenbaum is president of Database Design Solutions, a New Jersey–based consulting firm specializing in the revitalization of corporate databases. She has almost 20 years of experience in all phases of systems development, concentrating specifically in the database area.

Her interests in repositories began several years ago when one of her major clients agreed to become an early support program (ESP) partner with IBM during the development of IBM's Repository Manager (RM/MVS). She has specialized in repository technology ever since and has implemented several corporate repositories for major U.S. clients.

Adrienne has published articles on most aspects of information management (including repositories) in major U.S. and international publications. She has also lectured at various national technical conferences.

Her firm, Database Design Solutions, has assisted major corporations with their information management problems. The firm's services include:

- Database/application reengineering
- Systems integration
- Corporate repository implementation
- Strategic information management advice
- Development of enterprise data resource architectures
- Corporate database revitalization

Adrienne holds an MBA in information systems from Rutgers Graduate School of Management.

PREFACE

When a consultant is retained by an organization, she often needs to wear several hats. Although often hired to either introduce a new technology or improve the deployment of an existing one, the actual tasks accomplished most commonly involve the catalytic rework of some of the organization's application development practices. Regardless of the nature of the client's business, the "application inventory" always falls short—it is never easy to get an accurate picture of what each application does, how it relates to other applications, and what the application's role in the business actually is.

At best, this information is available for a small subset of an organization's MIS world. But when this subset delves into another technical horizon, all surrounding information is only available via interviews and detective work. It is this consistent interclient similarity that focused my interests toward a uniform solution.

The *repository* is the underlying backbone that can tie the business world to the reality of MIS applications and their data. As information engineering and CASE-based application development continue, the repository's importance continues to increase. As the underlying tool set used to build today's applications becomes more and more diversified in terms of vendor and execution platforms, the repository becomes the only common source of communication between all components. This book addresses the building of this bridge, that is, the implementation of a corporate repository.

This book introduces practicality to the repository concept. Readers will gain a hands-on flavor of what repositories are all about and what they can do for an application development environment. More important, they will understand what is involved in setting one up and gain from the practical experiences of the author and other repository implementers.

The book's intended audience includes most categories of information systems professionals.

- At the topmost level, information systems management is sure to benefit by receiving an honest assessment of what it takes to prepare for and set up a working corporate repository. Specifically, after reading this book, management should be able to decide whether or not the effort is worth pursuing within its own MIS organization based on current organizational characteristics and the most likely benefits to be realized by repository implementation.

- Systems analysts, data modelers, and information engineers, most notably those with CASE tool experience, should read this book regardless of whether or not their organizations are headed toward a repository. *Part One* of the book discusses today's models, *Part Two* discusses the modeling environment, and both parts may provide a new perspective into the evaluation of how CASE tools are being used to create them. *Part Three* compares some popular CASE tools by attempting to depict the same model with each of them. Although the models are evaluated with "repository eyes," modelers everywhere are sure to benefit with an improved CASE tool usage scenario.
- Database and data administrators are already quite familiar with the need for a repository as well as its potential benefits. Aside from giving them practical repository implementation advice, this book should increase the scope of their intended solution to include areas that go well beyond data-specific issues.
- Consultants, regardless of specialty, will benefit with an increased awareness of how their specialty relates to the entire MIS application development world. Because repositories touch all application development arenas and delve beyond MIS into the end-user business arena, this book presents the so-called "enterprise" perspective to all potential repository suppliers.

It is my intent that regardless of the reader's specific specialty interests, this book should open his or her eyes to the realities of today's application development practices and why a repository should be the gateway between today's scattered application world and tomorrow's world of uniformly accessible and perhaps reusable application components.

Adrienne Tannenbaum

ACKNOWLEDGMENTS

There is no author, first-time or experienced, who can create a book without relying on the assistance of other professionals. Regardless of whether these professionals provided expertise in specific technical areas, contacts that eventually led to technical information, or book production support, my gratitude cannot be overstated.

My first acknowledgment goes to Bob Gordon, a long-time acquaintance. Ironically, his massive network of contacts led to the publication of this book. Related to this acknowledgment, my editor, Terri Hudson, of John Wiley & Sons, Inc., should be thanked for finding me.

The creation of this book relied on multiple information suppliers. Most notably, I would like to thank all of my case study suppliers, many of whom cannot be mentioned by name due to the nondisclosure requirements of their employers. In addition, many CASE tool vendors were paramount in their assistance. Specifically, I would like to thank John Grant of Texas Instruments, Inc., Cindy Rosenbloom of Intersolv, Inc., and Marsha Sherwin of Knowledgeware, Inc. Many repository vendors also need to be acknowledged. Barry Brown and Mike Collier of BrownStone Solutions, Inc., Harjinder Gill of InfoSpan, Graham Thompson of R & O, Inc., and Tom DePasquale and Sanders Partee of Reltech, Inc., were noteworthy in their support and assistance. Of course, I cannot forget to thank Mary Ann Solimine for her verification of my card catalog–metadata comparison.

Finally, I would like to thank my reviewers. Bob Holland and Paul Barlage should especially be thanked for their support and review of the entire manuscript. In addition, many other reviewers evaluated pieces of this manuscript ranging from chapter sections to book sections. Included are Chris Loosley of DataBase Associates, Jerry Winkler of ASYSA, Inc., Christian Bremeau of Stanford Management Group Mary Lomas of Oracle Corp., Bob Mathews of IBM Corp., and Jack Liu of Digital Equipment Corp.

And most important, I would like to thank my family: Jim, Christopher, and Nicole, for living without a wife and a mother during the book creation process!

INTRODUCTION

Implementing a Corporate Repository is unique in that it addresses the prerepository world, the repository implementation process, and the postrepository world. Because repositories have the potential to affect virtually every aspect of an organization's application process as well as the impact these applications have on the business, a discussion of these organizational aspects is a mandatory beginning.

The book begins in *Part One* by discussing the natural prerequisites to a corporate repository: good models and standard use and depiction of these models. Although repositories can be used to depict and integrate information beyond and perhaps not including application models, the existence of these models as well as the understanding of how they relate to the live application world is a definite advantage in the repository arena. In addition, most initial repository implementations concerned themselves with some aspects of CASE tool integration. For this reason, today's models are evaluated in this book as the primary focus of the corporate repository. They are evaluated first as standalone representations of an application and later as participants in a wider, more integrated model. Many CASE experts may not see the need to pursue Part One. However, as discussed in the preface, some eyes may be opened, particularly in Chaps. 2 through 4. Anyone contemplating repository implementation must be prepared to evaluate the information targeted for repository load, and Part One provides the essentials required to do this.

Part Two discusses the "people issues," or the need for a model supportive organization. I urge everyone to read this short but important part.

Part Three begins the discussion of the repository bridge—why it is needed, the issues surrounding its implementation, what it is, and what functions it should serve. It discusses models from a tool perspective instead of an application perspective. Those readers who are already "CASE experts" will find Part Three a reminder of all of the tool-specific modeling issues they have encountered. Although Part Three does not address repositories specifically, it is important in that it depicts life without them (according to the underlying modeling tools) and gives the reader a "repository perspective" regardless of whether or not his or her organization is headed that way.

Part Four defines the repository in terms of its fulfillment of all requirements depicted in Parts One through Three. The repository definition begins with a depiction of its purpose as the integrated application holding area. Repository molding standards efforts are discussed, and this part ends with an illustration of repository-based application development.

Finally, *Part Five* discusses the steps to implementing a corporate repository: from getting ready through short- and long-term implementation strategies. Both centralized and distributed repositories are discussed. The practical experiences of many repository implementing organizations are included—both successes and failures—and the case studies depicted include organizations at virtually every phase of the repository implementation process.

Readers of this book, regardless of whether they ever implement a repository, will surely understand why one is needed, and, more important, why it is so important to begin planning for one immediately. Despite the fact that Parts One through Three do not address the repository specifically, they are important in that a repository is only as good as its contents and its organizational priority. Too many organizations fail by jumping prematurely into a new technology when they have not yet optimized their deployment of the current transitional technology.

IMPLEMENTING A CORPORATE REPOSITORY

PART ONE
TODAY'S MODELS AND THEIR ROLE IN APPLICATION DEVELOPMENT

1

MODELS, REPOSITORIES, AND CASE: PUTTING THEM INTO PERSPECTIVE

The world of repositories has always been one of undefined boundary. Repositories almost certainly exist as part of every developer's vocabulary, but may not be a tangible part of every developer's workday. Their theoretical life therefore requires much clarification in terms of what they are and how they relate to the many other facets of the development world.

The repository *holding area* is this book's focus. However, because repositories can be representative of virtually any aspect of an organization's information, the topic's discussion can be quite complex. In order to add practicality and common understanding to repository implementation, the subject's presentation must first address many *nonrepository* areas. Because the close relationship between repositories, application models, and modeling tools has been the starting point of many early repository implementations, it is important for the reader to understand the multiple perspectives of each of these development aids—individually and as part of the repository arena.

We begin this section with a discussion of today's models and the tools with which they are created, most notably CASE tools. These discussion areas provide an evolutionary perspective to today's repository. As each aspect of the CASE-based modeling environment is detailed, it would be helpful for the reader to consider the potential role of an integrated holding area and the different perspectives that could be placed on each CASE-resident model. Of course, as the book progresses, these perspectives will all be clarified.

This chapter opens the repository background discussion. We will begin with a brief discussion of CASE—its original marketplace niche and how it has affected today's repository ideas. We will consider the fact that repositories are often viewed as the means to a CASE rebirth: the way to leverage the investment made in CASE-based modeling. Because the heart of CASE is really its outputs (i.e., models), we place a model focus on the entire discussion. Finally, we will see at the end of this chapter, why repositories are so closely linked to the CASE-based modeling arena and how they fit in with an organization's application strategy, regardless of the maturity of the organization's CASE deployment.

■ CASE DEFINED

The term *computer-aided software engineering* (CASE) can be generically defined as any piece of software used to develop an application. Early CASE tools tended to concentrate on the graphical representation of an application's requirements. They were based for the most part on structured methodologies (DeMarco, Gane and Sarson, etc.) and provided a way of consistently diagramming and relating the specifications for a new application to the recipient programmer. As initial CASE offerings became popular, the definition of CASE expanded. Soon tools that addressed postmodeling application efforts (test case generation and execution, configuration management, code analyzers, etc.) became part of the CASE product family. CASE therefore can be defined as follows:

1. *The philosophy that encourages the standardized capture of the application development process by documenting the application from conception through coding in a reusable, accessible automated tool.*
2. *Any software product that helps to implement the preceding philosophy.*

■ THE ORIGINAL INTENTIONS OF CASE

Based on the definition dichotomy, a historical perspective tells us that CASE was originally designed to be a set of independent tools, each striving to accommodate the noted philosophy. A narrow reinterpretation of this original intention resulted in first-generation CASE tools, which were, for the most part, mechanized system documentation aids. Tool vendors may tell us in retrospect that their initial tools assumed a well-deployed in-house structured methodology, and therefore the tools

The Impacts of CASE		
Items Measured	Able to Quantify Improvement	Level of Improvement
Time Savings	54%	31%
Application Quality	47	31
Development Productivity	47	37
Maintenance Efforts	40	47
User Satisfaction	39	40
Financial Savings	32	31

Figure 1.1 The impacts of CASE (©1991 Sentry Market Research)

themselves were not created to be the enforcers of the methodology. But back then, vendor claims of major productivity improvements and resulting decreases in application development backlogs were based on the correct deployment of these tools, not (as many vendors wanted us to believe) solely on the acquisition of the tools. In any case, those development organizations that pursued CASE deployment pursued it with high hopes.

CASE expectations differed depending on the relationship of the Management Information Systems (MIS) employee to the tool. MIS management (typically involved in the decision to bring CASE into its application development environment) usually expected budget-impacting savings. As initial project work continued, management's expectations subsided slightly with the realization that an investment in terms of time and resources was required before savings would result (see Fig. 1.1). Analysts, however, were the typical initial users of the tool. Most analysts were initially excited about the tools because they made the tasks of developing data models, data flow diagrams, and so on, substantially easier and quicker. What used to be a manual task aided only by the IBM systems analysis template was now driven by a mouse, and, more important, easily altered. What annoyed many initial analysts was the requirement of some tools to follow certain methodology constraints that were perhaps new to them. Because systems development methodology enforcement was never a presale requirement, many "methodology naive" analysts created their own versions of application models and the tools did not object. Typically, those tools with the least amount of methodology-based restrictions received the highest initial success ratings from the analyst user base. Those tools that attempted to enforce rules from an information engineering perspective were often labeled "hard to use." The real issue was the qualification of the tool's user as an analyst—with a knowledge of information engineering concepts and the ability to apply them to application development.

■ THE ORIGINAL INTENTIONS OF CASE-BASED MODELS

Assuming a satisfied analyst as the initial CASE user (probably the only category that pursued the development of CASE-based models), the resulting models were geared to application developers. Most CASE tools operated on a project definition level, the project being equivalent to the application. Models developed within the tool represented the application perspective in terms of data (usually logical data models) and functional (process flows, process specification diagrams, etc.) requirements.

The resulting application models, however, rarely depicted the entire set of requirements. Early CASE tools, especially those without required information engineering rule adherence, usually did not allow sufficient constructs to fully depict an application's specification set. Typically, an analyst would graphically depict data and process models, and supplement the illustrations with word processor–based text. Thus, the intent of these models was illustrative; the heart of the specifications often remained in word processing documents.

As model-based code generation became most prevalent, the process models became more detailed. Rules were enforced by the CASE tools themselves and model integrity, which ensured the commonality of construct definition regardless of the model in which it resided, became a requirement. Data models became related to process models within the tools. The relationship between the models and the delivered application grew stronger. Still, initial code generators lacked sophistication. Generated code rarely took performance into consideration, and tweaking was often necessary. Again, the models alone did not represent the entire application definition, and were not intended to.

■ BARRIERS TO CASE MODELING SUCCESS

Considering the objective of CASE deployment, that is, documented system models that eventually lead to the generation of some application code, the satisfaction of this objective requires some characteristics within the CASE user organization. In most installations involved in early CASE usage, expectations exceeded results. Companies that have stayed with CASE since its inception now have realistic expectations of what the tools can and cannot do for their application development process. Recent polls gauged the MIS CASE satisfaction level (see Figs. 1.2 and 1.3).

Because the Very Satisfied category in Fig. 1.2 is by no means representative of the majority of those surveyed, it is important to consider typical development organization characteristics and how they often become barriers to effective CASE deployment. More important, the barriers to CASE success can directly parallel potential barriers to repository success, and hence the need for up-front discussion.

Lack of Adherence to a Systems Development Methodology With or without CASE tools, the way in which new applications are currently developed often prevents successful CASE penetration. Does a set of standards exist that must be adhered to throughout the system development life cycle? Does the standard methodology require a set of standard deliverables?

Methodology adherence is an important consideration. An honest assessment of how standards in this area are enforced, if at all, should result in an accurate depiction of how successful CASE deployment has been or could be in your organization. The existence of a methodology does not imply its enforcement. For

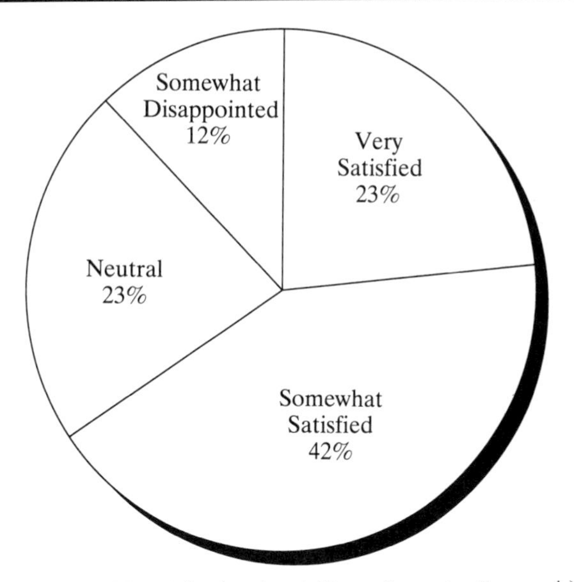

Figure 1.2 MIS executive CASE satisfaction level (From Forrester Research)

example, methodologies are only methodologies when they are effectively, consistently, and globally deployed. Consider the fact that I have consulted for numerous organizations where upper management tells me during initial interviews that it follows "Methodology X" (insert any popular methodology). As the consulting engagement progresses and actual client systems analysts and/or developers are involved, the reality of methodology adherence often unfolds to a methodology that

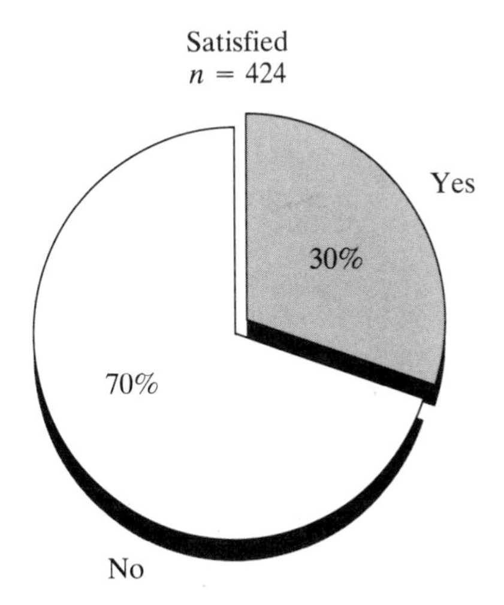

Figure 1.3 Organization satisfaction with CASE (©1991 Sentry Market Research)

belongs in one of the following categories:

The dust collectors. In these installations major deliverables, usually in three-ring binders at least three inches thick, appear in major bookcases throughout the department, sometimes in the bookcase of every analyst. Opening one up reveals its lack of use (sometimes they are even dusty, hence the name!). It becomes obvious to the outside consultant that this methodology is not followed in the least, despite the beliefs of upper management.

Rubber stamp methodologies. Here methodology adherence requires deliverables, but nobody checks them for accuracy or standard contents. Deliverables are okayed based on quantity (one entity-relationship E–R diagram, one data flow diagram, etc.), but the reviewer does not check for accurate depiction of the system's data or process descriptions. In most cases they are not updated as the application is enhanced.

Workaround methodologies. The best category of the three, these installations do have a standard, enforced application development methodology. The methodology existed long before the deployment of CASE and was followed consistently. However, the CASE tool(s) deployed do not have the facilities in terms of model constructs, for example, to support the methodology 100%, hence, the name "workarounds." What is crucial here is whether the workarounds are consistently deployed.

So what does all of this have to do with repositories? Putting a practical perspective on the importance of methodology adherence, it is important to consider my favorite example, that of *subtypes*. In some CASE tools subtypes do not exist as an object construct, or at least did not exist in initial versions. Look at the different ways modelers can depict the existence of a subtype, as shown in Figs. 1.4 through 1.6.

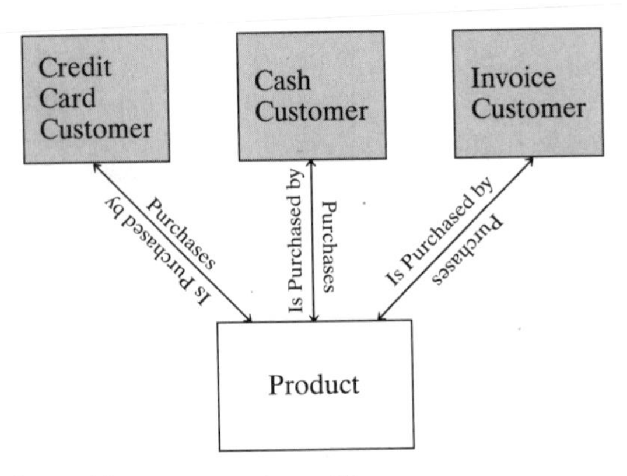

Figure 1.4 Representing subtypes as regular entities

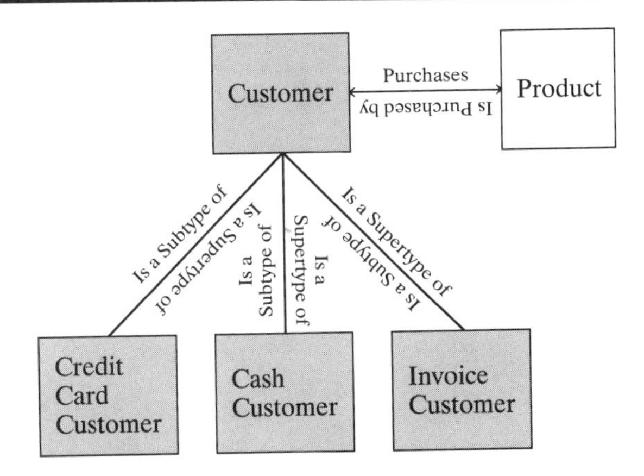

Figure 1.5 Representing subtypes as regular entities with "special relationships"

As we will see later, placing a repository perspective on existing models will demonstrate why standard methodology adherence is not only a crucial CASE success factor but a major factor in the readiness of an organization for repository implementation. In terms of our preceding example, consider the fun to be had when the multiple renditions of nonstandard subtype depictions need to be put together for the purposes of repository population.

Size of Initial and Subsequent CASE Investments Typically, initial CASE deployment is small (e.g., pilot projects). For CASE to be successful, its deployment must go beyond initial pilots to major application development efforts. Assess your expenditures on CASE and relate them to expenditures on other new technology products (e.g., workstation-based compilers). Where does it fit? In most installations CASE does not represent a major portion of the MIS budget (see Fig. 1.7).

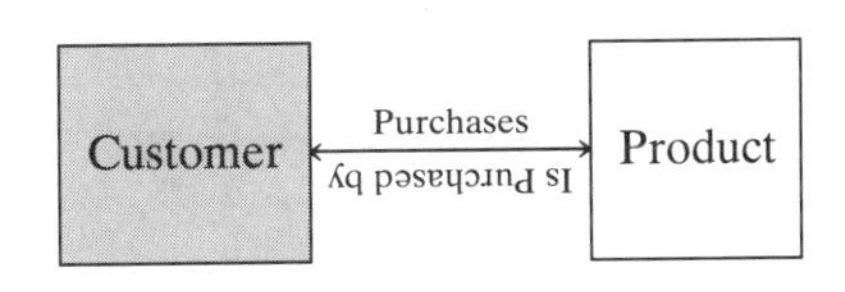

Customer Description

**Note:* We will be processing customer product purchases based on the customer/payment relationship code.

Values are as follows:

R = CREDIT CARD CUSTOMER
C = CASH CUSTOMER
I = INVOICE CUSTOMER

Figure 1.6 Relying on textual comments

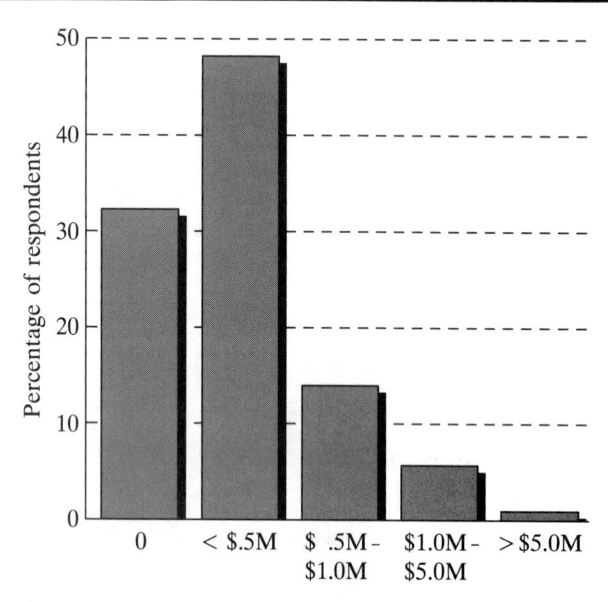

Figure 1.7 Expected 1992 – 1993 CASE expenditures (From Forrester Research)

Placing a repository perspective on CASE investment size gives us an idea of how well received and anticipated the repository population of CASE-based models would be by the non-CASE developer faction. In fact, it may even change the original objectives of an organization's repository efforts.

Inadequate CASE Training Is the amount of money spent on CASE software substantiated by an equivalent investment in tool-specific training? Specifically, has each developer granted access to the tool been offered the requiring tool training? Many CASE installations do not invest in vendor-offered tool training. There is a belief among some MIS management that because CASE tools operate on a workstation, they are equivalent to other workstation-based tools (spreadsheets, word processing packages, etc.) in terms of complexity. I have consulted for companies where investment in the initial CASE software alone reached $250,000, yet "there was no money in the budget" for training. Without training, CASE users may not be optimally representing the application within the domain of the tool's constructs. Training is important, especially if the tool represents the user's first experience with CASE. Again, consider the accuracy of a developer's models before considering whether they should be opened up for access via a repository.

Ineffective Managment Support Is management really supportive of CASE? Most new technologies are initially feared by those who must use them. Also, CASE in and of itself may put a new flavor on how applications are developed in a particular MIS installation. Developers may not be eager to work with the unknown to produce the same end result (the coded application). A 1991 Sentry Market Research poll shows that one out of three of those MIS personnel surveyed were unwilling to try CASE (see Fig. 1.8).

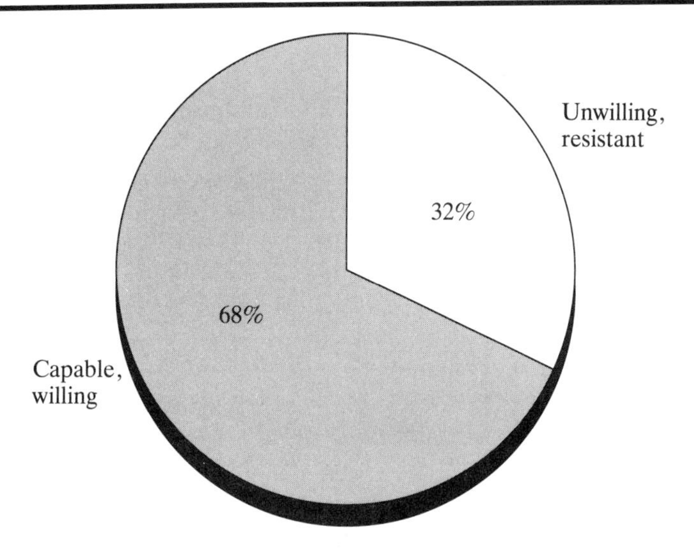

Figure 1.8 CASE readiness (©1991 Sentry Market Research)

Management support is critical. By requiring CASE-based deliverables, evaluating developers based on their timely adherence to delivery requirements, and constantly praising the potential merits of the tools, CASE is sure to be off to a better start. If, instead, management constantly reallocates resources from CASE-based development projects to other areas, the perceptions of where CASE fits in terms of organizational priority will be based on actions rather than words. For CASE deployment to be successful, management should impress on developers that CASE is a desired skill, more organizational opportunity results from successful CASE usage, and the support will always be there in terms of resources.

Unqualified CASE Users Finally, one of the largest potential barriers to modeling success with CASE is the type of person who uses the tool. This may seem like common sense, but many MIS installations assume that their best programmers will feel at home with a CASE tool. This is not necessarily true. Technical strengths do not imply logical analysis capability. The most successful CASE modeler has skills that cross both camps; he or she is able to recognize the business problem being addressed by the application (and each application component) and relate it to the technical details of the application's specifications. The ideal candidate is a good analyst who was once a programmer. If the programmer uses the CASE tool to document the requirement which he or she will eventually code, much is apt to fall through the cracks!

■ THE LIMITED EFFECTS OF GOOD MODELS

The preceding barriers are common in even the best development organizations. Despite these impediments, many developers can and do create excellent application models by optimally deploying the chosen CASE tool. However, even the best models are limited in their MIS impact when they are evaluated in terms of the ideal environment.

First, consider the impact that a uniform systems development methodology would have on today's models. At best, models would conform to a set of company standards and their depiction within the deployed CASE tool set would be consistent. Interpreting the effect of this well-implemented set of models, the following benefits would have resulted, over time:

1. Substantial proportion of applications are documented.
2. Application documentation covers the entire life cycle—analysis through coding.
3. Those models used for code generation result in more timely delivery of the applications into production.
4. Application developers have increased business analysis skills.

These benefits certainly would have a positive impact on the MIS environment. However, they are limited when we evaluate the MIS environment without a single application perspective. What is unclear is how well the preceding benefits can be leveraged beyond the application level. For example:

Shareability. For ideal impact on application development, existing models should be shareable among application development efforts. Depending on the existence of a shareable encyclopedia, this may or may not be the case. Shareable application models imply reusable application models.

Accessibility. Again, assuming the existence of an encyclopedia, how accessible is it? If the encyclopedia exists on mainframe Multiple Virtual tasking System (MVS) and most application development occurs on Unix workstations, the models may not be reaching the audience that needs them the most.

Logical vs. physical connections. Depending on whether or not the existing CASE environment included the use of capture products (discussed in Chapter 6), most models probably represent new application development. The modeling efforts began when new applications were conceived, and ended as they were completed. If the CASE tools deployed consisted solely of upper-end CASE tools (no program design, construction, or code generation capability), chances are their links to the physical programs and databases were not documented as part of the modeling effort.

Application vs. enterprise perspective. Existing models depict existing and proposed applications. Often, these models reflect that perspective as opposed to that of the business or enterprise. The different perspectives are usually indicated by redundant data and process names, definitions, and occurrences. Assuming an accessible set of models, it is possible that an application manager looking to see all database sources

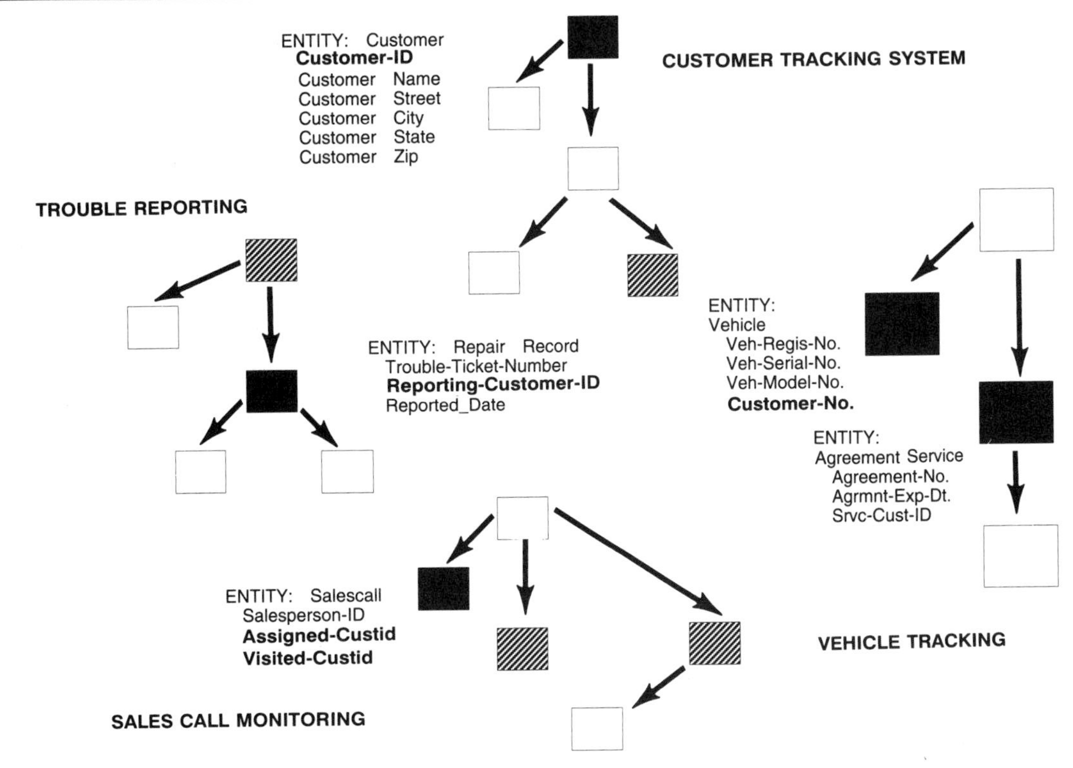

Figure 1.9 Result of Customer ID "search" query

of "Customer ID" may receive a fruit bowl of apples and oranges with each result representative of one application's way of identifying its rendition of customer, not all inclusive and not necessarily correct (see Fig. 1.9). So, at best, good models have had a limited effect when viewed against their potential impact.

■ THE ROLE OF A REPOSITORY

Repositories can and do go well beyond CASE. The repository achieved its reputation as the integrated holding area by being the first place where tool-independent views of information could be related and accessed. Initial repositories concentrated on the integration of application models coming from distinct vendor CASE offerings. However, the architecture of a repository tool permits the integration of any suite of tools, provided that the underlying structure of the information stored in each tool is defined to the repository and related to any other pertinent repository definitions.

Because the use of CASE is responsible for the majority of today's models, it has been chosen as the focus of the initial sections of the book. In contrast, detailed repository discussion is postponed until after the nonrepository application development environment is sufficiently uncovered. As today's environment (with and without today's models) is discussed, it will become clear that a need exists for the fulfillment of the following independent functional roles:

- The ability to define just what constitutes an organization's information
- The relating and cross-referencing of an organizations' information, regardless of its source
- The indexing and cataloging of an organization's information
- The accessibility of the organization's information, with or without a front-end index, regardless of the accessing tool, user skill level, or technical platform
- The ability to version any combination of an organization's information, and hence store and relate the multiple versions

All of the preceding roles can and should be fulfilled by the existence of a corporate repository. This book will uncover the way to make this happen, beginning first with a detailed discussion of why these needs exist. Those considering repository implementation should seriously evaluate their own organizations in terms of the characteristics unfolded in the initial sections of this book. Then, with a slate of repository objectives, and reader will see the *why's* complemented with the *how's* in the later book sections.

2

GOOD CASE ENVIRONMENTS

We begin our discussion of the model-based application development environment with a depiction of the success stories. By realizing where CASE helps and where it typically does not, the reader will appreciate the realistic definition of success as depicted in this chapter. More important, the live success stories depicted in this chapter's case studies will provide a practical barometer against which any organization's CASE deployment can be gauged. Remember also that the makings of a workable repository environment often begin here.

GOOD CASE-BASED APPLICATION DEVELOPMENT

CASE has typically been used for new application development. Although one could argue that applications are never really "new" anymore (they are often rewrites of existing applications), the application engineering and development processes still require full life cycle definition. In a good environment, CASE should fit in minimally as a tool to assist the documentation process throughout the application development life cycle. Depending on the tool's integrity check capabilities, it can also serve to validate the documented models and their relationships to each other.

THE AVAILABLE TOOL SET

In a typical good environment, the available tool set does not span a wide diversity of vendors. Tool evaluation is based on the company's generic application development requirements, most probably considering the target platform of the to-be-developed application, the accessible platform of the developer, and the existing application development methodology to be the most important aspects. Because selection results in a limited set of available CASE tools (ideally no more than three), developers have become experienced and well versed in the strengths and weaknesses of each product. Standardized modeling conventions have also been developed for each tool.

■ THE RIGHT TOOL FOR THE RIGHT JOB

In a multitool environment, each tool services a particular application development need. Good CASE environments do not force a tool's use in situations where it is not merited. For example, requiring the use of an OS/2-based CASE tool in an organization of Unix developers would most likely be unsuccessful. Those using the tool would use it minimally while concentrating on the Unix development platform for most of the application's requirements.

The available tool set and associated capabilities are public knowledge in a good CASE environment. When new applications are considering CASE, their guidance should come from within the organization rather than from particular CASE vendors.

■ CONSISTENT TOOL USAGE

Because good CASE environments use the tools for their intended functions, CASE users learn through experience how best to leverage a tool's strengths. They also learn through experience how misuse of a tool can render the resulting model's usefulness less than optimal. The result is a set of CASE usage standards that itemize how to represent an application's models within the tool while conforming to internal application development standards.

■ CASE CASE STUDIES

Yes, there are organizations that have successfully implemented CASE within MIS. These organizations did not attain instant success, nor did they immediately reap the rewards of their initial investment. As with most new technologies, their use of CASE represented an initial plunge into a new, unproven territory (unproven to those involved). The initial implementations were not perfect. In fact, the success that these organizations enjoy is based almost entirely on the fact that initial mistakes have been corrected.

CASE STUDY 1 *British Columbia Systems Corporation**

British Columbia Systems (BC Systems) is a service organization providing data processing, telecommunications, professional consulting services, and information access to public organizations in British Columbia, Canada. Most of its customers receive an integrated set of services which typically include the use of BC Systems–developed software or installed packages.

The internal service organizations within BC Systems suffered from the typical application nightmare—most of the applications in use were inaccurately documented and contained redundant and conflicting data. In fact, BC Systems

---

*Frank Rusman, Director MIS, BC Systems, Victoria, BC, phone interview, December 11, 1992.

employees were beginning to view the use of many of these applications as an obstacle rather than an aid to productivity. Based on the increased disability being caused by its application environment, BC Systems decided to embark on a major reengineering effort by establishing a model-driven application development methodology via the use of CASE tools.

In 1987, BC Systems brought in its first upper-level CASE tool. At the same time it developed an internal methodology and began the development of an Information Systems Plan (ISP). Upon completion of the plan, the initial application reengineering efforts concentrated on customer tracking (*Customer Information System*). At this point, BC Systems had already used the planning workstation of IEW (Knowledgeware) to complete the ISP, the analysis workstation of IEW to begin the modeling of the *Customer Information System*, and Texas Instruments' IEF to reengineer another application, the *Product/Service Database*. The biggest issue BC Systems had to face was the retrofitting of these tools to its internal methodology. Based on this number one need, BC Systems found that the Knowledgeware products did not meet its methodology's process definition requirements, and that IEF required the definition of too many physical qualities in the analysis component of the tool. These conclusions took approximately 2 years to reach.

In 1989, BC Systems purchased the Bachman DBA and Analyst products. Using the tools for a new application development effort (an on-line user-id query system used by the data center), the Bachman products were used for the development of the data model, process models, and process specifications. As the tool matured, other applications had their code generated by IBM's Cross Systems Product (CSP) Via a Bachman-supplied interface with its Designer product. BC Systems found the need to retrofit some of its internal development methodology based on the type of application, whether it was a new development effort, a purchased package, or the reengineering of an old application. This revised methodology, PIM (Pacific Information Management), involved three major phases:

- Business area analysis (BAA)
- Business systems design (BSD)
- Construction

For new application development and new package purchases, the business requirements are modeled in Bachman as part of the BAA phase. Existing applications are not required to participate in BAA. Using the methodology to drive the use of the Bachman tool, BC Systems has developed a set of Bachman modeling standards in order to ensure consistency across applications.

Today, Bachman is installed on a LAN and the Shared Work Manager allows the cross development and access of application models. BC Systems expects a total of 15 Bachman users. Its success with the tool is directly attributable to its willingness to try a select grouping of products, its adherence to a standard methodology, and its willingness to retrofit the methodology based on the type of application being modeled.

CASE STUDY 2 *CSX Technology**

CSX Technology is a Jacksonville, Florida–based information services organization which supports the needs of CSX Transportation, a global transportation company. Many of its developed systems involve complicated transportation scheduling algorithms that are supported by huge databases (as many as 108 million rows) with complicated designs.

Based on the desire to increase programmer productivity, MIS management requested a team of CSX developers to research and acquire a "COBOL program generator" back in 1985. Over 20 packages were researched and compared, and four were brought in house for a detailed structured test. CA-TELON, a Computer Associates product, was chosen based on its best adherence to CSX internal requirements.

CA-TELON has been the standard deployed lower CASE tool since 1986. CSX developers have use this product to generate approximately 4500 production programs. The tool is in use by 50 percent of the 500 developer organizations. Most of its new application development is accomplished in two-thirds of the time coding would have taken using traditional methods. Within each application developed with CA-TELON, approximately 88 percent of the finished product is CA-TELON-generated code.

In conjunction with the growth in the use of CA-TELON, coding standards were minimally modified to incorporate its use in program development. These standards are available in hard-copy format or on line in a FOCUS database. In addition, an entire Customer Information Control System (CICS) application has been developed which interactively depicts the proper deployment of these standards in a CA-TELON development session. For example, a developer can easily view standard screen formats and the associated standard edits, use them as part of an under-development application definition, and execute the edits in order to view the results.

CSX Technology attributes its success with CA-TELON to the fact that it was the best fit with its development environment. Being primarily a CICS shop, CA-TELON'S mainframe execution platform did not require a major culture change. In addition, the code that is generated by CA-TELON has surpassed manually generated code in terms of accuracy and structure. There is no management mandate to use CA-TELON, yet it is the favored tool with 50 percent of the organization.

CSX Technology continues to investigate ways in which to increase programmer productivity. It is currently investigating upper CASE tools as a way in

---

*Peggy Hall, and Ron Prybis, "CSX Technology Case Study," write-up and follow-up phone interview, December 29, 1992.

which to mechanize the analysis and system design that precedes the CA-TELON-based program development. In addition, Reltech's DB Excel has been deployed as a data dictionary supporting DB2 and IMS database development. Currently, any CA-TELON program development effort that requires IMS database definitions receives a standard export file from DB Excel containing the required IMS source definitions. This prevents the need to reinput existing data definitions and ensures the accuracy of database/program interaction.

CASE STUDY 3 *United Kingdom–based Insurance Company**

A major U.K.-based insurance company, which chooses not to be mentioned by name, has an application development staff of approximately 250 people. It supports a network of over 6000 user terminals throughout 60 U.K. offices. David Lodge, the computer systems manager, has been a "convinced downsizer" since the 1970s. Half of the application development resource is the direct responsibility of the actual business lines (Information Technology maintains control of the IT infrastructure). It made sense in 1981 for the firm to deploy Softlab's Maestro I as a way of moving a substantial portion of the development process off of the mainframe while preserving the tie between the application and its associated business requirements and adhering to internal development standards.

During the deployment of this first CASE tool (early 1980s), the firm developed a "paper methodology" which was based on SSADM (a commonly deployed structured systems application development methodology). The methodology was very loosely supported by Maestro I, and it became apparent by 1987 that the insurance company's developers needed an enterprise-wide development environment, and perhaps a relook at their internal development methodology. David Lodge decided to evaluate Softlab's upgrade offering (Maestro II) as well as System Engineer, a CASE offering from Learmonth and Burchett Management Systems, Inc. (LBMS). System Engineer was ruled out based on its underlying architecture which conflicted with the needs of Lodges's organization. A 3-month test of Maestro II, involving 10 licenses resulted.

It became apparent to David Lodge that separate methodologies were needed depending on the size and type of each application development effort. His developers established models within the tool that reflect each distinct methodology requirement, ranging from the requirements for a small enhancement to those of a major project development effort. As developers begin their work, they pick one of these existing Maestro II models and tailor it to meet their individual specification needs. In this sense, the development methodology has been standardized, and redundancy between application development efforts is minimized. All of the older application models (developed in Maestro I) can also be accessed.

*David Lodge, phone interview, December 11, 1992.

Developers have undergone a cultural change as they moved their efforts off of the mainframe. However, David Lodge's support for the effort is recognized throughout the department. He has allowed for a 5 percent drop in productivity attributed to the learning curve required as developers are trained in the use of the new tool. Despite this, he expects a 10 percent gain in overall developer productivity.

This insurance company is continuing its IT productivity improvements. A project scheduling package is in the process of being integrated with the company's CASE platform. This will allow the tracking in terms of time and resources of all project development efforts. The company is also pursuing object-oriented methodologies. Another model is currently being built in Maestro II as a prototype for a new development methodology. David Lodge sees this as a better means of supporting client/server-based applications. Finally, the company is in the process of developing a corporate data model which will be integrated into its CASE tool set.

Here, the successful deployment of CASE can be attributed to two major factors: the foresight of the IT management and its willingness to support (with resources) the trial and error that were necessary in order to establish a complete development methodology backed by CASE tool support.

■ COMMON CASE BENEFITS

In the successful CASE installation, whether CASE is deployed consistently throughout the application development arena or narrowly for specific application development tasks, there are common enjoyed benefits. The extent of CASE deployment directly parallels the impact of these benefits within the MIS organization.

The most obvious benefit is that of *accurate and accessible application specifications*. As discussed earlier, proper CASE deployment requires the use of the tool throughout the application development life cycle. The immediate benefit is the capture of all development-related documentation. Installations that go beyond the record-keeping aspects of CASE make sure this information is used. The CASE-based diagrams are part of the application specification set—they are used by the programmers and referred to by the application testers. More important, they are referred to and updated as application enhancements are performed. Like architectural blueprints, they remain alive as long as the original structure (the application) remains in production.

Another common benefit of CASE-based application development is that of *consistency in application development specifications*. Unlike pre-CASE specifications, the use of a limited tool set mandates the use of a limited set of tool constructs and diagram styles. In properly deployed CASE scenarios, a set of standards, often implemented via application development templates, ensures consistency even further. The benefits are obvious—application developers become used to standard terminology and expect standardized deployment of the objects. MIS personnel can move from project to project and come on board relatively quickly by reviewing a set of CASE-based application definitions.

Many installations have reported *increased application quality*. The definitions of "increased" and "quality" are totally dependent on the pre-CASE state of application development when compared to the delivered product. Because CASE serves as a documentation holding area, the application specifications are stored and subject to consistency checks. Internal tool syntax checks point out incompleteness within the total set of specifications. Perhaps the increased quality is based on the fact that specifications were not always complete before the use of CASE. Or perhaps the tool-specific consistency checks eliminate occasional simple errors in the specifications, which when implemented result in the need for immediate "maintenance."

Finally, depending on the personnel traits and skills of those involved, consistent use of CASE has led to *improved analysis and application development skills* in some installations. Although this is more true of installations with deployed standards that require a standard set of application deliverables, many programmers become more "analytical" upon receipt and review of structured CASE-based application requirements. Their ability to read and interpret logical requirements increases with time. Some actually cross paths into the "analyst" camp. The CASE tool often serves as the catalyst.

■ COMMON CASE DEPLOYMENT SHORTCOMINGS

The best of CASE implementations still have their weaknesses. Success with CASE requires a scoping of the tool's role in application development. The reason for setting a boundary on the tool's role is based on the inability of most major CASE tools to cover all aspects of the application development process. A 1991 study by Sentry Market Research cited "Incomplete Tool Solutions" as the major reason for dissatisfaction with CASE.* Putting the blame on the tools themselves aside, *the scoping by the MIS user is often narrower than it should be.*

For example, a major corporate advocate of CASE (they are cited quite frequently by one of the major CASE vendors as one of their "success stories") has mandated the use of a particular tool for all new DB2-based application development. The scoping of this tool's role was based on the initially limited code generation capabilities of the tool—its initial target platform was limited to COBOL/DB2. In addition, an upper-management mandate dictated the scope before the tool was even brought in house. So the CASE tool has been successfully used to create and maintain all DB2 applications created after the initial mandate.

Why limit the CASE scope based on target platforms? It is probably quite accurate to say that the depicted applications were getting their data from somewhere other than DB2 to begin with. The "load" processes was not considered part of the CASE-based application scope. Stepping backward, the data being retrieved and consolidated was not modeled within the CASE tool. A greater boundary on the initial CASE scope would have reaped larger long-term rewards for MIS. A more lucrative return would have been gained by modeling the source data (as it

---

**1991 CASE Market Study*, Sentry Market Research, Westboro, MA.

was) as well as the edit/consolidate/load routines. Because the data being targeted for DB2 is obviously key corporate data, its modeling is crucial for accurate reuse. From a repository perspective, the application takes on a larger scope—its predeveloped state must also be included. By only modeling the DB2-targeted arena, data redundancy is sure to compound itself. The source data could be replicated and loaded into several "new" databases. The eventual decision support user is bound to be confused without easy access to the origin and original characteristics of the data being analyzed.

Another common shortcoming in CASE deployment is its *limited cross-functional infiltration*. Even MIS organizations with CASE installations in the 100+ seat range do not commonly deploy CASE beyond immediate application developers. For example, the end-users who may be responsible for testing the application typically do not have access to the application's design via CASE. Hence, they are testing the application based on what they remember as a design requirement. When test results conflict with expected results, it is reported to the MIS application developer who often responds with a copy of the application design specifications. Allowing CASE access to at least one member of the application end-user community (usually an MIS liaison) could save valuable time in the requirement/design translation process.

Within MIS, the specific application models, as depicted in the associated CASE tool, also do not typically rate cross-functional access. All new databases typically require database administrator (DBA) review before implementation. The logical data model as well as data security and access requirements are among the information submitted to a DBA. Even good CASE installations handle this transaction via paper. DBAs, although most likely using a tool suite of their own to mechanize the creation of the database definition language (DDL) and the calculation of the Direct Access Storage Device (DASD) requirements, often do not have access to the CASE tool that originated the application level models. Despite the minor inconvenience of reporting and manual paper shuffling, the lack of tool access prevents the automatic integration of the logical data model (in this example) to its physical implementation.

Another common CASE deployment shortcoming is the *lack of tool integration*. Although most of this can be blamed on the CASE vendors (second most cited reason for dissatisfaction with CASE*), the lack of deployed tool integration is usually related to the lack of MIS function integration. Using the previous example, the application developers' tool may not interface at all with the tools used by the database administration group. If the CASE tool is to be used to its ultimate advantage, its models should be shareable with those who benefit directly. If the vendors do not provide direct interface, simple extract and load programs could be written to ensure the model's continuity across organizational responsibilities.

CASE deployment often neglects the life and after-life of its models. When an application is retired, what happens to its CASE history? Usually, it is not even a

---

**1991 CASE Market Study*, Sentry Market Research, Westboro, MA.

concern. Although program libraries always contain source code and its multiple versions, CASE tools rarely are used to track the multiple versions of the application models. Besides the fact that the tools themselves do not usually offer versioning capability, the tool users rarely track and store multiple versions of an application model. At best, there is always one "production" set of models that depicts the application in use as well as one "under development" set of models that may depict the next release. When the next release becomes implemented, it is unlikely that the CASE user will be able to distinguish the current release from its predecessor by accessing the CASE tool's encyclopedia.

Finally, another shortcoming of good CASE deployment is the unenforced requirement of the CASE-based modeler to follow standards that may originate outside of the application development arena. Take naming standards for example. Typically, these standards cover many aspects of the MIS arena, most relating to the physical applications: program naming, data element naming, database naming, application naming, and so on. The enforcement of these standards is usually left to a "production control" organization, but some naming standards (such as data element names) may be the responsibility of a data administration group. Where does the CASE-based modeling fit in, and how do the naming standards become enforced? Typically, the logical/physical correlation, if it does occur in the CASE tool, does not require integrity checking. If data element names require a four-character abbreviation on the table name to precede all column names, it is unlikely that the CASE tool was used to enforce this requirement. It is unlikely that the tool even allowed this naming standard enforcement capability. So, again, the tool's use serves its intended functional scope, but the remaining application requirements are not considered during the CASE-based application development process.

■ COMMON MISPERCEPTIONS OF CASE "SUCCESS"

When we read CASE success stories, we generally see the vendor's rendition. Typical statements cover the reduced time it takes to develop an application (start to finish), or the fact that resulting code is error free. When we delve into the realities of the CASE-based projects, the definition of *success* varies. If you as a reader consider your CASE involvement successful, it is essential that the following areas be investigated if you are looking forward to a repository in the near future:

- *The scope of CASE infiltration*. Because those installations that have reaped benefit from CASE defined and followed an initial boundary of tasks for their CASE deployment, it is almost acceptable to have low CASE infiltration. Consider the eventual role existing models would play in a repository. Perhaps they would serve as an index into the what, where, why, and how of each modeled application. Assuming model completeness and accuracy, this role could be well served. However, what proportion of the existing application world is represented by these models? 10 percent? If so, evaluate whether or not CASE usage is "successful." Before preparing for repository implementation, decide whether the time would be better spent modeling the rest of the application world, or at least the crucial business-sustaining applications. The emphasis should rest on whether or not the existing models alone would make repository-based model access and relatability worthwhile.

- *The scope of CASE knowledge/experience.* Continuing the infiltration issue, assume that a fair amount of the existing and planned application world has been represented via CASE-based models. Evaluate whether this effort was accomplished by a consolidated set of a few MIS members or by a member of each modeled application. Most industry studies gauge CASE infiltration by counting the number of CASE seats within an organization. The real issue behind CASE penetration, however, is how (functionally) the deployed seats are represented. The important aspect of this evaluation is a determination of how fluent the organization is with CASE concepts and modeling constructs. Again, when each existing world model is repositioned as a potential repository piece, the terminology used to depict the models becomes a language in and of itself. It may not be necessary for the whole world to understand the contents of a process specification diagram for example, but consider who the potential repository users will be and evaluate their need to access existing CASE-based constructs. Many options exist for dealing with the wide diversity of interests and needs that could arise from the access of a CASE-modeled world, but the issue is one to consider when strategizing based on existing perceptions of CASE success.
- *The CASE cost/benefit.* If you are a successful deployer of CASE, your success may have been defined without any attention to money. For the purposes of the application developer whose workload may have been eased or shortened due to the assistance of a CASE tool, the money costs associated with CASE software are not usually a direct issue. However, the application development manager is always directly responsible for project-related costs. If the project was the first (pilot) involved with CASE in the organization, the software and hardware costs may have come directly out of the project budget. How does one quantify the benefits that result from CASE-based success? It is a known fact that the acquisition of a $25,000 set of CASE tools and the $10,000 upgrade of existing hardware required to set up one CASE seat will not result in immediate, measurable savings of at least $35,000. If management publically acknowledges success with CASE, the issue to consider is whether the advertised CASE success includes cost/benefit analysis. Common areas of cost savings occur after a CASE-developed application is implemented. Typically, the amount of maintenance required is lessened based on the use of a CASE tool for reasons mentioned earlier.

Money must be a consideration of the CASE success definition, especially if a repository is being considered. The money measurement, if it is performed, must include cost avoidance as opposed to bottom-line savings. Successful CASE implementation, especially if acknowledged by MIS management, includes backup cost/benefit figures.

Another variable that can usually be considered as part of the success perception is budget item allocations for continued CASE deployment. Actions generally speak louder than words, so rather than believing a verbal management commitment to CASE, evaluate its allocated budget amounts. Verbally committing to CASE and allocating the money to deploy it correctly are often two different sets of activities in some MIS organizations. Success with CASE implies continued financial commitment to CASE, not just verbal commitment.

■ MISSING LINKS: WHERE EVEN GOOD CASE DEPLOYMENT FALLS SHORT

To conclude this chapter on a note of pessimism is self-defeating. However, it is essential that those installations proud of CASE inroads realize their limitations when their accomplishments are viewed from a different perspective (perhaps an eventual repository perspective).

The first area in which even successful CASE-based organizations fall short is *model relatibility and integration*. Organizations with high levels of CASE penetration (both functionally and across applications) typically treat each project as an island unto itself. Each application is a separate defined "project" within the CASE encyclopedia, regardless of whether the encyclopedia is centralized. The implications are reflected by several key areas:

1. *Model redundancy*. Many models (applications) probably have common data and processes. Their definition and representation are most likely inconsistent from model to model. Inconsistencies are represented by simple name differences or by more detailed discrepancies in the object definitions themselves.
2. *Lack of model connection*. Integration of existing application models is a major undertaking in any organization. However, keeping an eye toward integration alleviates the effort by relating each application model to a higher-level (enterprise) view through commonalities in names and definitions of "enterprise" objects. When applications are developed in isolation, even in a common tool with a common encyclopedia, it is difficult to realize where applications come together and how they relate to the business tasks they help perform.
3. *No model sharing*. Model and submodel reusability is unlikely when models are separate, distinct, and unconnected. The redundancy mentioned previously is eliminated when a common set of data and process models are used throughout the application models.

Next, *the tools themselves are often not integrated*. As discussed earlier, this is primarily the fault of the vendors. However, by not connecting tools, application development phases are most likely unconnected. The logical models of CASE Tool A are not connected or related to the physical models in CASE Tool B or to the actual code as stored in program library X. The original objectives of an organization's CASE deployment in all likelihood did not even consider this aspect of CASE-based modeling as a requirement. Use repository foresight and decide where models residing in each tool would connect with their counterparts in other tools. Or, more important, identify which counterparts are not available and might be worth developing.

Finally, even good CASE deployment does not usually take into account *long-term goals*. CASE begins with an application perspective, and its use parallels the life of each developed application. Its usage as a tool may have been planned for long periods of time, but the long time frames were expected to cover multiple, distinct applications. At the application model level, CASE was not planned as a resting place for the inactive model or as the reference point for investigating the way an application was developed. Now, as the needs arise to "go back and see how it was done in application X," CASE-based model backup, versioning, and accessibility are usually less than ideal.

Correction of the preceding CASE deployment deficiencies involves both short and long-term tasks. We begin the next chapter by discussing today's models in detail. This discussion will be used as the basis for the remainder of Part One, which will enumerate how to build upon today's good models. As the repository world becomes defined and uncovered in later parts of the book, the long-term tasks involved in enhancing today's CASE-based models in a world that extends well beyond CASE are also presented. Keep your organization's models, modeling practices, and CASE deployment specifics in mind as you read the following chapters.

3

EVALUATING TODAY'S MODELS

The greatest difficulties lie where we are not looking for them.

Goethe

Of crucial importance to repository-targeted models is their accuracy and relevance. Consider the state of your current models. An evaluation of each model in terms of its role within a repository should consider the following questions:

1. Why was the model developed?
2. Who developed the model (as in the MIS role of the modeler)?
3. When was the model developed (where in the application life cycle)?
4. Has the model been kept up to date? By whom?
5. What is the model used for today?
6. How often is the model accessed? For what reasons? By whom?
7. Does the model conform to a standard methodology?
8. Where does the model reside? Has it been copied/transferred to other platforms?

The majority of today's models were created as part of new application development. Therefore, they began as models of the precoded application. In this chapter we will discuss and evaluate the types of models created during application development in terms of their suitability for a repository. Models will be considered as blueprints of the precoded application.

Before evaluating each type of model in terms of its potential for repository residence, the previous questions can be used as clues generically. Consider each individually:

Why was the model developed? Often, the answer to this question is not readily apparent (it is certainly not documented). Ideally, the model was developed as part of the application development process as a means of graphically depicting the application's functional and/or data requirements. If not (the model was developed after the application was completed), its main objective was probably documentation. Remember the perspective when it comes to evaluating the model's contents.

Who developed the model? Check the user id associated with the model within its CASE tool. The role of the model author sometimes reveals the perspective of the model: Programmers may relate physical requirements, whereas analysts may relate logical (business) requirements.

When was the model developed? Ideally model development occurs during the initial stages of application development. Models should be used to convey application requirements, starting with the user or business perspective and eventually progressing to the physical requirements of target database management systems (DBMS), programming languages, physical architectures, and operating systems. Although this sequence represents the intended and natural flow of events in model-driven development, many organizations are lax in its adherence. If, for example, application development began with the creation of a logical data model and moved into coding from user-written specifications, the existence of process models should raise a red flag. When were these models created? Since the coding was underway before they existed, they may very well represent after-the-fact pieces of documentation, as discussed earlier. If the model creation process was not representative of a logical application development sequence, the various models are most likely disjointed in terms of intermodel relationships. Compare the various models and determine their relative suitability for a repository. If major gaps exist (e.g., the process models seem skimpy when compared with the actual implemented application), some advance model clean-up and expansion may be worthy.

Has the model been kept up to date? By whom? Compare the model to the production implementation. Are they different? Where are the differences? Is there a relationship between application releases and inaccuracies in the model? Are there several models, one for each application release? Ideally, the model is accurate and has been maintained by a member of the original application team. If the model has been maintained (meaning there are model versions, or the latest differs from the original) by someone who was not part of the initial team, it is possible that some of the original application perspective was lost in translation. If the model has not been maintained at all, consider the remaining questions as a way of gauging the model role within MIS development.

What is the model used for today? The model's accuracy is a direct factor in the answer to this question. If it has not been kept current, chances are it is not used for much today. Typical minimal uses would be as a reference depicting certain modeling constructs within a particular tool, as a source for data administration efforts to identify application data sources, and so on. If the model is current, it continues to serve its intended role—it aids the application development process.

How often is the model accessed? For what reasons? By whom? Obviously related to the previous question, the answers to these questions provide concrete examples of model usage within the organization (and perhaps outside, depending on who has been accessing it). Unfortunately, in many installations, the requestor/recipient of the model may not have been the actual person who extracted it. For example, an end-user without CASE tool access may have requested the model for purposes not known to the actual CASE user. Again, for repository-targeted models, access reasons are a key perspective in determining how the models fit within a repository architecture.

Does the model conform to a standard methodology? Systems methodologies are quite complex and certainly beyond the scope of this book.* In terms of model evaluation, methodology adherence provides a perspective on the set of modeling constructs deployed within and across models and whether or not they are consistently used. Ideally, a methodology exists, is followed, and a set of standards as to how the CASE tool of selection should be used in conformance is followed.

Where does the model reside? Has it been copied / transferred to other platforms? The operating platform of model residence brings another aspect of reality to repository implementation. Those models targeted for repository population will need to either reside or be accessible by the repository's operating platform. Consider also additional platforms that may have already required access to these models; they will most likely require access to the repository.

Aside from the generic questions noted previously, each type of model must be evaluated on its own merits. Keep these perspectives in mind, however, while reading the rest of this chapter. The reader should leave this chapter with a good idea of where his or her installation's models are strong and where additional work may be needed before repository implementation.

*For a list of methodology-specific books, see the References at the end of this book.

■ LOGICAL DATA MODEL

Most CASE users begin the incorporation of the tool into the application development process by developing a logical data model. A data-oriented approach is usually the first perspective that represents an application's requirements without considering its physical processing platform. Data models are the single most likely type of model, however, to go beyond the application perspective. The types of logical data models that are developed over time can represent one or all of the following perspectives.

The Application Perspective Although logical data models should in theory be developed at a level above the application (i.e., they should represent the data and its relationships without respect to application or functional use and access), most of today's models represent the data targeted to become an application-specific database. For example, a *Customer Order* data model may represent the data as it is used by an order processing system. At some sites I have seen data models that represent order processing for one type of customer (e.g., wholesale buyers) only.

The Departmental (Functional) Perspective As application-specific data models become implemented, redundancy multiplies. Sometimes the redundancy is vague. A customer's id differs from one application to another depending on how that customer is viewed by the application (as a wholesale buyer, a retail walk-in customer, etc.) or on which part of the installation the customer representation is needed for the application (headquarters, field sites, individual managers). Departmental data models represent the first level of integration among these application level data models. They represent the major subject areas of a company, but with a departmental flavor. See Fig. 3.1 for an example. Here, "customer" may represent only those customers of concern to the marketing department. If the same customer is also tracked by a customer service organization based on products purchased, its identification (keys), relationships, and attributes may differ.

The Enterprise Perspective The third level in the data model hierarchy, this data model was never the first to be developed by organizations with progressive modeling experience. Enterprise models represent the company's data without respect to departmental, functional, or application processing requirements. Think of them as the data for data's sake alone. Organizations that are just embarking on CASE tools and modeling today may start by developing an enterprise model first, and then relating it to the many data implementations that exist in the company's application world. However, few organizations can afford the major investment in time and resources required for such an undertaking. Those organizations that are pursuing the creation of an enterprise data model usually take one of the following practical approaches:

1. The enterprise data model represents major subject areas only (usually no more than 30 entities).
2. A data administration effort sets out to integrate the many application and departmental level data models existing in a company. That is, an organiza-

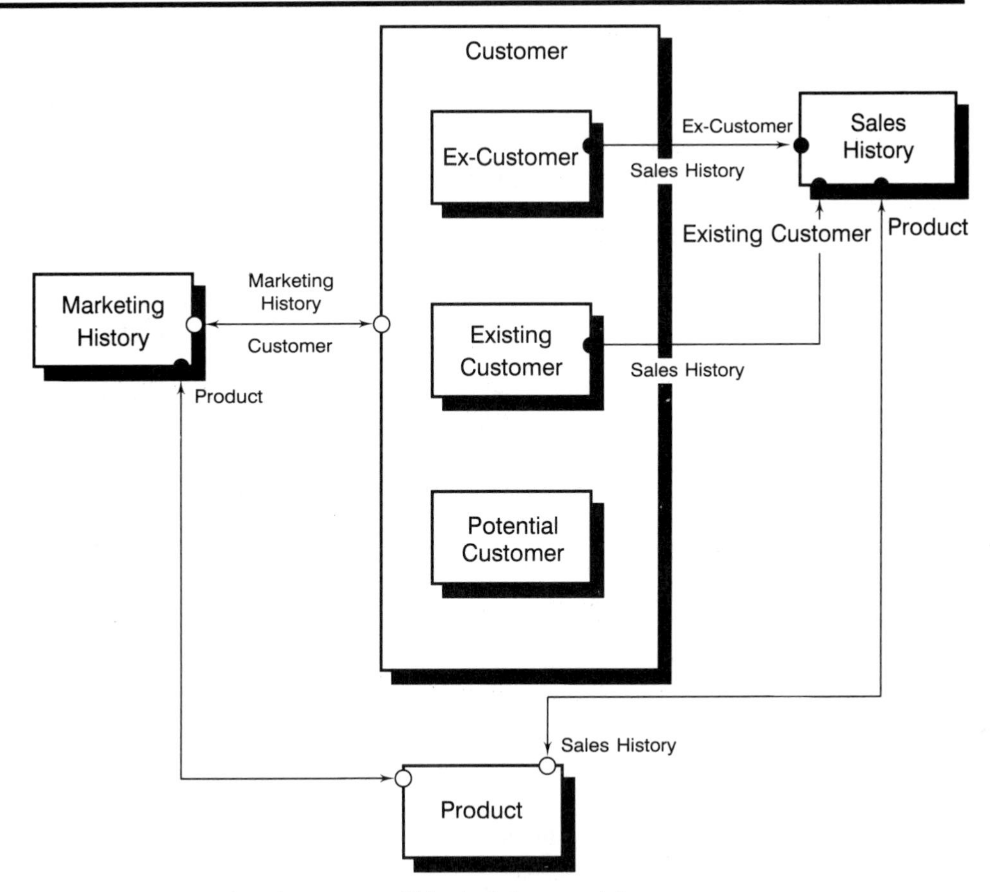

Figure 3.1 A sample "departmental" logical data model

tion is dedicated to creating this model from a corporate perspective while integrating the existing data models (a "bottom-up" approach). This is usually a long-term effort with defined milestones (see Fig. 3.2).

The fully implemented enterprise model, in any case, may be viewed by many as theoretical in that it rarely represents a specific implementation. However, from a repository perspective, it often represents the entry way into the lower-level models. The details of enterprise modeling will be covered in Chap. 4.

When evaluating a logical data model in terms of its accuracy and applicability to a corporate repository, consider the questions at the beginning of this chapter, but consider them with respect to the model's perspective. Because departmental and enterprise data models, as discussed previously, typically result from efforts outside of specific application development, their evaluation in terms of potential repository residence is saved for a later chapter.

```
1. Completion of application / database inventory identifying
   all major corporate applications
2. Development of integrated data models representing the de-
   partmental and / or functional views of the data
3. Development of process flows representing the corporate
   work flow without respect to departmental responsibility
4. Development of an enterprise process model covering the
   corporate line of business
5. Development of an enterprise data model covering the
   major data subject areas
6. Completion of first level model integration:
   • Relating the enterprise data model to departmental data
     models
   • Relating departmental (or functional) work flows to the
     enterprise process model
7. Completion of second level model integration:
   • Labeling existing applications and databases based on
     their relationship to the enterprise model
   • Relating existing application and database models to the
     correct departmental (functional) model entries
```

Figure 3.2 Sample enterprise data modeling milestones

Application level data models should have been developed as one of the first major deliverables of the application development process. When evaluating the quality of each model, it should be evaluated against its physical implementation.

1. *Consider the entity and attribute names*. Logical data models, when developed at the appropriate stage of the application development life cycle, should reflect business definitions as opposed to application or physical DBMS implementation-specific restrictions. Names that are specific or similar to the implemented versions may be indicative of "after the fact" or physical data models. That is, the models may represent the physical implementation of the application database rather than a business representation of the logical data relationships. This is not necessarily bad, but it is a fact that needs to be known when the model becomes repository resident. Figure 3.3 illustrates some sample logical and physical name differences.

2. *Consider the relationship of the logical design to the actual physical implementation*. A well-designed logical data model should represent a normalized (third normal form) version of the data and its relationships. Logical data models, being implementation independent, represent an ideal design which allows access to all data in a nonredundant fashion.* However, in the real world of database administration, normalized databases are rarely implemented. Instead, redundancy is added in a controlled fashion, usually for performance reasons. For a comparison of a normalized database and an implemented database, see Figs. 3.4 and 3.5.

Evaluate the relationships between entities and compare them to the physical tables (files) and their primary and foreign keys. For each modeled entity (including

* For more information on data modeling, see the References at the end of this book.

Logical Entity/ Attribute Name	Physical File/ Table, Field/ Column Name
Customer	MKTG.RD43.CUST
Customer Name	CUSTNAME
Order Number	Ordno
Customer Address Line 1	CUSTADDR1
Employee Hire Date	Emp_Hir_Dt
Employee YTD Federal Tax	EMP_YTD_FTX

Figure 3.3 Logical/physical data name differences

associative entities), does a table (file) exist? If so, one of two possibilities exists:

1. The physical implementation is fully normalized.
2. The logical data model does not represent third normal form, but a mirror image of the physical database design.

Continue the comparison further and look at the attributes within each entity and compare them to the columns (fields) within each physically implemented table

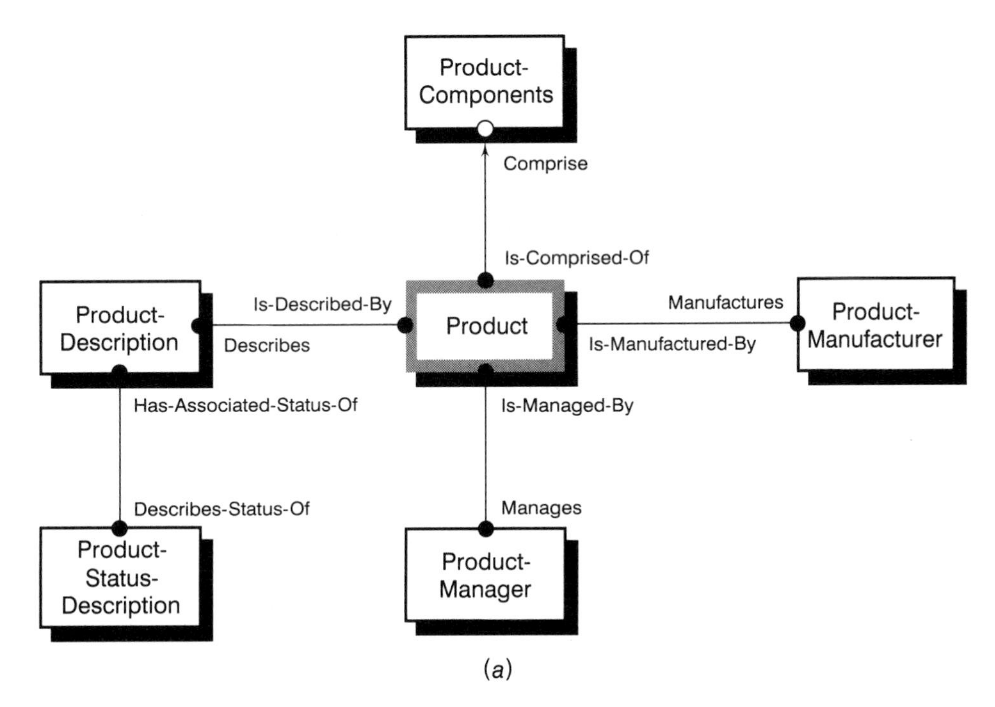

Figure 3.4 A normalized data model

```
Entity: PRODUCT

  DESCRIPTION:  THE PACKAGED VERSION OF A COMPANY OFFERING

  Foreign Key Attributes (PSet.FKAttr / (Entity.Attr))
    MANUFACTURES.MANUFACTURER-ID
      (PRODUCT-MANUFACTURER.MANUFACTURER-ID)
    DESCRIBES.PRODUCT-ID
      (PRODUCT-DESCRIPTION.PRODUCT-ID)
    MANAGES.PRODUCT-MANAGER-ID
      (PRODUCT-MANAGER.PRODUCT-MANAGER-ID)

  Entity MIN Vol=250,    Entity MAX Vol = 9999999

Attribute:  PRODUCT.PRODUCT-ID

  Nulls not allowed
  Storable;  Source type: Manual
PSet:  PRODUCT.IS-COMPRISED-OF

  Joins:
   PRODUCT-COMPONENTS.COMPRISE

  PSet MIN Vol = 1,    PSet MAX Vol = 8

PSet:  PRODUCT.IS-DESCRIBED-BY

  Joins:
   PRODUCT-DESCRIPTION.DESCRIBES

  PSet MIN Vol = 1,    PSet MAX Vol = 1

PSet:  PRODUCT.IS-MANAGED-BY

  Joins:
   PRODUCT-MANAGER.MANAGES

  PSet MIN Vol = 1,    PSet MAX Vol = 1

PSet:  PRODUCT.IS-MANUFACTURED-BY

  Joins:
   PRODUCT-MANUFACTURER.MANUFACTURES

  PSet MIN Vol = 1,    PSet MAX Vol = 1
Key:  PRODUCT.PRODUCT-KEY (PRIMARY)

  CONSISTS OF:
   PRODUCT.PRODUCT-ID  ATTR

Entity:  PRODUCT-STATUS-DESCRIPTION

  DESCRIPTION:  THE STATUS CODES AND DESCRIPTIONS ASSOCIATED
      WITH A PARTICULAR PRODUCT

  Foreign Key Attributes (PSet.FKAttr / (Entity.Attr))
   DESCRIBES-STATUS-OF.PRODUCT-ID
     (PRODUCT-DESCRIPTION.PRODUCT-ID)
```

(*b*)

Figure 3.4 (Continued) Normalized Model Details

```
  Entity MIN Vol = 0, Entity MAX Vol = 9999999

Attribute:  PRODUCT-STATUS-DESCRIPTION.PRODUCT-STATUS-CODE
  Nulls not allowed
  Storable;   Source type:   System

Attribute:  PRODUCT-STATUS-DESCRIPTION.PRODUCT-STATUS-
     DESCRIPTION
  Nulls not allowed
  Storable;   Source type:   System

PSet:  PRODUCT-STATUS-DESCRIPTION.DESCRIBES-STATUS-OF

  Joins:
   PRODUCT-DESCRIPTION.HAS-ASSOCIATED-STATUS-OF

  PSet MIN Vol = 1,    PSet MAX Vol = 1

Key:  PRODUCT-STATUS-DESCRIPTION.PRODUCT-STATUS-KEY
     (PRIMARY)

  CONSISTS OF:
   PRODUCT-STATUS-DESCRIPTION.PRODUCT-STATUS-CODE ATTR

Summary Information for C: \BACHMAN\DESIGNS\BOOK.AN

    Total Entities:                  6
    Total Free Attributes:           0
    Total Entity Attributes:        23      ( 3.83 per Entity)
    Total PSets:                    10      ( 1.67 per Entity)
    Total Keys:                      5      ( 0.83 per Entity)
    Total FK Attributes:             9      ( 1.50 per Entity)
    Total Notes:                     0
    Total Lines of Desc/Notes:      10      ( 1.67 per Entity)


SET:  PRODUCT-MANUFACTURER.MANUFACTURES

  Joins:
   PRODUCT.IS-MANUFACTURED-BY

  PSet MIN Vol = 1,    PSet MAX Vol = 1

Key:  PRODUCT-MANUFACTURER.PRODUCT-MANUFACTURER-KEY
     (PRIMARY)

  CONSISTS OF:
   PRODUCT-MANUFACTURER.MANUFACTURER-ID    ATTR

Entity:   PRODUCT-DESCRIPTION

  DESCRIPTION:   THE DETAILS BEHIND EACH PRODUCT CODE

  Foreign Key Attributes (PSet.FKAttr / (Entity.Attr))
    DESCRIBES.PRODUCT-ID
      (PRODUCT.PRODUCT-ID)
    DESCRIBES-STATUS-OF.PRODUCT-STATUS-CODE
      (PRODUCT-STATUS-DESCRIPTION.PRODUCT-STATUS-CODE)
```

Figure 3.4 (Continued)

```
  Entity MIN Vol =250,    Entity MAX Vol = 9999999

Attribute:   PRODUCT-DESCRIPTION.PRODUCT-ID
  Nulls not allowed
  Storable;     Source Type:   Manual

Attribute:   PRODUCT-DESCRIPTION.PRODUCT-DESCRIPTION
  Nulls not allowed
  Storable;     Source type:   Manual

Attribute:   PRODUCT-DESCRIPTION.PRODUCT-WHOLESALE-PRICE
  Nulls not allowed
  Storable;     Source type:   System

PSet:   PRODUCT-DESCRIPTION.DESCRIBES

  Joins:
   PRODUCT.IS-DESCRIBED-BY

  PSet MIN Vol = 1,   PSet MAX Vol = 1

PSet:   PRODUCT-DESCRIPTION.HAS-ASSOCIATED-STATUS-OF

  Joins:
   PRODUCT-STATUS-DESCRIPTION.DESCRIBES-STATUS-OF

  PSet MIN Vol = 1,   PSet MAX Vol = 1

Key:   PRODUCT-DESCRIPTION.PRODUCT-DESCRIPTION-KEY
     (PRIMARY)

  CONSISTS OF:
   PRODUCT-DESCRIPTION.PRODUCT-ID   ATTR

Entity:   PRODUCT-COMPONENTS

  DESCRIPTION:   THE LIST OF ALL PRODUCT COMPONENTS THAT
     COMPRISE THE PACKAGED PRODUCT

  Foreign Key Attributes (PSet.FKAttr / (Entity.Attr))
   COMPRISE.PRODUCT-ID
     (PRODUCT.PRODUCT-ID)

  Entity MIN Vol = 0,    Entity MAX Vol = 9999999

Attribute:    PRODUCT-COMPONENTS.PRODUCT-ID
  Nulls not allowed
  Storable;     Source type:   Manual

Attribute:   PRODUCT-COMPONENTS.PRODUCT-COMPONENT-ID
  Nulls not allowed
  Storable;     Source type:   Manual

PSet:   PRODUCT-COMPONENTS.COMPRISE

  Joins:
   PRODUCT.IS-COMPRISED-OF

  PSet MIN Vol = 0,    PSet MAX Vol = 1
```

Figure 3.4 (Continued)

Entity: PRODUCT-MANAGER

DESCRIPTION: THE COMPANY EMPLOYEE RESPONSIBLE FOR THE PRODUCT'S INTRODUCTION AND MAINTENANCE

Foreign Key Attributes (PSet.FKAttr / (Entity.Attr))
MANAGES.PRODUCT-ID
(PRODUCT.PRODUCT-D)

Entity MIN Vol =10, Entity MAX Vol = 100

Attribute: PRODUCT-MANAGER.PRODUCT-MANAGER-ID
Nulls not allowed
Storable; Source type: Manual

Attribute: PRODUCT-MANAGER.PRODUCT-MANAGER-NAME
Nulls not allowed
Storable; Source type: Manual

Attribute: PRODUCT-MANAGER.PRODUCT-MANAGER-PHONE-NUMBER
Nulls not allowed
Storable; Source type: Manual

Attribute: PRODUCT-MANAGER.PRODUCT-MANAGER-DEPARTMENT-CODE
Nulls not allowed
Storable; Source type: Manual

PSet: PRODUCT-MANAGER.MANAGES

Joins:
PRODUCT.IS-MANAGED-BY

PSet MIN Vol = 1, PSet MAX Vol = 1

Key: PRODUCT-MANAGER.PRODUCT-MANAGER-KEY (PRIMARY)

CONSISTS OF:
PRODUCT-MANAGER.PRODUCT-MANAGER-ID ATTR

Entity: PRODUCT-MANUFACTURER

DESCRIPTION: THE EXTERNAL OR INTERNAL ORGANIZATION RESPONSIBLE FOR MANUFACTURING THE PARTICULAR PRODUCT OR COMPONENT

Foreign Key Attributes (PSet.FKAttr / (Entity.Attr))
MANUFACTURES.PRODUCT-ID
(PRODUCT.PRODUCT-ID)

Entity MIN Vol = 10, Entity MAX Vol = 9999999

Attribute: PRODUCT-MANUFACTURER.MANUFACTURER-ID
Nulls not allowed
Storable; Source type: Manual

Attribute: PRODUCT-MANUFACTURER.MANUFACTURER-NAME
Nulls not allowed
Storable; Source type: Manual

Attribute: PRODUCT-MANUFACTURER.MANUFACTURER-CONTACT-NAME
Nulls not allowed
Storable; Source type: Manual

```
Attribute:   PRODUCT-MANUFACTURER.MANUFACTURER-ADDRESS-
     LINE-1
  Nulls not allowed
  Storable;     Source type:   Manual

Attribute:   PRODUCT-MANUFACTURER.MANUFACTURER-ADDRESS-
     LINE-2
  Nulls not allowed
  Storable;     Source type:   Manual

Attribute:   PRODUCT-MANUFACTURER.MANUFACTURER-CITY
  Nulls not allowed
  Storable;     Source type:   Manual

Attribute:   PRODUCT-MANUFACTURER.MANUFACTURER-STATE
  Nulls not allowed
  Storable;     Source type:   Manual

Attribute:   PRODUCT-MANUFACTURER.MANUFACTURER-PHONE-AREA-
     CODE
  Nulls not allowed
  Storable;    Source type:   Manual

Attribute:   PRODUCT-MANUFACTURER.MANUFACTURER-PHONE-
     EXCHANGE
  Nulls not allowed
  Storable;     Source type:   Manual

Attribute:   PRODUCT-MANUFACTURER.MANUFACTURER-PHONE-NUMBER
  Nulls not allowed
  Storable;    Source type:   Manual

Attribute:   PRODUCT-MANUFACTURER.MANUFACTURER-PHONE-
     EXTENSION
  Nulls not allowed
  Storable;     Source type:   Manual

PSet:   PRODUCT-MANUFACTURER.MANUFACTURES

  Joins:
   PRODUCT.IS-MANUFACTURED-BY

  PSet MIN Vol = 1,    PSet MAX Vol = 1

Key:   PRODUCT-MANUFACTURER.PRODUCT-MANUFACTURER-KEY
       (PRIMARY)

  Summary Information

  CONSISTS OF:
   PRODUCT-MANUFACTURER.MANUFACTURER-ID   ATTR

      Total Entities:                  4
      Total Entity Attributes:        22      ( 5.50 per Entity)
      Total PSets:                     6      ( 1.50 per Entity)
      Total Keys:                      3      ( 0.75 per Entity)
      Total FK Attributes:             5      ( 1.25 per Entity)
      Total Notes:                     0
      Total Lines of Desc / Notes:     7      ( 1.75 per Entity)
```

Figure 3.4 (Continued)

(file). One-for-one correlation would validate one of the preceding conclusions. Again, this is not necessarily incorrect (every model serves a purpose!), but it focuses the model into the right category—logical or physical design.

By determining whether or not the supplied data model is indicative of the logical business relationships or the physical database implementation, a flavor of the level of analyst skill inherent in the original modeler becomes clearer. Many *analysts* receive this job title based on their experience with a CASE tool. That is, the ability to input and define objects to a modeling tool is enough to merit the label. Although Chap. 10 will explore the people side of modeling in depth, it is important to mention modeler talents (or lack thereof) during model evaluation. Chances are great that if the models for a particular application are not representative of the application's role in the business, any other models authored by the same *analyst* will also be lacking. Although model evaluation is not presented here as a means of employee performance scoping, it does result in an indication of modeler skill level and perhaps the organization's readiness on the whole for repository implementation.

■ PROCESS MODELS

Obviously, the other half of the application involves the *processing* of the data represented in the logical data model. Process models take on many flavors, ranging from the logical (functional and process decomposition diagrams) through

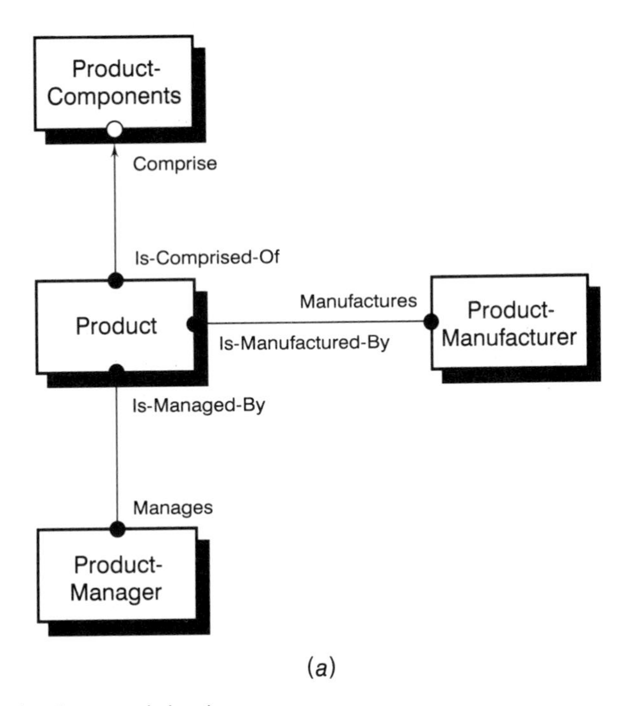

Figure 3.5 The implemented database

```
Entity:   PRODUCT
  DESCRIPTION:   THE PACKAGED VERSION OF A COMPANY OFFERING

  Foreign Key Attributes (PSet.FKAttr / (Entity.Attr))
    MANUFACTURES.MANUFACTURER-ID
      (PRODUCT-MANUFACTURER.MANUFACTURER-ID)
    MANAGES.PRODUCT-MANAGER-ID
      (PRODUCT-MANAGER.PRODUCT-MANAGER-ID)

  Entity MIN Vol = 250,   Entity MAX Vol = 9999999

 Attribute:   PRODUCT.PRODUCT-ID
  Nulls not allowed
  Storable;     Source type:   Manual

 Attribute:   PRODUCT.PRODUCT-STATUS-CODE
  Nulls not allowed
  Storable;    Source type:   System

 Attribute:   PRODUCT.PRODUCT-STATUS-DESCRIPTION
  Nulls not allowed
  Storable;     Source type:   System

 Attribute:   PRODUCT.PRODUCT-DESCRIPTION
  Nulls not allowed
  Storable;    Source type:   Manual

 Attribute:   PRODUCT.PRODUCT-WHOLESALE-PRICE
  Nulls not allowed
  Storable;     Source type:   System

 PSet:   PRODUCT.IS-COMPRISED-OF

  Joins:
   PRODUCT-COMPONENTS.COMPRISE

  PSet MIN Vol = 1,    PSet MAX Vol = 8

 PSet:   PRODUCT.IS-MANAGED-BY

  Joins:
   PRODUCT-MANAGER.MANAGES

  PSet MIN Vol = 1,    Pset MAX Vol = 1

 PSet:   PRODUCT.IS-MANUFACTURED-BY

  Joins:
   PRODUCT-MANUFACTURER.MANUFACTURES

  PSet MIN Vol = 1,    PSet MAX Vol = 1

 Key:   PRODUCT.PRODUCT-KEY   (PRIMARY)

  CONSISTS OF:
   PRODUCT.PRODUCT-ID   ATTR
```

(*b*)

Figure 3.5 (Continued) Implemented Database Details

```
ENTITY:   PRODUCT-COMPONENTS

  DESCRIPTION:   THE LIST OF ALL PRODUCT COMPONENTS THAT
      COMPRISE THE PACKAGED PRODUCT

  Foreign Key Attributes (PSet.FKAttr / (Entity.Attr))
    COMPRISE.PRODUCT-ID
      (PRODUCT.PRODUCT-ID)

 Entity MIN Vol = 0,   Entity MAX Vol = 9999999

Attribute:   PRODUCT-COMPONENTS.PRODUCT-ID
  Nulls not allowed
  Storable;     Source type:   Manual

Attribute:   PRODUCT-COMPONENTS.PRODUCT-COMPONENT-ID
  Nulls not allowed
  Storable;     Source type:   Manual

PSet:   PRODUCT-COMPONENTS.COMPRISE

  Joins:
   PRODUCT.IS-COMPRISED-OF

  PSet MIN VOl = 0,   PSet MAX Vol = 1

Entity:   PRODUCT-MANAGER

  DESCRIPTION:   THE COMPANY EMPLOYEE RESPONSIBLE FOR THE
     PRODUCT'S INTRODUCTION AND MAINTENANCE

  Foreign Key Attributes (PSet.FKAttr / (Entity.Attr))
    MANAGES.PRODUCT-ID
      (PRODUCT.PRODUCT-ID)

  Entity MIN Vol = 0,   Entity MAX Vol = 9999999

Attribute:    PRODUCT-MANAGER.PRODUCT-MANAGER-ID
  Nulls not allowed
  Storable;     Source type:   Manual

Attribute:   PRODUCT-MANAGER.PRODUCT-MANAGER-NAME
  Nulls not allowed
  Storable;     Source type:   Manual

Attribute:   PRODUCT-MANAGER.PRODUCT-MANAGER-PHONE-NUMBER
  Nulls not allowed
  Storable;     Source type:   Manual

Attribute:   PRODUCT-MANAGER.PRODUCT-MANAGER-DEPARTMENT-CODE
  Nulls not allowed
  Storable;     Source type:   Manual
```

Figure 3.5 (Continued)

```
PSet:    PRODUCT-MANAGER.MANAGES

  Joins:
   PRODUCT.IS-MANAGED-BY

  PSet MIN Vol = 1,     PSet MAX Vol = 1

Key:    PRODUCT-MANAGER.PRODUCT-MANAGER-KEY    (PRIMARY)

  CONSISTS OF:
   PRODUCT-MANAGER.PRODUCT-MANAGER-ID    ATTR

Entity:    PRODUCT-MANUFACTURER

  DESCRIPTION:    THE EXTERNAL OR INTERNAL ORGANIZATION
      RESPONSIBLE FOR MANUFACTURING THE PARTICULAR PRODUCT OR
      COMPONENT

  Foreign Key Attributes (PSet.FKAttr / (Entity.Attr))
    MANUFACTURES.PRODUCT-ID

      (PRODUCT.PRODUCT-ID)

  Entity MIN Vol = 0,     Entity MAX Vol = 9999999

Attribute:    PRODUCT-MANUFACTURER.MANUFACTURER-ID
  Nulls not allowed
  Storable;      Source type:    Manual

Attribute:    PRODUCT-MANUFACTURER.MANUFACTURER-NAME
  Nulls not allowed
  Storable;      Source type:    Manual

Attribute:    PRODUCT-MANUFACTURER.MANUFACTURER-CONTACT-NAME
  Nulls not allowed
  Storable;      Source type:    Manual

Attribute:    PRODUCT-MANUFACTURER.MANUFACTURER-ADDRESS-
      LINE-1
  Nulls not allowed
  Storable;      Source type:    Manual

Attribute:    PRODUCT-MANUFACTURER.MANUFACTURER-ADDRESS-
      LINE-2
  Nulls not allowed
  Storable;      Source type:    Manual

Attribute:    PRODUCT-MANUFACTURER.MANUFACTURER-CITY
  Nulls not allowed
  Storable;      Source type:    Manual

Attribute:    PRODUCT-MANUFACTURER.MANUFACTURER-STATE
  Nulls not allowed
  Storable;      Source type:    Manual
```

Figure 3.5 (Continued)

```
Attribute:   PRODUCT-MANUFACTURER.MANUFACTURER-PHONE-AREA-
      CODE
  Nulls not allowed
  Storable;     Source type:   Manual

Attribute:   PRODUCT-MANUFACTURER.MANUFACTURER-PHONE-
      EXCHANGE
  Nulls not allowed
  Storable;     Source type:   Manual

Attribute:   PRODUCT-MANUFACTURER.MANUFACTURER-PHONE-NUMBER
  Nulls not allowed
  Storable;     Source type:   Manual

Attribute:   PRODUCT-MANUFACTURER.MANUFACTURER-PHONE-
      EXTENSION
  Nulls not allowed
  Storable;     Source type:   Manual

PSet:   PRODUCT-MANUFACTURER.MANUFACTURES

  Joins:
   PRODUCT.IS-MANUFACTURED-BY

  PSet MIN Vol = 1,    PSet MAX Vol = 1

Key:   PRODUCT-MANUFACTURER.PRODUCT-MANUFACTURER-KEY
      (PRIMARY)

  CONSISTS OF:

   PRODUCT-MANUFACTURER.MANUFACTURER-ID   ATTR

Summary Information

     Total Entities:                  4
     Total Entity Attributes:        22      ( 5.50 per Entity)
     Total PSets:                     6      ( 1.50 per Entity)
     Total Keys:                      3      ( 0.75 per Entity)
     Total FK Attributes:             5      ( 1.25 per Entity)
     Total Notes:                     0
     Total Lines of Desc/Notes:       7      ( 1.75 per Entity)
```

Figure 3.5 (Continued)

the programming spec (process specification diagrams) through the physical (structure charts). Process modeling is geared to the development of applications. It is unlikely for "enterprise process models" to exist or even be planned. Despite the closer tie of the process models to the physical applications, some organizations develop "high-level" process flows that represent organizational or departmental processing, with or without supporting applications. These are often developed as a way of identifying redundant processing of data across departments or across applications.

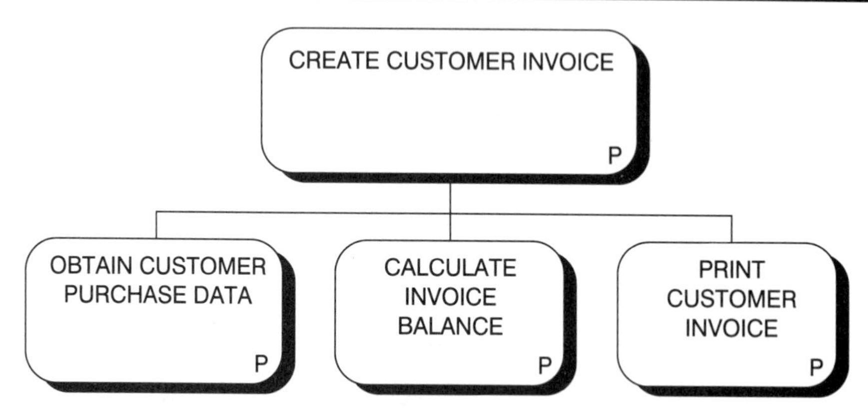

Figure 3.6 A process decomposition diagram

We will begin by discussing the "logical" process models. These models represent the application functionality in structured hierarchical diagrams. The full range of application processing usually spans several diagrams, each representing a more detailed breakdown of a process in a previous related diagram.

Process Decomposition (Process Hierarchy)

In process decomposition diagrams the modeler is setting the stage for a structured application architecture and structured programming (see Figs. 3.6 and 3.7). Each named box (or row of boxes) on a chart can translate to a module of code once implemented. When evaluating a process decomposition diagram in terms of its suitability for eventual repository population, process names and their associated functionality often take on a larger scope.

Consider the name of each identified process within one application set of process models. A name like *Calculate Gross Return* may be representative of an application process. Consider the fact that another application may have an

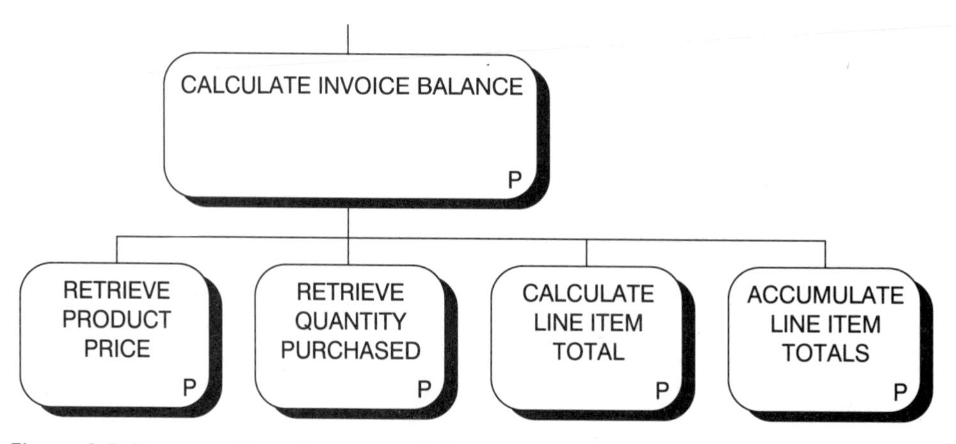

Figure 3.7 Decomposition of an expanded process

identical process name. This is fine (even preferred) if the processes are identical in terms of functionality. But if they are not, one (or both) should change by becoming more specific—*Calculate Gross Return on Investment*, for example. Process names will be critical once the repository becomes the major source of identifying application functionality. Perhaps a new application is looking to reuse as much existing code as possible. When searching for applications that calculate gross return on investment, the underlying process name labels are key to a successful query.

It should be noted that names need not be unique across applications. If identification of the specific process within the specific application would be a common query into the repository, remember that each function (process) will be related to the particular application to which it belongs. For optimal repository usage, processes that perform identical functions should be named identically, regardless of their resident application.

The goal of process reusability has opened up the scope of process naming, identification, and categorization as discussed previously. But processes are virtually useless without the associated data upon which they operate. Traditional information engineering (and traditional CASE) has kept process apart from data in terms of its identification and specification. Some models (e.g., data flow diagrams, to be discussed later) do bridge the process and data worlds. However, these models are not the main identification required to access process details; the process names (or the data/entity names) are, as mentioned earlier.

Object-oriented analysis and design methods* are an attempt at identifying data and its associated behavior together, as an object. Objects such as *Employee* become associated with *behaviors* like *Delete Employee* as a way of representing the process of deleting an employee record (row) despite the application under which the process is occurring. Object orientation is relatively new as of the writing of this book and has not yet become standardized from a methodology perspective. Furthermore, object-oriented repositories are just appearing and few address the relationship of their object-oriented metadata to traditional systems engineering metadata. If the goal of process identification is geared at reusability and minimal process redesign and recoding, installations should consider using one of the object-oriented CASE tools (OOCASE) available today.

Process Specification Diagram

Processing details are covered here, and the term *diagram* is used extremely loosely. The best example of a process specification is pseudocode. A process specification diagram displays the pseudocode in a hierarchical fashion (see Fig. 3.8).

At this level, although still logical, the "model" purpose is the relaying of specifications. Because its association with a process name is key to its repository-based usefulness, evaluation of this type of model's accuracy is based on delivered results (the actual code). Compare the code to the process specifications. If there is

*See the References at the end of this book for object-oriented methodology reading.

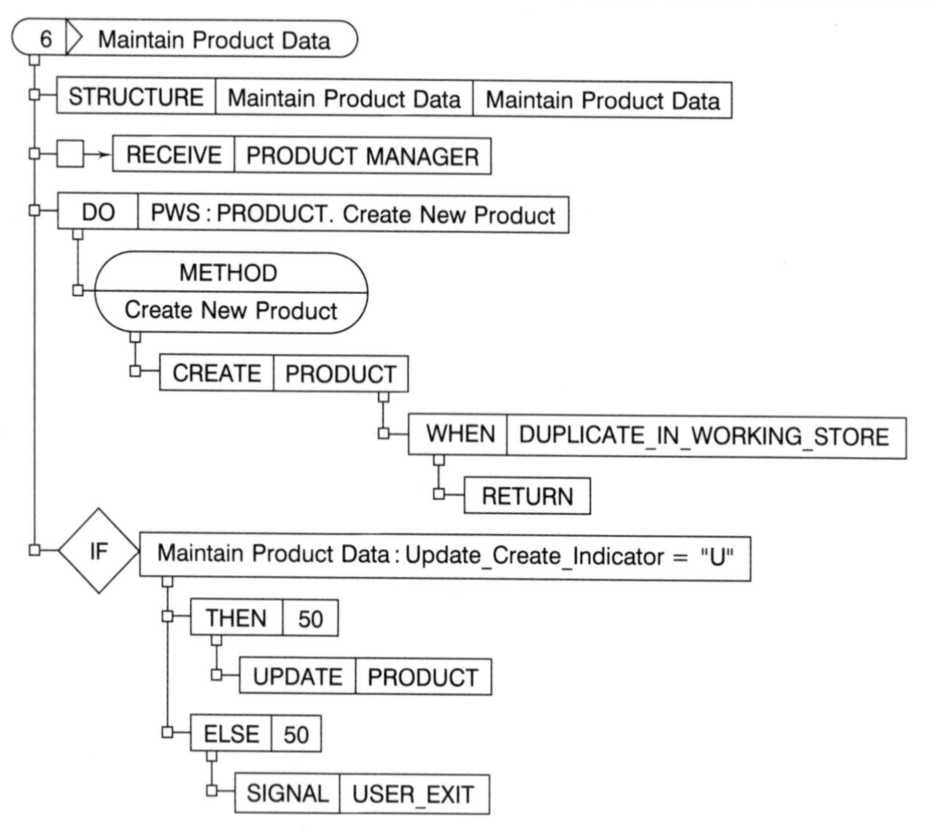

Figure 3.8 A process specification diagram

more to the code than is itemized in the process specifications, then much of the program specifications came from elsewhere (supplemental meetings, documents, etc.). Evaluate the relationship of your installation's modeling with the delivered results and decide whether or not to scope repository contents based on existing model contents, or whether to improve existing model contents via detailed expansion. In Chap. 4 we will discuss model improvement possibilities.

Before leaving the discussion of logical process models, it is important to consider their accuracy in terms of representing their physical implementations. As with the data models discussed earlier, an evaluation of the physical code should provide an indication as to whether or not CASE-based development continues through the maintenance cycle. Remember to keep the role of the existing models in perspective when planning your repository.

■ DATA FLOW DIAGRAM

Still at the logical level, this model ties the process and data sides of an application together. There are differences in opinion as to when in the CASE-based application development life cycle these diagrams are first developed. Some analysts develop these first, even before the logical data model, as a way of portraying the different process views that the application's data must support. Others develop them as a way of tying process together with data and ensuring that all data is represented and accommodated by the proposed application processes.

Evaluation of data flows must consider the diagram's intent. The collection of diagrams (and there should be more than one) represents an application perspective. Each diagram most likely depicts a different level of data flow. For example, the highest level of data flow (as depicted in Fig. 3.9) portrays the application and its relationship to external agents (sources/recipients of data beyond the scope of the application). Each successive level of data flow would portray the data and process interaction within the application itself, starting at the highest level in the process hierarchy and exploding to lower levels as necessary.

Consider the data flow diagram set when evaluating potential for repository residence.

1. Each level in the process hierarchy should have a corresponding data flow diagram whenever the inputs and/or outputs of a subordinate process differ from those of its parent.
2. Objects (either data or process) that are common to more than one data flow diagram should not be represented in conflicting scenarios. For example, data stores that exist in one data flow diagram should not contain data that is not accounted for either by a previous data flow or by an incoming process.

The source tool of the data flow diagram is also a factor in evaluating the models. If the diagrams were created with an integrated CASE tool (ICASE is covered in Chap. 9), all data and process objects referenced in the data flow diagrams are resident in the ICASE encyclopedia. Nonintegrated, standalone upper-end CASE tools often allow data flow diagramming without validation or prior definition of the diagram objects. More important, many CASE tools in this category do not require syntactical validation of data flows either. It would be possible in this scenario to have "illegal" or incorrect data flow diagrams (e.g., a data store connected to another data store without process intervention).

Weigh the source of the data flows (as in the tool) with the role of the diagrams as discussed in the beginning of this chapter. The data flow diagram is often supplemental in intent. The diagram in and of itself does not convey enough information for the systems implementer. Its role in the repository is directly relatable to its accuracy and original intent. Perhaps the identification of external agents is the only additional application data worth preserving in a repository. Decide whether the data flow diagrams are accurate and complete enough to add to the application's depiction of requirements. Then decide whether this additional flavor is worth saving in the planned repository.

■ PHYSICAL MODELS

The remaining models to be discussed in this chapter relate to the physical design of the application. These models extend the logical requirements through the

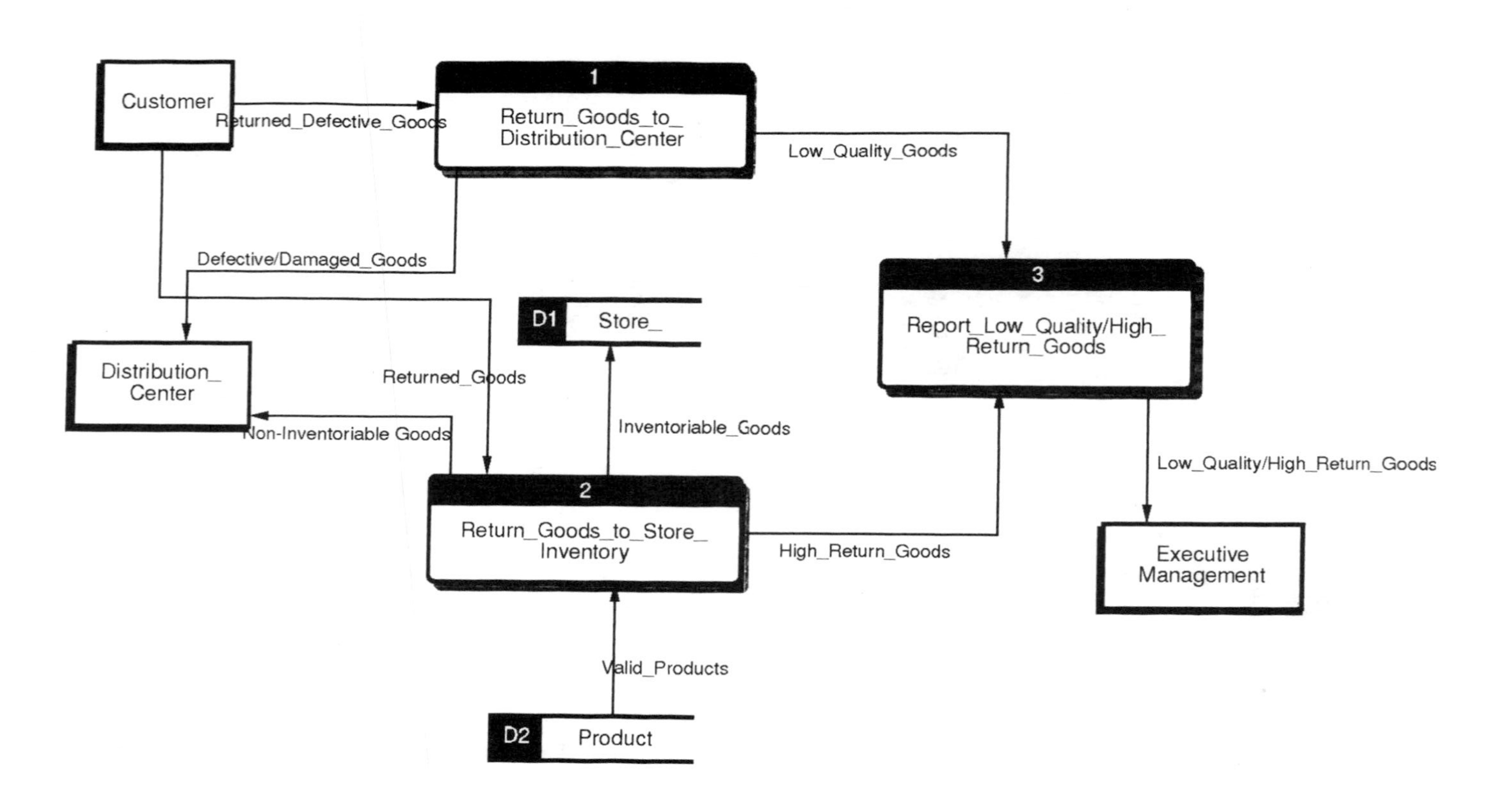

Figure 3.9 A data flow diagram

physical design. As with logical models, physical models for the most part represent either the data or process application perspective. When evaluating physical models, their relationship to the coded application as well as the corresponding logical models in terms of accurate depiction is the primary evaluation standard.

Application Architecture

On large application development projects, major applications are often broken into subsystems. Subsystems are usually the level at which development work is assigned, with a further distribution of effort occurring within the subsystem hierarchy. The application architecture diagrams the subsystem relationships (see Fig. 3.10). In simpler applications, it can be thought of as the physical implementation of the highest level of the process hierarchy.

The existence of the application architecture diagram implies a large development effort. Its role as a model within the larger set of application models is as an arranger of modules (the physical implementation of the process). From a repository perspective, the high-level architecture could provide the gateway into the actual modules. When related to the process hierarchy, it provides the first physical depiction of the logical process specifications.

Determination of its suitably for repository residency should consider its role as an index from the logical process hierarchy to the physical code structure:

1. Is the architectural organization based on functional division? If so, is the functional division directly related to the functional division of the process hierarchy?
2. Does each coded program relate to one of the major boxes on the application architecture?
3. Are different tools used to depict the process specification diagrams and the physical architecture?

The relationship of the logical process to the physical module is key to repository suitability. If different tools are involved, the metadata of each tool may have prevented the documentation of this connection. If "workaround" documentation exists (e.g., using a comment of text to track the logical/physical connection), be sure to identify its location as part of the repository targeting process.

Structure Charts

At the physical program level, the structure chart is a key part of programmer-supplied documentation (see Fig. 3.11). Here, the "main" module is broken down into all of its "subroutines." Development tools often allow the easy graphical depiction of the structure chart, but its relationship to the appropriate box on the application architecture, or even more distantly, to the appropriate box on the process specification diagram is not always a standard feature.

While considering whether or not the structure chart has a home in the planned repository, consider the tool of depiction and the role that is played by the structure chart within the tool. Programmer productivity tools often use structure

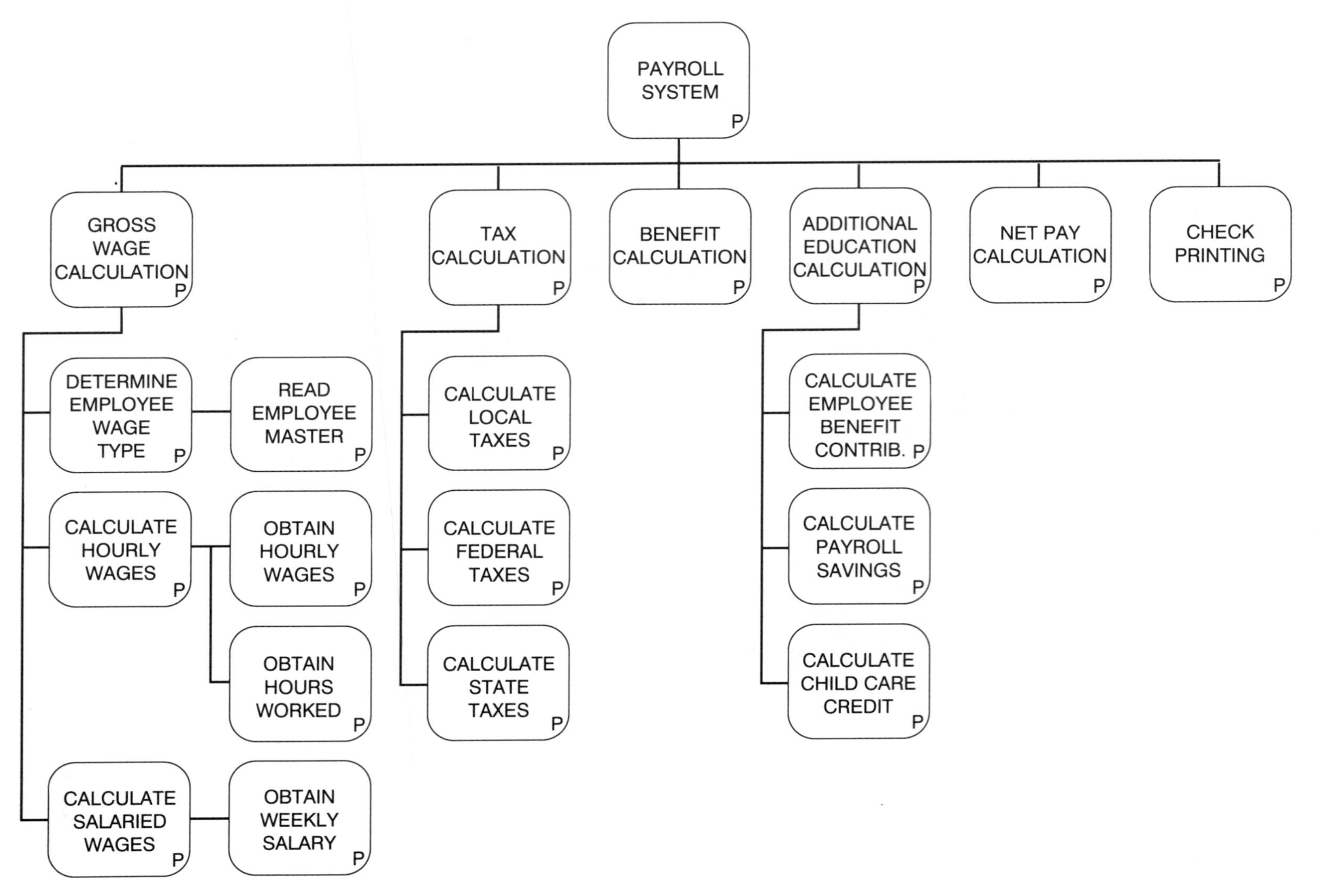

Figure 3.10 An application architecture

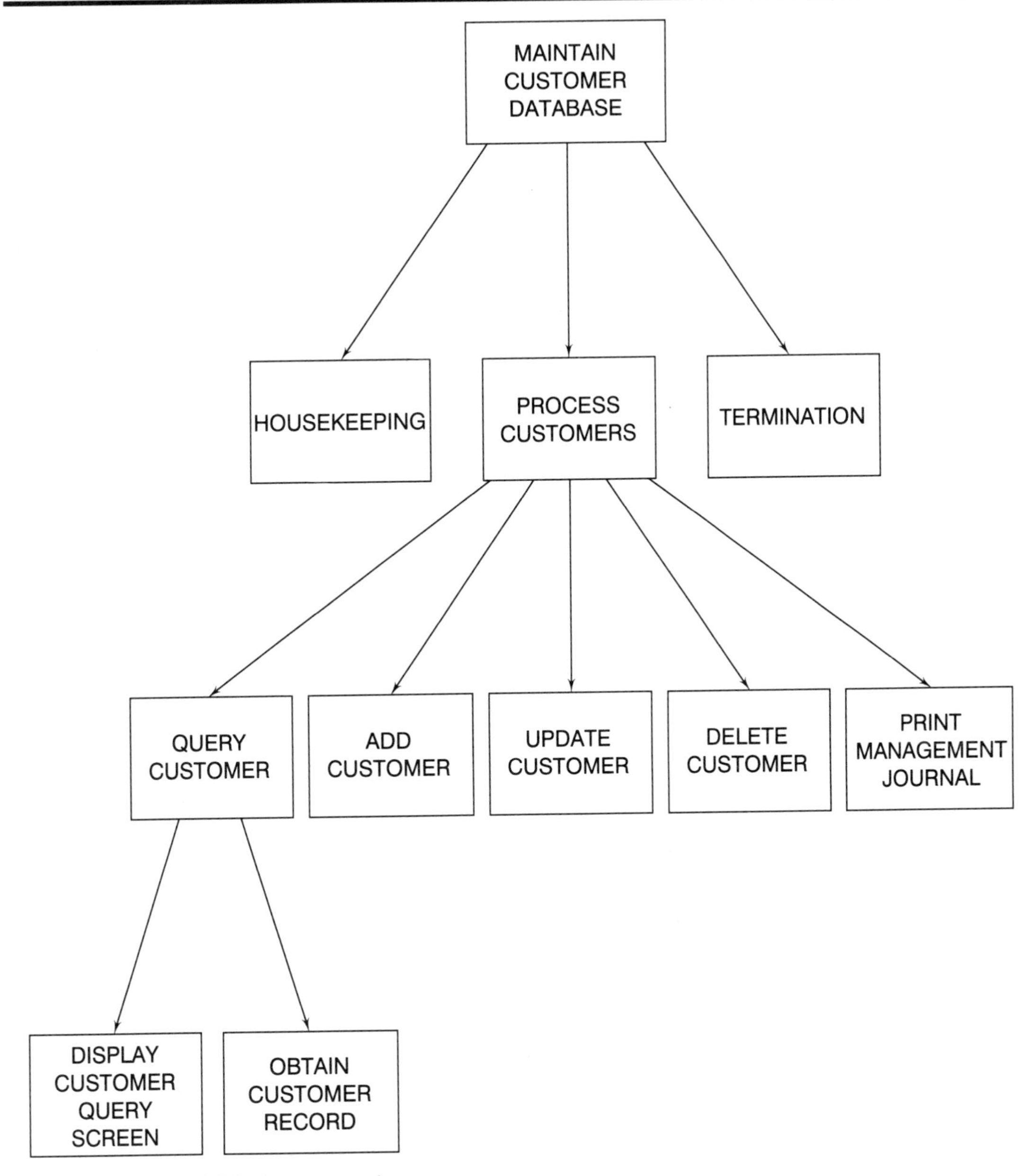

Figure 3.11 A structure chart

charts as the backbone for tests of program complexity or as logic paths to generate test data and test cases. These objectives may not be directly comparable to those of the planned repository. ICASE tools, on the other hand, use structure charts as the representative template of generated code, and are therefore fully related to the logical process specifications.

Whether the code depicted by the structure chart was generated or manually developed, the key issue as to where the structure chart fits in a repository centers

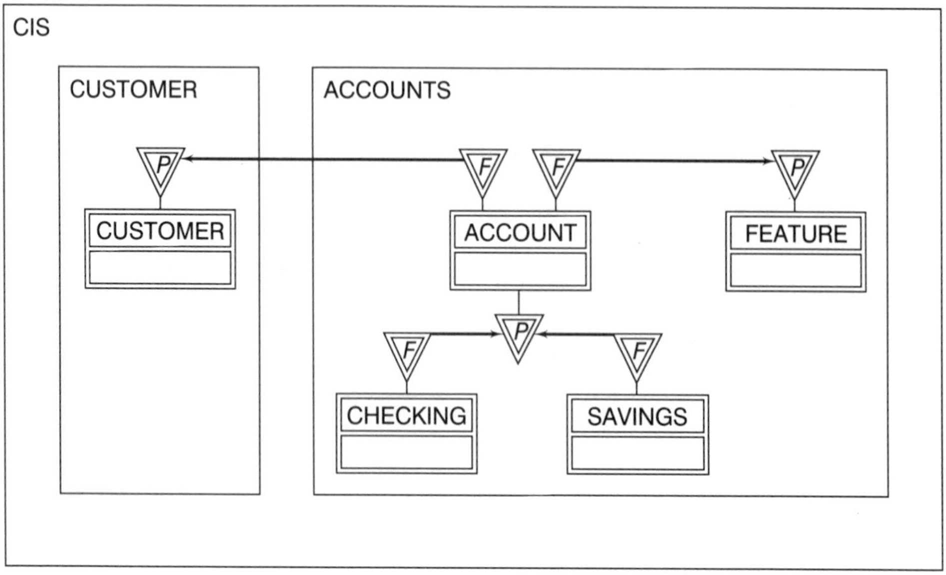

Figure 3.12 A physical data model

around whether the actual code will be related to the repository-based models, and if so, at what level. For example, the structure chart may represent the lowest level of detail you wish to track in your repository. Or you may wish to track all program library resident data and relate it to its originating business requirements.

Physical Data Model

Contrary to the logical data model, the physical data model more likely represents an application's specific implementation of its logical data requirements (see Fig. 3.12). If the physical model represents a further refinement of the associated logical data model within the same tool, it provides physical characteristics to the entities by representing them as physical tables (or files) and introduces redundancy into the normalized model for performance reasons. Attributes become columns or fields. Indexes relate to their logical keys. Technology-specific features appear within the models depending on the target DBMs. Many CASE-based physical data models result from the input logical data model, and DDL generation is often a side benefit.

The source tool of the physical model is an important factor in assessing the readiness and role of the physical model within a target repository. Many DBA aids offer database design advice geared to performance. The physical data model is evaluated in terms of storage requirements. Attribute names are evaluated based on DBMS restrictions in length. Relationships between tables are evaluated in terms of access paths. Little or no weight is placed on the business aspects of the data or its relationships to a logical data model. CASE tools, in contrast, usually require the logical data model before the physical data model. In many ICASE scenarios the physical model results from the logical model.

Consider how the physical data model relates to the logical set of application requirements (including the logical data model) if at all. If there is no correlation (e.g., no logical data model exists), then one will need to be created if the physical model is going to be used to help identify occurrences of corporate data across applications. If not all physical data models will represent the same aspect of the repository's focus, the logical/physical connection may not be necessary in all cases. For example, some physical data models (often developed in DBA tools) exist purely for the purpose of storage planning. New databases are input into the particular tool by a member of the DBA staff as a way of mechanizing the DASD calculations and ensuring their sizing for growth. These physical data models may not have been derived from an associated set of application models. For example, they may be representative of an IMS to DB2 conversion.

While determining the intended purpose of each physical data model, decide whether or not it is worth leveraging into a model of more global scope. Locate other application documentation. Determine its accuracy and role as mentioned throughout this chapter. Evaluate the tasks and effort that would be necessary to relate the physical data model to its logical application counterparts.

Screen and Report Specifications

Finally, we must address CASE-based screen and report specifications. Although the specifications in and of themselves are not usually considered "models," they are such a common part of most CASE tools that they deserve mention. Typically, objects that are already defined in the CASE encyclopedia are accessible as fields to be defined on either a screen, a report, or both. Their existence as an alphanumeric field with a length of 8, with a set of domain values defined within the same encyclopedia, is carried through to the screen definition module of the tool. The analyst is saved a great deal of typing and explanation in terms of user validation routines if all of the associated data values exist in the encyclopedia.

Are these specifications worthy of loading into a repository? That is up to each installation and based entirely on how large a scope the repository is to fulfill. The screen and report specifications are a crucial part of code generation, so if model-driven development is an eventual goal of the repository, these specs need to be tracked somewhere. Consider the original role of these specifications and how much they would need to be leveraged for reusability. More detail on this topic is presented in Chap. 4.

■ TOOL-SPECIFIC CONSIDERATIONS

The evaluation guidelines of the preceding models should be considered tool independent. That is, the depiction of each model should be consistent despite its source tool. Users of multiple tools already know that not all tools share the same metadata construct set, and therefore the reality of consistency becomes tainted when multiple tools are involved. Tools become an important part of the repository implementation process, and the tool-tainted model perspective is discussed in great detail in Part Three. However, there are some commonsense standards that should be followed despite the tool in use.

Probably the most obvious rule is that of *using the tool's metadata for its intended purpose*. Simply speaking, put alternate names in the *alternate name* field, default values in the *default value* field, and so on. Although this advice is obvious, I have rarely encountered a model in which this was entirely true. The problem arises when there is a need to document a situation that goes beyond the tool's metadata (e.g., more than one alternate name). Fudging of metadata intentions is a problem that was surely characteristic of some of the repository-targeted models.

Continuing the tool-specific rules, consider the second rule: *Assuming the need to fudge metadata, do it consistently—both within the tool and across other tools.* When evaluating models for repository readiness, look at the tool constructs and the associated values. Does an alternate name field always contain alternate names? Or does it also contain the physical lengths of the alternate name occurrences? What about models depicted in tools without alternate name fields? Is the alternate name stored as part of the description?

When preparing for repository implementation, the reality of the tools' metadata plays a major role. Inconsistent use of metadata makes the job even more difficult. This topic will be discussed in great detail in *Part Three*. For now be aware of where metadata is misused and whether or not the misuse is consistent. Consider the effort involved in correcting the misuse before repository loading. Contrast that effort with the effort required to programmatically translate and retarget the misplaced data during the loading process. Available alternatives will be discussed in *Part Five*.

■ RELATING MODELS TO THE CODED APPLICATION

We have considered most of the models (both logical and physical) used to represent an application. Their importance and usage require an association with the physical world. Evaluation of today's models must also include evaluation of today's programs and databases. Where are they? How are they tracked? How are version control and deployment handled? Quite often, many of the functions related to application deployment (version control, configuration management, etc.) are handled outside of the modeling environment via other nonconnected tools.

When preparing for a repository, the repository's scope should be targeted to include representations of the physical world. Although repositories often begin as a place for model consolidation, a well-implemented repository relates these models to their physical representations, both programs and data. Depending on the desired scope and the repository tool selected, the connection can continue and include application deployment information (configuration management). All of these connections require an evaluation of how the "physical application world" is currently tracked and maintained. This physical application world includes all applications running in a production mode, regardless of whether or not they have the benefit of the associated logical models discussed throughout this chapter.

■ PROGRAM LIBRARIES

Determine the accuracy of the current program library. Source code control is a major aspect of most application development organizations. Verify the attainability of each production and test version of a particular program and the set of programs that constitute an application. If the maintenance of source code libraries received lax attention over the years, it is essential that the libraries be brought up to date. More important, determine whether or not more than one library management tool is in use. If so, are applications tracked in more than one place? Why? There must be a firmly followed policy that depicts how and where program source code is tracked. Any misconstrued implementations must be corrected if the repository is to be used for accurate model/program tracking.

■ FILE DESCRIPTIONS, DATABASE DEFINITIONS

The onset of DB2 has required DBA functions in most organizations. These database administrators are usually the sole possessors of the authority required to establish and define the physical database. The database definition language is often accessible by physical database name regardless of whether or not an associated physical database model exists. How are changes to original database definitions implemented? Is the original DDL updated, or is a new "version" created and related to all of its previous versions (similar to source code)? If only the latest DDL is available, evaluate how this would impact the planned scope of the repository. Determine whether or not new DBA procedures should be required.

Determine where the physical attributes of nonrelational data exist. Hopefully, COPYLIBS (or their equivalent) are used for major common data areas. How are they maintained? Is versioning functional? Does existence as a COPYLIB member ensure its uniqueness in terms of definition?

Finally, evaluate the usage of all defined data. In the database arena each database is most likely associated with a single application. Files, however, are more commonly accessed by more than one application. Determine the difficulty involved in inventorying existing data usage. At a minimum, key data should be tracked for relatability within a repository.

■ PRODUCTION CONTROL

Job control language (JCL) streams are usually the most likely aspect of the physical application world to be intensely monitored. Product abends are the most visible application problem in that they require immediate attention. Most organizations require the strict documentation of application run-time requirements, JCL, abends and associated actions, restart and recovery procedures, and emergency call-out lists. Unfortunately, many organizations do not store this information in a mechanized tool or database. The relevance of production control documentation to a repository project is dependent on the planned scope. Often, its accessibility determines whether or not it should be included.

A brief evaluation of the accuracy and accessibility of the physical MIS environment is necessary in order to scope the effort required to relate it to its logical counterparts (when they exist). For those production applications that do not have the benefit of associated logical depiction via models, determine whether creation of these models is a worthwhile endeavor. Most installations base this decision on the criticality of the application to the organization as well as its expected life. Obviously, if an existing payroll application is scheduled for rewrite, its modeling

Category Type	Examples
Function	Payroll, Order Processing, Commission Calculation
Responsible Organization	Personnel, Catalog Sales, Management Recruiting
Production Category	Nightly Batch, Monthly, Online
Operating Environment	MVS, Unix, OS / 2
Implemented DBMS	DB2, IDMS
Development Status	Production, Test, Development
Enterprise Data Used	Customer, Purchase Order, Employee
Security Level	User Read-only, Dept. Confidential
Implemented Language	COBOL, PL / I

Figure 3.13 Sample application categories

for the purposes of repository loading may not be timely (however, modeling will preserve and document its functionality for the purposes of inclusion or enhancement by the new application!).

If modeling the existing application world is impractical (and it often is), consider categorizing the applications. Application categories can range from the names of the business functions that they fulfill, to their physical characteristics (e.g., processor name). These categories can be related to appropriate applications within the repository. See Fig. 3.13 for some suggestions as to how applications can be related via categorization.

■ SUMMARY

In this chapter we have presented a lengthy set of evaluation criteria for models being considered as potential repository residents. We have provided the reader with a repository perspective on existing CASE-based models. The book continues expanding on today's models by increasing their usability. The next chapter depicts the necessary steps required to build upon today's good models.

4

BUILDING UPON TODAY'S GOOD MODELS

As discussed previously, most CASE deployment to date has concentrated on the development of new applications. In these start-to-finish scenarios, the CASE tool served its secretarial role, and the models functioned as blueprints which eventually became the coded application and supporting database structure. As the models improved, so did the resulting applications. Considering the investment required to make CASE work, the deliverables resulting from CASE usage should be used for maximum benefit. Initiatives outside of the application arena can often serve to complement the CASE-based results. Or, more directly, the CASE-based results can be used for initiatives that may not have been originally planned for.

WHAT IS NEEDED FOR IMPROVED MODEL IMPACT?

It is clear that today's models have not yet reached their potential in terms of usefulness. Even the best models can be made better. Areas in which to concentrate include:

1. Keeping models accurate
2. Making accurate models easily accessible to the right people
3. Maintaining both logical and physical application models as well as their relationships
4. Using models that represent both the enterprise and the application perspectives as well as their relationships
5. Instituting a standardized set of common modeling constructs

■ THE CASE ROLE IN APPLICATION MAINTENANCE

Consider postdevelopment application efforts—changes, enhancements, corrections, design improvements, and "*maintenance*." CASE vendors have always touted lower maintenance costs as a direct benefit of CASE deployment. The theory always was that the delivered applications would be of better quality; hence, less maintenance would be required. But what about the maintenance that is required anyway: the enhancements that come about irrespective of good and complete design? An unforseeable decision to purchase customer rating data can have major enhancement requirements on applications that use the "customer master." With or without a CASE tool, this maintenance is a necessary fact.

Today's good models should continue serving as blueprints throughout application maintenance. In typical installations models get updated after the fact. In other words, enhancements are planned and designed. The CASE tool is used to document the design changes and specifications, but the enhancement-specific models are usually tracked separately. The record-keeping methods range from defining separate projects within the tool for each maintenance-specific release (each "project" contains only the models necessary to implement the specific enhancement) to updating the original models (in the original project) after the enhancement design has been finalized (or in the worst case, implemented).

When defining the role of CASE in application maintenance, consider the role played by program libraries in an application's life cycle. Each release and its component programs are stored and retrievable along with associated optional comments explaining the release and its intentions. The same capabilities should be characteristic of the application life cycle models. Each application release should contain associated models that completely represent the implemented enhanced version of the application. The releases should also be related to each other so that retrieval based on the application itself is also possible.

The functional role of the tool during application maintenance should be no different from its role during the initial development of the application. The role of the originally developed models, however, will change during application maintenance. Each existing model will serve as a reference point for the definition and design of the subsequent release. Even when entirely new functionality is added to an existing application, the existing models will need to be updated to include their interaction with the new application processes and data. As depicted in Fig. 4.1, CASE-based models should parallel the delivered applications, even into the maintenance cycle.

The CASE-experienced reader is probably wondering how anyone could possibly establish a CASE-oriented maintenance cycle within the functionality constraints of the currently available tool set. Ideally, models within projects should have version control features. An umbrella project should contain all models. The models themselves should be relatable to specific application releases (each release can be viewed as a submodel of the umbrella project). Model components in turn should be relatable to one or more application releases. Implementing this flexibility does require some imagination when dealing with some of the major CASE tools available as of this writing. However, it *can* be done.

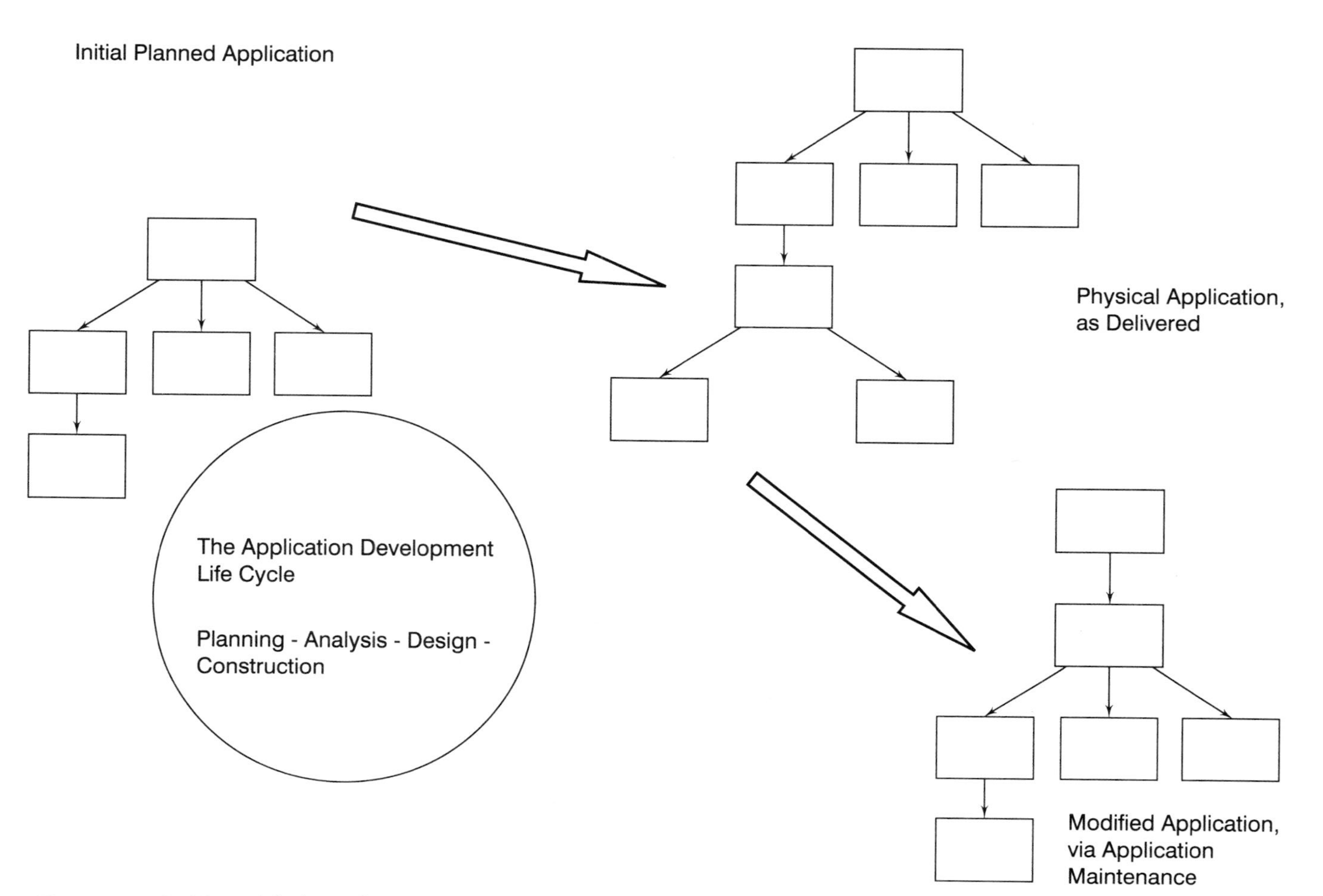

Figure 4.1 CASE models throughout an application life cycle

Consider your plan of attack. The existing application models should be evaluated as to what they represent in terms of the current, previous, and planned application implementations. Evaluate the amount of effort required to backtrack and recreate models of each application release against the resulting benefits. Then assess the ability of your deployed CASE tool to support the multiple relationships and versioning requirements involved.

A simple solution is the establishment of keyword values to represent each application release and the subsequent association with each model component as necessary. Obviously, the maximum number of keywords relatable within the tool to a CASE construct would determine whether or not this is a feasible approach. Whatever the method deployed within the tool to identify each model component as being part of an application release, the CASE tool's reporting and/or export capabilities would have to be used to identify specific release components.

The approach is dependent on the CASE tool's versioning capabilities. Some CASE tools, being inherently weak in this area, offer interfaces to source code libraries. In this scenario the models and the appropriate release-specific components would be exported to the library, where the library's version control features would then be available.

With or without repository intentions, today's models can become much more resourceful when they can detail the specifics of an application over time. Application maintenance is sure to prove more accurate and resourceful when the existing blueprints are used as a foundation for additional designs. Impact analysis will become a subconscious first step because the existing design will always be the backbone for each enhancement. Application costs can be directly attributable to the application's complexity when the entire model view is available. Consider the perhaps different perspective that your application models may serve.

■ REUSING TODAY'S MODELS

Because today's models are so good and complete, we certainly want to reuse them. I am sure we can all remember a situation where another application designer/developer had already modeled a similar function within a separate application, but it was not readily available or suitable for incorporation into the new model under construction. There were probably multiple stumbling blocks involved, some directly attributable to the implemented tool sets involved. Putting these aside, first consider how and why existing models could be reused.

Application Maintenance As discussed previously models are reused when the entire application maintenance cycle is tracked and modeled. Each release builds upon the previous; hence, a simple "project copy" could get the release-specific modeling into play. The use of CASE-based models for application maintenance would not be practical without model reuse.

Application Similarities Most corporate applications have commonalities. In most situations the commonalities revolve around the use of common data. If the databases involved have similarities or are identical, then the processes used to read and update them are most likely similar. There is no reason why each application should have to build the logical data model from scratch when parts (or all) of it already exist. The same is true for common processes. In the old (current?) COBOL days, copybooks and copylibs served this need. Here, the actual code was reused from application to application. Take this practice to the design level and application development is sure to benefit.

Data Model Consolidation A major initiative in most corporate MIS organizations has been data administration. The need for data administration arose primarily based on the inability of most upper-level executives to get their hands on the right data within the right time frame. As part of the attempt to correct data-related inadequacies, corporate data is being modeled (in many cases for the first time) by members of data administration as a means of identifying where the data is and how it relates to its probable multiple occurrences across the application world. Unless none of this data was ever modeled (implying there are no existing models anywhere), the ability to reuse the data models within already modeled applications is sure to be a timesaver. First, existing models could reduce the initial modeling effort to some degree. More important, the inclusion of existing models provides a starting point for the consolidation of the multiple views of particular pieces of corporate data.

Cross-Functional Model Reference Considering the original model was developed to serve application development needs, its reuse to serve other objectives should not be ruled out. Most of the potential will reside in information systems (IS) planning areas. Application development managers often receive requests for supportive data relating to their development efforts—questions relating to estimated staffing requirements, estimated target platform hardware requirements, the need for new software or software upgrades, and so on. Although most of these questions are answered without reference to the application models within the CASE tool, it is often true that a direct correlation exists between some aspects of the model and the resulting implementation requirements, predicted and actual. If the model is not referenced, it should at least be expanded to include the associated "planning" figures. Planning models will be discussed in more detail at the end of this chapter.

■ WHAT A GOOD MODEL NEEDS TO BECOME REUSABLE

Reusability seems to be a new buzzword. It is already obvious why one would want to reuse existing models. The ability to do so, however, is dependent on reusability qualities within the model. What makes a model reusable? Two primary areas need to be addressed when discussing reusability: the model itself and the model's identification. Other issues, such as accessibility, are reserved for later chapters.

The Model Itself When thinking about model reusability, the model must be considered modular. Like program code, reusability occurs most often at the lowest level. In fact, one could consider program functions (read, write, open, close) to be reusable code, depending on the defined level of reusability. When the reusability occurs at the design level, the same principle applies.

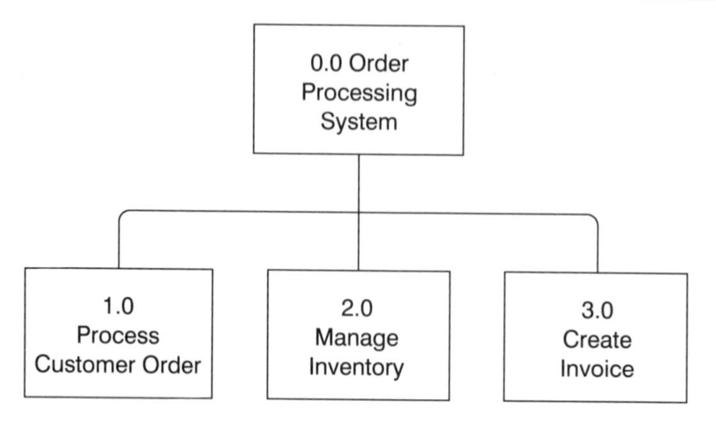

Figure 4.2 Functional areas within a sample application architecture

The CASE-based application model was segmented into functional areas. These areas most likely represented a box within the high-level-system application architecture. Subsequent models broke each box down into further components as the process specifications became more detailed. When evaluating the functional breakdown of an application model, consider how the segmentation occurred, that is, what functional differences determined the architectural differentiation.

As shown in Fig. 4.2, segmentation does imply functional differences. For example, Process Customer Order (1.0) will contain all design relating to the processing of the application request (*customer order* in this case) as it relates to the data appearing on the order itself. The next functional segment, Manage Inventory (2.0), continues the processing, but concentrates on inventory levels as dictated by the incoming customer orders. Finally, Create Invoice (3.0) is concerned with all billing-specific processing.

When studying this functional division, we get the impression that the dividing lines are based primarily on the data involved in each function—customer orders, inventory masters, and invoices. Although there is data commonality across the three areas, the commonality is represented by related key fields (customer id, order line item, inventory number). Consider the potential for reusability of this design. The determining factors revolve around:

1. *Customer*. Generic customer, or only a specific type in this application (e.g., corporate customers only)
2. *Order*. Generic order (all orders for this company's products are identical), or a specific category (e.g., phone orders only). If only a specific category, are its processing qualities truly unique?
3. *Inventory*. Centralized corporate inventory vs. inventory of a particular product type. Again, if the inventory referenced by this application has specific characteristics (e.g., foreign manufactured, long delivery time), determine whether they are specific only to this application.

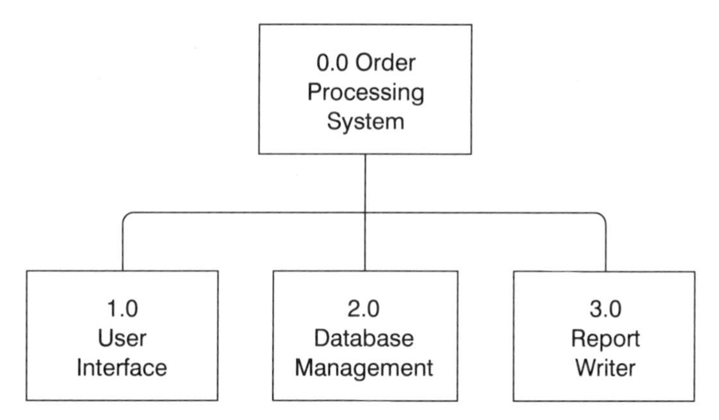

Figure 4.3 Another view of the same application architecture

4. *Invoice*. If all invoices generated by the organization are identical, then chances are this aspect of the design merits reusability. However, is the processing within this function correlated with specifics related only to the unique types of orders and/or customers dealt with by this application? How separable are the invoice-specific aspects of the design from the other nongeneric processes?

Evaluating the previous design for potential reusability starts by determining whether the design itself is modular and general enough to provide benefit to other application development efforts. Consider the design shown in Fig. 4.3, which could also be used to represent the previous application.

In this scenario there is no argument as to whether or not this design is generic enough to merit reuse. Practically all applications could fit into this architecture. But the question is, Is it worth it?. What benefits would a typical application merit by conforming to this generic architecture? Again, going down to the program code level, the benefits become clearer. Just as common program libraries include standard user interface modules (standard screen designs, error handling, etc.), standard DBMS routines (open, close, read, write, select, etc.), and standard reporting routines, their design can also be standardized.

Obviously, an application's architecture loses substantial detail when it is "standardized" to the generic representation shown in Fig. 4.3. The ideal design for reuse is a mixture of both. The designs represented in the generic architecture can be included, where necessary, in the specific functions itemized in Fig. 4.2. Generic user interface designs, DBMS interface routines, and report designs can be integrated with the application-specific functions.

To evaluate a model as a candidate for reusability, look for the following characteristics in the overall design:

Modularity. Identify many distinct functions, each with specific processing characteristics and little or no process redundancy.

Common data definition. Where data is modeled, its naming and definition should be clear enough (hopefully standardized) for other interested applications to understand and benefit from reuse of the data model components.

Use of generic design modules, where appropriate. As discussed previously, consider where aspects of the design belong in a common library. Standard user interface designs, database procedures, and transaction logging are just a few examples.

The Model's Identification The other major aspect of making models reusable is how they are identified. The best models in the world are worthless if no one can remember what they are called. The naming of models and their components is crucial to the goal of reuse. Aside from a full understandable name for the application model itself, each component must be identified with an equally meaningful name. In addition, they must be named in such a way that each component implies a relationship to the application *and* its functionality. The typical CASE tool does have name length restrictions on both the model and its components. However, other constructs within the tool can be used to identify the features that would be in demand by those looking for existing designs.

Determine the goal of design reusability. If, for example, an attempt at standardizing all application user interfaces is a major priority, concentrate on identifying those existing designs that merit participation in a reusability scheme. Perhaps they should be copied to the "common" project. Their reuse is dependent on how easily identifiable they are. Identify them as completely and specifically as possible. Names such as *Determine User Permissions* are better than *Verify User*. Relate each component to as many other components as necessary to keep a functional design set complete. For example, a name such as *User Interface Design* should be associated with all pertinent components.

Reusability is not an overnight accomplishment. However, good models deserve revisit in order to maximize their benefit potential. It may be determined that in order to reuse a particular set of models, additional models need to be developed. Like all development efforts, a cost/benefit analysis can determine whether the undertaking is worth pursuing. If repository plans are being considered, models targeted for the repository should be evaluated for their reuse potential.

■ PREPARING FOR MODEL-DRIVEN DEVELOPMENT

Perhaps one of the most common goals of CASE advocates is to become an application development shop that creates and maintains application models rather than application code. Since code generation became viable, many installations have been experiencing the model-driven development of new applications. These applications are usually free of complexity in that they typically consist of a relational DBMS (usually DB2) and surrounding menu-based access and update. The data model is typically the central focus of the application, and with an integrated CASE tool as the modeling aid and code generator, the data objects are intertwined into the process descriptions.

As code generators have improved (performance considerations are now included in some of the generated code), generated applications have become more complex in terms of application size. It is now feasible for large corporate applications to result from model-based code generation. Even when manual supplementation of the generated code was required, developers have found that the result was more accurate and was developed in a shorter time frame.

If your organization desires a move toward model-driven development, the transition will require a change in application development practices and the management attitudes that surround them.

For example, I remember a client of mine who headed an internal MIS organization. This organization was charged with the development of internal tools to support the application development process. The supported developers, although quite technically superior in terms of application development skills, had not embraced information engineering, CASE, or modeling in general. Instead, most applications were developed from written requirements, with architectures developed during subsequent small work sessions and documented in the continued series of technical requirements documents. We had talked about bringing in CASE and a required application development methodology. We also talked about code generation as a by-product of this change in application development practice. I remember his response to the potential of automatic code generation:

> Code generation sounds like an interesting opportunity, but the best I could hope for is that the developers would take the code and run with it. I know the generated code will need modification, so if we save time by getting 65 percent of the code generated, and then only have to recode the other 35 percent we're ahead of the game.

We had several discussions about how code generation and model-driven development should be deployed. But our basic differences in philosophy convinced me that model-driven development would never be a reality at this company. Despite the fact that upper management constantly expressed a publicized commitment toward "model-driven development," the behind-the-scenes discussions with the same people resulted in mixed reviews of how and where the technology would be deployed. The person quoted previously, for example, did not see merit in the models themselves. Instead, he saw them only as a required step in getting cleaner code delivered more quickly. What he refused to admit, even after substantial evidence of other company's successes and failures with code generation, was that the models were the most important part of the entire code generation process. In fact, models that function as input to code generators, whether the generators are part of the same CASE tool set or not, are extremely detailed. Many developers cynically comment that they practically coded the application via pseudo-English in their process specification models. What does save time is the means by which these models are created—everything defined to the CASE tool is available via a "point-and-click" action. Hence, the model's input and continued refinement become easier and easier.

The moral to this story is that management attitudes toward model-driven development may not always be what they appear. It is essential that management understand the implications of emphasizing the development of models as opposed to the development of code. Assuming that modeling has been around at your organization (unlike the cited example), the move toward model-based development implies the elimination of the person who codes for a living. Now, it is quite unlikely that programmers will go the way of elevator operators, but what will be inevitable is a change in the skill set required to perform the job as well as a change in the nature of the job itself.

When the MIS organization becomes an organization of modelers, everyone must understand modeling constructs. Obviously, an understanding of modeling does not always imply the ability to construct a model. However, if models are to be the key to the generation of complete and accurate code, everyone involved in their interpretation and supplementation must be able to read them. Just as construction workers must be able to follow blueprints, programmers must be able to read CASE-based models. Begin the education process now by requiring a course in your modeling methodology, the deployed tool set, and how the two are used together.

The existing job functions—programmer, programmer/analyst, analyst—can remain. The analyst, already the modeler, will continue to be the creator and maintainer of models. This person can translate business requirements into application models. The programmer/analyst, instead of taking business requirements and coding them, will be looking at an application model, as changed by the analyst, filling in the technical details, and generating the code. There will be a fine line of distinction, if none at all, between the programmer/analyst and the programmer. Both job responsibilities will require the ability to interpret a logical model, interpret and/or change physical models, generate code, and validate the generated code. When manual supplementation of the code is necessary, it will still need to start with model-based definitions. In some cases the model will merely need to include a "Call external routine" type statement in the process specifications. This indicates the existence of code that falls outside the realm of the application model. However, its development and maintenance must be closely monitored and related to the rest of the model-driven application.

Finally, if models are to become the main deliverable of an MIS organization (code will be a by-product), there must be a place to store all of them! By reading this book, I know you are thinking repository, but I mention the point as one that will need addressing in any model-based development organization. Keeping the models, as good as they may be, in isolated workstation-based CASE tools will not be sufficient if all developers need access to them.

■ THE DEFINED STRATEGIC ROLE OF CASE

We have covered a lot of ground so far in this chapter, all of which concentrates on ways to make the most of today's good models. As the models gain in functional role, so must the modeling tool.

When the decision to acquire CASE was first made, its functional role was defined based on vendor information and possibly the experience of other installations. As CASE usage matured, its role was most likely narrowed and hopefully standardized. As the models are reevaluated for potential repository residence, they are most likely going to gain in functionality based on their enhancement. In order to continue the persistent upgrade of application models and their infiltration beyond application developers, the role of CASE must also be revisited.

In the majority of situations, CASE was initially purchased as an aid to new application development. In more focused situations, CASE use concentrated on the data side of the application. As discussed in this chapter, many of the existing models can be used for a more sizable charter without major effort. In order to focus CASE usage on its most practical yet beneficial purpose, consider how the role of application models will change once they are enhanced and accessible (e.g, via a repository). Then evaluate how the model-depicting tool set should be used as this new model role becomes a way of life. The new CASE role is initially strategic; but as existing models become "role models," the strategic role must become practical in order for new applications to maintain this expanded role.

■ MODELING THE ENTERPRISE

An effort that has been underway in many MIS modeling organizations is that of enterprise modeling. In fact, information engineering methodology advocates this effort as a way of maximizing the CASE benefit. In a massive enterprise modeling effort, the business is modeled from several perspectives:

> *The organizational perspective.* Like an organization chart, this model looks at the business from the viewpoint of its physical organization divisions. Functions performed within each organization are depicted. This effort is usually one of the first involved in identifying organization inefficiencies.
>
> *The functional perspective.* This model depicts the functions performed by the enterprise. This view of the organization most closely resembles the content of a work flow diagram in that it depicts organizational processes without respect to physical organization structure. The attributes of the depicted processes are indicative of the organizations responsible for performing those functions.
>
> *The information perspective.* The stream of information throughout the enterprise is modeled in this view. Often considered an enterprise data model, it depicts the relationships between all corporate information.
>
> *The application perspective.* Relating all corporate applications, this model illustrates the application view. All corporate applications are related via inputs and outputs, resulting in one large data flow diagram.

The enterprise model, despite its various perspectives, is integrated. Once complete, the tracing of a particular type of corporate data (e.g., customer data) throughout the business functional flow, the organizational hierarchy, or corporate applications is feasible and directly attainable. Many repository advocates stress the need for an enterprise model as the way to relate the massive amounts and types of models that exist in today's corporations.

Enterprise modeling, in enough detail to satisfy the multiplicity of relationships that exist between business functions and their respective implementations across organizations and applications, is a multiyear effort. It is mentioned here as a way of discovering the multiple ways of indexing access to existing models. Given adequate resources to begin modeling the enterprise, it can only benefit any planned repository role. However, if resources are scarce or unsupported, consider the exercise of indexing existing models from each of the enterprise modeling perspectives. For example, take an existing payroll application and assign keywords that represent the associated organizations, functions, types of corporate information, and applications that would be related as a means of indexed access into the application's models.

In most installations enterprise modeling is undertaken by a centralized group (most typically data administration). However, if each application modeling effort were to assess the application's corporate role and relationship, good models would become more available.

■ PLANNING MODELS

As a final way to build upon today's application models, consider the model of what is to be, rather than what is, otherwise known as the *planning model*. Planning models typically represent a strategic view of the enterprise. Many CASE vendors offer planning components as a separately packaged product which can be integrated with the application modeling products.

In a correctly implemented scenario, strategic planners model the business as it is targeted (short and long term). Perhaps the organization's goals and objectives are depicted as they relate to an anticipated organizational restructuring. Continuing this strategy, each goal is related to application models, both existing and planned. MIS planners represent the application planning view and continue to refine the planning models. The end result provides a better view of the role of each application model within the enterprise, both current and future. It also allows the model user to see what lies ahead in terms of planned organization changes and to relate these changes to any planned application enhancements. Finally, by viewing the goals and objectives of planned applications, application managers can assess the impact of the eventual replacement of interfacing applications before the new applications are implemented. See Fig. 4.4 for an illustration of a sample planning model.

■ SUMMARY

In this chapter we discussed the multiple ways of improving the use and validity of today's models. To briefly recap, the areas discussed include:

- Using the models throughout application maintenance
- Reusing existing models
- Preparing for model-driven development

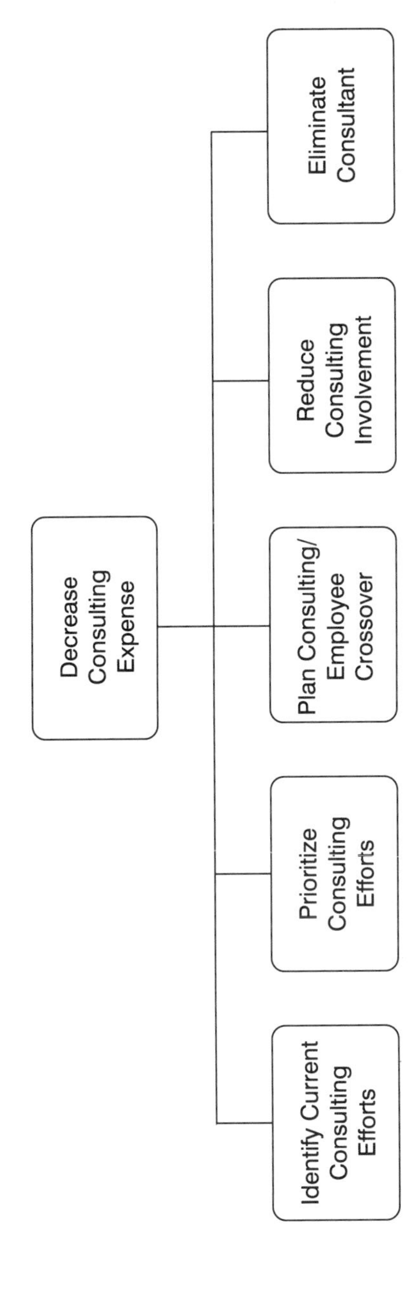

Figure 4.4 A sample planning model

- Reassessing the CASE strategy
- Modeling the enterprise
- Incorporating the use of planning models

These areas were all presented as a way of introducing the reader to perspectives that may not have been considered when the idea of centralizing access to application models was first contemplated.

5

MODELS AND FORWARD ENGINEERING

In most things success depends on knowing how long it takes to succeed.

Montesquieu

Forward engineering, the art of taking logical models and automatically creating their physical implementations, covers two major functional areas: data and process. The data side of forward engineering is in a more mature state of evolution. In fact, the technology itself has been delivering its promises since its initial offerings. Process forward engineering (typically called "code generation") does not share the same glory.

The reasons are simple. In the data world the specifications in terms of modeling required to constitute the logical representation of a database can be made extremely close to its physical implementation. In fact, it is quite simple to generate the DDL for a fully normalized (third normal form) relational database from a logical data model in most tools. When fully normalized databases are not the way to go (as they most often are not), the changes to the logical model (e.g., adding redundancy) result in the direct change to the generated physical definitions.

Considering the fact that the rest of the application constitutes the process world, the direct correlation between modeling constructs and the actual programming code required to implement them are not all necessarily there. To begin, some program code often has nothing to do with the logic of an application, but is directly related to the physical environment in which the program will reside. One example that comes to mind is that of restart and recovery procedures. One could argue that they are not to be considered within the modeling framework, but the fact is they are required for the implemented application to function. Also, when performance becomes an issue (and when doesn't it?), the direct translation of process model logic to code is not often the most efficient. There are many other factors which will be covered within this chapter, but the general opinion regarding code generation remains skeptical both within and outside of the CASE user community.

Reverting back to the data side of forward engineering, consider the amount of detail that your CASE-based logical data models currently contain.

■ CASE-BASED SCHEMA GENERATION

Database Schemas Database schemas are not very complicated once they have been designed. The design determines the number of entities (correlating to tables in the perfect world), each of which has its associated attributes (columns) with respective physical requirements (name, length, storage type, default value, value range, etc.). The entities are related to each other via identifiers (primary and foreign keys), and the relationships are controlled via referential integrity constraints. Most data modeling tools allow for the input and definition of all of the aforementioned constructs. The real question at the heart of forward engineering is whether these constructs are required inputs, and how accurate any semantic checking actually is.

In typical CASE tools the tool is designed to be just that—a tool. From an implementation perspective, this means that most of the physical database-specific constructs are not required to be input into a logical data model. I think back to the early days of commercial CASE (approximately mid to late 1980s) and how it was deployed in many eager MIS organizations. Many had been using PC-based graphics packages to draw their E–R diagrams and had become tired of their limitations (they needed to create their own double-arrow icons, moving entities required redrawing the connecting lines, deletions required multiple inputs, etc.). With the advent of CASE, all of these graphics package limitations were taken care of automatically. So, analysts were immediately sold and loved the ease in which data models could be "drawn" and updated in the CASE world. Most of the remaining application documentation did not occur within the CASE tool; it was still word processed. In fact, many of the early CASE tools did not have the capacity to allow full application specification anyway. So CASE tool vendors, looking for sales, made their input requirements as loose as possible. Requiring inputs that did not directly appear in graphical outputs would probably have been viewed as a tool hindrance by many of the initial CASE users.

As user demands progressed, the CASE tools progressed. Analysts interested in using the tools for more than just graphics wanted the ability to accurately store their modeling constructs along with their graphical depiction. CASE vendors had always allowed the capability within the tools, but without the intent that these constructs generate their physical definition requirements.

CASE began to function as a holding area for data models and their related constructs. Soon forward engineering capabilities appeared, the first being that of data definition language generation. Initial market leaders in this area assumed that all new databases were targeted for mainframe DB2. Early releases of DB2, not concerned with referential integrity, required only the barebones data definitions in order to establish a database. Entity names became table names (some tools allowed the input of a physical name along with the entity's logical name), and each attribute within the entity became a column. Lengths and data types resulted from the same information, as stored with each attribute. Perhaps the only other requirement instilled by the tool, which was most likely followed anyway, was the identification of primary and foreign keys. These were used to establish the intertable relationships.

As DB2 matured, so too did those tools used to design for it as a target environment. Referential integrity, always a consideration in logical data models, became definable with a database's data definition language. Now, the model constructs were required to include optional/mandatory indications with the relationship definitions as well as a host of other insert/delete constraints and characteristics. Again, as long as the modeler accurately depicted the requirements, the generated DDL was accurate (see Fig 5.1).

Through trial and error modelers, who may not have been as conscientious about covering all of the details required for a fully documented database design, learned via the tool what was missing. When the "generate" function was triggered by the modeler, the tool notified the user of any missing factors (e.g., the lack of identified foreign keys) that prevented DDL generation. Some modelers, who were conscientious enough to know the details required for the physical database, resented the

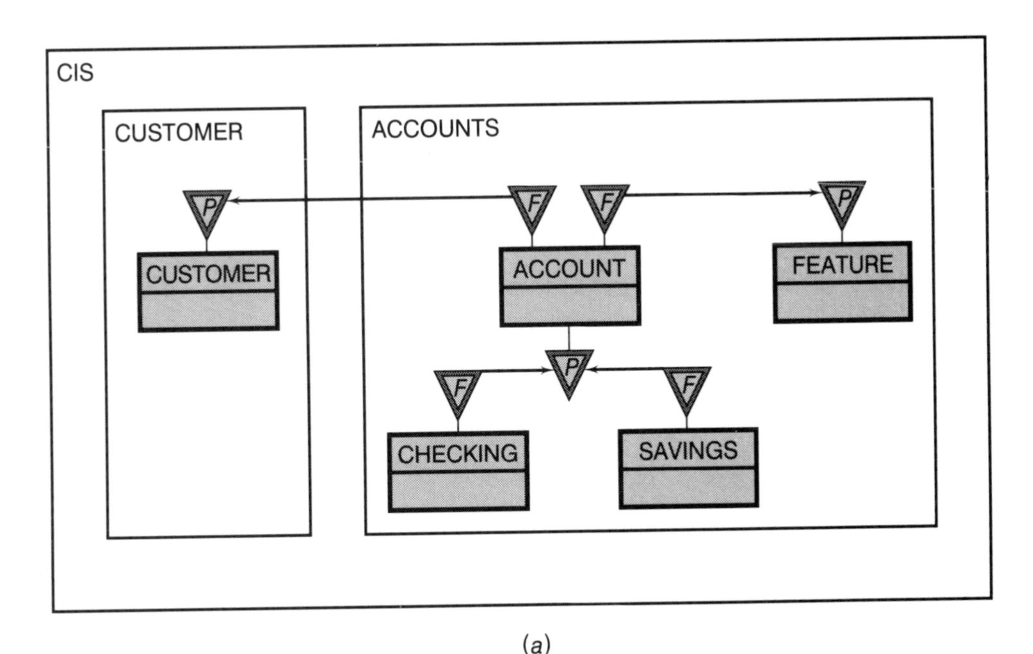

(*a*)

Figure 5.1 A DDL generation example

need to input every little requirement. Many felt that they could have input the DDL in less time! The fact remained, however, that by inputting the logical side of a database, the business became linked to the physical world. Many developers would say, "So what?," but the perspective repository implementer already knows the advantages.

Also, many conscientious modelers did identify the full requirements for a relational database within their data model and still received error messages when the "generate" function was initiated. In their minds the tool was the only factor to blame. The reality often centered around the names of the constructs themselves. Tools could not relate an entity with a primary key of *Product-ID* to another entity with a primary key of *Part-ID*, for example, without being told that the two attributes are in fact the same, despite their names. These trivialities can become annoying to the sophisticated analyst, and the more there are, the more (useless?) time the analyst must spend to get the models in the right shape for schema generation.

The fact remains, however, that once the model and its contents conform to the intricacies required for database schema generation, accurate and complete DDL will result.

Process Schemas Schemas that result from models are not limited to the database world, however. Many alleged "forward engineering" tools handle the

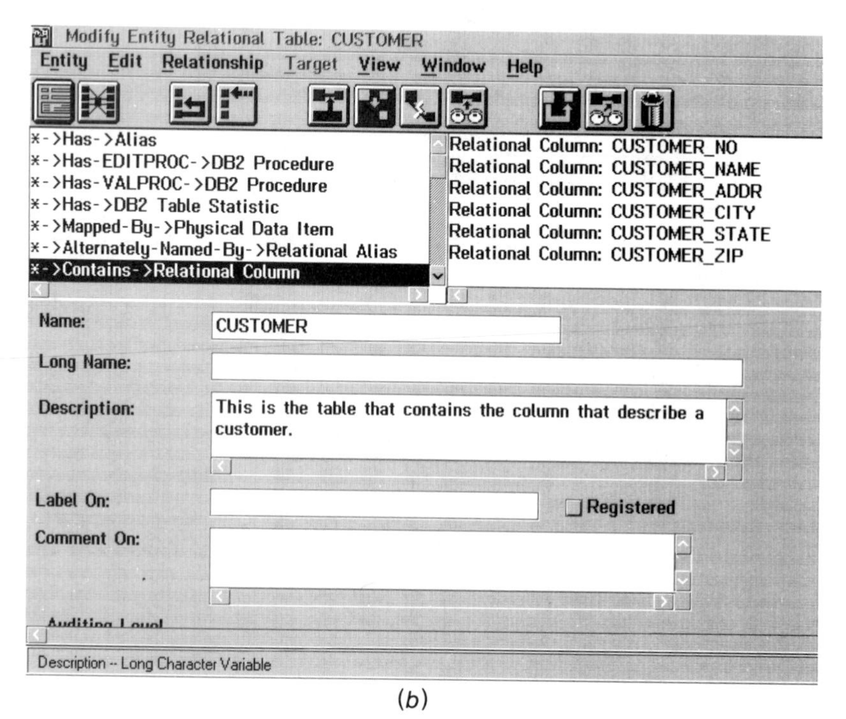

(*b*)

Figure 5.1 (Continued)

```
------------------------------------------------------------
-- EXCELERATOR - SQL / DDL GENERATE
============================================================
-- DATE: 03 / 21 / 93    USER    : CINDYR
-- TIME: 02:47:30        PROJECT: Customer Information System
------------------------------------------------------------
CREATE STOGROUP CIS ;

CREATE DATABASE CIS
   STOGROUP CIS
   BUFFERPOOL BP0 ;

CREATE TABLESPACE ACCOUNTS
   FREEPAGE 10
   BUFFERPOOL BP0
   LOCKSIZE ANY
   CLOSE YES ;

CREATE TABLESPACE CUSTOMER
   FREEPAGE 10
   BUFFERPOOL BP0
   LOCKSIZE ANY
   CLOSE YES ;

CREATE TABLE ACCOUNT
   ( ACCOUNT_NUMBER       CHAR           (010)  NOT NULL,
     ACCOUNT_CUST_NO      CHAR           (006)  NOT NULL,
     ACCOUNT_TYPE         CHAR           (002)  NOT NULL,
     ACCOUNT_BALANCE      DECIMAL    (012,002)  NOT NULL,
     ACCOUNT_ACT DATE     DATE                  NOT NULL,
     ACCOUNT_MINIMUM_DA   DECIMAL    (012,002)  NOT NULL,
     ACCOUNT_DESC         CHAR           (040)  NOT NULL,
     ACCOUNT_FEATURE_CO   CHAR           (003)  NOT NULL,
     PRIMARY KEY
       ( ACCOUNT_NUMBER
       )
   )
 IN DATABASE CIS;

 CREATE TABLE CHECKING
   ( ACCOUNT_NUMBER       CHAR           (010)  NOT NULL,
     CHECK_FEES           DECIMAL    (006,002)  NOT NULL,
     OVERDRAFT_PROTECT    DECIMAL        (005)  NOT NULL,
     PRIMARY KEY
       ( ACCOUNT_NUMBER
       )
   )
 IN DATABASE CIS;
```

(c)

Figure 5.1 (Continued)

```
CREATE TABLE CUSTOMER
   ( CUSTOMER_NO          CHAR        (006)  NOT NULL,
     CUSTOMER_NAME        CHAR        (020)  NOT NULL,
     FREEPAGE 10
     PCTFREE 5
     SUBPAGES 4
     BUFFERPOOL BP0
     CLOSE NO ;

CREATE UNIQUE INDEX SAVINGS ON SAVINGS
   ( ACCOUNT_NUMBER     ASC
   )
   FREEPAGE 10
   PCTFREE 5
   SUBPAGES 4
   BUFFERPOOL BP0
   CLOSE NO ;

ALTER TABLE ACCOUNT
      FOREIGN KEY
        ( ACCOUNT_CUSTOMER_NO
        )
      REFERENCES CUSTOMER ON DELETE RESTRICT;

ALTER TABLE ACCOUNT
      FOREIGN KEY
        ( ACCOUNT_FEATURE_CO
        )
      REFERENCES FEATURE ON DELETE RESTRICT;

ALTER TABLE CHECKING
      FOREIGN KEY
        ( ACCOUNT_NUMBER
        )
      REFERENCES ACCOUNT ON DELETE RESTRICT;

ALTER TABLE SAVINGS
      FOREIGN KEY
        ( ACCOUNT_NUMBER
        )
      REFERENCES ACCOUNT ON DELETE RESTRICT;
      :
     CUSTOMER_ADDR        VARCHAR     (032)  NOT NULL,
     CUSTOMER_CITY        CHAR        (020)  NOT NULL,
     CUSTOMER_STATE       CHAR        (003)  NOT NULL,
     CUSTOMER_ZIP         CHAR        (010)  NOT NULL,
     PRIMARY KEY
       ( CUSTOMER_NO
       )
   )
IN DATABASE CIS;
```

Figure 5.1 (Continued)

```
CREATE TABLE FEATURE
   ( FEATURE_CODE         CHAR          (003)  NOT NULL,
     FEATURE_DESC         CHAR          (050)  NOT NULL,
     SUGGESTION_MSG       CHAR          (050)  NOT NULL,
     FEATURE_COST         DECIMAL (007,002)  NOT NULL,
     PRIMARY KEY
       ( FEATURE_CODE
       )
   )
IN DATABASE CIS;

CREATE TABLE SAVINGS
   ( ACCOUNT_NUMBER       CHAR          (010)  NOT NULL,
     ACCOUNT_INT_YTD      DECIMAL (027,020)  NOT NULL,
     ACCOUNT_INTEREST_P   DECIMAL (003,001)  NOT NULL,
     ACCOUNT_INTEREST_A   DECIMAL (027,020)  NOT NULL,
     PRIMARY KEY
       ( ACCOUNT_NUMBER
       )
   )
IN DATABASE CIS;
CREATE UNIQUE INDEX ACCOUNT ON ACCOUNT
   ( ACCOUNT_NUMBER  ASC
   )
   FREEPAGE 10
   PCTFREE 5
   SUBPAGES 4
   BUFFERPOOL BP0
   CLOSE NO ;

CREATE UNIQUE INDEX CHECKING ON CHECKING
   ( ACCOUNT_NUMBER  ASC
   )
   FREEPAGE 10
   PCTFREE 5
   SUBPAGES 4
   BUFFERPOOL BP0
   CLOSE NO ;

CREATE UNIQUE INDEX CUSTOMER ON CUSTOMER
   ( CUSTOMER_NO    ASC
   )
     FREEPAGE 10
     PCTFREE 5
     SUBPAGES 4
     BUFFERPOOL BP0
     CLOSE NO ;
```

Figure 5.1 (Continued)

```
CREATE UNIQUE INDEX SAVINGS ON SAVINGS
     ( ACCOUNT_NUMBER     ASC
     )
     FREEPAGE 10
     PCTFREE 5
     SUBPAGES 4
     BUFFERPOOL BP0
     CLOSE NO ;

ALTER TABLE ACCOUNT
     FOREIGN KEY
       ( ACCOUNT_CUSTOMER_NO
       )
     REFERENCES CUSTOMER ON DELETE RESTRICT;

ALTER TABLE ACCOUNT
       ( ACCOUNT_FEATURE_CO
       )
     REFERENCES FEATURE ON DELETE RESTRICT;

ALTER TABLE CHECKING
     FOREIGN KEY
       ( ACCOUNT_NUMBER
       )
     REFERENCES ACCOUNT ON DELETE RESTRICT;

ALTER TABLE SAVINGS
     FOREIGN KEY
       ( ACCOUNT_NUMBER
       )
     REFERENCES ACCOUNT ON DELETE RESTRICT;
     .
     .
     .
```

Figure 5.1 (Continued)

process world by generating code skeletons. These skeletons are derived from process models (usually process decomposition diagrams), the defined process hierarchy resulting in a one-to-one program hierarchy member.

To the application developer, resulting code skeletons do not rate any major appreciation factor. Any developer can take a process hierarchy and copy the process and subprocess names into a file of to-be-written application code. However, as with database schemas, by allowing the tool to create these skeletons, the relationship between the logical and the physical is automatically created and maintained within the tool's encyclopedia. Consistent deployment of this relationship saves a major amount of correlation work when preparing for a repository. In fact, some installations with "design and code" developers responsible for the application design *and* implementation often store the actual program code within the tool (disguised as process specifications). This practice is often indicative of the lack of an integrated documentation holding area and a lack of foresight as to the purpose of process specifications. It also violates the intended relationship between the specifications and the actual code. However, when these process models are evaluated for repository load, the process/program connection will be easily identifiable.

■ CASE-BASED CODE GENERATION

Taking process schema generation one step further implies the generation of fully executable application code. Developers are already aware of the intricacies and detail required to code an application, regardless of whether or not the supplied specifications included all of the necessary particulars. For a CASE tool to generate code from application models, the models must be substantially detailed. Tools that generate code provide integrity check features which validate all designs throughout the application specification cycle. It is important to note, however, that some tools do not include their own code generators. These tools allege the ability to use the complete design, as input and validated by the CASE tool, as input to a code generator. The code generator then generates code for the specified target platform.

The code generator, regardless of whether or not it is an integral part of the designing CASE tool set, usually derives its requirements from several of the CASE-resident models. Although ideal, this is not always the case, however. Some code generators are designed to meet the needs of both the modeling and the nonmodeling camps. For nonmodelers, the code generator itself creates a "behind the scenes" model via developer inputs to generator-initiated prompts. When the models originate in an interfacing CASE tool, they are then often tied together in the model that directly precedes the generation of code (often called the process specification diagram, or program action diagram). Data models (logical E–R diagrams as well as database schemas), data flow diagrams, screen and report layouts, screen (dialog) hierarchies, structure charts, and the intricacies of any decision trees are all referenced in the process specifications.

Figure 5.2 shows a simple code generation result. In this example a non-model-driven code generator was used as input. The code was generated based on a series of user inputs, the order of which was controlled by the tool.

■ IS MODEL-DRIVEN DEVELOPMENT REALLY HERE?

One of the CASE like/dislike controversies centers around the ability of CASE tools to generate usable code. The fact is CASE tools can and do generate code. The issue then centers on what the CASE tools define as code and how it relates to the finished application as it runs in production.

Many vendor-provided success stories talk about organizations generating applications for target platforms on which their developers have no experience. The MIS management views this as a real cost saver in that inexperienced developers become immediately productive. In fact, many of these organizations staff their MIS development function with a majority of junior programmer/analysts trained in information engineering. These developers are trained in the CASE tool specifics as they apply to the internal system development methodology. In addition, a few technical specialists are maintained to modify generated code that does not meet

```
   EVALUATE DUPDT-FUNCTION                                     PG
      WHEN ‡Q‡                                                 PG
          MOVE ‡QUERY FUNCTION COMPLETE‡                       PG
              TO DUPDT-MESSAGE                                 PG
          PERFORM QUERY-LOGIC
      WHEN ‡U‡                                                 PG
          MOVE ‡UPDATE FUNCTION COMPLETE‡                      PG
              TO DUPDT-MESSAGE                                 PG
          PERFORM UPDATE-LOGIC
      WHEN ‡A‡                                                 PR
          MOVE ‡ADD FUNCTION COMPLETE‡                         PG
              TO DUPDT-MESSAGE                                 PG
          PERFORM ADD-LOGIC
      WHEN ‡D‡                                                 PG
          MOVE ‡DELETE FUNCTION COMPLETE‡                      PG
              TO DUPDT-MESSAGE                                 PG
          PERFORM DELETE-LOGIC
      WHEN ‡C‡                                                 PG
          MOVE SPACES TO DUPDT-FUNCTION-INPT
          MOVE SPACES TO DUPDT-CUSTOMER-NO-INPT
          MOVE SPACES TO DUPDT-SAVEKEY-INPT
          MOVE SPACES TO DUPDT-CUSTOMER-NAME-INPT
          MOVE SPACES TO DUPDT-CUSTOMER-ADDR-INPT
          MOVE SPACES TO DUPDT-CUSTOMER-CITY-INPT
          MOVE SPACES TO DUPDT-CUSTOMER-ZIP-INPT
          MOVE SPACES TO DUPDT-GEORGE-INPT
          MOVE SPACES TO DUPDT-MESSAGE-INPT
  ELSE IF ( PF3 OR PF15 )                                      PG
      MOVE ‡S‡ TO TP-INVOCATION-MODE
      MOVE ‡DMENU‡ TO TP-CALLING-PROGRAM-ID
      IF NOT DMENU-CURSOR-POS
         MOVE -1 TO DMENU-SELECTION-LEN
             END-IF
      EXEC CICS SEND MAP(‡DMENU‡)
         FROM(DMENU-RECORD)
         MAPSET(‡DMENU$‡)
         CURSOR
         ERASE
         FREEKB
      END-EXEC
      EXEC CICS RETURN
         TRANSID(‡DMEN‡)
         COMMAREA(TP-COMMAREA)
         LENGTH(200)
      END-EXEC
  ELSE IF ( PF4 OR PF16 )                                      PR
      MOVE ‡P‡ TO TP-INVOCATION-MODE
      MOVE LOW-VALUES TO TP-ADDR-TABLE
      MOVE 0 TO TP-ADDR-COUNT
      EXEC CICS XCTL PROGRAM(‡DUPDT‡)
         COMMAREA(TP-COMMAREA)
         LENGTH(200)
      END-EXEC
      MOVE EIBFN  TO APS-EIBFN
         MOVE EIBRCODE TO APS-EIBRCODE
```

Figure 5.2 A simple code generation result

```
QUERY-LOGIC.                                                    PG
    PERFORM CUSTOMER-01-READ
    PERFORM MOVE-REC-TO-SCREEN.
ADD-LOGIC.                                                      PG
    PERFORM MOVE-SCREEN-TO-REC
    PERFORM CUSTOMER-01-STORE.
UPDATE-LOGIC.                                                   PG
    PERFORM CUSTOMER-01-SETKEY
    PERFORM CUSTOMER-01-READUPDT
    PERFORM MOVE-SCREEN-TO-REC
DELETE-LOGIC.                                                   PG

    PERFORM CUSTOMER-01-SETKEY
    PERFORM CUSTOMER-01-READUPDT
    PERFORM MOVE-SCREEN-TO-REC

** START OF DATABASE ACCESS ROUTINES                            PG
     ************************************************************
**  BEGIN DB-OBTAIN CUSTOMER-REC                                **
     ************************************************************

      EXEC SQL SELECT
           CUSTOMER_NO,
           CUSTOMER_NAME,
           CUSTOMER_ADDR,
           CUSTOMER_CITY,
           CUSTOMER_STATE,
           CUSTOMER ZIP
           INTO
           :CUSTOMER-REC.CUSTOMER-NO,
           :CUSTOMER-REC.CUSTOMER-NAME
           :IND-CUSTOMER-REC.IND-CUSTOMER-NAME,
           :CUSTOMER-REC.CUSTOMER-ADDR
           :IND-CUSTOMER-REC.IND-CUSTOMER-ADDR,
           :CUSTOMER-REC.CUSTOMER-CITY
           :IND-CUSTOMER-REC.IND-CUSTOMER-CITY,
           :CUSTOMER-REC.CUSTOMER-STATE
           :IND-CUSTOMER-REC.IND-CUSTOMER-STATE,
           :CUSTOMER-REC.CUSTOMER-ZIP
           :IND-CUSTOMER-REC.IND-CUSTOMER-ZIP
           FROM
           USERID.CUSTOMER
           WHERE
           CUSTOMER_NO = :DUPDT-CUSTOMER-NO
      END-EXEC
```

Figure 5.2 (Continued)

```
CUSTOMER-01-READUPDT.                                                   PG

    ***************************************************************
**   BEGIN DB-OBTAIN CUSTOMER-REC                                     **
    ***************************************************************

     EXEC SQL SELECT
          CUSTOMER_NO.
          CUSTOMER_NAME,
          CUSTOMER_ADDR,
          CUSTOMER_CITY,
          CUSTOMER_STATE,
          CUSTOMER_ZIP
          INTO
          :CUSTOMER-REC.CUSTOMER-NO,
          :CUSTOMER-REC.CUSTOMER-NAME
          :IND-CUSTOMER-REC.IND-CUSTOMER-NAME,
          :CUSTOMER-REC.CUSTOMER-ADDR
          :IND-CUSTOMER-REC.IND-CUSTOMER-ADDR,
          :CUSTOMER-REC.CUSTOMER-CITY
          :IND-CUSTOMER-REC.IND-CUSTOMER-CITY,
          :CUSTOMER-REC.CUSTOMER-STATE
          :IND-CUSTOMER-REC.IND-CUSTOMER-STATE,
          :CUSTOMER-REC.CUSTOMER-ZIP
          :IND-CUSTOMER-REC.IND-CUSTOMER-ZIP
          FROM
          USERID.CUSTOMER
          WHERE
          CUSTOMER_NO = :PX-CUSTOMER-01-SKX-0001
     END-EXEC
CUSTOMER-01-STORE.                                                      PG
    ***************************************************************
**   BEGIN DB-STORE CUSTOMER-REC                                      **
    ***************************************************************

        EXEC SQL INSERT
            INTO USERID.CUSTOMER
            (CUSTOMER_NO,
            CUSTOMER_NAME,
            CUSTOMER_ADDR,
            CUSTOMER_CITY,
            CUSTOMER_STATE,
            CUSTOMER_ZIP)
            VALUES
            (:CUSTOMER-REC.CUSTOMER-NO,
            :CUSTOMER-REC.CUSTOMER-NAME
            :IND-CUSTOMER-REC.IND-CUSTOMER-NAME,
            :CUSTOMER-REC.CUSTOMER-ADDR
            :IND-CUSTOMER-REC.IND-CUSTOMER-ADDR,
            :CUSTOMER-REC.CUSTOMER-CITY
            :IND-CUSTOMER-REC.IND-CUSTOMER-CITY,
            :CUSTOMER-REC.CUSTOMER-STATE
            :CUSTOMER-REC.CUSTOMER-ZIP
            :IND-CUSTOMER-REC.IND-CUSTOMER-ZIP)
        END-EXEC
*****************************************************
    PG
```

Figure 5.2 (Continued)

```
CUSTOMER-01-MODIFY.                                              PG
    ****************************************************************
**   BEGIN DB-MODIFY CUSTOMER-REC                                **
    ****************************************************************

       EXEC SQL UPDATE
            USERID.CUSTOMER
            SET CUSTOMER_NO =
                :CUSTOMER-REC.CUSTOMER-NO,
                CUSTOMER_NAME =
                :CUSTOMER-REC.CUSTOMER-NAME
                :IND-CUSTOMER-REC.IND-CUSTOMER-NAME,
                CUSTOMER_ADDR =
                :CUSTOMER-REC.CUSTOMER-ADDR
                :IND-CUSTOMER-REC.IND-CUSTOMER-ADDR,
                CUSTOMER CITY =
                :CUSTOMER-REC.CUSTOMER-CITY
                :IND-CUSTOMER-REC.IND-CUSTOMER-CITY,
                CUSTOMER STATE =
                :CUSTOMER-REC.CUSTOMER-STATE
                :IND-CUSTOMER-REC.IND-CUSTOMER-STATE,
                CUSTOMER_ZIP =
                :CUSTOMER-REC.CUSTOMER-ZIP
                :IND-CUSTOMER-REC.IND-CUSTOMER-ZIP
            WHERE
            CUSTOMER_NO = :PX-CUSTOMER-01-SKX-0001
       END-EXEC
*************************************************************   PG
CUSTOMER-01-ERASE.                                               PG
    ****************************************************************
**   BEGIN DB-ERASE CUSTOMER-REC                                 **
    ****************************************************************

       EXEC SQL DELETE
            FROM USERID.CUSTOMER
            WHERE
            CUSTOMER NO = :PX-CUSTOMER-01-SKX-0001
       END-EXEC

MOVE-SCREEN-TO-REC.                                              PG
    MOVE DUPDT-CUSTOMER-NO                                       PG
         TO CUSTOMER-NO                                          PG
    MOVE DUPDT-CUSTOMER-NAME                                     PG
         TO CUSTOMER-NAME                                        PG
    MOVE DUPDT-CUSTOMER-ADDR                                     PG
         TO CUSTOMER-ADDR                                        PG
    MOVE DUPDT-CUSTOMER-CITY                                     PG
         TO CUSTOMER-CITY                                        PG
    MOVE DUPDT-CUSTOMER-ZIP                                      PG
         TO CUSTOMER-ZIP.                                        PG
```

Figure 5.2 (Continued)

```
MOVE-REC-TO-SCREEN.                                          PG
    MOVE CUSTOMER-NO                                         PG
         TO DUPDT-CUSTOMER-NO                                PG
    MOVE CUSTOMER-NAME                                       PG
         TO DUPDT-CUSTOMER-NAME                              PG
    MOVE CUSTOMER-ADDR                                       PG
         TO DUPDT-CUSTOMER-ADDR                              PG
    MOVE CUSTOMER-CITY                                       PG
         TO DUPDT-CUSTOMER-CITY                              PG
    MOVE CUSTOMER-ZIP                                        PG
         TO DUPDT-CUSTOMER-ZIP.                              PG
```

Figure 5.2 (Continued)

performance expectations or that needs some "tweaking" here and there. These organizations consider their code generation experiences successful, but a determination as to whether they are deploying *model-driven development* requires a closer look.

Just what is meant by *tweaking*? Based on developer experiences, it can be defined as any non-model-based coding that becomes part of the delivered application. There are many examples.

CASE STUDY 1 State Court System

The first example is an image processing system that was implemented by a court system which chooses to remain anonymous. This application was designed as a record keeper for all court cases. It provides real-time court support; court clerks are able to pull up documents as needed during a trial. They are also able to capture documents via a scanner and log and index them as they are presented as evidence. Finally, they can print documents on an as-needed basis. The entire application was "developed" in an integrated CASE tool, complete with a code generator for a Unix/C target platform. However, the scanner calls were obviously not a part of the application design. In order to incorporate the hardware-dependent code that was required to incorporate scanner processing into the application, "external action blocks" were incorporated into the application design. Most CASE tools with code generation capabilities have the ability to go outside of the model for just this reason. This application represents a successful code generation experience, but because the model alone did not result in the fully generated application, it does not truly represent model-driven development.

CASE STUDY 2 Dylex, LTD.

A more direct success story is that of Dylex, Ltd., Canada's largest fashion retailer.* Using PACLAN from CGI Systems, the Model Allocation Program

*As submitted by Allen Thomerson, Dylex, Ltd., September 30, 1992.

(MAP) was fully generated based on the design models that were input into the tool. The application allocates "large ticket items" (such as coats) across one of Dylex's retail chains. Buyers use the system to distribute an even mixture of styles, sizes, and colors for new items. MAP interfaces with the Dylex purchase order system as well as its national distribution center.

All design and construction were accomplished within Dylex's OS/2 PACLAN configuration. The COBOL/VSAM/CICS application was targeted for an IBM mainframe running VM/VSE. Although the system was relatively small (total development time was 4 months), Dylex estimates a 43 percent improvement in existing developer productivity. Since the development of MAP, 12 additional systems have been generated using PACLAN over the last 2 years. Developer productivity has steadily increased, and at last estimate it had increased almost 200 percent.

Dylex considers itself a model-driven development organization. The MAP application code was 100 percent generated from the design models, and no performance problems have arisen. Maintenance on all PACLAN-generated systems is accomplished by changing the models—developers are not allowed to touch generated COBOL code. When evaluating the nature of Dylex's model-driven development, it is important to consider the breakdown in terms of time of the application development life cycle of MAP:

Design: 25 days
Construction: 75 days
Testing: 20 days
Implementation: 5 days

Considering that "construction" in a forward engineering tool typically involves executing a "generate" option that translates the models into code, it is likely that Dylex's "construction" phase did in fact include some design and redesign. What typically occurs with code generation tools is the discovery of model semantic specifics that become requirements in order to generate certain types of code constructs. Often, the designer cannot possibly be aware of these specific syntaxes until the results are not quite what the modeler wants. However, once the tool's semantics are understood and the resulting generated code is exactly what the designer wants, true model-driven development does occur in subsequent applications.

6

CREATING MODELS FROM CODE

CASE and its resulting models have their advantages for new application development, as we have discussed throughout the book thus far. Unfortunately, as most readers are well aware, most major applications have been in existence for awhile, dating back to the days before CASE or even modeling was commonplace. Those of us who are contemplating the implementation of a corporate repository realize that these applications must be represented.

Representation of unmodeled applications starts with the application code and its hopefully accurate documentation. The older the application, the less structured its code is likely to be. In some cases it is also true that older applications are less likely to have accurate and complete documentation—which brings us back to the code, which is often the only realistic depiction of the application.

Creating models of existing applications is initiated with a set objective in mind. If an inventory of existing applications is the needed objective, it is essential that the effort be scoped. Determine which applications must be modeled, then evaluate the state of their technical implementations. There are basically two ways to model an existing application:

1. Manually, that is, by reading the code, reading the documentation, drawing and documenting the "pictures"
2. Manually, with the aid of a mechanized capture tool

The appropriate method is dependent on each application's code structure and its resident technical platform.

Manual creation of application models requires the ability to read code (even so-called "spaghetti" code), determine its functionality, and supplement that functionality with the business role the application performs. In addition, it requires the ability to relate a usually flat file record layout (or in more recent years a hierarchical database schema) to entities in a data model. Some organizations are only interested at first in the data side of existing applications; others consider the code as an equal contender. In either case the code will have to be reviewed—most old unstructured application code contains a substantial amount of hard-coded data values.

If a mechanized capture tool is being considered, manual effort will still be required. To begin, capture tools are not smart enough to unravel spaghetti code into structured process models. In short, most current tools are still unable to extract design level requirements from physical code (i.e., they are not able to raise physical code to the next higher level of abstraction). The technology is improving, but humans still do much better. Second, most capture products recommend some manual changes to existing code in order to get the best capture results. Finally, as we will see later in this chapter, the resulting model is often only as good as the underlying application code structure.

Another aspect of the modeling effort to consider is the role the resulting model(s) will play. Models that are targeted for application and/or data inventories serve different functional needs than those that will be part of a reengineering effort. Reengineering requires the use of a CASE tool, and ideally a capture result can serve as the starting point for the model's enhancement. Inventories, however, do not necessarily require a CASE tool—many dictionaries/repositories offer a front end which allows input right into the underlying database. Others read existing database catalogs (such as the DB2 catalog) and load the physical database constructs directly. Although this input and its result may not be graphical, the constructs can arrive directly into the dictionary, making for a faster inventory preparation process.

Considering the added value graphical depiction of a model represents, this chapter will concentrate on the role of a CASE tool in the creation of models from existing applications.

■ CASE-BASED REVERSE/REENGINEERING

Reverse engineering is the first step in the CASE-based initiation of application rebuilding. The process typically begins with a capture of the existing data and/or program structures. In many circles the capture itself is often labeled a "reverse engineering" effort. As we will see, captures are the easiest and simplest aspect of the reverse engineering process, and alone they will not result in an accurately reverse engineered application.

The reverse engineering process typically consists of a series of reiterative steps. These steps are common to both the data and process components of the reverse engineering effort. The repetitiveness of the reverse engineering process is directly proportional to the complexity and architectural stability of the item being captured (either data structures or program code or both).

Consider the Requirements of the Capture Tool The first step in reverse engineering is an analysis of how the to-be-used capture tool can yield optimal

```
01 VENDOR.
   03 VENDOR-ID
       05 VENDOR-STATE-CODE          PIC 9(2).
       05 VENDOR-ORG-CODE            PIC 9(5).
       05 VENDOR-TYPE                PIC X(20).
   03 VENDOR-NAME                    PIC X(20).
   03 VENDOR-ADDRESS.
       05 VENDOR-STREET              PIC X(15).
       05 VENDOR-STREET2             PIC X(15).
       05 VENDOR-CITY                PIC X(15).
       05 VENDOR-STATE               PIC X(2).
       05 VENDOR-ZIP                 PIC 9(5).
   03 FILLER                         PIC X(8).
   03 VENDOR-STATUS REDEFINES FILLER.
       05 VENDOR-CREDIT-CODE         PIC X(1).
       05 VENDOR-OLD-CREDIT-CODE     PIC X(1).
       05 FILLER                     PIC X(6).
   03 VENDOR-PAYMENT OCCURS 5.
       05 PAYMENT-DATE               PIC 9(6).
       05 PAYMENT-AMOUNT             PIC 9(7)V99.
   03 FILLER                         PIC X(10).
```

Figure 6.1 Sample Pre-Capture COBOL Structures

results. In every CASE capture tool, the documentation specifically addresses which aspects of the source code or data structures will not be captured. In addition, each tool expects its source code to be in a certain format. The documentation typically advises the user to eliminate certain aspects of the source code or replace them with a clearer representation. For example, many COBOL capture products simply do not translate FILLER when creating a first-cut data model of an existing COBOL structure. This concept makes good logical sense because FILLER is not supposed to represent anything at all. However, we all know what happens to FILLER fields over time—they become populated with data that was not part of the original file design. In the worst scenario the same FILLER field is used to represent many different data fields—the first byte usually indicates what follows. In the best scenario FILLER is renamed to something more meaningful, and appropriate REDEFINES clauses follow. However, many installations are strict about changing COBOL COPYBOOK members. The programmer with a rapidly approaching deadline does not have the time for bureaucratic red tape and library updates. The fudging begins. Figure 6.1 illustrates a typical mediocre compromise.

As illustrated in Fig. 6.1, the REDEFINES clause represents a way of life in application development organizations maintaining massive COBOL-based applications. How does the capture tool handle a REDEFINES clause? Some require their elimination; others may capture the REDEFINES statement as another separate data element. In either scenario determine the role to be played by the captured model and evaluate how the tool's constraints will play a part.

Modify the Source Code as Appropriate Continuing our example, it will most likely be necessary to modify the source code based on the constraints of the capture tool. If a FILLER field is not really a FILLER field anymore, it should be renamed to a meaningful substitute. The new name will be reflected in the captured model. Some data administration advocates may insist on capturing reality as opposed to ideal reality. That is, the renaming of FILLER for the purposes of an accurate capture is only necessary in the input file to be used by the capture tool. If reality still identifies this data as FILLER, perhaps reality should be changed also (even if it involves changing a COPYBOOK and the multiple application programs that use it!).

Identify the Capture Tool's Option Settings Because of the multiple ways in which data and process can be represented in a programming language, many capture tools offer the user a series of options as to how certain constructs should be represented once captured. Consider group level data items (in our example, VENDOR-STATUS, VENDOR-ID, VENDOR-ADDRESS, and VENDOR-PAYMENT). Many capture tools give the user the option of identifying these as either entities or attributes. Maybe this is not an option that can apply globally. In our example VENDOR-PAYMENT and perhaps VENDOR-STATUS are the only group items with entity characteristics. It might be decided that options need to be decided on an object-by-object basis. Other definable options allow the definition of prefixes and suffixes for data items. If, for example, all customer-related data begins with a CUST prefix, CUST should be defined to the capture tool as a prefix. The result would be a capture of the actual data names that follow the defined prefix (e.g., NAME as opposed to CUST-NAME). The treatment of name components as prefixes or suffixes generally requires a data administration oriented strategy. Continuing out example, CUST would need to be defined as an owning entity so to speak, and this is typically a data administration responsibility.

Run the Capture This is the easiest and fastest step in the reverse engineering process. Assuming all tool input requirements were adhered to, the capture can be run in a batch or interactive fashion. In an interactive capture options can be decided as each conflict arises, and the capture can become time consuming. Appreciate the fact that the first capture execution will most likely not be the last.

Evaluate the Resulting Model Figure 6.2 shows the result of our sample COBOL data structure as it was input into the Bachman/Analyst Capture for COBOL. First, note the contents of the Capture Log File. In this file the options used during the capture as well as the capture statistics are saved. Note that we chose to identify all group level elements as entities. In our COBOL data structure, this applied to VENDOR-PAYMENT. The other options pertain to the automatic creation of dimensions and domains based on field name contents (e.g., inclusion of the word DATE) and data types. For the purposes of this illustration, we chose not to execute that ability.

The resulting data model shows two entities, VENDOR and VENDOR-PAYMENT. The relationship between them, an optional one to many, was automatically created by the tool. By obtaining a Bachman Entity Detail report, we can see the details behind the created model. Note that the tool automatically made some assumptions on the minimum and maximum volume of occurrences of each

```
Capture Options:
----------------
Dimension assignment is off.
Group level elements are entities.
The dimension match strategy is not applicable.
Group Domains by data type is off.

A:\PART1\6-1.CBL captured successfully. Elapsed time:
0:01:27
Capture Statistics:
-------------------
The number of entities created is 2.
The number of attributes created is 16.
The number of partnership sets created is 2.
The number of partnerships created is 1.
The number of dimensions created is 0.
The number of domains created is 13.
```

(a)

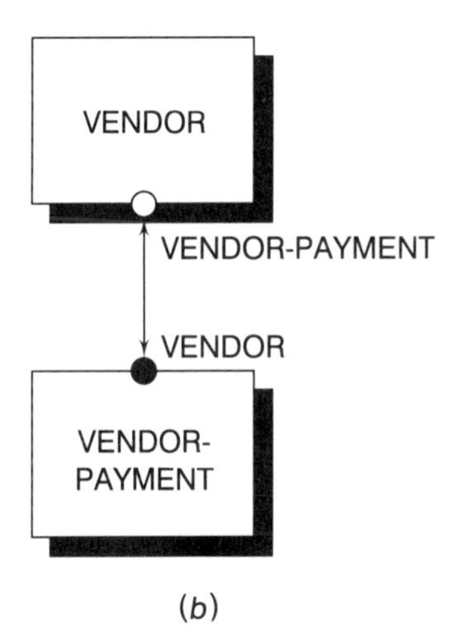

(b)

Figure 6.2 The capture result: (a) capture log file. (b) Resulting data model. (c) Model details.

attribute. It also defaulted each attribute to not allowing nulls and to be sourced from manual input. Component attributes were created where appropriate (see VENDOR-ADDRESS). The partnership set that relates VENDOR to VENDOR-PAYMENT correctly shows a maximum occurrence of 5.

In our simple example we could credit the capture with saving us some time in terms of model creation. However, whether or not the initial captured result needs modification depends on whether or not the Bachman-initiated defaults are satisfactory, and whether or not the model is to be expanded or enhanced as part of a reengineering effort. It may be possible that the capture needs to be redone with

```
Entity:  VENDOR

  Entity MIN Vol = 0,    Entity MAX Vol = 9999999

Attribute:   VENDOR.VENDOR-ID (Owner)
  Nulls not allowed
  Storable;     Source type:   Manual

  Component Attributes:
    VENDOR-STATE-CODE
    VENDOR-ORG-CODE
    VENDOR-TYPE

Attribute:   VENDOR.VENDOR-STATE-CODE (Component)
  Nulls not allowed
  Storable;     Source type:   Manual

  Domain    = VENDOR-STATE-CODE
    Datatype = Integer;  Min Val = 0, Max Val = 99

  Owner Attributes:
    VENDOR-ID

Attribute:   VENDOR.VENDOR-ORG-CODE (Component)
  Nulls not allowed
  Storable;     Source type:   Manual

  Domain     = VENDOR-ORG-CODE
    Datatype = Integer; Min Val = 0, Max Val = 99999

  Owner Attributes:
    VENDOR-ID

Attribute:   VENDOR.VENDOR-TYPE (Component)
  Nulls not allowed
  Storable;     Source Type:   Manual

  Domain     = VENDOR-TYPE
    Datatype = Alphanumeric;  Min Len = 1, Max Len = 20,
     Exp Len = 20

  Owner Attributes:
    VENDOR-ID

Attribute:   VENDOR.VENDOR-NAME
  Nulls not allowed
  Storable;     Source type:   Manual

  Domain     = VENDOR-NAME
    Datatype = Alphanumeric;   Min Len = 1, Max Len = 20,
     Exp Len = 20
```

(c)

Figure 6.2 (Continued)

```
Attribute:   VENDOR.VENDOR-ADDRESS (Owner)
  Nulls not allowed
  Storable;     Source type:   Manual

  Component Attributes:
    VENDOR-STREET
    VENDOR-STREET2
    VENDOR-CITY
    VENDOR-STATE
    VENDOR-ZIP

Attribute:   VENDOR.VENDOR-STREET (Component)
  Nulls not allowed
  Storable;     Source type:   Manual

  Domain     = VENDOR-STREET
    Datatype = Alphanumeric;   Min Len = 1, Max Len = 15,
     Exp Len = 15

  Owner Attributes:
    VENDOR-ADDRESS

Attribute:   VENDOR.VENDOR-STREET2 (Component)
  Nulls not allowed
  Storable;     Source type:   Manual

  Domain     = VENDOR-STREET2
    Datatype = Alphanumeric;  Min Len = 1, Max Len = 15,
     Exp Len = 15
  Owner Attributes:
    VENDOR-ADDRESS

Attribute:   VENDOR.VENDOR-CITY (Component)
  Nulls not allowed
  Storable;     Source type:   Manual

  Domain     = VENDOR-CITY
    Datatype = Alphanumeric;  Min Len = 1, Max Len = 15,
     Exp Len = 15

  Owner Attributes:
    VENDOR-ADDRESS

Attribute:   VENDOR.VENDOR-STATE (Component)
  Nulls not allowed
  Storable;     Source type:   Manual

  Domain     = VENDOR-STATE
    Datatype = Alphanumeric;  Min Len = 1, Max Len = 2,
     Exp Len 2
```

Figure 6.2 (Continued)

```
    Owner Attributes:
      VENDOR-ADDRESS

Attribute:    VENDOR.VENDOR-ZIP (Component)
    Nulls not allowed
    Storable;      Source type:    Manual

    Domain      = VENDOR-ZIP
      Datatype = Integer;   Min Val = 0, Max Val = 99999

    Owner Attributes:
      VENDOR-ADDRESS

Attribute:    VENDOR.VENDOR-STATUS (Owner)
    Nulls not allowed
    Storable;      Source type:    Manual

    Component Attributes:
      VENDOR-CREDIT-CODE
      VENDOR-OLD-CREDIT-CODE

Attribute:    VENDOR.VENDOR-CREDIT-CODE (Component)
    Nulls not allowed
    Storable;      Source type:    Manual

    Domain      = VENDOR-CREDIT-CODE
      Datatype = Alphanumeric;   Min Len = 1, Max Len = 1,
        Exp Len = 1

    Owner Attributes:
      VENDOR-STATUS

    Attribute:    VENDOR.VENDOR-OLD-CREDIT-CODE (Component)
    Nulls not allowed
    Storable;      Source type:    Manual

    Domain      = VENDOR-OLD-CREDIT-CODE
      Datatype = Alphanumeric;   Min Len = 1, Max Len = 1,
        Exp Len = 1

    Owner Attributes:
      VENDOR-STATUS
PSet:    VENDOR.VENDOR-PAYMENT

    Joins:
      VENDOR-PAYMENT.VENDOR

    PSet MIN Vol = 0,     PSet MAX Vol = 5

Entity:     VENDOR-PAYMENT

    Entity MIN Vol = 0,     Entity MAX Vol = 9999999
```

Figure 6.2 (Continued)

```
Attribute:    VENDOR-PAYMENT.PAYMENT-DATE
  Nulls not allowed
  Storable;     Source type:   Manual

  Domain     = PAYMENT-DATE
    Datatype = Integer;  Min Val = 0, Max Val = 999999

Attribute:    VENDOR-PAYMENT.PAYMENT-AMOUNT
  Nulls not allowed
  Storable;     Source type:   Manual

  Domain:     = PAYMENT-AMOUNT
    Datatype = Real;  Min Val = 0.0, Max Val = 9999999.99

PSet:   VENDOR-PAYMENT.VENDOR

  Joins:
    VENDOR.VENDOR-PAYMENT

  PSet MIN Vol = 1,    PSet MAX Vol = 1

Summary Information for C:\BACHMAN\DESIGNS\VENDORS.AN
  Total Entities:                2
  Total Free attributes:         0
  Total Entity Attributes:       16 ( 8.00 per Entity)
  Total PSets:                   2 (1 1.00 per Entity)
  Total Keys:                    0
  Total FK Attributes:           0
  Total Notes:                   0
  Total Lines of Desc/Notes:     0
```

Figure 6.2 (Continued)

different option settings. Perhaps, for example, VENDOR-ADDRESS is best labeled as another entity despite the current design. Perhaps knowledge of the actual data reveals the fact that some vendors are stored twice (with different vendor id's?) because they have multiple addresses. The real issue is whether or not the VENDOR-ID applies to a vendor or to a vendor/address combination.

Refining the Resulting Model Depending on the ultimate objective of the reengineering effort, the next tasks involve possible recaptures or refinement of the model within the respective CASE tool (in our case, the Bachman Analyst). It is at this stage that the reengineering process actually begins.

The reengineering of existing applications and/or their associated databases is a major effort. Most organizations do not reengineer for the sake of improving existing code structure; instead they usually intend to increase or modify the existing application's functionality. In this respect reverse engineering has immense similarities to traditional information engineering in that new requirements need to be defined and modeled in order to eventually result in revised application designs.

A major difference lies in the fact that a substantial part of the detective work is aided by the existence of first-cut capture results.

CASE STUDY New York City Transit Authority

One example of a major reverse engineering project is the State of Good Repair (SOGR) project which was started by the New York City Transit Authority (NYCTA) in the first quarter of 1991.*All public bus and subway systems within New York City are governed and operated by NYCTA.

Consistent IS production interruptions resulted in a needed evaluation of the existing mainframe environment. It was determined that less than 5 percent of production jobs had adequate operating instructions. In addition, software modules were redundantly populated across multiple development libraries, which were often being used for production runs. Other problems included insufficient management control and security, poorly structured code, and the lack of a data dictionary.

A decision was made to undertake a 2.5-year effort to revitalize the existing production applications. Old, undocumented COBOL applications were to be fully documented as well as analyzed to determine the degree of reengineering that would be required to correct existing deficiencies. The documentation objective also included the population of a data dictionary.

This effort was divided into several phases. The first phase, discussed here, concentrates only on the capture, analysis, and documentation of existing applications. Later phases will determine which applications should be reengineered and result in the beginning of the reengineering process. Figure 6.3 depicts an overview of the entire reverse engineering project.

The data dictionary deployed by the NYCTA was Computer Associates' IDMS/IDD. This decision was based on the preexistence of IDMS databases. Adpac's PM/SS was chosen as the data capture and analysis tool. The data being analyzed existed primarily in sequential VSAM files. Program analysis was targeted for PathVu from XA Systems.

Because the capture and analysis of data results in quicker and more accurate results than the same task performed on application programs, efforts in phase 1 have concentrated on the data portion of existing applications.

Results have exceeded expectations. Using Adpac's PM/SS, the capture results have represented the underlying data with 98 percent accuracy. In fact, the only problem experienced during this data capture phase was the loss of some aliases. Apparently, NYCTA applications exceeded the maximum number of aliases that could be handled by Adpac's tool. When the data capture process is completed, NYCTA expects to download the captured data definitions into a PC-based tool (most probably Knowledgeware's ADW). The tool will be used to complete the documentation process via the creation of data models, data flow diagrams, and so on.

---

*Louis J. Marcoccia, "Reverse Engineering," paper and followup phone interview, September 30, 1992.

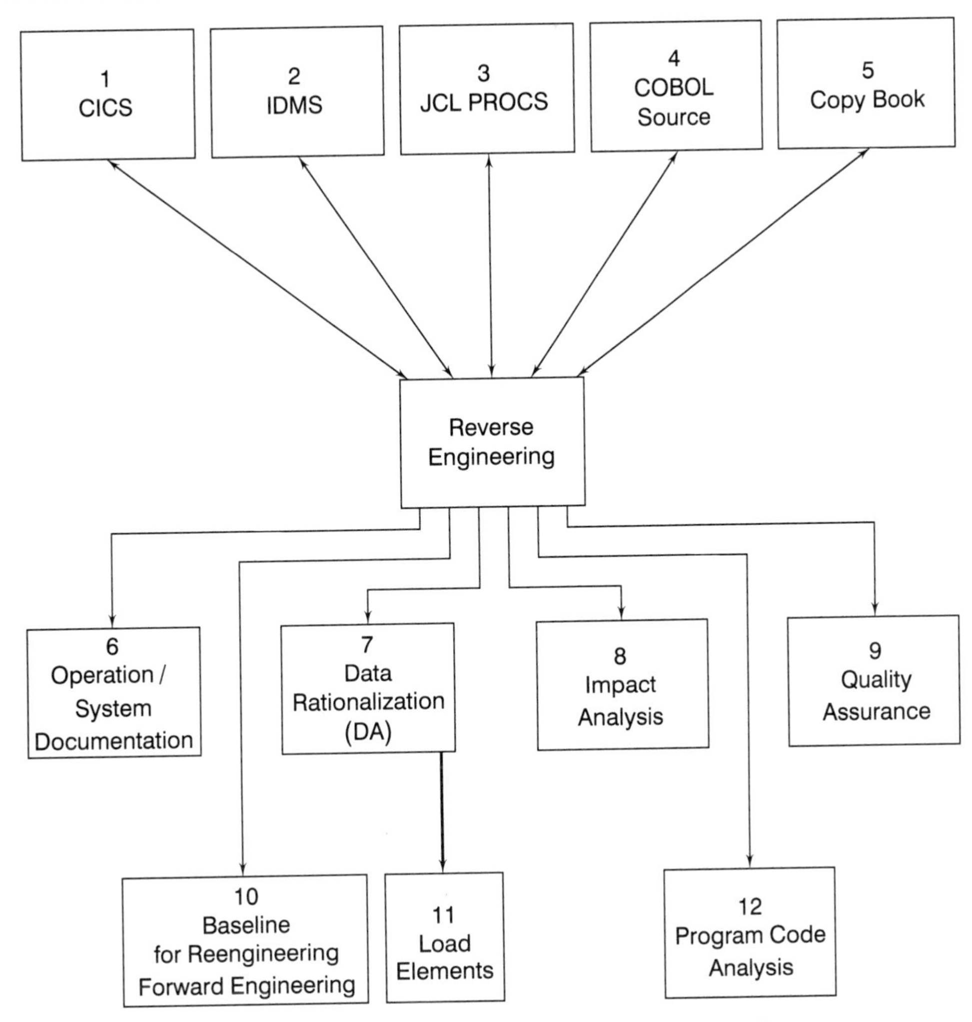

Figure 6.3 The New York City Transit Authority. Reverse Engineering Effort.

Process capture (program analysis) results have not been as accurate. As of September 1992, only 6 of the 40 applications targeted for analysis by PathVu had been completed. Expectations have become more realistic, and PathVu's primary role will be the identification of "dirty" code. The documentation effort will require manual intervention.

The NYCTA agrees that the use of its selected reverse engineering tools has saved considerable time and money. Its estimate of cost savings due to reduced maintenance time is an average of $200,000 per year. The amount of annual increased maintenance required on the analyzed applications has decreased from 9 to 7 percent. The documentation effort associated with the reverse engineering process has also saved an average of $175,000 in operating costs. The effort was so well received that it has now become part of standard developer training. The NYCTA expects to train 200 people in reverse engineering procedures, as well as the use of Adpac's PM/SS.

Once existing applications have been documented, PM/SS will continue to be functional in the analysis and capture of purchased software packages.

7

SHARING TODAY'S GOOD MODELS

With or without the improvements cited thus far, good models become better work savers when they are shared. Sharing can be as simple as the passing of paper reports among project members or as complicated as on-line access to a centralized repository. Model sharing can require its own distributed architecture if the "sharers" are distributed across multiple platforms and locations. In any event the way models are shared can almost become secondary to the reason models are shared.

■ THE CODEVELOPED APPLICATION

The primary reason model sharing came to be is the nature of CASE (in terms of installation expense) and the size of most corporate development projects. Aside from initial pilot projects, most application efforts involve a multiperson team. The team usually is functionally divided, and people may be pulled from separate physical organizations for the purposes of knowledge pooling. The models therefore often represent a collection of viewpoints or functional roles. Resource constraints usually prevent each developer from having a dedicated copy of the modeling tool. So, not only is model sharing a required aspect of the project's development, but so is sharing of the tool itself in many cases.

Sharing of the tool simplifies sharing of the models. In the simplest of cases, one standalone copy of the tool implies one standalone copy of each model. Developer A, responsible for the database design, creates a logical data model. Developer B accesses and references the same data model when developing process models. All models reside in the same location. The sharing of updates depends on the integrity within the tool itself (if a centralized dictionary/encyclopedia is the backbone of all models, then updates are obviously automatically shared) and how it is implemented. For example, the data modeler changes the data model by eliminating the

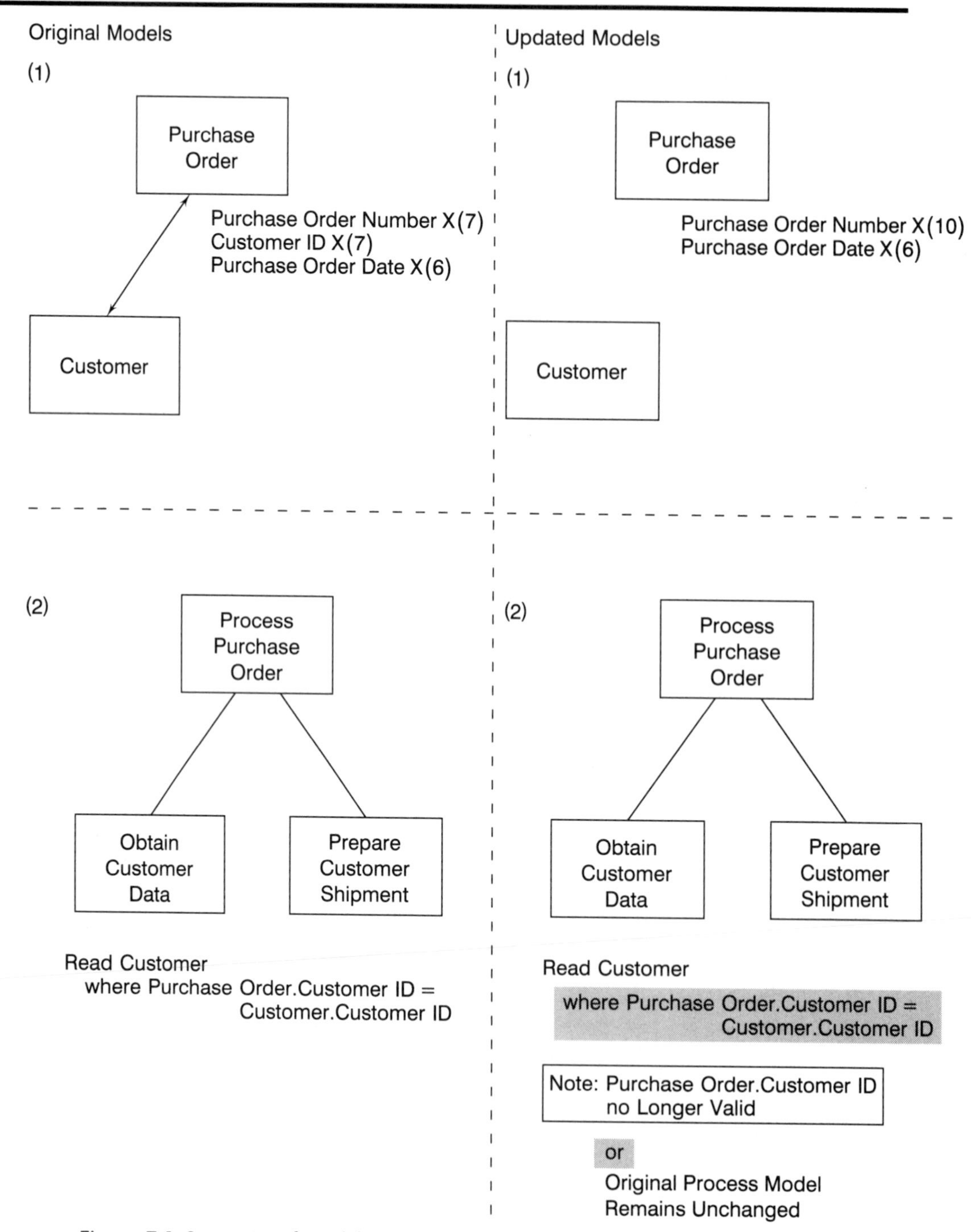

Figure 7.1 Semantics of model update in a standalone environment

foreign key *Customer ID* from the entity *Purchase Order* (see Fig. 7.1). This attribute was already referenced in a process model that used it to access customer data for the purposes of preparing the customer shipment. After the change to the data model–based attribute (the source of the original object), some CASE tools notify the process modeler that one of the referenced objects has changed, and leave an option with the process modeler–the modeler can accept the change by modifying any dependent internal items (e.g., the temporary file) or the modeler can ignore it by creating another internal object (a substring of the modified 10-character key attribute, in this case). Other CASE tools do nothing automatically, but leave the update validation to user-initiated execution of the tool's integrity checking capabilities. In either scenario verbal communication among the project members is mandatory to prevent the development of a set of isolated, conflicting models. Figure 7.1 illustrates the possibilities of model update semantics in a standalone copy of a tool, shared among project members.

The model sharing situation becomes a little more complicated when additional copies of the tool are purchased. Each copy still operates in a standalone mode, yet the same application is being developed across the multiple copies. Each workstation has its own encyclopedia, and any interencyclopedia communication occurs outside of the tool. Following the preceding example, it is quite feasible that Developer A changes the data model on his or her workstation and Developer B continues process model development unaware of the change. Typically, when multiple encyclopedias are involved, weekly encyclopedia consolidation is usually a required routine. However, consolidation could mean overwrite of incompatible model components if the proper communication did not occur among the application developers.

As the proliferation of multiple encyclopedias became a maintenance headache, CASE vendors introduced LAN versions of their products. The problem of multiple encyclopedias was eliminated by the existence of one server-based encyclopedia which was accessed by all client CASE tool users. However, model sharing for the purposes of application codevelopment was still difficult, depending on how update and access locking were handled by the tool. Continuing our example, in the worst scenario Developer A's update resulted in the same scenario as that depicted in Fig. 7.1, the standalone environment. Also, depending on the timing of Developer A's update, Developer B could have locked Developer A out and prevented the update from taking priority over its use in referencing process models. Fortunately, most LAN versions of CASE encyclopedias do allow user-id-based priority at the element level, some allow ownership even at the element attribute level (e.g., the entity description could be owned by a different user than the entity itself).

With all of the options available to enable model sharing within an application, this issue becomes focused more on how the model should be segmented for sharing and how common model components should be updated.

■ HOW A CASE MODEL IS SHARED TODAY

Despite the physical configurations discussed previously, successful model sharing among application developers is based on successful partitioning of the application modeling process. From a project role point of view, the modeling task is often divided based on developer responsibility. At the highest level the analysts are separated from the programmers. Even when project members function as programmer/analysts, they participate first as analysts and later as programmers.

Model Sharing Among Analysts / Designers Beginning with the multiple types of models developed by the application analyst, the analyst role is often further divided between data and process responsibilities. To begin, it is quite typical for one designer (or a subgroup of designers) to have responsibility for the application's data. This effort, usually one of the first to be assigned, is often the focal point for remaining process-oriented development.

The complexity of the data model's shareability grows when the data model itself is developed by more than one analyst. This is often true in major corporate applications. Today, the data modeling responsibility is divided among participating analysts in one of several ways:

By subject area. Based on data expertise, data modelers are often assigned their responsibility areas by major entity categories (subject areas). For example, a data analyst who has worked on a major billing application has most likely gained experience with the types of customer data found in the company's major applications. This data analyst, now assigned to this application, would be a logical choice for modeling the customer-specific areas within the application's data model. Other analysts are assigned subject areas based on their relevant experience. A senior data modeler, experienced in multiple areas of corporate data, is then responsible for integrating the multiple subject areas. Figure 7.2 illustrates the semantics of how such a data modeling approach would work.

By data source. In major application consolidation efforts, the data comes from several sources. Typically, representatives from each supplying application are gathered as part of the data modeling effort for the new application. Individual responsibilities cover the data by application source. This division is not as clean cut as the previous in that many overlapping subject areas will exist among the source-based models. In more complicated situations the details of each application-sourced subject area will differ between applications (they may not even share the same primary identifiers). The logical data modelers work separately, modeling the data to be extracted from their individual application areas. When these separate models become integrated, many of the source application-specific contradictions must be addressed. It is often at this stage of the application consolidation effort that "surprises" are uncovered.

By user-specific function. Another data modeling task separation can occur based on the way in which the data is used. For example, consider

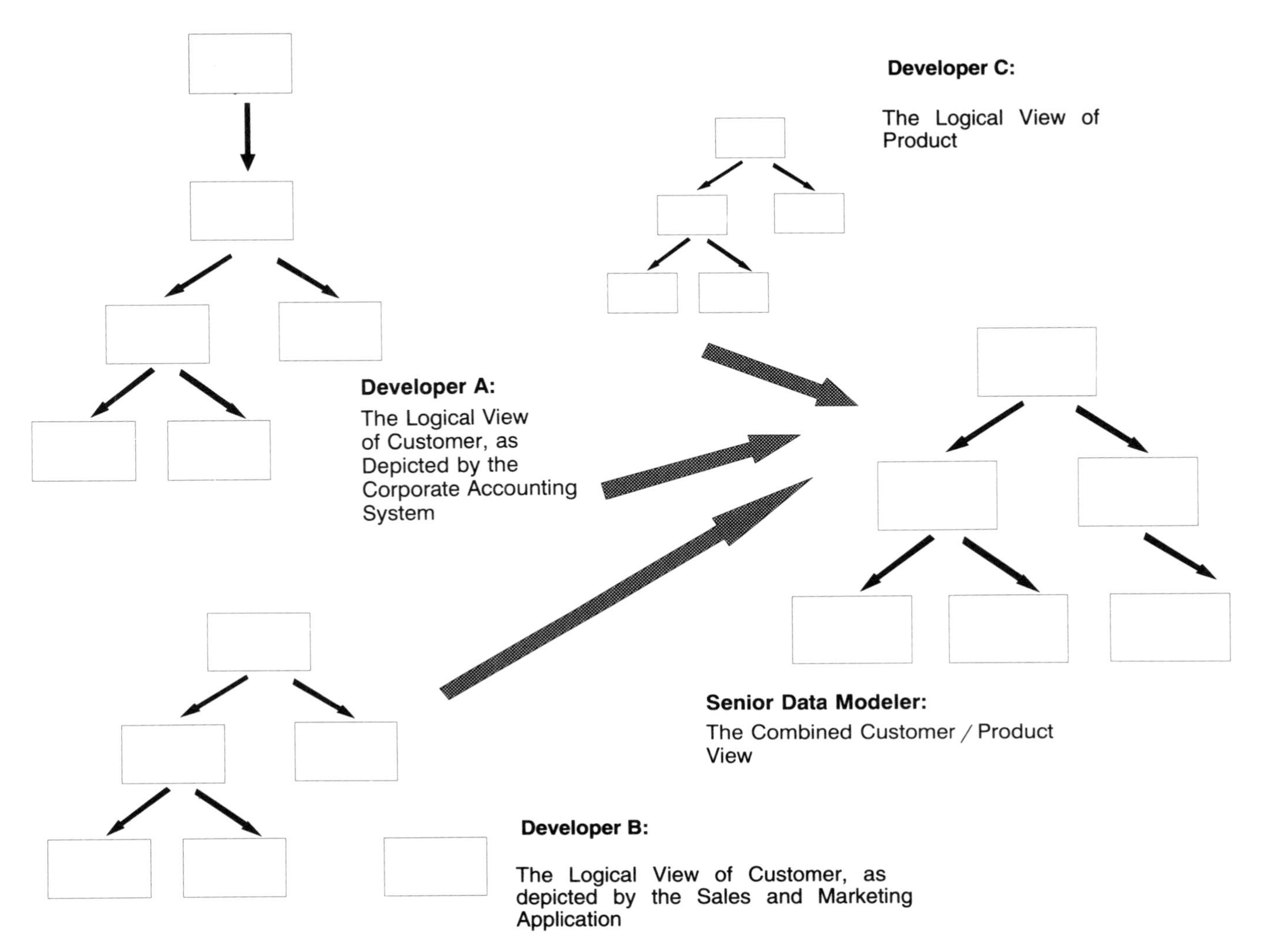

Figure 7.2 Codevelopment of the logical data model

the processing of an insurance claim. The basic steps include (not necessarily in order):

- The input and tracking of the reported claim
- The verification of the claimant's coverage
- Claim approval or denial
- Calculation of the monetary value of the claim
- Payment of the claim (or notification of claim rejection)
- Closing of the reported claim

The subject areas involved include: *policy*, *policyholder*, (customer), *claimant*, and *claim*. The data modeling effort could be divided such that one modeler models the data from a policy perspective. In typical insurance companies a department exists solely for the purpose of marketing policies and establishing coverage. Data included in this data submodel would cross the policy, policyholder, and claim subject areas. Another data model could represent the claim payment perspective. In this view all subject areas would be touched. Finally, another modeler could also represent claim payment, but from an actuarial perspective. This model would look at the claim payment as a statistical event needed to calculate policy premiums by comparing the statistics surrounding the claim and the involved claimant. This data model subdivision has more of a process-oriented flavor. When the models are integrated, it is likely that data existing in one data model will not exist in another and the integrated model will represent a composite view of all process-specific needs.

Once the integrated data model exists, it is a required resource for all process modelers. Today, CASE-based multideveloper projects require its storage within an accessible encyclopedia.

As the logical data model is completed, the data side of the application development process moves toward physical design. Process design uses the data model as a basis for all of its data-specific processing. Depending on whether or not the CASE tool contains an integrated encyclopedia, each process model accesses and refers to the same data objects existing in the completed data model. When the CASE tool is not integrated, it is possible for process modelers to use the same names and terms to refer to their process-specific data regardless of whether or not they conflict with the centralized data model. The strategy for sharing a data model among application analysts should depend on whether or not the underlying CASE tool is truly integrated.

In the easier scenario assume the existence once and only once of each object belonging to the data model. As the process designs are developed, each by a member of the application development team, reference to data is required to be consistent (by the tool) as long as the same names are used by the process modelers. The process modeler must use the tool's "look-up" feature if the data object name is uncertain. Otherwise, most tools would simply create a new object if the name mentioned in the process model did not already exist. In order to ensure the use of the application's data model where appropriate, process modelers should have immediate access to the data model constructs. Depending on the tool set deployed, this access could be available via a menu-driven encyclopedia access function, or, worst case, a hard copy of the encyclopedia's contents should be immediately accessible as a reference.

When the tool does not guarantee the integrated access of its encyclopedia constructs across models, the modelers themselves must ensure that objects are consistently deployed and referenced. Hard copies of the encyclopedia's contents must be a part of each modeler's resources. Then, at regular intervals, depending on the rate of model completion, integrity checks must be made against all process models and their referenced data.

Finally, just as integration testing is a standard part of a programmer's job, integration of separately developed process models is also required. Many CASE tools themselves provide utilities to ensure that named processes have defined inputs and outputs, or that processes that are called by a particular process do in fact exist in the encyclopedia. However, just as walkthroughs are used to validate pretested code, walkthroughs (or design reviews) should be used to validate the application's design. Discrepancies among process models can be corrected when the entire team of analysts has a chance to review the full application design.

To summarize, model sharing among analysts and designers should concentrate on the following objectives:

- A centralized, shareable data model
- Process and data model integration
- Process model connection and integration
- Elimination of process model redundancy

Model Sharing Among Developers Continuing the application development life cycle, the models created and validated by the analysts, once accessible by the developers, increase the accuracy of analyst/programmer communication. Typically, developers should have access to the data and process models, because, when combined, they should represent the application specifications. Depending on the deployed tool, however, the modeling constructs within the tool may not have been sufficient enough to relay the full set of application requirements. In many situations the CASE-based models needed supplementation via word processing documents, graphical depictions of system icons, and detailed output layouts for example.

When the full set of application specifications is submitted to the developer, the proportion that originated in a CASE tool should indicate whether or not direct developer access to the models would result in immediate benefit. If the CASE-based models alone are not specific or complete enough for an application developer to complete the coding effort, then model sharing among developers can be made functional via paper copies of the CASE-originated specifications along with the supplemental documents. If the tool's models do cover the entire gamut of application specs, the sharing of the models among developers would serve to ensure the correct interpretation of all models by each developer regardless of whether the particular model is being implemented by the accessing developer.

For example, assume developers have been assigned distinct functional application pieces based on the process specifications. As each developer codes his or her application section, questions about the interface to and from other processes as well as database access are common. By sharing the full set of models with the developers, answers to these questions can be resolved almost instantly via model access and validation.

In a fully functional model-based development environment, some of the physical implementation of the design models is also accomplished via a CASE tool. Obviously, model sharing among developers would be a normal activity in this scenario. Many installations let the analyst/designer generate the code and then pass it to a developer for testing and validation. The interaction of model and code is always model driven, so developer-recommended changes to the code are referred to the modeling analyst. In the worst case an external subroutine is coded and simply included in the design via a "call."

Therefore, sharing among developers can achieve the following:

- Design/specification validation within the programming project team
- Validation of model-generated code, easy interaction between developer and designer
- Increased analyst/programmer communication via common knowledge of the application design

Model sharing serves different audiences when the model creators are not the model interpreters. Original CASE covered only the logical aspects of application development; hence, sharing these models with developers aids more as a communication medium than anything else. The advent of integrated CASE (ICASE) has brought the logical models down to a much more detailed physical level. The next chapter summarizes today's models by putting them into the broader context of MIS deliverables.

8

A SUMMARIZED VIEW OF TODAY'S MODELS

As we begin to consider models from a repository perspective, it is important to always be aware of the major evaluative aspects that place the repository tag on today's application models. Despite the original purpose under which each model was developed, once part of an accessible repository, contents are bound to take on different perspectives.

Perhaps an entity–relationship (E–R) model represents the logical data picture of an order entry system. It was used many years ago by developers as a backbone for the implemented physical database. Today, it resides in its originating CASE tool and remains relatively stagnant (the order entry database has not changed in quite some time). Consider its role as a repository member. It now serves a variety of potential purposes:

- It identifies the data that exists in the order entry database (by logical business name).
- It potentially relates order entry data to similar data in other application models or to an enterprise data model.
- It shows the decision support end-user where order-specific data originates.

When the original E–R model was developed, and throughout its life cycle tenure, it was most likely not intended for access or reference by anyone other than its immediate application development team. Once a repository is implemented, its contents most likely become accessible to audiences that expand beyond any model's original recipients. This chapter summarizes the necessary perspectives under which repository-targeted models, either developed or to be developed, should be evaluated.

■ MODEL ACCURACY AND ACCESSIBILITY

Of most obvious consideration is the model's accuracy. If your organization does not currently have a quality control function which evaluates models against their production implementations, it may be a necessary addition once the decision has been made to implement a repository. Once a model becomes available to a larger audience, it must remain accurate. The most obvious way to ensure this accuracy is via direct interface between the repository and the modeling tool. But does this really ensure accuracy? What it does ensure is that the repository contains an exact copy of the model as depicted in the interfacing tool! Accuracy from a repository perspective means a precise representation of reality, regardless of the level of abstraction. If the models have already been implemented, their physical counterparts must not contradict the models themselves. If the models are part of a current development effort, their accuracy can only be gauged by a clear vision of the system's requirements. Models which were themselves used to generate application code are more likely to be accurate representations of their physical reality. However, once the code is modified without its backbone model, the same problem ensues. Quality control is a natural fit within a repository administration function. Unless the repository models are to be the direct producers of their physical implementations, even throughout application maintenance, manual or "nonrepository" inspection will be necessary as models and their subsequent updates are loaded. More detail on how models can become validated as part of the repository population will be provided in Part Five.

One major improvement a repository provides for today's models is increased accessibility. As discussed previously, it is this very reason that demands model accuracy. Evaluate the availability of your models against several potential audiences:

- Developers and maintainers of their source application
- End-users of their source application
- Other developers
- MIS management
- MIS planners
- Data administration personnel
- Decision support analysts
- Database administrators
- Data processing operations

If, in fact, the preceding functional areas are already requesting and receiving models, how is it happening? Model access can range from the printing of CASE encyclopedia reports and graphical diagrams to actual on-line query of the base encyclopedia. As we will discuss later in Part Five, repository-based access to today's models will most likely require the addition of categorical indexes which will classify a model and many of its components into the areas that will most likely be of interest to its accessing user base. As models become considered for the repository, examine how they should be classified. Then consider how often these classifications will be queried and by what functional areas. Strive to make your repository-based models accessible to those who want them for the purposes for which they are seeking assistance. Begin now by centralizing model requests (perhaps the beginnings of a repository administration function). Many applications are already doing this with requests for database extacts. The same principles apply. As requests get logged, they can more easily be analyzed in terms of similarities: the same types of requests by the same types of people, or different types of requests by the same types of people, and so on.

As model requests are categorized, evaluate the frequency with which they occur. Also consider how long it takes to fulfill these requests and whether or not the time lag is hindering the analysis that will take place with the delivered model components. Common sense will reveal the most common types of requests and identify the need for each requestor to have on-line access to the planned repository.

Today's models should be accurate and accessible if they are to benefit from implementation in a repository. Even if today's accessibility is not as polished as it would be with an on-line distributed repository, the fact that models are desired implies their worth.

■ THE MODEL AS A MAINSTREAM MIS DELIVERABLE

Once today's models are geared toward accuracy and accessibility, the next step is an evaluation of the proportion of MIS development that is represented. If modeling has become a required aspect of all new application development (*new* usually implies all application development after a certain date), eventually modeled applications will become more common than unmodeled applications. If modeling is not a required part of applicatin development, it is likely that models will never become commonplace.

There are many ways in which the model becomes a mainstream MIS deliverable. The easiest (we all have different definitions of *easy*) is via mandate. Just as JCL streams are a requirement for batch applications before they are turned over to production operations, applications that are in development could be required to have the full set of CASE-based models "approved" before coding begins. Approval could mean many things, depending on the scope under which application models are being evaluated. If they are being evaluated purely as models of the to-be-coded application, their approval will more likely involve adherence to modeling methodology constructs and evaluations for completeness. If the models are also being targeted for residence in a repository, their approval could also involve integration points with a corporate or departmental model, ensuring the maximum use of common data and processes and the proper indexing and labeling of the model and its key components to allow maximum user access at a later date. Of course, if CASE tools are also generating the code, the models are already a required deliverable in the application development process. The difference, however, can lie in the different objectives that a model could have—one immediate objective, the generation of efficient, executable application code; another, perhaps secondary, objective, the graphical and backup dictionary depiction of an application's functionality, data, and business role.

How does one mandate model delivery? In most MIS organizations standards that cover one or more aspects of application development, delivery, and execution are in existence. Whether or not the standards are followed is most likely dependent on whether or not they are mandatory. Mandatory adherence to any standard implies the "no exceptions" mentality. If, for example, applications cannot be moved over to production without the input of their JCL run stream, backup, and recovery procedures into a central dictionary, a mandatory standard guarantees that all production applications are documented the same way and in the same place (the central dictionary). Operations management ensures adherence to this standard by refusing to run an application unless the documentation was entered. As soon as one application slips through this mandatory process, the standard is no longer mandatory. The secret to success in this area is strong management that has the authority to say "no." Operations management, in this example, in not the only involved management function. Application management, and perhaps at times even user management, must be aware of this policy and not expect to be granted an "exception."

Getting back to our original question regarding the mandated delivery of application models, the same principles apply. Perhaps application coding cannot begin until the application has been fully modeled. There are many ways to implement a rule like this, but the application development resource and the way it is assigned are directly impacted. Typically, development efforts are staffed on a project-by-project basis. When an end-user (or at times an MIS) idea for a new development effort originates, an approval process usually begins. This process includes the submission of a project plan, project schedule, project budget, and optional technical addendum to an internal project steering committee. Here, the project is approved or denied, and money is allocated. At this point the project is assigned a project manager, and staffing on the MIS side includes analysts and developers. Perhaps the approval process should deliver a *phased* budget allocation. Phase 1 of the project could involve analysis and require the delivery of detailed application models. These models would be the prerequisite to approval of phase 2 development. Many readers may already be skeptical, because this approach resembles the typical waterfall development process where applications are developed via a similar approach. What we all know from experience is that applications are usually more successful when the development process is iterative; that is, we do not travel from one phase to the next without ever looking back (see Fig. 8.1).

Iterative development does not prevent the mandatory delivery of application models, as proposed. Once a set of models is delivered, it is not barred from modification. However, the *initial* set must be relatively complete. An "outsider," one who was not part of the initial application team should be able to understand the system's functionality with enough technical detail via the presented models. Then, as changes ensue, the impact on the original design is more clearly understood via the required submission of model revisions. The mandated delivery of

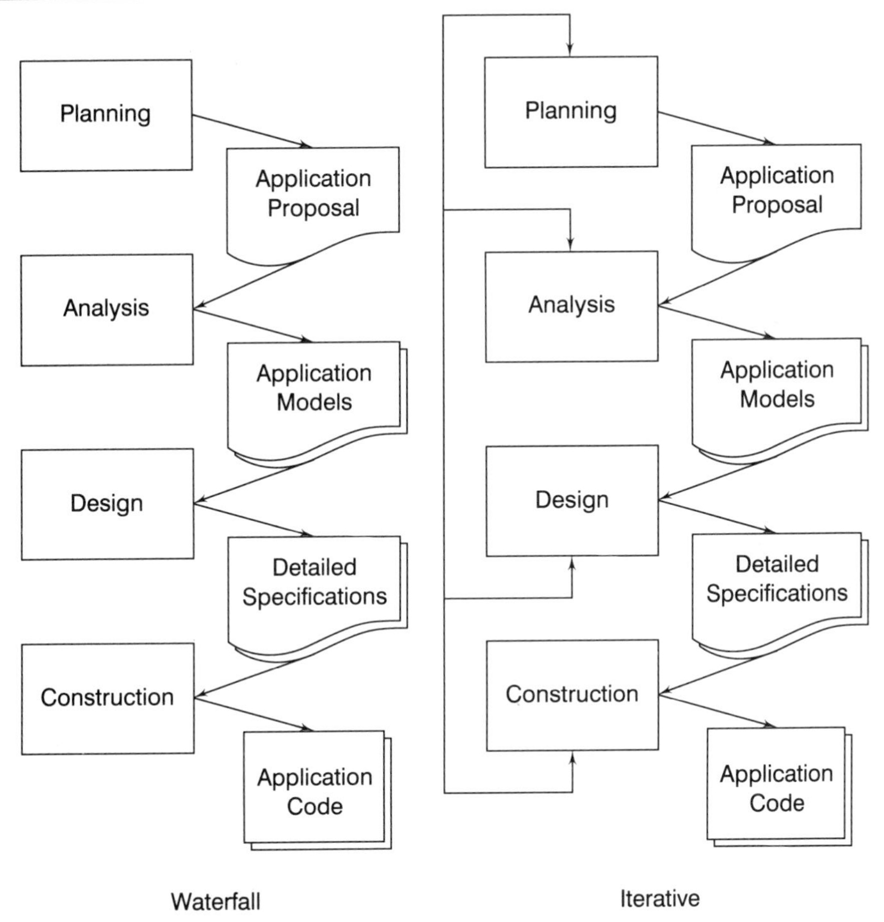

Figure 8.1 Waterfall vs. iterative application development

models does not guarantee improved application delivery. However, it does guarantee a more complete analysis step in that models themselves, once related, will require a CASE-initiated sanity check. These sanity checks often point out inconsistencies which traditionally have led to faulty application logic. Furthermore, mandated application models will lead to more complete repositories.

There are other mandated practices for ensuring delivery of accurate application models. The best are dependent on many installation-specific factors, including how well current standards are adhered to and how often "exceptions" are granted. Consider the following requirements for transitioning the model into a mainstream MIS deliverable:

1. The delivery of application models must be a universal requirement—no exceptions!

2. The timeliness of mandated model delivery within the application development cycle must prevent after-the-fact modeling. Models should not be created after applications have been coded.
3. Submitted models should go through a quality assurance check. As discussed previously, this functional area could be the beginning of the repository administration function. The check would ensure adherence to modeling standards as well as an attempt to eliminate redundancy across application models. As models are reviewed they should be evaluated for repository readiness.

■ THE MODEL'S ROLE IN THE APPLICATION LIFE CYCLE

Mandatory delivery of application models does not guarantee that the models are used for the best intentions. Unless the models are part of a new model-driven application, the hooks between the models and the actual code and databases exist on faith. In order for repository-resident models to serve as accurate maps of their implementations, the link between the models and reality should ideally be physical; that is, the models either directly create their physical implementations or are directly linked via repositoy relationships (Part Five will detail how the logical and physical worlds relate within a repository). More important, the logical/physical connection must be accurately preserved throughout the application's life cycle, including maintenance.

Continuing the concept of an application model delivery mandate, consider postproduction application changes and how models currently participate in the process. In many installations CASE-based models often freeze well before the code does. Star analysts rarely stay on projects once they are cut over, unless the cutover was functionally minimal compared to the overall application (in other words, the cutover was not really a cutover, but a first-phase delivery). Maintenance (or in many cases, "corrections") usually carries a negative professional stigma—programmers are forced to retrofit their ideas into existing designs, and their creativity is hindered. In fact, in many organizations, maintenance (whether it is during the analysis/design or programming phase) is the starting point for new MIS recruits (often right out of college). Based on the professional experience level of the maintenance programmer, modeling is not usually a part of the preexisting skill set. However, it is this fact alone (the typical business acumen of the new maintenance programmer) that reinforces the need for the model's role in application maintenance.

If you once were a maintenance programmer (and most of us started that way), think back to your first assignment. How was most of your time spent? If you worked on a typical major application, you probably went through the following steps (see Fig. 8.2):

1. *Evaluation of the maintenance request*. The maintenance request was most likely presented in textural form. If inputs or outputs were being modified, they may also have been included as attachments (record and report layouts —existing and/or proposed). If you were lucky, a flowchart or data flow

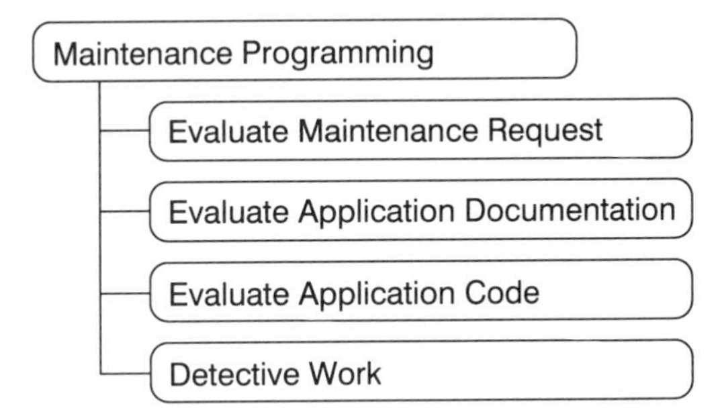

Figure 8.2 Typical implementation of a maintenance request

diagram accompanied the package. Your task at this point involved acquiring an understanding of what was requested. Perhaps phone calls and/or meetings were held with the requestor.

2. *Evaluation of the application documentation.* Once the request was understood, the fun began. Implementing the request involved figuring out the functionality of the existing application as well as how and where to best implement the change. In most cases the application documentation did not help much. It was either out of date or not detailed enough to convey which modules performed which functions and how the modules interrelated.
3. *Evaluation of the application code.* The next step involved actual reading of the code. In all likelihood the code was not structured and contained many poorly named temporary fields which were crucial parts of each implemented postproduction maintenance request. Sporadic comments might have helped, but the code did not render itself completely understandable—at least not for the purposes of your immediate assignment.
4. *Detective work.* By now, at least one week had passed and your coding had not yet begun. The next source of information was the experienced programmer—one who had worked on this application before. In many cases this person had the answers to your questions, and you were now ready to code. If not, your detective work became "trial-and-error" work. You implemented the request in what seemed the most logical place, and then when it affected other existing application processing, or it did not work as expected, you tried something else. This iterative cycle continued until either success or location of the source of knowledge—usually someone who had been through this before or your supervisor.

In retrospect, consider the time savings and efficiencies that would have been realized if the application was accurately modeled. Step 3 would most likely have been eliminated, and step 4 would have been renamed *Implementation*. However, additional steps would have been changed, altering the nature of the original steps

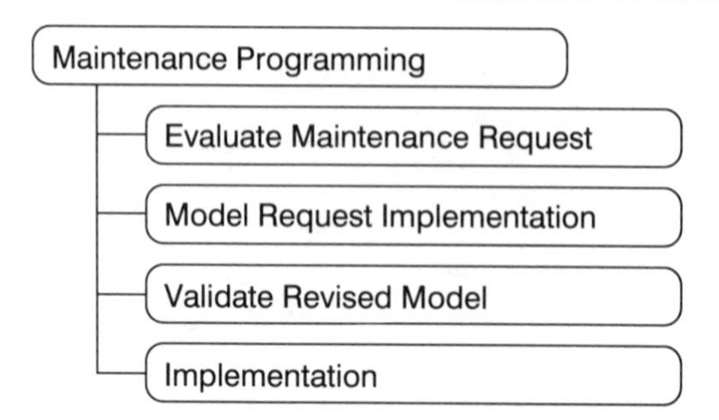

Figure 8.3 Model-based maintenance Implementation

2 through 4 as follows (see Fig 8.3):

2. *Modeling the request's implementation*. Depending on how models were deployed, the model of the request's impact could have accompanied the request itself. However, if the request came from an end-user, and you are the application analyst, this responsibility comes with the implementation of the maintenance request. Here, the existing model is changed, incorporating the functionality of the requested enhancement. The impact of the enhancement could have involved the modification of one or several application models. In an organization with deployed model-driven development, model enhancement *is* request implementation (or a substantial portion of it). In an organization with required model delivery, the model modification serves as the design of the maintenance request's implementation.
3. *Validating the revised model*. Going back to the requestor with what is proposed as well as how it will be done and how long it will take requires usable documentation. The model serves as the common ground for these discussions.
4. *Implementation*. Implementation is now more straightforward. Detective work is unnecessary with a good, detailed, accurate model of the application as it existed before the change as well as how it will exist after the implementation of the requested maintenance.

This cyclical model-driven maintenance process keeps the application tied to the CASE-based model. Mandating model enhancement as part of the maintenance cycle should be a part of mandated model delivery. As repository implementation approaches, models that have been included in the application maintenance cycle stand a better chance of being repository assets.

Creating accurate models as part of a new application development is now not the only goal of successful CASE-based modeling. Using these models throughout the application life cycle as the functional roadmaps that they are and keeping them accurate throughout the application life cycle are just as crucial when the models are headed for a repository.

9

A LOOK AT INTEGRATED CASE

If you think you can, you can. And if you think you can't, you're right.

Mary Kay Ash, 1985

We will end our discussion of today's models with a brief look at ICASE (integrated CASE). Perhaps the first "repository" tendency was introduced with integrated CASE. In the integrated CASE arena, the same tool, by the same vendor is used throughout the application development life cycle. The simple impact of this single-tool, single-vendor approach is that constructs defined in one phase of application development (e.g., planning) are accessible throughout the remainder of the applications's continued design and definition. In fact, most object instances input into ICASE are immediately accessible throughout the remainder of the tool set, regardless of whether or not the object's qualities have been finalized by the modeler.

ICASE VS. CASE

How does ICASE distinguish itself from traditional CASE? With the early introduction of ICASE, the major distinguishing quality was very simply that the entire life cycle was covered by the tool set. The first model-driven code generators were part of an ICASE offering. Here, for the first time, the models that had already been developed as a means of documenting application requirements were used to generate the actual application code. The key factor that distinguished ICASE from CASE was that the same tool was used for all required tasks—from modeling through code generation.

The backbone of ICASE is the encyclopedia. Here, all defined objects are instantly resident, regardless of the model in which they initiate (see Fig. 9.1). In a typical ICASE product the mere naming of an object creates an entry into the encyclopedia. Many products do not require any other information (definition, attributes, etc.) at this early stage of input. Once the graphical depiction of the object appears on the screen, its encyclopedia entry backs it up.

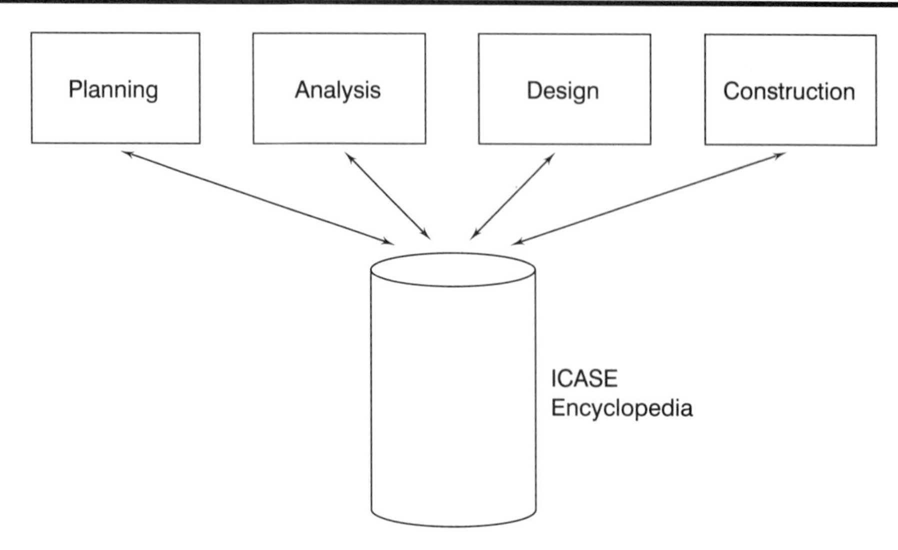

Figure 9.1 The ICASE encyclopedia

With traditional CASE, in contrast, the encyclopedia population is often an optional task. Although models and their component constructs must indeed be saved in order to be referenced and updated, the way in which they are saved as well as the place in which they are saved are often left to user discretion in a nonintegrated CASE tool.

For example, many nonintegrated CASE tools offer the user a multiplicity of diagram creation options. Many users of these tools utilize them primarily for the ease in which graphic depictions of system diagrams can be entered and displayed (when compared to a traditional graphics package or the old-fashioned plastic systems development template). Some tools make distinctions between the "for presentation only" diagrams and the true models that are used to convey system requirements, graphically and via textual description. In a sense, by creating a presentation diagram, the user is choosing to circumvent the CASE tool's encyclopedia and any embedded syntax checking. The "models" in this category are not really models, but presentation graphs. When and if the time comes for these diagrams to evolve into models, the CASE tool user is required to start from scratch. Any process that appeared on a presentation "data flow diagram" is not automatically retrievable when the true data flow diagram is created as part of system design. Once system design is underway, the extent of integration from diagram to diagram also varies among CASE tools.

In many nonintegrated CASE tools, different levels of model definition and therefore integration exist. For example, some CASE tools use the enterprise as the uppermost level of definition. The user can define as many *enterprises* as he or she wants, but within each enterprise, only one of each application-wide model type (e.g., entity–relationship diagram, data flow diagram) is allowed. The "integration" at best occurs within each enterprise. That is, an object that is defined in an

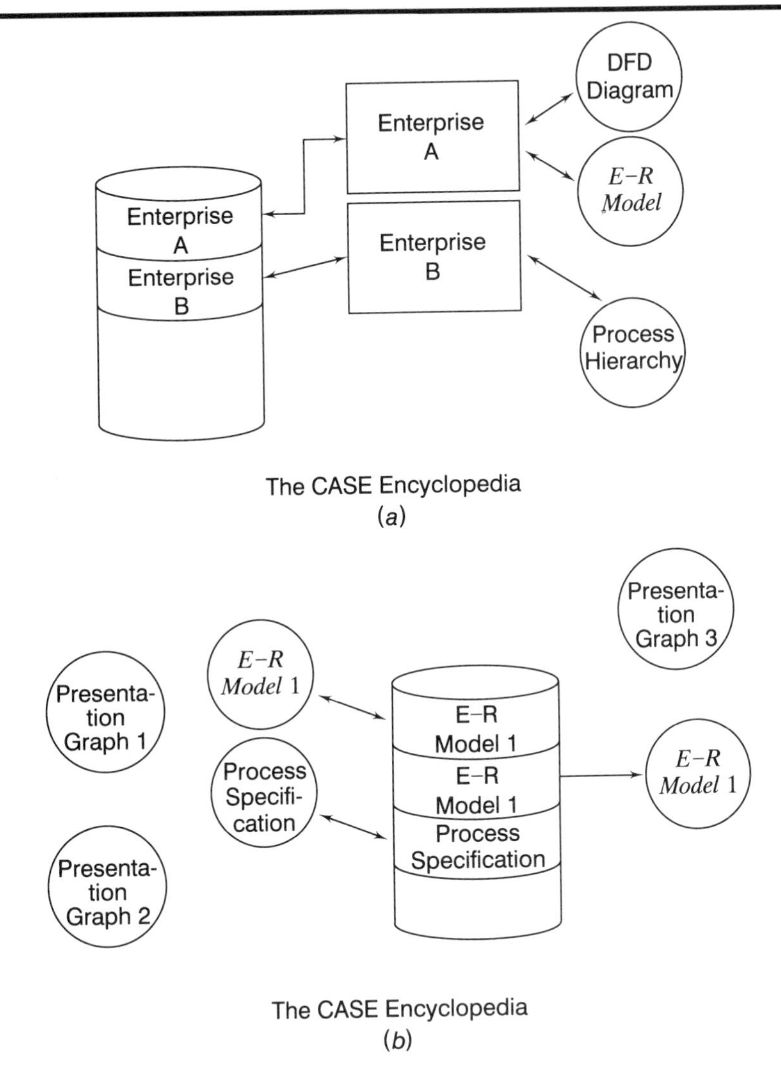

Figure 9.2 Non-ICASE encyclopedia integration examples: (a) Partial encyclopedia integration. (b) No encyclopedia integration.

enterprise's data flow diagram is accessible and relatable within that enterprise's E–R diagram. Other CASE tools do not even offer this level of integration. Each diagram (or model type) contains its own constructs. The level of integration is the model itself, and constructs cannot be accessed or related from one model to another. Figure 9.2 shows the different ways integration does and does not happen in the non-ICASE arena.

The second major factor that distinguishes ICASE from CASE is that the encyclopedia backbone of ICASE is truly integrated from one design phase to the other, and from one model (diagram, screen definition, report definition, etc.) to another. An entity defined in the E–R diagram is accessible in the database schema. An attribute that exists within the entity is accessible when the screen to be used for its input is being defined.

As a final distinguishing characteristic, it is important to consider the evolution of ICASE and how it has affected CASE in general. As stated previously, when ICASE was first introduced, it was truly the only total tool solution for application model definition and subsequent construction. Traditional CASE did not cover the entire application life cycle, and its models were not the prerequisites to code generation. ICASE was geared toward eventual code generation. Its models required more detailed specifications as the modeler approached the code construction phase. Many modelers with analysis backgrounds (as opposed to recent coding experience) found it difficult to express application process details in the syntax required by the ICASE tool for subsequent code generation. Initial ICASE offerings far outpriced their CASE competitors, but the functionality could not even be compared. Users looking to mechanize the application development process rather than simply document it were the initial consumers of these ICASE offerings.

As the initial ICASE market was penetrated by the few ICASE offerings, non-ICASE offerings began to cross over into the ICASE arena by offering more integration within their encyclopedias. Tools that did not have encyclopedia backbones began offering them. Tools that did not cover the entire application development life cycle started offering additional package components (planning, analysis, design, construction) which could be optionally purchased and tied to existing analysis-only tools via their "integrated" encyclopedia. Likewise, ICASE offerings began to cross over into the CASE arena. Tools that covered the entire application development life cycle began to "break up" into life cycle components (planning, analysis, design, construction) which could be packaged by the ICASE consumer in any combination. No longer were planning models required before application analysis could begin. Similarly, not all design models had to be used to generate code.

What has happened over time is that today there may be little distinction between CASE and ICASE. In fact, when evaluating a particular CASE product in terms of its integration capability, the following criteria should be considered:

1. Does the tool have a backbone encyclopedia?
2. If so, is the encyclopedia integrated? At what level of definition?
3. Does the tool cover all aspects of the application development life cycle? Is each phase mandatory?

■ ICASE ADVANTAGES

Model Continuity The clearest advantage ICASE has over CASE is its model continuity across the application development life cycle. With traditional CASE, many designers often found the need to export models from one tool in order to load them into another tool for the purpose of continuing application development. Perhaps the data model's attribute names had to be loaded into a corporate data dictionary. The dictionary may have been the required holding area for any proposed database before it was reviewed by an internal DBA group.

With ICASE, the backbone encyclopedia as well as the tool components can be used by more than one functional application development area. There is no reason why the DBA group cannot access the logical data model created by the application analyst and use the database definition portions of the "construction" component to finalize and therefore generate the physical database definition (in fact they *should*!). Likewise, the application analyst should access the physical database definition (as proposed by the DBA) before it is "implemented" as a means of final verification.

Model Object Integration Continuing the same benefit, once an object is defined as a component of a particular model, it is accessible throughout all downstream modeling efforts. A CUSTOMER entity is accessible in the planning model, the analysis data model, and the design database structure definitions. The integrated CASE tool prohibits the definition of another CUSTOMER entity within the application model.

Indirect Enforcement of Modeling Standards As the ICASE-based model gets closer and closer to code generation in the construction component, its modeling constructs become more detailed and more conformant to the tool's standard syntax. In fact, many designers trifle with the details of the specifications in order to get the desired code semantics. Once the specification/code construct combination is discovered, it is likely to infiltrate other similar application development efforts. Depending on the organization and how methodologies are deployed, the modeling specifics could very likely evolve into a tool usage standard.

▪ ICASE SHORTCOMINGS

As with most technologies, the advantages brought to the market can sometimes backfire when implemented without the proper planning and foresight. Many organizations view ICASE advantages, as discussed in the preceding section, to be the specific shortcomings that keep them from moving away from existing multitool platforms.

Limited Target Code Generation Platforms Few ICASE tools can generate code for all target execution platforms. Initial ICASE offerings concentrated on COBOL applications targeted for the traditional IBM mainframe platform. Since their inception, many have expanded into minicomputer and workstation targets (DEC/VAX, the multiple renditions of Unix, and limited client-server). When this limitation is considered in the context of an ICASE tool, the analysis and design that is required within the tool in order to generate application code may not fully suit a particular MIS implementation strategy if the full set of target platforms cannot be accomodated.

Mandatory Functionality Limitations Although the types of process specifications that can be modeled and depicted within a preconstruction ICASE design component have increased since the introduction of ICASE, there are still some types of code that simply cannot be generated. The impact of this on the ICASE user (or potential user) is knowledge in advance that some of the application code will not be model driven and will have to be accounted for in the overall application design. Most ICASE tools allow the definition of "external action blocks" which fall outside of the model's code generation. However, the ICASE user has to immediately decide how maintenance of the non-model-based code will be handled and how its releases will relate to the releases tracked by the application's model versions. Many view this additional effort as an immediate negative impact on any of the benefits that are realized by the use of ICASE for application development.

Uneven Tool Capabilities Particularly with those tools that originate as separate components, many ICASE offerings are stronger (functionally) in one major component. For example, some ICASE tools offer very strong data modeling functionality, but are weak, in contrast, on the process modeling side. They still generate "code" but only for data-intensive applications.

Inaccessibility of Encyclopedia Most ICASE encyclopedias are relatively closed as of this writing. That is, they cannot be accessed by tools that are not part of the same vendor's ICASE offering. With the advent of "generic" code generators, some ICASE encyclopedias allow the export of models into a receiving code generator. However, what is to be exported is usually not a user option.

Limited Integration of Encyclopedia-Resident Constructs Finally, the major benefit that ICASE brought to the marketplace, that of model integration throughout the application development life cycle, is only worthwhile when the focus is on one application. All encyclopedias require an uppermost model level under which integration occurs. As discussed previously, it is usually an application (often called the model name) but can sometimes be considered an enterprise. The constructs within this encyclopedia level are truly accessible and shared by all models that fall under its realm. But when we consider the encyclopedia as a potential repository, how beneficial is this integration across different applications? If an *Order Entry* system is the first application to define a CUSTOMER entity, this definition should be reusable when the *Order Processing* system development effort begins. In most ICASE tools another application would have to be defined (another model, another enterprise, etc.), and the components of the existing *Order Entry* models that pertain to *Order Processing* would have to be copied or merged into the "new" encyclopedia. Or, an effort that is now underway in some organizations is the definition of yet another "application" (model, enterprise, etc.) that reflects the *corporate* (or departmental) view of applications and their data. In this scenario CUSTOMER is resident in this model and can be copied (extracted, downloaded) to any application levels with a need to use the model. Security can be imposed which prevents models from updating aspects of the corporate models that are truly "corporate." Figure 9.3 illustrates the ways in which ICASE encyclopedias can result in reusability, but, in any case, the effort involves manual control in most ICASE offerings.

CASE STUDY Banc One Services Corporation

Whether or not ICASE has proven to be a major benefit to organizations can only be determined by actual experiences. This case study cites the experience on Banc One Services Corporation (herein referred to as *The Services*

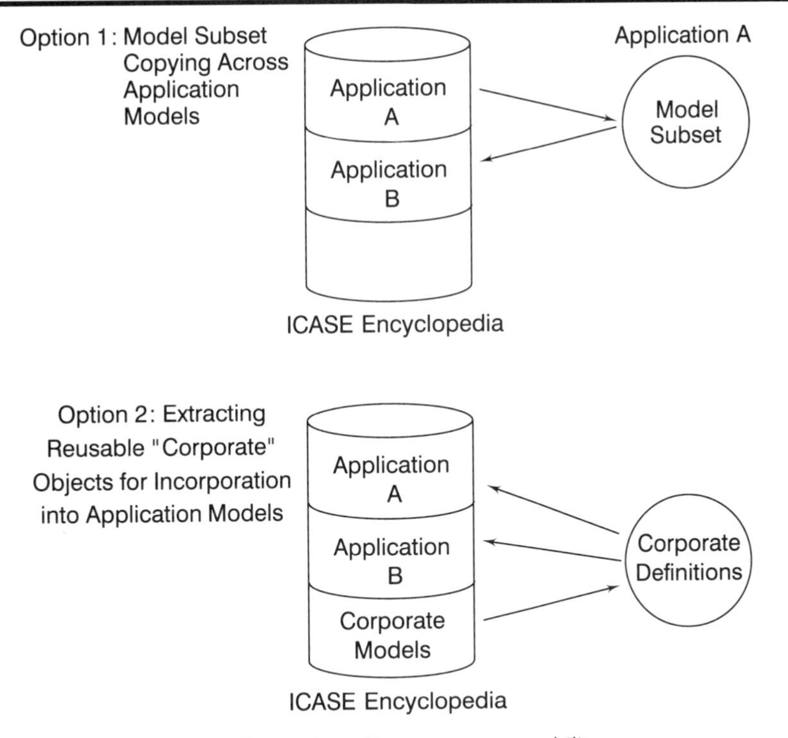

Figure 9.3 Implementing ICASE encyclopedia construct reusability

Corporation), the data processing service arm of all Banc One affiliates.* As of this writing, Banc One is the twelfth largest bank in the United States.

The Services Corporation has been using PACBASE, an ICASE offering from CGI Systems, Inc., for over 6 years. The deployed suite of tools also includes other complementary CGI products: DSMS (Development and Support Management System) for event tracking and change control, PEI (Production Environment Interface) for versioning, and PACDESIGN/PACBENCH, the workstation-based analysis/design components. Thus far, applications developed using the PACBASE suite are mainframe CICS, IMS/DC, and batch. They have varying underlying DBMS's, including DB2, VSAM and sequential files, and IMS/DB. Although these applications all consist of code that was generated by the PACBASE suite of tools, not all applications were supported by the tools throughout the entire information engineering life cycle. Specifically, in some cases the analysis and logical design occurred outside of PACBASE (e.g., manual diagrams); PACBASE did not become a supporting factor until the logical specification/physical design phase (immediately preceding code generation, also known as construction).

*David Rosky, Advisory CASE Consultant, Banc One Services Corp., Columbus, OH, phone interview, February 4, 1993.

The Service Corporation's PACBASE configuration involves a mainframe CICS copy with the supporting encyclopedia implemented in VSAM files. Approximately 125 users have access to the tool. Most developers access the tool via dumb terminals (mainframe interactive devices, or MFIs). Those developers with intelligent workstations use the PACDESIGN/PACBENCH packages and interface with the mainframe encyclopedia when necessary. Based on this hardware configuration, most developers (those without intelligent workstations) are not currently developing logical designs with the PACBASE tool set. The deployed PACBASE architecture is illustrated in Fig. 9.4.

The Services Corporation considers its ICASE experience a successful one. Its major benefits have resulted from an integrated encyclopedia which is the backbone of all PACBASE components. Specifically, any constructs defined, regardless of the associated application, are available for reuse by subsequent modeling/development efforts. This reusability has led to a great reduction in the redundancy of definition among applications. Banc One credits this success to its having organized the underlying encyclopedia structure. Various "libraries" have been established, each representing a distinct level of application development and/or enterprise integration. The lowest level contains all under-development applications. As applications are completed, they are "promoted" to a higher level. The uppermost level in this encyclopedia structure represents "corporate" definitions. As new applications are developed, developers are encouraged to check this upper level for potentially reusable definitions that could pertain to their particular application needs.

The encyclopedia is truly integrated, according to David Rosky (an internal CASE consultant). When model construct instances are changed, the changes do potentially impact all dependent objects, regardless of application. It should be noted that the scope of impact is dependent on the setup of the encyclopedia structure. At *The Services Corporation*, because reusability and shareability were the two major benefits being sought by ICASE, an object's scope extends to all PACBASE-developed applications. The key to update management and tracking rests with the tool set's *impact analysis* feature which is provided via automatic management of entity cross references. Modelers/developers are encouraged to conduct an impact analysis before changing a particular object. Once the change is made, it will not impact dependent code until the applications are regenerated. However, once regenerated, any program, and so forth that was dependent on this object is automatically updated. In this sense the impact of the changes to the integrated encyclopedia is dependent on manual verification.

The Services Corporation's ICASE success was not without its challenges. The most obvious issue was the cost of implementing such a technology. Aside from the pricing of the tool set, most developers considered the tools to be quite complex. Special training was required for all involved (application developers, DBAs, etc). In addition, *The Services Corporation* had to establish an internal consulting organization to provide continuing support, training, and advice. To date, *The Services Corporation* has been satisfied with its return on investment.

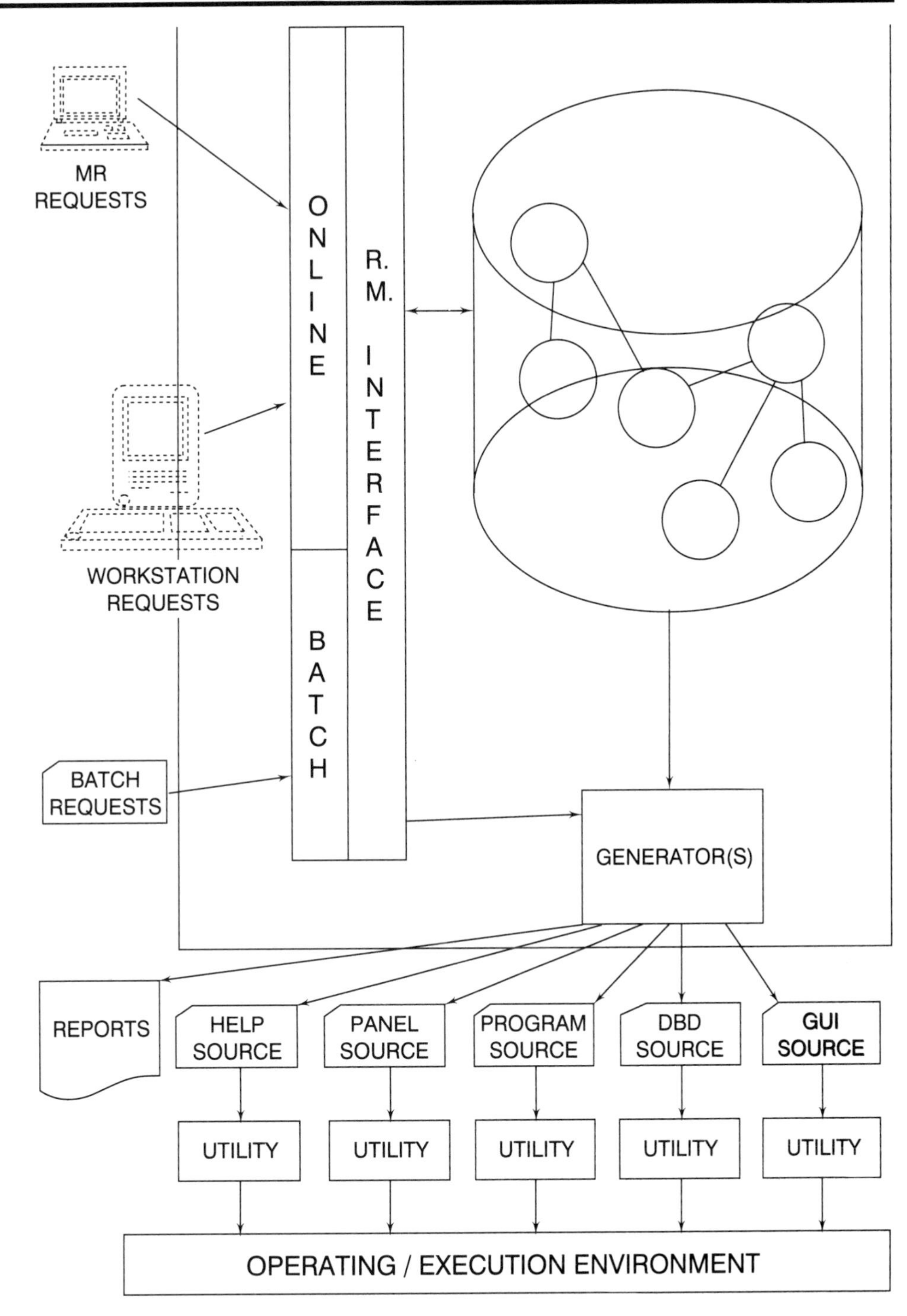

Figure 9.4 The Banc One Services Corp. ICASE environment

When evaluating the applications that result from the ICASE platform, it is important to note that entire applications are not fully supported by the tool. Specifically, JCL is developed and maintained outside of the tool set, and its existence is not necessarily tracked or noted within the PACBASE encyclopedia. A recent development effort (a cost tracking system) was conceived using the entire PACBASE tool set. Development began in May 1992, and the application went into production in February 1993. This DB2 application consists of a standalone database that is accessed both on line (IMS/DC) and in batch mode. The delivered application is of very high quality when compared to other non-ICASE-developed internal applications.

When evaluating the experience of *The Services Corporation*, one can consider the use of ICASE beneficial. It is important to note the considerable investment that was required, however, and to remember that the tool's usage within this organization involves the majority of the developer population. This usage, although limited in terms of development life cycle stages (most developers begin using the tool at the specification stage of an application), has encouraged the reusability of data and program structures.

PART TWO
THE MODELING ENVIRONMENT

10
THE PEOPLE SIDE OF CASE-BASED MODELING

A cynic is not merely one who reads bitter lessons from the past; he is one who is prematurely disappointed in the future.

Sydney J. Harris, 1962

As we have discussed today's model's, so too have we discussed today's tools and the role that they play. The other crucial parts of corporate modeling are the people themselves. Being only human, we do have traits that affect the role modeling plays in an organization. In addition, our behavior is influenced by that of others, most notably our superiors. The human aspects of modeling are indeed quite influential when it comes to model quality and penetration.

QUALIFICATIONS OF THE CASE PRACTITIONER

The most obvious influential aspect of a modeler is his or her qualification to perform modeling. Yes, an obvious point. But as a consultant, I have encountered some organizations where qualifications are more perceived than real.

As discussed in the preceding chapters, the models themselves are directly reflective of modeler personality and objectives. For example, some "logical" data models may in fact be quite "physical." Perhaps an ex-application programmer or ex-DBA authored the model. Since the inception of CASE, modeling has expanded to become a recognized specialty in the MIS arena. However, early CASE involvement at organizations often requires the use of human resources previously unfamiliar with modeling or its intent.

What makes a good CASE practitioner? Perhaps the most important quality is a solid understanding of the corporate function being addressed by the to-be-modeled application. This understanding must be translatable and approached from several perspectives:

The Business Perspective A good modeler can take an application and consider its role in a particular corporate function or set of functions. The role is not a mere input/output data passthrough function. Instead, it should cover and include the corporate activities that require the execution and/or access of the application and its data. In integrated CASE tools all of this information initially appears within the enterprise perspective and becomes further refined as the application models expand upon the business enterprise objects. However, when the application models predate the introduction of integrated CASE, it is important that this perspective be maintained despite the lack of tool-based requirements to do so.

The Application Perspective Continuing the previous line of reasoning, the business function must also be translatable into the view of the application. Immediately, the business, broken down already into a series of functions, becomes represented at the process specification level. However, the qualified CASE practitioner now brings the first technical details into the model. Subject areas such as *customer* are now thought of as a collection of entities, attributes, and relationships. This perspective views the business in terms of the application being modeled and relates this view to those of other interfacing and downstream applications. The functional requirements must be translated and modeled with the intention of eventual translation into a working set of databases and application code.

The Technical Perspective Finally, the technical details must be considered and conveyed. It is only at this level that actual database layouts are uncovered, performance issues are taken into consideration, and the execution platform is targeted. The qualified CASE practitioner has the experience required to consider these technicalities. Because it is common for ex-programmers to grow into analyst/designers, their experience is often old or outdated or not applicable to the current application's target platform. The important factor to consider is how adaptable previous development experience can be to the current environment. Training in new technology areas should be a constant offering to the qualified CASE modeler.

The preceding perspectives are hard to find encompassed in one individual. In the ideal scenario all CASE modelers have at their disposal accurate enterprise models that depict the various relationships in which the modeled application must participate. Without an accessible integrated scenario, most of the enterprise modeling is left to the CASE application modeler's interpreted view. It is this interpretation that makes or breaks successful CASE-based modeling. In more common scenarios the models are developed from the technical perspective, with touches of the business perspective added in later.

Following the common technical deployment viewpoint often results in a cynical perspective toward application integration, data consolidation, and enterprise modeling in general. These opinions can often be inferred via the role and priority CASE plays in the modeler's daily activities. As application enhancements become required and hence delivered, they are rarely evaluated in terms of whether or not more thorough up-front analysis would have resulted in an earlier delivery of the same functionality.

The preceding perspectives demand good communication skills. Successful CASE practitioners, aside from being able to view and interpret needs on the various levels, must be able to translate and represent them to associate project developers and the targeted user community. It follows naturally that the ability to translate the multiple sets of requirements also requires the ability to communicate and represent each "translated" version.

It is essential to consider the profile of your average CASE user. It is unlikely that they all meet the ideal requirements itemized previously. Scope the disparities between the ideal and the real. Be prepared to either supplement missing skills where needed or to evolve into a broader set of modeler skills over time. Many organizations begin anew when CASE is introduced in that they hire new recruits and put them through CASE-specific training, including perhaps lessons covering an internal methodology. In fact, one theory considers business- and technology-naive modelers to be the best option in terms of delivering impartial user-driven application models. This theory is only practical when, despite the impartiality of the CASE modeler, he or she is an excellent analyst. This excellent analytical skill is required as the means to separate user biases from true business-specific requirements. In other words, it is not always the best idea to take user-stated requirements verbatim—an amount of "requirement" evaluation is always worthwhile, particularly in today's environment where everything new needs to be retrofitted with what already exists. Consider how those with excellent analytical skills compare to those with excellent technical skills, and divide CASE modeling responsibilities appropriately.

■ INSPIRING THE USE OF CASE

The success of CASE as well as the breadth of its deployment across the total application development function is often directly dependent on how the tool set was brought in house. In a study by International Data Corporation, CASE sites were asked if CASE usage had been inspired by corporate mandate. Of the sites polled, 22 percent reported an existing corporate mandate, and 42.2 percent expected a mandate to exist by 1994.*

In my own personal experience, many CASE sites without mandated CASE usage were always "piloting" its usefulness. When a CASE-based application was

---

*"1990 to 1994 Computer-Aided Software Engineering (CASE) User Requirements," International Data Corporation, Framingham, MA., March 1991

	NON-CASE		CASE	
Activity	Frequency	%	Frequency	%
Documented procedures	7	4	10	19
Information engineering, IRM	1	1	2	4
Rapid iterative prototyping	2	1	4	8
Structured design, waterfall	6	3	10	19
Other	1	1	1	2
No process	163	91	25	48
Total*	180	100	52	100

*Multiple responses allowed

Figure 10.1 Types of formal software development processes deployed with and without CASE (From International Data Corp.).

successful, its success was often attributed to the application's lack of complexity. When a CASE-based application development effort did not result in timely accurate delivery, the tool often received a substantial portion of the blame. The pilots at some sites were never completed. Because pilots were always a lower priority than true application production problems, the resources allocated to their completion were often reassigned during peak workload periods. This often became a cyclical process with the result being very limited penetration of CASE outside of the research and development area.

Continuing with my own experience, consider the organizations that have not even reached the stage of piloting CASE. Without a *corporate mandate* so to speak, the decision as to whether or not CASE is appropriate is considered quite often. Skeptics who have not yet concluded that CASE has any worth in their organizations probably spend a substantial amount of time looking for specific qualities within their application development environments that would prevent CASE benefit. For example, organizations often complain that applications are "too scientific," "very specialized," or "noncentralized." In many cases mandates often result in semirebellion following the same line of reasoning. Regardless of what the typical application looks like in these non-CASE organizations, there is always one clear similarity among all of them—the lack of a standardized application development methodology. Figure 10.1 shows the results of an International Data Corporation survey on formal software engineering practices and how they differ in CASE and non-CASE environments. The interesting fact, despite the type of practices deployed, is that in non-CASE sites only 8.6 percent had formal software engineering practices.

Inspiring the use of CASE in organizations unaccustomed to formal software engineering and documentation standards cannot be done too hastily. Many developers would view the required use of a CASE tool as an unnecessary documentation hindrance and therefore would give its use the lowest priority in the development task list. When CASE is to be instilled, it is essential that a methodology or set of usage standards accompany it. If not, the usage and applicability of the selected CASE tool will be left to individual creativity to the greatest degree allowed by the tool and/or the developer management.

When CASE is to play a role within a repository framework, it is essential that its use is inspired to the greatest degree possible. It is also essential that once deployed, CASE usage is consistently geared toward reusability. The use of CASE should not be perceived as a hindrance by the application developer. Management attitudes are important, but actions in terms of appropriate resource allocation ensure the appropriate follow-through within the development community.

■ CASE MODEL QUALITY CONTROL

In a chapter dealing with people issues, model quality is directly related. As discussed previously, it is the job of management to inspire the use of CASE. This inspiration should also cover the necessity to use the tool according to a set of modeling standards as required. Organizations concerned with data problems typically have well-supported data administration functions. These functions usually "rubber stamp" proposed database designs relatively early in the application development life cycle. They also oversee or coordinate DBA activities on the same database. When CASE is introduced into this entire process, the tool's usage should also be monitored from a standardization viewpoint.

Unlike data administration, however, CASE usage delves beyond the data side of applications. A fully integrated tool is used for full application definition which includes everything from screens to reports as well as the processing and data required to get from one to the other. In a repository-targeted environment, CASE-based models must be consistent enough to be readable by nonauthors, regardless of their project affiliation. As we will see in Part Five, in many installations a "repository administration" group is established as the quality check for any model before it is loaded into the repository. At this stage in our discussion, model quality control should happen as early as possible, with or without a repository tool.

Consider the modelers, the modelers' objectives, and how the infusion of model quality control could taint their perceptions of CASE as an ease to their workloads. To accommodate the egos and requirements of the multiple parties involved, it may be best to jointly develop the modeling standards. Also, to prevent the common view that standards do nothing but ensure the existence of quality-assurance (QA) organizations, present the objectives early on—model shareability, accessibility, and reusability. For a sure buy-in from application modelers, take two or more existing models and demonstrate their different "styles." Explain where standards can help and where they cannot.

■ EXECUTIVE CASE RESPONSIBILITY

The most obvious responsibility relating to CASE-based modeling is that of commitment. This commitment must be verbal, financial, and consistent. Many organizations tout devotion to CASE, information engineering, and general data

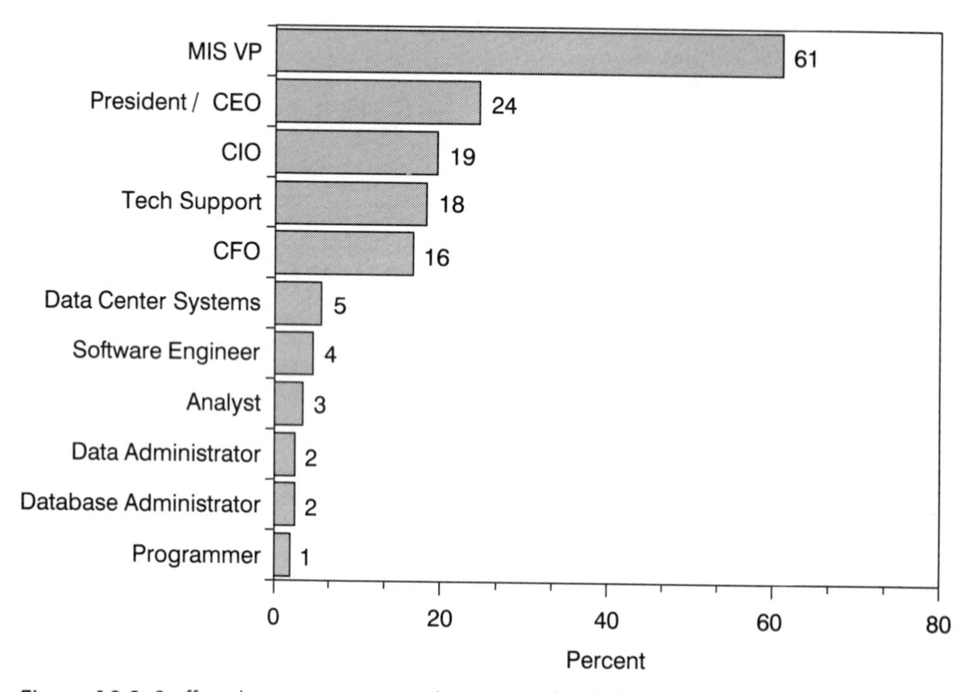

Figure 10.2 Staff and management involvement in the CASE purchase process (by job title) (© 1991 Sentry Market Research).

quality. The true assessment of commitment is measured, however, in the "trenches."

Because CASE is not a trivial financial purchase, the purchase decision authority typically rests at the executive level. Figure 10.2 depicts the involvement in the CASE purchase decision by job function.

Thinking back to when CASE was first introduced to your organization, executive involvement was most likely required if CASE has penetrated beyond a few isolated copies. However, because of the technical complexity that surrounds CASE and its associated modeling techniques, executives were not necessarily the most qualified people to select a particular tool. As Fig. 10.3 illustrates, tool specifics are typically handled at the technical level.

Executive responsibility in this area should ideally have resulted in the following sequence of events:

1. Executive decision to evaluate CASE
2. Technical staff evaluation of CASE tool subset with follow-up recommendation

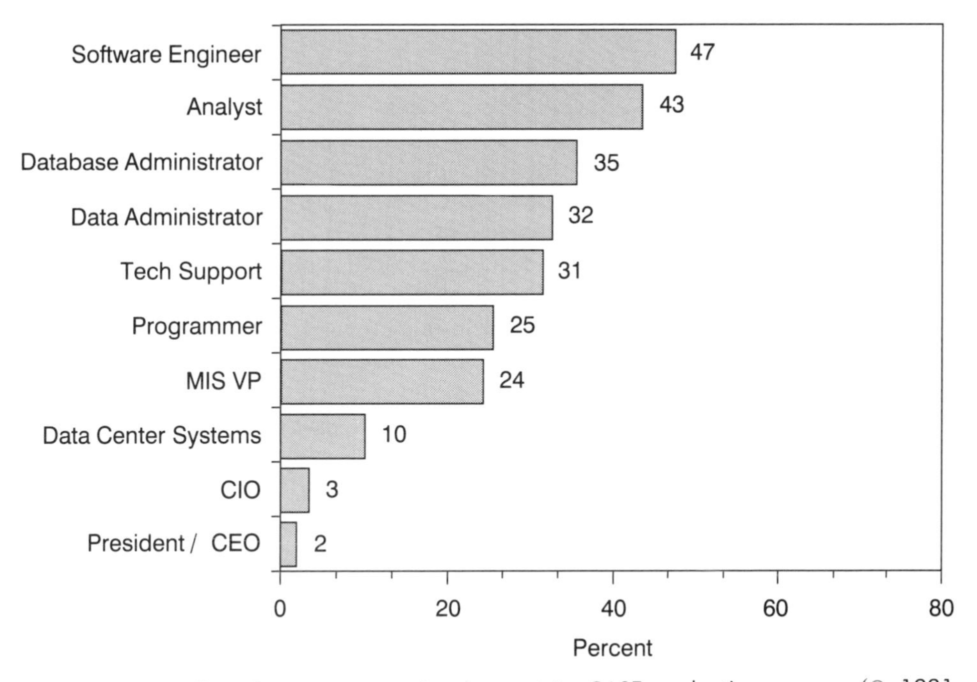

Figure 10.3 Staff and management involvement in CASE evaluation process (© 1991 Sentry Market Research).

3. Executive review of recommendation, technical staff feedback as required
4. Executive financial and resource commitment
5. Technical staff introduction of the tool into mainstream application development and support

In some installations the reality of CASE instillment is actually quite different. The decision to bring CASE in, as well as the decisions as to (1) which tool(s) to deploy and (2) how they are to be deployed, all occur at the executive level. The technical analysts are then told (or mandated) to use the selected tool as directed. In many scenarios existing project deadlines are not padded to allow for the delays common to the introduction of new product technologies. The introduction of CASE is therefore not viewed as advantageous by any of the involved technical developers. In fact, any problems inherent in the selected tool are typically used as reasons for project deadline slips.

Executive responsibility requires the financial and professional commitment to CASE as a developer aid. It also requires the delegation CASE implementation requirements and strategies to those "in the trenches" so to speak. If CASE is to flourish and be used consistently among the MIS development community, developers must perceive its value as beneficial to both the immediate project at hand as well as their corporate careers.

■ JUSTIFYING THE CASE INVESTMENT

It has always been hard to put a dollar amount on the savings that result from successful CASE deployment. There are many reasons for this, but most relate to the fact that application development is always funded on a user-chargeback basis. Once applications are approved, billing codes are assigned to all related expenses, including the acquisition of the CASE tool and its associated hardware.

Why does user chargeback make CASE justification difficult? First, the initial cash outlay required to establish more than a mere prototype CASE operation is quite substantial. Second, CASE benefit is typically measured in terms of cost avoidance as opposed to actual savings. When cost/benefit analysis demonstrates CASE to be a worthwhile investment, it typically puts a dollar value on a more timely and accurate application delivery. Then, if the application *is* delivered in a more timely (and accurate) fashion, the actual savings (as compared to the predicted dollar value) rarely equate to dollars in hand so to speak. The predicted vs. actual savings were both intangible because actual costs never played a part; hence, even savings that appear monstrous on paper are hard to believe.

A more verifiable cost justification for CASE would involve actual cost figures. It has always been my contention that the use of CASE for application development results in a greater reduction of design oversights. By documenting an application via a CASE tool throughout the development process, developers as well as end-users have access to the recorded plan. Many miscommunications are more easily cleared up when the blueprint is available and maintained. When this basic development philosophy is compared against the amount of "maintenance" required for the CASE-developed application, the benefits of CASE become more evident. How does one put a dollar value on prevented maintenance?

In today's world of project chargeback, all "maintenance" has an associated billing code. My definition of maintenance is different, however, from the current deployed definition. Today, anything that happens to change or enhance an application once it is in production is considered maintenance. In my definition, however, there are actually quite a few categories that cover MIS "maintenance":

> *Corrections.* In this category fits all "maintenance" that reflects an error in the original design. Examples include corrections to existing report formats and the recalculation of a mathematical result.
>
> *Oversights.* These "maintenance" changes are also based on the incomplete original design. Perhaps the designer forgot that the nightly feeds to the accounting system had to be processed differently at the end of each month (or perhaps the accounting manager forgot to tell the designer, and the analyst/designer forgot to ask!).
>
> *Technical revisions.* Application changes that are necessary because of unforeseen technical constraints (database size limitation, excessive

user access contention, limited CPU resource availability) often require the initiation of "maintenance."

Technical upgrades. These are changes that are required because of the installation of a new release of underlying software (DBMS, application language, operating system, etc.).

Enhancements. This category encompasses additional functionality that was not part of the base application. Many enhancements are scheduled based on the inability of the initial development team to deliver them in a timely manner for the first production release. In this scenario they are not really enhancements, but "delayed required functionality."

The preceding categories represent a clearer picture of how the maintenance dollar is spent. If one were able to categorize each maintenance effort associated with a particular project over time, it would become clearer exactly where most of the money is being spent. The first three categories listed previously are the ones that should be minimized with consistent use of CASE. Compare the maintenance dollar of a CASE-based application with one of the same complexity that did not involve a CASE tool. In this type of analysis, dollars being referenced would be real, not imagined.

■ SUMMARY

When considering the people side of CASE-based modeling, its importance becomes clearer when CASE usage is compared to the usage of other application development aids. In the ideal, repository-targeted environment, CASE tools should play as much of a role in application development as compilers. Every developer should either be using a CASE tool as models are authored, or accessing the CASE-based models of others. Strive for this objective and implement any necessary cultural changes over time. Do not prematurely begin repository implementation without first addressing the needs of those who will populate and access the planned repository.

11

THE CURRENT MIS PERSPECTIVE ON MODELING

It is not solutions that make ideas attractive. It is unsolved possibilities. . . .

Russell W. Davenport, 1954

The modeling environment controls the general view of the MIS organization toward today's models and their potential. The organization's perspective is often not the same as the people's perspective.

Organizational perspectives always exist in several forms. One format is the set of documented organizational objectives. In these popular bullet lists, MIS talks about strategic goals—some are long term (with no dates or dates extending beyond 2 years), some are immediate (within the next year). These goals are rarely controversial—everyone agrees, for example, that MIS should integrate its major sources of corporate decision support data. Another form of organizational perspective is the MIS budget. Here, based on funding and resource allocation, one can view which goals are important and which are merely bullet list members. Yet another form of the MIS perspective, and perhaps the most accurate, are MIS purchase orders (or MIS spending records). Here, the reality of how money was spent (despite budget allocations) gives us a real picture of where the MIS perspective meets the day-to-day workings of the MIS department.

MIS objectives, whether short term, long term, perceived, or actual, are closely related to the role models play (or can play) in an organization. Furthermore the role models play can be a direct indication of the role a potential repository will play.

Evaluation of the organizational perspective requires a look at several organizational factors:

- The nature of organizational planning
- The organization's attitude toward structure
- The organization's personality, also known as the *corporate culture*

As we will see in this chapter, models themselves are affected by each of these organizational traits.

■ THE MODEL'S ROLE IN MIS PLANNING: SHORT TERM VS. LONG TERM

Consider the state of MIS planning in your organization. In most organizations a box on an organization chart is attributed to this function within MIS. Depending on the vision of the overseer, subboxes divide the planning function into distinct technical areas (see Fig. 11.1).

Planning functions vary in their implementations. In some organizations planners deliver massive "plans" that occupy several binders. As discussed in a previous chapter, many of these have the same characteristics as "dust collector" methodologies. They are rarely implemented. Plans that are always paid attention to are *capacity plans*—specifically, those that relate to network and hardware usage and planned usage. Few things draw more immediate attention to MIS than the inability of an internal network to handle user and programmer processing. Capacity plans, although part of MIS planning in some instances, are often a deliverable of the MIS technical services organization. It is common knowledge that these plans are crucial to MIS viability and are typically short term in nature.

Strategic plans, in contrast, rarely get beyond MIS upper management. In many organizations they are authored by outside consultants and are usually "confidential." How does the average developer become aware of the department's strategic objectives? Or, more important, how does the average developer relate his or her functional goals to those of MIS or to those of the business?

When evaluating the worth and applicability of the planning function, consider the potential role CASE-based models can play. For example, technology planners often concentrate on target computing architectures which may differ from the

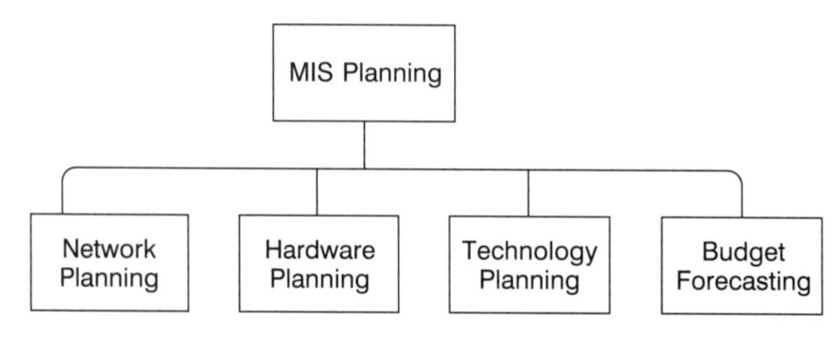

Figure 11.1 A typical MIS planning organization hierarchy

deployed architecture in use by developers and end-users alike. Many technology planners are in the process of evaluating ways to move application development off of the mainframe. Yet their concentration most likely begins with the selection of software tools (PC-based compilers, workstation-based development tools, etc.). The target hardware and network architectures are determined based on specific tool requirements. What is typically overlooked in architectural planning efforts is the current environment and how it can be retrofitted or phased into the planned evolutionary target.

Today's models represent today's and tomorrow's applications. In many situations the CASE tools that depict these models will also generate the executable code depending on the target execution platform. Short and long term architectures should be considered when modeled applications are scoped for their suitability to either architecture. For example, if existing models were developed in an integrated CASE tool with a mainframe encyclopedia, the existing target environments for code generation may or may not include sub-mainframe execution platforms. The planners should be communicating with the application development managers and determining how a short-term strategy can relate mainframe-based models to planned targets that exist on sub-mainframe platforms. Other related discussions should include how these models will be accessed once application development moves off of the mainframe. The short- and long-term plans for model viability should directly correlate with the short- and long-term target computing architectures.

Aside from application models, today's data models (both logical and physical) should also play a part in MIS planning. As discussed in previous chapters, many organizations have begun this effort via the creation of enterprise data models. In these scenarios a data administration function, not usually part of an MIS planning organization, begins to tackle the arduous task of integrating corporate data. The target plan in this scenario is the enterprise data model—the model of how all corporate data logically relates. It is every data administrator's dream to actually implement a physically relatable version of this model. But what impact does this effort have on MIS planning efforts? Hopefully, the planners consider the state and resting place of corporate data when target platforms for end-user computing are planned.

Finally, the piece of the planned architecture that should ideally relate the present application world with the planned target environment for both developers and end-users is the corporate repository. Whether a repository is a short- or long-term objective for an organization, it brings many issues to the planners as we will discuss in later chapters. Short- and long-term MIS plans should account for it as a piece of software with possible unique hardware and user access requirements. More important, its contents should reflect (or plan on reflecting) the long-term MIS plan. Planning models are important aspects of a repository's overall architecture.

■ ALIGNING MIS PLANNING WITH BUSINESS PLANNING

The model as a component of the MIS planning process becomes more of an integrated part of the business when MIS plans ally with the plans of the business.

Most corporations become aware of the lack of MIS/business planning integration when the first symptoms of an information crisis occur. Typically, end-user analysts need certain types of data for decision support. When they find that the data is simply not there or not compatible with the type of analysis they intend to do, joint problem-solving efforts begin.

If the data crisis alluded to previously is handled correctly, the objectives of the to-be-analyzed data should be reflective of a business plan. Perhaps a particular product line is being evaluated to determine whether it should be discontinued. The marketing analyst needs access to all product-specific purchases made over the past 3 years, by customer type. In order to supply this data, an application programmer has to access three distinct databases and consolidate incompatible customer id's. The effort is slated to take 3 weeks. In most short-sighted, implementation-oriented MIS installations, this would be the end of the business/MIS collaboration.

In well-aligned, business-driven MIS organizations, the effort to deliver the needed data would result in more than just the data. It would result in the following:

- A short-term strategy for ensuring the immediate availability, without programmer intervention, of the types of data needed by the marketing analyst
- A long-term collaborative plan that details the types of data that are of key importance to strategic business decisions and how they will become part of an end-user-accessible decision support platform
- They types of strategic business decisions that are currently under consideration and how they could impact current applications and their data

It should be noted that delivery of the preceding in and of itself does not constitute a business/MIS partnership. The implementation plan that covers MIS projects, their budgets, and their schedules should be a direct descendant. It is crucial that technical input as to how best to implement is received early on. The input should be derived not just from MIS planners, but from the developers responsible for day-to-day application, database, and network solutions.

In many organizations MIS functions as a reactive implementer. When the business needs demand a certain type of technological solution, MIS responds. The cycle continues. A collaborative working relationship puts the implementation responsibility in both camps. Corporate functions request MIS advice. MIS requests corporate advice. The result is a plan reflective of the business needs and MIS capabilities.

The amount of impact that a planning function has had on MIS effort in the past should be an indicator as to how well attuned planners are to the operational business needs of the company as well as the value placed on planning in general. When looking toward a repository objective, the business goals to be fulfilled by the repository must be itemized in advance and scoped to ensure they will be met.

■ STRUCTURE IN THE ORGANIZATION: THE EFFECT OF METHODOLOGY

Structure implies methodological approaches to standard organizational tasks. When we look at structure from a modeling perspective, the issue of methodology again returns. Although we discussed methodology earlier in this chapter when looking at the role (and potential role) of CASE, it deserves revisit as an organizational quality. Although the issue of methodology is always a topic of interest when discussing CASE, CASE-based modeling, and repositories, it is never a popular topic among programmers. In fact, programmers often view standards as required annoyances, similar to filing federal and state income tax forms. There is one difference, however. If filing taxes is really an annoyance to some , they can always hire an accountant. With standard methodology adherence, how do those who are not anxious to comply deal with the requirement?

Many debates can be held as to the value of methodology deployment and standards enforcement. In the ideal scenario the methodology and the standards in force by an organization are practical enough so that ignorance of them results in immediate disadvantage to even the programmer. As discussed previously, many methodologies function merely as documented deliverables of a standards organization. For everyone else, they are dust collectors.

The real value of standards to the organization becomes increasingly evident when models, programs, databases, and plans become evaluated as potential repository participants. Here, an organization may for the first time realize that its methodology deployment is academic as opposed to actual. If a standards organization had evaluated deliverables for methodology adherence and the reality of the model-based implementations shows otherwise, this could be perceived as another academic instance of methodology deployment. The issues surrounding the enforcement of methodology standards often revolve around the following organization-specific areas:

Practicality As a consultant, I see volumes (in terms of quantity as well as in terms of thickness!) of methodologies. There are some that literally are academic. That is, they discuss methodology requirements at such a high level that it is clear the authors never had a chance (or maybe a desire) to test them out.

EXAMPLE 1

I once consulted for a major research company with a separate organization responsible for the development of standards. Here, employees were developing standards for the use of CASE tools to which they had no access. They literally borrowed the documentation from company developers and read it. This was the only source of tool-specific experience they used for the development of these standards! Were the standards followed? Well, the first problem was the fact that some aspects of the standards could not be followed based on tool limitations. Of course, these limitations were not documented in user guides, but known to most actual users of the tool. Needless to say, standards were not given much credibility by those in the trenches.

EXAMPLE 2

In another consulting engagement a pharmaceutical company had hired a prestigious management consulting organization to deliver systems development standards for use in its MIS organization. Volumes resulted. Were they ever followed? Were the volumes ever opened? No. Why? The standards described an information engineering methodology with practical guidelines for the development of deliverables within each application development life cycle phase. The problem was that application developers were not *at all* familiar with information engineering. The terms *data flow diagrams* and *E–R models* were foreign to all employee developers. In addition, the only previous developer requirement was the input of batch job stream procedures into a central dictionary. Some conscientious developers actually drew flowcharts of the production job flow with pencil and systems template. But these diagrams remained with them. So when management hired a team to develop a methodology, its vision was extremely shortsighted. The developers also needed guidance or at least training as to what methodologies were and how they could be applied.

Enforcement Practical methodologies should imply adherence, but deadlines sometimes put standards into a lower implementation priority. Standards organizations chartered with the enforcement of their deployment should have the power to ensure it. No ifs, ands, or buts. Anyone granted a "temporary restraining order" is an immediate public exception.

Completeness Another reason why methodologies are not consistently deployed is their lack of coverage. Does the methodology cover the different types of application development efforts currently underway in the organization? If not, does it clearly state why not? When the developer of a fourth-generation language (4GL) does not see standards in the manuals covering the naming of elements in his database, he assumes they do not exist. Maybe he is right, but maybe he should be following the same naming standards used by COBOL developers. Does the methodology make this issue clear? What about other organizational policies—are they complete? Does the personnel policy that addresses maternity leave also address employee families who choose to adopt? What does this have to do with models? If your organizations's policies have never been complete in terms of their coverage and expected adherence, why should a developer expect a methodology to be any different? Surely there must be some way of getting out of this one (like all the others)!

Support Upper management, when targeting a corporate repository goal, must be aware of the important role standards play in such an effort. It is much easier to populate models and their implementations when the same rules are displayed the same way from application to application.

Take a close look at the realities behind your methodology. Consider these realities in terms of the effect structure has (or does not have) on your organization's operation. Determine how modeling varies from application to application, be tween life cycle phases, and between MIS functional areas. If the differences outnumber the similarities, consider another review of how *actual* your methodology really is. Then consider whether structure in general is an organizational quality, an organizational objective, or an organizational opposition.

■ MIS CULTURAL BELIEFS

Finally, the perspective organizations have on modeling is directly influenced by the internal culture of the MIS organization. How are applications developed in your organization? Are they planned, designed, and then implemented? Are they implemented and then replanned and redesigned? Does the culture support new technologies? Would the advent of stricter standards be interpreted by some as a hindrance to their creativity? How would required access of repository constructs before application design be interpreted?

Would the establishment of a powerful repository administration function be immediately resented by database administrators? Do database administrators already hate data administration? Does data administration already hate database administrators? The questions go on and on . . . .

Culture has roots, and, as we all know, roots always remain for years after the tree is chopped down unless the initial job goes beneath the surface. If a repository is the first attempt at consolidating the many distinct aspects of your MIS organization, the existing culture must be ready and willing. If you are already planning to allocate major financial support to a repository effort, the culture may resist its implementation if simple financial requests such as the establishment of a local area network for a small development group have been consistently denied. In order to gain cultural acceptance, the proposal must be presented as a means of accomplishing multiple objectives, including those that may not have previously been attained through simpler solutions (such as the LAN example). Begin an "under the surface" evaluation of your MIS culture. Today's models, today's applications, and tomorrow's repository are all directly impacted.

PART THREE

INTEGRATING TODAY'S MODELS: THE NEED FOR A BRIDGE

12

VIEWING MODELS THROUGH THE EYES OF THE TOOL

Incomprehensible jargon is the hallmark of a profession

Kingman Brewster, December 1977

Aside from viewing today's models through the eyes of their creators, their target applications, and their benefiting organizations, we need to consider an additional model perspective—that of the underlying deployed tool set. Modeling, CASE, code generation, reverse engineering, and even modelers themselves are affected by tool-specific usage requirements. The tool vendors advertise their methodology independence; yet their tools usually require adherence to at least some specific methods. Once the tools in use expand to include components from a suite of distinct vendors (or sometimes from the same vendor!), the tool-specific requirements begin to add slightly different perspectives to similar tool-based results.

Those readers anxious to get to our repository discussion (which beings in Part Four) should consider this part as a prerequisite. As Part Three unfolds, we will be delving underneath today's models by considering the tool's perspective. As many may already be aware, how a model is created (within a modeling tool) affects how a model is accessed. More important, how the model is stored (within the same modeling tool) affects how easily it can be made accessible to others. Before looking at the repository as the "silver bullet," we must first look at what the repository will be required to deal with.

■ WHY THE DEPLOYED TOOL SET IS SO IMPORTANT

Model quality and depth, as we discussed previously, is directly dependent on modeler quality and depth. Assuming a qualified modeler with the ability to delve beyond the obvious, to seek clarification when varying perspectives are presented as requirements, and to consolidate the necessary components of an otherwise segmented set of application models, the tool's ability to support this excellence is the next factor affecting the resulting models. Experience has proven that virtually any modeling tool can support the need to convey virtually any type of model requirement depiction. However, the best way in which requirements need to be depicted from tool to tool, or from tool component to tool component, is not always obvious or even universally agreed upon. In fact, many developers have differing favorites based merely on the ease in which their particular modeling needs are met by each vendor offering.

Consider this example:

A data administration function in a major corporate MIS organization considers itself the pioneer responsible for introducing CASE into the organization. Well before application developers were even aware of modeling as a part of application development, data administrators had begun using and sharing a particular CASE tool to model the company's major application databases. Most application developers often wondered what data administration personnel did with their time (the only data administration interface with the typical application developer involved the official granting of names for application database elements). More astute application developers visited the data administration members and questioned the use of CASE. Data administration personnel often demonstrated their chosen tool by displaying an in-progress model and explaining the benefits the tool offered in terms of model creation and maintenance. Some value may have been perceived by the astute developer at this point, but still the role of the tool as deployed by data administration was not quite what the developer had in mind. The world of the developer consisted of much more than data!

Continuing the example, data administration persisted with its deployment of the selected CASE tool. The major application databases had been modeled: Stating that a logical data model existed for each major application was a fair statement. The underlying tool had been selected based on its seemingly wider collection of data modeling constructs when compared with other available modeling tools. The successful and consistent use of the tool by data administrators had resulted in a visible and beneficial data administration function. In fact, the existence of accurate data models had saved an application development effort considerable expense by avoiding the need to recreate data that already existed in other applications. Instead, a database extract was performed based on information supplied by data administration—the application developers had no idea that data items similar to those being requested by their eventual users already existed in another department's database. Based on the visible success data administration enjoyed with its usage of CASE, developers decided to put CASE to a trial as part of the development of this new application.

The tool used by data administration had shortcomings in the process arena. This new application involved event-driven processing and therefore the ability to depict real-time system requirements was essential. The involved application developers, after some research, chose a different CASE tool to support their effort.

For the specifics of the application's process models, the two tools did not compare. In fact, data administration was not even taking advantage of the process modeling components of its deployed tool. But what about the data models? The tool used by data administration contained 50 percent more data modeling constructs than the one chosen by the application developers. It was decided that data administration would oversee and advise the application data modeling efforts in the new tool.

This involvement of data administration proved to avoid many integration issues that could have been obstacles to the eventual integration of models originating from either tool. Instead, data administration continued the use of its tool, with its wide array of data modeling constructs, while the tool deployed by this trialing application spread to other applications throughout the department. Application modelers handled their data models at the high level (modeling entities, attributes, and relationships) and then forwarded this model to data administration where the models were refined and incorporated into its more detailed view (which included subtypes, complex relationships, and consistent sets of codes and value sets). This organization's modeling *integration* made its transition to a repository a much smoother process.

■ WHAT IS MEANT BY INTEGRATION?

Speaking of industry jargon, the word *integration* certainly belongs to this category. Like *repository* (as we will see later), practically all tool vendors allege compliance. Yet compliance itself can vary by level, and the vendor interpretation and definition of integration can vary substantially throughout the industry.

If we look to *Webster's Dictionary* for clarification, *integration*, is defined as

> ...the act or process of forming or blending into a whole...to unite with something else...to incorporate into a larger unit.

Probably the last aspect of the definition, *to incorporate into a larger unit*, is the only universally agreed upon perspective to integration. But how the *incorporation* is implemented or attained, as well as the definition of the *larger unit*, are merely replacement ambiguities.

Consider the model, its components, and the relationships from one to the other (and back). See Fig. 12.1 for a simple clarification of model vs. model component. When a tool is integrated, model components are accessible from within their associated model as well as from the outside. For example, the access of a *Customer* entity, which is part of the *Accounts Receivable* data model, should be

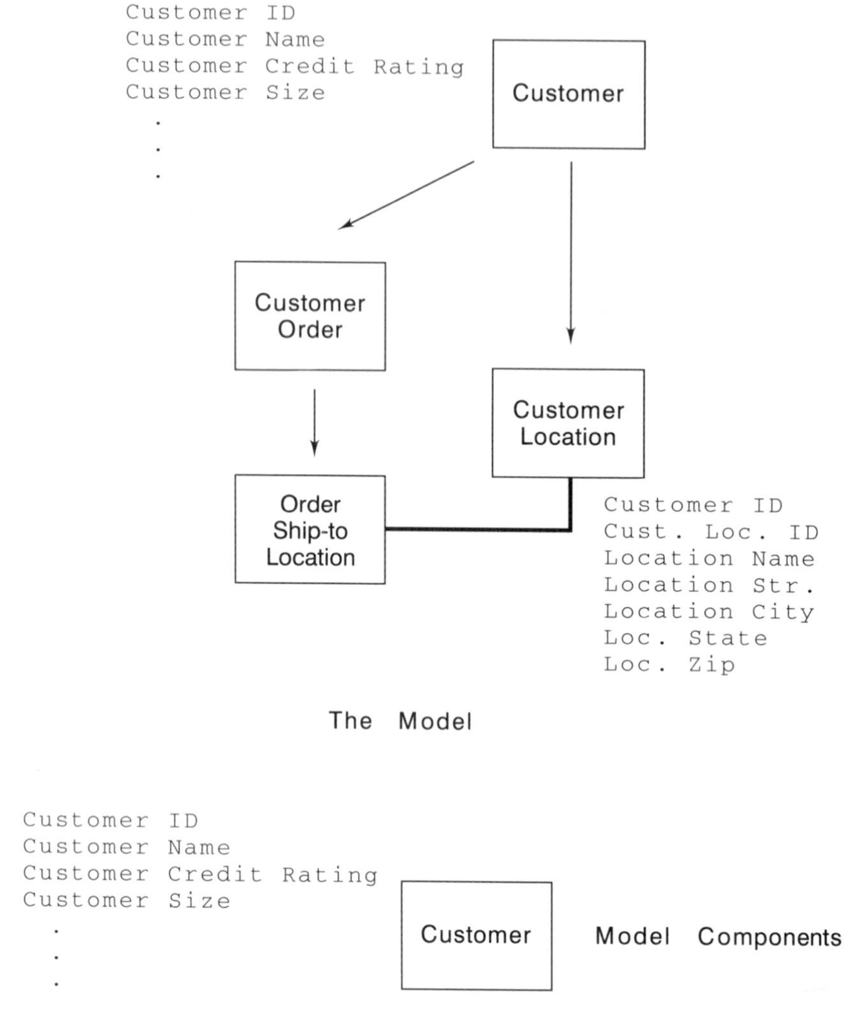

Figure 12.1 A simple clarification of model vs. model component.

allowed without knowledge of the model name (simply by referencing the *Customer* entity). Now, to make issues more complicated, the *incorporation* that was referred to in *Webster's* definition dictates how the *Customer* entity can be accessed without respect to its parent model and whether or not this *access* is for reference, reuse, or copying.

Putting the model aside, the model-independent access within a tool may also have further restrictions. Here, the ambiguity of the *larger unit* is interpreted by each vendor. In the simplest scenario the larger unit is the diagram itself (the model in many cases). Following our previous example, if model equated to diagram, the *Customer* entity would only be part of the *Accounts Receivable* data model. If the *larger unit* equates to a diagram collection, that is, the *larger unit*

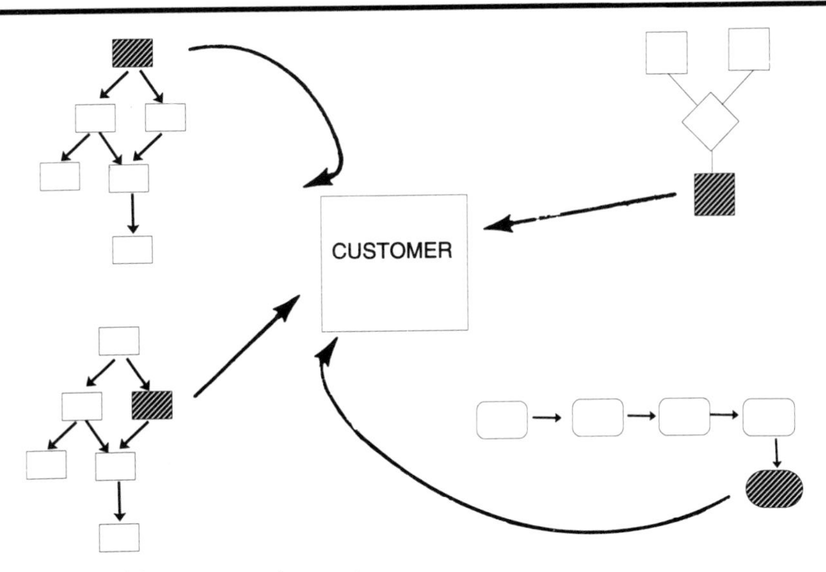

Figure 12.2 Model component integration.

equals the *model* (the data model, as discussed previously, and any other *Accounts Receivable* models that may be developed), then the *Customer* entity is consistently part of all diagrams (data flow diagrams, process specifications, etc.) under the *Accounts Receivable* umbrella (see Fig. 12.2). If this collection is truly integrated, the tool component used to depict the respective diagram should not be a factor in how or whether the model component can be accessed by an *Accounts Receivable* model.

As experienced readers may already be aware, many vendors do restrict access to model components based on the modeling tool component with which it was originally created. In other words, components of an accounts receivable planning model, created with a planning tool component, are not always accessible for incorporation into design models being worked on by the same vendor's design component.

The *integration* issue gets even more complicated when the *larger unit* goes beyond the model (beyond *Accounts Receivable* in our example). Here, despite the fact that the *Customer* entity may be incorporated into all *Accounts Receivable* models, it may need to be redefined (copied?) if it is to be incorporated into other application models (e.g., *Accounts Payable*). Again, the issue of *incorporation* and the definition of the *larger unit* must be considered in parallel. Finally, the ultimate integration puzzle involves all previously discussed levels of incorporation and larger units across multiple vendor tools.

Integration is the primary factor that forces us to look at repositories. The integration is not limited to CASE tools either. As we will see in later chapters, integration can be horizontally or vertically focused. In fact, the definition of horizontal and vertical integration is often dependent on where (which tool, which application development life cycle phase) the model originally started. When models and their components need to be related, reused, and bound to the realities (code, databases, etc.) that they depict, they need a neutral representation in a neutral location. Integration should allow the access of a model component despite its source:

- Diagram
- Model
- Modeling tool component
- Tool vendor

As we will see throughout Part Three, the last two tool-specific model aspects bring quite a perspective to the complexity of intermodel integration.

WHY A BRIDGE BETWEEN TOOLS IS NECESSARY

Looking back to the previous example which cited the use of distinct tools by an application development team and the centralized data administration group, it is obvious that many organizations can benefit by the use of different tools for different purposes. Aside from modeling tools, many other tools are part of the application delivery process: Testing tools, configuration management packages, source code libraries, and data dictionaries are just a few of the many tools that contain and represent aspects of MIS. As each MIS function mechanizes aspects of its regular routine, the tools that are used to assist the process begin to contain and reference the data items that describe and document the MIS world. Each tool and its associated underlying database typically exist in their own isolated area.

Consider the amount of duplication or contradiction that becomes part of each tool's domain. For example, a software testing tool, in order to generate test cases, needs to know the physical characteristics and value ranges of all data that needs to be input to each application test. Similarly, the application's models and specifications (if they were input to a CASE tool) contain the names and qualities of all application data. Without integration, it is likely that the testing tool did not interface with the CASE tool in order to obtain the data definitions. In fact, in most situations, it probably would have been a much greater effort to develop an interface between the two packages than to manually reinput the information in the format required by the testing package.

The situation perpetuates itself as more and more tools become part of the application delivery process in an organization. Redundancy grows exponentially, but the redundancy is usually not simple duplication. Redundancy across tools is based on *what* is being identified and named rather than *how* it is named. That is, the name *Product-Code* may or may not exist across development tools, the number *459-4* may or may not exist identically among the tools, but the product that is being identified is sure to be a part of many of the tool's representations of the company's products, the application databases, the test data, report formats, and so on, which are part of each tool's view of a company's MIS picture. More important, the concept of *Product* (not necessarily the same particular product) is sure to be a

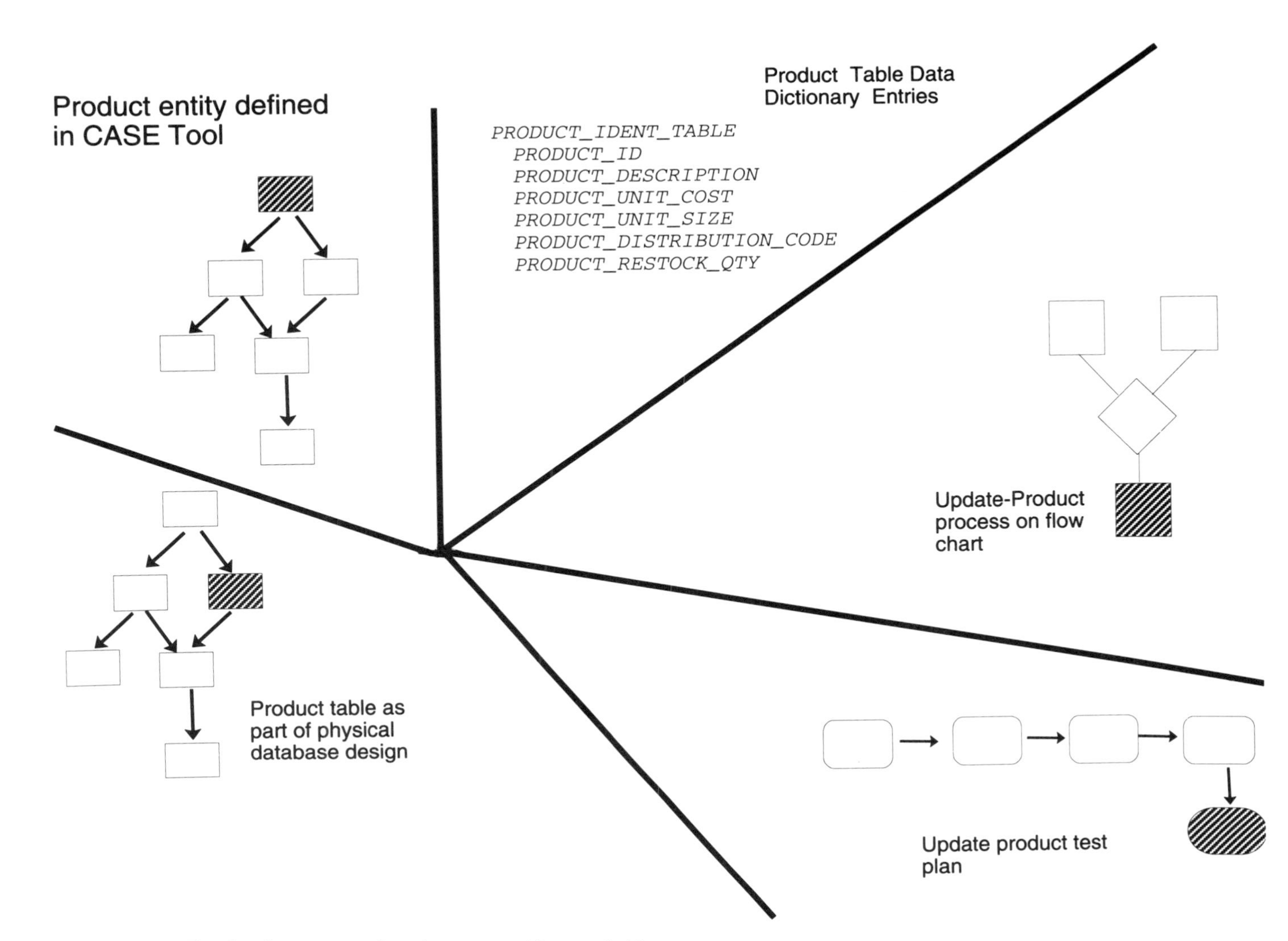

Figure 12.3 The development tool environment without a bridge.

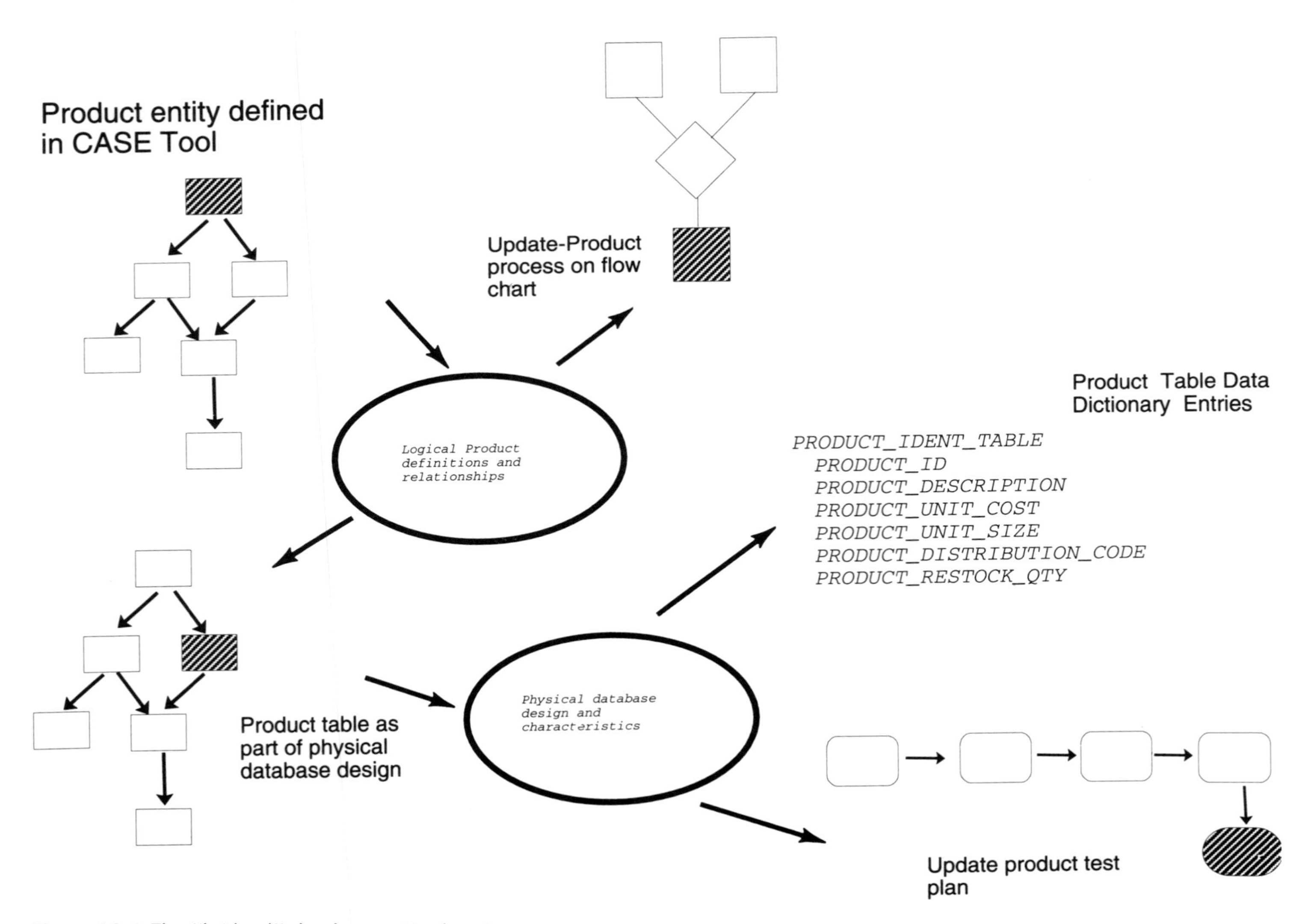

Figure 12.4 The "bridged" development tool environment.

universal component of many MIS applications in an organization, and therefore many of the supporting development tools (See Fig. 12.3).

The need for a bridge becomes obvious after a developer notices that the required critical information does in fact exist already. The hardship then becomes getting the information into the required place and format. In many situations the forward-looking developer plans a workable interface between the information-supplying components and the recipient process or package. However, in most cases, the pressure of deadlines forces the developer to pursue a "one-time" quick solution, and redundancy continues.

With a bridge between development tools, development objects are defined once, in the most logical place. In the case of databases, for example, an entity–relationship (E–R) modeling tool, the DBMS itself, and a database tuning package are logical places for database definition. The E–R modeling tool may contain the definitions from a logical business perspective (e.g., in the logical data model), the DBMS requires the names of the physical databases, and the database tuning package most likely needs to access the same physical database names. Figure 12.4 shows a simple intertool bridge and how *Product* definition traverses the bridge depending on the developments tool's needs.

With an available connection between development tools, the developer avoids the constant need to duplicate and translate data from one tool to another. Application development benefits from the mechanized quality control features, which are resident in each available development aid, and the execution of different tools as part of the delivery of a single application would not be considered a major handicap.

■ WHY A BRIDGE BETWEEN TOOL COMPONENTS IS NECESSARY

What about tool components that originate from the same vendor? As discussed in Part One, many integrated CASE (ICASE) tools offer the availability of modular tool units, each representing a distinct functional aspect of the application development process. Componentized tools originated in one of two distinct camps:

1. Tools in the first category began as *pioneer ICASE offerings*. They were the first tools to cover the entire application development process (minimally from planning through construction, or beyond construction through testing and configuration management). Although they were technical breakthroughs when first offered, they were limited in that the entire application (models and their relationships) was restricted to depiction within the tool itself. Getting other models into the tool or getting the tool-resident models out of the tool was often an arduous task, and in many situations a fully functional interface was not included with the tool.
2. The second category represents tools that originated as *component offerings*. In most situations the vendor's product line began with a modeling tool, most typically one that represented aspects of the *analysis* phase. As modeling's role penetrated beyond that of the graphical depiction of application specifications, vendors began offering complementary tool components—design

tools that allowed for the refinement of logical models into physical models and, in many cases, construction tools that generated code from the physical design models.

Despite the originating category, all ICASE offerings are now available in modular components. Based purely on marketing considerations, tools in the first category, having reached their initial level of market saturation, decided to tap other segments of the CASE market. By segmenting their product offering, the component price was low compared to that of the original full life cycle modeling tool. In addition, the reputation that had been attained via the full ICASE product carried over to the new component offerings. Tools in the second category functionally expanded their component line as a way of attaining increased market share. Now, customers who had to go elsewhere to purchase code generators could in theory feed their existing analysis component originating models into generators that originated from the same vendor.

The result over time is a series of application development aids, each packaged as a tool component that represents a distinct functional piece of the traditional information engineering life cycle. The historical beginnings of the associated vendor's initial tool offerings indicate whether today's particular component product represents an entirely new functional add-on or a functional slice of a much larger original offering. In either situation it is important to realize that today's product components were most likely not originally architected as pieces designed to smoothly fit together.

In most scenarios a central encyclopedia serves as the backbone of each component. When a model construct is updated in the analysis tool component, the updated version is accessible from the design tool component. However, is it only accessible upon request? Or do the dependent design constructs automatically become apprised of or attached to the update based on the way in which the construct is accessed?

Figure 12.5 represents the practical semantics involved when tool components truly share the underlying model, despite the tool component under which it originated. However, as many readers may already be aware, reality is often quite different. At the beginning of an application, tool components appear to flow together smoothly. A planning model, developed with the planning component, is accessible for refinement by the analysis tool. The models created by the analysis tool can be refined by the design component, and so on. At this early stage of development, each tool is creating new model instances that are related to the instances that were created by the preceding component in the application engineering life cycle chain.

Complexity arises when models need to be updated. For example, the more dependencies on a particular entity, the more impact the elimination of a particular attribute may have. In the truly integrated scenario depicted in Fig. 12.5, each tool component is always accessing the underlying encyclopedia and is therefore always accessing the most recent version of every component instance. Update of a component (the entity/attribute relationship in our example) must be evaluated in terms of impact analysis. If code was already generated which assumed the

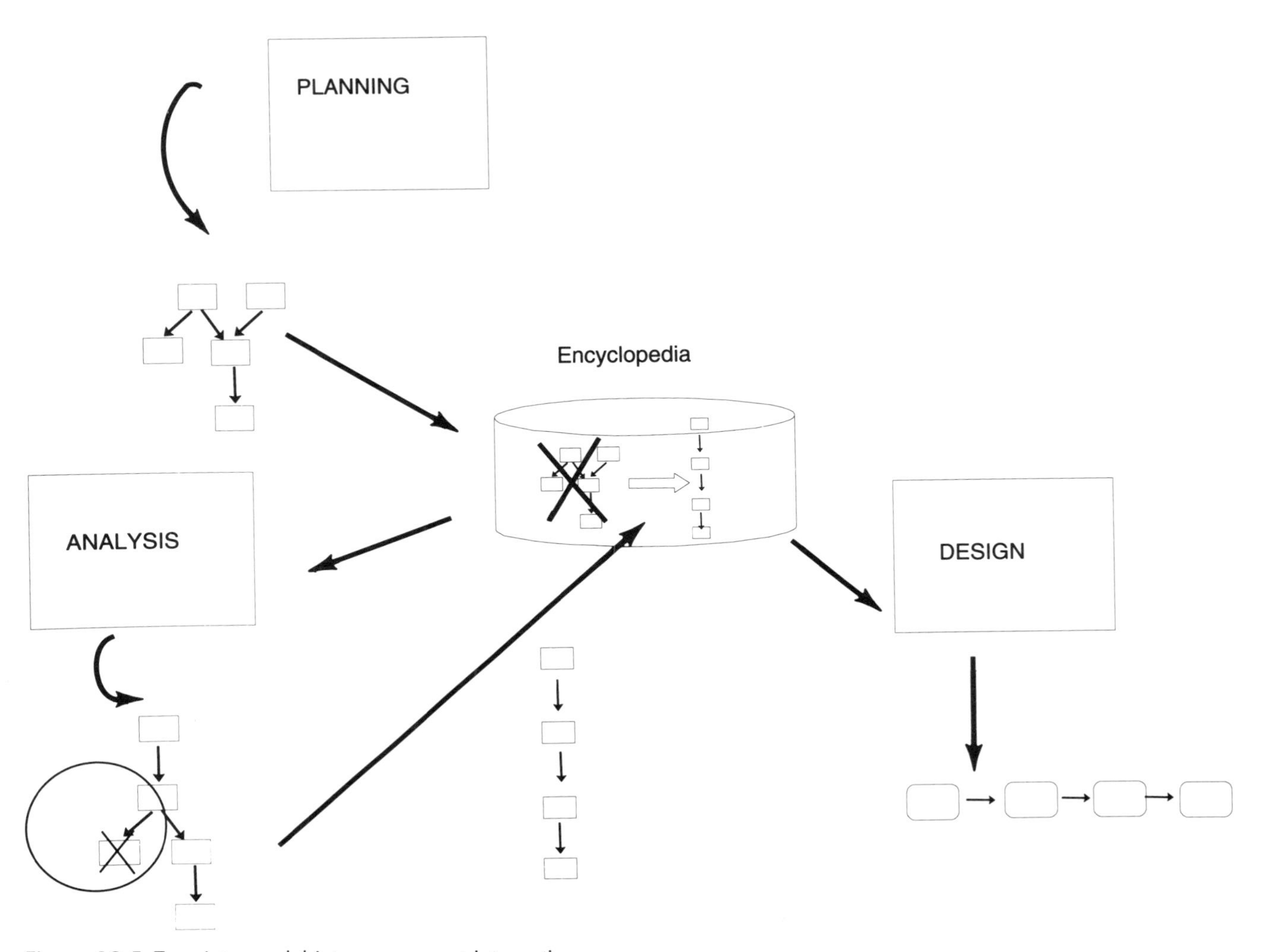

Figure 12.5 True intermodel intercomponent integration.

existence of the deleted attribute within the original entity's framework, the tool should inform the user, require a regeneration of all dependent constructs and code, and result in an integrity check before committing the change. In most existing scenarios the tool checks dependencies and warns the user of potential inconsistencies that could arise if the change is implemented. In other scenarios the change is accepted and the inconsistencies are not pointed out until an attempt at code regeneration ensues.

It is unfortunate that these dilemmas exist in today's tools, particularly in today's "integrated" tools. Putting reality into perspective, it is clear why a bridge is needed—even between tool components that may belong to the same vendor's integrated framework.

■ THE ISSUES INVOLVED IN BUILDING BRIDGES

Inter (or intra) package communication is never an easy task. Many issues come into play when products that represent a diversity of vendors and a diversity of hardware/software combinations attempt to communicate with each other. Attempts at standardizing the protocol and contents of interpackage communication generally result in a limited set of standard choices, but these choices usually conflict with each other in some interface aspect. As we will see in later chapters, standards are not truly standard when they consist of a collection of choices.

Putting "standards" aside, consider the compromise that would be necessary when two packages, each representing the primary revenue source for a different vendor, decide to establish a two-way interface. The following issues are guaranteed to surface:

The elements that each vendor offers as ingredients for modeling vary from tool to tool and from vendor to vendor. A model that was composed in a tool from Vendor A was developed using seven of the tool's available modeling constructs. The model could be further enhanced in a tool offering from another vendor; yet its transfer would involve translation issues with two of the seven modeling constructs because equivalents do not exist in the other vendor's tool. What is the best way of handling the transfer of uncommon model components?

Common model components differ from tool to tool. One tool may offer a 30-character maximum length for the names of logical attributes. Another tool may allow a maximum of 45 characters. If a model developed in the second tool takes advantage of the 45-character length, what do we do when we transfer this model to the first tool? Do we simply truncate the last 15 characters? Or do we create another field in which to store them? Reverse the scenario, and the issue becomes where to pad the 30-character name to expand its length to the 45-character equivalent in the second tool. The multiple scenarios that exist today are discussed in Chap. 14.

There are basic differences in the operating system platforms under which particular modeling tools execute, the organization's applications are developed, and the completed applications eventually reside for end-user access. In Fig. 12.6 a 1991 survey conducted by International Data Corporation shows the distribution of application

Use of Operating Systems for Application Development

	CASE USERS				NON-CASE USERS			
	HOST		CLIENT		HOST		CLIENT	
Operating System	Now	1994	Now	1994	Now	1994	Now	1994
Macintosh	3.2	—	9.5	3.1	11.8	9.7	6.7	6.7
MS / DOS	25.8	23.5	47.6	34.4	2.5	3.1	10.0	7.9
OS / 2	3.2	2.9	19.0	25.0	6.4	6.2	17.8	18.0
Unix	6.5	2.9	9.5	12.5	8.9	10.8	35.6	33.7
MVS	22.6	29.4	—	3.1	8.9	8.2	—	—
VM	6.5	5.9	—	—	31.5	29.7	—	—
VMS	16.1	14.7	4.8	6.3	13.8	13.8	—	—
DOS / VSE	3.2	5.9	—	—	14.8	17.4	—	—
OS / 400	6.5	5.9	4.8	9.4	1.5	0.5	—	—
Other	6.5	8.8	4.8	3.1	—	0.5	6.7	5.6
X-Terminal	—	—	—	—	—	—	22.2	27.0
MS / Windows	—	—	—	3.1	—	—	1.1	1.1
Total	100.0	100.0	100.0	100.0	100.0	100.0	100.0	100.0

Source: International Data Corp., 1991.

Figure 12.6 Use of operating systems for application development by CASE status (from International Data Corp., 1991).

development environments among CASE and non-CASE users as it existed in 1991 and as it is intended for 1994.*

It is important to consider the fact that CASE users are already developing a substantially equivalent amount of application on workstation-based operating systems (MSDOS, OS/2) as on the mainframe (MVS, VM). However, non-CASE users, currently developing an equivalent amount of applications on mainframe platforms (primarily VM) and Unix-based clients, are gearing more of their application development toward Unix. When existing models need to be accessible from the application development environment, bridges now need to consider the fact that CASE tools may not exist on both sides.

Application development tools, aside from CASE, may be functionally disparate yet still need access to CASE-based models. Models that reside in CASE tools could be beneficial to corporate data dictionaries, physical database design evaluators, graphic presentation packages, and application testing packages, to name a few.

The bridge must be built to be executable with standard application restrictions. Consider the bridge that could be built between a model or its components and the end-user. In many scenarios the end-user may benefit from this bridge when it exists as part of the finished application. For example, an end-user may generate a canned report request, view the output on line, and question the definition of one of the report columns. A bridge from the application to the application model

*"1990 to 1994 Computer-Aided Software Engineering (CASE) User Requirements," International Data Corporation, Framingham, MA, March 1991.

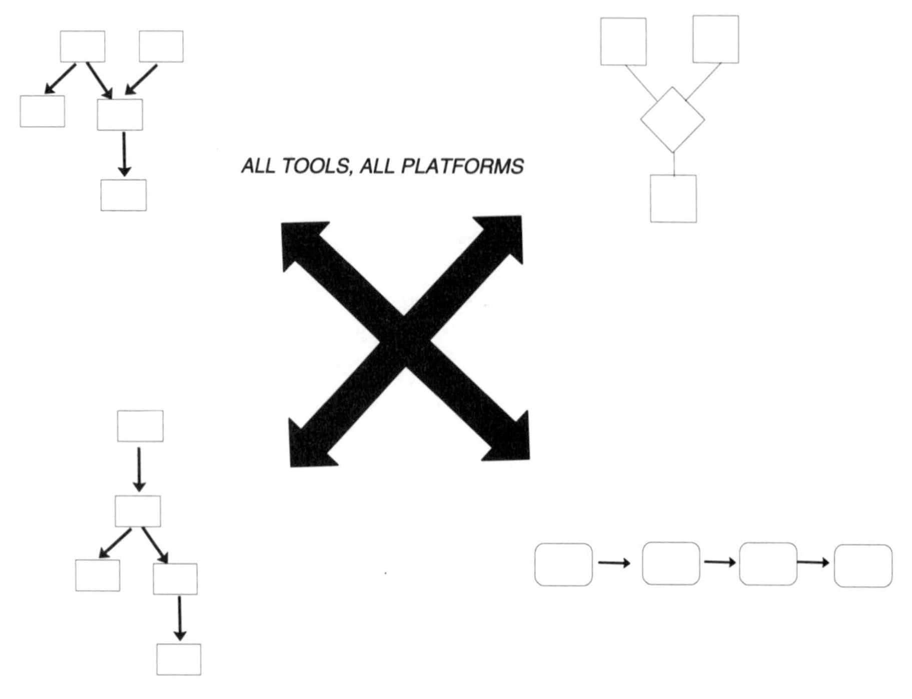

Figure 12.7 An illustration of an implemented bridge.

could immediately answer the question. Without a bridge the solution could involve several phone calls or, at best, the access of a developer-input user-help facility.

The architecture of the bridge itself lends many options. Batch file transfer, on-line access to a transfer process, on-line access to the source of the model, or the bridge as an entire independent application are just a few options. The bridge can provide limited functionality (e.g., connect only one internal application database with a CASE tool) or expand to include the entire application development world. (See Fig. 12.7 for an illustration of an implemented bridge).

Some organizations build their own bridges; yet they usually start as simple file transfer import/export mechanisms. When a visionary realizes how beneficial increased capability would be to a development organization, a developer realizes how complicated the execution of such a plan would be. Custom interfaces usually do not go beyond simple short-term fixes that were developed to meet an immediate need.

The reader should conclude this chapter with an appreciation of the complexity that can be involved when we begin to view models through the eyes of both the originating tool and those of the target model users. Because the targets as well as the originations can be multiple and diverse in terms of how the model was depicted, the platforms on which the model resides and needs to be accessed, and the functional roles played by the model on either end of the bridge, bridges are often not the best solution.

13

CASE METADATA CONSTRUCTS

"Incomprehensible jargon" continues its penetration when we begin discussing *metadata*. Everyone involved in dictionaries and repositories considers metadata to be a primary buzzword. In fact, many discussions get as theoretical as meta-metadata and meta-meta-metadata. These extra dimensions can get deep enough to confuse even the best dictionary administrator, let alone a sophisticated CASE modeler. For the purposes of this chapter, we will concentrate only on metadata, the data about the data (as opposed to the data about the metadata, or the data about the data about the metadata). Knowing that you are already confused, consider that each "definition" so to speak is entirely and strictly dependent on your level of concern and perspective within the application world.

■ METADATA DEFINED

When a standard definition requires additional clarification, it is safe to say that the standard definition is, in fact, not a definition, but a memorized phrase. Continuing our metadata discussion, members of our profession are always quick with their instantaneous "*data about the data*" retort. The key component of everyone's definition is *data*, and it is here (in both pieces of the metadata definition) that the multiple perspectives and concerns flourish.

Position yourself, as a reader, within the perspective of CASE integration for the purposes of Part Three. As we get beyond CASE in the later chapters of this book, your perspective and concerns will not change, but will become wider. As a CASE model integrator, your beginning area of concentration is the CASE-based model, as depicted in the underlying encyclopedia of each modeling tool. Therefore, your *data* can be thought of as a model itself, and the *describing data* (the data *about* your data) is the set of constructs that are used to store and relate the model within the CASE tool's internal encyclopedia.

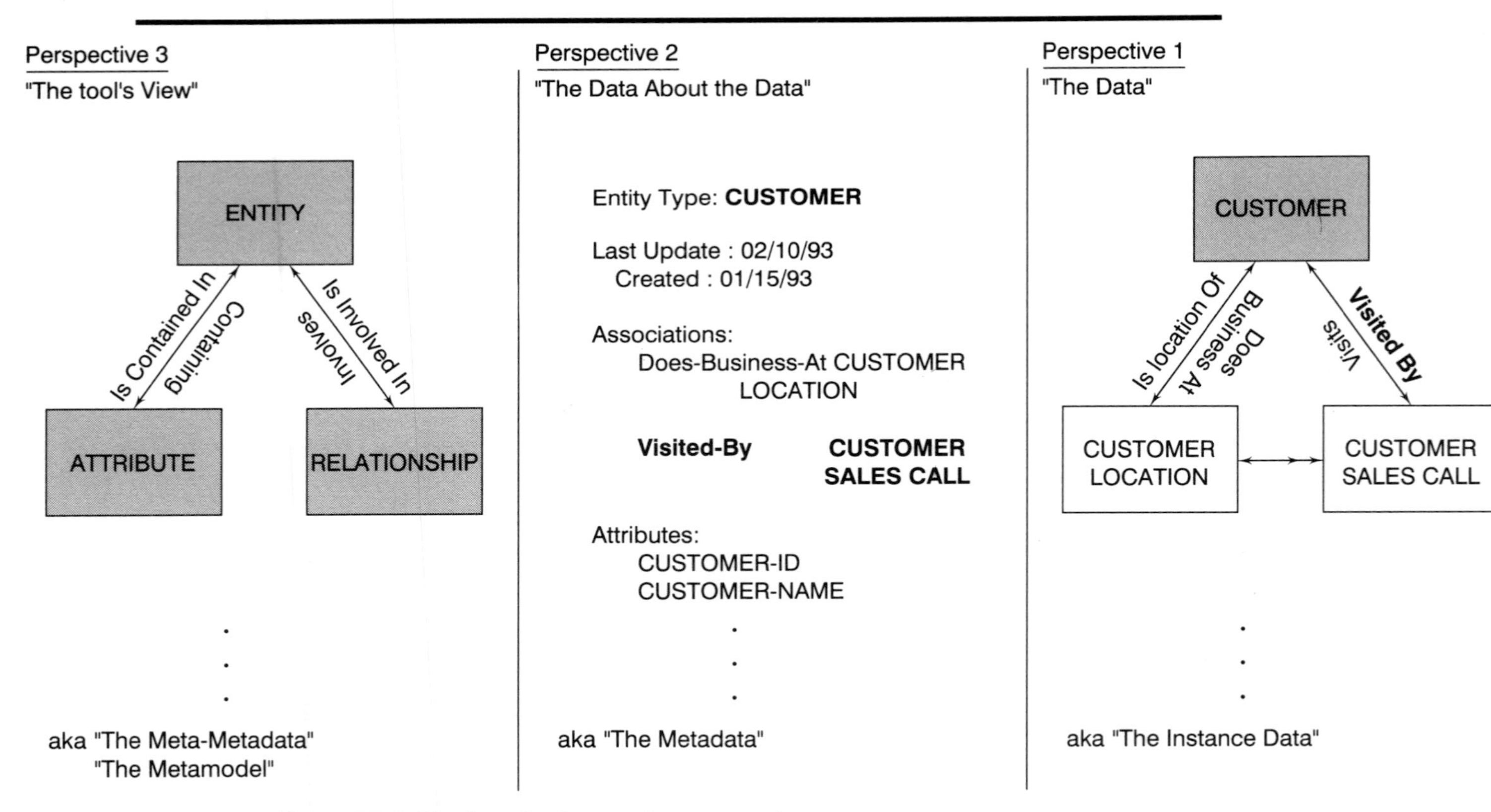

Figure 13.1 The three basic metadata perspectives

In a generic sense, all *data*, when being considered for residence in an underlying dictionary or encyclopedia, must be viewable and definable in a minimum of three perspectives. Figure 13.1 illustrates (from right to left) these perspectives and how they relate. At the rightmost segment is an illustration of the first perspective, that of "the data." In this example, because we are discussing CASE-based models, the data is in fact the model. The data is that which is input into the tool by the CASE user. To a database developer, this CASE model can be considered "metadata" (as we will discuss later), because it is a description of the developer's physical environment (in his or her world, the application database definition can be considered "the data"). Consider the relationship—a logical E–R data model describes (logically) the physical database. In this respect the CASE-based E–R model is the metadata; the physical database definition (e.g., the DDL) is the data! Finally, the developer's "data" can be considered "metadata" to the application user. The application user considers the actual database contents to be the data. Anything that describes or defines this "data" (such as a database schema or definition) is therefore "metadata" to the end-user.

Confused? The simplest way to define the first perspective, or "the data," is as follows:

> The data is that which is being input by the user/developer. Inside a dictionary/repository/modeling tool, data can take on several forms—models, dictionary entries, graphic representations. Outside the world of modeling tools and model storage mediums, but still within the realm of MIS, data can refer to application code, database definition language, or test data. Outside of MIS, data refers to the values stored within an application database, viewed on an application screen, or presented on an application's report.

The multiple perspectives that can belong to this first level of data definition are important baselines to remember. The definition and/or perspective of each successive level directly depends on where and how "data" becomes a part of the hierarchy. As the saying goes, "One person's data is another person's metadata."

In our simple example the data consists of a simple E–R model segment: three entities, three binary relationships, and the attributes associated with all entities. A clearer name for the data is the *instance data*.

Continuing our example, each succeeding perspective (in our case, the second) details that of the preceding viewpoint. Perspective 2 therefore depicts *the data about the data*, otherwise known as *the metadata*. Consider the example depicted in Fig. 13.1, and move to the middle column. When we view the middle or second perspective, we are concentrating on the descriptive details of the instance data supplied in perspective 1. For example, additional descriptive data such as the last-update and creation dates are now a part of every defined instance. In addition, the relationships between and among all populated instances are now also considered as instances regardless of whether or not they were user populated or automatically generated by the tool. Some metadata is also directly attributable to the tool itself and was originally intended for use only by the tool. For example, graphic positioning data (usually in the form of x and y coordinates) is often stored with the names of entities and relationships so that they can be redrawn by the tool. Metadata can also be organized by the tool into various groupings. Many of these groupings (often called submodels) may be invisible to the supplier of instance data, or even irrelevant. However, once the metadata perspective is placed on a set of data, the groupings typically affect tool-generated metadata and its relationships to the populated instances.

Not all metadata is necessarily retrievable or even viewable by the user of the modeling tool. When using the tool-supplied reports or utilities to look at a model's underlying metadata, some of the metadata (e.g., x, y coordinates) may not be output. Some tools feature proprietary database backbones and may internalize even more. The advent of repositories has opened up many previously "closed" tools, and hence the popularity of metadata.

To maintain our perspective, it is important to remember the different potential viewpoints that could represent our baseline data (as discussed previously). In our example a CASE-based model represents the data, the metadata is therefore represented as the underlying CASE database backbone, as it is populated by the tool upon model creation and update. If the baseline data is a database definition, our data (the model) can be considered metadata. Finally, to an end-user, the database definition (the DBA's data) is metadata. A generic metadata definition can be summarized as follows:

> The detailed description of data instances. Depending on the types of data populated, metadata can range from simple database field names, lengths, and characteristics, to the underlying tool constructs used to support a populated process model. Metadata, simply stated, is the definition, format, and characteristics of populated data.

Finally, to complete our definitions, the third metadata perspective needs to be clarified. Here, the details behind *metadata* (as discussed previously) form yet another set of constructs. These constructs are often called a *metamodel*. A tool's metamodel is often proprietary and untouchable by the tool user. Consider the metamodel to be the equivalent of the tool's view of the data. That is, to a tool developer, the model that depicts the underlying database behind the internal encyclopedia represents the tool metamodel. In most scenarios only tool-specific software needs to be concerned with the metamodel. However, once the issue of intertool communication becomes crucial, each involved tool must be evaluated and approached from a metamodel perspective.

Metamodels will be discussed in more detail in Part Five. For now, as a "bridge builder," the reader should be aware of their existence and how they relate to the other previously discussed data perspectives.

The leftmost viewpoint in Fig. 13.1 represents that of the metamodel (the tool's view). Notice that metamodels are often much simpler than the metadata depiction itself. It can be said (if we dwell in theory for a second) that every metamodel is the same: It consists of entities, attributes, and relationships. At the highest level this is true.

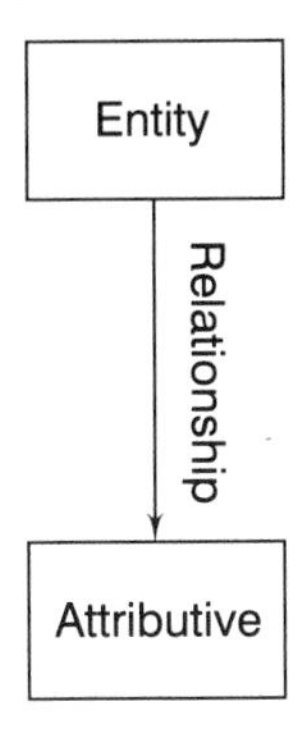

Figure 13.2 The generic metamodel

As illustrated in Fig. 13.2, every construct in an E–R-based modeling tool is eventually either an entity, an attribute, or a relationship. For example, an entity is obviously an entity, but an attribute can also be viewed as an entity type in that it has its own identifier and describing "attributes" when you look at it from inside the tool. Most repositories deal with this confusion by differentiating between entities at this level (perspective 3) and those at the instance level (perspective 1) with different naming conventions (e.g., ENTITY-TYPE vs. ENTITY). A great academic exercise which takes metadata to all levels of representation and understanding is the depiction of E–R constructs (as they exist in your favorite CASE tool, for example) as instances of the generic metamodel. This exercise has proven to be well worth its invested time when the objective was the understanding of metadata, its multiple perspectives, and their interrelationships. Those able to perform the task are well on their way to repository implementation!

But what about the object-oriented (OO) metamodel?* Another excellent academic exercise (which many of our existing CASE vendors are in the process of doing as of this writing) is the depiction of OO constructs in the generic metamodel illustrated in Fig. 13.2. Obviously, an *object* can be depicted as an entity. We could also view *classes* as entities. Their associated qualities and characteristics can be depicted as attributes. *Associations* can be mapped to relationships. Where the generic metamodel begins to fall apart is in the depiction of behavioral constructs such as services. Behavioral characteristics and event-driven modeling are not often easy to depict in an underlying E–R framework. However, all OO constructs do share similarities with the E–R basic components.

■ A REAL-LIFE METADATA ANALOGY

Those readers who are new to metadata internals are most likely scratching their heads now and may therefore appreciate this non-MIS example. Let us consider the public library in terms of its role as a holding area (a repository?) for books, magazines, films, and so on. We will define the various "metadata" perspectives in

---

*For a list of object-oriented readings, see the References at the end of this book.

two ways: first in terms of what the "repository user" (the library borrower) needs to know, and then in terms of what the "repository administrator" (the librarian) needs to know. We will not consider the many other perspectives (publishers, authors, etc.).

To the user, the item being borrowed (whether it is a book, magazine, video, or whatever) represents data. Using a book as an example, the user's metadata can be found in several places—the most accessible is within the book itself. The title and the author are probably the most useful pieces of metadata in that they describe and identify (immediately) the book (data) itself. Because they are within the book, they are also part of the data, event though they also represent a metadata perspective. But what if the title were not known to the user, that is, the user does not have the book in hand? Then the user must access the next perspective (perspective 2, the metadata). In a library this is the card catalog entry. The card catalog itself is considered metadata to the library borrower. The Dewey decimal system call number links the card catalog nonfiction entry (the metadata) to the actual data (the book) via the little tag taped to the outside of each book. The borrower's perspective is not necessarily this simple, however. We naively assumed that the borrower went right to the appropriate card within the card catalog. As experienced library users, we know the metadata gets a little more sophisticated, by necessity. Other categories (subject or author) also identify the data (books) within a card catalog. Although all of this is still metadata to the library borrower, it begins our bridge to the next perspective in that it is all part of a metamodel (that of the card catalog itself) and its internals so to speak. Only the librarian is concerned with this perspective (perspective 3).

Now, we revisit this example using the librarian perspective. First, to keep matters simple, we will consider this library to be the equivalent of a local repository (i.e., we are not "integrating" multiple libraries yet... more on that in upcoming chapters). In addition, we will consider the card catalog to be the equivalent of a single metamodel (one tool's view so to speak). The library does of course have other "metamodels"—an on-line computer indexing system, microfiche, and the physical ordering of the library shelves to name a few. But here, the card catalog will provide our repository administrator perspective.

To the librarian, each card within the card catalog can be considered data (perspective 1, the instance data). The books themselves are not her concern, only their entries within the catalog. So when she needs to get to her instance data, she always starts at the card catalog. Likewise, because she is responsible for maintaining the card catalog, she is always involved with perspective 3 in that she must consider how each card relates to all of the others and how it is referenced within the context of the entire catalog. This higher perspective is that of the metamodel, and, to a librarian, it would appear as shown in Fig. 13.3.

Hopefully, you can now imagine the differences in perspectives that are required. To the repository administrator (the librarian), everything represents an instance of the metamodel. New instance data is always evaluated in terms of its metamodel relationships. If a new way of indexing things is being proposed (e.g., beyond the Dewey Decimal system), the librarian immediately ponders how to

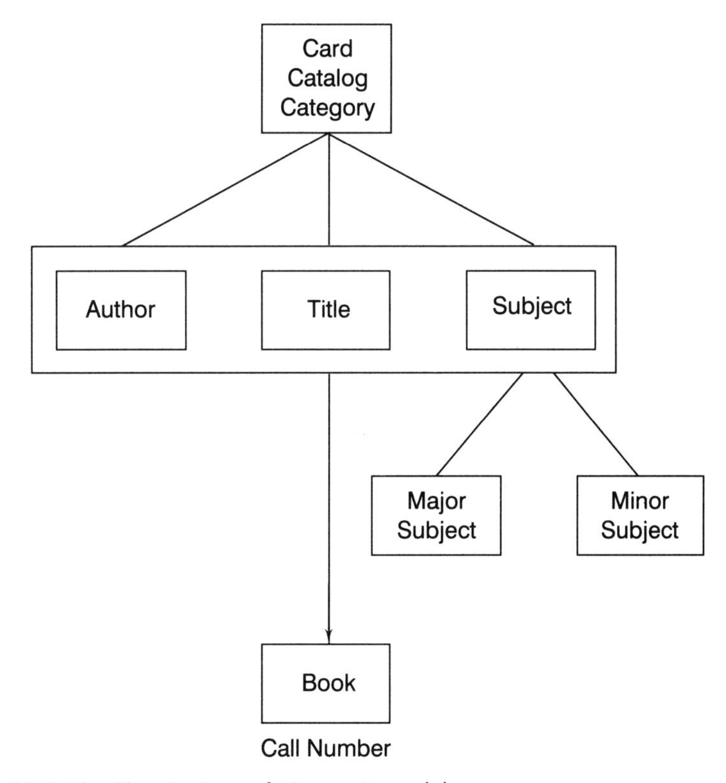

Figure 13.3 The librarian's nonfiction metamodel

retrofit this new perspective into the existing metamodel. Repository administration is no different!

Returning to our MIS focus, our metadata discussion continues in this chapter with a *submodel* flavor. As discussed previously, most CASE metadata is grouped in many ways. To the user, the models are often grouped by application. To the tool, the models are grouped by source tool component, and then by whatever user-initiated grouping names each set of instance data. Each source tool component is often a separate submodel to the encyclopedia. However, integrated CASE tools are integrated in one sense through common submodel usage by each component. Typically, the submodels are reflective of the information engineering stage in which the associated constructs are populated (planning, analysis, design, construction). In addition, there are common submodels (e.g., logical data model) that are accessible by multiple tool components.

■ COMMON METADATA CONSTRUCTS BY SUBMODEL

CASE-experienced readers most probably accomplish most of their CASE work using one main tool. Perhaps CASE usage is standardized in the organization and

Entity Model
- Attribute Type
- Entity Type
- Data Type
- Relationship Type

Data Structure Model
- Attribute Type
- Data Type
- Entity Type
- File Record
- Relation
- Relationship Type
- Segment
- Template Data Structure

Figure 13.4 Typical submodel examples

there is no option to employ a diversified tool suite. Or perhaps the choice is merely reflective of a favorite. The deployed tool is therefore the metadata template under which each reader is most probably operating. Depending on the types of models authored within and/or the functionality fulfilled by the used tool, each CASE user is accustomed to one or more subsets of metadata constructs, each referred to as a *submodel*.

Submodel is often a logical term in that it merely represents a logical grouping of a subset of a tool's underlying metamodel. In many cases not every submodel is represented by a distinct physical database within the tool's encyclopedia. The submodel then represents a "view" of the underlying data.

In Fig. 13.4 two submodels taken from a major CASE tool's planning module are depicted. The Entity Model consists here of the constructs listed previously. In essence, it is a logical, high-level representation of a potential database. The Data Structure Model contains all of the entity model constructs plus additional qualifying constructs to add a physical nature to the defined logical grouping.

In a competing vendor's CASE tool, Data Models consist of:

- Subject areas
- Entity types
- Partitioning
- Subtypes
- Relationships

The second tool allows more diversity in the construction of logical models, whereas the first tool combines some physical characteristics with logical constructs early on.

Regardless of the type of submodel being considered, it is obvious that the base set of constructs will vary from tool to tool. In fact, what is considered a submodel, as well as how each submodel is represented (physically and logically), will also vary among tools.

Based on these dichotomies, we will now attempt to standardize major submodel categories by depicting the common constructs that can be found in each, regardless of the underlying CASE tool.

Planning Submodels

Because planning implies the description of something that does not yet exist, most constructs that are resident in planning submodels do not contain detailed or in-depth attribute characteristics. They typically represent a high-level capture of a to-be-implemented idea. These ideas range from business objectives to proposed application processes. In general, planning constructs consist of the following:

Goal. A nameable, described objective

Problem. A nameable, identifiable situation that requires correction

Organization. A named physical unit within a business

Subject area. A high-level category of business-critical information

Project. A nameable work effort

Process. A nameable task or set of tasks

Relationship. A nameable association between two or more of the preceding constructs or between multiple occurrences of one of the previous constructs

Logical Data Models

Continuing the identification of common submodels and their standard components, the next major category of metadata is that comprising the logical data model. This collection of metadata is generally not considered a submodel in itself, because it usually spans most of the application development life cycle. In many tools the development of the logical data model begins early on, in the planning phase. The model is then further refined through analysis and becomes physically attributed in the design phase. Depending on whether the underlying tool has a heavy data orientation, the supporting constructs for logical data models can be extensive. The logical data model depicts the data needs of an application, their characteristics, and their interrelationships. All logical data models, despite the underlying CASE tool, consist of the following constructs:

Entity. Any nameable person, place, thing, or event about which information will be stored

Attribute. A nameable quality or characteristic of an entity

Primary and foreign keys. An attribute or group of attributes that can uniquely identify an occurrence of an entity or an occurrence of a related entity (foreign key)

Relationship. A nameable association between two or more entities or between multiple occurrences of a single entity

The preceding list is seemingly small. Most tools offer a more extensive list of metadata constructs. However, when describing the common intersection without regard to the underlying tool base, the preceding list results.

Process Models

Process models (or submodels) represent the processes within an application. They are typically distinct and apart from associated application data models. The data and process models usually come together in some diagrams (e.g., data flow diagrams) or in the actual specifications. The number of constructs belonging to the process model umbrella is dependent on whether or not the underlying CASE tool is involved in code generation. Again, because we are depicting common process submodel constructs across the tool universe, the following list represents a common intersection:

Process. A nameable function or operation that has an effect on data

Subprocess. A nameable subordinate process that belongs to a process hierarchy

*Data store.** A nameable temporary holding area for data that is part of process input/output (I/O)

*External agent.** A process, application, or organization that is outside the scope of the particular process model, yet affects the process as either a supplier or receiver of information, or as an event trigger

Like logical data models, process models are not complex in terms of their common construct set. The three submodel categories mentioned previously constitute the majority of the commonality among tools.

Continuing the identification of commonality requires the identification of the following implementation-oriented submodels. At this level of modeling, constructs are relatively common among tools because they are being used to represent, and in some cases generate, specific hardware/software requirements for an application. However, whether or not they need to be addressed as part of an intertool bridge is dependent on whether the source of these submodels will differ from the recipient user (e.g., code generation tool). In addition, the scope of a target repository should also consider where physical design models are best resident. Assuming the need to transfer physical design models, we will discuss next the physical models and their common constructs.

Process Specification Models

Process specifications supply what is often called the *pseudocode* for a particular process. In standard English-like terminology, the processing required is depicted in a structured format. Because the process specifications are often eventually fed

*These process model components are not usually illustrated in the process model diagrams, but in data flow diagrams.

as input to a code generator, most of the statement types (DO, IF, READ, LOOP, etc.) are relatively standard. The main, relatively standard components of process specification models are as follows:

Statement. The actual pseudocode-like logic that describes each step of a process

Block. A nameable group of statements, usually performed as a unit

Condition. If/else logic that optionally precedes a statement or block

Call. A transfer of processing to another process, either external (often called an external procedure) or internal to the application

When evaluating process specifications in terms of CASE tool bridging, it is important to be aware of how the specifications are stored within the depicting tool and how they relate from a storage perspective to the affected construct instances in other submodels (e.g., entities, attributes, information stores). It may not be practical to export process specifications from their originating tool.

Physical Data Models

As CASE usage extends deeper into the application development process, design modules further refine the preexisting logical data models into more specific physical, implementation-oriented models. Typically, performance-affecting criteria are input into the depicting tool, and the tool recommends or generates particular physical designs. The criteria that affect physical database design are directly dependent on the target DBMS platform. The following constructs assume the existence of a logical data model and a relational DBMS target:

Database name. The name of the physical database

DBMS type. The name of the target DBMS

DBMS-specific constructs. Using DB2 as an example, names of each physical implementation-specific database construct (Buffer Pool, Storage Group, VCAT, Table, Column, etc.). IMS would require different constructs (Database, Segment, Index, Program Specification Block, etc.) and so on

Index. The name and correlated attributes of each data structure index

The preceding list represents a common set of implementation-specific requirements that translate a logical model into a to-be-implemented physical database design.

Physical Design Models

The remaining aspects of an application are derived from the already established process and data models. Examples include screens (or windows) and reports. Each of these represents a way of viewing or supplying information that may or may not be a part of the application database. Depending on whether or not the depicting tool will actually generate the code required to construct these application components, the list of CASE-based inputs can be quite lengthy. Also, because there is little variation in how the resulting code must be represented, most of the required constructs are standard.

Screen- and window-specific constructs include anything that will appear on the screen (window) that was not previously defined in any model as well as the physical representation qualities of all screen components despite their existence as named constructs within other models. Any reader familiar with the programming required to establish screens and windows should realize the types and categories of additional information required above and beyond already defined CASE-based models. Without going into the enormous detail that would be required to list these constructs, it is sufficient to remind the potential CASE integrator that the only variability between tools is how the physical programming-specific constructs relate to any already defined model instances. In addition, many new processing requirements are introduced via the definition of screens and windows. For example, PF (program function) key definitions, displayed text, and executed procedures may or may not relate to other application processes already represented in other models. Similarly, help messages, error messages, and screen-to-screen execution order (also called dialog design) also become part of these physical submodels.

Like screens and windows, reports require the definition of all components and the associated physical qualities, as they will appear on paper. Aside from the obvious field names, report-specific processing requirements include header and detail definition, total and subtotal processing requirements, sort order, and carriage control. Again, similar to screen and window definition, additional logic (in the form of additional process specifications) is often required to generate and/or calculate reports and report sections. The integration issues relate again to how the underlying tool stores and depicts report generation requirements and how they relate (if at all) to existing constructs in other models.

■ WHERE COMMON CONSTRUCTS BECOME UNCOMMON

Experienced CASE users have already noticed the disparity between constructs that are common to other tools and constructs that are in use in their own individual tool set. Many "best of breed" CASE tool contenders are justified in their belief that different tools are the best for different aspects of software engineering. There are many reasons for the various renditions of CASE tool metadata:

- The tool's underlying methodology
- The tool's primary function (e.g., drawing diagrams vs. code generation)
- The timing and degree of the tool's consistency checking
- The tool's "operating level" (e.g., conceptual analysis vs. physical database design)

For example, some CASE tools are known for their excellent code generation capabilities (when compared to competitors). This implies excellent process model support, allowing the detail necessary to express the constructs necessary to generate specific and accurate code. On the other hand, this same tool may not be a favorite with data administrators who have the need to represent detailed relationships between and within major aspects of corporate data. Hence, the divergent tool selection paths.

Realizing that each tool has its area of specialty, few CASE users expect the exact same set of metadata constructs to exist from tool to tool. The previous section highlighted those constructs that are relatively standard among the CASE tool marketplace. But what does *standard* imply? The mere existence of a construct does not imply a standard meaning, usage, or relationship to other constructs within the submodel. Also, the purpose of the immediate submodel within the entire model framework has a direct effect on how powerful the particular construct is when viewed from a reusability perspective.

There is no easier way to prove the point that even common constructs are uncommon than to look at the *entity* construct. Every CASE tool must have this construct as part of its logical data model. Figure 13.5 shows the required inputs from two major CASE tools. In one example the Information Engineering Facility

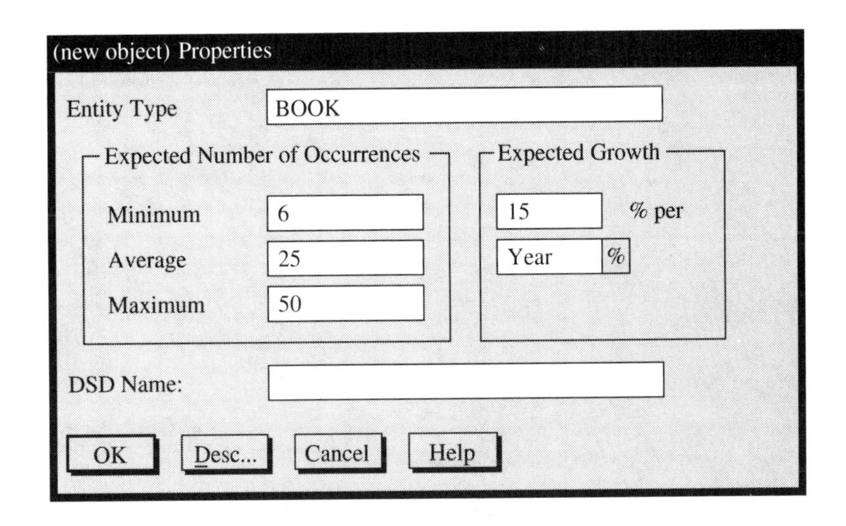

Model : BOOK
Subset : (Complete model)

Entity Definition

Entity:	BOOK			
Description:	ANY PUBLISHED WORK WITH AN ASSOCIATED AUTHOR AND ISBN NUMBER			
Subject area:	BOOK			
Properties:	Min Occ:	6	Avg Occ:	25
	Max Occ:	50	Growth Rate:	15% per year

Figure 13.5 The definition of an entity in two popular CASE tools: (a) the entity *Book* as defined in Texas Instruments IEF (Version 5.1).

Create/Find

Create or find Entity Types

Names:

BOOK

Fundamental
Attributive
Associative
Other

Create | Find | Cancel | Help

NAME

BOOK

PURPOSE

FUNDAMENTAL

(FUNDAMENTAL, ASSOCIATIVE, ATTRIBUTIVE, OTHER)

DEFINITION

ANY PUBLISHED WORK WITH AN
ASSOCIATED AUTHOR AND ISBN
NUMBER

COMMENTS

LAST UPDATE
01-08-1993 03:42:50 PM ABT

CREATED
01-08-1993 03:42:50 PM ABT

(b)

Figure 13.5 (b) the entity ***Book*** as defined in Knowledgeware's ADW Analysis Workstation (Version 1.6).

(IEF) was used to define the entity *book*. In the other example the Application Development Workbench (ADW)'s Analysis Workstation was used to define the same entity.

The first obvious difference is the type of information requested by each tool. The *Expected Number of Occurrences* seems to be of importance in IEF, whereas ADW categories entities into types (fundamental, associative, etc.) upon creation. In the next chapter we will discuss metadata attributes in detail, covering the differences in attributes associated with each metadata construct and the impact this could have on repository implementation. For now, we will concentrate on the role the entity plays within each of the sample tools.

In our simple example each entity has been depicted as a standalone instance. It is obvious that tools (such as the ones used in the previous example) with implementation in mind view each entity as an eventual file, table, or database segment. What does vary with each tool is whether or not the entity can exist with only a logical flavor, and, if not, when the physical characteristics must be introduced. In the IEF example (Fig. 13.5*a*), an optional entry is a *DSD name*. This name is used by the code generator as the name of the generated database structure. The ADW example (Fig. 13.5*b*), on the other hand, has no physical references at all in the entity definition. Although this may seem like a trivial point, the implications in usage across multiple projects in an organization can affect the ease in which data models from either tool can be cross referenced. It is likely that those developers working on an immediate application placed as much physical quality as possible, as early as possible in the IEF tool. For example, the *DSD name* is probably populated in most entities, implying that the data model is more physical than logical. Developers using ADW, on the other hand, have the option of using the entity to represent a logical occurrence (only). The physical redesign and association with the logical entities happen further in the development life cycle.

Neither option is necessarily inferior. However, the problems in model integration across tools arise when different goals were depicted by different developers. For example, an IEF entity named CUSTOMER-RECEIPT could represent the implemented DB2 table in terms of its related attributes. An ADW entity named RECEIPT may represent the same table from a logical viewpoint. How is the tool integrator to know this? Most likely, the two entities do not consist of the same attributes. Furthermore, each entity is probably not related to the same set of entities (CUSTOMER-RECEIPT most likely relates to a smaller universe of entities). Of course, other issues such as modeling and methodology standards (as discussed in previous sections) affect the accuracy and reusability of models within each deployed tool. The point to remember, however, is that when different tools have different sets of metadata, the intended use of even the common metadata constructs can differ.

■ EXAMPLE: A MODEL REPRESENTED IN VARIOUS TOOLS

The discrepancies cited previously with common constructs can take a back seat to the most obvious concern when dealing with multiple tools: that of uncommon metadata. Any integration of models that were depicted with a varying tool set will have to deal with two issues: (1) combining apples with apples of a different variety and (2) translating apples into substitute oranges.

The easiest way to depict the integration issue is via an example. In the following discussion, a simple Customer/Purchase-Order data model with a subset of its associated process models is illustrated in a few CASE tools. The model, although simple, concentrates on the use of constructs that are particular to the depiction of specific requirements in either the data or process characteristics of the model. All of the models try to convey all or some of the following business rules:

1. Our company sells directly to four types of customers: retail outlets, wholesale distributors, end-consumers, and practicing professionals.
2. Each customer type has its own unique identification algorithm.
3. The identification of practicing professionals is controlled by outside licensing agencies.

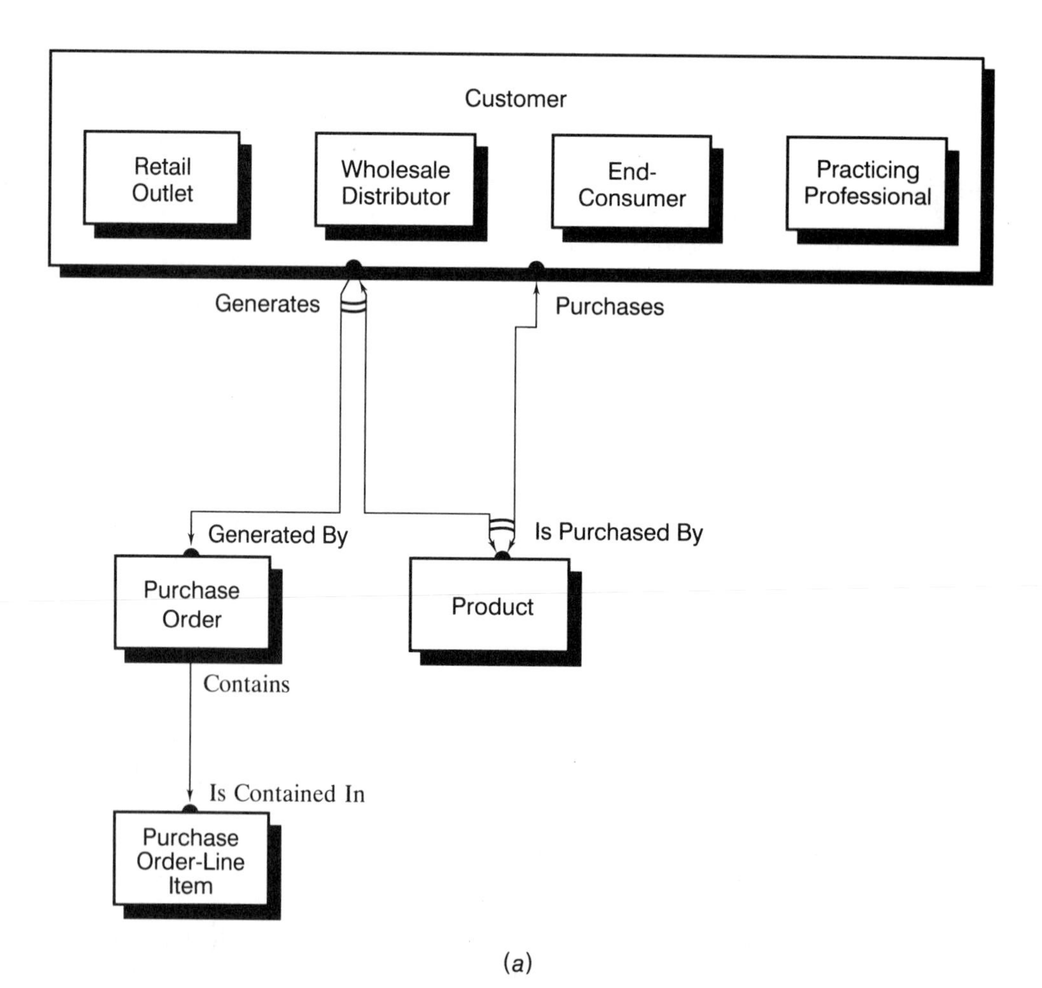

Figure 13.6 A simple E–R model depicted by the Bachman Analyst (Version 4.1)

```
   Entity Detail Report Created at: 1-11-93 10:41:49AM

   Enterprise Model:  part2
     File is C:\BACHMAN\DESIGNS\PART2B.AN

   Information Model:  part2

   Free Attribute: TODAY
     Nulls not allowed
     Storable;  Source type:   System

   Entity:   CUSTOMER

   DESCRIPTION:   The buyer of company goods. Currently, customers
    are one of four basic types:  Practicing Professionals,
    End-Consumers, Wholesale Distributors, or Retail Outlets

1    Subtypes:
1     END-CONSUMER
1     PRACTICING PROFESSIONAL
1     RETAIL OUTLET
1     WHOLESALE DISTRIBUTOR

     Entity MIN Vol = 200,    Entity MAX Vol = 39999996

   Attribute:    CUSTOMER.CUSTOMER-ID
     Nulls not allowed
     Storable;     Source type:    System

     DESCRIPTION:   A SYSTEM-GENERATED IDENTIFIER THAT UNIQUELY
      TAGS EACH CUSTOMER, CUSTOMER-IDS ARE ASSIGNED BASED ON THE
    LEGAL
      IDENTITY OF EACH CUSTOMER, IRRESPECTIVE OF THE NUMBER OF
      ASSOCIATED LOCATIONS.

2    Dimension = IDENTIFIER
     Domain    = GENERATED-NUMERIC
      Datatype = Integer;  Min Val = 1, Max Val = 99999

   Attribute:   CUSTOMER.CUSTOMER-NAME
     Nulls not allowed
     Storable;     Source type:   Manual

   Attribute:   CUSTOMER.CUSTOMER-TYPE
     Nulls not allowed
     Storable;     Source type:   Manual

   Attribute:   CUSTOMER.CUSTOMER-CREDIT-RATING
     Nulls not allowed
     Storable;     Source type:    Manual
```

Key: 1 = Subtypes / Supertypes
2 = Dimensions
3 = Complex Relationships
4 = Domains / Subdomains
5 = Allowed Value Table
6 = Compound Attributes
7 = Compound Identifiers
8 = Note

Figure 13.6b (Continued).

```
DESCRIPTION:   A ONE-DIGIT ENCODED NUMBER THAT DEPICTS THE
 CUSTOMER 'S CREDIT.  THE CREDIT RATING IS DETERMINED BY
 PAYMENT HISTORY ACQUIRED BY US OVER THE YEARS. ALL NEW
 CUSTOMERS ARE GIVEN A FAIR CREDIT RATING. AFTER ONE YEAR OF
 ON-TIME PAYMENTS, THE RATING IS ELEVATED TO GOOD. CUSTOMERS
 WITH TWO OR MORE YEARS OF GOOD PAYMENT HISTORY RECEIVE
EXCELLENT CREDIT RATINGS.
 CUSTOMERS WHO MISS AT LEAST TWO PAYMENTS IN A YEAR 'S TIME HAVE
 THEIR CREDIT RATING LOWERED TO 'BELOW AVERAGE.' UNLESS A FULL
 YEAR OF ON-TIME PAYMENTS RESULTS, THE CREDIT RATING IS THEN
 LOWERED TO 'POOR.'

2    Dimension = CODE
4    Domain    = INTEGER1
       Datatype = Alphabetic;  Min Len = 1, Max Len = 1, Exp Len = 1

  PSet:   CUSTOMER.GENERATES

    Joins:
     PRODUCT.IS PURCHASED BY
     (AND) PURCHASE ORDER.GENERATED BY

    PSet MIN Vol = 125,    PSet MAX Vol = 9999999

  PSet:   CUSTOMER.PURCHASES

    Joins:
     PRODUCT.IS PURCHASED BY

    PSet MIN Vol = 1,    PSet MAX Vol = 500

  Key:   CUSTOMER.CUSTOMER-IDENTIFIER  (PRIMARY)

    CONSISTS OF:
     CUSTOMER.CUSTOMER-ID   ATTR

  Entity:   END=CONSUMER

    DESCRIPTION:   The type of customer who purchases a product
     directly. CURRENTLY, this purchase option is only available
     via mail-order or telephone.

1    Supertype:
      CUSTOMER
6   Inherited from:  CUSTOMER
6    Inherited Attrs:
6     CUSTOMER-ID
6     CUSTOMER-NAME
6     CUSTOMER-TYPE
6     CUSTOMER-CREDIT-RATING
6    Inherited PSets:
6      GENERATES
6      PURCHASES
6    Inherited Keys:
6      CUSTOMER-IDENTIFIER
```

```
     Entity MIN Vol = 0,    Entity MAX Vol = 9999999

   Attribute:   END-CONSUMER.CUSTOMER-SHIP-TO-STREET
     Nulls not allowed
     Storable;     Source type:   Manual

   Attribute:   END-CONSUMER.CUSTOMER-SHIP-TO-CITY
     Nulls not allowed
     Storable;     Source type:   Manual

   Attribute:   END-CONSUMER.CUSTOMER-SHIP-TO-STATE
     Nulls not allowed
     Storable;     Source type:   Manual

   Attribute:   END-CONSUMER.CUSTOMER-SHIP-TO-ZIP
     Nulls not allowed
     Storable;     Source type:   Manual

   Entity:   PRACTICING PROFESSIONAL

     DESCRIPTION:   The customer subtype who is a licensed health
      care practitioner.

1    Supertype:
      CUSTOMER

6    Inherited from:  CUSTOMER
6     Inherited Attrs:
6      CUSTOMER-ID
6      CUSTOMER-NAME
6      CUSTOMER-TYPE
6      CUSTOMER-CREDIT-RATING
6     Inherited PSets:
6       GENERATES
6       PURCHASES
6     Inherited Keys:
6     CUSTOMER-IDENTIFIER

     Entity MIN Vol = 0,    Entity MAX Vol = 9999999

   Attribute:   PRACTICING PROFESSIONAL.PROFESSIONAL-LICENSE-NO
     Nulls not allowed
     Storable;     Source type:   Manual

   Attribute:  PRACTICING PROFESSIONAL.PROFESSIONAL-SPECIALTY-CODE
     Nulls not allowed
     Storable;     Source type:    System

     DESCRIPTION:   THE TWO-DIGIT CODE INDICATING THE TYPE OF
      MEDICAL SPECIALITY FOR WHICH THE PROFESSIONAL IS LICENSED

2    Dimension = CODE
4    Domain    = INTEGER1
       Datatype = Alphabetic;  Min Len = 1, Max Len = 1, Exp Len = 1
```

```
8     NOTE:    VALID SPECIALTY CODE VALUES:  HOW CURRENT ARE THE
       SPECIALTY CODES THAT EXIST IN THE PROFESSIONAL LICENSING
       APPLICATION 'S DATABASE? DO WE NEED TO UPDATE THEM WITH
       A NEW TAPE?

   Entity:   PRODUCT

      DESCRIPTION:   ANY PACKAGED, SELLABLE, DISTRIBUTABLE VERSION
       OF OUR COMPANY 'S MANUFACTURED ITEMS

      Entity MIN Vol = 0,    Entity MAX Vol = 9999999

   Attribute:   PRODUCT.PRODUCT-NUMBER (Owner)
      Nulls not allowed
      Storable;     Source type:   System

      DESCRIPTION:   AN INTERNALLY GENERATED IDENTIFIER FOR EACH
       PACKAGED PRODUCT OFFERING

6     Component Attributes:
6       PRODUCT-CATEGORY
6       PRODUCT-PACKAGE-TYPE
6       PRODUCT-MAIN-INGREDIENT-CODE
6       PRODUCT-NUMBER-OF-UNITS

   Attribute:   PRODUCT.PRODUCT-CATEGORY (Component)
      Nulls not allowed
      Storable;     Source type:   System

6     Owner Attributes:
        PRODUCT-NUMBER

   Attribute:   PRODUCT.PRODUCT-PACKAGE-TYPE (Component)
      Nulls not allowed
      Storable;     Source type:   System

6     Owner Attributes:
        PRODUCT-NUMBER

   Attribute:   PRODUCT.PRODUCT-MAIN-INGREDIENT-CODE (Component)
      Nulls not allowed
      Storable;     Source type:   System

6     Owner Attributes:
        PRODUCT-NUMBER

   Attribute:   PRODUCT.PRODUCT-NUMBER-OF-UNITS (Component)
      Nulls not allowed
      Storable;     Source type:   System

6     Owner Attributes:
        PRODUCT-NUMBER
```

```
Attribute:   PRODUCT.PRODUCT-PACKAGE-PRICE
  Nulls not allowed
  Storable;     Source type:   System

Attribute:   PRODUCT.PRODUCT-LIFE-CYCLE-TERMINATION-DATE
  Nulls not allowed
  Storable;     Source type:   System

PSet:   PRODUCT.IS PURCHASED BY

  Joins:
   CUSTOMER.GENERATES
   (AND) CUSTOMER.PURCHASES

  PSet MIN Vol = 2,    PSet MAX Vol = 9999999

Key:   PRODUCT.PRODUCT-IDENTIFIER  (PRIMARY)

  CONSISTS OF:
   PRODUCT.PRODUCT-NUMBER   ATTR

Entity:   PURCHASE ORDER

  DESCRIPTION:   THE RESULT OF A PURCHASE TRANSACTION. UNITES A
   CUSTOMER WITH PURCHASED PRODUCTS

  Foreign Key Attributes (PSet.FKAttr / (Entity.Attr))
    GENERATED BY.CUSTOMER-ID
     (CUSTOMER. CUSTOMER-ID)

  Entity MIN Vol = 0,    Entity MAX Vol = 9999999

Attribute:   PURCHASE ORDER.CUSTOMER-ID
  Nulls not allowed
  Storable;    Source type:   System
  DESCRIPTION:   A SYSTEM-GENERATED IDENTIFIER THAT UNIQUELY TAGS
   EACH CUSTOMER, CUSTOMER-IDS ARE ASSIGNED BASED ON THE LEGAL IDENTITY
   OF EACH CUSTOMER, IRRESPECTIVE OF THE NUMBER OF ASSOCIATED
   LOCATIONS.

2   Dimension = IDENTIFIER
4   Domain    = GENERATED-NUMERIC
      Datatype = Integer;  Min Val = 1, Max Val = 99999

Attribute:   PURCHASE ORDER.ORDER-NUMBER
  Nulls not allowed
  Storable;     Source type:   System
 Source name:   GENERATE-ORDER-NUMBER

  DESCRIPTION:   THE SEQUENTIALLY GENERATED NUMBER ASSOCIATED
   WITH EACH CUSTOMER'S ORDER PLACEMENT
```

```
2    Dimension = IDENTIFIER
4    Domain    = GENERATED-NUMERIC
       Datatype = Integer;  Min Val = 1, Max Val = 99999

  Attribute:   PURCHASE ORDER.ORDER-DATE
     Nulls not allowed
     Storable;     Source type:   Manual

     DESCRIPTION:   DATE ORDER WAS PLACED

2    Dimension = DATE
4    Domain    = MMDDYY
4      Has 3 Subdomains

  Attribute:   PURCHASE ORDER.ORDER-DOLLAR-TOTAL
     Nulls not allowed
     Storable;     Source type:   System

     DESCRIPTION:   THE TOTAL DOLLAR AMOUNT OF THIS ORDER

2    Dimension = MONEY
4    Domain    = DOLLARS AND-CENTS
       Datatype = None

  PSet:   PURCHASE ORDER.CONTAINS

     Joins:
      PURCHASE-ORDER-LINE-ITEM.IS CONTAINED IN

     PSet MIN VOL = 1,    PSet MAX VOL = 60

  PSet:  PURCHASE ORDER.GENERATED BY

     Joins:
      CUSTOMER.GENERATES

     PSET MIN VOL = 1,    PSET MAX VOL = 1

7    KEY:   PURCHASE ORDER.PURCHASE-ORDER-NUMBER  (PRIMARY)

7    CONSISTS OF:
7     PURCHASE ORDER.CUSTOMER-ID   ATTR
7     PURCHASE ORDER.ORDER-NUMBER   ATTR

  Entity:   PURCHASE-ORDER-LINE-ITEM

  DESCRIPTION:   EACH PRODUCT/QUANTITY COMBINATION THAT
   CONSTITUTES A PURCHASE ORDER

  Foreign Key Attributes (PSet.FKAttr / (Entity.Attr))
    IS CONTAINED IN.CUSTOMER-ID
      (PURCHASE ORDER.CUSTOMER-ID)
    IS CONTAINED IN.ORDER-NUMBER
      (PURCHASE ORDER.ORDER-NUMBER)
```

```
     Entity MIN Vol = 1,    Entity MAX Vol = 9999999

   Attribute:   PURCHASE-ORDER-LINE-ITEM.LINE-NUMBER
     Nulls not allowed
     Storable;     Source type:   Manual

   Attribute:   PURCHASE-ORDER-LINE-ITEM.PRODUCT-NUMBER
     Nulls not allowed
     Storable;     Source type:   Manual

   Attribute:   PURCHASE-ORDER-LINE-ITEM.PRODUCT-QUANTITY
     Nulls not allowed
     Storable;     Source type:   Manual

7    PSet:   PURCHASE-ORDER-LINE-ITEM.IS CONTAINED IN

     Joins:
      PURCHASE ORDER.CONTAINS

     PSet MIN Vol = 1,    PSet MAX Vol = 1

7    Key:   PURCHASE-ORDER-LINE-ITEM.LINE-NUMBER  (PRIMARY)

     CONSISTS OF:
      PURCHASE-ORDER-LINE-ITEM.LINE-NUMBER   ATTR

   Entity:   RETAIL OUTLET

     DESCRIPTION:  A bulk purchaser of our products with facilities
      directly accessible to the end-consumer. Retail outlets
    purchase
      our products at wholesale prices and resell them directly to
      the end-consumer at mark-up prices.

1    Supertype:
      CUSTOMER

6    Inherited from:  CUSTOMER
6     Inherited Attrs:
6      CUSTOMER-ID
6      CUSTOMER-NAME
6      CUSTOMER-TYPE
6      CUSTOMER-CREDIT-RATING
6     Inherited PSets:
6       GENERATES
6       PURCHASES
6     Inherited Keys:
6       CUSTOMER-IDENTIFIER

     Entity MIN Vol = 0,    Entity MAX Vol = 9999999

   Attribute:   RETAIL OUTLET.RETAIL-SPECIALTY-CODE
     Nulls not allowed
     Storable;     Source type:   Manual
```

```
     DESCRIPTION:   CODE DESCRIBING THE MAJOR PRODUCT LINE OF THE
      RETAIL OUTLET

2    Dimension = CODE
4    Domain    = INTEGER1
       Datatype = Alphabetic;  Min Len = 1, Max Len = 1, Exp Len = 1

   Entity:   WHOLESALE DISTRIBUTOR

     DESCRIPTION:  Bulk buyers of our products. Distributors resell
      our products at mark-up prices. Distributors can only
      purchase from us via prearranged contractual agreements.

1    Supertype:
      CUSTOMER

6    Inherited from:  CUSTOMER
6     Inherited Attrs:
6      CUSTOMER-ID
6      CUSTOMER-NAME
6      CUSTOMER-TYPE
6      CUSTOMER-CREDIT-RATING
6     Inherited PSets:
6       GENERATES
6       PURCHASES
6     Inherited Keys:
6       CUSTOMER-IDENTIFIER

     Entity MIN Vol = 0,    Entity MAX Vol = 9999999

   Attribute: WHOLESALE DISTRIBUTOR.DISTRIBUTORSHIP-EXPIRATION-DATE
     Nulls not allowed
     Storable;     Source type:   Derived

     DESCRIPTION:   DATE ON WHICH DISTRIBUTORSHIP EXPIRES

2    Dimension = DATE
4    Domain    = MMDDYY
4      Has 3 Subdomains

   Attribute:   WHOLESALE DISTRIBUTOR.CENTRALIZED-WAREHOUSE-
    INDICATOR
     Nulls not allowed
     Storable;     Source type:   Manual

     DESCRIPTION:   A ONE-CHARACTER INDICATOR THAT DETERMINES
      WHETHER OR NOT THIS WHOLESALE DISTRIBUTOR REPRESENTS A
      CENTRALIZED WAREHOUSE

2    Dimension = INDICATOR
4    Domain    = YES-NO
       Datatype = Alphabetic;   Min Len = 1, Max Len = 1, Exp Len = 1
```

(b)

```
   **** Dimensions with Domains ****

2    Dimension:    CODE

2    DESCRIPTION:    ANY ENCODED VALUE BELONGS TO THIS DIMENSION

     Associated Attributes:
       CUSTOMER.CUSTOMER-CREDIT-RATING
       PRACTICING PROFESSIONAL.PROFESSIONAL-SPECIALTY-CODE
       RETAIL OUTLET.RETAIL-SPECIALTY-CODE

4    Domain:   INTEGRAL1   (Default)

4    DESCRIPTION:   ONE DIGIT INTEGER CODES FALL INTO THIS DOMAIN
      CATEGORY

     Associated Attributes:
       CUSTOMER.CUSTOMER-CREDIT-RATING
       PRACTICING PROFESSIONAL.PROFESSIONAL-SPECIALTY-CODE
       RETAIL OUTLET.RETAIL-SPECIALTY-CODE

     Datatype = Alphabetic;  Min Len = 1, Max Len = 1, Exp Len = 1

     Allowed Value Table:  CREDIT-RATING-CODES
       Exclude = NO

       DESCRIPTION:   ONE DIGIT INTEGERS AND THEIR ASSOCIATED
        CREDIT RATINGS

       Begin Value:  0
       End Value:    0

         DESCRIPTION:  FAIR

       Begin Value:  1
       End Value:    1

         DESCRIPTION:  GOOD

       Begin Value:   2
       End Value:    2

         DESCRIPTION:  EXCELLENT

       Begin Value:   3
       End Value:   3

         DESCRIPTION:  BELOW AVERAGE

       Begin Value:  4
       End Value:    4

         DESCRIPTION:  POOR
```

```
2     Dimension:   DATE

      Associated Attributes:
        PURCHASE ORDER.ORDER-DATE
        WHOLESALE DISTRIBUTOR.DISTRIBUTORSHIP-EXPIRATION-DATE

4     Domain:   MMDDYY    (Default)

4     DESCRIPTION:   THE STANDARD DATE FORMAT FOR ALL USER-INPUT
       DATES

      Associated Attributes:
        PURCHASE ORDER.ORDER-DATE

4     Subdomain:   MONTH (Level 1, # 1)

        Datatype = None

4     Subdomain:   DAY (Level 1, # 2)

        Datatype = None

4     Subdomain:   YEAR (Level 1, # 3)

        Datatype = None

2     Dimension:    IDENTIFIER

2     DESCRIPTION:   ALL NUMERIC IDENTIFIERS BELONG TO THIS DIMENSION

      Associated Attributes:
        CUSTOMER.CUSTOMER-ID
        PURCHASE ORDER.CUSTOMER-ID
        PURCHASE ORDER.ORDER-NUMBER

4     Domain:   GENERATED-NUMERIC   (Default)

4     DESCRIPTION:   ALL PRIMARY IDENTIFIERS THAT ARE NUMERIC
     (INTEGER) AND GENERATED BY THE SYSTEM BELONG TO THIS DOMAIN

      Associated Attributes:
        CUSTOMER.CUSTOMER-ID
        PURCHASE ORDER.CUSTOMER-ID
        PURCHASE ORDER.ORDER-NUMBER

      Datatype = Integer;  Min Val = 1, Max Val = 99999

2     Dimension:   INDICATOR

2     DESCRIPTION:   ANY FLAG VALUE BELONGS TO THIS DIMENSION.
       TYPICALLY, ONLY TWO VALUES ARE POSSIBLE.
```

```
      Associated Attributes:
        WHOLESALE DISTRIBUTOR.CENTRALIZED-WAREHOUSE-INDICATOR

4     Domain:   YES-NO    (Default)

      Associated Attributes:
        WHOLESALE DISTRIBUTOR.CENTRALIZED-WAREHOUSE-INDICATOR

      Datatype = Alphabetic;  Min Len = 1, Max Len = 1, Exp Len = 1

5     Allowed Value Table:   Y-OR-N
        Exclude = NO

        Begin Value:  Y
        End Value:    Y

          DESCRIPTION:  YES

        Begin Value:  N
        End Value:    N

          DESCRIPTION:   NO

2     Dimension:   MONEY

      Associated Attributes:
        PURCHASE ORDER.ORDER-DOLLAR-TOTAL

4     Domain:   DOLLARS-AND-CENTS    (Default)

      Associated Attributes:
        PURCHASE ORDER.ORDER-DOLLAR-TOTAL

      Datatype = None
```

(c)

4. The purchase of a product by any type of customer requires the generation of a purchase order. Each purchase transaction, regardless of whether or not it occurred on the same day and/or by the same customer, requires the generation of a unique purchase order.
5. Customers must have customer numbers before they can purchase products.
6. Every product available for purchase must exist in the product master. The product master is updated daily with price, availability, and product description data.
7. There is a need to query, on a daily basis, which customer purchased which products, or which products were the most heavily purchased, and so on for decision support reasons.
8. A purchase order can request the purchase of multiple products. Each product ordered represents a distinct line item on a purchase order.

```
Domain Detail Report Created at: 11-29-92 3:02:10PM

Enterprise Model:   part2
  File is C:\BACHMAN\DESIGNS\PART2B.AN

Information Model:   part2

**** Dimensions with Domains ****

Dimension:   CODE

  DESCRIPTION:   ANY ENCODED VALUE BELONGS TO THIS DIMENSION

  Associated Attributes:
    CUSTOMER.CUSTOMER-CREDIT-RATING
    PRACTICING PROFESSIONAL.PROFESSIONAL-SPECIALITY-CODE
    RETAIL OUTLET.RETAIL-SPECIALITY-CODE

Domain:   INTEGER1   (Default)

  DESCRIPTION:   ONE DIGIT INTEGER CODES FALL INTO THIS DOMAIN
                 CATEGORY

  Associated Attributes:
    CUSTOMER.CUSTOMER-CREDIT-RATING
    PRACTICING PROFESSIONAL.PROFESSIONAL-SPECIALITY-CODE
    RETAIL OUTLET.RETAIL-SPECIALITY-CODE

  Datatype = Alphabetic;  Min Len = 1, Max Len = 1, Exp Len = 1

  Allowed Value Table:   CREDIT-RATING-CODES
    Exclude = NO

  DESCRIPTION:   ONE DIGIT INTEGERS AND THEIR ASSOCIATED CREDIT
                 RATINGS

  Begin Value:  0
  End Value:    0
    DESCRIPTION:   FAIR

  Begin Value:  1
  End Value:    1

    DESCRIPTION:   GOOD

  Begin Value:  2
  End Value:    2

    DESCRIPTION:   EXCELLENT

  Begin Value:  3
  End Value:    3
```

Figure 13.6c (Continued).

```
  DESCRIPTION:   BELOW AVERAGE

Begin Value:  4
End Value:    4

  DESCRIPTION:   POOR
 Dimension:   IDENTIFIER

   Associated Attributes:
     PURCHASE ORDER.ORDER- DATE
     WHOLE DISTRIBUTOR.DISTRIBUTORSHIP- EXPIRATION- DATE

 DOmain:   MMDDYY   (Default)

   DESCRIPTION:   THE STANDARD DATE FORMAT FOR ALL USER- INPUT
                  DATES

   Associated Attributes:
     PURCHASES ORDER.ORDER- DATE

   Subdomain:   MONTH (Level 1, # 1)

     Datatype = None

   Subdomain:   DAY (Level 1, # 2)

     Datatype = None

   Subdomain:   YEAR (Level 1, # 3)

     Datatype = None

 Dimension:   IDENTIFIER

   DESCRIPTION:   ALL NUMERIC IDENTIFIERS BELONG TO THIS
                  DIMENSION

   Associated Attributes:
     CUSTOMER.CUSTOMER- ID
     PURCHASE ORDER.CUSTOMER- ID
     PURCHASE ORDER.ORDER- NUMBER

 Domain:   GENERATED- NUMERIC   (Default)

   DESCRIPTION:   ALL PRIMARY IDENTIFIERS WHICH ARE NUMERIC
                  (INTEGER) AND GENERATED BY THE SYSTEM BELONG
                  TO THIS DOMAIN
```

```
    Associated Attributes:
      CUSTOMER.CUSTOMER-ID
      PURCHASE ORDER.CUSTOMER-ID
      PURCHASE ORDER.ORDER-NUMBER

    Datatype = Integer;  Min Val = 1, Max Val = 99999

  Dimension:   INDICATOR

    DESCRIPTION:   ANY FLAG VALUE BELONGS TO THIS DIMENSION.
                   TYPICALLY, ONLY TWO VALUES ARE POSSIBLE.

    Associated Attributes:
      WHOLESALE DISTRIBUTOR.CENTRALIZED-WAREHOUSE-INDICATOR

  Domain:   YES-NO   (Default)

    Associated Attributes:
      WHOLESALE DISTRIBUTOR.CENTRALIZED-WAREHOUSE-INDICATOR

    Datatype = Alphabetic;  Min Len = 1, Max Len = 1, Exp Len = 1
    Allowed Value Table:   Y-OR-N
      Exclude = NO

      Begin Value:  Y
      End Value:    Y

      DESCRIPTION:   YES

      Begin Value:  N
      End Value:    N

      DESCRIPTION:  NO

  Dimension:   MONEY

    Associated Attributes:
      PURCHASE ORDER.ORDER-DOLLAR-TOTAL

  Domain:   DOLLARS-AND-CENTS   (Default)

    Associated Attributes:
      PURCHASE ORDER.ORDER-DOLLAR-TOTAL

    Datatype = None
```

9. The price paid by a customer for a product is dependent on several factors: the quantity purchased, the type of customer, and the customer's credit rating.
10. Customers with poor credit ratings must pay before receiving their ordered products.

We begin our model depiction by illustrating the data side of our requirements via an entity–relationship (E–R) model in the Bachman Analyst. In Fig. 13.6*a* we see the graphical depiction as well as the elements and metadata attributes behind the picture. The highlights of the Bachman model include the following:

Subtypes. Customers have been separated into four distinct subtypes based on the unique processing requirements and/or data characteristics on each subtype. The supertype *Customer* contains the generic "category-neutral" attributes. The subtype/supertype functionality of the Bachman Analyst causes all of the subtypes to inherit the generic attributes that are part of the supertype.

Complex relationship. The relationship between *Customer*, *Purchase Order*, and *Product* is considered complex in that more than two entities are involved. When a customer makes a purchase, a purchase order is *generated*, and the relationship between the customer and the *purchased* product must be maintained elsewhere in order to satisfy the decision support requirements listed previously.

Dimensions. Looking at the diagram's details as depicted in Figs. 13.6*b* and *c*, note the presence of dimensions. Dimensions are used to classify attributes with common characteristics (usually physical). With the emphasis on reusability, they have become popular data model integration aids. In our model CODE, DATE, INDICATOR, and MONEY have been defined based on the similarities that exist among several attributes.

Domains/subdomains. Domains are associated with dimensions and represent physical data types. They can also be broken down into subdomains, as illustrated. In our model INTEGER1, GENERATED-NUMERIC, MMDDYY, DOLLARS-AND-CENTS, and YES-NO are defined domains.

Allowed value tables. All valid values for attributes that belong to a domain are defined in this construct. CREDIT-RATING-CODES and Y-OR-N are examples within this model.

Compound attributes. Attributes that can be sub-defined into separate components are illustrated in this model; an example is PRODUCT-NUMBER.

Compound identifiers. Like compound attributes, compound identifiers consist of multiple component attributes. An example is PURCHASE-ORDER-NUMBER.

Notes. Notes represent a way of tagging particular model components with some type of text. An example is the text assigned to attribute PROFESSIONAL-SPECIALTY-CODE.

There are many other components to this model, but this chapter concentrates on those components that require extra attention when being considered for integration.

Continuing the depiction of data, Fig. 13.7 is an attempt at representing the previous model in Knowledgeware's ADW (Analysis Workstation, Release 1.6). Many of the constructs depicted in the previous model are identically represented, some are depicted via different constructs or a set of constructs, and some cannot be represented at all. The major areas to be noticed are as follows:

Subtypes. As of this writing, ADW does not have a subtype construct. Instead, two relationships, IS-A-SUBTYPE-OF and IS-A-SUPERTYPE-OF, have been created and used to associate each CUSTOMER subtype.

Associative entity. PURCHASE-ORDER-LINE-ITEM is depicted as an associative entity, one that exists to relate other entities. In this example it relates PRODUCT and PURCHASE-ORDER. Another associative entity could be established to meet the requirements of the complex relationship between PRODUCT, CUSTOMER, and PURCHASE-ORDER as depicted in the first example. However, because the relationship exists as a relationship in the first model, this illustration did not depict the concept as an entity (see the following entry).

Complex relationship. No direct means of representation. Mapped to associative entity for the purposes of illustration.

Data type. The use of global data types to ADW is similar to the *dimension* concept in the Bachman model. However, here the data types are defined with their physical qualities. Data types therefore are analogous to Bachman dimensions *with their associated domains*.

Domains / subdomains. See *data type* given previously.

Allowed value tables. No equivalent construct. Values can be itemized as text in the description associated with each attribute.

Concatenations. The ADW equivalent of *compound attributes*.

Compound identifiers. Although not depicted in the preceding illustration, this concept is supported, and identifiers are visibly noted by an *ID* prefix which precedes each so-labeled attribute. However, there is no separate logical name for the identifier.

Having discussed the data side of each CASE tool's modeling constructs, differences are paramount even in our simple model. Now, to complete the analysis, consider these simple process specification models—first as standalone

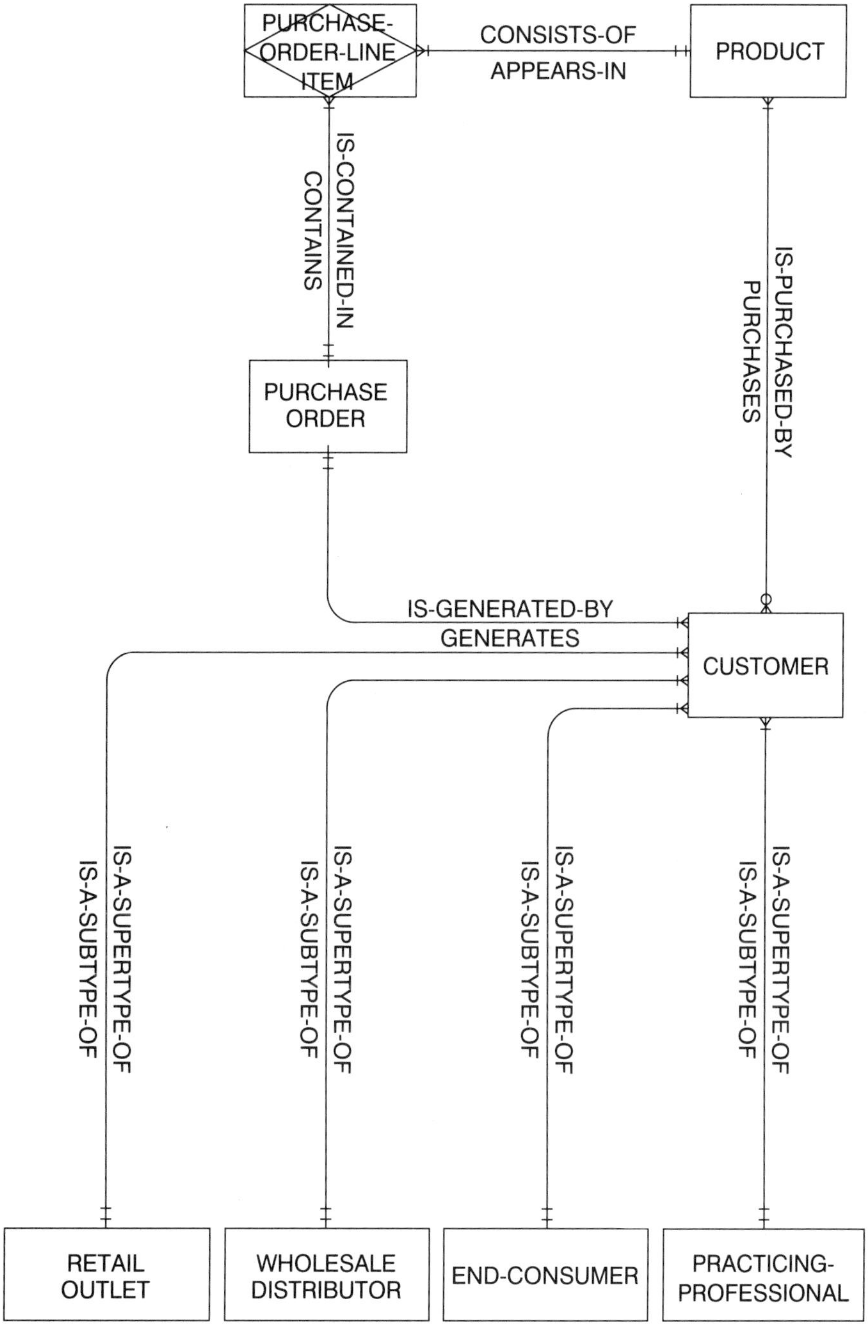

(a)

Figure 13.7 The same model represented in Knowledgeware's ADW Analysis Workstation (Version 1.6)

```
Object Summary Report

Attribute Type: WHOLESALE DISTRIBUTOR.CENTRALIZED-WAREHOUSE-
   INDICATOR

  Definition
  A ONE-CHARACTER INDICATOR THAT DETERMINES WHETHER OR NOT THIS
  WHOLESALE DISTRIBUTOR REPRESENTS A CENTRALIZED WAREHOUSE

  PROPERTY             VALUE                     Key: 1 = Subtypes / Supertype
                                                      2 = Dimensions
  Minimum per Subject  1                              3 = Complex Relationshi
  Maximum per Subject  450                            4 = Domains / Subdomains
  Maximum per Value    1                              5 = Allowed Value Table
  Last Update          1992/11/30 16:50:40 ABT        6 = Compound Attributes
  Created              1992/11/30 16:48:31 ABT        7 = Compound Identifier
  Type                 ELEMENTARY                     8 = Note
  Item Type            ALPHA
  Format               A
  External Length      1
  Internal Length      1

  ASSOCIATION          TYPE                      NAME

2 Has                  Data Type                 INDICATOR

Attribute Type: CUSTOMER.CUSTOMER-CREDIT-RATING

  Definition
  A ONE-DIGIT ENCODED NUMBER THAT DEPICTS THE CUSTOMER'S CREDIT.
  THE CREDIT RATING IS DETERMINED BY PAYMENT HISTORY ACQUIRED
  BY US OVER THE YEARS. ALL NEW CUSTOMERS ARE GIVEN A FAIR
  CREDIT RATING. AFTER ONE YEAR OF ON-TIME PAYMENTS, THE RATING
  IS ELEVATED TO GOOD. CUSTOMERS WITH TWO OR MORE YEARS OF GOOD
  PAYMENT HISTORY RECEIVE EXCELLENT CREDIT RATINGS.

  CUSTOMERS WHO MISS AT LEAST TWO PAYMENTS IN A YEAR'S TIME HAVE
  THEIR CREDIT RATING LOWERED TO `BELOW AVERAGE.' UNLESS A FULL
  YEAR OF ON-TIME PAYMENTS RESULTS, THE CREDIT RATING IS THEN
  LOWERED TO `POOR.'

  PROPERTY             VALUE

  Minimum per Subject  200
  Maximum per Subject  M
  Maximum per Value    1
  Last Update          1992/11/30 14:37:09 ABT
  Created              1992/11/30 13:55:34 ABT
  Type                 ELEMENTARY
  Item Type            EXTERNAL DECIMAL
  Format               9(1)
  External Length      1
  Internal Length      1
```

```
     ASSOCIATION          TYPE                 NAME
2    Has                  Data Type            CODE

   Attribute Type: PRACTICING-PROFESSIONAL.CUSTOMER-CREDIT-RATING

     PROPERTY             VALUE
   Minimum per Subject  20
   Maximum per Subject  2000
   Maximum per Value    1
   Last Update          1992/11/30 15:48:54 ABT
   Created              1992/11/30 15:48:54 ABT

   ASSOCIATION          TYPE                 NAME

Attribute Type: END-CONSUMER.CUSTOMER-CREDIT-RATING

   PROPERTY             VALUE

   Minimum per Subject  1000
   Maximum per Subject  9999
   Maximum per Value    1
   Last Update          1992/11/30 15:57:59 ABT
   Created              1992/11/30 15:57:59 ABT

   ASSOCIATION          TYPE                 NAME

Attribute Type: RETAIL OUTLET.CUSTOMER-CREDIT-RATING

   PROPERTY             VALUE

   Minimum per Subject  1
   Maximum per Subject  300
   Maximum per Value    1
   Last Update          1992/11/30 16:44:41 ABT
   Created              1992/11/30 16:44:41 ABT

   ASSOCIATION          TYPE                 NAME

Attribute Type: WHOLESALE DISTRIBUTOR.CUSTOMER-CREDIT-RATING

   PROPERTY             VALUE

   Minimum per Subject  1
   Maximum per Subject  450
   Maximum per Value    1
   Last Update          1992/11/30 16:48:34 ABT
   Created              1992/11/30 16:48:34 ABT

   Association          TYPE                 NAME
```

```
Attribute Type: CUSTOMER.CUSTOMER-ID

  Definition
  A SYSTEM-GENERATED IDENTIFIER THAT UNIQUELY TAGS EACH
  CUSTOMER.CUSTOMER-IDS ARE ASSIGNED BASED ON THE LEGAL
  IDENTITY OF EACH CUSTOMER, IRRESPECTIVE OF THE NUMBER OF
  ASSOCIATED LOCATIONS.

  PROPERTY              VALUE

  Minimum per Subject   200
  Maximum per Subject   M
  Maximum per Value     1
  Last Update           1992/11/30 13:57:23 ABT
  Created               1992/11/30 13:55:30 ABT
  Type                  ELEMENTARY
  Item Type             EXTERNAL DECIMAL
  Format                9(5)
  External Length       5
  Internal Length       5

  ASSOCIATION           TYPE                   NAME

  Has                   Data Type              IDENTIFIER

2 Attribute Type: PRACTICING-PROFESSIONAL.CUSTOMER-ID

  PROPERTY              VALUE

  Minimum per Subject   20
  Maximum per Subject   2000
  Maximum per Value     1
  Last Update           1992/11/30 15:48:49 ABT
  Created               1992/11/30 15:48:49 ABT

  ASSOCIATION           TYPE                   NAME

Attribute Type: END-CONSUMER.CUSTOMER-ID

PROPERTY                VALUE

  Minimum per Subject   1000
  Maximum per Subject   9999
  Maximum per Value     1
  Last Update           1992/11/30 15:57:55 ABT
  Created               1992/11/30 15:57:55 ABT

  ASSOCIATION           TYPE                   NAME
```

Attribute Type: PURCHASE ORDER.CUSTOMER-ID

Definition
A SYSTEM-GENERATED IDENTIFIER THAT UNIQUELY TAGS EACH CUSTOMER. CUSTOMER-IDS ARE ASSIGNED BASED ON THE LEGAL IDENTITY OF EACH CUSTOMER, IRRESPECTIVE OF THE NUMBER OF ASSOCIATED LOCATIONS.

PROPERTY	VALUE
Minimum per Subject	1
Maximum per Subject	9999
Maximum per Value	1
Last Update	1992/11/30 16:20:52 ABT
Created	1992/11/30 16:18:21 ABT
Type	ELEMENTARY
Item Type	EXTERNAL DECIMAL
Format	9(5)
External Length	5
Internal Length	5

ASSOCIATION	TYPE	NAME
Has	Data Type	IDENTIFIER

7

Attribute Type: PURCHASE-ORDER-LINE-ITEM.CUSTOMER-ID

PROPERTY	VALUE
Minimum per Subject	1
Maximum per Subject	100
Maximum per Value	100
Last Update	1992/11/30 16:37:34 ABT
Created	1992/11/30 16:37:34 ABT

ASSOCIATION	TYPE	NAME

Attribute Type: RETAIL OUTLET.CUSTOMER-ID

PROPERTY	VALUE
Minimum per Subject	1
Maximum per Subject	300
Maximum per Value	1
Last Update	1992/11/30 16:44:36 ABT
Created	1992/11/30 16:44:36 ABT

ASSOCIATION	TYPE	NAME

Attribute Type: WHOLESALE DISTRIBUTOR.CUSTOMER-ID

PROPERTY	VALUE
Minimum per Subject	1
Maximum per Subject	450
Maximum per Value	1
Last Update	1992/11/30 16:48:39 ABT
Created	1992/11/30 16:48:39 ABT

ASSOCIATION	TYPE	NAME

```
Attribute Type: CUSTOMER.CUSTOMER-NAME

   PROPERTY                 VALUE

   Minimum per Subject  200
   Maximum per Subject  M
   Maximum per Value    1
   Last Update          1992/11/30 13:55:31 ABT
   Created              1992/11/30 13:55:31 ABT

   ASSOCIATION          TYPE                        NAME

Attribute Type: PRACTICING-PROFESSIONAL.CUSTOMER-NAME

   PROPERTY                 VALUE

   Minimum per Subject  20
   Maximum per Subject  2000
   Maximum per Value    1
   Last Update          1992/11/30 15:48:51 ABT
   Created              1992/11/30 15:48:51 ABT

   ASSOCIATION          TYPE                        NAME

Attribute Type: END-CONSUMER.CUSTOMER-NAME

   PROPERTY                 VALUE

   Minimum per Subject  1000
   Maximum per Subject  9999
   Maximum per Value    1
   Last Update          1992/11/30 15:57:56 ABT
   Created              1992/11/30 15:57:56 ABT

   ASSOCIATION          TYPE                        NAME

Attribute Type: RETAIL OUTLET.CUSTOMER-NAME

   PROPERTY                 VALUE

   Minimum per Subject  1
   Maximum per Subject  300
   Maximum per Value    1
   Last Update          1992/11/30 16:44:38 ABT
   Created              1992/11/30 16:44:38 ABT

   ASSOCIATION          TYPE                        NAME
```

```
Attribute Type: WHOLESALE DISTRIBUTOR.CUSTOMER-NAME

  PROPERTY             VALUE

  Minimum per Subject  1
  Maximum per Subject  450
  Maximum per Value    1
  Last Update          1992/11/30 16:48:37 ABT
  Created              1992/11/30 16:48:37 ABT

  ASSOCIATION          TYPE                     NAME

Attribute Type: END-CONSUMER.CUSTOMER-SHIP-TO-CITY

  PROPERTY             VALUE

  Minimum per Subject  1000
  Maximum per Subject  9999
  Maximum per Value    1
  Last Update          1992/11/30 15:58:03 ABT
  Created              1992/11/30 15:58:03 ABT

  ASSOCIATION          TYPE                     NAME

Attribute Type: END-CONSUMER.CUSTOMER-SHIP-TO-STATE

  PROPERTY             VALUE

  Minimum per Subject  1000
  Maximum per Subject  9999
  Maximum per Value    1
  Last Update          1992/11/30 15:58:04 ABT
  Created              1992/11/30 15:58:04 ABT

  ASSOCIATION          TYPE                     NAME

Attribute Type: END-CONSUMER.CUSTOMER-SHIP-TO-STREET

  PROPERTY             VALUE

  Minimum per Subject  1000
  Maximum per Subject  9999
  Maximum per Value    1
  Last Update          1992/11/30 15:58:01 ABT
  Created              1992/11/30 15:58:01 ABT

  ASSOCIATION          TYPE                     NAME

Attribute Type: END-CONSUMER.CUSTOMER-SHIP-TO-ZIP

  PROPERTY             VALUE

  Minimum per Subject  1000
  Maximum per Subject  9999
  Maximum per Value    1
  Last Update          1992/11/30 15:58:06 ABT
```

```
   Created                 1992/11/30 15:58:06 ABT

   ASSOCIATION             TYPE                      NAME

Attribute Type: CUSTOMER.CUSTOMER-TYPE

   PROPERTY                VALUE

   Minimum per Subject     200
   Maximum per Subject     M
   Maximum per Value       1
   Last Update             1992/11/30 13:55:33 ABT
   Created                 1992/11/30 13:55:33 ABT

   ASSOCIATION             TYPE                      NAME

Attribute Type: PRACTICING-PROFESSIONAL.CUSTOMER-TYPE

   PROPERTY                VALUE

   Minimum per Subject     20
   Maximum per Subject     2000
   Maximum per Value       1
   Last Update             1992/11/30 15:48:52 ABT
   Created                 1992/11/30 15:48:52 ABT

   ASSOCIATION             TYPE                      NAME

Attribute Type: END-CONSUMER.CUSTOMER-TYPE

   PROPERTY                VALUE

   Minimum per Subject     1000
   Maximum per Subject     9999
   Maximum per Value       1
   Last Update             1992/11/30 15:57:58 ABT
   Created                 1992/11/30 15:57:58 ABT

   ASSOCIATION             TYPE                      NAME

Attribute Type: RETAIL OUTLET.CUSTOMER-TYPE

   PROPERTY                VALUE

   Minimum per Subject     1
   Maximum per Subject     300
   Maximum per Value       1
   Last Update             1992/11/30 16:44:39 ABT
   Created                 1992/11/30 16:44:39 ABT
```

```
     ASSOCIATION          TYPE                    NAME

   Attribute Type: WHOLESALE DISTRIBUTOR.CUSTOMER-TYPE

     PROPERTY             VALUE

     Minimum per Subject  1
     Maximum per Subject  450
     Maximum per Value    1
     Last Update          1992/11/30 16:48:35 ABT
     Created              1992/11/30 16:48:35 ABT

     ASSOCIATION          TYPE                    NAME

   Attribute Type: WHOLESALE DISTRIBUTOR.DISTRIBUTORSHIP-
     EXPIRATION-DATE

     Definition
     DATE ON WHICH DISTRIBUTORSHIP EXPIRES

     PROPERTY             VALUE

     Minimum per Subject  1
     Maximum per Subject  450
     Maximum per Value    1
     Last Update          1992/11/30 16:49:39 ABT
     Created              1992/11/30 16:48:33 ABT
     Type                 ELEMENTARY
     Item Type            DATE
     External Length      0
     Internal Length      0

     ASSOCIATION          TYPE                    NAME

2    Has                  Data Type               DATE

   Attribute Type: PURCHASE-ORDER-LINE-ITEM.LINE-NUMBER

     PROPERTY             VALUE

     Minimum per Subject  1
     Maximum per Subject  100
     Maximum per Value    100
     Last Update          1992/11/30 16:37:37 ABT
     Created              1992/11/30 16:37:37 ABT

     ASSOCIATION          TYPE                    NAME

   Attribute Type: PURCHASE ORDER.ORDER-DATE

     Definition
     DATE ORDER WAS PLACED
```

PROPERTY	VALUE
Minimum per Subject	1
Maximum per Subject	9999
Maximum per Value	1
Last Update	1992/11/30 16:25:49 ABT
Created	1992/11/30 16:19:27 ABT
Type	ELEMENTARY
Item Type	DATE
External Length	0
Internal Length	0

	ASSOCIATION	TYPE	NAME
2	Has	Data Type	DATE

Attribute Type: PURCHASE ORDER.ORDER-DOLLAR-TOTAL

Definition
THE TOTAL DOLLAR AMOUNT OF THIS ORDER

PROPERTY	VALUE
Minimum per Subject	1
Maximum per Subject	9999
Maximum per Value	1
Last Update	1992/11/30 16:31:26 ABT
Created	1992/11/30 16:19:29 ABT

ASSOCIATION	TYPE	NAME

Attribute Type: PURCHASE ORDER.ORDER-NUMBER

Definition
THE SEQUENTIALLY GENERATED NUMBER ASSOCIATED WITH EACH CUSTOMER'S ORDER PLACEMENT

PROPERTY	VALUE
Minimum per Subject	1
Maximum per Subject	9999
Maximum per Value	1
Last Update	1992/11/30 16:22:51 ABT
Created	1992/11/30 16:19:26 ABT

ASSOCIATION	TYPE	NAME

```
Attribute Type: PURCHASE-ORDER-LINE-ITEM.ORDER-NUMBER

   PROPERTY               VALUE

   Minimum per Subject    1
   Maximum per Subject    100
   Maximum per Value      100
   Last Update            1992/11/30 16:37:36 ABT
   Created                1992/11/30 16:37:36 ABT

   ASSOCIATION            TYPE                    NAME

Attribute Type: PRODUCT.PRODUCT-CATEGORY

   PROPERTY               VALUE

   Minimum per Subject    1
   Maximum per Subject    M
   Maximum per Value      M
   Last Update            1992/11/30 13:46:42 ABT
   Created                1992/11/30 13:46:42 ABT

   ASSOCIATION            TYPE                    NAME

   Is Part of             Attribute Type          PRODUCT-NUMBER

Attribute Type: PRODUCT.PRODUCT-LIFE-CYCLE-TERM-DATE

   PROPERTY               VALUE

   Minimum per Subject    500
   Maximum per Subject    M
   Maximum per Value      1
   Last Update            1992/11/30 13:30:21 ABT
   Created                1992/11/30 13:30:21 ABT

   ASSOCIATION            TYPE                    NAME

Attribute Type: PRODUCT.PRODUCT-MAIN-INGREDIENT-CODE

   PROPERTY               VALUE

   Minimum per Subject    500
   Maximum per Subject    M
   Maximum per Value      1
   Last Update            1992/11/30 13:30:16 ABT
   Created                1992/11/30 13:30:16 ABT

   ASSOCIATION            TYPE                    NAME

   Is Part of             Attribute Type          PRODUCT-NUMBER
```

```
Attribute Type: PRODUCT.PRODUCT-NUMBER

   PROPERTY               VALUE

   Minimum per Subject  1
   Maximum per Subject  M
   Maximum per Value    1
   Last Update          1992/11/30 13:42:35 ABT
   Created              1992/11/30 13:42:35 ABT

   ASSOCIATION       TYPE               NAME

7  Consists of       Attribute Type     PRODUCT-NUMBER-OF-UNITS
7                                       PRODUCT-MAIN-INGREDIENT-CODE
7                                       PRODUCT-PACKAGE-TYPE
7                                       PRODUCT-CATEGORY

Attribute Type: PURCHASE-ORDER-LINE-ITEM.PRODUCT-NUMBER

   PROPERTY               VALUE

   Minimum per Subject  1
   Maximum per Subject  100
   Maximum per Value    100
   Last Update          1992/11/30 16:37:39 ABT
   Created              1992/11/30 16:37:39 ABT

   ASSOCIATION            TYPE                   NAME

Attribute Type: PRODUCT.PRODUCT-NUMBER-OF-UNITS

   PROPERTY               VALUE

   Minimum per Subject  500
   Maximum per Subject  M
   Maximum per Value    1
   Last Update          1992/11/30 13:30:18 ABT
   Created              1992/11/30 13:30:18 ABT

   ASSOCIATION            TYPE                   NAME

Is Part of                Attribute Type         PRODUCT-NUMBER

Attribute Type: PRODUCT.PRODUCT-PACKAGE-PRICE

   PROPERTY               VALUE

   Minimum per Subject  500
   Maximum per Subject  M
   Maximum per Value    1
   Last Update          1992/11/30 13:30:20 ABT
```

```
  Created              1992/11/30 13:30:20 ABT

  ASSOCIATION          TYPE                 NAME

Attribute Type: PRODUCT.PRODUCT-PACKAGE-TYPE

  PROPERTY             VALUE

  Minimum per Subject  500
  Maximum per Subject  M
  Maximum per Value    1
  Last Update          1992/11/30 13:30:15 ABT
  Created              1992/11/30 13:30:15 ABT

  ASSOCIATION          TYPE                 NAME

  Is Part of           Attribute Type       PRODUCT-NUMBER

Attribute Type: PURCHASE-ORDER-LINE-ITEM.PRODUCT-QUANTITY

  PROPERTY             VALUE

  Minimum per Subject  1
  Maximum per Subject  100
  Maximum per Value    100
  Last Update          1992/11/30 16:37:40 ABT
  Created              1992/11/30 16:37:40 ABT

  ASSOCIATION          TYPE                 NAME

Attribute Type: PRACTICING-PROFESSIONAL.PROFESSIONAL-LICENSE-NO

  PROPERTY             VALUE

  Minimum per Subject  20
  Maximum per Subject  2000
  Maximum per Value    1
  Last Update          1992/11/30 15:48:55 ABT
  Created              1992/11/30 15:48:55 ABT

  ASSOCIATION          TYPE                 NAME

Attribute Type: PRACTICING-PROFESSIONAL.PROFESSIONAL-SPECIALTY-CODE

Definition
THE TWO-DIGIT CODE INDICATING THE TYPE OF MEDICAL SPECIALTY
FOR WHICH THE PROFESSIONAL IS LICENSED.

Comments
VALID SPECIALTY CODE VALUES: HOW CURRENT ARE THE SPECIALTY
CODES THAT EXIST IN THE PROFESSIONAL LICENSING APPLICATION'S
DATABASE? DO WE NEED TO UPDATE THEM WITH A NEW TAPE?
```

```
        PROPERTY                VALUE

        Minimum per Subject     20
        Maximum per Subject     2000
        Maximum per Value       1
        Last Update             1992/11/30 15:52:35 ABT
        Created                 1992/11/30 15:48:57 ABT
        Type                    ELEMENTARY
        Item Type               EXTERNAL DECIMAL
        Format                  9(1)
        External Length         1
        Internal Length         1

        ASSOCIATION             TYPE                   NAME

2       Has                     Data Type              CODE

    Attribute Type: RETAIL OUTLET.RETAIL-SPECIALTY-CODE

        Definition
        CODE DESCRIBING THE MAJOR PRODUCT LINE OF THE RETAIL OUTLET

        PROPERTY                VALUE

        Minimum per Subject     1
        Maximum per Subject     10
        Maximum per Value       1
        Last Update             1992/11/30 16:45:27 ABT
        Created                 1992/11/30 16:43:52 ABT
        Type                    ELEMENTARY
        Item Type               EXTERNAL DECIMAL
        Format                  9(1)
        External Length         1
        Internal Length         1

        ASSOCIATION             TYPE                   NAME

2       Has                     Data Type              CODE

    Data Type: CODE

        Definition
4       ONE-DIGIT INTEGER CODES BELONG TO THIS DATA TYPE

        PROPERTY                VALUE

        Last Update             1992/11/30 14:44:13 ABT
        Format                  9(1)
        Created                 1992/11/30 14:37:41 ABT
6       Internal Length         1
6       External Length         1
6       Type                    ELEMENTARY
6       Item Type               EXTERNAL DECIMAL
```

ASSOCIATION	TYPE	NAME
Is Data Type of	Attribute Type	CUSTOMER . CUSTOMER-CREDIT-RATING PRACTICING-PROFESSIONAL . PROFESSIONAL-SPECIALTY-CODE RETAIL OUTLET . RETAIL-SPECIALTY-CODE

2 Data Type: DATE

Definition
ALL SYSTEM-GENERATED DATES IN THE FORM MMDDYY BELONG TO THIS DATA TYPE

	PROPERTY	VALUE
	Last Update	1992/11/30 16:30:39 ABT
	Created	1992/11/30 16:26:01 ABT
6	Internal Length	0
6	External Length	0
6	Type	ELEMENTARY
6	Item Type	DATE

ASSOCIATION	TYPE	NAME
Is Data Type of DATE	Attribute Type	PURCHASE ORDER . ORDER- WHOLESALE DISTRIBUTOR . DISTRIBUTORSHIP-EXPIRATION-DATE

2 Data Type: IDENTIFIER

Definition
4 ALL PRIMARY IDENTIFIERS THAT ARE NUMERIC (INTEGER) AND GENERATED BY THE SYSTEM BELONG TO THIS DATA TYPE

	PROPERTY	VALUE
	Last Update	1992/11/30 14:12:43 ABT
	Format	9(5)
	Created	1992/11/30 14:03:20 ABT
6	Internal Length	5
6	External Length	5
6	Type	ELEMENTARY
6	Item Type	EXTERNAL DECIMAL

ASSOCIATION	TYPE	NAME
Is Data Type of	Attribute Type	CUSTOMER . CUSTOMER-ID
		PURCHASE ORDER . CUSTOMER-ID

2 Data Type: INDICATOR

	PROPERTY	VALUE
	Last Update	1992/11/30 16:51:48 ABT
	Format	A
	Created	1992/11/30 16:50:53 ABT
6	Internal Length	1
6	External Length	1
6	Type	ELEMENTARY
6	Item Type	ALPHA

ASSOCIATION	TYPE	NAME
Is Data Type of	Attribute Type	WHOLESALE DISTRIBUTOR . CENTRALIZED-WAREHOUSE-INDICATOR

Entity Type: CUSTOMER

PROPERTY	VALUE
Purpose	FUNDAMENTAL
Last Update	1992/11/30 13:53:12 ABT
Created	1992/11/30 13:53:12 ABT

ASSOCIATION	TYPE	NAME
PURCHASES	Entity Type	PRODUCT
IS-A-SUPERTYPE-OF	Entity Type	RETAIL OUTLET
		WHOLESALE DISTRIBUTOR
		END-CONSUMER
		PRACTICING-PROFESSIONAL
GENERATES	Entity Type	PURCHASE ORDER
Is Described by	Attribute Type	CUSTOMER-ID
		CUSTOMER-NAME
		CUSTOMER-TYPE
		CUSTOMER-CREDIT-RATING

```
Entity Type: END-CONSUMER

   PROPERTY                               VALUE

   Purpose              FUNDAMENTAL
   Last Update          1992/11/30 15:16:31 ABT
   Created              1992/11/30 15:16:31 ABT

   ASSOCIATION          TYPE              NAME

   IS-A-SUBTYPE-OF      Entity Type       CUSTOMER
   Is Described by      Attribute Type    CUSTOMER-ID
                                          CUSTOMER-NAME
                                          CUSTOMER-TYPE
                                          CUSTOMER-CREDIT-RATING
                                          CUSTOMER-SHIP-TO-STREET
                                          CUSTOMER-SHIP-TO-CITY
                                          CUSTOMER-SHIP-TO-STATE
                                          CUSTOMER-SHIP-TO-ZIP

Entity Type: PRACTICING-PROFESSIONAL

   PROPERTY             VALUE

   Purpose              FUNDAMENTAL
   Last Update          1992/11/30 15:16:32 ABT
   Created              1992/11/30 15:16:32 ABT

   ASSOCIATION          TYPE              NAME

   IS-A-SUBTYPE-OF      Entity Type       CUSTOMER
   Is Described by      Attributed Type   CUSTOMER-ID
                                          CUSTOMER-NAME
                                          CUSTOMER-TYPE
                                          CUSTOMER-CREDIT-RATING
                                          PROFESSIONAL-LICENSE-NO
                                          PROFESSIONAL-SPECIALTY-CODE
```

Entity Type: PRODUCT

Definition
ANY PACKAGED, SELLABLE, DISTRIBUTABLE VERSION OF OUR COMPANY'S MANUFACTURED ITEMS

PROPERTY	VALUE
Purpose	FUNDAMENTAL
Last Update	1992/11/30 13:15:38 ABT
Created	1992/09/21 09:41:25 ABT

ASSOCIATION	TYPE	NAME
IS-PURCHASED-BY	Entity Type	CUSTOMER
APPEARS-IN ITEM	Entity Type	PURCHASE-ORDER-LINE-
Is Described by	Attribute Type	PRODUCT-PACKAGE-TYPE
		PRODUCT-MAIN-INGREDIENT-CODE
		PRODUCT-NUMBER-OF-UNITS
		PRODUCT-PACKAGE-PRICE
		PRODUCT-LIFE-CYCLE-TERM-DATE
		PRODUCT-NUMBER
		PRODUCT-CATEGORY

Entity Type: PURCHASE ORDER

PROPERTY	VALUE
Purpose	FUNDAMENTAL
Last Update	1992/11/30 16:17:03 ABT
Created	1992/11/30 16:17:03 ABT

ASSOCIATION	TYPE	NAME
IS-GENERATED-BY	Entity Type	CUSTOMER
CONTAINS	Entity Type	PURCHASE-ORDER-LINE-ITEM
Is Described by	Attribute Type	CUSTOMER-ID
		ORDER-NUMBER
		ORDER-DATE
		ORDER-DOLLAR-TOTAL

Entity Type: PURCHASE-ORDER-LINE-ITEM

Definition
EACH PRODUCT/QUANTITY COMBINATION THAT CONSTITUTES A PURCHASE ORDER

PROPERTY	VALUE
Purpose	ASSOCIATIVE
Last Update	1992/11/30 16:39:13 ABT
Created	1992/11/30 16:35:22 ABT

ASSOCIATION	TYPE	NAME
IS-CONTAINED-IN	Entity Type	PURCHASE ORDER
CONSISTS-of	Entity Type	PRODUCT
Is Described by	Attribute Type	CUSTOMER-ID
		ORDER-NUMBER
		LINE-NUMBER
		PRODUCT-NUMBER
		PRODUCT-QUANTITY

Entity Type: RETAIL OUTLET

PROPERTY	VALUE
Purpose	FUNDAMENTAL
Last Update	1992/11/30 15:16:33 ABT
Created	1992/11/30 15:16:33 ABT

ASSOCIATION	TYPE	NAME
IS-A-SUBTYPE-OF	Entity Type	CUSTOMER
Is Described by	Attribute Type	RETAIL-SPECIALTY-CODE
		CUSTOMER-ID
		CUSTOMER-NAME
		CUSTOMER-TYPE
		CUSTOMER-CREDIT-RATING

Entity Type: WHOLESALE DISTRIBUTOR

PROPERTY	VALUE
Purpose	FUNDAMENTAL
Last Update	1992/11/30 15:16:34 ABT
Created	1992/11/30 15:16:34 ABT

ASSOCIATION	TYPE	NAME

```
   IS-A-SUBTYPE-OF       Entity Type       CUSTOMER
   Is Described by       Attribute Type    CENTRALIZED-WAREHOUSE-INDICATO
                                           DISTRIBUTORSHIP-EXPIRATION-DAT
                                           CUSTOMER-CREDIT-RATING
                                           CUSTOMER-TYPE
                                           CUSTOMER-NAME
                                           CUSTOMER-ID

Relationship Type: PURCHASE-ORDER-LINE-ITEM.CONSISTS-OF.PRODUCT

   PROPERTY              VALUE

   To From Name          APPEARS-IN
   From To Minimum       1
   From To Maximum       1
   To From Minimum       1
   To From Maximum       M
   Last Update           1992/11/30 16:42:32 ABT
   Created               1992/11/30 16:42:32 ABT

   ASSOCIATION           TYPE              NAME

Relationship Type: RETAIL OUTLET.IS-A-SUBTYPE-OF.CUSTOMER

   PROPERTY              VALUE

   To From Name          IS-A-SUPERTYPE-OF
   From To Minimum       1
   From To Maximum       10
   To From Minimum       1
   To From Maximum       M
   Last Update           1992/11/30 15:20:59 ABT
   Created               1992/11/30 15:19:54 ABT

   ASSOCIATION           TYPE              NAME

Relationship Type: WHOLESALE DISTRIBUTOR.IS-A-SUBTYPE-
   OF.CUSTOMER

   PROPERTY              VALUE

   To From Name          IS-A-SUPERTYPE-OF
   From To Minimum       1
   From To Maximum       M
   To From Minimum       1
   To From Maximum       1
   Last Update           1992/11/30 15:22:42 ABT
   Created               1992/11/30 15:21:54 ABT

   ASSOCIATION           TYPE              NAME
```

```
Relationship Type: END-CONSUMER.IS-A-SUBTYPE-OF.CUSTOMER

   PROPERTY              VALUE

   To From Name          IS-A-SUPERTYPE-OF
   From To Minimum       1
   From To Maximum       M
   To From Minimum       1
   To From Maximum       1
   Last Update           1992/11/30 15:55:53 ABT
   Created               1992/11/30 15:23:26 ABT

   ASSOCIATION           TYPE             NAME

Relationship Type: PRACTICING-PROFESSIONAL.IS-A-SUBTYPE-
   OF.CUSTOMER

   PROPERTY              VALUE

   To From Name          IS-A-SUPERTYPE-OF
   From To Minimum       1
   From To Maximum       M
   To From Minimum       1
   To From Maximum       1
   Last Update           1992/11/30 15:41:11 ABT
   Created               1992/11/30 15:24:08 ABT

   ASSOCIATION           TYPE             NAME

Relationship Type: PURCHASE-ORDER-LINE-ITEM.IS-CONTAINED-
   IN.PURCHASE ORDER

   PROPERTY              VALUE

   To From Name          CONTAINS
   From To Minimum       1
   From To Maximum       1
   To From Minimum       1
   To From Maximum       M
   Last Update           1992/11/30 16:40:11 ABT
   Created               1992/11/30 16:40:11 ABT

   ASSOCIATION           TYPE             NAME

Relationship Type: PURCHASE ORDER.IS-GENERATED-BY.CUSTOMER
```

```
   PROPERTY                 VALUE

   To From Name             GENERATES
   From To Minimum          1
   From To Maximum          M
   To From Minimum          1
   To From Maximum          1
   Last Update              1992/11/30 16:33:53 ABT
   Created                  1992/11/30 16:33:53 ABT

   ASSOCIATION              TYPE             NAME

Relationship Type: CUSTOMER.PURCHASES.PRODUCT

   PROPERTY                 VALUE

   To From Name             IS-PURCHASED-BY
   From To Minimum          1
   From To Maximum          M
   To From Minimum          0
   To From Maximum          M
   Last Update              1992/11/30 16:06:25 ABT
   Created                  1992/11/30 16:06:25 ABT

   ASSOCIATION              TYPE             NAME
```

(*b*)

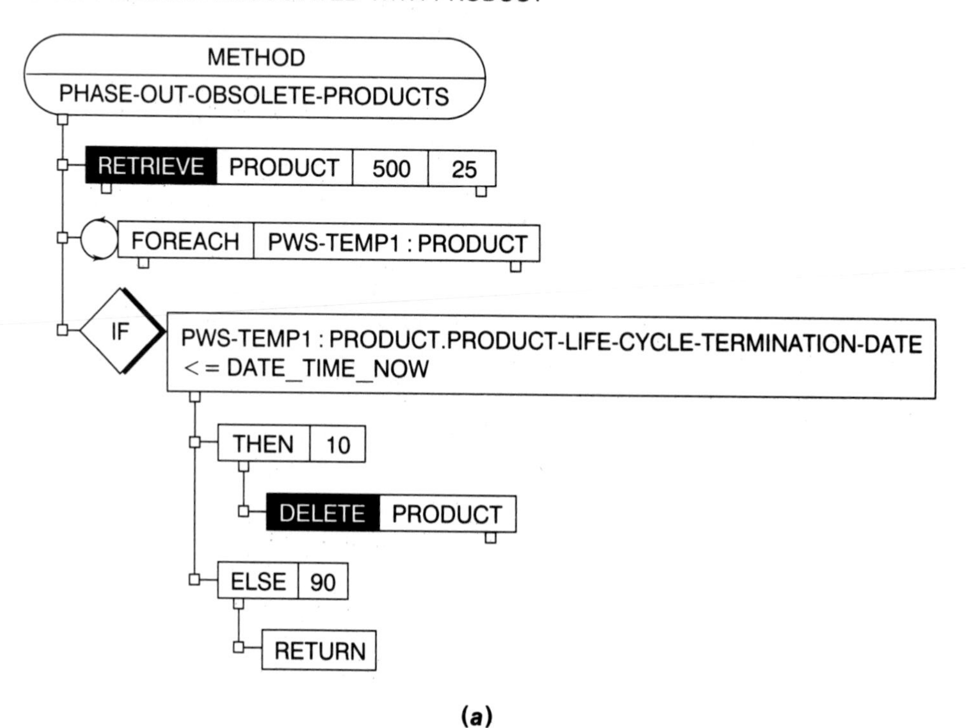

(*a*)

Figure 13.8 An "entity method" depicted in the Bachman Analyst (Version 4.1)

```
METHOD PHASE-OUT-OBSOLETE-PRODUCTS
  STRUCTURE PHASE-OUT-OBSOLETE-PRODUCTS PHASE-OUT-OBSOLETE-
     PRODUCTS
    RETRIEVE PRODUCT . PRODUCT-LIFE-CYCLE-TERMINATION-DATE
      FROM PRODUCT
      STRUCTURE ISDATE-COMP PWS-TEMP1
      VOLUME 500 , 25
    END RETRIEVE

    FOREACH PWS-TEMP1 : PRODUCT
    END FOREACH

    IF PWS-TEMP1 : PRODUCT . PRODUCT-LIFE-CYCLE-TERMINATION-DATE <=
    DATE_TIME_NOW 10 %
        THEN
            DELETE PRODUCT
              STRUCTURE IS-OBSOLETE-PROD PWS-OBS-PROD
            END DELETE

        ELSE
              RETURN

        END IF

   END PHASE-OUT-OBSOLETE-PRODUCTS
```

(*b*)

Figure 13.8 (Continued).

sets of modeling constructs and next as they relate to their counterpart data models.

In Fig. 13.8 specifications for a routine that cleans up the PRODUCT master (PRODUCT entity) by eliminating products deemed obsolete are considered an "Entity Method," because they are related directly to the PRODUCT entity. There are few constructs deployed in this illustration; yet the method itself is associated with an entity occurrence.

In contrast, a much more simplified equivalent is illustrated in Fig. 13.9 in a *Minispec Action Diagram*. From a CASE tool integration perspective, this specifica-

```
  Read PRODUCT

For each PRODUCT-NUMBER

If PRODUCT-LIFE-CYCLE-TERM-DATE LE TODAY

  Delete PRODUCT

  RETURN
```

Figure 13.9 An equivalent process, as depicted in the ADW Analysis Workstation

tion contains minimal tool-specific constructs. Like the Bachman Analyst example, the minispec, too, can be related to specific entities in the tool's data models. The relatability of the minispec, however, can extend beyond particular entity instances. The entity itself can appear in multiple models throughout the CASE tool (aside from the E–R model). Once the relationship between the minispec and the entity is identified, this relationship can pertain to all entity occurrences (data flows, etc.). The same functionality can also be duplicated in the Bachman Analyst via *External Procedures*.

The issues in these process specification examples then revolve around the impact that each specification was intended to have on the overall application, and whether or not that impact was accurately maintained by the CASE tool's internal relationships and integrity checks. Experienced CASE modelers may have "fudged" process specifications to eliminate the automatic integrity that the tool guarantees via the process specification/data relationships. When models from different tools are pulled together, it is important to assesss how these specifications are depicted compared to how they are (or will be) actually implemented in the application.

■ SUMMARY

In this chapter we defined metadata from a CASE perspective. In keeping with the theme of Part Three, metadata differences were illustrated as important considerations in determining the need for an intertool bridge. Metadata constructs themselves, however, are not the true obstacles in bringing models together. As we will see in the next chapter, tool metadata representations simply serve as modeling materials. The ways in which the materials are put together and built upon, both within the CASE tool architecture and by the modelers themselves, serve as equally important considerations.

14

THE ATTRIBUTES OF CASE METADATA

Based on the metadata perspective presented in the previous chapter, models can be considered direct representations of the resident constructs in the underlying tool. But these constructs are only a part of the metadata story. Each metadata construct, despite similarities in name and/or function, can be represented and detailed differently from tool to tool. In addition, the use and population of metadata via the user of the tool requires further analysis into metadata characteristics.

■ METADATA ATTRIBUTES DEFINED

Metadata attributes are the describing fields (elements) associated with each metadata object. These attributes, their associated objects, and the relationships between constructs all constitute a tool's metamodel. The attributes associated with each metadata construct often vary from tool to tool, or sometimes from submodel to submodel within different components of one tool.

If we take a common metadata construct, ENTITY, as an example, standard metadata attributes include the following:

Name. The entity's name

Description. A textual description/definition of the entity

Creator. The user id of the person who originally input the entity instance

Creation date. The date and time of the entity's creation

Graphical coordinates. Numbers (usually x, y coordinates) that represent the physical location of the entity on an E–R diagram

Internal key. A number generated by the tool which represents a unique index to this entity occurrence

The preceding set of attributes is common to practically every metadata construct in CASE metamodels. The set is also relatively standard in that CASE tool representation and use of the model component instances require this minimal set of characteristics.

Tool depiction and use of these construct instances results in an expanded set of attributes, dependent exclusively on the particular tool's architecture and functional purpose as an application development aid. Continuing our example, many CASE tools also track the following additional attributes as part of the entity representation:

Normalization flag. Whether or not the entity is currently in third normal form

Modified by. The user id responsible for the last modification of this entity instance

Modify date. The date and time of the last update

Minimum volume. The minimum number of expected occurrences of this entity in the implemented database

Maximum volume. The maximum number of expected occurrences of this entity in the implemented database

Most of these attributes have little bearing on the use of the instance by embedded functions within the tool; they merely serve as additional requirements documentation.

Typically, there is not much more to entity attributes. Experienced CASE users realize that their use and description of entities within a CASE tool requires much more input on their part, and they are probably pondering the fate of other entity-specific data (such as the attributes, keys, etc.). In relationally backboned encyclopedias these additional entity characteristics are representative of relationships between the defined entity instance and the other populated constructs. For example, the entity/attribute connection is diagrammed in Fig. 14.1. It is important to note that although the attributes may have been input and originally defined in a

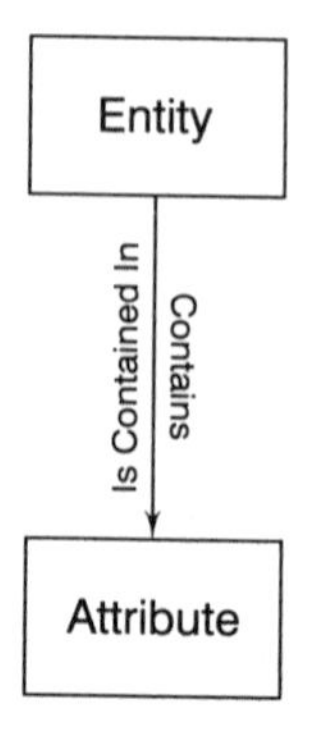

Figure 14.1 How entities and attributes relate in typical encyclopedia metamodels.

"Create Entity" window, they are not necessarily stored as attributes of the entity instance. This type of design allows the flexibility of associating a given attribute with more than one entity, for example.

■ COMMON METADATA ATTRIBUTES, UNCOMMON REPRESENTATIONS

The evaluation of those attributes commonly stored with certain metadata constructs does not necessarily result in standard depictions from tool to tool. The most obvious example, as we discussed previously, is the *description field*. The length allowed for descriptions typically ranges from 80 characters to unlimited lengths.

Using *description* as an example, most tool interfaces that are offered by CASE vendors (usually as a way to get models from a competitive CASE tool into theirs) deal with the "extra text" in one of the following ways:

1. *Truncation*. Truncation involves simply importing the amount of text that the receiving metamodel can handle (e.g., 80 characters), as stored in the originating tool's first 80 characters, and ignoring the rest.
2. *Truncation plus redirection*. The extra text that is not stored in the target tool's description field is stored in an outside area, usually an external ASCII file. The text is available for manual cut and paste by the target CASE tool user, if desired.
3. *Generation of an import error*. In rare instances some interfaces generate a warning and require the user of the interface to establish a description field (in the extract file) that meets the metadata attribute requirements of the target tool. This is not typical treatment for description fields, but is common in more important CASE constructs.

The means by which CASE interfaces implement the translation of differing metadata attribute representations can become an issue when the target tool's representation of the particular value changes its meaning. For example, consider Fig. 14.2, where a set of descriptive text was truncated. After truncation of the excessive *description* text, much of the original meaning was lost. Probably the most important aspect of the original definition was the business rule which determined when credit ratings can be established. It is not the intention of this chapter to evaluate whether or not business rules belong in a description field. However, assuming the existence of critical information in a description field, its preservation after transfer to a new home (whether it is a repository or simply another CASE tool) is crucial.

Continuing the analysis of the impact of intertool transfers, consider Fig. 14.3. A more significant implication of truncation is the elimination of key values, for example, the truncation of the attribute *name* as depicted in Fig. 14.3. After the name was transferred to the target tool, it has become impossible to determine its true meaning from the name alone.

Clearly, before embarking on the transfer of models from one tool to the other, it is important to assess whether the transfer will be beneficial. In most situations

```
ATTRIBUTE NAME:    CUSTOMER-CREDIT-RATING-CODE
DESCRIPTION:       The coded value which determines a customer's
                   standing wrt credit-based purchases. Credit
                   ratings are achieved after 1 year of solid
                   payment history based on purchases that
                   exceeded $25,000. Code values and their
                   meaning are stored in the CUSTOMER-CREDIT-
                   RATING-TABLE.

Description as stored in source CASE tool, before transfer.

ATTRIBUTE NAME:    CUSTOMER-CREDIT-RATING-CODE
DESCRIPTION:       The coded value which determines a customer's
                   standing wrt credit-based purchases. Credit

Description as stored in target CASE tool, after transfer.
```

Figure 14.2 Intertool transfer of a metadata attribute instance.

```
ATTRIBUTE NAME:   CALCULATED-DAYS-REMAINING-TILL-RETIREMENT

    Name as stored in source CASE tool, before transfer.

ATTRIBUTE NAME:   CALCULATED-DAYS-REMAINING-TILL-RE

    Name as stored in target CASE tool, after transfer.
```

Figure 14.3 Another intertool transfer example.

the target tool contains functionality that is not part of the current model's source tool, hence the desire for transfer. However, if a substantial portion of the base model's integrity and/or meaning will be lost upon transfer, productive gains would most likely be hindered by the manual effort required to replace lost data.

There are solutions to this problem, but they involve the existence and interoperability of the diverse tool set. The details behind this type of arrangement require the existence of an interfacing repository, which will be introduced and explored in Part Four.

■ UNCOMMON METADATA ATTRIBUTES

What about metadata attributes that exist in one tool, but not in the other? A very common situation, it presents a problem when the attributes are populated in the source model and have no corresponding equivalent in the metadata of the target tool. Complexity also arises when the metadata attributes of the source tool have "functionally close" substitutions in the target tool.

Consider the definition of a subordinate process, *RECEIVE_PAYMENT_ENVELOPE*. This process, a manual process, is being documented as the initial process in a *PROCESS_PAYMENTS* process definition. Figure 14.4 depicts the definition of this process in Texas Instruments' IEF. Key descriptive attributes in

RECEIVE_PAYMENT_ENVELOPE Properties

Process Name: RECEIVE_PAYMENT_ENVELOPE

Elemenatry

Repetitive

Suggested Mechanism

Online

Manual

Batch

Other

OK Desc... Cancel Help

(*a*)

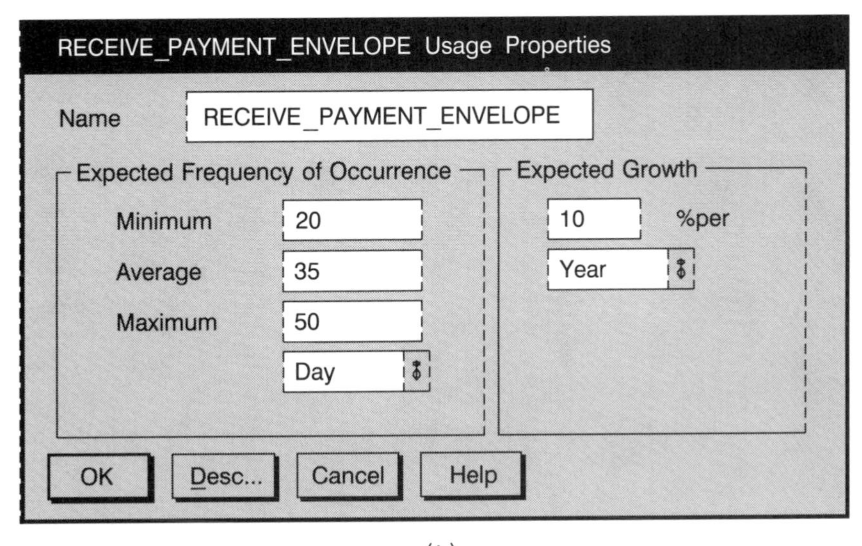

(*b*)

```
Model : PART2
Subset : (Complete model)
                 Activity Definition


  NAME:             RECEIVE__PAYMENT__ENVELOPE

  DESCRIPTION:      PROCESS BEGINS WITH THE RECEIPT OF A CUS
     TOMER
                    PAYMENT, VIA MAIL

  TYPE:             Process
                    Repetitive
                    Manual Implementation Suggested

  SUBORDINATE OF:  PROCESS__PAYMENTS
```

(*c*)

Figure 14.4 The depiction of a manual process in IEF (Version 5.1).

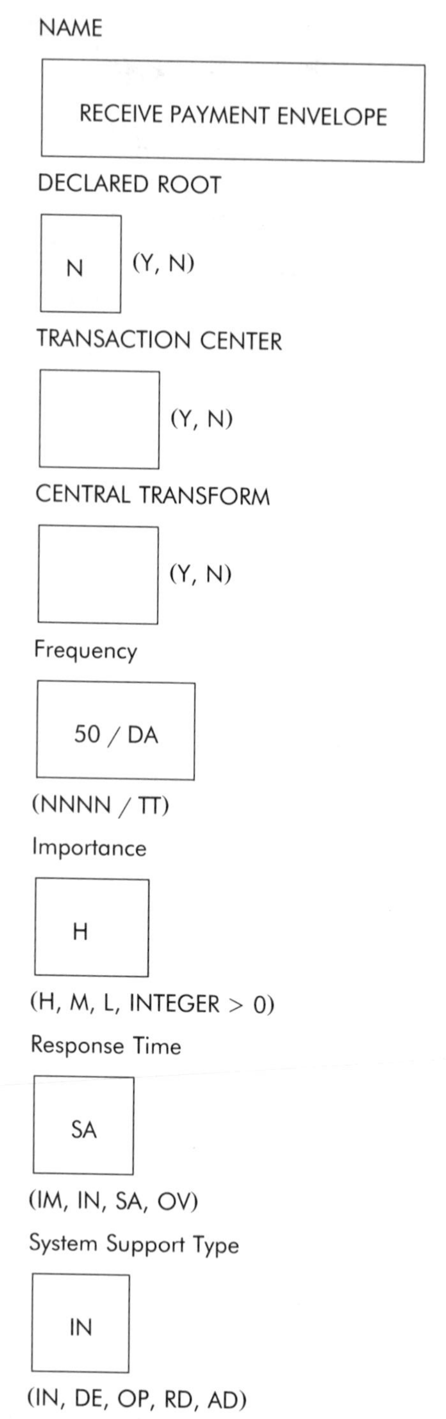

Figure 14.5 Depiction of the same process in ADW (Version 1.6).

DEFINITION

PROCESS BEGINS WITH THE
RECEIPT OF A CUSTOMER PAYMENT,
VIA MAIL.

COMMENTS

LAST UPDATE

01-14-1993 03:06:05 PM ABT

CREATED

01-14-1993 03:06:04 PM ABT

RECEIVE PAYMENT ENVELOPE

01-14-1993 03:18:38 PM

Figure 14.5 (Continued).

the IEF definition include:

- Suggested mechanism
- Elementary vs. repetitive
- Frequency of occurrence
- Expected growth

Because the depicted process is expected to be manual, it is not directly tied to any code generation requirements. The preceding documentation will be used to assess the resources required to process received payments and plan the staffing requirements and/or structural reorganization that may be necessary once the new payment processing system is in place.

In comparison, the same process has been depicted in Knowledgeware's ADW Planning Workstation. (see Fig. 14.5) Notable points include the fact that there are no metadata attributes to depict the fact that this process is manual (the *suggested mechanism*), repetitive, or to depict a more detailed accounting of the process execution frequency (minimum, maximum, average, and expected growth). On the other hand, there are additional attributes that do not appear in the IEF process depiction set:

- Transaction center
- Central transform

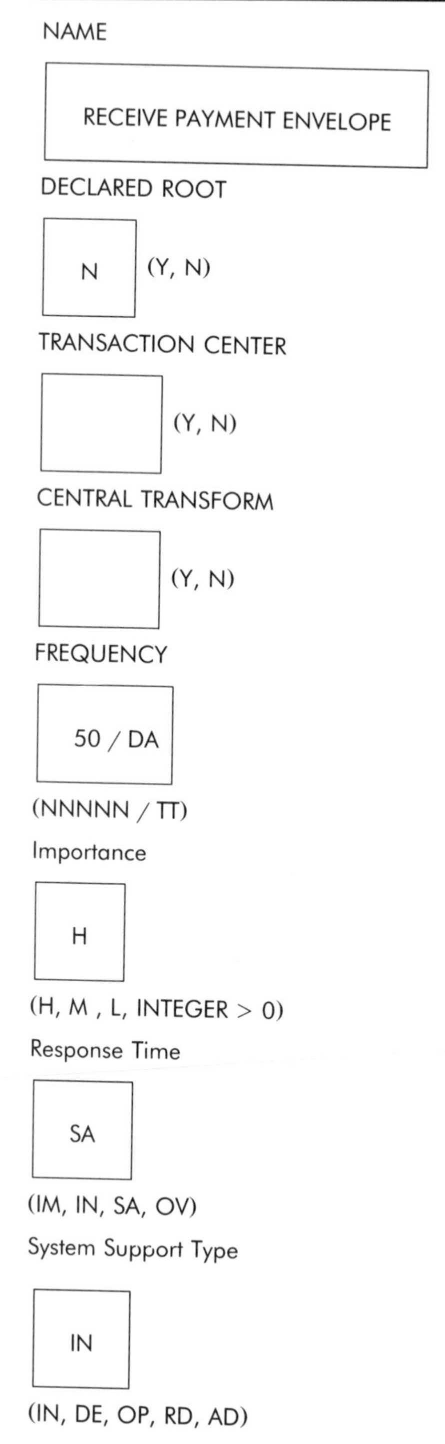

Figure 14.6 "Fudging" the ADW (Version 1.6) depiction.

DEFINITION

PROCESS BEGINS WITH THE RECEIPT OF A CUSTOMER PAYMENT, VIA MAIL. THIS IS A MANUAL PROCESS.

COMMENTS

ONCE THE NEW PAYMENT PROCESSING SYSTEM IS ON LINE, THE NUMBER OF ENVELOPES RECEIVED IS EXPECTED TO REACH 50 PER DAY. THEREAFTER, EXPECT A 10% ANNUAL INCREASE.

LAST UPDATE

01-14-1993 03:1851 PM ABT

CREATED

01-14-1993 03:06:04 PM ABT

RECEIVE PAYMENT ENVELOPE

01-15-1993 02:28:39 PM

Figure 14.6 (Continued).

- Importance
- Response time (amount of time process takes to execute)—we selected SA for *same* day
- System support type (classification of support necessary)—we selected IN for *information system*

It is not the purpose of this chapter to favor one tool's depiction over the other. In fact, depending on the intended use of the process documentation, either tool could potentially be more appropriate. However, we can see that despite the existence of common metadata (the *process* construct) in both tools, the metadata attributes are not identical.

REPRESENTING UNCOMMON METADATA ATTRIBUTES (FUDGING THE DESCRIPTIONS)

Assume for the purposes of an example that the process description depicted in Figs. 14.4 and 14.5 needed to universally convey the following facts:

- The process RECEIVE_PAYMENT_ENVELOPE is a manual process.
- Currently 40 envelopes are received daily, with the number expected to increase to 50 once the new payment processing system is on line. Thereafter, a

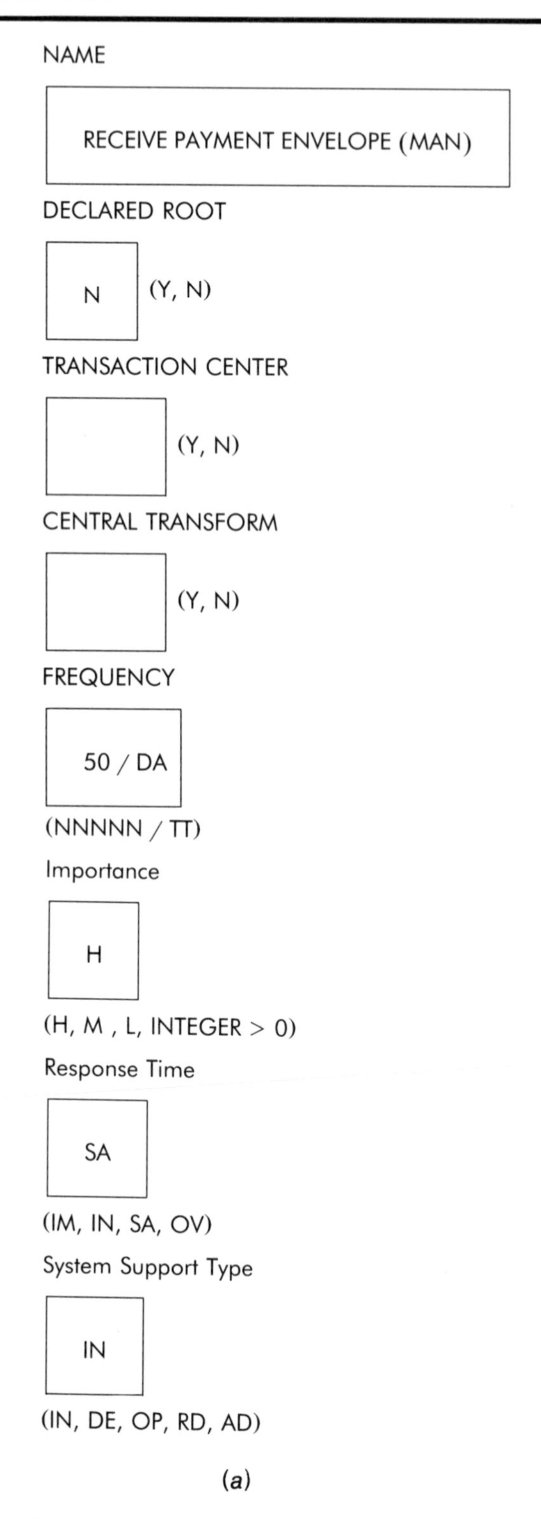

Figure 14.7 A better ''fudging'' alternative.

DEFINITION

PROCESS BEGINS WITH THE
RECEIPT OF A CUSTOMER PAYMENT,
VIA MAIL. THIS IS A MANUAL
PROCESS.

COMMENTS

ONCE THE NEW PAYMENT PROCESSING
SYSTEM IS ON LINE, THE NUMBER
OF ENVELOPES RECEIVED IS
EXPECTED TO REACH 50 PER DAY.
THEREAFTER, EXPECT A 10% ANNUAL
INCREASE.

LAST UPDATE

01-15-1993 02:29:29 PM ABT

CREATED

01-14-1993 03:06:04 PM ABT

RECEIVE PAYMENT ENVELOPE

01-15-1993 02:42:30 PM

```
Model: PART2
Subset: (Complete model)
                Activity Definition
```

```
Name:                 RECEIVE__PAYMENT__ENVELOPE (MAN)

Description:          PROCESS BEGINS WITH THE RECEIPT OF A CUSTOMER
                      PAYMENT, VIA MAIL
Type:                 Process
                      Repetitive
                      Manual implementation suggested
Subordinate of :      PROCESS__PAYMENTS
```

(*b*)

Figure 14.7 (Continued).

10 percent annual increase in the amount of envelopes (payments) received daily is expected.

The preceding information has been conveyed in the IEF example. Conveying the same facts in ADW would require some "fudging." Typically, the extra information would be conveyed in either the *definition* or the *comments* fields. If so, the ability to then query this process instance based on its assessment as a manual process would not be an easy task.

As illustrated in Fig. 14.6, extra clarification has been added to both the *definition* and *comments* attributes. Figure 14.7 presents a better alternative. Here, we are changing the *meaning* of an already existing attribute, *NAME*. By adding the suffix (MAN) to the process name (as depicted in both tools: IEF and ADW), we are not only using this attribute to convey the process name, but also to indicate the fact that the process is manual. If this "fudging" is a more desirable alternative, it can only be effective if it is implemented consistently (in all tools if your organization is moving toward a repository implementation).

Consistent implementation of any type of metadata fudging (either to the use of the metadata constructs themselves or to the population of their attributes) generally requires adherence to a set of CASE modeling standards. As discussed in Part One, consistent usage of even one vendor tool leaves an organization more prepared for a repository than the existence of individualized modeling styles. Standards become even more important when multiple tools constitute the modeling environment.

The recommendations presented in this chapter are not ideal. However, if tools are to be bridged without a repository, they are really the best practical solution. As we will see in later chapters, a "vendor-neutral" repository provides better ways of handling metadata conflicts.

15

VERTICAL CASE INTEGRATION

Don't throw a monkey-wrench into the machinery.

Philander Chase Johnson, May 1920

Integration, as we saw in Chap. 12, is a partially nebulous concept. For this reason *integration categories* exist as a means of clarifying the many scopes that can have an "integration" flavor. In this chapter we will concentrate on one specific integration category, that of *vertical* integration.

VERTICAL INTEGRATION DEFINED

In the early days of information engineering, the tasks involved in the development of an application were organized into several phases: planning, analysis, design, and construction. Each phase built upon the previous by virtually requiring the output of the previous phase as its own input, and expanding upon it via the addition of more application-specific details.

These methodology-related phases formed the framework for today's CASE tools. As discussed previously, most CASE tools are componentized, each component being geared to a specific aspect (phase) of the information engineering life cycle. In a single vendor's tool set, vertical integration implies the access of any model component from within any tool component.

As depicted in Fig. 15.1 *vertical* refers to the relationship between each development phase, or, from the tool's perspective, between each tool component. Figure 15.1 depicts the implementation of vertical integration within one vendor's tool set. Each component has access to encyclopedia constructs that may have initiated from a preceding life cycle phase component. The implications of vertical integration, as we will see later in this chapter, can be both good and bad, depending on the type of access permitted by nonowning tool components.

Vertical integration can get complicated when multiple tools (from multiple vendors) are involved. Figure 15.2 depicts the implementation of vertical integration across and within multiple tool sets. In keeping with our previous definition,

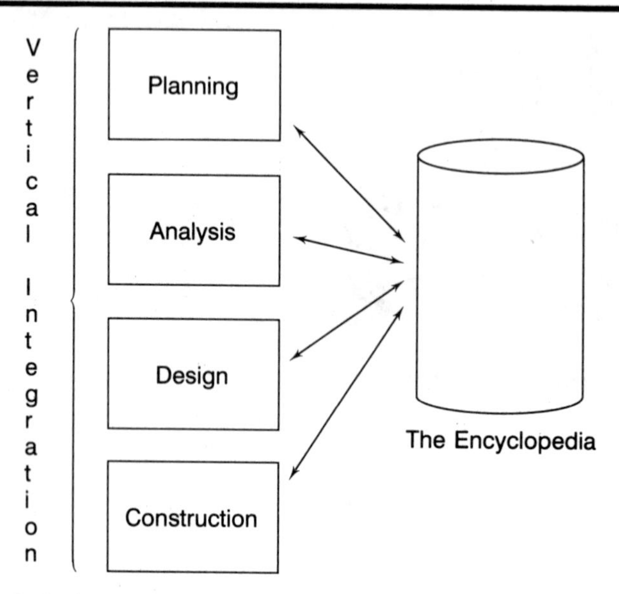

Figure 15.1 Single-tool vertical integration.

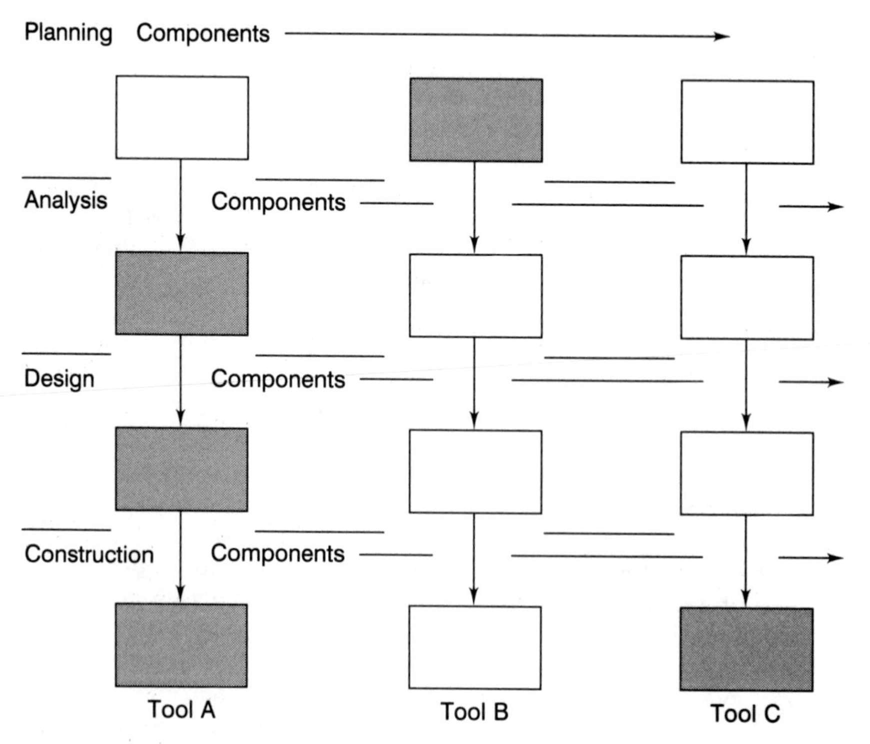

Figure 15.2 Multiple-tool vertical integration.

each tool's component would have access to the constructs defined by the previous phase's component. In Fig. 15.2, the shaded boxes represent the actual components deployed in the development of our application models and the subsequent generated application. Tool B was used only to depict the planning models. It was likely therefore that the concept of this particular application originated in an organization that used this tool, or by a developer/planner who had access to or was the most familiar with this particular tool. Once the planned application became more than a plan, its refinement and further definition became the responsibility of the MIS development organization, the users of Tool A. Finally, when the time came to actually generate the application, another tool, Tool C, was necessary due to the disparity in the target platforms generated by Tool A vs. the actual execution platform in use by the target user community. The practicality of such an approach (without a repository) is questionable, as we will see later. However, true vertical integration allows this setup and implies relatively seamless transfer of the models from one tool to the other, from one vertical life cycle to the next. Many issues come to mind in this scenario, some of which will be covered in the next chapter.

Vertical integration therefore can be defined as

> The access, by nonoriginating CASE tool modules, of model components throughout the application development life cycle by chronological (vertical) application development life cycle successor modules.

Before leaving the definition of vertical integration, we should consider Zachman's Information Systems Architecture* as another means of defining the concept of *vertical*. His framework complements the traditional information engineering life cycle by defining the deliverables in terms of their place in the application development chronology and their relationship to enterprise resources. In his scenario vertical still implies application development life cycle phases. However, its definition in terms of deliverable models simply validates our definition in terms of CASE-based model components.

As depicted in Fig. 15.3, the first two rows generally constitute deliverables from a CASE tool's *planning* component. The next row represents *analysis* deliverables, the next two rows (Technology Models and Detailed Representations) are *design* component deliverables, and finally the Functioning System is the output of the *construction* component. A vertically integrated tool considers each cell in terms of its originating tool component and meets our previously stated definition.

■ MODEL ACCESS WITHIN A SINGLE VENDOR'S VERTICAL TOOL SET

Continuing with our refinement of integration, the issue of *access* reappears. As discussed previously, there are many types of access, ranging from read-only access to the ability to update (write access) to the ability to delete an object. Within a single vendor's tool set, model access is typically dependent on the user id

---

*John Zachman, *Information Systems Architecture—A Framework*.

Information Systems Architecture - A Framework

	Data	Function	Network
Objectives / Scope	List of Things Important to the Business Entity = Class of Business Thing	List of Processess the Business Performs Process = Class of Business Process	List of Locations in Which the Business Operates Node = Major Business Location
Model of the Business	e.g., "Ent/Rel Diagram" Ent = Business Entity Rein = Business Rule	e.g., "Funct. Flow Diagram" Proc. = Bus. Process I/O = Bus. Resources	e.g., Logistics Network Node = Business Location Link = Business Linkeage
Model of the Information System	e.g., "Data Model" Ent = Data Entity Rein = Data Relationship	e.g., "Data Flow Diagram" Proc. = Application Function I/O = User Views (Set of Data Elements)	e.g., Distributed System Architecture Node = I/S Function (Processor, Storage, etc.) Link = Line Characteristics
Technology Models	e.g., Data Design Description Ent. = Segment/Row Rein = Pointer/Key	e.g., "Structure Chart" Proc. = Computer Function I/O = Screen/Device Formats	e.g., "System Architecture Node = Hardware/System Software Link = Line Specifications
Detailed Represen-tations	e.g., Data Design Ent. = Field Rein = Addresse	e.g., "Program" Proc. = Language\ Statement I/O = Control Block	e.g., Network Architecture Node = Address Link = Protocol
Functioning System	e.g., Data	e.g., Function	e.g., Network

Figure 15.3 Vertical integration in the John Zachman framework. © 1987 International Business Machines Corp. Reprinted with permission from IBM Systems Journal, Vol. 26, No. 3.

associated with each model component instance or is at least dependent on the user id associated with the respective application model.

True vertical integration within a single vendor's domain implies the accessibility of all model element instances from within any CASE tool component regardless of where, when, and how the instance was originally created. For example, a CASE modeler may be editing a physical database design and realize that one of the attributes that was defined in the logical data model needs to be split into two distinct attributes based on access considerations. Perhaps most users are concerned with net expenses (after taxes), as defined in the logical model but one distinct view of the data requires several definitions and renditions of "net" expenses. In a vertically integrated tool, the *design* component should be able to access the attribute NET EXPENSES, as originally defined in the *analysis* component of the tool; update its definition to very specifically reflect the correct derivation of "net"; and, while in the *analysis* component, the modeler should be able to create the other attributes as required. After this attribute clarification is complete, the modeler should be able to return to his or her in-progress physical database design model and reference these newly created logical attribute definitions as new components of the physical database model.

The reality of such an example varies among vendor offerings. In some scenarios the newly created logical attributes may not be immediately accessible to an under-development design model; it may be necessary to "save" the underlying encyclopedia before its instances become universally accessible, or it may even be necessary to "close" and "reopen" the tool component window before a new "view" of the encyclopedia becomes available. Regardless, vertical integration within a single-vendor tool set requires an encyclopedia as part of the vendor-developed offering. The encyclopedia's metadata directly represents the metadata of each tool component, and its stored relationships should allow the accessibility depicted earlier.

Vertical integration can get complicated when the access of model elements crosses "projects" in addition to life cycle phase tool components. Most CASE tools require the definition of some model level boundary (most typically a *project*, *enterprise*, *model*, or *encyclopedia* name) which usually relates to a to-be-developed application. When modelers are diagramming a multiple-application view (e.g., the enterprise), the "enterprise" itself is usually defined as an application level equivalent.

As depicted in Fig. 15.4 the existence of multiple projects within a single encyclopedia typically requires the creation (by the tool) of a project id which functions as the major key (and sometimes the *only* key) into the identification and access of the particular project's model constructs. If a model element was defined as part of a *Customer* project, in the supporting tool's *planning* component, can it be accessed (for reuse?) by an *Accounts Receivable* project's *analysis* component–based model? In most cases it cannot be directly accessed. Some tools do let you open other projects while you are working within one project, the type of access you as a modeler have into the secondary project is not always the same as the access you have into your primary project. In many cases the secondary project's models are available only for scanning (i.e., *read* access). In better

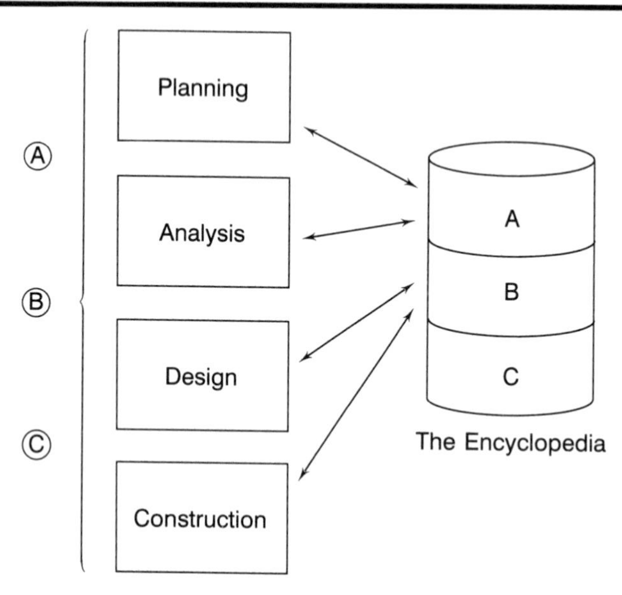

Figure 15.4 Multiple projects within a single-vendor tool set.

situations a model element in the secondary project can be "copied" (e.g., via a *cut-and-paste* operation) based on the base operating system's windowing and multiprocess capabilities.

The point to be realized is that *vertical integration* is not consistently realized among vendor offerings. Even within a single vendor's multicomponent tool set, the *integration* usually has its limitations. When dealing with these restrictions in the tool domain of one vendor, there typically is not much that can be easily done to get around this dilemma. Model export and subsequent reimport certainly do not help because the export and import functions all work within and around the same central encyclopedia backbone, regardless of the model element's parent project or originating CASE tool component. Many CASE vendors offer *model consolidation* utilities as a way of combining and/or copying model components from one project to another, or simply as a way to consolidate (combine) multiple projects. These utilities, however, occur outside of the functional boundaries of the modeler's authorship. In most scenarios the models (projects) must be saved and closed, the modeler must exit the appropriate tool component, and then begin execution of the consolidation utilities. To truly benefit from this arrangement, the need for model element "reuse" must be realized in advance, and the actual consolidation routine (which elements from which source projects become which elements in which target projects) must be preliminarily planned.

■ MODEL ACCESS/TRANSFER ACROSS MULTIPLE VENDOR TOOLS

Realizing now that vertical integration may not be as simple and universal as vendors may allege, consider the complexity that enters the picture when tool components from multiple vendors become part of the integration framework. Perhaps one CASE tool is used strictly for analysis; the models developed in that tool then become the base for detailed application design and development in a different tool. The design tool is selected in this example based on its ability to generate code for this organization's particular target execution environment. The source analysis tool does not have a design component and therefore could not have been considered suitable for continued application development. However, its supportive metadata constructs are one of the most diverse among similar vendor offerings, and customization of the metadata (to conform with this company's modeling methodology) is another key advantage.

How is vertical integration handled in this scenario? To begin, model export from the originating analysis tool is a requirement. The subsequent import of this model into the target design/construction tool set is the next step. But what about constructs that exist in the source analysis tool that have no counterparts in the target design tool? This issue will be discussed in detail in Chap. 16. In fact, the issue of incompatible metadata is one of the primary reasons repositories became popular as inter-CASE transfer mechanisms. For now, a simple answer to this question is my favorite retort: *It depends*! The importance of the source metadata is directly related to how the target tool generates code. Specifically,

- Which constructs in the target tool's analysis metamodel directly relate and/or become physical constructs in the target tool's design models?
- Do constructs in the target tool's metamodel have the same functionality/role as those in the source tool, but merely have different names? In this case a simple mapping (translation) could solve the problem.
- Are the extra constructs in the source tool used primarily for documentation, or are they necessary prerequisites to a more specific physical implementation?
- Where do the majority of the noncompatible constructs reside—in the source tool or the target tool?

As illustrated in Fig. 15.5, successful vertical integration, when multiple vendor tools are involved, requires the existence of an interface/translation function. Some vendors offer this feature as an extra-price option. Those who do typically realize the benefits of a competitor offering and are willing to acknowledge the need for many customers (existing and potential) to move models from or to the other vendor's product. Or, more simply, their tool may lack the functionality of the other vendor offering (maybe their tool does not have code generation capability), and the availability of an interface to a tool equipped with the extra feature makes their tool a more marketable option. In many situations vendors began to offer this feature after their customers requested and/or demanded it. Progressive organizations utilizing the "best of breed" CASE tool philosophy built their own custom translation/interface programs. In either circumstance additional programming was a required part of the intervendor vertical integration framework.

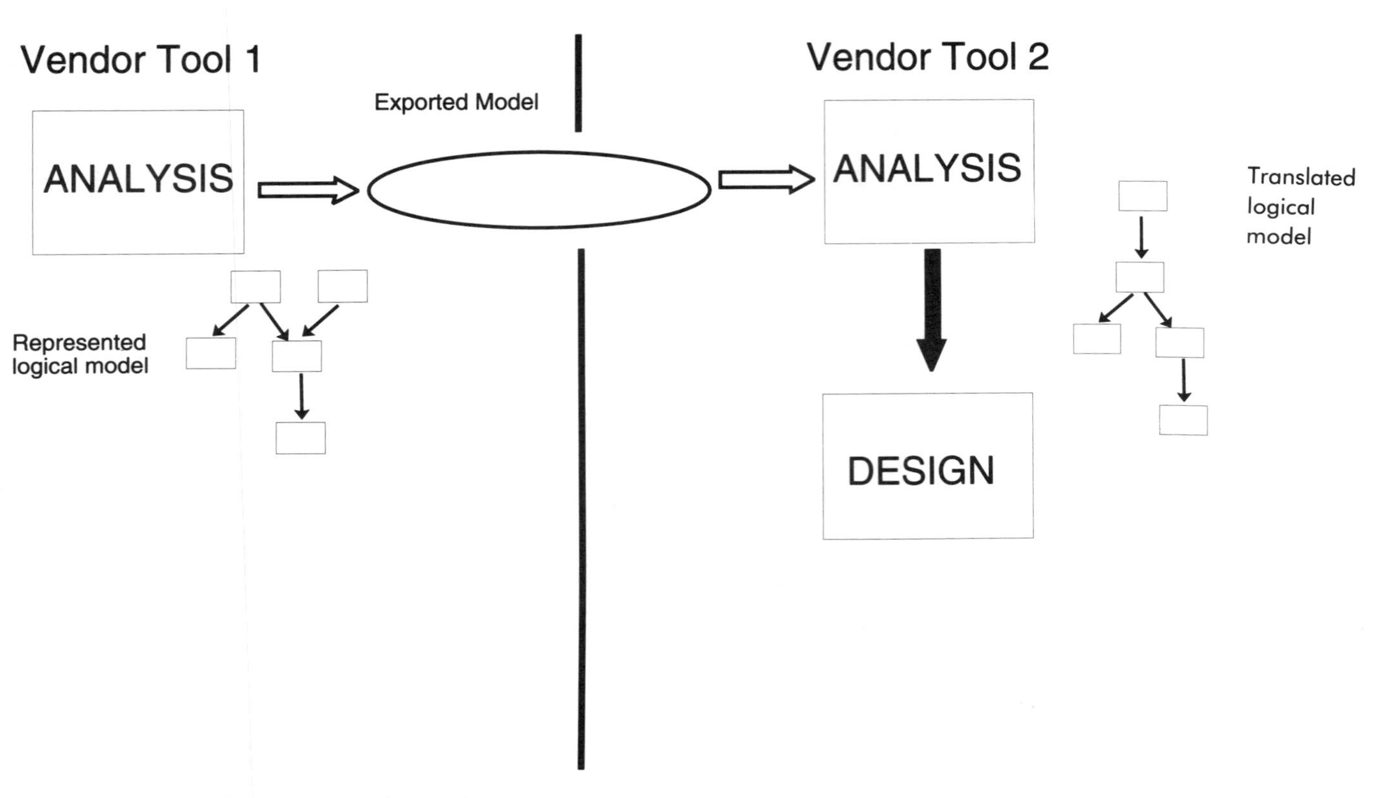

Figure 15.5 Vertical integration with a multi-vendor tool architecture.

■ EXAMPLES

Vertical integration is more commonly a part of a single vendor's integrated tool set (e.g., ICASE). In this scenario a modeling effort begins with a business level definition (sometimes in a tool's planning component, but more typically in a tool's analysis component) and becomes further refined and more specific throughout the lower-level components. Consider Fig. 15.6, where a set of planning model constructs is accessed from the same tool's analysis component. Here, subject areas were defined in the tool's planning component. As the modeling effort progressed, some subject areas became entities (one to one), some became multiple entities (one to many), and some were simply not implemented in the E–R diagram at all

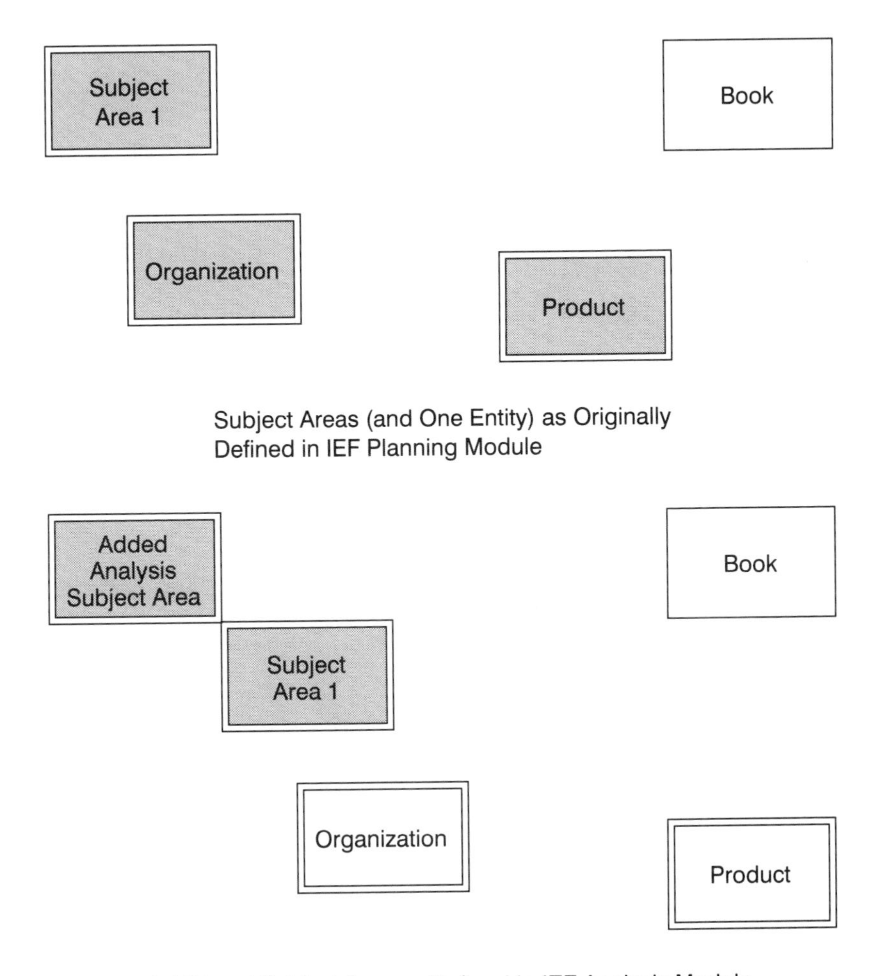

Figure 15.6 A planning / analysis vertical integration example.

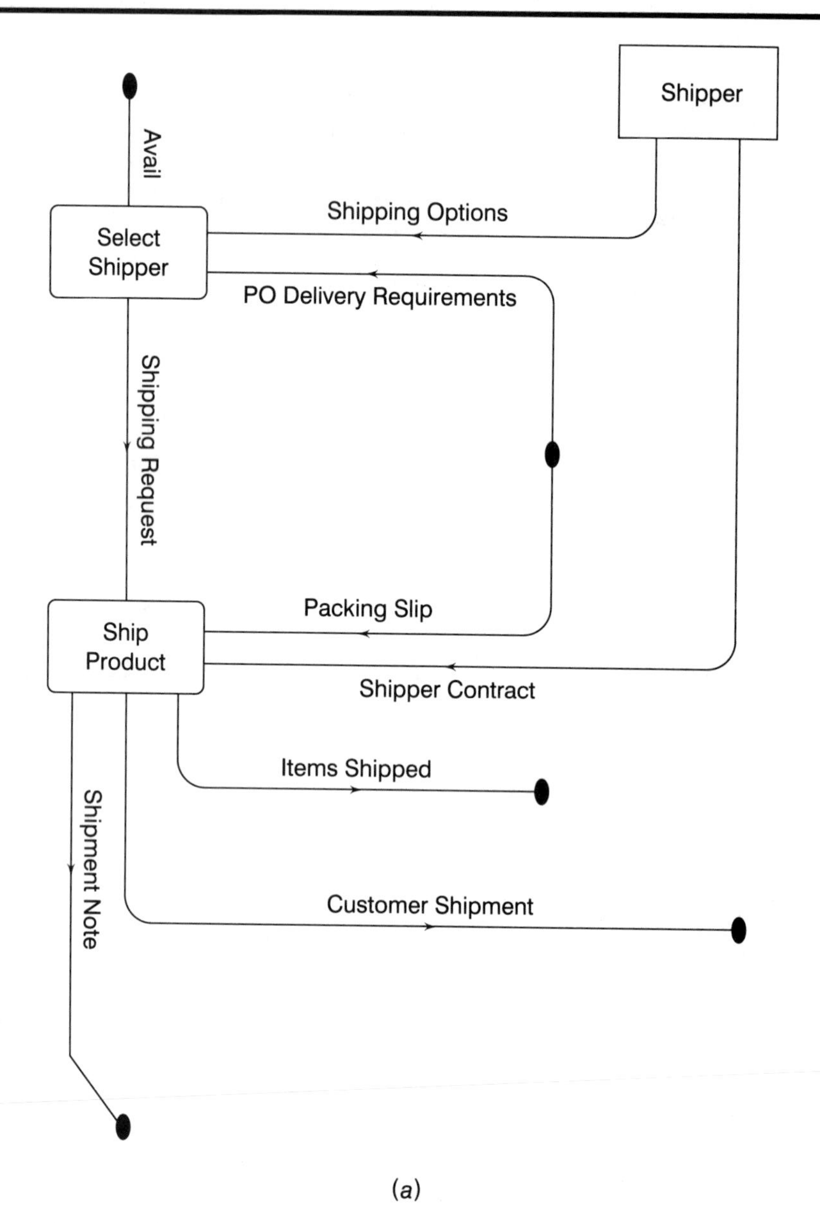

(*a*)

Figure 15.7 An analysis / design vertical integration example.

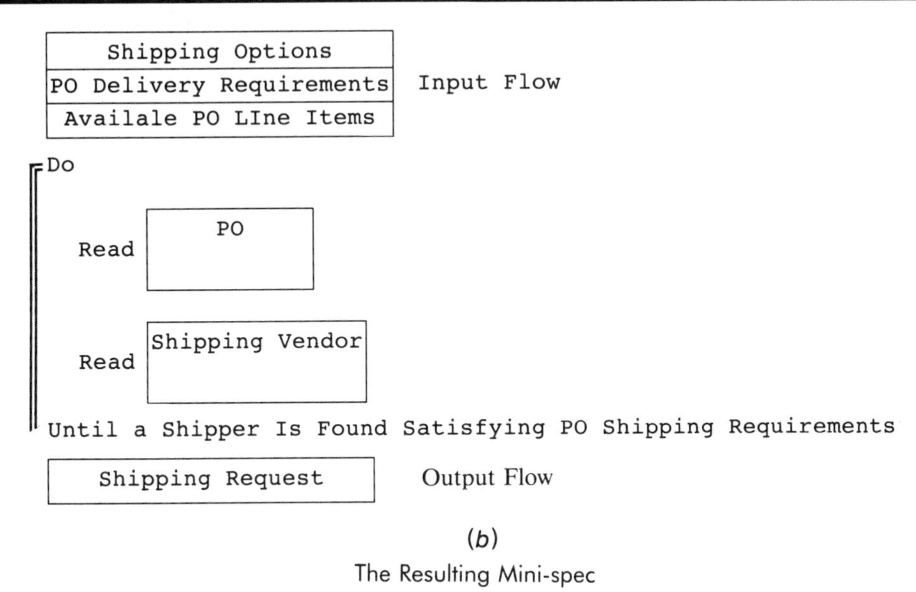

(*b*)
The Resulting Mini-spec

Figure 15.7 (Continued).

(one to none). While working on the E–R diagram, the accessibility of the previously defined subject areas is almost a must. What about afterthoughts? The modeler realizes a subject area was overlooked and should have been previously defined. Vertical integration does not necessarily imply the ability to postdefine an object that should have been defined in a previous life cycle phase. In our example, using Texas Instruments' IEF, the ability to define subject areas is part of both the *planning* and *analysis* modules of the tool. Based on the accessibility of the same metadata, despite the originating tool component, the newly created subject area (created via the *analysis* module) was just as accessible from the *planning* module.

Consider another example. A process defined in a data flow diagram (via a tool's analysis component) receives further definition in the tool's design component. As the process definition becomes more refined in design, the modeler realizes an error in the logical data model that needs to be corrected. She tries to access the logical data model while positioned in the tool's design section. From Fig. 15.7 we can see that the type of access granted when accessing a model component defined in an earlier development life cycle phase (which means, in effect, in another tool part) does not necessarily permit this. It is necessary to reopen the original model, from within the analysis segment. Once the logical data model is revised, what impact do the changes have on already defined design elements which may have been dependent on their previous versions? Every tool handles this differently. In optimum situations the modeler is advised that the affected design components are no longer "kosher" (obviously my term). In the less than ideal situations, the inconsistencies are not identified until the modeler runs a tool-supplied model integrity check, or, in the worst case, when the model is used to generate code and/or DDL.

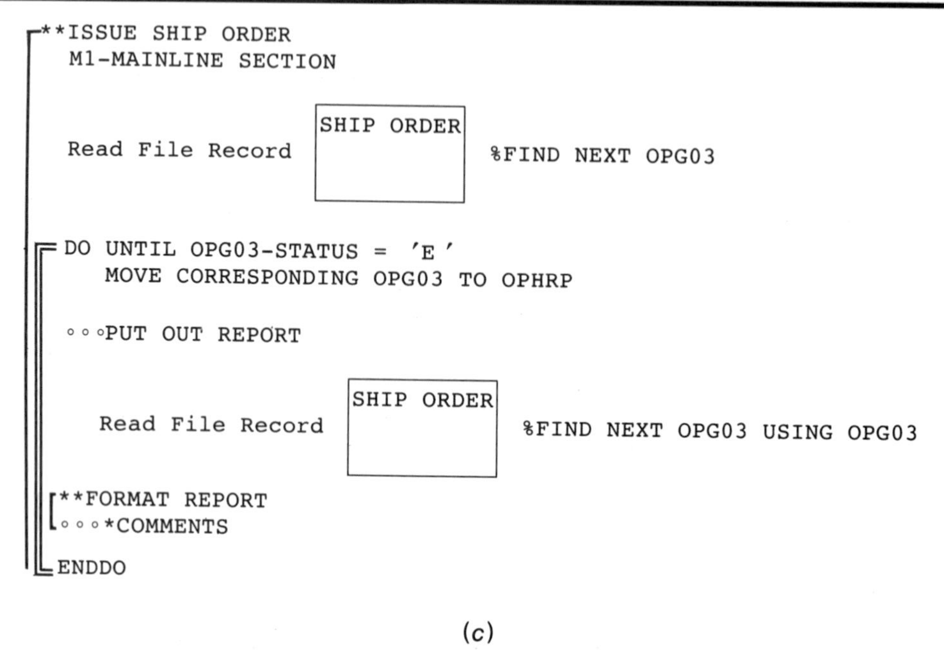

(*c*)

Detailed definition of a subordinate module (Design Component) reveals the need to 're-look' the E-R diagram Component which addresses SHIP ORDER. Not allowed from the Design Component.

Figure 15.7 (Continued).

As the opening quote of this chapter implies, vertical integration functions best in tools that were originally designed with multiple life cycle components. Some of these tools, when originally offered, were offered as one tool set, take it or leave it (e.g., there was no option to buy only the planning component). As the CASE market changed, so too did the vendor tool purchase options. Tools that covered the whole information engineering life cycle became "componentized" and those that only covered single phases of information engineering expanded by banding with other vendor's offerings or by building their own supplemental products. What we have now, in my opinion, is less vertical integration. In any case (no pun intended), vertical integration still implies a single vendor's set of tools.The Result-

16
HORIZONTAL CASE INTEGRATION

After discussing vertical integration in the previous chapter and realizing that it works best in a single vendor's tool set, it is necessary to address the integration that is necessary when more than one vendor tool is part of the integration scene. When discussing the requirements involved in horizontal integration, it is important to realize how far the framework of integration extends within a horizontal plateau. As we will see in this chapter, once multiple vendors (platforms, methodologies, etc.) populate this horizontal line, the issues can become quite interesting.

■ HORIZONTAL INTEGRATION DEFINED

Horizontal integration refers to the transfer and relating of models within the same life cycle phase. Obviously, this involves more than one vendor tool. As Fig. 16.1 illustrates, the horizontal nature of our integration refers to each horizontal line in the figure. For example, a planning model from Tool A could be transferred to Tool B across a horizontal path. The integration aspects imply the accessibility of those constructs that were part of Tool A's model despite the fact that they now reside in Tool B. Like vertical integration, the integration is forward, not backward. In theory, the same definition of horizontal integration should apply to all phases of the application development life cycle. That is, no matter where we are on our "*y* axis"—*planning*, *analysis*, *design*, or *construction*—horizontal integration implies the same functionality.

However, as we began to see in previous chapters, not all tools define the boundaries of each life cycle phase consistently. What one vendor may consider to be part of the analysis metamodel may not show up at all in another vendor's tool until the design component. Some tools do not expect or require the use of a planning component and therefore offer equivalent metadata constructs in their analysis component. Finally, those tools that have construction components (code generators) expect specific metadata constructs to be populated. "Generic" code generators do exist today. Theoretically, any export file that meets the code

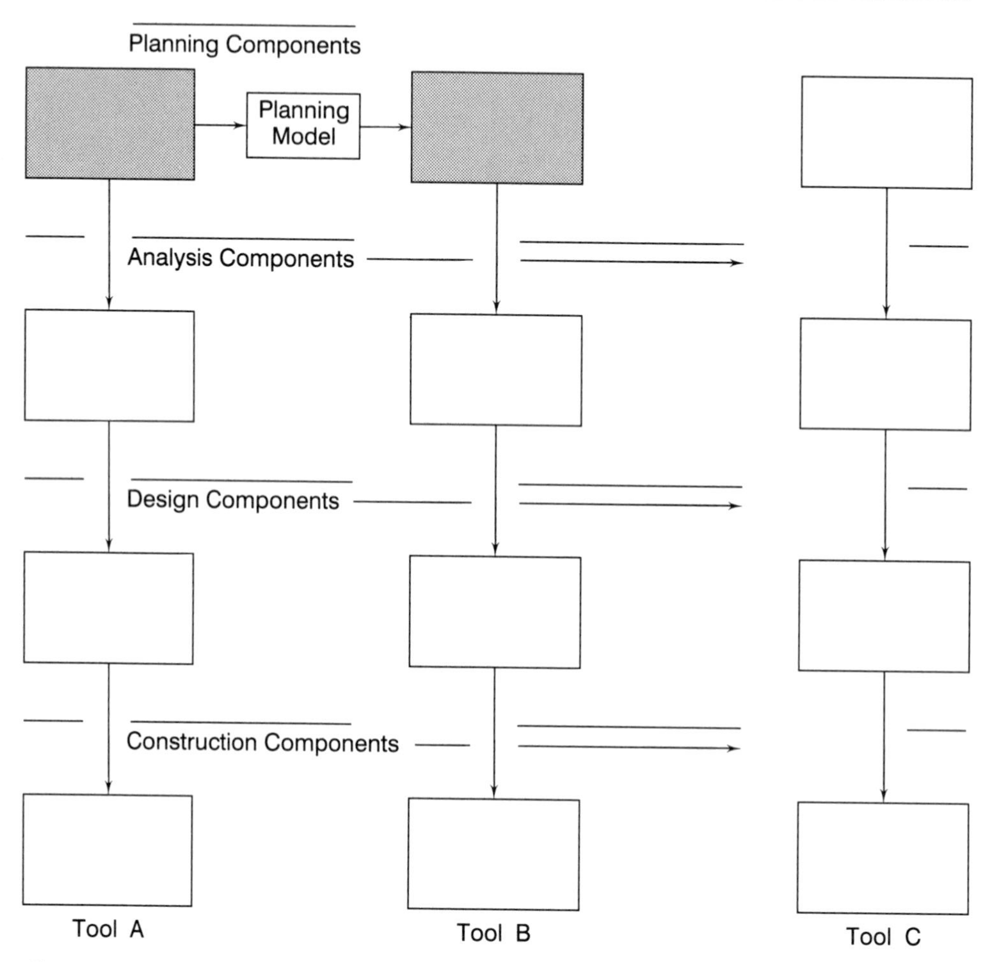

Figure 16.1 Illustrated horizontal integration.

generator's requirements can be considered to have originated from an "interfacing" tool. What we have been finding, as skeptical consumers, is a proliferation of "new releases" on both sides of the fence. Aspects of Vendor A's modeling metadata need to either expand, contract, or be substituted in order to meet the needs of Vendor B's code generator. Vendor B's code generator increases its functionality to handle metadata constructs in Vendor A's tool that were not part of the original realm of generation capabilities.

As discussed previously, the scope of horizontal integration relies on the boundary of a defined model in most cases. Some tools do allow the export of model components based on user/tool-defined selection criteria. In most of these situations, however, the tool-supplied utility allows the extract of all instances (within a model) of a defined set of metadata types (e.g., all entities in the *Customer Model*). The internal encyclopedias of integrated tools often contain query mechanisms that may allow customized export. However, unless a commercial DBMS is the backbone of the tool's encyclopedia, some limitations (most likely the constraint of remaining within a particular model) are likely to exist.

The issues get complicated as we will explore throughout this chapter. For this reason the definition of *horizontal integration* can be viewed, to some degree, as theoretical (as opposed to practical):

> Horizontal integration refers to the ability to access model components, despite their originating tool, by a tool or tool component that represents the equivalent life cycle phase.

In the simplest scenario a model is exported from Tool A and imported into Tool B. In some cases the import into Tool B involves a merge with a preexisting model. Many tools can handle this feature. The issue of metadata conflicts remains, however, regardless of whether the import results in a merge, update, creation, or replacement.

Horizontal integration without an intermediary repository can be more than tricky. Because different CASE tools imply differing metamodels, differing import/export formats, and sometimes redundant and/or overlying functionality despite their similar perceived role in the information engineering life cycle, the tying together of their various outputs can be exceedingly difficult and expensive. Because these conflicts are not unknown to vendors, it has always been in their best interest to deal with them. However, the objectives of each vendor's offered solutions often conflict with those of the multitool user determined to create the optimal model and/or generated application.

Because the building of an inter-CASE tool bridge should not be considered a minor undertaking, the following "tips" (from an experienced "bridge builder") are worth mentioning as a means of assessing the involved complexity:

- *Avoid bridge building whenever possible.* How's that for a tip? According to an experienced developer, the acquisition of an ICASE tool with one or more "weak" components is preferred over a set of diverse, "strong" tools that require an intertool bridge. In retrospect, the bridge built by this organization between two data modeling tools took over one person-year of work!
- *Make the bridge one way if possible.* This avoids as much as 50 percent of the maintenance problems.
- *Retain control over one side of the interface.* Control implies the fact that one side of the interface is built in house and therefore you are fully familiar with its functionality. It could also imply, when the interface is acquired from a vendor, that one side has a "frozen" release level in that maintenance releases are not going to be applied anymore, based on the existence of this bridge. This avoids 50 percent of the bridge changes that would be required based on new vendor releases, but of course prevents you from taking advantage of increased functionality that comes with new releases.

- *Extract from the tool with the most processed metadata and import into the tool with the least processed metadata.* If one tool provides extensive edits, the data exported from it will be purer, so to speak. Likewise, the target tool can be used for validation internally, because the tool itself "does not care" about the quality of the imported data.
- *Consider building a minirepository as the intermediary between the two tools.* This minirepository would only be populated during transfer and would be based on a composite metamodel of the two tools. No permanent data would be resident.

The previous "tips" should render the reader with a bit of queasiness. None are ideal, and, if anything, they will result in limited functionality once implemented.

■ THE CASE IMPORT/EXPORT DILEMMA

Without a repository horizontal integration requires the transfer of models. We already discussed why it is not a good idea to build your own bridge. It would be great if one tool could request and receive data on demand from another tool via a user-initiated request. However, as of this writing, this functionality implies the existence of an intermediate "repository," as we alluded to previously. Because the lack of a repository requires us to rely on file transfer, one would expect some standard treatment in this area. Well, as I said previously, when the word *standards* is a plural (as it is here), they become guidelines rather than requirements. There are multiple standards that define the format of CASE export files. The next section will discuss these and provide examples.

The dilemma focuses more on metadata conflicts and inconsistencies than on the existence of multiple (and perhaps incomplete) standards. Even with standardized record layouts and file structures, some things that exist in one tool but not the other will be exported. The conflict then arises in the target tool—how and whether to import those constructs that are "foreign" to the target tool's metamodel.

And how do we define *foreign*? In a simplistic, mechanized sense, a construct labeled A in one tool and B in the other creates a clash. To each tool, the other's construct is foreign. Depending on which tool is the target tool in a model transfer, either A or B could conceivably be ignored. This simplistic approach exists in the purest file transfer mechanisms. These simple export/imports operate in an obvious fashion: Exports take *everything* that has been defined in the tool (for a particular model) out. Imports search the "to be imported" file for *all constructs that exist within its own metamodel* and bring them in. Remember, as illustrated in Fig. 16.2, that the name we are referring to in this simple example is the name of the *metadata construct*, not the *metadata instance* (*Entity* as a name vs. *Customer* as a name). Names of metadata instances can also provide conflicts when they exist as part of multiple models being combined. This type of conflict is usually handled within the tool itself as part of the merge process.

So what happens when a construct exists as part of an exported model and has no equivalent in the target metamodel? The answer revolves around the word

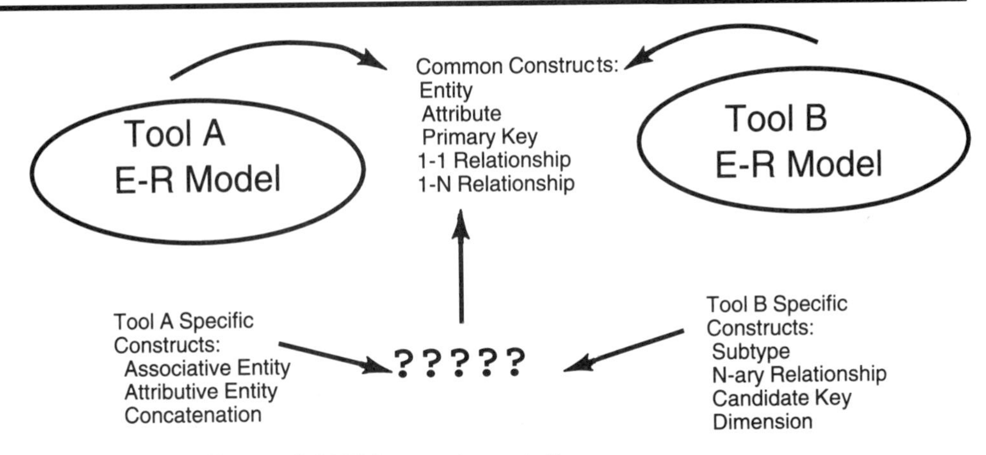

Figure 16.2 An illustrated CASE import / export dilemma.

equivalent. When vendors offer "interfaces" between their tool and those of other vendors, "equivalents" are often handled. For example, suppose Tool A's model contains a construct called *primary key*. As such, it is exported as an instance of that metadata type. Tool B has a construct called *identifier*, but no metadata construct called *primary key*. Vendors realize the equivalence, and typically translate the *primary keys* of the source tool into *identifiers* for the second tool. Sounds like a logical transition, right? The determination of *equivalence* in this situation rests with how *identifiers* are handled in the target tool. Can there be more than one in existence for a particular entity? If so, how does the modeler mark one of them as *primary*? Assume this example involved the transfer of a model from one vendor's analysis component to that of another vendor. The lack of a *primary* classification implies the existence of only one *identifier* per entity in the target tool. Or, if this is not the case (multiple identifiers are allowed), the designation of the *primary* classification may not occur until use of the *design* component. We determine equivalence from an overall application perspective to be practical. However, if the model(s) being transferred between vendor offerings is not going to remain in one particular vendor's ICASE tool for further refinement and eventual conversion into application code, the overall application perspective may not be suitable.

This perspective and the translations that occur between vendor metadata constructs typically support the target tool's best interests. In other words, the vendor assumes that once a model has been imported into its tool offering, it is going to stay there. Although this assumption is not necessarily incorrect, it is one that should be appreciated when intervendor tool interfaces are purchased. In our illustrated example, assuming the residency of our transferred model within the target tool for the remainder of the application development life cycle (and of course our intended use of the target tool's *design* component), the translation given previously is sufficient.

Metadata conflicts do not only occur at the construct level, as identified previously. They also occur at the *metadata attribute* level. For example, consider the two sets of attributes that describe entities within two tools as shown in Fig. 16.3. We already see discrepancies. Again, as with metadata constructs, the attributes of each construct are not necessarily consistent from tool to tool. Model export brings all of the resident attributes out as part of the overall model. The import of this model into the target tool typically addresses conflicts of metadata attributes in the same way metadata conflicts are handled. The issue of *equivalence* and how it is treated appears again.

In both of these situations, when a target tool makes assumptions about which of its own metadata constructs (and their associated attributes) are equivalent, the "conversions" are generally documented in a supplied user manual. It is in the user's best interest to seriously evaluate whether or not these conversions serve the same general purpose in the target model as was originally outlined in the source model. Any potential problems should be identified before major model transfers occur. Perhaps the vendor-supplied "interface" does not meet the particular needs of the multitool user.

Another simple aspect of the import/export dilemma involves the issue of truncation. As discussed in Chap. 14, when the source tool allows 120 characters for a field value and the target tool only allows 80, the disposition of the used additional 40 characters must be addressed. Most supplied inter-CASE interfaces do not eliminate the extra values (as discussed in a previous chapter). However, because they cannot be placed where you would like them (in the shortened target field), they are usually placed in an interface-created "holding area," available for later disposition by the user/modeler. Again, this treatment by the target vendor is usually documented in the interface user manual.

Finally, conflicts can also exist beyond the scope of equivalence and truncation. Questioning simply, What happens to constructs that exist in the source tool's metamodel but have no equivalents in the target tool's metamodel (at all)? It is hard to generalize a treatment that will fit all situations. The disposition is totally dependent on what the construct was used for in the source model and whether or not it becomes part of the target tool's functionality at any development point. If a construct existed in the source tool and has no equivalent at all in the target tool, there are only a few possible solutions that can be used:

1. The easiest is simply dropping the concept from the target model (a supplied vendor interface would most likely do this anyway). If severe meaning is lost, then reconsider why you are moving to the target tool in the first place.
2. Another possibility is the creation of "equivalence" via instance data. For example, if your source tool had metadata that contained different types of relationships between entities (mutually exclusive, *n*-ary, etc.) and your target metamodel contains only the simple categories of one to one and one to many, instance data would have to be created as shown in Fig. 16.4. Notice the creation of a relationship instance with a "metadata flavor."

ENTITY

This table lists the entities in the data model.

Column Name	Description	Enter Data As
mcode	Unique number among all the enterprise models in the database	
entitykey	Unique number that identifies this object	
createdby	Log-in name of the person who created this object	0 – 9 alphanumeric characters
createdtime	Time at which this object was created	Zero
modifiedby	Log-in name of the person who last modified this object	0 – 9 alphanumeric characters
modifiedtime	Time at which this object was last modified	Zero
name	Name of this object	1 – 75 characters
minvol	Lowest possible number of occurrences for this entity	
maxvol	Highest possible number of occurrences for this entity	
expvol	Expected number of occurrences for this entity	
grwpct	Expected growth percentage for this entity	
gptu	Character representing the growth rate period for this entity	
normlvl	Character representing the normalization level	1 for first normal form; 2 for second normal form; 3 for third normal form; 4 for fourth normal form; C for none
normok	Character indicates that the entity is sufficiently normalized	Y for yes; N for no
entity	ENTITY.entitykey value that identifies the parent entity	Zero if there is no parent entity
outline	Eight numbers (*outline, outline2, . . . , outline8*) that define the location of the entity within the entity – relationship (E – R) diagram	
valbits	Array of eight validation bits (*valbits, valbit2, . . . , valbits8*) that is used during the design task to determine if this object is marked as correct	Zeros
text	TEXT.textkey value that identifies the object's description (the description is defined as a separate text object)	
namebreaks	Used by the system	

(*a*)

Figure 16.3 Entity attributes as they exist in two CASE tools.

```
Entity Type
10007
Comments
30077

Creation Date
30110

Definition
30076

Purpose
30025

Entity Type in Entity Model Entity Diagram Position
30028

Last Update
30075
```

(*b*)

Figure 16.3 (*Continued*).

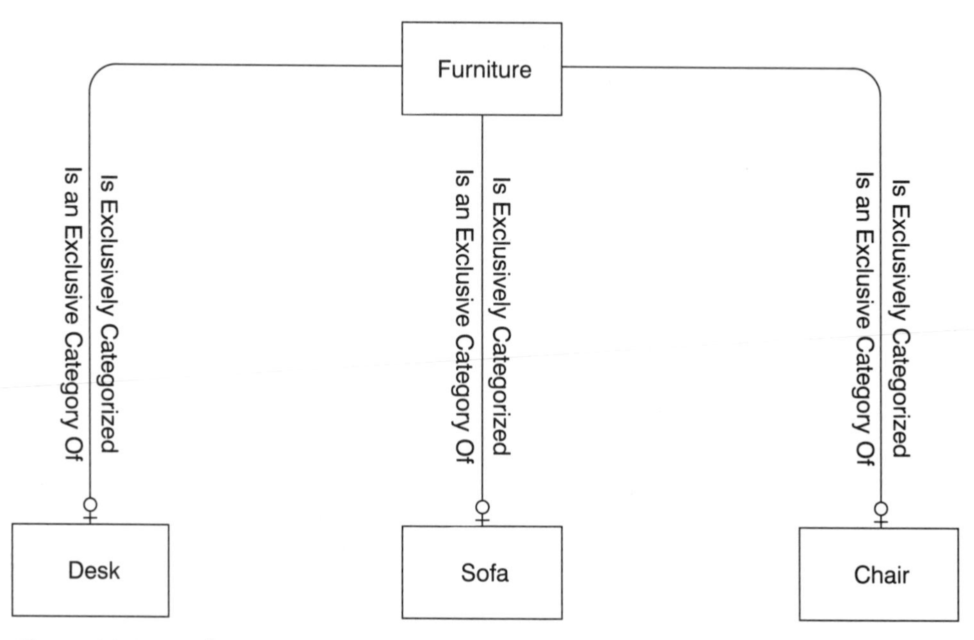

Figure 16.4 Handling metadata conflicts via the creation of instance data.

3. The final and least desirable possibility is the fudged use of a different metadata construct in the target model for something other than its original intent. This can be acceptable if it is done consistently among all target tool models, and the chosen metadata construct is not used for anything else.

The dilemma then is based on the lack of a standard metamodel that covers each application development stage across all vendor offerings. Later in this chapter we will address the implications of importing nonexisting metadata constructs into a target tool's metamodel.

■ SAMPLE MODEL IMPORT/EXPORT FORMATS

As discussed previously, multiple "standards" exist to define the ways in which multitool import/export should be implemented.* Specifically, they either address the format and contents of the export file (the earlier contenders) or the means and format of any direct communication between the tool and other operating system-resident applications (the more recent participants). Import utilities that conform to a particular standard will only import files that are formatted properly. Major contenders in the standards area which deal with intertool transfer are:

CDIF (CASE Data Interchange Format)
PCTE (Portable Common Tool Environment)
IRDS (Information Resource Dictionary System)

CDIF is the oldest of the three and originated in the computer-aided-design/computer-aided-manufacture (CAD/CAM) tool arena. It basically covers the format and order of an ASCII text file's contents as well as a defined set of tool architectures. The ASCII text file is deemed to be the way to transfer information between tools. Within this file exist the actual model instance data, organized by metadata construct type, the "links" between each instance and other instances, and the necessary graphical positioning coordinates.

PCTE originated as a standard that addressed the use of and communication between tools in a Unix environment. The interface consists of a set of defined function calls. The theory behind this standard is that if all tools called PCTE-defined functions to perform the generic routines covered by the standard, tools would be portable across multiple operating systems and platforms. The standard addresses much more functionality than model import/export.

IRDS addresses a substantial amount of the dictionary/repository tool environment. A section of the standard addresses interface, but it is geared toward repository interface as opposed to CASE tool interface. In short, it is geared toward dealing with conflicting metamodels in both the source and target repositories by requiring the exporter (importer) to define and customize the items to be exported.

*All of these standards (and others) will be discussed in detail in Part Four.

object instance token	object type code	object instance name

An object instance record

association instance token	assoc type code	From token	To token

An association instance record

subject token	prop. type code	rep. no.	property value

subject token	prop. type code	rep. no.	long textual property value

There are two kinds of property instance records: one for short property values and one for comments and definitions.

Figure 16.5 Knowledgeware's ADW model export file formats.

Putting theoretical standards aside (they must be considered theoretical because they are all always "evolving" and therefore no tools can possibly conform to them), we can look at the actual export formats that exist today in some major CASE tools.

In Knowledgeware's ADW the export of a model results in the creation of four text files (see Fig. 16.5):

1. An *object instance* file contains each object type and instance name, identified by an internal token.
2. An *association instance* file contains each association instance type identified by an internal token, as well as the tokens of the *from* and *to* object instances.
3. A *property instance* file, for "short" properties, contains the token of the object to which the properties pertain, a property type code, a repetition number (for multiple lines), and the actual property value.
4. A *textual instance* file pertains to long, textual property values.

The Bachman Analyst also produces ASCII text when a model is exported. As with Knowledgeware's ADW, internal identifiers are produced by the tool, and they precede each comma-delimited line of model instance data. Unlike Knowledgeware's ADW, the exported model resides on one file, and each "metadata construct grouping" is preceded by the textual name of that object within the Bachman metamodel (see Fig. 16.6).

```
Bachman Analyst V2.21 715634473 0 "vendors" " "
**ENTERPRISE_MODEL**
7,"AB",1992-09-04-15.21.18.000000,"ABT",1992-09-04-
15.21.18.000000,0,"vendors",0,0,0
**ENTERPRISE_MODELKE**
**ENTERPRISE_MODELSY**
**ENTERPRISE_MODELMA**
**DATA_MODEL**
1,"ABT",1992-09-04-15.21.16.000000,"ABT",1992-09-04-
15.30.01.000000,0,"vendor",0,0,0,0," ",0,7,0,0,0,0,0,0,0,0,0,0,
0,0,0,0,0,0,0,"
",0,0,0,0,0,0,2,2,3,4,5,6,0,0,0,0,0,0,0,0,0,0,0,0,0,0,
0,0,0,0,0,0,0,0,0,0,0,0,0,0,0,0,0,0,0,0,0,0,0,0,1,0,0,0
**DATA_MODELTEXT**
**DATA_MODELSYNONYM_**
**DATA_MODELER_NOTES**
**DATA_MODELATTRIBUT**
**DATA_MODELMAP_NAME**
**SWS_CONTROL**
**TEXT**
**SYNONYM_OBJECT**
**KEYWORD**
**PLACEKEEPER**
**PLACEKEEPERATTRIBU**
**ER_NOTES**
**ENTITY**
68,"ABT",1992-09-04-15.28.38.000000,"ABT",1992-09-04-
15.30.01.000000,0,"VENDOR",0,9999999,0,0,"Y","C","N",0,-550,
-100,-150,100,0,0,0,0,0,0,0,0,0,0,0,0,0
119,"ABT",1992-09-04-15.30.01.000000,"ABT",1992-09-04-
15.30.01.000000,
0,"VENDOR-PAYMENT",0,9999999,0,0,"Y","C","N",0,150,150,
550,3,50,0,0,0,0,0,0,0,0,0,0,0,0,0
**ENTITYSYNONYM__OBJE**
**ENTITYKEYWORD**
**ENTITYER_NOTES**
**ENTITYMAP_SYSTEM_M**
**ENTITYATTRIBUTE**
68,70
68,84
68,87
68,109
119,124
119,127
**ENTITYALLOWED_VAL_**
**ENTITYMAP_SYSTEM_2**
**ENTITYBUSINESS_SJ_**
**ENTITYSUBSET_DEF**
**ENTITYMAP_NAME_TAB**
**ENT_KEY**
**ENT_KEYSYNONYM_OBJ**
**ENT_KEYKEYWORD**
**ENT_KEYER_NOTES**
**ENT_KEYMAP_SYSTEM_**
**ENT_KEYMAP_NAME_TA**
**ATTR_JUNCTION**
```


Figure 16.6 Bachman Analyst model export file format.

```
73,"ABT",1992-09-04-15.29.02.000000,"ABT",1992-09-04-
15.29.02.000000,0,1,70,72
77,"ABT",1992-09-04-15.29.02.000000,"ABT",1992-09-04-
15.29.02.000000,0,2,70,76
81,"ABT",1992-09-04-15.29.02.000000,"ABT",1992-09-04-
15.29.02.000000,0,4,70,80
90,"ABT",1992-09-04-15.29.15.000000,"ABT",1992-09-04-
15.29.15.000000,0,1,87,89
94,"ABT",1992-09-04-15.29.15.000000,"ABT",1992-09-04-
15.29.15.000000,0,2,87,93
98,"ABT",1992-09-04-15.29.15.000000,"ABT",1992-09-04-
15.29.15.000000,0,3,87,97
102,"ABT",1992-09-04-15.29.15.000000,"ABT",1992-09-04-
15.29.15.000000,0,4,87,101
106,"ABT",1992-09-04-15.29.15.000000,"ABT",1992-09-04-
15.29.15.000000,0,6,87,105
112,"ABT",1992-09-04-15.30.00.000000,"ABT",1992-09-04-
15.30.01.000000,0,1,109,111
116,"ABT",1992-09-04-15.30.01.000000,"ABT",1992-09-04-
15.30.01.000000,0,3,109,115
**ATTR_JUNCTIONMAP_N**
**PARTNERSHIP_SET**
121,"ABT",1992-09-04-15.30.01.000000,"ABT",1992-09-04-
15.30.01.000000,0,68,"VENDOR-PAYMENT",0,5,5,"I",0,0,0,0,-150,
-40,0,-124,-99,0,0,0,0,0,0,"S",0,0,0,0,0
122,"ABT",1992-09-04-15.30.01.000000,"ABT",1992-09-04-
15.30.01.000000,0,119,"VENDOR",1,1,1,"I",0,0,0,0,400,150,0,406,
71,0,0,0,0,0,0,"S",0,0,0,0,0
**PARNTERSHIP_SETENT**
**PARTNERSHIP_SETSYN**
**PARTNERSHIP_SETKEY**
**PARTNERSHIP_SETER_**
**PARTNERSHIP_SETFOR**
**PARTNERSHIP_SETMAP**
**PARTNERSHIP_SETN_S**
**PARTNERSHIP_SETN_U**
**PARTNERSHIP_SETN_D**
**PARTNERSHIP_SETSUB**
**PARTNERSHIP_SETMAP**
**COMB_PSET**
**PARTNERSHIP**
123,"ABT",1992-09-04-15.30.01.000000,"ABT",1992-09-04-
15.30.01.000000,1,121,122,0,5,5,1,1,1,0,0,0,0,0,0,0,-40,-40,
400,-40,400,40,-284905481,61118,76489042,135589354,3,0
**PARTNERSHIPER_NOTE**
**PARTNERSHIPN_SEL**
**PARTNERSHIPN_UPD**
**PARTNERSHIPN_DEL**
**PARTNERSHIPFOREIGN**
**PARTNERSHIPFOREIG2**
**PARTNERSHIPMAP_NAM**
**COMB_PSHIP**
**DIMENSION**
**DIMENSIONSYNONYM_0**
**DIMENSIONER_NOTES**
```


Figure 16.6 (*Continued*).

```
**DIMENSIONKEYWORD**
**DIMENSIONSUBSET_DE**
**DIMENSIONMAP_NAME_**
**DOMAINS**
75,"ABT",1992-09-04-15.29.02.000000,"ABT",1992-09-04-
15.29.02.000000,0,0,1,0,"VENDOR-STATE-CODE",0,"I","0.","99.",
0,0,0,0,0,0,0,0,0,0,0,0,0
79,"ABT",1992-09-04-15.29.02.000000,"ABT",1992-09-04-
15.29.02.000000,0,0,1,0,"VENDOR-ORG-CODE",0,"I","0.","99999.",
0,0,0,0,0,0,0,0,0,0,0,0,0
83,"ABT",1992-09-04-15.29.02.000000,"ABT",1992-09-04-
15.29.02.000000,0,0,1,0,"VENDOR-TYPE",0,"N","0.","0.",
1,20,0,0,0,0,20,0,0,0,0,0,0
86,"ABT",1992-09-04-15.29.02.000000,"ABT",1992-09-04-
15.29.02.000000,0,0,1,0,"VENDOR-NAME",0,"N","0.","0.",
1,20,0,0,0,0,20,0,0,0,0,0,0
92,"ABT",1992-09-04-15.29.15.000000,"ABT",1992-09-04-
15.29.15.000000,0,0,1,0,"VENDOR-STREET",0,"N","0.",
"0.",1,15,0,0,0,0,15,0,0,0,0,0,0
96,"ABT",1992-09-04-15.29.15.000000,"ABT",1992-09-04-
15.29.15.000000,0,0,1,0,"VENDOR-STREET2",0,"N","0.",
"0."1,15,0,0,0,0,15,0,0,0,0,0,0
100,"ABT",1992-09-04-15.29.15.000000,"ABT",1992-09-04-
15.29.15.000000,0,0,1,0,"VENDOR-CITY",0,"N","0.","0.",
1,15,0,0,0,0,15,0,0,0,0,0,0
104,"ABT",1992-09-04-15.29.15.000000,"ABT",1992-09-04-
15.29.15.000000,0,0,1,0,"VENDOR-STATE",0,"N","0.",
"0."1,2,0,0,0,0,2,0,0,0,0,0,0
108,"ABT",1992-09-04-15.29.15.000000,"ABT",1992-09-04-
15.29.16.000000,0,0,1,0,"VENDOR-ZIP",0,"I","0.","99999.",
0,0,0,0,0,0,0,0,0,0,0,0,0
114,"ABT",1992-09-04-15.30.01.000000,"ABT",1992-09-04-
15.30.01.000000,0,0,1,0,"VENDOR-CREDIT-CODE",0,"N","0.","0.",
1,1,0,0,0,0,1,0,0,0,0,0,0
118,"ABT",1992-09-04-15.30.01.000000,"ABT",1992-09-04-
15.30.01.000000,0,0,1,0,"VENDOR-OLD-CREDIT-CODE",0,"N","0.","0.",
1,1,0,0,0,0,1,0,0,0,0,0,0
126,"ABT",1992-09-04-15.30.01.000000,"ABT",1992-09-04-
15.30.01.000000,0,0,1,0,"PAYMENT-DATE",0,"I","0.","999999.",
0,0,0,0,0,0,0,0,0,0,0,0,0
129,"ABT",1992-09-04-15.30.01.000000,"ABT",1992-09-04-
15.30.02.000000,0,0,1,0,"PAYMENT-AMOUNT",0,"R","0.0",
"9999999.99",0,0,0,0,0,0,0,0,0,0,2,9,0
**DOMAINSSYNONYM_OBJ**
**DOMAINSKEYWORD**
**DOMAINSER_NOTES**
DOMAINSSUBSET_DEF**
**DOMAINSMAP_NAME_TA**
**ATTRIBUTE**
70,"ABT",1992-09-04-15.29.02.000000,"ABT",1992-09-04-
15.29.02.000000,0,68,0,"VENDOR-ID",1,"N"," ","M","S",0,0,0,
0,0,0,0,0,0,0,-25896,0,0
72,"ABT",1992-09-04-15.29.02.000000,"ABT",1992-09-04-
15.29.29.02000000,68,0,"VENDOR-STATE-CODE",0,"N"," ",M"M","S",0,
75,0,0,0,0,0,0,0,0,7680,0,0
```

Figure 16.6 (*Continued*).

```
76,"ABT",1992-09-04-15.29.02.000000,"ABT",1992-09-04-
15.29.02.000000,0,68,0,"VENDOR-ORG-CODE",0,"N"," ","M","S",0,
79,0,0,0,0,0,0,0,0,-29186,0,0
80,"ABT",1992-09-04-15.29.02.000000,"ABT",1992-09-04-
15.29.02.000000,0,68,0,"VENDOR-TYPE",0,"N" "","S",
0,83,0,0,0,0,0,0,0,0,-1
9691,0,0
84,"ABT",1992-09-04-15.29.02.000000,"ABT",1992-09-04-
15.29.02.000000,0,68,0,"VENDOR-NAME",2,"N"," ","M",
"S",0,86,0,0,0,0,0,0,0,0,-2
0471,0,0
87,"ABT",1992-09-04-15.29.15.000000,"ABT",1992-09-04-
15.29.15.000000,0,68,0,"VENDOR-ADDRESS",3,"N"," ","M",
"S",0,0,0,0,0,0,0,0,0,0,22121,0,0
89,"ABT",1992-09-04-15.29.15.000000,"ABT",1992-09-04-
15.29.15.000000,0,68,0,"VENDOR-STREET",0,"N"," ","M","S",0,
92,0,0,0,0,0,0,0,0,13877,0,0
93,"ABT",1992-09-04-15.29.15.000000,"ABT",1992-09-04-
15.29.15.000000,0,68,0,"VENDOR-STREET2",0,"N"," ","M",
"S",0,96,0,0,0,0,0,0,0,0,-16116,0,0
97,"ABT",1992-09-04-15.29.15.000000,"ABT",1992-09-04-
15.29.15.000000,0,68,0,"VENDOR-CITY",0,"N"," ","M",
"S",0,100,0,0,0,0,0,0,0,0,-20999,0,0
101,"ABT",1992-09-04-15.29.15.000000,"ABT",1992-09-04-
15.29.15.000000,0,68,0,"VENDOR-STATE",0,"N"," ","M",
"S",0,104,0,0,0,0,0,0,0,0,-13915,0,0
105,"ABT",1992-09-04-15.29.15.000000,"ABT",1992-09-04-
15.29.16.000000,0,68,0,"VENDOR-ZIP",0,"N"," ","M","S",0,108,
0,0,0,0,0,0,0,0,2,7860,0,0
109,"ABT",1992-09-04-15.30.00.000000,"ABT",1992-09-04-
15.30.01.000000,0,68,"VENDOR-STATUS",4,"N"," ","M",
"S",0,0,0,0,0,0,0,0,0,0,13092,0,0
111,"ABT",1992-09-04-15.30.00.000000,"ABT",1992-09-04-
15.30.01.000000,0,68,0,"VENDOR-CREDIT-CODE",0,"N"," ","M",
"S",0,114,0,0,0,0,0,0,0,0,25090,0,0
115,"ABT",1992-09-04-15.30.01.000000,"ABT",1992-09-04-
15.30.01.000000,0,68,0,"VENDOR-OLD-CREDIT-CODE",0,"N"," ","M",
"S",0,118,0,0,0,0,0,0,0,0,24067,0,0
124,"ABT",1992-09-04-15.30.01.000000,"ABT",1992-09-04-
15.30.01.000000,0,119,0,"PAYMENT-DATE",1,"N"," ","M","S",0,
126,0,0,0,0,0,0,0,0,-6747,0,0
127,"ABT",1992-09-04-15.30.01.000000,"ABT",1992-09-04-
15.30.02.000000,0,119,0,"PAYMENT-AMOUNT",2,"N"," ","M","S",
0,129,0,0,0,0,0,0,0,0,28567,0,0
**ATTRIBUTEENT_KEY**
**ATTRIBUTESYNONYM_0**
**ATTRIBUTEKEYWORD**
**ATTRIBUTEER_NOTES**
**ATTRIBUTEATTRIBUTE**
**ATTRIBUTEALLOWED_V**
**ATTRIBUTEMAP_SYSTE**
**ATTRIBUTEN_SEL**
**ATTRIBUTEN_UPD**
**ATTRIBUTEN_DEL**
**ATTRIBUTEBUSINESS_**
**ATTRIBUTESUBSET_DE**
```

Figure 16.6 (*Continued*).

```
**ATTRIBUTEMAP_NAME_**
**METHOD**
**METHODSUBSET_DEF**
**METHODMAP_NAME_TAB**
**FOREIGN_KEY_ATTR**
**FOREIGN_KEY_ATTRSY**
**FOREIGN_KEY_ATTRMA**
**MAP_EXT_DESIGN**
**MAP_NAME_TABLE**
**MAP_SYSTEM_MAP**
**MAP_USER_MAP**
69,"ABT",1992-09-04-15.28.38.000000,"ABT",1992-09-04-
15.28.38.000000,0,0,"VENDOR",15,"VENDOR",21,
715634473,68,68,0,0,0,0
71,"ABT",1992-09-04-15.29.02.000000,"ABT",1992-09-04-
15.29.02.000000,0,0,"VENDOR-ID",11,"VENDOR",21,
715634473,70,0,70,0,0,0
74,"ABT",1992-09-04-15.29.02.000000,"ABT",1992-09-04-
15.29.02.000000,0,0,"VENDOR-STATE-CODE",11,"VENDOR",21,
715634473,72,0,72,0,0,0
78,"ABT",1992-09-04-15.29.02.000000,"ABT",1992-09-04-
15.29.02.000000,0,0,"VENDOR-ORG-CODE",11,"VENDOR",21,
7156344673,76,0,76,0,0,0
82,"ABT",1992-09-04-15.29.02.000000,"ABT",1992-09-04-
15.29.02.000000,0,0,"VENDOR-TYPE",11,"VENDOR",21,
715634473,80,0,80,0,0,0
85,"ABT",1992-09-04-15.29.02.000000,"ABT",1992-09-04-
15.29.02.000000,0,0,"VENDOR-NAME",11,"VENDOR",21,
715634473,84,0,84,0,0,0
88,"ABT",1992-09-04-15.29.15.000000,"ABT",1992-09-04-
15.29.15.000000,0,0,"VENDOR-ADDRESS",11,"VENDOR",21,
715634473,87,0,87,0,0,0
91,"ABT",1992-09-04-15.29.15.000000,"ABT",1992-09-04-
15.29.15.000000,0,0,"VENDOR-STREET",11,"VENDOR",21,
715634473,89,0,89,0,0,0
95,"ABT",1992-09-04-15.29.15.000000,"ABT",1992-09-04-
15.29.15.000000,0,0,"VENDOR-STREET2",11,"VENDOR",21,
715634473,93,0,93,0,0,0
99,"ABT",1992-09-04-15.29.15.000000,"ABT",1992-09-04-
15.29.15.000000,0,0,"VENDOR-CITY",11,"VENDOR",21,
715634473,97,0,97,0,0,0
103,"ABT",1992-09-04-15.29.15.000000,"ABT",1992-09-04-
15.29.15.000000,0,0,"VENDOR-STATE",11,"VENDOR",21,
715634473,101,0,101,0,0,0
107,"ABT",1992-09-04-15.29.15.000000,"ABT",1992-09-04-
15.29.15.000000,0,0,"VENDOR-ZIP",11,"VENDOR",21,
715634473,105,0,105,0,0,0
110,"ABT",1992-09-04-15.30.00.000000,"ABT",1992-09-04-
15.30.00.000000,0,0,"VENDOR-STATUS",11,"VENDOR",21,
715634473,109,0,109,0,0,0
113,"ABT",1992-09-04-15.30.01.000000,"ABT",1992-09-04-
15.30.01.000000,0,0,"VENDOR-CREDIT-CODE",11,"VENDOR",21,
715634473,111,0,111,0,0,0
117,"ABT",1992-09-04-15.30.01.000000,"ABT",1992-09-04-
15.30.01.000000,0,0,"VENDOR-OLD-CREDIT-CODE",11,"VENDOR",21,
```

Figure 16.6 (*Continued*).

```
715634473,115,0,115,0,0,0
120,"ABT",1992-09-04-15.30.01.000000,"ABT",1992-09-04-
15.30.01.000000,0,0,"VENDOR-PAYMENT",11,"VENDOR",21,
715634473,119,119,0,0,0,0
125,"ABT",1992-09-04-15.30.01.000000,"ABT",1992-09-04-
15.30.01.000000,0,0,"PAYMENT-DATE",11,"VENDOR",21,
715634473,124,0,124,0,0,0
128,"ABT",1992-09-04-15.30.01.000000,"ABT",1992-09-04-
15.30.01.000000,0,0,"PAYMENT-AMOUNT",11,"VENDOR",21,
715634473,127,0,127,0,0,0
**BUSINESS_SJ_AREA**
**BUSINESS_SJ_AREAEX**
**BUSINESS_SJ_AREAMA**
**SUBSET_DEF**
**SUBSET_DEFMAP_NAME**
**DATA_MDL_SBS_RUL**
**PROC_MDL_SBS_RUL**
**BSA_SUBSET_RULE**
**STRUCTURE**
**STRUCTURESYNONYM_0**
**STRUCTUREKEYWORD**
**STRUCTUREINFO_FLOW**
**STRUCTUREPROCESS_M**
**STRUCTUREMAP_NAME_**
**STRUCT_ENT**
**STRUCT_ENTMAP_NAME**
**STRUCT_ATTR**
**STRUCT_ATTRSTRUCT_**
**STRUCT_ATTRMAP_NAM**
**STRUCT_PSET**
**STRUCT_PSETMAP_NAM**
**STRUCT_PSHP**
**STRUCT_PSHPMAP_NAM**
**ALLOWED_VAL_TBL**
**ALLOWED_VAL_TBLSYN**
**ALLOWED_VAL_TBLKEY**
**ALLOWED_VAL_TBLSUB**
**ALLOWED_VAL_TBLMAP**
**ALLOWABLE_VALUE**
**ALLOWABLE_VALUEMAP**
**SYMBOLIC_CONSTANT**
**SYMBOLIC_CONSTANTM**
**DA_FREE_TEXT_BLOCK**
**EXTENSION_OBJECT**
**ROUTE_OBJECT**
**EXTENSION_RTE_OBJ**
**FILTERS**
**VIEWS**
**DGM_TEXT**
**DIAGRAM_PROPERTIES**
2,"ABT",1992-09-04-15.21.18.000000,"ABT",1992-09-04-
15.21.18.000000,0,1,1,1,1,1,1,0
3,"ABT",1992-09-04-15.21.18.000000,"ABT",1992-09-04-
15.21.18.000000,0,1,1,1,1,1,1,0
4,"ABT",1992-09-04-15.21.18.000000,"ABT",1992-09-04-
```

Figure 16.6 (*Continued*).

```
15.21.18.000000,0,1,1,1,1,1,1,0
5,"ABT",1992-09-04-15.21.18.000000,"ABT",1992-09-04-
15.21.18.000000,0,1,1,1,1,1,1,0
6,"ABT",1992-09-04-15.21.18.000000,"ABT",1992-09-04-
15.21.18.000000,0,1,1,1,1,1,1,0
**PROCESS_MODEL**
8,"ABT",1992-09-04-15.21.18.000000,"ABT",1992-09-04-
15.21.18.000000,0,7.1,"vendorsale",0,0,0,0,0,1,0
**PROCESS_MODELKEYWO**
**PROCESS_MODELTEXT**
**PROCESS_MODELSYNON**
**PROCESS_MODELSUBSE**
**PROCESS_MODELMAP_N**
**PROCESS**
**PROCESSTEXT**
**PROCESSKEYWORD**
**PROCESSSYNONYM_OBJ**
**PROCESSPERSON_EVEN**
**PROCESSCLOCK_EVENT**
**PROCESSSTORAGE_EVE**
**PROCESSFLOW_EVENT**
**PROCESSMAP_NAME_TA**
**EXTERNAL_AGENT**
**EXTERNAL_AGENTKEYW**
**EXTERNAL_AGENTSYNO**
**EXTERNAL_AGENTMAP_**
10**
```

Figure 16.6 (*Continued*).

Based on Figs. 16.5 and 16.6, we get the sense that major CASE vendors follow similar philosophies. First, they all generate their own internal identifiers as a way of tracking and relating populated instance data. These identifiers cannot be changed by the user without potentially damaging the integrity of a model and its components. Next, each "record" within the export file or files follows a predefined, nonstandard "field" order.

Considering the commonalities identified previously, it is difficult to bring models into a tool on your own. The major issue is that of identifier values. In order to create your own identifiers, you must ensure their nonexistence across all models within the target tool. Briefly, this involves an overall "behind-the-scenes" query into all populated models, as they are stored in the target tool. Or, as CASE vendors most likely prefer, it involves the purchase of their intertool interface packages.

■ IMPORTING NONEXISTENT METADATA CONSTRUCTS

As a final note, when discussing the issue of horizontal CASE integration, we must consider the implications of importing metadata constructs that simply do not exist in the target tool. As we will see later on, when the target tool is a repository, more options are available. However, when discussing intertool bridges, a practical approach must be addressed.

As we itemized previously, there are few "generic" solutions to this problem. This section assumes the following:

1. The CASE user absolutely needs the instance data associated with the source tool's unique metadata.
2. There are no "functional equivalents" in the target tool's metamodel.
3. The CASE user is willing to perform some custom programming in order to maintain the meaning and integrity of the populated source metadata.

First, in order to import the nonexisting metadata, custom programming is an absolute necessity. No target tools (that I am aware of) have an import function that brings in constructs that are not part of their underlying database design, unless the import is part of an add-on interface with a specific tool. Recently, the introduction of meta-CASE tools has begun to identify the need for a user to set up his or her own metamodel within a CASE tool. However, this metamodel is not one that can change constantly depending on the changing needs of its interfacing tools.

Realizing the need for customization, the required programming must consider these areas:

- The built-in functionality of the target tool's import mechanism
- Where the "new" metadata will fit into the target tool's architecture
- How the target tool's functionality may need to change to encompass the added metadata instances

Target Tool Import Functionality

It is hard to get a full understanding of how a tool's import function operates without seeing the actual source code. Yet, by executing the function and evaluating the resulting model's integrity as compared to its original source tool version as well as to the models that were created within the target tool itself, a decent impression of how source tool constructs and their instances are translated and subsequently related can be appreciated. The important factors to consider are how the import function relates imported model instances to those that already exist in the tool, if at all, and, if so, whether or not the import allows the setting of options to determine at what level (model, diagram, construct, etc.) the integration of imported instances can occur.

In order to modify (or more likely supplement) the existing import function with a custom program, it is necessary to plan how your imported metadata will relate to the already residing set of models in the target tool. This relationship requires the ability of your import function to be aware of and/or access certain existing target tool metadata.

As illustrated in Fig. 16.7, there ideally should be an overlap between the functionality of the two imports (yours and theirs). Regardless of whether this overlap is perceived (via user interface) or actual, it is important for the extraneous import function to build upon rather than restrict the target tool's built-in import capabilities.

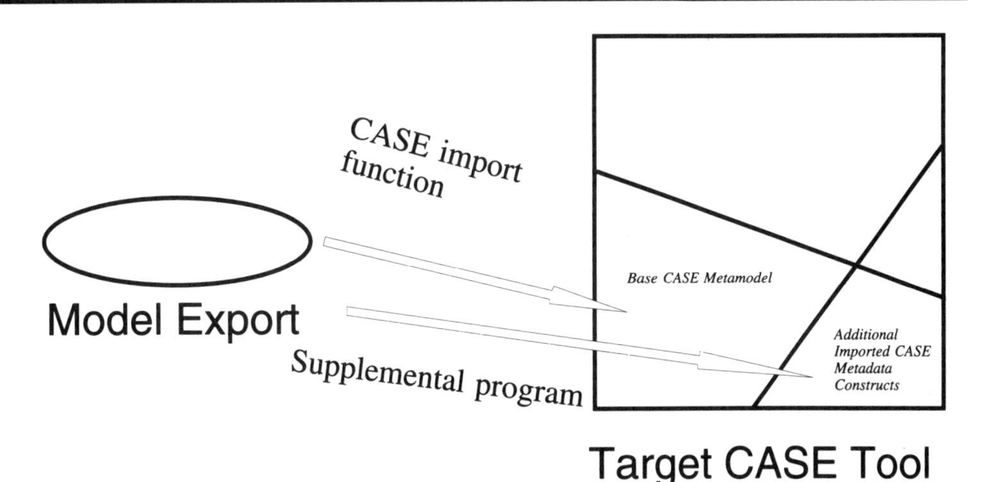

Figure 16.7 The supplemented CASE tool import.

New Metadata / Old Metadata

Where do we put the new metadata? A crucial prerequisite to the addition of new metadata is an underlying target tool DBMS which is not proprietary. If new constructs need to be added, they need to be added as tables, columns, files, fields, and/or segments in the target tool's database. It is obvious that the addition of new database structures immediately renders all tool-based reporting slightly obsolete. However, many CASE tools (even those with proprietary DBMS's) offer interfaces with commercial databases for the purposes of custom reporting. Typically, for example, a model can be "exported" and loaded into the respective database for SQL access.

In the less than ideal scenario being presented here, the base metamodel exists as designed by the CASE vendor. The user/developer then expands this DBMS design by adding the required additional database physical schemas and relating them to the base database design. Access to the populated instance data is then dependent on custom reporting, again developed by the user/developer. It is important to realize that the functions that exist in the target tool will not be aware of this newly created data.

Expanding the Base Tool Functionality

With the newly created and populated DBMS constructs, the target tool is now no longer sufficient. Diagramming and the related supplemental documentation are not aware of the additional metadata constructs. It is quite impractical to rewrite the target CASE tool in order to accommodate your specific metadata needs.

The only practical approach requires a slight amount of fudging. Keep the target tool's functionality as is (as if you have a choice!). Consider how and when the additional metadata needs to play role in your modeling. (An obvious practical note: The "new" metadata cannot play a major role in your use of the target CASE

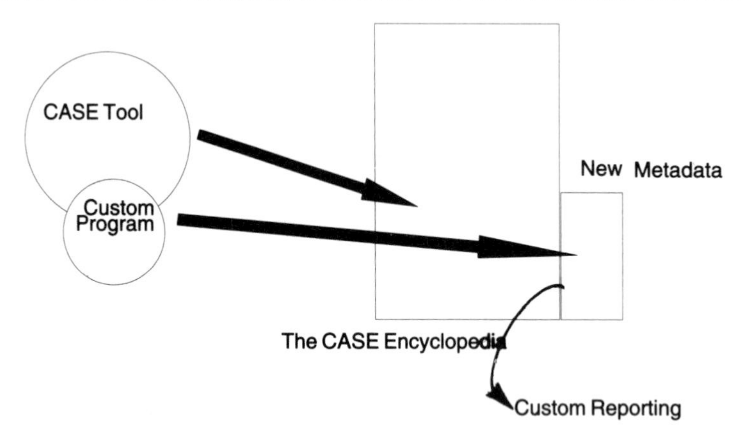

Figure 16.8 Incorporating new metadata.

tool. If this is necessary, you are probably better off with a different tool set.) In most situations the additional metadata will serve as a clarification or broadening of the target tool's underlying constructs. Identify those base metadata constructs that closely relate to the custom "extensions." Via their description, or ideally, via an existing related metadata construct (keywords, labels, etc.), identify, via populated instance data, the additional information that exists in "outside" metadata. The outside metadata, which is based on earlier work, exists in a related database construct and needs to be populated outside of the tool.

In an ideal scenario a callable routine (executable from within the target tool) would be used to populate the extra metadata instances. Otherwise, it is always possible that the additional metadata never becomes populated and/or updated in a timely fashion. What ties the extra metadata to the basic metadata is the custom reporting that will access and relate both. As illustrated in Fig. 16.8, the new metadata is only loadable via a custom program and only viewable via custom reporting. The CASE tool, in and of itself, has no knowledge of its existence.

It should be obvious that there must be a better way. Well, there is—it is called a repository!

17

MODEL MANAGEMENT

The final topic to be addressed in this part affects all modelers, with or without integration. Whenever modeling becomes part of an application development effort, the models have the same needs as the other documentation deliverables and the delivered program source. Specifically, models can be thought of as applications themselves, being eventually related to live, running applications that are associated with actual business functions within an organization. Like all applications, they need to be managed.

■ MODEL MANAGEMENT DEFINED

When we consider what is involved in managing an application, the management of associated models seems quite similar. Models share many application characteristics. However, because they are application blueprints that directly affect the delivered nature and structure of an application, many model management needs also pertain to the role and impact of the models as well as their many relationships to actual application deliverables.

Model management pertains to:

> the accurate development, delivery, and maintenance of a model or set of models despite the number of developers, application viewpoints, physical application configurations, or application/model changes.

Modeling tools along with all other tools used to develop an application should allow the tracking and relating of all deliverables necessary to support the defined multiple renditions. In order to clarify what is involved in the practical implementation of model management, it is necessary to divide its aspects into their functional categories. Each of the following categories cannot be considered in isolation. However, they represent distinct requirements of successful model management. The elimination of one affects the overall impact of them all.

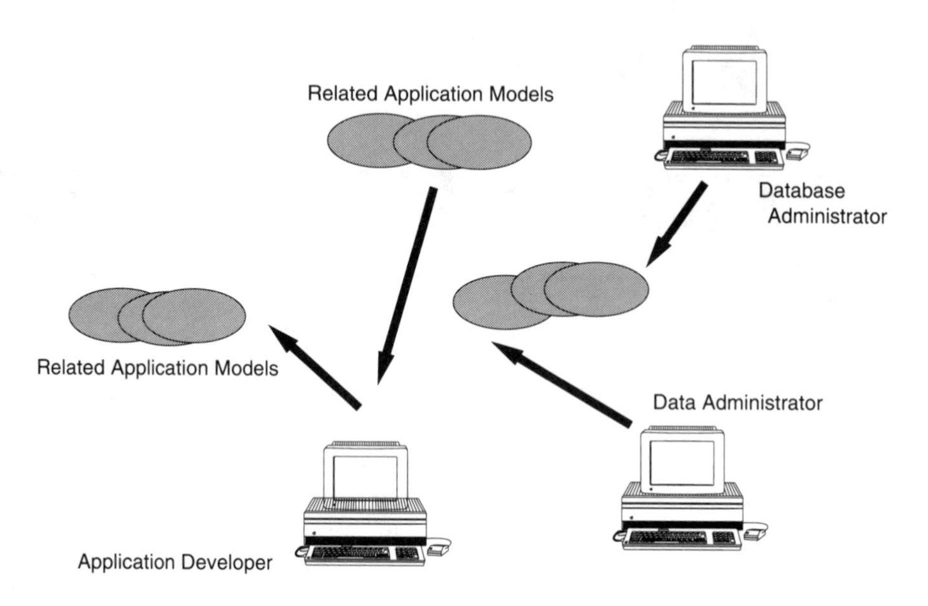

Figure 17.1 Multiuser model access requirements.

■ MULTIUSER ACCESS TO SPECIFIC MODELS AND SUBMODELS

Often not considered an aspect of model management, model access is a frequently overlooked specific that can make or break a model's success as an application development aid. When a model is under development, it often starts as a single-person effort. Even large application development efforts are functionally divided so that individuals can work on submodels (or models) independently of their coworkers. Sooner or later, the need for multideveloper access becomes a requirement.

As illustrated in Fig. 17.1, models become much more useful when they are viewed and related to other models. It is typical for an application developer to refer to and/or copy elements from one application model in order to create another. In addition, for example, nonapplication developer "forces" often need access to application models for the purposes of data administration. The need for a bridge becomes obvious when the issue of model access extends beyond the model author.

The importance of multiuser access should be taken into account up front when various tool architectures are being considered. In the simplest scenario a server-based CASE tool is set up with access to its models distributed according to the LAN configuration. In more complicated scenarios multiuser access becomes an afterthought and standalone modeling tools then need to become more integrated into a multiuser framework. Aside from the accessibility of the existing models, the architecture should also consider at what level (multiple models, single model, submodel, model component) most of the access is needed. It is common for model

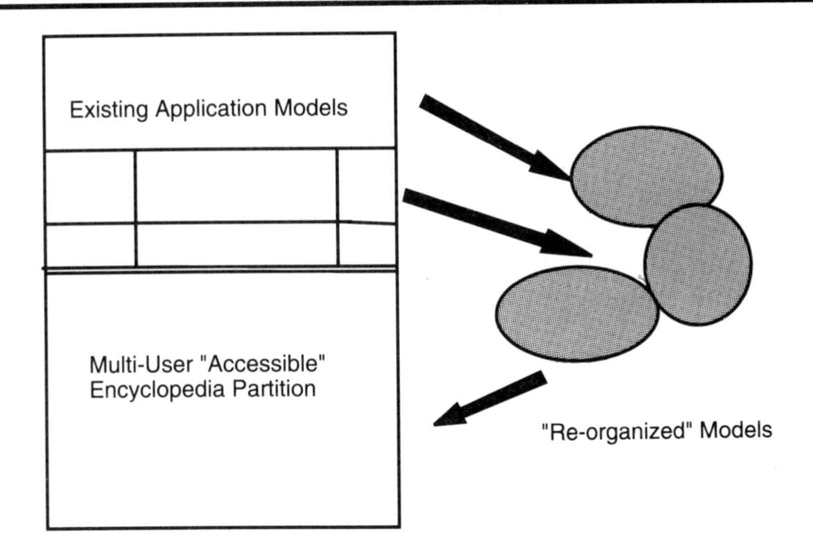

Figure 17.2 Expanding the CASE encyclopedia for multiuser access.

extracts, merges, and reorganizations to become a prerequisite to multiuser access. Many CASE encyclopedias, already holding the various application models, become expanded in order to meet multiuser access requirements. Existing models are reconsidered based on the needs of those requesting access to their contents. Then entire models, model components, or merged models are copied to another part of the encyclopedia which is established as the place for multiuser access (see Fig. 17.2).

In addition, the difficulty involved in establishing multiuser access is directly dependent on the tool's platform. With interactive mainframe tools, locking is often allowed while a particular entity instance, for example, is being updated. This locking usually does not disturb concurrent users. Complexity arises when the tool is operating on multiple workstations with models being stored on a server. Particular models are then usually "checked out" to one or more users at the same time. Consolidating the multiple versions that result later usually requires some manual effort.

■ READ/WRITE PROTECTION

Once multiuser access becomes an addressed requirement of model management, the issue of read/write protection follows as a model management security issue. Most nonoriginator access to models will not require write permission. However, if the access is for "copying" purposes (e.g., integrating an existing model into one under development), the access requirements include the ability to execute some built-in tool functions.

In the ideal situation some users may need the ability to update only certain aspects of certain model(s). Inherent tool security mechanisms usually do not allow model component level security definition unless they offer a server-based, shareable encyclopedia as part of the tool set. Even with a shareable encyclopedia, security levels usually stop at the model itself in most tools. True model management requires the ability to establish access security (by user id) by model component instance and/or by model metadata construct. For example, it may not be desirable for database administrators to have write access to any attribute names. Yet the ability to update attribute lengths and/or physical characteristics (e.g., data types) would be quite desirable. In contrast, data administration needs write access to attribute names, but not to process-related information.

In many of today's practical situations, when there are no shareable encyclopedias, repositories, or the like, most "multiuser" model access is accomplished via paper copies. Changes are made either verbally (in meetings) or with a pencil. The "modified" model is given back to its originator, and the originator, being the only one with the capability to do so, then makes the changes in the modeling tool. The need to do better should be obvious.

■ UPDATE/VERSION MANAGEMENT

Often the only aspects that are considered when model management is discussed, the manipulation and handling of the multiple model versions that become a part of application development are crucial aspects of model maintenance. Without trying to generalize too much, version control seems to be an available feature primarily in Unix-based CASE tools, presumably because of the inbred capabilities of many Unix features, such as *sccs* (source code control system). Using *sccs* as an example, version control becomes second nature once the structure and relationships of all application members are defined. Having done this, *sccs* allows the creation of "releases" under user control at various levels. For example, one particular file (which typically translates to a program, subroutine, or data structure definition) can have multiple versions. The entire application is itself "versionable" and contains differing versions of its many contributing members.

When we relate the preceding *sccs* example to the modeling world, it is clear that models and their components could have differing "versions." It would be nice if an entity could change its contents several times without the modeler losing the ability to retrieve the previous versions. The ability to access these various renditions should also not require the modeler to have multiple versions of the model itself. In summary, versioning should allow the tracking and relating of multiple versions of:

- The *models* themselves
- The *model components* (irrespective of the model versions)
- The *model component attributes* (irrespective of their associated model component versions)
- The *metadata* used to describe any of the preceding. (For example, there may be multiple renditions within a tool's metamodel of the *Subject Area* construct. Typically, the new renditions come with a new tool release, and the incorpora-

tion of the old metadata into the new metadata format is handled by vendor-supplied conversion routines.) At thispoint, this is wishful thinking. Even in the repository arena, versioning of the metamodel is not under user control.

As we will illustrate in the following discussion, the implementation of version control applies to how and when models and their associated components are updated. When developers are modeling an application (or even an enterprise), changes occur constantly during the initial stages. Sooner or later, some stability occurs. This is typically viewed as a *version* or *release* of the models. As we all know, changes do not stop at the first onset of stability. As with delivered applications, models continue to evolve. The evolution is based at times on incomplete initial analysis or simply on changing business and/or technical requirements. Application releases are a way of life in the MIS development world. So, too, should be model releases. Simply speaking, the applications, as they exist, whether they were generated from a CASE tool or coded from specification

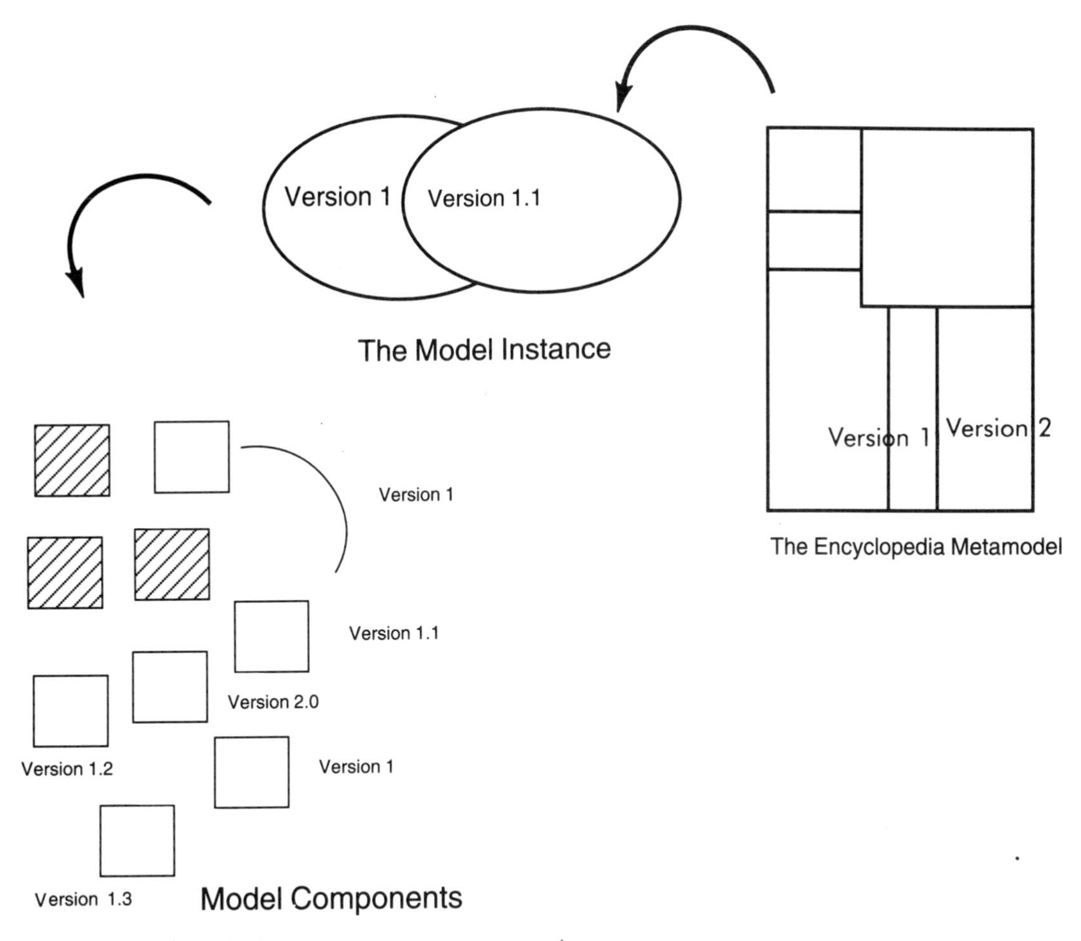

Figure 17.3 Ideal version management at work.

models, should relate to logical constructs at the high end. The tracking of these model releases should not require the constant creation of new models.

Tools are often required to support several different "versions" of a model concurrently, based on various stages of application development. For example, multiple environments (development, unit test, integration test, production, etc.) may each require the existence of a different version of the same model. In the ideal scenario, as depicted in Fig. 17.3, model *components* are associated with one or more model versions. Each model instance, having its own associated version, becomes a collection of independently versioned model components.

■ CONFIGURATION MANAGEMENT

Along the lines of versioning requirements, application configurations can also have several variations which need to be tracked and related. Consider a common situation involving the deployment of an application across the multiple field sites of an organization. It is reasonable to expect the needs of some field sites to differ in terms of their actual deployed application configurations. For example, perhaps each field site has its own local database structure, customized based on specific data access needs. Model management should allow the tracking of the various renditions of a delivered application as they may be depicted in various models or model viewpoints. Specifically, using the varying database structures as an example, the ability to track the E–R model aspects that pertain to each deployed application site (by application site) is a standard requirement.

As illustrated in Fig. 17.4, despite each deployed application being based on the same set of application models, each illustrated configuration varies slightly in terms of its pertinent model components. In many cases these differences may simply refer to different physical configurations (e.g., different execution platforms), and therefore the modeling subtleties may pertain only to physical models. However, sometimes the differences in application deployment requirements are based on distinct business differences. The differences are distinct enough to require different application code, but not so distinct as to require entirely different application models. True model management should address these subtleties at the logical model level and relate these differences to the different configurations that result.

■ BACKUP/RESTORE

Finally, model management is not complete without a discussion of model backup. Many vendors leave this responsibility to the tool user, based on the resident operating system in which the tool resides. Workstation-based CASE tool vendors simply advise the modeler to back up directories in which the models reside. When and if corruption occurs, the modeler simply restores everything from his or her backup disk/cassette into the model directory.

Backup at this level is usually sufficient but does not provide for an audit trail, because most tools store only the latest version. However, many tools offer alternatives via import/export functions. In this scenario multiple models or model components, as well as user-defined model component sets, can be exported. The backup is then left to the modeler, as discussed. The difference here is that the

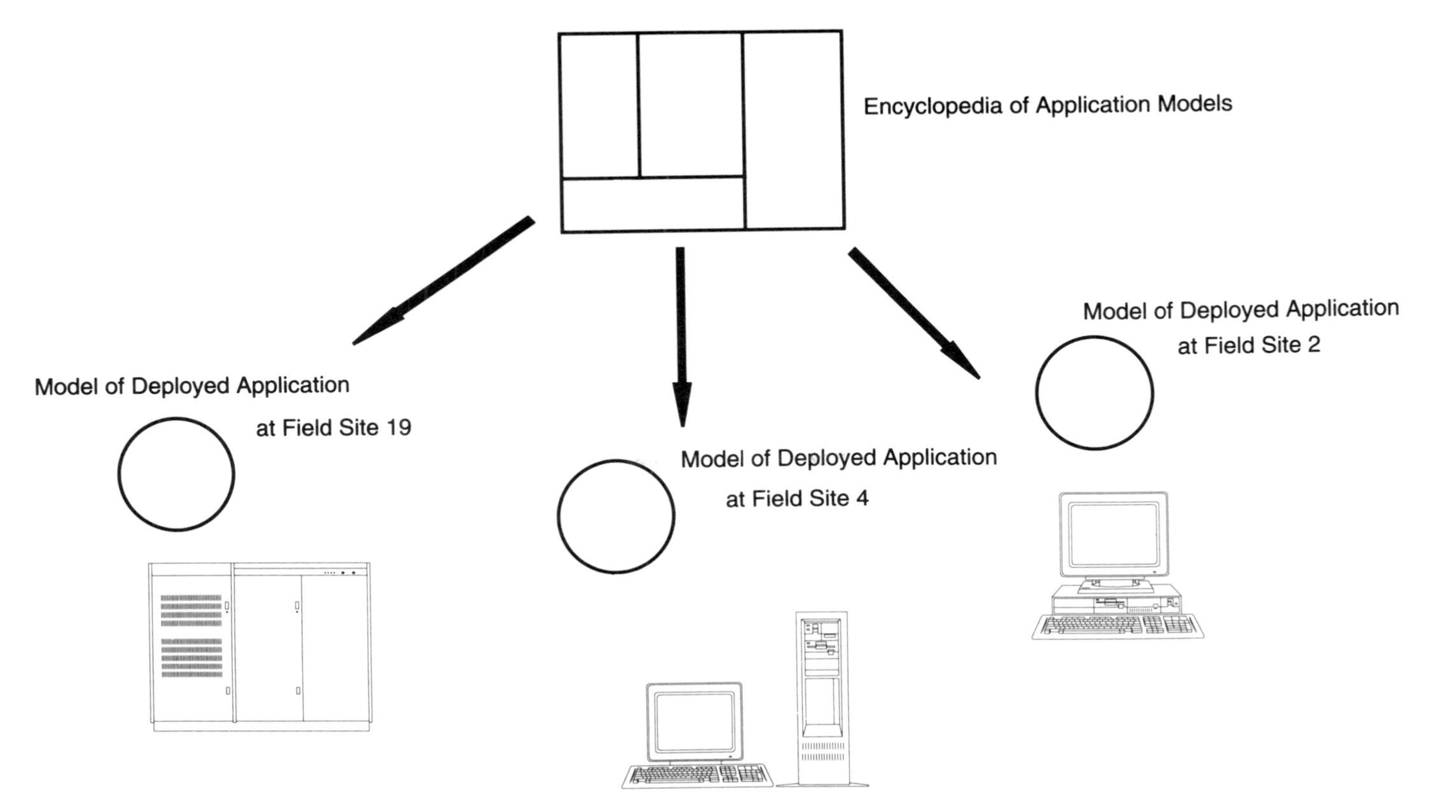

Figure 17.4 Tracking models for configuration management.

modeler is controlling the scope of the backup, as opposed to simply backing up an entire model.

Restoring models is directly dependent on how they were backed up. Because it is impossible to predict where corruption will occur, it is always wise to back up entire models. However, what about backing up a day's worth of model updates? This ensures the ability to restore at least a daily picture of model progress. Few tools have a built-in feature that allows this (directly related to their version management capabilities as discussed previously). A practical solution therefore involves the daily backup of the entire model.

■ SUMMARY

In Part Three we pointed out why today's models need integration (with each other and with the rest of the MIS world) and how limited integration really is without a tool-independent bridge. By now, readers should be getting an idea of how repositories can hopefully help. In the next part of this book, we will introduce the repository by defining it, detailing its role, and explaining its benefits.

PART FOUR

THE REPOSITORY AS THE BRIDGE

18

WHAT IS A REPOSITORY?

If you are sure you understand everything that is going on, you are hopelessly confused.

Walter Mondale, March 1978

After appreciating the issues that surround the optimization and integration of today's models, we are now ready to discuss the repository. Like many buzzwords in our profession, the repository is truly understood by few in terms of its scope. Few even agree on its basic definition! This chapter will concentrate on the specific delineation of a repository: a discussion of what it is and what it is not. The remainder of Part Four will clarify repositories by discussing their purpose (practically) and giving some coverage to the multiple standards that are shaping repository architectures. Repository architectures (both centralized and distributed) will be covered in Chap. 21. Finally, Part Four will end with a practical example of repository benefits.

■ THE DICTIONARY DEFINITION

What better place to start our clarification of what a repository is than *Webster's* dictionary?

> ...a place, room, or container where something is deposited or stored...one that contains or stores something nonmaterial... .

With a definition as generic as this one, inconsistency in interpretation is certainly excusable. In fact, any tool deployed for any purpose in the MIS world could allege the existence of a repository based on the preceding definition. In a sense any database can be considered an instance of *Webster's* defined repository. Because tools all require inputs, as long as these inputs are stored somewhere, the tool has a vanilla repository as its heart.

Consider the second part of the dictionary definition, the reference to "nonmaterial" repository contents. Virtually all of our repositories can be considered nonmaterial in that we cannot touch them or their contents. But in the MIS world, can we really touch anything? In order for our applications and their data to become material, they have to be transferred to material objects, such as paper, magnetic tape, floppy disks, CRT screens, or any I/O media. Even still, it is the medium that is material rather than the internal contents. In order to be more specific as to the interpretation of an implemented repository, the definition must also be considered from an MIS perspective.

■ THE MIS DEFINITION

In the MIS world, inconsistency abounds. As with any industry that has a major trend-inducing marketing force, the interpretation of what constitutes a repository seems to be quite loose. Because repository has been (and still is) an industry buzzword, it is to each vendor's advantage to tout the existence of one in its product line. As I have often stated, vendors seem to interchange the words *dictionary*, *encyclopedia*, and *repository*. Because *dictionary* and *encyclopedia* were never marketing buzzwords, they are virtually not spoken of in the MIS community. Everyone has a *repository*. Or do they?

Dictionary vs. Encyclopedia vs. Repository

Before the advent of CASE, many data administration organizations began tracking their data resources with *dictionaries*. For the most part, early dictionaries simply tracked the multiple occurrences of specific element names, across all applications and databases. Progressive organizations linked them to a common "DA name," and the instances were all required to follow a data administration–originating naming standard. Once hierarchical databases (such as Information Management System [IMS]) became common, the functionality of dictionaries expanded to include the automatic generation of database descriptors (DBDs), program specification blocks (PSBs), and I/O areas from dictionary-resident constructs. Dictionaries became categorized based on their relationship to the database world as follows:

Passive Here, the dictionary has no direct relationship to the physical database world. Any documented applications and/or databases are manually populated into the dictionary, usually after development is complete. Updates to the physical environment are not automatically reflected in the dictionary; they, too, must be manually input. The limitations of a dictionary are therefore based on the fact that dictionary input is manual and dictionary output is not directly usable by any other applications.

Active in Development Some software engineering steps are automated based on populated dictionary contents. Using our preceding example, the automatic generation of database definitions (DBDs for IMS, or DDL for SQL-based databases) would place a dictionary in this category. The key aspect of this mode of dictionary usage is that the dictionary's existence is not essential to the completion of the production runs. That is, production could be completed in other ways (e.g., through the manual entry of DDL).

Active in Production Few dictionaries ever reached this category. Here, the dictionary is more than just a development aid. It is actually the means by which a user accesses an enterprise's applications and resources. For example, by accessing an entity named CUSTOMER, as represented in the dictionary, the user should be able to view the actual physical implementations of the logical CUSTOMER that exist in the modeled application world. In addition, further delving should result in the set of retrieved application programs that access these physical CUSTOMER implementations. In this scenario the dictionary is the gateway to the application world, as it exists. The dictionary's contents not only generate the application world, they also retrieve and relate it to its logical business requirements. With active production dictionaries, production comes to a halt when the dictionary is unavailable.

As illustrated in Fig. 18.1, whether or not a dictionary is active or passive, in development or production, affects its relationship to the live application world. Most dictionaries never got beyond the second category, *active in development*.

Perhaps the drawing line between the end of the dictionary era and the beginning of the *encyclopedia* era was the advent of the CASE tool. Although most data-related constructs had always been resident in a dictionary, their access was limited to basic reporting. In order to retrieve a particular instance, it was usually essential to know where that instance resided (as in which metadata construct type). Simply speaking, if you wanted to see the details of the CUSTOMER entity, you did a 'LIST Entity CUSTOMER' (or some similar rendition) request. True, some dictionaries allowed you to search the entire set of dictionary constructs by populated instance name (e.g., LIST CUSTOMER), but the amount of time spent waiting for a response was often unbelievable. Retrieval of dictionary instance data typically has the following restrictions:

- The dictionary's own retrieval language must be used.
- Construct instances are retrievable only by knowing in which construct they reside.
- Requests cannot relate different construct types. For example, it is usually not possible to see all attributes by entity without requesting a standard report, as opposed to executing a simple dictionary access request. An illustration of typical dictionary-based access appears in Fig. 18.2.
- Most dictionary output is textual only; no graphical depiction of the dictionary's contents is possible through resident dictionary access functions.

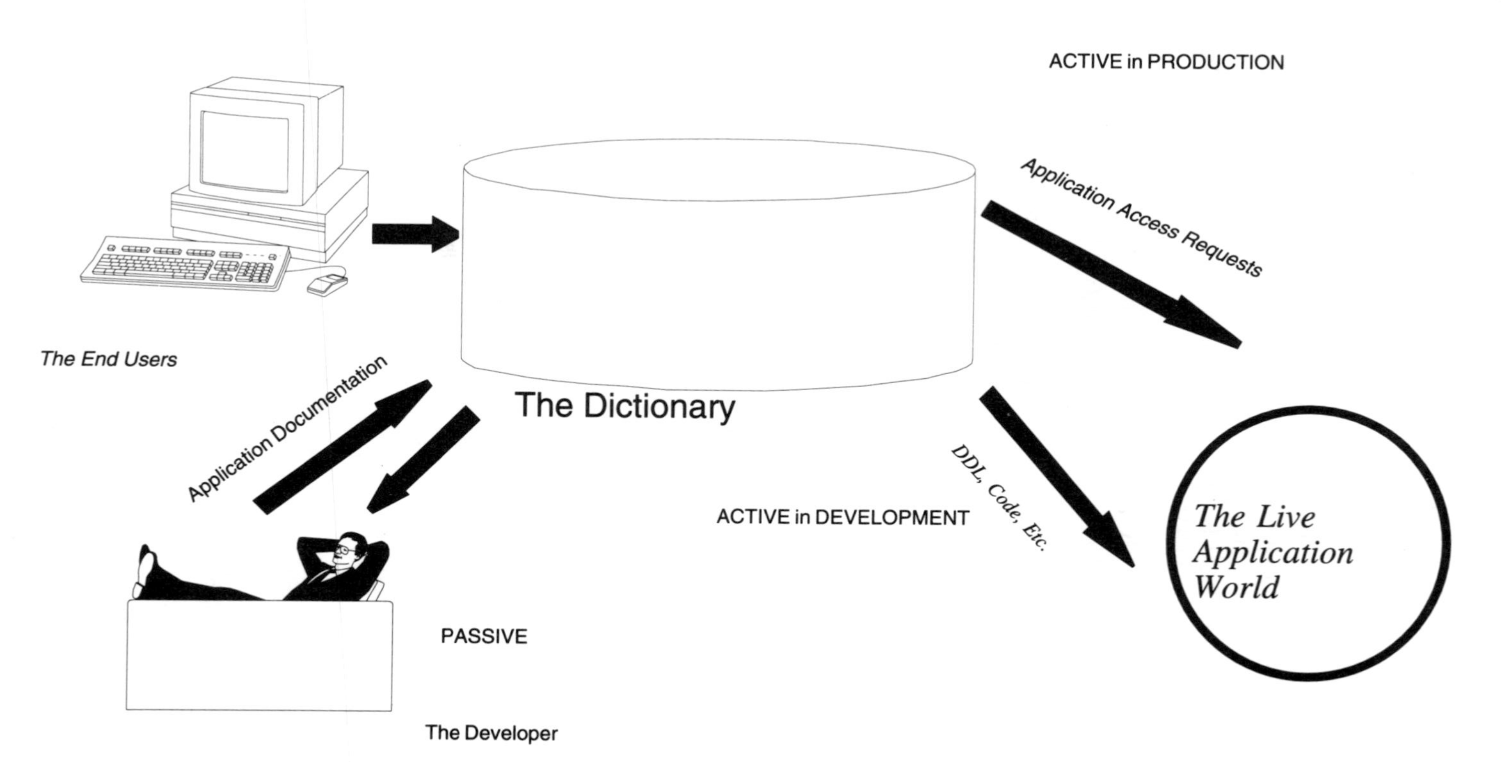

Figure 18.1 Dictionary usage modes.

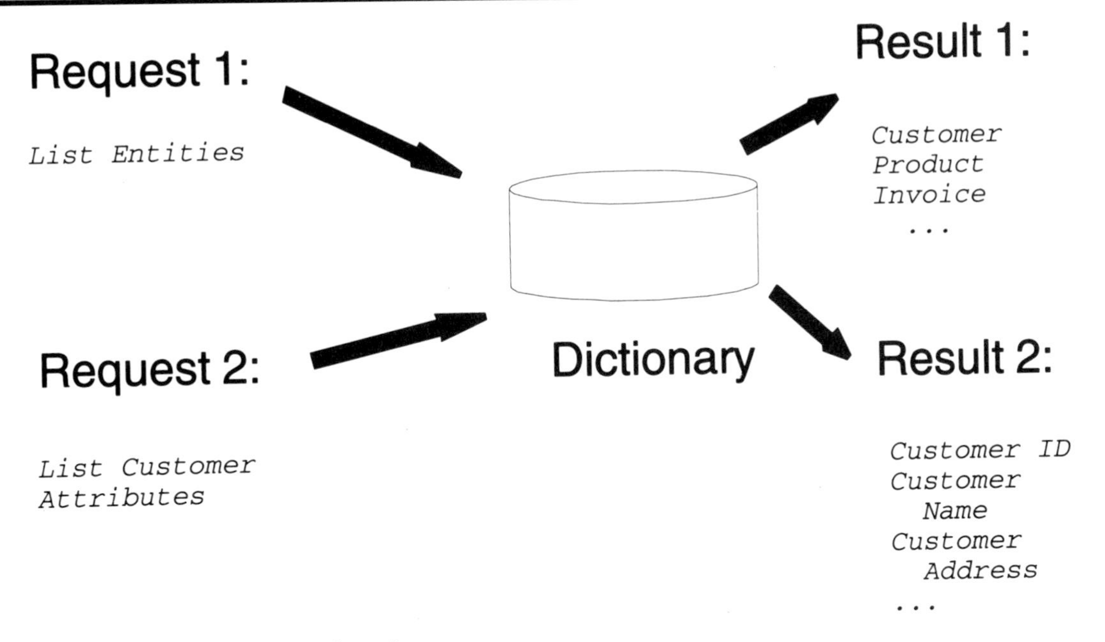

Figure 18.2 Dictionary-based access.

Encyclopedias replaced dictionaries once the advent of graphic model depiction became the norm. Encyclopedias are often thought of as performing dictionaries. All dictionary functionality is included in most encyclopedias, when they are viewed along with their complementary access tools. With encyclopedias, access includes the ability to cross reference related encyclopedia constructs. For example, requesting all entities that contain the EMPLOYEE-NAME attribute is a standard feature. Encyclopedias are the backbone of most major CASE tools, particularly ICASE tools. Typically, regardless of the component in which a model instance originated, any tool component can access that instance. For example, the entity INVOICE, although initially defined in a CASE tool's *planning* component, should be retrievable by the *analysis* component. Figure 18.3 illustrates encyclopedia-based access.

Encyclopedias do have their limitations. The contents of the encyclopedia are indeed accessible by varying tool components, despite their origination. However, all tool components typically represent products from the same vendor. In that sense, the encyclopedia is *closed* to access from outside the particular vendor's tool suite. True, there are usually export functions that are part of the resident encyclopedia utilities, but they are not usually very flexible in terms of custom export requests. Typically, an entire "model" must be exported. Also, as we discussed in Chap. 16, despite the fact that vendor encyclopedias now offer import utilities that allow models resident in other vendor encyclopedias to be brought into the target vendor's encyclopedia, conflicts in metadata constructs are often ignored. Therefore, the two major limitations of an encyclopedia can be summarized as follows:

1. Constructs can only be accessed by tools architected by the same vendor.
2. The underlying encyclopedia metamodel is frozen; that is, the encyclopedia user cannot add to or detract from the encyclopedia's database structure.

Now, hopefully the reader is beginning to appreciate what the MIS definition of a repository should be. Repositories should be thought of as integrated encyclopedias. They encompass all of the functionality of an encyclopedia, but do not restrict access to construct instances based on their originating tool. As illustrated in Fig. 18.4, the user of Tool A should be able to access a construct instance that originated in Tool B.

Perhaps the major difference between encyclopedias and repositories rests with their ability (or inability) to *extend* the underlying metamodel. Extensibility is a feature of virtually all true repository products. Extensions are additional constructs that a repository administrator can add to a repository's underlying metamodel. For example, if an organization's internal methodology requires the use of metadata constructs to differentiate between multiple subtype/supertype relationship categories (e.g., exclusive, nonexclusive), this relationship attribute can be implemented as an addition in an extensible repository. Although this is not always an ideal solution,* the capability is usually a requirement for multitool integration. Ideally, extensions should share the same capabilities as all base metamodel constructs in terms of supported repository functions. As we will see in Part Five, this is not always the case.

Therefore, in MIS, the accepted definition of a repository should be as follows:

> Integrated holding areas for enterprise metadata. The contents should be definable, loadable, and retrievable regardless of the originating tool, platform, progamming language, or DBMS.

■ THE IRDS DEFINITION

Although we will discuss the major repository standards in more detail in Chap. 20, the definition of a repository is in fact shaped by many of these standards. One standard, the Information Resource Dictionary System (IRDS) standard, was the first recognized attempt at standardizing the architecture and functionality of data dictionary systems. Although the term *repository* is only alluded to within the standard itself, its equivalent is the Information Resource Dictionary System (also referred to as an *information repository*). To round out this standard's interpretation, it is necessary to cite two of its base definitions:†

> *Information Resource Dictionary (IRD).* A collection of entities, relationships, and attributes used by an organization to model its information environment.

*Extensions will be discussed in detail in Part Five.

†"Information Resource Dictionary System," Federal Information Processing Standards Publication 156, American National Standards Institute, Inc., April 5, 1989.

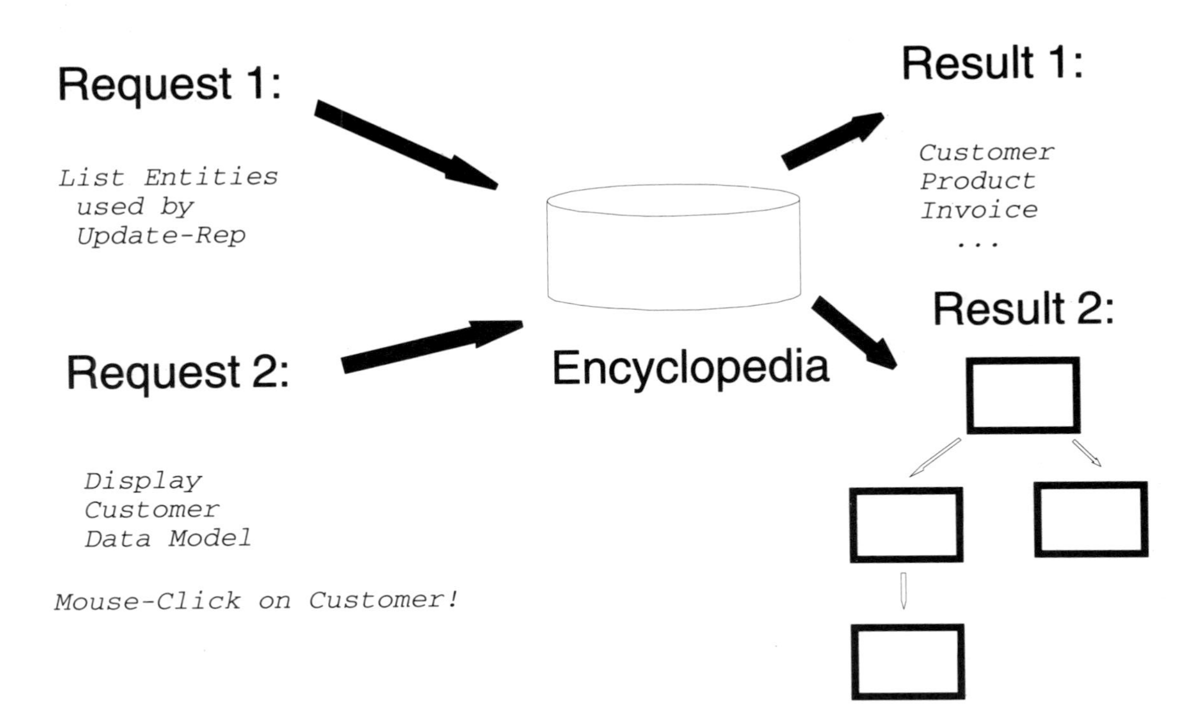

Figure 18.3 Encyclopedia-based access.

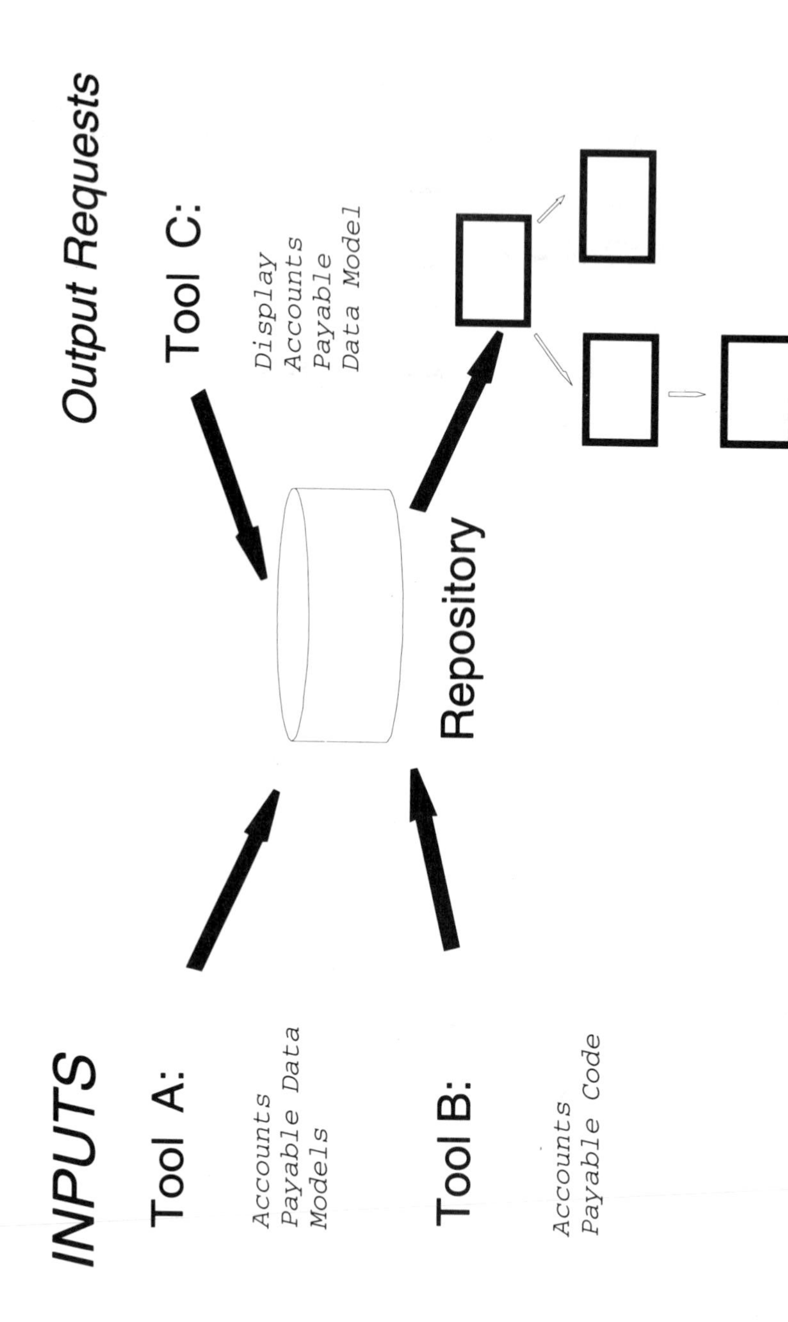

Figure 18.4 Repository-based access.

Information Resource Dictionary System (IRDS). (1) A computer software system that provides facilities for recording, storing, and processing descriptions of an organization's significant information and information processing resources. (2) A computer software system that maintains and manages an information resource dictionary.

The important aspects of the preceding definitions center around the following assumptions:

1. The underlying metamodel is based on an E–R approach.
2. The contents of the dictionary alone are not enough. The maintenance and management of this information are also a base functional requirement.

Therefore, when putting the IRDS standard into the context of a repository definition, its impact resides in the scoping of a repository's responsibility—that of storing and caring for an organization's information.

■ THE DEFINITION AS SHAPED BY OTHER STANDARDS

In addition to IRDS, other standards efforts rely on a preconceived definition of repository. PCTE (Portable Common Tool Environment), a tool interface standard geared toward tool developers, relies on an object management system (OMS) as its "information repository."* Its underlying metamodel is also based on an E–R representation. ATIS (A Tools Integration Standard) is yet another standard, targeted also toward intertool communication. It advocates an object-oriented interface to its E–R-based underlying metamodel.† Finally, IBM's work with AD/Cycle and AD/Platform has certainly been influential in shaping the definition of a repository as the heart of an integrated application development environment (ADE). As stated previously, all of these standards will be discussed in more detail in Chap. 20. For the purposes of repository definition, it is important to note, however, that even the standards community does not wholeheartedly agree upon where a repository's role as an intertool communication enabler starts and stops.

■ MY DEFINITION

Finally, to uniformly set the boundaries of repository definition, it is essential that *I* define *repository*. The remainder of this book assumes and relies on the repository characteristics itemized as follows:

- *A repository is an integrated holding area.* Despite the type of model being stored (logical data model, physical program structures, etc.), it can be related to other distinctly different model types that exist elsewhere in the repository.

*G. Boudier, F. Gallo, R. Minot, and I. Thomas, "An Overview of PCTE and PCTE+," *ACM Software Engineering Notes*, Vol. 13, No. 5, November 1988.

†"Digital's Distributed Repository: Blueprint for Managing Enterprise-Wide Information," Digital Equipment Corporation.

Models can also be related to their physical implementations, which will exist outside of the repository. For example, the logical definition of a process, when related properly, can be the input to a request that retrieves all physical implementations (program names) of that process across an MIS application environment.

- *The input, access, and structure of a repository and its contents are vendor independent*. Simply speaking, a repository must be open. It should not be a requirement that a model be depicted in Tool A in order for it to become part of the populated repository. Similarly, it should not be a requirement for a model to originate in Tool B in order for a user of Tool B to access a repository-populated model. The repository's underlying structure (often called the *metamodel*) should not be dependent on or representative of any particular vendor tool's metamodel.
- *The repository's metamodel should be extensible*. As discussed previously, this is a crucial feature of any repository.
- *The contents of a repository should be retrievable via predefined "views" or "templates*." Because the repository can contain multiple related views of an organization's metadata, ranging from the metadata that describe the implementation of a DBMS to the metadata that describe a department's objectives, it is necessary that the access of this metadata be tailorable. Similar to the concept of database views, repository views must definable and maintainable.
- *Repository contents must be versionable and subject to user-implemented security restrictions*. Like any corporate DBMS, and probably more so, repositories need to be protected and well managed. Versioning, which will be discussed in detail in Part Five, is a necessary feature as are model, submodel, and model component level security.
- *The repository product should include the capabilities required to perform all of the preceding essential functionality on a highly functional basis*. That is, if the repository implementer is required to custom-code most of the preceding functionality via interfacing programs in order to get the product of choice fully repository operational, maybe the product is not really a repository.

THE GENERIC REPOSITORY ARCHITECTURE

Although the underlying architecture of a repository is to some degree dependent on the implementing vendor, it is safe to consider it as *generically* consisting of the following components:

The Repository Metamodel As we will see in Chap. 20, the repository metamodel represents the underlying description of all information that is accessible via the repository. This metamodel consists of various levels (remember our metadata definitions), ranging from the uppermost repository-specific view to the lowest instance data view.

An Underlying DBMS Described via the various metamodels, the repository's contents are stored in an underlying database. Again, depending on the vendor offering, this DBMS can be proprietary, based on a major vendor offering (e.g.,

IBM's DB2), or flexible in that the repository offers the capability to run "on top of" a variety of available vendor DBMS's.

Repository-Supplied Utilities Depending on the level of dependency of the repository on a particular DBMS, many repository-specific functions are often part of the base repository offering. An example of a repository utility is that of repository load.

Repository Interface The implemented repository's usefulness is totally dependent on its relationship to an organization's information and its ability to take advantage of that relationship for repository user benefit. Repository interface therefore includes many architectural components:

- Access views, or templates
- Tool interfaces
- APIs (application program interfaces)

Repository Security Very architecturally dependent, the implementation of repository security, as we will see in Part Five, is dependent on how the tool separates repository processing from underlying database processing. In a generic sense the architectural components dedicated to repository security could consist of one or more of the following:

- Access views, as before
- Repository policies
- Repository-supplied utilities, as before
- DBMS-specific security features

All of the preceding components of the repository's underlying architecture will be unfolded in more detail throughout the remainder of the book. Specifically, Chap. 20 will give the reader an appreciation of how much of the repository architecture has been addressed by existing and upcoming repository standards. Chapter 21, which covers distributed repositories, will address the impact of distribution on the generic architecture. Of course, all of Part Five, concerned with the how-tos of setting up a repository, will expand upon all of the preceding architectural components.

It is unfortunate that the definition of a repository requires so much substantiation. However, when so many misinterpretations exist in both the vendor and the user communities, it is important to itemize the reality of what is required of repository tools. Assuming the preceding capabilities, the potential impact of a well-implemented repository is virtually limitless.

19

A REPOSITORY'S PURPOSE

Clarifying the definition of a repository does not automatically clarify its intended role and usage. Because of the flexibility that is inherent in repository structures and functionality, the roles a repository can play in the application world are quite varied and almost directly dependent on the amount of resources attributed to their setup. We will begin here by discussing the basic position fulfilled by the generic repository. As the discussion progresses, this role will become as enhanced as the reader desires to make it.

■ THE INTEGRATED HOLDING AREA

The previous chapter clarified what is meant by *integrated*. Without respect to tool origination, everything that is loaded into or defined by a repository is potentially related to everything else that exists in the repository. The repository is a *holding area* in that the creation and maintenance of repository-populated models typically occurs outside of the repository in a workstation-based CASE tool, for example. The model's residence in the repository fulfills the need to make the model, once in a relatively stable state, accessible beyond the development workstation. In this respect the repository serves as the "holding area," otherwise known as the permanent residence. This residence is also typically the place in which the multiple renditions, or versions, of the models are stored. It is important to note, as illustrated in Fig. 19.1, that the holding area's role should be independent of its physical execution platform as well as the execution platforms of the interfacing developers.

What is stored in this holding area as well as how "integrated" it truly becomes with the nonrepository outside world is dependent on several factors:

- The amount of setup time and resources dedicated to the repository's initiation
- The amount of interface between the repository and other application development tools

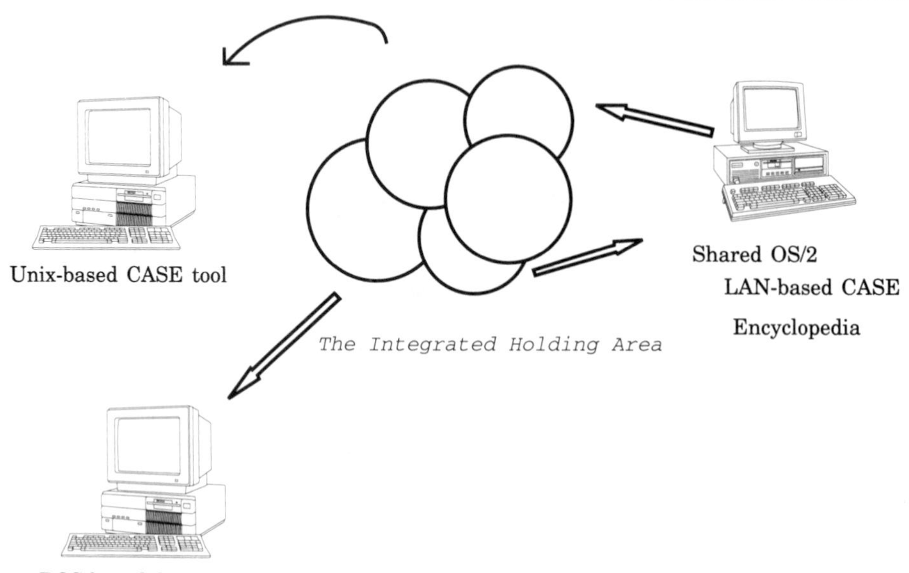

Figure 19.1 The integrated holding area.

- The extent to which current application development practices are dependent on the aforementioned tools
- The extent of interface that nonapplication developers can realistically be expected to achieve with an MIS-controlled resource, such as a repository

As we will continue to see, the preceding issues will directly impact the realization of a repository's role in any organization.

■ THE REPOSITORY ROLE IN APPLICATION DEVELOPMENT

Because the role a repository plays is directly affected by the amount and quality of the efforts involved in its establishment, this section will portray the ideal scenario. Assuming the proper starting point (accurate and ready to-be-loaded models) and a well-established application development process which resulted in standardized implementations, the role of a repository should affect new application development practices as follows:

Application Definition/Scoping During the initial phase of application definition, where we are concerned with establishing the boundaries of a to-be-developed application, a populated repository can serve as the source of answers to many of the questions that are part of the application definition process. Typically, research into the sources of data to be used by the new application as well as into those applications that will be using data that is processed and/or generated by this application will need to be conducted. Of course, once the application's functionality has been defined, its place of record should be the corporate repository.

Regardless of the tool used to document the initial application's scope, be it a CASE tool or a simple word processor, the application's planned functionality and objectives should become part of a permanent application record. Also, depending on the impact existing applications have (or would have) on the planned application, relationships may also be populated in the repository which reflect the connections between the new application's elements and any existing application components.

Application Analysis Most of this phase will occur in some type of development tool (usually a CASE tool). While the application is being defined and the various diagrams (data flow diagrams, E–R models, functional decomposition diagrams, etc.) are being developed, the repository again serves as a source of look-up information. Is there an existing database that is the master source of product id's? How accessible is it? Is it implemented in a relationally backboned DBMS? How often is it updated? What about this application's processing? Do any of the base functions exist in other applications? If so, what language are they coded in? What platforms do their associated applications execute on? All of these questions would be answered based on a repository query. Also, as with the previous phase, the application diagrams, once relatively firm, belong in the repository. They would be related to their higher-level definitions as appropriate, and therefore would be accessible via associated planning models, for example.

Application Design Continuing the refinement of the analysis-produced specifications, the populated repository's role in this phase serves as the recorder of design decisions. With properly recorded decisions, a clear path from the logical model to the actual physical design is possible. Finalized design would be populated into the repository and related to any or all of the previously populated models and model components, as appropriate.

Application Coding / Construction Depending on whether or not code is being generated from detailed design models that exist in a CASE tool, the construction phase could be relatively simplified. In any case construction does involve testing and debugging. Once major bugs have been worked out, the full set of application code is often ready for beta testing. Perhaps different versions of code are tested at different trial sites. Here, the repository's role is that of version tracking and configuration management. The actual code, although not necessarily resident in the repository, should be related to its repository-resident design models. In addition, the configured test application code, assigned a version, should also be traced and related appropriately by test site within the repository. During application testing, a fully populated repository will prove to be an invaluable resource. Imagine discovering a design flaw (e.g., incomplete logic) and being able to determine immediately which programs need to be revised. Based on repository-populated relationships, this answer results from a simple "impact analysis" type of request. Obviously, any updates to existing models (regardless of the development phase under which they initiated) should be reflected within the repository versions of these models.

Production Once an application is in production, the repository continues to serve as an information source. Perhaps the production application is now a supplier of data used in upper management's decision support systems. Queries regarding data definition and source, as input by the end-users of these decision support applications, are made against repository-populated data. In addition, the recording of all installed versions (by site, as appropriate) of the application is retrievable based on the repository's role as the tracker of configurations.

Project Management Throughout the application development process a series of tasks require management. Specifically, the development of the application, as discussed in all of the preceding phases, involves the assignment and monitoring of project resources as well as quality checking of each deliverable. In an ideal repository environment the deliverables of each project phase, as discussed previously, are related to their assigned resources and associated deadlines. The project management function can access the repository and determine which deliverables are complete, when they were completed (and by who). In addition, the deliverable contents (e.g., the actual data flow diagram) can be perused at the same time. Finally, the actual tasks involved in the completion of the project should be recorded as metric equivalents. Function points, person-hours, and other measurements of involved tasks could therefore be associated with each level of the involved application—everything from its logical models to its actual programs. Project management information, once loaded, could aid in the estimation of subsequent similar development efforts.

But what about application maintenance? In Part One (Chap. 8 to be specific), we discussed the model's role in the application life cycle. When the issue of maintenance was discussed, it was presented as involving a series of tasks, ending with a repetitive *Detective Work* function. With the advent of an accurate model, maintenance became a much more managed process. Continuing along the same functional track, consider that the models now reside in the repository and are related to all dependent instances, including their upper-level business and organizational requirements, other applications, and their physical implementations. The repository's role in application maintenance would involve the following (see Fig. 19.2):

1. *Impact analysis*. Impact analysis involves querying the repository for all models, programs, files/databases, screens/reports/windows, and so on that would be impacted by the maintenance request.
2. *Storage and relatability of the revised application model*. Once the maintenance request is accurately reflected in revised application models, these models represent a new application *version*. The new version is of course related to the old version as well as to all of its dependent items.
3. *Configuration management*. As with the original application development effort, the construction, testing, and subsequent deployment of this "release" involve the repository as the holding and tracking area of all involved application items.

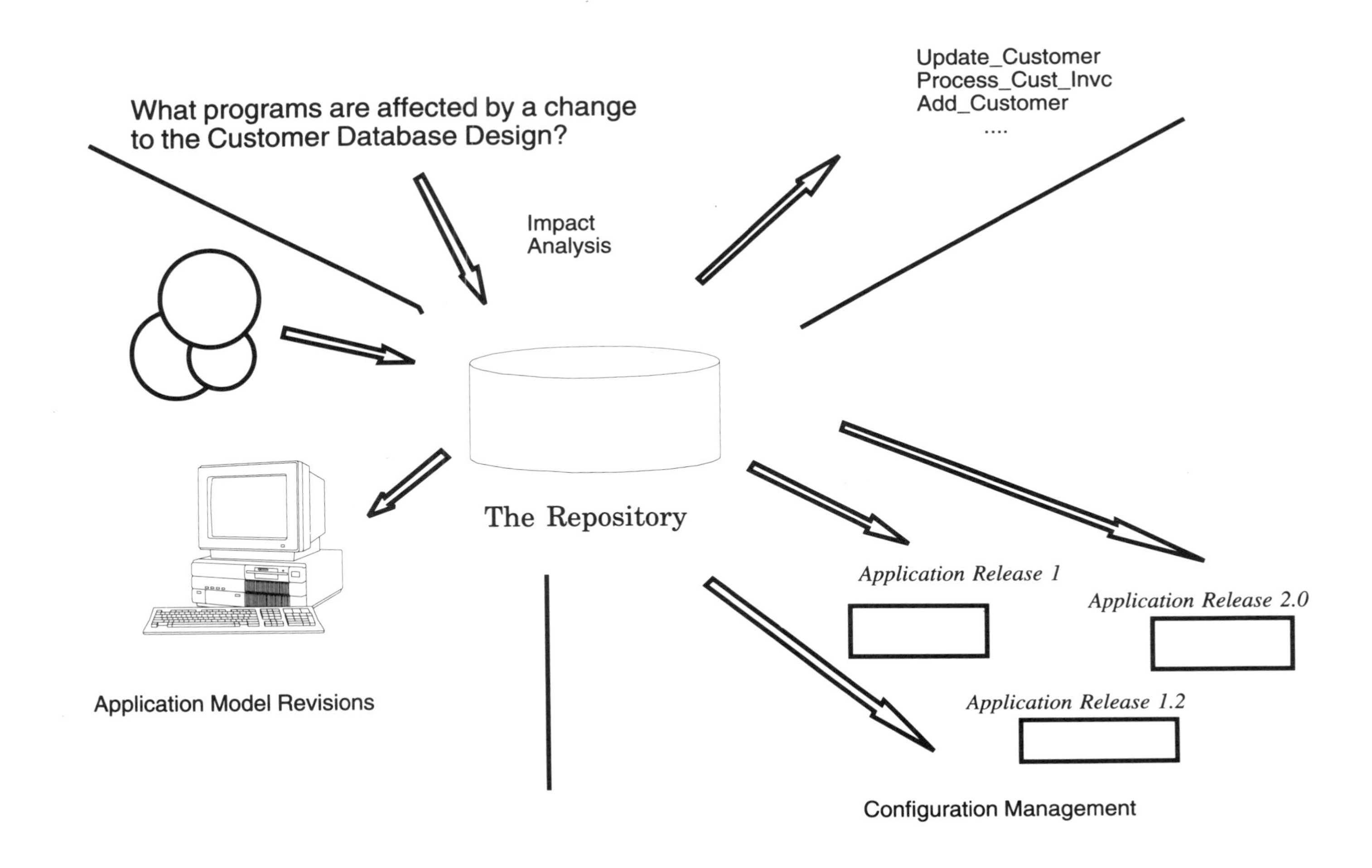

Figure 19.2 The repository's role in application maintenance.

■ REPOSITORIES AND CASE

Repositories originated as CASE tool integrators. Specifically, their original purpose was that of a permanent intermediary between CASE tools belonging to different vendors. As we discussed in Part Three, many problems existed with CASE import/export functions. Constructs that existed in the source tool, but not in the target, were not imported. Similarly, constructs that existed in the target tool, but not in the source tool, were never populated via the target tool's import utility. Despite the existence of interface standards, many holes remained in the inter-CASE transfer process.

In CASE-progressive organizations a "best of breed" philosophy was followed when deciding which application development aids to deploy. When it came to modeling, it was quite common for systems planners to use a tool with a wide variety of planning constructs. Application developers often chose tools of a different nature, often from different vendors. Systems analysts, requiring a wide range of diagramming constructs, may have picked analysis-based tools from a vendor specializing in logical systems design (as opposed to detailed physical implementation considerations). Programmer/analysts, or systems designers, being more concerned with how the specs will be implemented, tended to model the to-be-implemented representations of an application (physical program structure, physical database design, etc.) and may have needed a tool with a different set of modeling constructs. When an organization realizes the amount of time that is spent reinputting redundant aspects of each model from one tool to another, as well as the amount of extra translation that would be eliminated if the same model were reused from one project member to another, a repository begins to come into consideration.

The advent of the intermediary repository increased communication between CASE tools (see Fig. 19.3). A model developed in one vendor's tool would be placed in the repository. Another vendor's tool could access the same model via the repository. Of course, the implementation of such a scenario is not as problem-free as we would like. The issue of conflicting metadata constructs still comes into play with an intermediate repository. However, there are many ways of handling these conflicts, as we will see in Part Five. For now, the purpose of the repository is the preservation of the models, as they are stored in their originating tool and/or subsequently updated in another tool. In other words, constructs should not be lost because they do not uniformly exist in all interfacing tools.

In addition, as with application development, repositories also serve as the library for CASE-based models. Most CASE tools do not allow the existence and/or retrieval of multiple model versions. By storing the models in the vendor-neutral repository, versioning capability is acquired.

■ REPOSITORIES BEYOND CASE

Once CASE-based models become repository residents, many organizations make their CASE models part of the regular production MIS world. Instead of being limited to their precoding specification depiction role, the models continue serving a purpose throughout application development and well into the production and

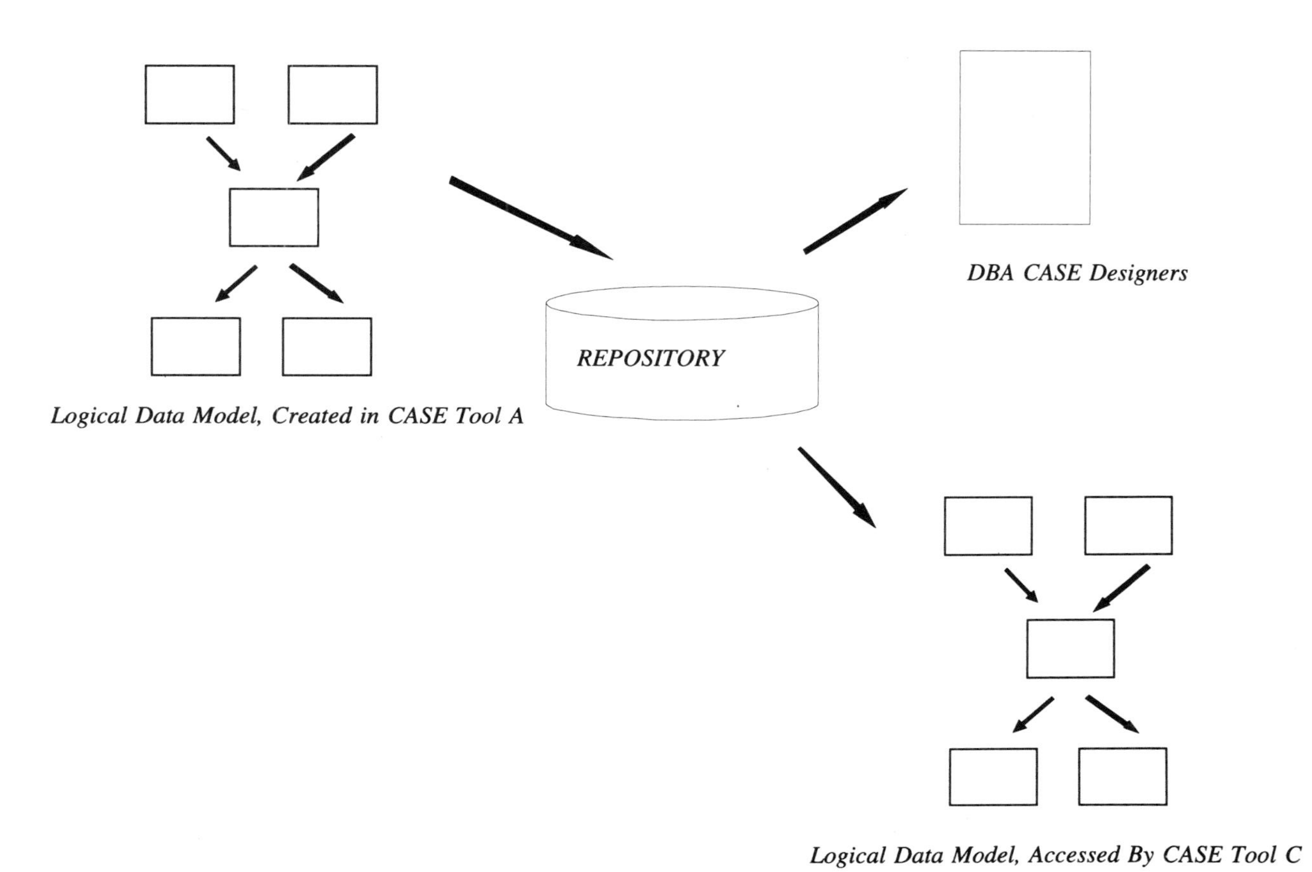

Figure 19.3 The repository as CASE intermediary.

maintenance cycles, as discussed previously. But the repository's contents need not be limited to CASE tool–initiated model components.

Many repositories began as data dictionaries. The data dictionary's purpose was the identification and administration of corporate data. Its actual implementation included the assignment of corporate data names (according to a predefined standard) and associated abbreviations (sometimes called synonyms) as needed based on the constraints of the physical implementation (the DBMS, the programming language, etc.). The purpose quickly expanded to include the automatic generation of the database's physical definition, as discussed in Chap. 18. Data-conscious organizations used their dictionaries as the controller of physical database implementations. Typically, database administration organizations were the only ones authorized to generate and subsequently implement the dictionary-based database definition. In the ideal situation DBAs served as a clearing house for the monitoring of preventable database changes and assured that database designs were optimally carried through. The dictionary functioned as the record keeper throughout the process.

As dictionaries became more functional, their contents expanded to include the tracking of programs, JCL run streams, and the like, as well as the relationships between these process-oriented constructs and their associated data. However, as discussed in Chap. 18, the relationship between the populated dictionary and reality was at best *active in development*.

Repositories bridge the development world with the production world by allowing an *active in production* role. End-user queries can initiate in the repository, with the repository generating the query and retrieving the data based on simple subject area selections, for example. The repository can go well beyond CASE integration by scoping the needs of the decision support user in terms of where and how to best retrieve the data needed.

■ EXAMPLES

An understanding of how a repository practically fits into an MIS environment requires the depiction of several practical examples.

ACCESSIBLE SYSTEMS PLANNING STRATEGY

The first example portrays a central repository as the official recorder of an organization's strategic application models. This organization, a consumer products manufacturing organization, plans all applications from a strategic perspective. A systems planning function uses the planning component of a major CASE tool to model the planned interrelationships between the organization's objectives and a strategic systems architecture. Most application developers were unaware of any strategic architectural plans, and, in many cases, they were unaware of corporate objectives, especially those that affected (or would affect) their application development work. Most of the developer naiveté was due to their lack of awareness of a systems planning function. The systems planners worked independently of the developers and did not share or publish their

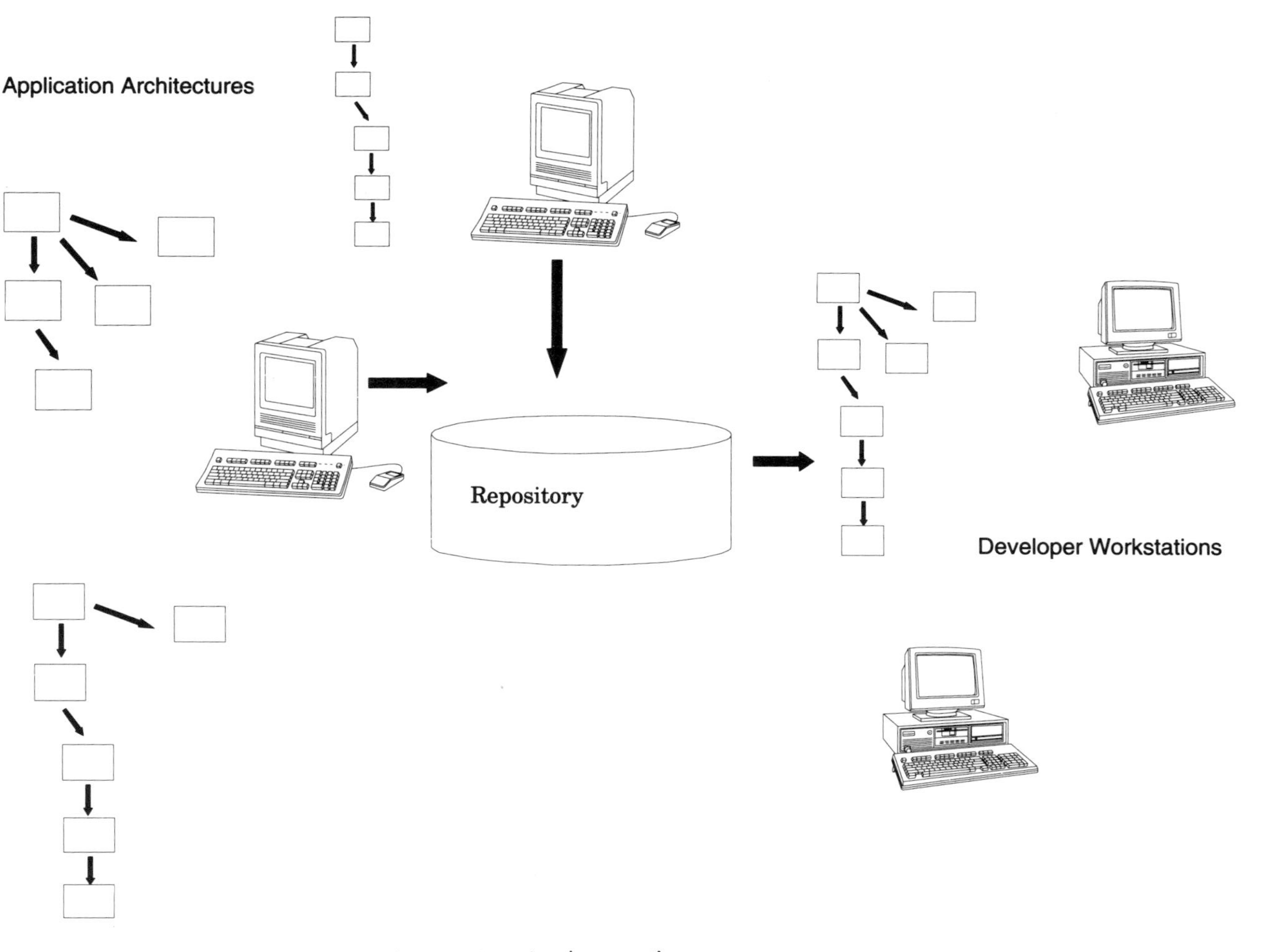

Figure 19.4 The first phase of a sample repository implementation.

architectural models beyond MIS management. Developers had no access to the CASE tool being deployed by the planners. Instead, their relatively specific design models were created with a desktop flowcharting tool and served primarily as documentation.

In order to make developers more aware of corporate strategy, particularly as it affected individual application design and implementation, the systems planners decided to make their strategic architectures available to all interested developers. In addition, planners felt that the architecture was more likely to be an influencing factor if developers could view their own applications as part of the overall MIS strategy. The planners then began a repository implementation effort. Initially, the repository was used to store all architectural blueprints. This was a relatively easy task, because the blueprints originated from the same CASE tool.

A repository was selected as the storage ground based on its vendor tool independence. Specifically, the scope of the repository was intended to extend beyond that of a holding area for system architectural plans and eventually to include the developer-created design models, too. As illustrated in Fig. 19.4, however, the first phase merely made these architectural plans accessible to every developer's workstation.

Once developers began to evaluate the system architectural plans, their individual application design intentions became evaluated in terms of their global impact. For example, a developer on the Inventory Tracking System never really questioned the potential effect of any changes to the Product Master, because its data originated within this application. Once he saw the impact that the Product Master had on the strategic systems plan (it was to be one of the primary sources of decision support data), he researched most requested data modifications extensively by talking to the project managers responsible for each dependent application as well as to the systems planners. This new "research first, design second, implement third" philosophy seemed to spread willingly among application developers. By merely making the corporate strategy available on the desktop, individual applications began to take on a corporate perspective.

EXPANDING THE CORPORATE DATA DICTIONARY

In another example an insurance company has a very strong data administration function. A heavily populated and accurate data dictionary has supported its intentions for approximately 10 years. No new data element is ever created without data administration approval. With the advent of end-user computing, much of the corporate data is being extracted and brought down to individual workstations. As the data becomes analyzed and reported, its original meaning tends to become lost.

Many end-user-created reports have been using data names such as *Net Revenue*, *Projected Sales*, and so on that need specific definitions as to how they are calculated and the extent of their scope (e.g., departmental vs. organizational). Data administration has decided to make its data dictionary accessible to

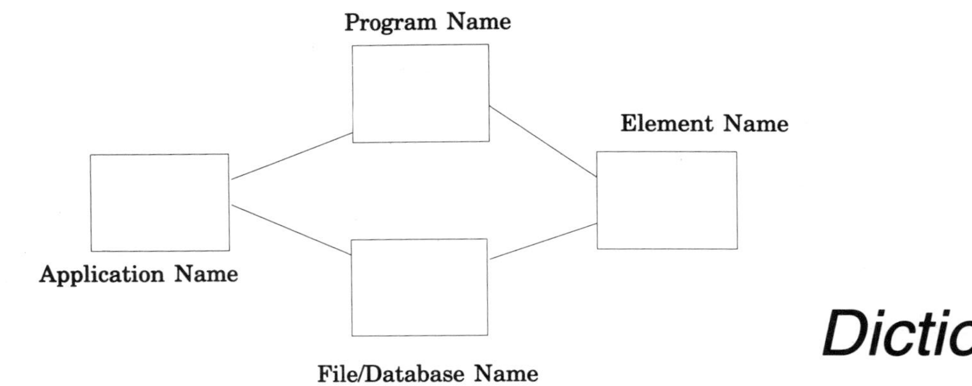

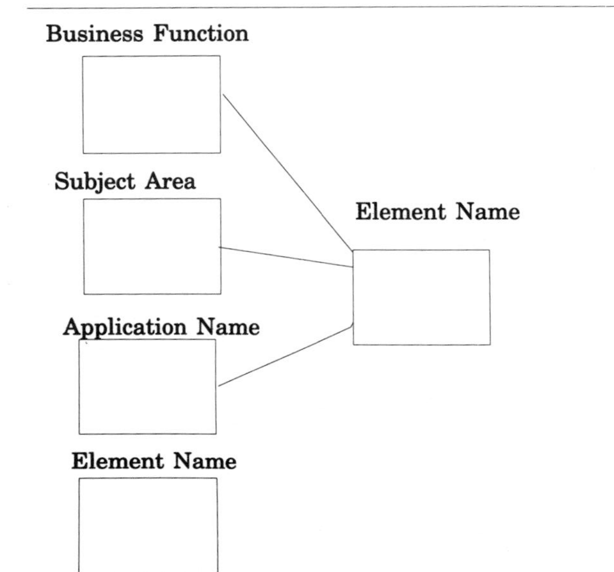

Figure 19.5 Accessing data definitions in a dictionary vs. in a repository.

these end-user decision support analysts. However, their current data dictionary, not intended for global access, does not have the flexibility that is required for end-user query based on element name, for example. For this reason, data administration began the conversion from a data dictionary to a flexible repository, with the primary objective being flexible end-user query access and reporting.

Here, the repository consists primarily of all populated data elements and definitions, related to specific business subject categories. The categories did not exist in the data dictionary and were created and related as part of the repository conversion effort. In addition, because most of the current data dictionary instance data is arranged by application (project name), a fair amount of reorganization was required in order to make end-user queries as flexible as possible. Figure 19.5 depicts accessing data definitions in a dictionary vs. in a repository.

As end-users become accustomed to repository access, data administration plans to increase the scope of the repository to go beyond that of a data dictionary. The first target is that of modeling existing data, as it is implemented across applications. Capture tools will be used to read the existing database and file structures and load first-cut data models into a CASE tool for further refinement. Eventually, physical data models will be loaded into the repository so that end-users (and developers) will be able to view the relationships between data items in addition to their names, definitions, and associated applications. Before these models become available in the repository, developers will still rely on their paper drawings.

■ SUMMARY

In this chapter we depicted the repository from a practical usage perspective. As was illustrated, although most repository implementations started out with a CASE integration objective, repository functionality should go well beyond CASE. The repository's purpose, simply speaking, is to organize a company's information by relating it to its various renditions, sources, and applications, and to make it accessible to all who need it, regardless of where they are and the means by which they must obtain it.

20

A LOOK AT REPOSITORY STANDARDS

As the repository marketplace continues to emerge, the issue of *standards* adherence is always a consideration. Before evaluating the major standards, we should consider the ways in which most standards originate. Standards in the MIS world typically originate in one of three ways.

The first, most common scenario results from the establishment of a new MIS product line. Specifically, most new marketplaces (and we can most likely consider the repository marketplace to be new during the 1990s) begin with a small set of distinct vendor offerings. Based on the functional completeness (or incompleteness) of each vendor offering, other vendors then offer tools of their own with varying degrees of complementary and/or redundant functionality. The consumers and potential consumers of these vendor offerings become confused and disheartened with the dichotomy of conflicting choices. They typically form "user groups" and discuss the multivendor similarities and differences. As a group they carry substantial weight within the new marketplace, and what may have begun as user-submitted requirements now become "standards efforts."

The second major method of standards origination usually begins in the academic or research-oriented world. Here, a research project typically involves the trial of new MIS-related functionality. The trial usually involves a "proof-of-concept" activity of a capability that is not currently available in the MIS hardware/software world. In the laboratory, so to speak, the concept is proven successful. Perhaps a PhD thesis results. Depending on the popularity of this research (once received and published outside the academic community), the research results fuel a standards effort. This effort, instead of working to fix existing software, works to define the ultimate software (because it does not yet exist). A highly respected organization that represents members of this category is the IEEE (the Institute of Electrical and Electronics Engineers).

Finally, the third method of standards origination involves hybrid origination. As with the first category, because new marketplaces typically involve the introduction of functionally incomplete and/or conflicting efforts, the consumers of these software products express their need for additional or differing functionality to the respective vendors. Each vendor, depending on the amount of architectural change that would be required in order to meet existing customer demands, has a vested interest in maintaining its current investment. Therefore, vendors may originate their own standards efforts by banding with other vendors that may not yet be participating in the new marketplace. In most scenarios multiple standards efforts soon result, each supported by one of the major early marketplace entrants. A good example of this type of standards body is ANSI (the American National Standards Institute), based in New York City.

The world of repository standards is no different. Currently, most of the existing repository standards began as a means of solving tool integration problems. The four major standards efforts that surround repositories are:

- CDIF (Case Data Interchange Format)
- IRDS (Information Resource Dictionary System)
- PCTE (Portable Common Tool Environment)
- ATIS (A Tools Integration Standard)

It should be noted that as of this writing, all of the preceding standards are still evolving and have not been finalized. In fact, many consider these efforts to be "moving targets" in that they are so involved in updates right now that much of the information in this chapter is sure to become outdated very quickly.

■ CDIF*

CDIF is an example of a standard that falls into the third category mentioned previously. The standard was originated by the major CASE vendors and some supporting major user organizations. The standards development effort was overseen by the Electronic Industries Association (EIA), and a subcommittee (the CDIF Technical Committee) resulted. The committee contains both U.S. and international members.

CDIF was developed as a standard way of transferring data between CASE tools. The standard was designed to be the guideline for a single-batch mechanism for inter-CASE file transfer. In this respect its originators considered the standard to be vendor and methodology independent. Vendors viewed the standard as a work saver in that it would free them of the requirement to develop multiple interfaces between their tool and those of other vendors.

The CDIF standard concentrates on CASE tool metadata. Its architecture consists of four layers (similar to IRDS as we will see next): the topmost representing the meta-metamodel, the lowest representing the instance data, as defined in each CASE tool and as represented in the real-world application (see Fig. 20.1).

---

*For a list of the CDIF standards numbers, as published by the EIA, see the References at the end of the book.

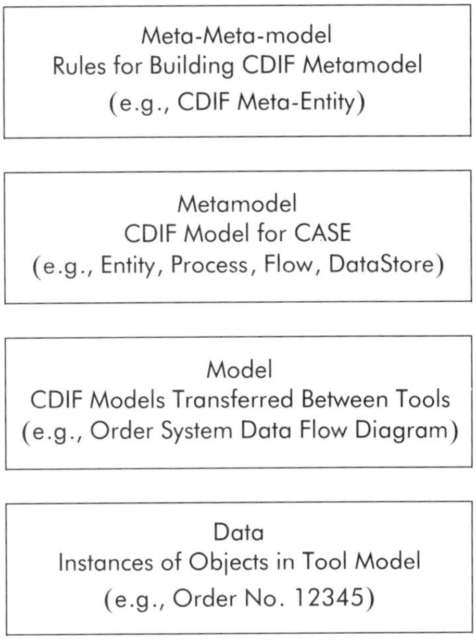

Meta-Meta-model
Rules for Building CDIF Metamodel
(e.g., CDIF Meta-Entity)

Metamodel
CDIF Model for CASE
(e.g., Entity, Process, Flow, DataStore)

Model
CDIF Models Transferred Between Tools
(e.g., Order System Data Flow Diagram)

Data
Instances of Objects in Tool Model
(e.g., Order No. 12345)

Figure 20.1 The CDIF four-level framework.

Similar to repository definition, the topmost level of the CDIF framework requires the definition of the meta-metamodel. Remember, as we stated previously, metamodels (and their associated metadata) are relative to where we sit on the horizontal scale of data definition (see Fig. 20.2).* When we discussed metadata in Chap. 13, we were looking at it from the point of view of a CASE tool. Therefore, our highest perspective (perspective 3) stopped at the metamodel (sometimes called the meta-metadata). Remembering that the third perspective represents the tool's perspective, we have to reorient ourselves a little higher (to perhaps a fourth perspective) when we are trying to integrate multiple tools. This fourth perspective (the meta-meta perspective) is that of the repository. For those readers who are still remembering our library analogy, this fourth perspective can represent that of the library itself (consolidating the views of the card catalog with the microfiche and the on-line computer directory into one overall directory or consolidating multiple libraries regardless of their internal indexing schemes!). This fourth perspective is an important concept that should be remembered throughout the remainder of this book! The four metadata perspectives are summarized in Fig. 20.3.

Therefore, when we look at the "meta-meta" level from the perspective of tool integration standards (such as CDIF), it is easier to see the purpose of this uppermost framework level. For the purposes of a standards discussion, consider it the place for the tool-independent metamodel. In other words, it is here where those rules that elaborate what can be defined and associated in individual metamodels are stored.

*See Chap. 13 for clarification.

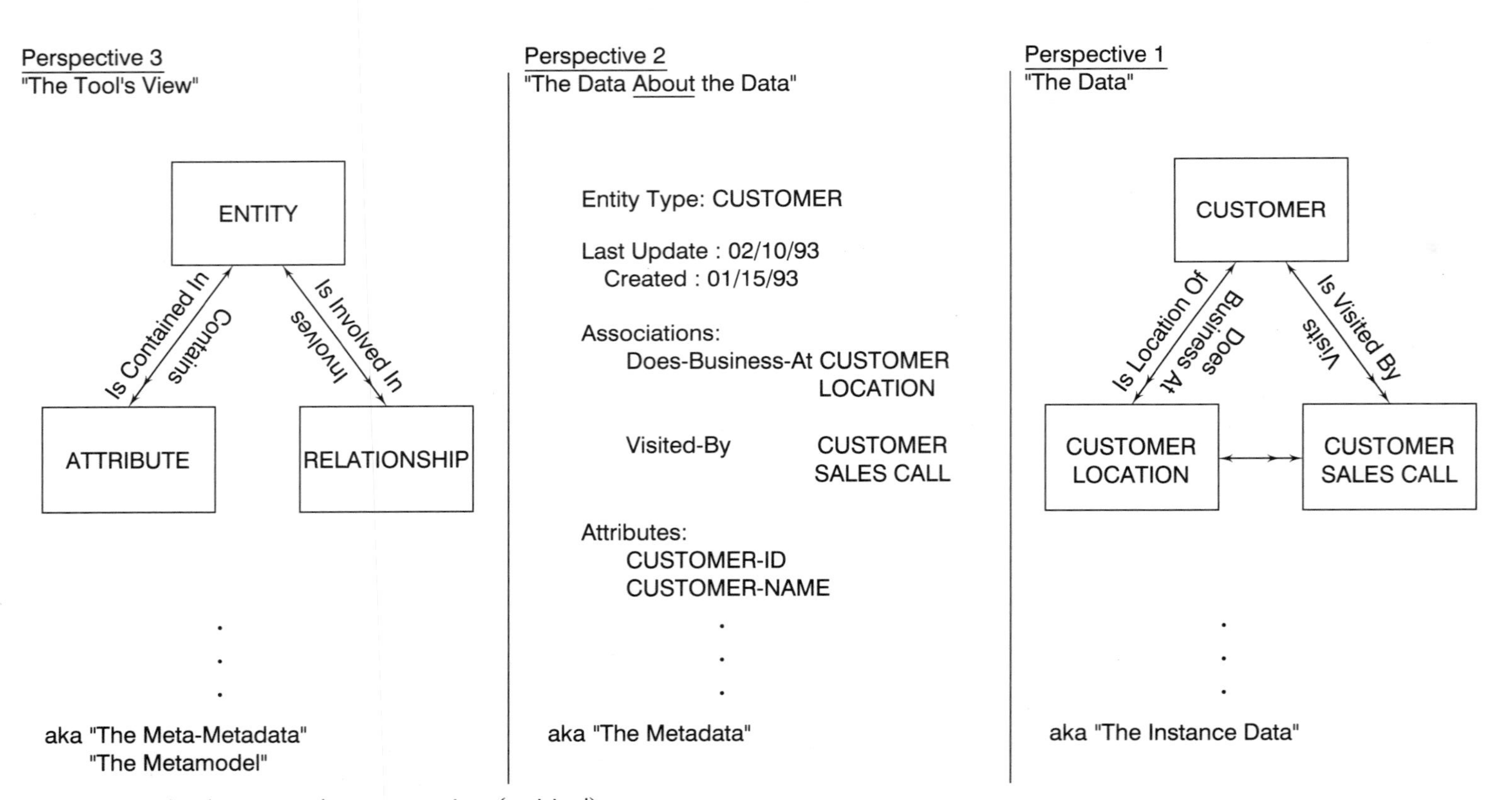

Figure 20.2 The three metadata perspectives (revisited).

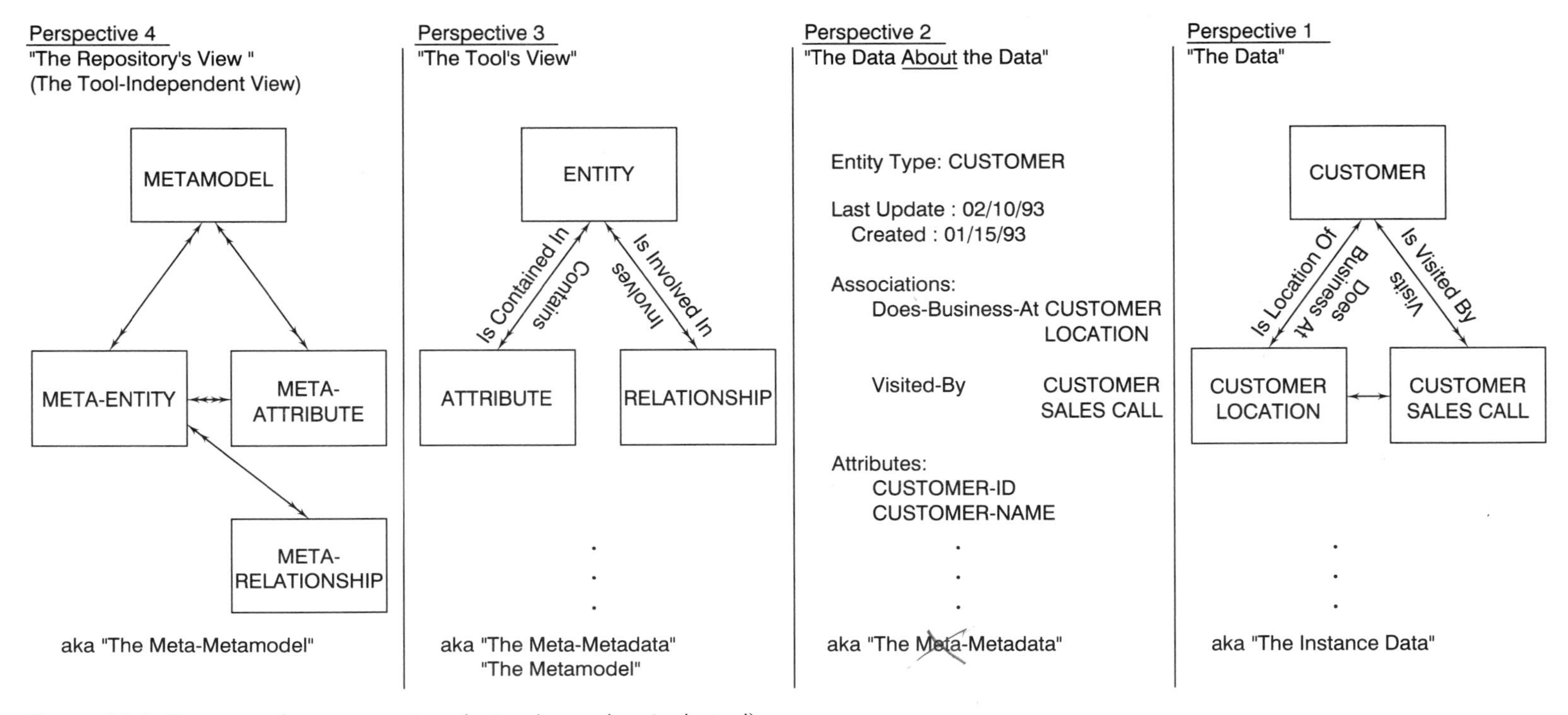

Figure 20.3 Four metadata perspectives (going beyond a single tool).

Today's CDIF consists of two major parts: the architecture, as discussed previously, of which a metamodel developed exclusively for CASE data transfer exists as a subset (the CASE information model); and a transfer format.

Within the CDIF transfer format, multiple syntaxes will eventually become standardized and acceptable. Within each syntax, multiple "encodings" will also be permitted. *Encodings* refer to the representation of the information being transferred according to the standard syntax (whether it is straight text, binary, or some type of symbolic keyword-based translation). Initial CDIF efforts revolve around a single syntax (SYNTAX.1) with straight text encoding (clear text encoding) called ENCODING.1. Simply speaking, CDIF currently contains a standardized ASCII text transfer format.

This transfer format specifies requirements for three parts of the transfer file: the *header*, the *metamodel* definition, and the *model* definitions. The header identifies the source tool, syntax, encoding, and general transfer audit information such as the date and time of the export. The metamodel definition identifies each construct type being used in the transfer (including extensions), as well as the version number of the CDIF standard metamodel being used. Finally, the model definitions contain the actual data (model instances) being transferred between the tools.

To complete our discussion of CDIF, we should briefly discuss the standardized CASE information model. The model's philosophy advocates the separation of presentation and content. Presentation deals with how a model is depicted in each tool (graphical positioning, symbol sets, colors, default fonts, etc.). These presentation details are then related to their actual to-be-displayed objects (the contents, as discussed next). For example, the way the entity CUSTOMER will appear in a particular diagram is stored and related with the actual CUSTOMER entity. The content (known as the *semantic model*) standardizes the definitions of the constructs that reside within each model. Four types of subject areas have been initially standardized:

- *Core.* Generic attributes that are required for all constructs, irrespective of which model they belong to [alternate names, user-id details, and general audit information (last update date, etc.)]
- *Data flow models.* Data flow diagram components
- *Entity–relationship models.* Entities, relationships (including *n*-ary vs. binary relationship depiction requirements), and attributes
- *Data inventory.* Characteristics of data type definitions (domains, structures, value tables, etc.)

Because the CDIF standard itself requires the definition of the metamodel constructs being transferred to be included as part of the transfer file, it can be considered relatively generic in that each transfer can represent virtually any combination of metamodel constructs. However, those subject areas that have been initially standardized represent only the analysis aspect of CASE-based system development. In addition, because of the wide range of metamodel adherence across today's CASE tools, CDIF compliance does not necessarily mean CASE tool to CASE tool compatibility. If a CASE tool receives a CDIF-compliant file to be processed for import, the file may contain metamodel constructs that are not resident within its own tool's metamodel (as we discussed in Chap. 16). Many CASE tools in this situation simply ignore constructs that they cannot handle.

To wrap up our discussion of CDIF, consider that it is not currently an all-encompassing standard by any means. It is important to note, however, that over 15 CDIF-related projects are currently in progress, under the direction of EIA. Each project's goal is the establishment of an additional ANSI standard that will cover the standard metadata requirements for the following areas:

- State/event processing (state transition diagrams, entity life histories)
- Logical and physical database design standards: relational, network, and hierarchical database designs, as well as the constructs necessary for the representation of files
- Process models
- Program structures
- Data structures
- CASE presentation information (This information is being addressed by subject area in order to make it easier for vendors to implement a minimum set of functionality which will allow the reproduction of a diagram with the same spatial layout and connectivity as its source tool.)

Some CDIF update to the July 1991 standard (the handling of subject area extensions) is expected to be complete by the end of 1993. In addition, further projects are underway to develop standards that will address the transfer of data from tools to repositories (as opposed to tool transfer only). All of these projects are expected to be completed by the end of 1994.

Because only analysis-based constructs have been addressed to date, any tool that goes beyond the analysis phase (and most do today) and claims CDIF compliance should be reconsidered. Also, even within the domain of analysis, compliance simply means adherence to a standardized import/export file format, not standardized processing of the transfer file. Therefore, the specifics of how each vendor complies with this standard need to be individually investigated. An important point to consider, however, is that CDIF committee members expect the existence of "compliance testing facilities" to be available some day.

■ IRDS*

Unlike the other standards described in this chapter, the IRDS (Information Resource Dictionary System) standard does not deal specifically with tool integration. Instead, it is a standard that addresses the requirements and architecture of any tool that describes (controls, protects, documents, and facilitates) an

*See the References at the end of the book for the official source of IRDS standard information.

installation's information resources.* Although the standard is based on an E–R approach, it does not require a relational database implementation. The standard, as written, is intended to be void of any particular hardware, software, or operating system requirements. It originated as a "category 2" standard, in that it attempts to describe the ultimate software, and was not initiated based on a set of existing products of the same functional category.

As published in 1988, the standard consists of seven modules:

Module 1—the core standard addresses the minimum requirements for IRDS compliance. It addresses the basic functionality required for operation of the IRD and the IRD schema. All subsequent modules assume compliance with the core standard and typically require extensions to the module 1 schema.

Module 2—the basic functional IRD schema extends the schema covered in module 1 by addressing the implementation of extensions to the metamodel discussed in module 1.

Module 3—IRDS security addresses the implementation of security in terms of access control to the IRDS contents and its supporting schema.

Module 4—extensible life cycle phase facility addresses life cycle management of the IRDS contents.

Module 5—procedure facility discusses the definition and execution of IRDS command procedures.

Module 6—application program interface defines an interface to the implemented IRDS via standard language "call" features.

Module 7—entity lists describes the ability to name a list or group of entities and details those commands and panels that are used for entity list manipulation.

The IRDS standard is based on a four-level architecture, as illustrated in Fig. 20.4. Each level in the architecture describes the requirements of the next level down. Therefore, in a sense, control based on what can and cannot exist within a particular architectural level is determined by a level's "parent."

The top level contains the types of all constructs that become part of the IRD schema (defined at the next level, level 2). Consistent with our way of thinking, the top level of the IRDS architecture contains meta-entity-*types*, meta-attribute-*types*, and meta-relationship-*types*. In a sense therefore *meta-types* share the characteristics of the *meta-meta* world. Placing practicality into the concept of the first level of the IRDS architecture, examples of some constructs that are defined at this level include:

- Entity-Type, Relationship-Type, Attribute-Type
- Relationship-Class-Type, Attribute-Group-Type

*"Information Resource Dictionary System," American National Standards Institute, Inc., October 19, 1988, p. 1.

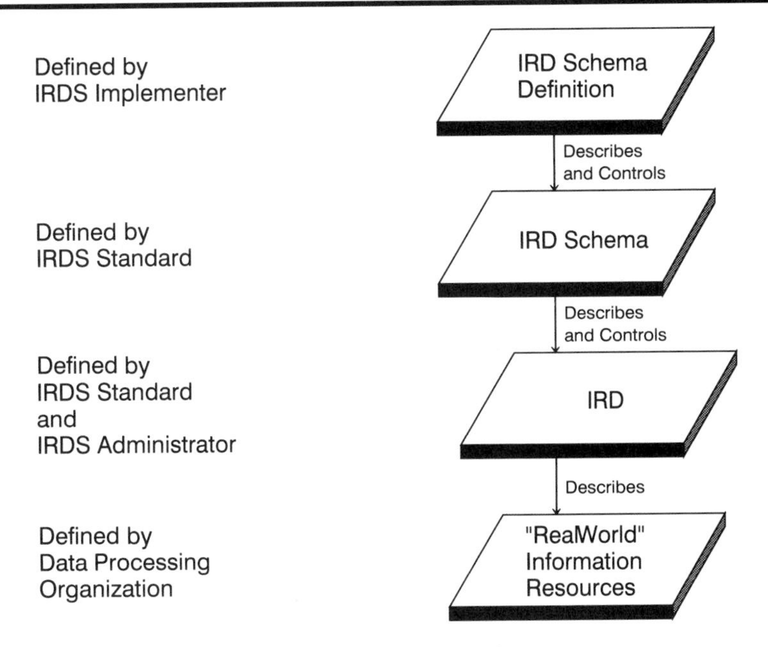

Figure 20.4 The four-level architecture of the IRDS database.

- Attribute-Type-Validation-Data, Attribute-Type-Validation-Procedure
- IRDS-Reserved-Names, IRDS-Defaults
- Names

The preceding list is by no means all inclusive. However, when evaluating the purpose of the topmost layer of the IRDS architecture, remember that the preceding constructs are setting the boundaries for those constructs that will actually exist as instances to be populated in the dictionary/repository. For example, LAST-MODIFICATION-DATE is an instance of the meta (or meta-meta) construct *Attribute-Type*. Remember again to consider the perspective under which your data (metadata) is being defined and populated. To put these levels into their appropriate perspectives via a practical example, consider the following:

- At *level 1* (the IRD schema definition, aka Meta-Entity types), the constructs Entity-Type and Attribute-Type are defined.
- At *level 2* (the IRD schema), instances of the preceding are established as follows:
  - Entity (an instance of Entity-Type)
    - Entity Name (an instance of Attribute-Type)
    - Entity Description (an instance of Attribute-Type)
    - Last Modification Date (an instance of Attribute-Type)

The second level therefore defines those constructs that will be populated in the dictionary/repository and some specific associated control mechanisms (defaults, etc.) of the repository tool.

The third level is the actual populated repository/dictionary. Here, the standard addresses the actual models. This level is equivalent to our "perspective 1" as illustrated in Fig. 20.2.

Finally, the fourth level is the real-world information environment. This level is not addressed at all in the IRDS standard. It pertains to those resources being modeled in the dictionary/repository (in the third level given previously). It is included in the standard as a way of putting the standard into its proper position.

In order to fully address the IRDS standard, a brief description of *module 1* (the core standard) is necessary.

The IRDS Core Standard

Aside from detailing the basic IRDS architecture and the IRD schema, the core standard addresses the requirements for a minimal IRD schema, as well as the requirements for the definition, access, maintenance, output, and transfer of the base IRD.

The Minimal IRD Schema The core standard takes a subset of those Meta-Entity types defined and implemented in the first two levels of the IRDS architecture and considers them required for minimal IRD compliance. In the 1988 version of the standard (being revised as of this writing), 14 Meta-Entity-Types were specified. The minimal standard also requires the definition of specific meta-entities (part of the level 2 IRD schema) as instances of the required Meta-Entity-Types. Figure 20.5 lists these meta-entities and their associated Meta-Entity-Types. The standard also lists specific relationship-types, relationship-class-types, and the meta-attributes required for all of the preceding.

When evaluating the preceding list for completeness, it is important to keep in mind the following points:

- The list is part of a standard published in 1988 which is currently being revised.
- The list represents the requirement for *minimal* compliance. It obviously does not include the many extensions that are required for IRDS features covered beyond the core standard (in modules 2 through 7 as of 1988, and beyond based on current standard revision efforts).

The IRD Command Language The core standard defines a generally syntax-neutral command language. Although each command does not have a required syntax, certain "command clauses" do require specific parameters to appear in a defined order. The command language is intended to be used for the following IRD functionality:

- *Schema maintenance* (addition, deletion, modification, etc. of meta-entities and meta-relationships)

```
Minimal IRD Schema Meta-Entity  Meta-Entity-Type

ADDED-BY............................... ATTRIBUTE-TYPE
ARCHIVED-LIFE-CYCLE-PHASE.............. IRD-PARTITION
CONTROLLED-LIFE-CYCLE-PHASE............ IRD-PARTITION
DATE-TIME-ADDED........................ ATTRIBUTE-GROUP-TYPE
DATE-TIME-LAST-MODIFIED................ ATTRIBUTE-GROUP-TYPE
DEFAULT-VIEW........................... ATTRIBUTE-TYPE
HAS.................................... RELATIONSHIP-CLASS-TYPE
IRD-PARTITION-NAME..................... ATTRIBUTE-TYPE
IRDS-USER.............................. ENTITY-TYPE
IRDS-USER-HAS-IRD-VIEW................. RELATIONSHIP-TYPE
IRDS-USER-HAS-IRD-SCHEMA-VIEW.......... RELATIONSHIP-TYPE
IRD-VIEW............................... ENTITY-TYPE
EXISTING-IRDS-DEFAULTS................. IRDS-DEFAULTS
EXISTING-IRDS-LIMITS................... IRDS-LIMITS
LAST-MODIFIED-BY....................... ATTRIBUTE-TYPE
NAMING-RULES........................... NAMES
NUMBER-OF-TIMES-MODIFIED............... ATTRIBUTE-TYPE
STANDARD-RESERVED-NAMES................ IRDS-RESERVED-NAMES
RANGE-VALIDATION....................... ATTRIBUTE-TYPE-VALIDATION-PROCEDURE
IRD-SCHEMA-PHASE-NAME.................. ATTRIBUTE-TYPE
IRD-SCHEMA-VIEW........................ ENTITY-TYPE
SECURITY............................... IRD-PARTITION
SYSTEM-DATE............................ ATTRIBUTE-TYPE
SYSTEM-GENERATED-NAME.................. ATTRIBUTE-TYPE
SYSTEM-TIME............................ ATTRIBUTE-TYPE
UNCONTROLLED-LIFE-CYCLE-PHASE.......... IRD-PARTITION
VALUE-VALIDATION....................... ATTRIBUTE-TYPE-VALIDATION-PROCEDURE
YES-OR-NO-VALUE........................ ATTRIBUTE-TYPE-VALIDATION-DATA
```

Figure 20.5 Meta-entities required for the minimal IRD schema.

- *IRD maintenance* (update of the *contents* of the IRD—addition, deletion, modification etc. of entities, attributes, relationships, etc.)
- *IRD output* (the query of the IRD contents—a specific syntax order is specified)
- *IRD interface* (the transfer of an IRD schema and its contents from one IRD to another)

The IRD Panel Interface Requirements for the contents of an interactive "screen-oriented" interface are covered here. The core standard addresses inter-panel structures (for traversal), panel trees (logical groupings of panels that are required for the execution of a particular IRD command), and panel types (IRD schema panels vs. IRD panels). Each panel type is also defined as consisting of distinct "panel areas." Depending on the contents of each area, specific operation requirements (COMMIT points, access, panel saving, security, etc.) are also covered.

A product is said to be IRDS "core compliant" if it follows the requirements for *either* the IRD command language *or* the IRD panel interface.

To summarize, the IRDS standard is the most complete in terms of its coverage of data dictionary/repository functionality as it pertains to the representation of the repository's contents. However, its scope as published is limited to a standalone centralized perspective. The published standard, official as of 1988, is already out of date. An update to the standard has been in progress for quite some time. Specifically, draft updates have been circulating which address the following additional capabilities:

> *Services interface.* This supplement (X3.185) addresses the requirements for an IRDS programming interface. Specifically, programs that are external to the IRDS will be allowed to maintain, populate, and access the contents and schema of an IRD. This standard would "open up" the repository to a host of other tools, including CASE tools, DBA tools, compilers, and other application development aids. The approval to begin work on this additional standard was granted in 1986. As we will see later in the chapter, the services interface is based in part on the original ATIS (A Tools Integration Standard).
>
> *Export / import file format.* This standard (X3.195) will address the requirements for batch transfer between the IRDS and other tools, as stated previously.
>
> *Object-oriented metamodel.* The capabilities and representation of an object-oriented perspective are being investigated.
>
> *Distributed capabilities.* The implications of a distributed IRDS are addressed in this update to the existing standard.

Therefore, as with CDIF, when a vendor alleges "IRDS compliance" it can only be based on the official published standard. In addition, compliance can be defined as pertaining only to the core standard, as illustrated previously.

■ PCTE*

The Portable Common Tool Environment (PCTE) represents a standard with a research-based origin (the second category of standard origination, as discussed previously). In 1983, a major research project began in Europe (the ESPRIT project). The project's objective was the definition and prototype of a set of interfaces which would form the basis for an integrated software engineering environment. Project participation consisted of six European information technology companies. The first phase of the project (PCTE 1.4) ended in 1986 with the publication of the requirements for a C language standard interface. Although this publication was not yet considered a "standard," its completion invoked the formation of the PCTE Interface Management Board (PIMB) whose objective was the conversion of these requirements into a standard. The "standard" (PCTE 1.5) was published in November 1988. The standard as published pertained only to Unix development environments and addressed both the C and Ada languages.

---

*See the References at the end of the book for a list of official PCTE standards publications.

Based on requests that stemmed primarily from European NATO members, the PCTE standard was modified to become more operating system independent. Unix dependencies were removed from the published PCTE 1.5. In addition, all of the PCTE concepts became representable within the standard's object base. Major enhancements in terms of security and versioning capabilities were also addressed and a revised standard (PCTE +) resulted. This standard was then examined by the European Computer Manufacturer's Association (ECMA), and it became a formal ECMA standard in December 1990.

The PCTE interface definition is broken down as follows:

- The *basic mechanisms* address the core architecture and functionality of the PCTE interface. Included are descriptions of the underlying "repository," process management facilities, interprocess communication facilities, concurrency control, input/output, and requirements for a distributed PCTE environment.
- The *user interface*, originally geared toward the developer of the PCTE-compliant tool (discusses user interface–specific issues such as fonts, icons, menus, cursors, etc.), has since been replaced by a statement that recommends the use of an X-Windows interface.

PCTE Basic Mechanisms

The heart of PCTE is the *object management system* (OMS). It is based on an E–R model and assumes a distributed LAN-based implementation. "Objects," the backbone of the data structure, are typed. Many "types" are predefined, including the obvious root type of *object*. Predefined types have predefined attributes. The schema of the OMS is hierarchical in that all types typically have subtypes and parent types. In addition to "typed" objects, the OMS also consists of links, relationships, and attributes. Subtypes inherit the attributes and links of their parents, and hence the concept of multiple inheritance is addressed in the underlying structure of the OMS.

The PCTE standard details the specific definitions of relationships, links, and attributes as follows:

Relationship A relationship represents a bidirectional association between two objects, or a pair of "links." The properties of a relationship are defined by the properties of the associated links.

Link Links represent the origin and destination of a relationship. Every relationship consists of two mutually inverse links. There are five categories of links—existence, composition, reference, implicit, and designation:

> *Existence links* represent links that are directly dependent on the existence of the destination object. For example, a link that represents the "participates in" aspect of an employee/meeting relationship makes a meeting meaningless without the existence of at least one participating employee. Representing the "participates in" aspect of the relationship as an existence link implies that meetings do not really "exist" without the participation of the employees. In other words, the meeting object

type is *created* once at least one employee participates (that person may officially start the meeting, so to speak), and it is *deleted* once the last "participates in" link has been removed (e.g., the last person leaves the meeting).

Composition links represent existence links where the link destination is already a component of the origin object. When this occurs the origin object is said to be the root of a composite object in which the destination object is also a component. For example, a composition link can be defined from a book object to many chapter objects. Each chapter can be allowed to "manipulate" the book object (e.g., by creating a new version) because it represents a component. The book, as it existed before the creation of each additional chapter link, was also a component of the newest version (it had less chapters so to speak).

Reference links represent links with the referential integrity quality. That is, the destination object cannot be deleted as long as a reference link points to it. Although both composition links and existence links also have this property, the reference link is different in that it does not also share the *existence* property. For example, consider a chapter that "refers to" another chapter. The target (destination) of this link (the referred-to chapter) cannot be deleted as long as this link (the referring chapter) still exists. This differs from the previously mentioned link types in that a referred-to chapter (the destination of this link) cannot be created—it must already exist!

Implicit links are limited in their functionality. They have no "relevance to the origin" in that their existence (as a link) does not in any way affect the origin of the link (in other words, the origin has an existence of its own). They are typically used to reverse other links. For example, if we look at the reverse of our previously cited chapter-to-chapter reference link, the fact that the destination chapter "is referred to by" the referring chapter does not in any way affect its existence as a chapter. That is, the *referred-to* chapter was not changed in any way by the fact that another chapter is referring to it. Hence, it is said to have no relevance to the link's origin.

Designation links represent links that only have relevance to the origin (they have no referential integrity). That is, the object that exists as the destination of this link *can* be deleted, despite its participation in this relationship. Designation links can be considered "virtual links" so to speak, in that they are implemented like pointers.

There are four basic link properties, as described in the PCTE standard:

1. The existence property
2. The composition property
3. The referential integrity property
4. The relevance to the origin property

The link categories discussed previously each represent a grouped collection of the preceding properties, as follows:

Composition links: all link properties
Existence links: all properties *except* composition
Reference links: referential integrity and relevance to the origin *only*
Implicit links: referential integrity *only*
Designation links: relevance to the origin *only*

Therefore, in order to appreciate the standard PCTE link categories, it is essential to evaluate each relationship in terms of its adherence to *all* of the official link properties.

Attributes Attributes are defined as characteristics, similar to all other standard definitions. They have a name (not necessarily globally unique), and they also have an associated *attribute type*. Currently, the allowed types include integer, string, Boolean, real numbers, enumeration types, and date. They can be applied to either objects or links.

The OMS is implemented based on a two-level schema. Unlike CDIF and IRDS, the schema is not centralized. It can be implemented in a distributed fashion with each local schema definition set (SDS) containing the relative subset of the overall schema. The two classes (levels) of schema definition are:

- *The "type" level.* Here, all of the base properties of objects, links, and attribute types are defined (the meta-metadata equivalent).
- *The "type in SDS" level.* This level specifies the actual application of each metadata type to each schema definition set. Specifically, the attributes of each object as well as the link types between objects are specified (the metamodel equivalent).

Because the schema definitions (SDSs) are implemented in a distributed local fashion, names may exist in many different SDSs without the potential of clashing. Working schemas, which are in fact a composition of multiple SDSs, are associated with implemented processes. Therefore, at any point in time, a process is aware of the types of objects, links, and attributes that can be accessed as well as which "applications" of these constructs are "visible." This working schema can be changed as often as desired, and, via standard calls, the application "views" are immediately updated.

In addition to the preceding services, the ECMA PCTE standard also provides for the following basic OMS capabilities:

- *Versioning facilities.* Via the use of composite entities, individual version schemas can be modeled. Standard calls (*revise*, *snapshot*) are used to create new versions. Versions can be related to each other via *predecessor* and *successor* relationships.

- *Usage mode facilities.* Here, in a sense, type level security is defined. These facilities are used to restrict the usage of an object.
- *Object content facilities.* Some PCTE objects (file, pipe, or device object types) can have associated contents.
- *OMS administration facilities.* The representation of PCTE types as part of the metabase as well as various distribution and replication facilities are provided.

Beyond the basic OMS services are the following additional PCTE capabilities:

Process Execution and Monitoring Services These services include the following:

The ability to represent processes as objects. By modeling processes as objects, they can also inherit properties from parent (calling) processes such as security restrictions.

The ability to model foreign systems and processes. Any system that will interface with a PCTE-compliant system via non-PCTE interfaces can be modeled as an object. Routines for the transfer of data between foreign objects and PCTE-defined objects are provided.

Interprocess Communication Services In order to ensure operating system independence, the management of signals (between processes) is not covered in the PCTE standard. However, message queues are represented as PCTE objects.

Concurrency and Integrity Control Services The protection of activities from concurrent access is controlled via the definition of activity classes (protected, unprotected, transaction).

Security Services Security can be implemented as *discretionary* (an access control ist that grants or denies over 20 types of elementary access rights is associated with each PCTE object) or mandatory (each PCTE object has associated confidentiality and integrity labels). In addition, an auditing mechanism allows the ability to record any operations that could impact implemented security.

It should be noted that PCTE's original intentions differ in scope from the standards discussed thus far (IRDS, CDIF). PCTE strives to describe the *basis* for a standard software engineering *environment*. The environment includes a base repository enhanced by the usual operating system services as well as a foundation for communication between tools. For this reason, its overall framework is substantially different. However, despite the differences in intent, basic similarities do exist in terms of requirements:

- An underlying, shareable "repository"
- The need for intertool communication, including the ability to transfer substantial amounts of "data"

As with the other standards discussed previously, PCTE is not officially complete. Therefore, vendors that allege compliance with the standard should be prepared to discuss which aspects of the standard their tools comply with, and how their tool architecture will conform as the standard evolves.

ATIS

ATIS (A Tools Integration Standard) began as a joint project between Digital Equipment Corporation (Digital) and Atherton Technologies. During the late 1980s, both Digital and Atherton agreed to use ATIS as the basis for their software tools. Being primarily vendor initiated, it falls into the third category of standards origination. ATIS was developed as the first repository standard geared toward object-oriented development. Based on the perceived need for a standardized repository-based object-oriented approach, ATIS was presented to the ANSI X3H4 committee. At that time the standard was accepted by ANSI as a base document for the X3H4.2 IRDS Services Interface Subcommittee, and a project was started to develop an object-oriented repository standard. ATIS has since been incorporated into the IRDS services interface proposal, as mentioned previously.

Because ATIS assumes an underlying object-oriented model, its incorporation into IRDS extends the IRDS data model and expands the core IRDS facilities. Briefly, the IRDS services interface proposal addresses the following major areas:*

The Base Object Model Using an object-oriented paradigm, the base object model is presented as a type hierarchy. Because in the OO world each object is an instance of a class (or type), these classes are related to each other via a hierarchy, with the hierarchy depicting the concept of inheritance. Objects can have various states (over time), and the current state of an object is determined by the values of the associated attributes. The IRDS services interface considers *elements* to be objects, whereas *types* correspond to classes. Elements are manipulated via *messages*, with part of the base element definition (which includes behavior) defined via associated *methods*.

Because the details of object-oriented analysis and design are beyond the scope of this book, many readers may not already be familiar with the basics of the methodology.† Most object-oriented models are represented via a *schema* (similar in concept to a data model). The IRDS services interface takes the concept of the object-oriented schema to its most flexible level in that it is self-defining. Similar to the concept of meta-metadata, the metaschema describes both the objects (elements) and the object types. Simply speaking, self-definition allows the actual object types to be manipulated via the same mechanisms as their actual instances—hence the ability to extend the metaschema with additional object types. In terms of tool interface and integration, self-defining schemas allow this self-definition to occur based on the receipt of messages from one tool to another.

---

*"Future Direction for Evolution of IRDS Services Interface," Draft Proposal Document X3H4/92-161, September 15, 1992.

†See the References at the end of the book for additional object-oriented reading.

The object-oriented concepts of the IRDS services interface meet the base IRD schema as follows:

- Objects correspond to entities *and* their associated relationships.
- Object types correspond to metaentities *and* metarelationships.
- Various new element types (using the IRD term) have been added to the base IRD schema, including *message*, *method*, and *type*.

The Versioning Model This model describes the extensions necessary to support versioning.

The Configuration Management Model Here, extensions depict the required support for configuration management, that is, the depiction of system configurations.

The Work Flow Control Model Extensions for life cycle management of a system are covered here.

Tool Integration Facilities This section defines the necessary schema definition steps required to incorporate a new tool. It essentially covers the *tool registration* model. In the IRDS services environment, tools communicate by sending messages to elements in the repository.

In addition to the preceding, a generic IRDS services interface specification is included in the proposed standard.

In summary, ATIS can now be considered a part of the IRDS standard world. Products that conform to the original ATIS are still paramount, however. In fact, an ATIS standards unification effort has been in progress since late 1992, with the ultimate goal being that of a uniform ATIS standard to ensure client application portability and interim operability, because multiple variations do exist. This unification effort was customer driven.

■ AD/CYCLE*

Another effort worth mentioning (in its own category) is that of AD/Cycle (Application Development Cycle). This philosophy touts a repository-based application development environment in which any participating tool becomes "plug compatible," so to speak. The effort was spearheaded by IBM several years ago, and many debates exist today as to whether or not AD/Cycle is a set of tangible products or a mere product philosophy. Regardless, its establishment (with a variable set of International Alliance partners) had a major impact on the repository marketplace, and merits discussion as a "standard," although it is not officially a standards effort.

AD/Cycle consists of two major components: the repository-based application development architecture, as discussed previously, and an AD/Cycle Information Model (also called the AD/Information Model), which represents the metamodel of the underlying repository. When AD/Cycle was first introduced, the repository

*For a list of AD/Cycle specific publications, see the References at the end of the book.

at the heart of its architecture was the mainframe-based IBM Repository Manager/MVS (RM/MVS). The structure has since been changed to incorporate workstation-based application development via the planned introduction of a LAN-based equivalent, the implementation details of which (other than its planned object-oriented structure) have not been announced as of this writing. Because it is not the objective of this book to discuss specific vendor offerings, the focus of our AD/Cycle discussion will be the underlying information model.

AD/Cycle's Information Model is quite extensive in that it addresses virtually all aspects of application development, across several technical platforms. Its complexity and thoroughness have been considered a major attribute in that they allow for the incorporation of many independent vendor tool offerings. In fact, many consider the AD/Information Model to be the forerunner of repository metamodel definition.

The AD/Cycle Information Model is divided into separate submodels for ease of functional understanding. These submodels constitute one of three submodel categories:

- The *enterprise submodel* which contains all information pertaining to an enterprise, its goals, resources, business models, and logical application models and is itself divided into several component models
- The *technology submodels* which represent distinct physical implementations as well as models for end-user interface (EUI) and application configuration (APT)
- A *global submodel* which contains constructs common to all submodels, such as the generic storage of text and object "control"

The Enterprise Submodel

The enterprise submodel (ENT) is used to identify all aspects of enterprise modeling. Because of the wide functional coverage of the enterprise submodel, it has been divided into the following component models:

- *General constructs* which allow for the bridging of multiple enterprise models via a generic common model
- *Mission* which holds goal statements for an entire enterprise or portion thereof
- *Planning* which defines both long- and short-term enterprise strategies
- *Problem* which identifies an enterprise's uncertainties, complexities, and difficulties
- *Resource* which pertains to the enterprise's assets (facilities, services, etc.) that are used (or will be used) to complete a particular task or set of tasks
- *Organization* which depicts the physical enterprise—its elements and management structure
- *Business rule* which identifies business policies and other constraints
- *Subject area* which allows for the creation of high-level enterprise data models
- *Entity definition* which is used for all enterprise entities and their associated attributes

- *Data value definition* which supports the definition of values and symbols that may be associated with entity attributes
- *Basic entity–relationship* which handles the standard E–R model structure through entity–relationship depiction
- *Process* which handles logical process definitions as well as the components of data flows between processes
- *Derived descriptors* which represent complex data situations (e.g., indirect relationships)
- *Model constraints* which define any restrictions on data components
- *Flow content* which is used to associate information flows
- *Info submodel* which is used to partition enterprise data
- *Annotation* which is used for additional information, when necessary, for entity instances
- *Extension* which handles any user-implemented model extensions
- *Mapping* which takes care of relationships between enterprise submodel–defined constructs and any technology submodel occurrences
- *Object oriented* which is used to support object-oriented analysis, design, and programming

It is important to realize that, despite the existence of multiple component models as identified previously, they are still all part of one physical enterprise submodel. In this respect, occurrences of each component model are quite related to occurrences of other component models, based on their relationships within the overall enterprise submodel. However, the reader should be able to get a feel for the potential coverage of a well-implemented rendition of this model. The enterprise submodel typically represents all analysis-based aspects of application development.

Technology Submodels

The physical world of application development (programming languages, databases, user interface protocols, etc.) is represented in the AD/Cycle Information Model via a set of technology submodels, as follows:

- *Application programming and test (APT).* This submodel contains the information relevant to an application's physical structure. That is, those application parts that are necessary for an application's "build" routine are identified via this submodel. It is closely related to the other technology submodels in that the definitions of the application parts identified in APT are typically resident in the other submodels. In a typical APT scenario, all activities, links, procedures, calls, source code modules, files, database definitions, and so on, which must be put together to generate or build the completed application, are identified in this submodel.
- *IMS / VS (DLI).* IMS data base descriptors (DBDs) and program specification blocks (PSBs), as required for their specification and maintenance, are represented in this submodel.

- *Common relational database* (*DRC*). Those constructs common to both DB2 and SQL/DS are stored here. Some definitions are obviously shared with the following submodel via connected relationships.
- *MVS relational database* (*DRM*). This submodel is intended to support the design of DB2 databases. It requires the existence of the DRC submodel in order to be complete. In general, the DRM submodel contains the constructs necessary to generate DB2 database definition language (DDL).
- *End-user interface* (*EUI*). All information necessary for the implementation of an application's end-user interface is supported here. EUI design is not tracked here—rather the components of the actual end-user interface. This submodel has close relationships with the APT submodel discussed previously and the GLO and HLL models discussed next.
- *Global* (*GLO*). Those constructs common to all models are resident here. Specifically, the handling of text as well as the control of repository constructs via associated methods are taken care of by this submodel. In addition, this submodel handles the relationships of repository instances to external non-repository resident pieces of data (i.e., the relationship of the entity CUSTOMER to an external IMS DBD).
- *High-level languages* (*HLL*). Source code data objects are defined in this submodel. As of this writing, only COBOL II is supported.

The reader's evaluation of the AD/Cycle Information Model should be based on the model's potential impact as the backbone of a well-implemented repository. Its high-level structure was presented as part of our standards chapter because efforts are currently underway to incorporate aspects of the model into the CDIF standard.

■ STANDARDS UNIFICATION?

Because of the obvious overlap that exists among all of the aforementioned "standards" efforts, it should come as no surprise that efforts are currently underway to consolidate many aspects into one universal standard. Of course, each standards committee has a vested interest in seeing that its standard becomes *the standard*. They do agree on one objective, however—the use of the same meta-model and export/import format!

■ SUMMARY

With the variety of repository-molding standards that currently exist in today's world, it is not surprising that vendors rarely devote themselves to full support of any one of them. However, each standards effort, despite its overlap with segments of other efforts, should be evaluated in terms of its intent. Repositories are only successful when they are consistently accessed and maintained within an organization. Imagine the exponential increase in their resourcefulness when this consistency crosses organizational boundaries. Standards are the only path to this ultimate goal.

21

DISTRIBUTED REPOSITORIES

If we are to perceive all the implications of the new, we must risk, at least temporarily, ambiguity and disorder.

J. J. Gordon, 1983

Repositories can be thought of in a different perspective when we consider the possibility that they do not necessarily have to consist of one centralized base. Because one of the major trends of the 1990's is the downsizing of the MIS application world, the repository must be evaluated as part of this trend. Even without this categorization, a distributed repository offers an organization the ability to start small by functionally segmenting the potential roles of a repository within the MIS organization.

MAINFRAME VS. LAN ARCHITECTURAL DIFFERENCES

When attempting to differentiate the distributed repository from the centralized mainframe repository, the first criterion is that of the repository architecture. Another 1990s buzzword is *client/server*, and similar to *repository*, it has yet to be defined consistently in the vendor community. Because any processor (regardless of size, operating platform, or processing capacity) can technically be either a client or a server (or both) in a systems architecture, immense flexibility exists when it comes to establishing an overall architecture for application development and execution as well as determining where a repository (or repositories) should fit in.

When discussing repository "architecture," it must be considered in terms of the components mentioned in our repository definition (see Chap. 18). Each component should be evaluated from these distinct functional perspectives:

- The architecture (centralized or distributed) of the repository's contents, including the metamodel
- The architecture of the functional processes required to use and access the repository's contents
- The logical point of control

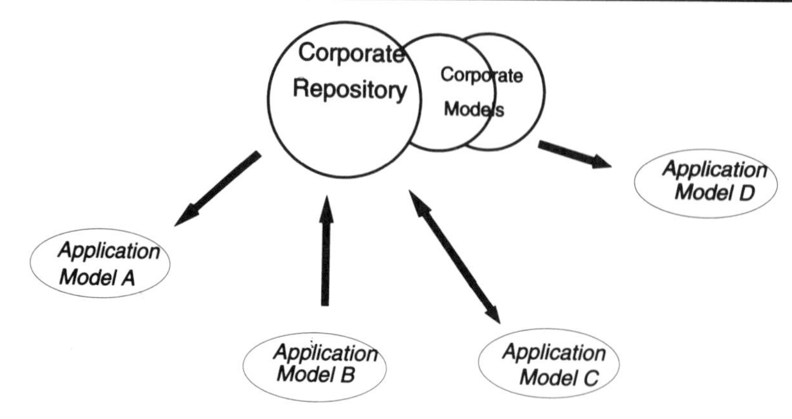

Figure 21.1 The centralized repository.

In a distributed repository the logical point of control gets the repository user from any one point within the distributed architecture to any other logical architectural location. This concept is the key to allowing true distributed repository access and functionality.

Repository Contents: Mainframe vs. LAN

Considering what is stored in a repository, perhaps the major difference between mainframe repositories and their sub-mainframe counterparts is that, from both an architectural as well as a "point of control" perspective, mainframe repositories offer few options.

As illustrated in Fig. 21.1, mainframe repositories were assumed to be the only game in town when they were first implemented. Before the advent of client/server technology, repositories were basically mainframe offerings only. They typically started as data dictionaries, and, as interfaces with other tools were built, dictionary contents expanded to describe aspects of the MIS world beyond data. Despite the enlarged coverage of the populated contents, the repository's design typically precluded the existence of complementary repositories. If any "complementary" storage areas interfaced with the central repository, they typically represented internal encyclopedias or databases of an interfacing tool. Figure 21.1 illustrates the average centralized repository architecture. In this example the mainframe serves as the resting place for corporate models, and individual application models, as they are being developed, reside on interfacing workstations.

As the current trend toward downsizing began to penetrate MIS, traditional repository vendors (those with mainframe offerings only) saw the need to refocus their market positions. With an installed base of mainframe repository clients moving application development and the applications themselves off of the mainframe, the vendors' perception of the mainframe as the only place for repository-based information was seen as a potential handicap. In addition, competing offerings of "sub-mainframe" LAN-based repositories were beginning to surface.

The era of client/server computing put the contents of mainframe repositories into a new architectural perspective.

The architectural role of the mainframe repository's contents changes when it coexists with other repositories. Instead of serving as the resting place for corporate models, the mainframe repository now serves as the *integrated* resting place for corporate models.

As illustrated in Fig. 21.2, the mainframe repository's purpose changes with the existence of local repositories. Consider Fig. 21.1 representative of a very large development organization. Each "local repository" was implemented as a necessity based purely on the number of developers involved with each major application. Local Repository A represents the integrated set of information which supports the reengineering on the company's accounting systems. Included in this repository are the multiple CASE-based models that depict the old systems as well as those that are currently being developed as blueprints for their replacement. The local repository will also be used to store code releases and track their effectiveness throughout the system testing and field trial processes. However, this repository is truly local. No one outside of the involved developers has access to its contents. In addition, it contains only the information of interest to those who are reengineering the accounting applications.

Local Repository B is used by the data administration group. It was implemented based on the need for multimodeler access to distinct application data models developed in several different CASE tools. The data administration group, which is in the process of developing a corporate data model, is constantly comparing models from tool users of differing originating skill sets.

Finally, Server C is not really a repository in that it represents a shareable decision support implementation. Executives use LAN-based decision support software to query a server-resident database that represents an integration of several daily extracts of select mainframe-based corporate databases.

In this illustrated scenario the mainframe repository is the only place where the relationships between all of these local implementations exist. The integrated corporate picture which relates the accounting system reengineering work to existing applications and interfacing databases can only be obtained via the mainframe repository. There are many other potential roles for the mainframe repository's contents when they are considered as adjuncts to their existing "local" sub-mainframe counterparts. As we will see in Part Five, the mainframe's role in a distributed architectural environment directly affects both short- and long-term repository implementation strategies.

The contents of mainframe repositories can therefore participate in distinctly different repository architectures:

- They can be part of the "only" repository; that is, they represent the centralized single source of information.
- They can represent the "integrated" repository; that is, they can coexist with the contents of subordinate repositories, each representing a distinct aspect of the bigger picture which only the mainframe repository contains. The implications of such an architecture will be covered later in the chapter.

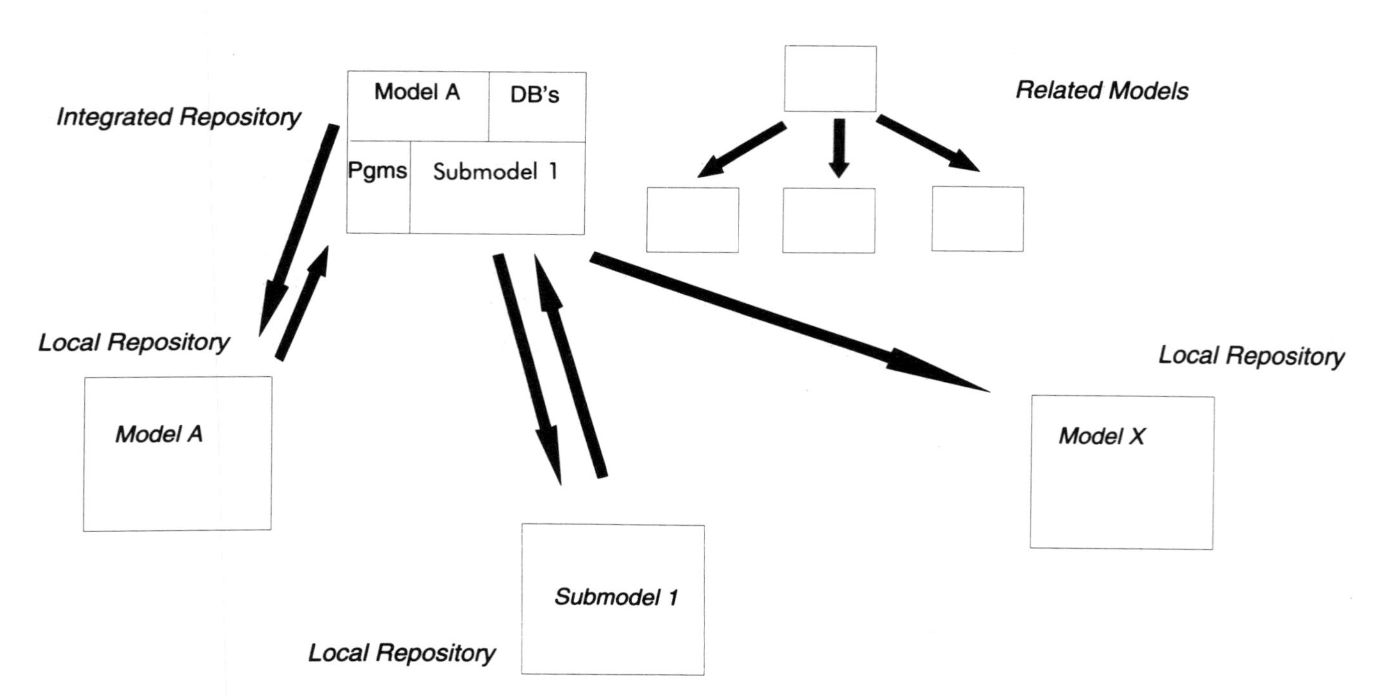

Figure 21.2 The mainframe integrated repository.

Supporting Repository Functionality: Mainframe vs. LAN

Aside from the distinct differences in the functional role of the repository contents, the supporting application functionality, which is required to use and access the repository's contents, has limited architectural options when the mainframe repository is the *only* repository. Most database applications are divided into four distinct architectural components when they are being considered for downsizing:

- The database itself
- Database-specific processing logic (the CRUD* of the database)
- Application logic (the actual application programs that process the data)
- Presentation logic (graphical user interfaces, menus, screens, and reports that represent the inputs and outputs to and from the application)

Early mainframe repository offerings handled all of the preceding supporting functionality themselves. Many, with proprietary databases, had no choice. Even the later product offerings, based on commercial relational databases, still handled all of the supporting logic via mainframe-based application code. As personal computers (PCs) became common desktop equipment, many of these mainframe dictionary/repository vendors began to offer PC-based "front ends." With this functionality the user had the option of handling the repository's presentation logic via workstation software. Still, the rest of the repository's functionality was handled on the mainframe. Every request for information, even though initiated at the workstation, involved the transmission of a request to the mainframe as well as the receipt of data from the mainframe.

As illustrated in Fig. 21.3, many mainframe repository products now offer compatible workstation (PC) software. However, this software is rarely representative of true client/server functionality. Typically, it is functionally equivalent to terminal emulation with a graphical user interface (GUI). For example, a workstation-initiated request for a subset of repository-resident data results ideally in a downloaded file, a display of the file's contents on the workstation, and the option to either save or delete the data. True client/server processing would allow the data to become the "substitute" database and therefore be available for subsequent repository queries. This client functionality would eliminate the need for constant mainframe-targeted requests. As of this writing most mainframe repositories do not allow this functionality. Therefore, today, the supporting processing for mainframe repositories is implemented in one of two ways:

- Entirely on the mainframe (all repository contents and the supporting process functionality)
- On the mainframe, with the exception of the presentation logic, which is handled via PC front ends.

---

*Create, read, update, delete.

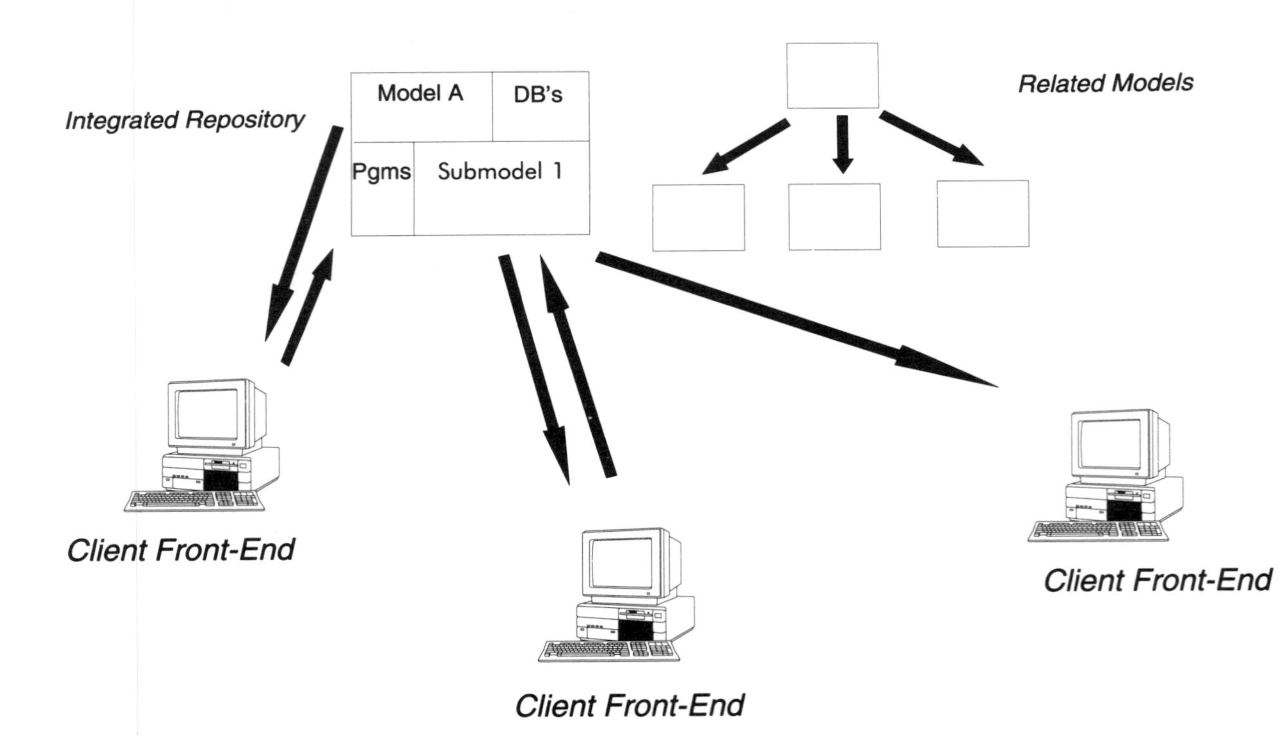

Figure 21.3 The mainframe repository with a "client" front end.

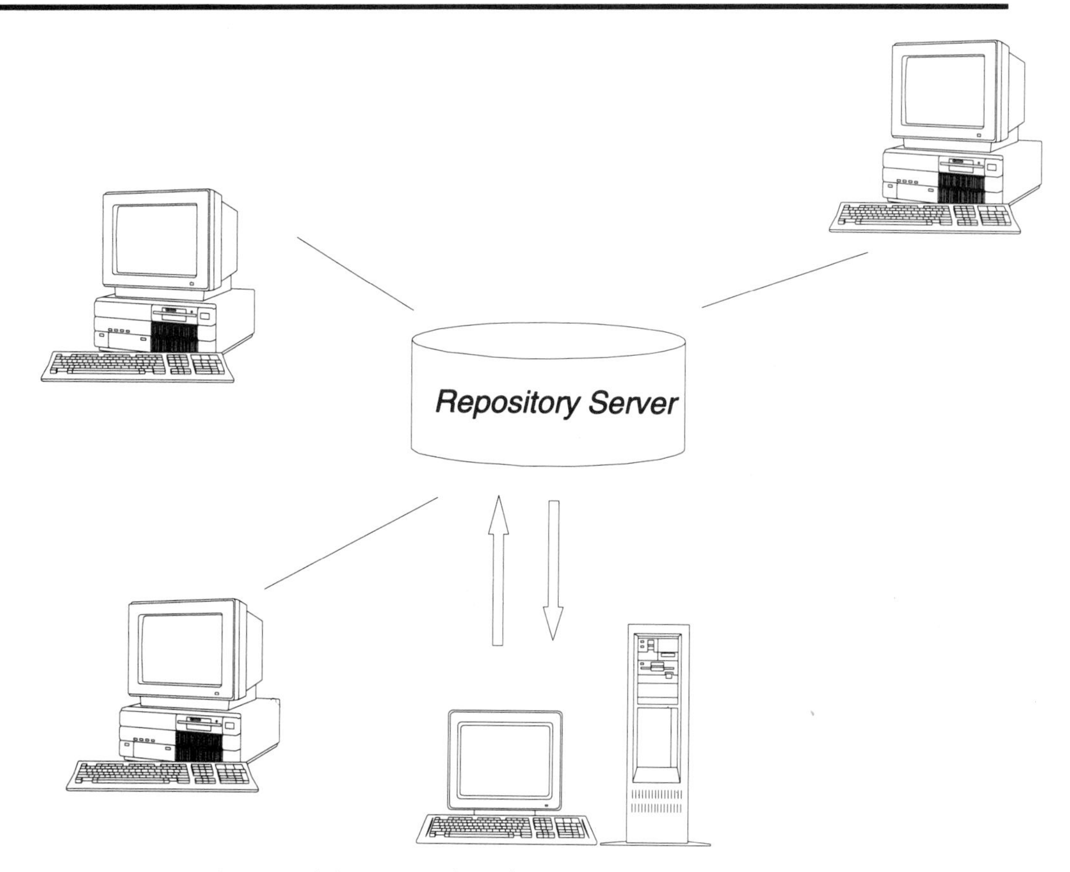

Figure 21.4 The "standalone" LAN-based repository.

LAN-Based Repository Contents

What about LAN-based repositories? From an architectural perspective, they can represent either standalone implementations (similar to a centralized mainframe architecture, only with a much smaller client scope) or part of a more widespread distributed implementation. As we discussed previously, the participation of a sub-mainframe repository can potentially affect the repository architecture in terms of the repository's contents and in terms of the supporting processing.

Before discussing the potential breakdown and distribution of the repository's functional roles, consider the multiple ways in which LAN-based repositories can physically exist. As illustrated in Fig. 21.4, a LAN-based repository can share the same perspective and position as a centralized mainframe repository. Perhaps the scope of the repository's contents may not be corporate; the repository could represent the holding area for a major application reengineering effort, for example. Or perhaps the scope *is* corporate; smaller businesses may not even be in the market or potential market for a mainframe.

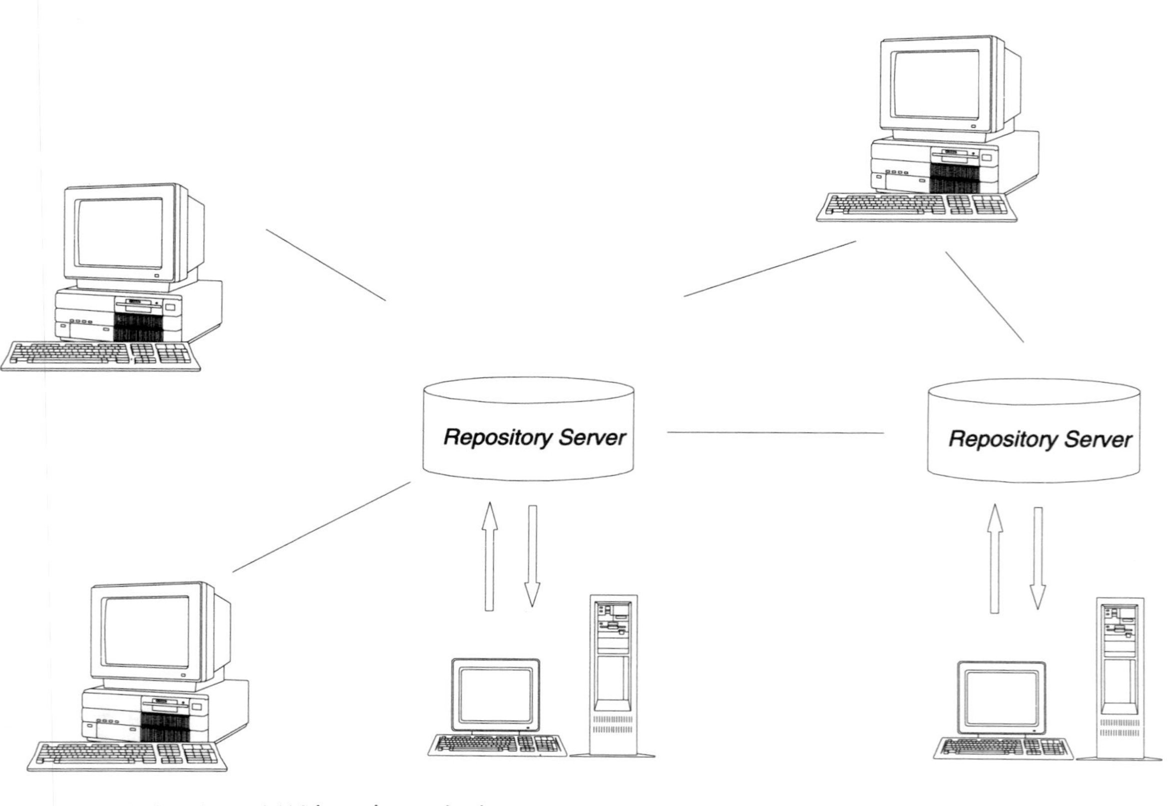

Figure 21.5 Coexistent LAN-based repositories.

Once the need to delve beyond a single-server implementation becomes apparent, as illustrated in Fig. 21.5 multiple repositories result.* Enter the complexity. As we will discuss at the end of this chapter, the issues of distributed data management now become a potential concern. Already, the contents of the repository can be spread across the multiple implementations in a variety of ways:

- In a *standalone* manner, that is, each repository contains information that exists nowhere else. The contents are separate, segmented, and not related to each other from either a functional or logical perspective.
- In a *linked* manner, that is, each repository contains unique information that is related to the contents of another repository of unique information.
- In a *redundant* manner, with separate repositories containing identical information. Each repository may or may not be related to any others aside from the existence of common data.

Aside from the data management issues which are obvious in all but the first of the preceding scenarios, the issue of whether or not the mainframe (or an equivalent *repository of record*) exists in the overall architecture is also a major consideration. Figure 21.6 illustrates the mainframe repository of record. Here, various local repositories are connected and managed through the mainframe repository. Each local repository represents a distinct functional use of a subset of the corporate models. Model components exist redundantly across the various local repositories. Yet, because the mainframe repository is the "official" repository, control and management require its participation as both a supplier and integrator of any local repository's contents.

Without a mainframe, data management and control are still issues when the various repositories are related or contain redundant data. Typically, one of the local repositories becomes "corporate" in this respect. At a minimum, it serves as the controller and overseer of the multiple repositories' contents. At its fullest functionality, it also represents the roadmap and integrator of the various subordinate repositories. The various data management issues will be discussed at the end of this chapter.

LAN-Based Repository Supporting Functionality

The scenarios depicted in the previous section focused on the repository's contents (the database itself) and the multiple ways in which they can be architectured on sub-mainframe server platforms. The supporting functionality (CRUD, application, and presentation logic) offers even more diverse scenarios in terms of distribution possibilities. This chapter will discuss the possibilities from a theoretical viewpoint. The practicalities will be covered in Part Five.

The most debated topic in distributed repository architectural implementation is the distribution of the database processing logic. Unfortunately, the decision as to

*The implementation specifics of distributed repositories will be discussed in Part Five.

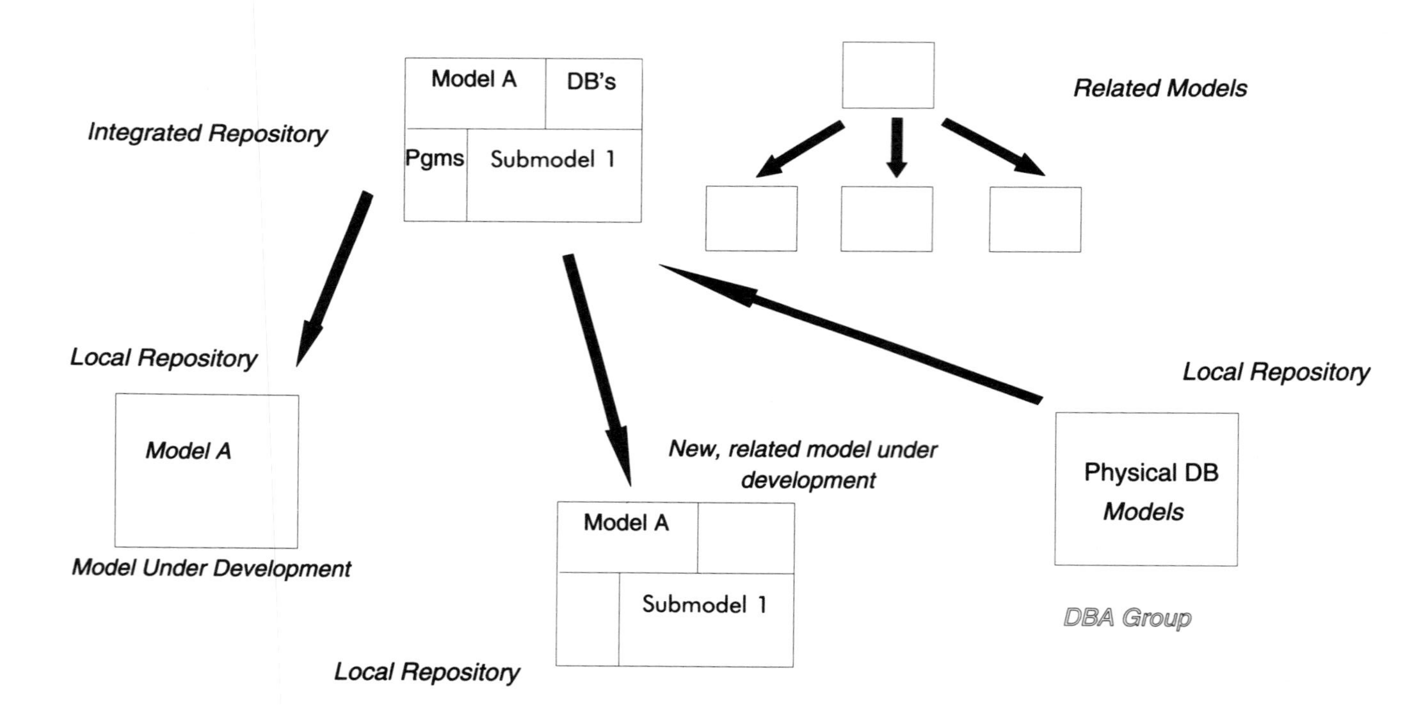

Figure 21.6 The mainframe repository of record.

whether it belongs on the client or the server depends on many factors, and may in fact not even be an option in some scenarios. Specifically, not all DBMSs (or proprietary databases) have the ability to separate the database from the associated access logic. If this is the case with the to-be-implemented repository package, then the decision has already been made. Wherever the database resides, the database processing logic will also reside.

If database access can exist remotely from the actual database, the access logic most typically is implemented at the client platform. This would be true regardless of how many distinct databases needed to be accessed by the client, and regardless of how the databases were physically distributed. Most repositories that are intended for a distributed architecture, however, rely on a commercial DBMS as their backbone. Distributed database products assume their implementation on a *database server*, that is, a server dedicated purely to the needs of the underlying database, including the associated processing logic. Simply speaking, the difference between client- and server-based database processing logic lies in where the actual request for data, as represented in the DBMS language, originates and where it is actually processed (see Fig. 21.7). For example, in client-based database processing, a user initiates a request for database access (not necessarily in the data manipulation language [DML] of the DBMS). It is translated, validated, and parsed, with only the native DBMS functions being sent to the server-resident DBMS. When the database processing logic is delegated to the remote database server, this entire process is handled at the server (as part of the database server architecture). This distinction is true regardless of how many distinct databases (and how many distinct servers) need to be accessed.

Application logic is hard to separate from database processing logic when discussing repositories. In typical database applications the application logic refers to the processing that occurs before or after database access. Assume the implementation of a commercial DBMS as the repository backbone. If this is the case, the application logic deals with the translation of a user-initiated repository access request into the multiple database processing requests that must result. For example, if a user requests a list of all programs that access the Customer database, application logic would be required to translate the request, as received from the tool interface or interfacing application, into the distinct and related database queries that would need to ensue. This translation does not necessarily immediately result in DBMS-specific language (e.g., SQL). Further translation may occur with database processing logic. Or, taking a few steps closer to the user-initiated request, application logic could be required to translate some of the presentation-specific request parameters into a more generic application-like set of "code."

Ideally, application logic should be functionally split between both clients and servers. The logic that is executed as a direct result of presentation-based requests obviously belongs with the client, whereas the application logic that is closely linked to the resulting database processing belongs with the database processing logic (which could reside on either the client or the server).

Finally, presentation logic deals with what the repository user sees—as repository inputs and repository outputs. Realizing that most repository users do not interface with the repository directly (they interface via tools), this aspect of the

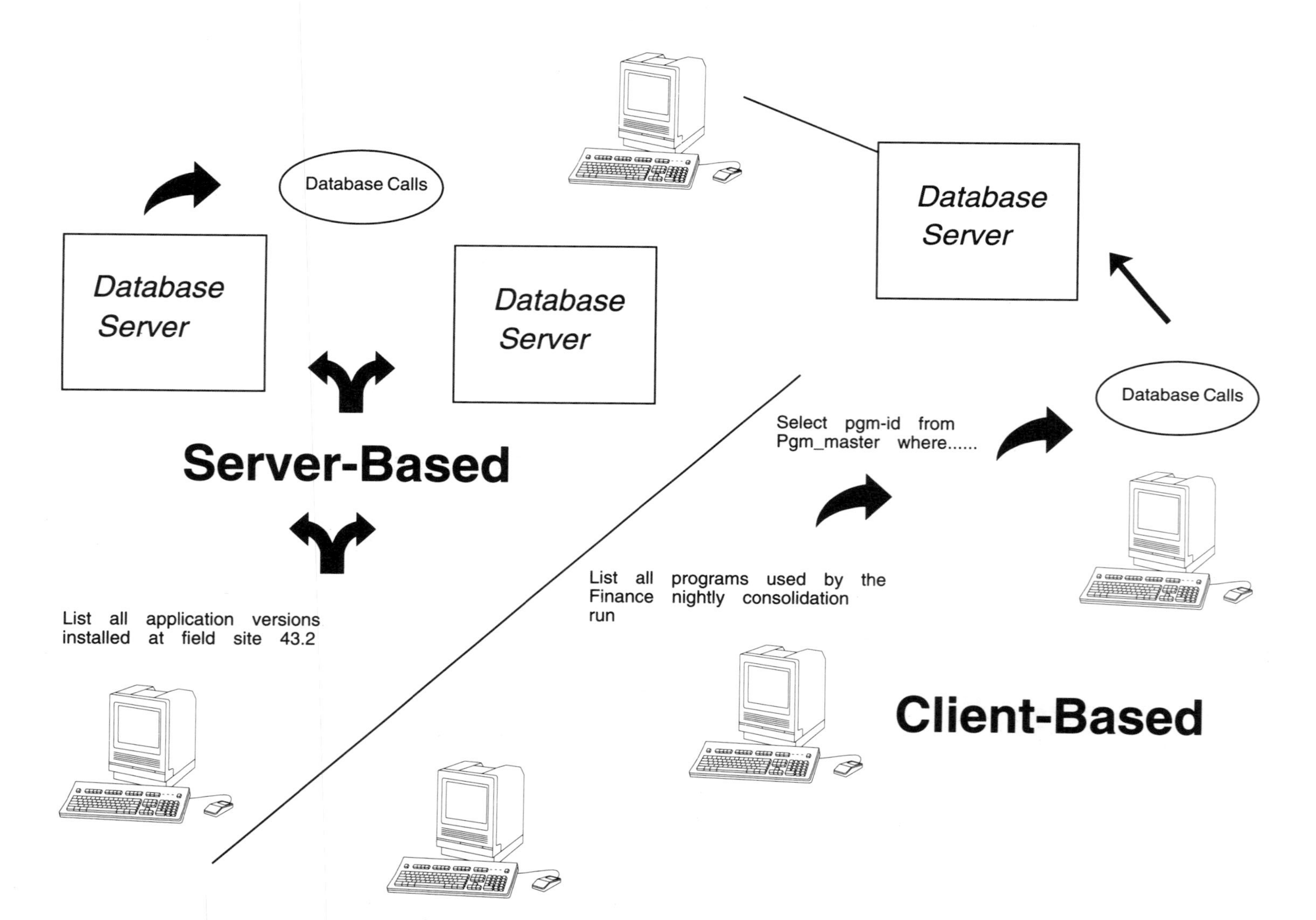

Figure 21.7 Client vs. server-based database processing logic.

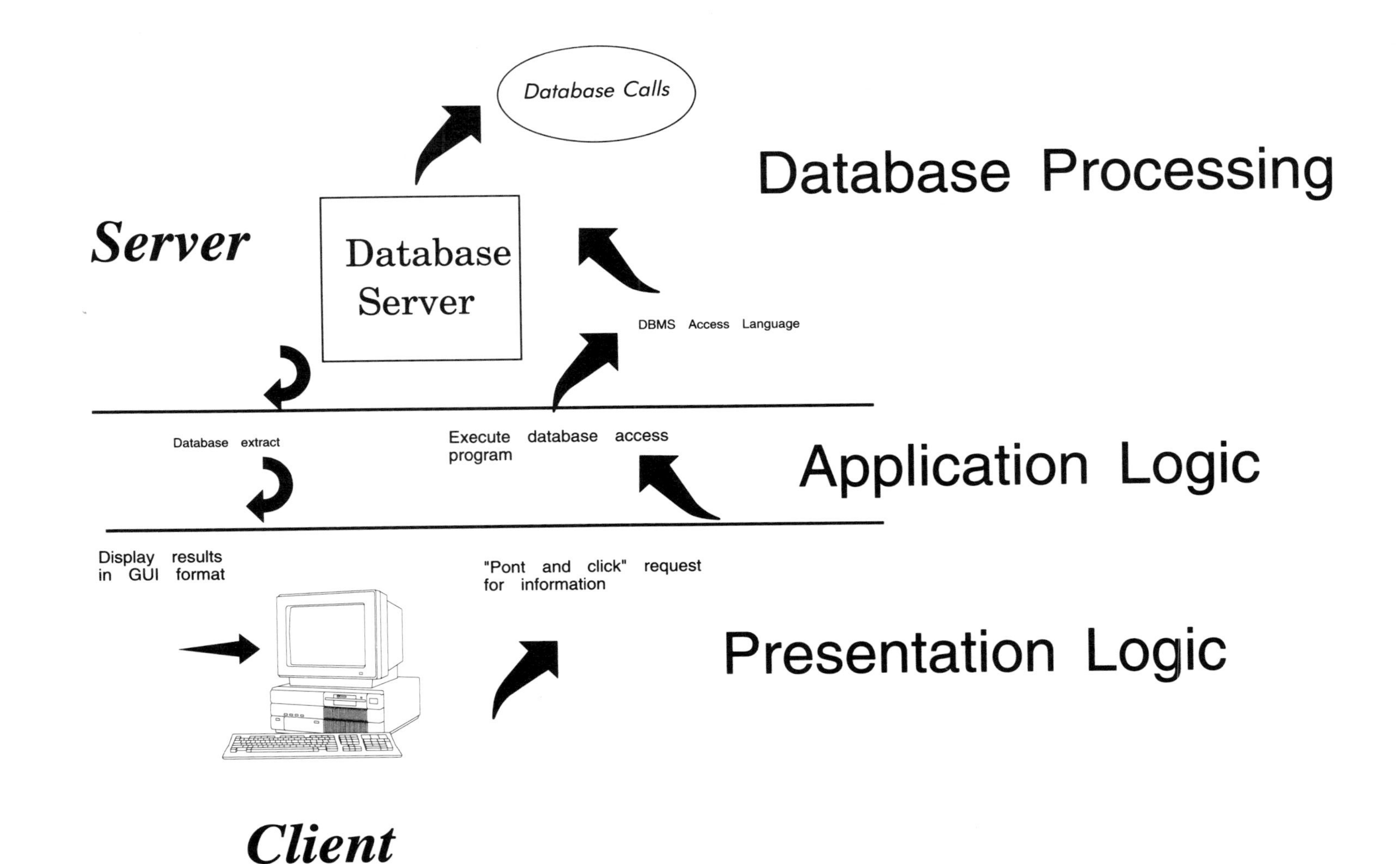

Figure 21.8 An example of a distributed repository support architecture.

distributed repository affects repository administrators primarily. Most presentation logic is implemented at the client side of the distributed architecture (see Fig. 21.8). In fact, the existing workstation-based front ends to mainframe repository offerings are perfect examples of this scenario.

Despite the fact that a theoretical discussion allows us to separate the multiple types of processing from the underlying database in client/server applications, the practical perspective reminds us that repositories generally come as packaged tools. Most of the architectural decisions (placing respective processing types at either the client level, the server level, or both) are made by the respective vendor. However, when implementing a corporate repository, as we will see in Part Five, many customization possibilities are left to the implementing organization. It is for this reason that we have discussed the theoretical issues involved.

■ LINKED VS. STANDALONE REPOSITORIES

Once repositories become part of a connected framework, data management issues must be considered. The types of data management problems that could arise are dependent on just how each repository's contents interrelate as well as the methods by which each repository is loaded and subsequently kept up to date. In addition, simple requests for multirepository sourced data can often prove to be a performance bottleneck in inadequately designed distributed repository architectures. Aside from the obvious concern of keeping the multiple repositories in sync with each other, the basic question of just where and how to distribute the company's information across multiple repositories is one that deserves considerable forethought.

Although distributed database design is beyond the scope of this book,* the same basic principles of how to best segment database contents apply equally to distributed repositories. Briefly, the repository should be evaluated in terms of its planned functional role. The information necessary to support this planned functionality will typically come from multiple sources. By creating a matrix that maps the type of information to be stored in the repository with its suppliers and its target users, functional groupings will result. A sample functional matrix is shown in Fig. 21.9. Consider each functional grouping as a potential local repository setup. In this way, those who are most concerned with specific aspects of the repository's overall contents have the subset within their realm of access. Next, consider the types of requests that would require the access of other member repositories. Consider the relationship between these requests, the "local" requests, and where the information becomes common. Depending on the expected frequency and volume of these distributed requests, the repository architect can appreciate the validity and potential usefulness of the planned repository segmentation. If most requests can be fulfilled "locally," the initial distribution plan is a worthy one.

---

*For additional readings on distributed database design, see the References at the end of the book.

Information Type	Suppliers	Target Users
Application documentation	Application developers	Application developers
Data element definitions	Data administration	Data administration, decision support end-users
Production abends	Application developers	DP operations
Organization charts	Personnel	Upper-level executives

Figure 21.9 A sample functional matrix for determining repository segmentation.

Linked repositories are related to each other in one or more of the following ways:

By Common Keys (or Indices) Following the well-respected rules for normalization, both primary and foreign keys can be used to relate multiple repositories from both a logical and a physical perspective. Although the concept is easy to envision in a distributed database scenario, it becomes slightly complicated when we are relating repositories. Depending on how the repository's underlying database is physically implemented (i.e., the underlying database design), a common key could be represented by any of the following:

- A metadata construct name (e.g., entity)
- A metadata construct instance (e.g., an entity name, such as CUSTOMER)
- A submodel name (e.g., an ACCTS-RCVBL application)

There are many more common "keys" that can be defined (see Fig. 21.10).

Although the specifics as to how repository segmentation relates to the underlying repository metamodel will be discussed in Part Five, it is important for the reader to appreciate the immense flexibility that exists in terms of commonality among the separate repositories.

Instance Data Segmentation Separate repositories can share identical designs in terms of both their metamodel and their actual database implementation. The differing aspects of each local implementation could be based entirely on the populated contents of each repository. For example, consider a large data administration organization. The assignment of data element names and the handling of all data requests are conducted on a departmental basis. Each department has a local data administration function and processes all requests based on the existence of a local repository which contains all pertinent information about that department's applications and databases. The departmental functional separation is centrally

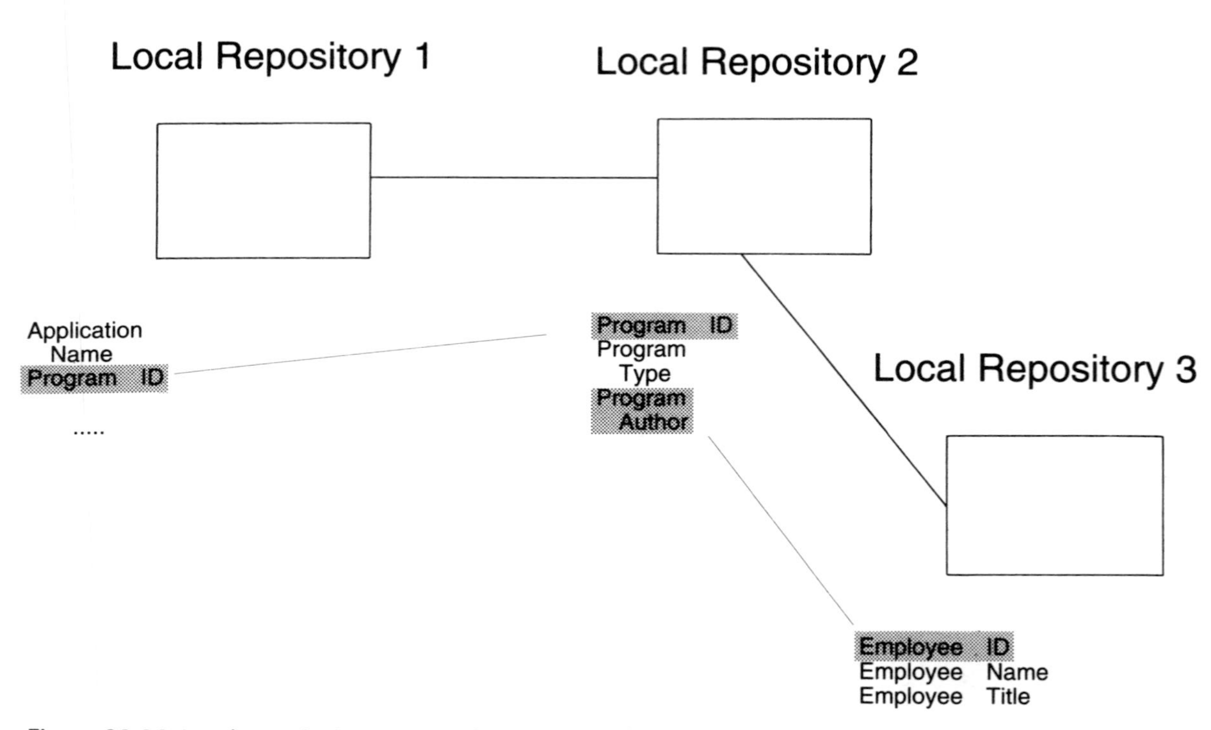

Figure 21.10 Local repositories connected via common keys.

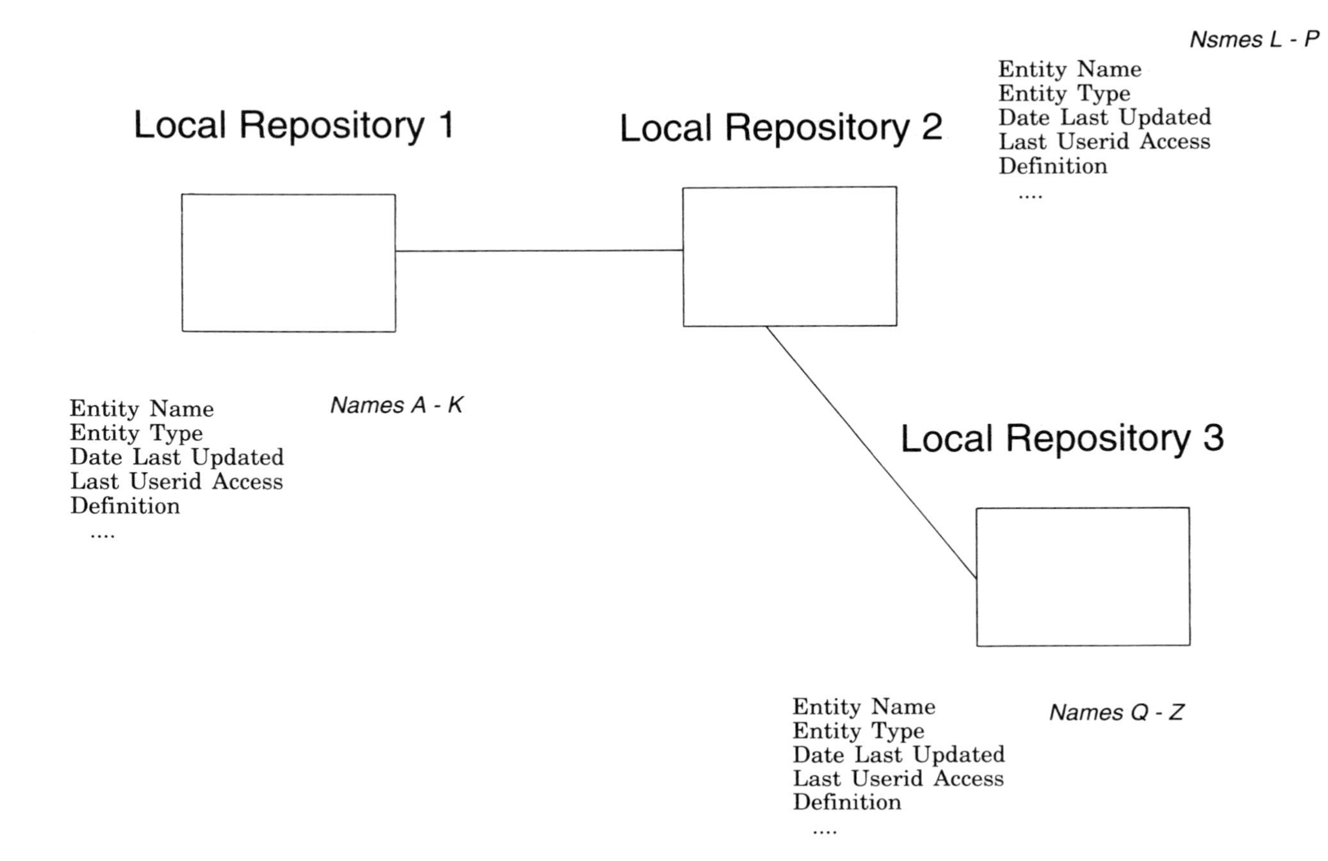

Figure 21.11 Local repositories segmented by value.

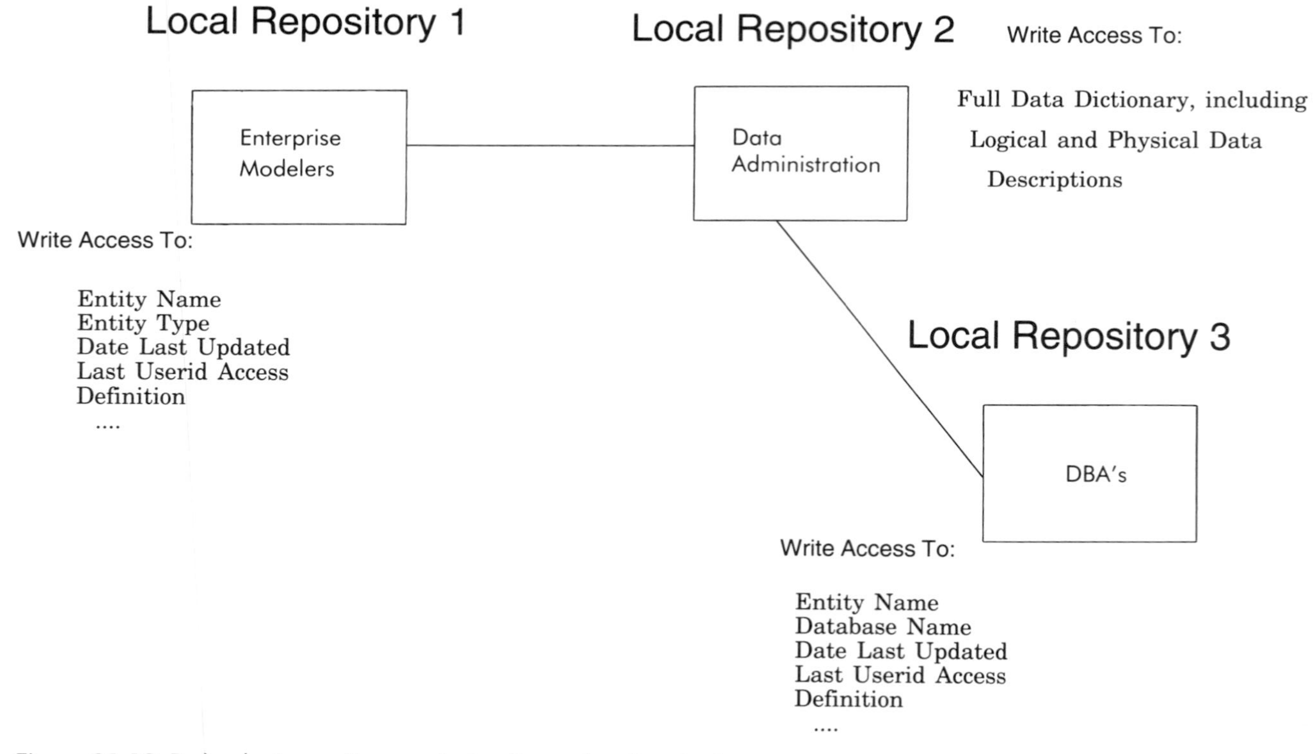

Figure 21.12 Redundant repository contents, diverse functional roles.

controlled, however. In fact, data element names are indicative of the responsible department based on the first three characters (ACT for accounting, PER for personnel, etc.). Without debating whether or not this is the ideal method of data administration, this naming convention provided an easy way of separating the repository contents into their distinct local components. Each department's repository is loaded with only those data element names for which it is responsible. When requests for new data elements are presented to the departmental representatives, or when the representatives receive requests for data that are not within their realm of control, the repositories of other departments are queried. An example appears in Fig. 21.11.

Diverse Functional Role / Redundant Data Segmentation As with the previous example, each repository in this situation shares the same metamodel and underlying database design. They also share the same instance data. What separates each implemented repository is the implemented security levels and integrity rules that are in effect at each local site. Perhaps one of the local repositories exists for read-only access by end-users, whereas another is maintained by the repository administration group with full update permission. The read-only local repository is updated at the end of each business day (see Fig. 21.12).

Once repositories are "linked," data management issues must be considered. Regardless of how the repositories relate to each other, there must be one master source of data (the controlling repository so to speak) which tracks and ensures the consistency among all populated interrepository relationships. It is not necessary for this "controlling repository" to contain the integrated copy of each local repository once connected. However, it must be aware of the following:

1. The distinctions between each local repository in terms of its implemented metamodels, the range and scope of its populated instance data, as well as the source(s) of the instance data
2. The relationships among the repositories as well as the rules for enforcing multirepository data integrity
3. The security levels in effect at each local repository implementation

In effect, the "controlling repository" tracks each local repository implementation as if it were a local application (similar to configuration management packages). The information is often tracked via the population of a controlling metamodel that contains submodels representative of each local repository's implementation.

■ SUMMARY

In this chapter we introduced the distributed repository. Its architectural flexibility allows organizations to begin their repository implementation efforts on a smaller, less expensive scale. However, as with centralized repositories, an overall plan is still a necessary prerequisite. The next chapter, the final chapter in Part Four, will portray the benefits of a well-implemented repository by depicting repository-based application development via an example.

22

REPOSITORY BENEFITS

The sad truth is that excellence makes people nervous.

Shana Alexander, 1970

Imagine the impact on the application development process when the answers to virtually all of the developer's questions are available on the desktop. No more phone calls to people who refer the developer to others who simply have no idea. No more interdepartmental "work sessions" where all those who simply have no idea band together to try and figure things out. As if this concept is too hard to believe, imagine further that the products of an application developer have a useful life that extends beyond a single application. Imagine the same application developer having access to the products that resulted from other application development efforts. Imagine an application being put together without every component being coded from scratch, in an enforced standardized manner.

If you have not decided to skip this chapter yet, keep imagining. The believers among us know that all of these concepts are not beyond the realm of reality. In fact, by considering application development as the business equivalent of any manufacturing process (e.g., automobile manufacturing), it would not be unusual for even the custom applications (the custom cars) to consist of common parts as well as some custom-developed components. What is missing in the MIS world and what makes us all snicker at the concept of "application assembly" is the inventory of all of the available "parts" and the schematic of how to put them all together. Perhaps we should consider the repository as the starting place and the holder of all of this information.

■ APPLICATION DEVELOPMENT USING A REPOSITORY

To bring our imaginations back to reality, our repository-based application development example is a practical one. We will start with a repository that becomes populated as each application becomes fully defined. In other words, the existing application world is not yet fully reflected in the repository.

The following example should serve to illustrate the practical benefits of repository-based application development. Specifically, readers should notice the effects of the following repository-oriented development characteristics:

- The repository as the only centrally accessible source of application documentation, including application models, designs, and specifications, program source, database definitions, logical data models, and physical design models, and production job streams
- The use and availability of "capture tools" to provide first-cut documentation of many undocumented legacy systems
- A repository-bridged set of development tools, that is, all tools that were part of standard application development practices with interfaces to and from the repository
- Accurate project time and cost estimates based on the use of repository-referenced application development actuals
- A standardized approach to application development and maintenance, with repository access as the first step

As you read through this example, consider how each step of the development process is aided by the existence of the repository. Consider also how the repository is improved as this application progresses. Finally, compare this hypothetical example with the process in place in your development organization.

The User Need

Begin with the user-initiated need for a new application. In our example the accounts-payable department has been under pressure due to its slowness in the payment of bills. The interest expense incurred last year due to late payments was the highest ever. In fact, an audit of this company's payments proved that 90 percent of its received invoices were not paid on time. Of the incurred late payments, 50 percent had accrued at least 2 months worth of interest charges. The director of finance has been instructed to reduce the incurred interest expense by at least 40 percent during the current year.

Based on an internal audit of the accounts-payable department's procedures, it became apparent that the processes involved in paying invoices were quite bureaucratic. In addition, very little of the process had been mechanized. The director of finance therefore approached the MIS department with the following requests:

1. Company employees responsible for authorizing payment of received invoices need the ability to enter their authorization on line, with the authorization containing the following information:

    - The date of the invoice, the invoice number, and the payee's name, address, and internal vendor number, if it exists

- The authorizing employee's employee number
- The invoice amount and the amount authorized for payment
- If the full invoice amount was not authorized, the reason (up to one page of text)

2. Accounts-payable clerks need to access all of this information in order to issue the appropriate checks. The accounts-payable clerk must also input the date of approval and the check amount and have this information associated with the same invoice record. Once an approval has been granted, a record will be created containing all of the necessary information required for the batch check-writing system. All records will be fed to the check-writing system on a nightly basis.
3. Once a check has been issued, the check-writing system will update the accounts-payable invoice record with the check number, amount, and date issued.
4. Accounts-payable clerks need on-line access to all information discussed thus far. The information should be available on line for a rolling period of 1 year. The clerks should have the ability to query this information based on variable inputs such as:

   - *Authorizing employee id.* A list of all invoices approved by a particular employee along with associated details such as date, invoice amount, and so forth
   - *Vendor number.* A list of invoices associated with a particular vendor along with the associated invoice details
   - *Check number.* All information pertaining to whether or not a particular check had been issued along with its associated invoice
   - *Invoice number.* Obvious requests, such as whether or not an invoice had been paid, if not, why not, and if so, the date, check number, and amount

The MIS Initiative

Upon receipt of this request, the MIS director delegated the design responsibility to the analyst responsible for financial systems. New MIS application development practices were evolving based on the existence of a repository. A repository administration group had been formed, and a phased implementation plan was in place for the repository's population. All analysts and developers had been instructed to refer to and use the repository as follows:

- Repository administrators were to be notified once the design models for new applications were completed. Likewise, once the coding phase was complete, repository administrators needed to be informed.
- Any development efforts (both new and maintenance) that required access to the contents of existing databases (either logical or physical contents) should depend on the repository for that information.

- Any changes to existing applications required repository update before moving into production. The program library was no longer directly accessible to developers. Access to the source code library was only via the repository.

As the request was evaluated by the assigned systems analyst, she realized the immediate need to do the following:

- Confirm that this request represented the best solution possible by reviewing the current invoice payment procedures and the role of the check-writing system.
- Determine the state of the check-writing system: its software and hardware platform as well as the existence of any scheduled enhancements.
- Establish an application development plan and schedule.

The remainder of this application development example will stress the repository-related activities. In fact, those steps that were aided by the repository's existence (the results obtained were more accurate and/or more timely because of it, or its impact would be felt by another benefactor down the line) have been typeset in *italics*. By no means should the reader get the impression that other application development steps were deliberately eliminated or minimized in terms of their importance.

The systems analyst reviewed current invoice payment procedures. She determined that the implementation of the requests presented by the director of finance would provide only a short-term solution in that the turnaround time for invoice payment would be shorter. However, what would be missing would be the long-term benefit of permanently capturing vendor- and service-specific payment totals. This information was of strategic value to upper management. In fact, the systems analyst had been involved in several decision support system proposal meetings where requests for this type of information had been initiated. Based on the immediate and short-term requirement of interest expense reduction, it was decided to postpone the "data capture" ability to a later phase of the project.

A repository request for information on the check-writing system returned the following facts:

- The check-writing system is a batch mainframe COBOL application consisting of 29 programs.
- It was moved into production in 1980. Maintenance requests were implemented through 1982, and the system has remained relatively stable since then.
- There are no plans for system upgrade.
- Logical design documents, specifications, and other application models do not exist in the repository.

The systems analyst discussed the status of the check-writing system with the repository administration group. Specifically, because she was interested in preserving some of the information that would potentially come from this application (for decision support purposes), she wanted it documented in the repository (at least a data model). *Repository administration agreed to run the source and file descriptions through its source code analysis and data capture tools. Because these tools had bridges to the repository, the results would be populated.* Repository administration reminded her that the results would be "first cut" and not necessarily 100 percent accurate. The systems analyst agreed that this was better than nothing.

The logical design of the new accounts-payable processing system was developed in the analyst's workstation-based CASE tool. The project plan and schedule were documented in her desktop word processor. When both were final (the director of finance had agreed to the design, scope, and duration of the project), they were presented to repository administration. *Repository administration suggested some changes to the CASE-based models in order to make them more consistent with others that had been developed by other application analysts. In addition, repository administration requested that the analyst relate each project step (as itemized in the project plan) and its associated time frame to the specific functions within the application that would result. All of this information was to be exported, using each tool's export mechanisms, and uploaded to the repository host when complete.*

As the design was completed, it was loaded (along with the project plan and its associations) into the repository. The analyst's application responsibilities had lessened. Some aspects of the application were generated by the CASE tool (e.g., the database design). A team of developers coded the necessary application programs and the bridge to the check-writing system. The request for update of the accounts-payable system by the check-writing system needed to be evaluated by check-writing systems analysts.

The analyst on the check-writing system requested the specifications for the check-writing/accounts-payable interface from the repository. He was not comfortable with the concept of on-line update of a new interactive application by an old batch system. He therefore proposed the generation of a completed transaction file which could be processed by the accounts-payable system. After receiving the okay from the accounts-payable analyst, *he downloaded the appropriate models from the repository into his workstation-based CASE tool and updated them appropriately. He then contacted repository administration, and the updates were loaded into the repository.*

When the application code had been tested, repository administration was notified. *Repository administration, based on the previously defined associations between project phases and application functions, related (with the assistance of the application developers) each program to its logical processes, as defined in the appropriate models.* The database physical/logical connections were already taken care of by the CASE tool. *The source code was loaded into the program library and a version was assigned. The repository-stored project that consisted of the associated application models was assigned the same version. The relationships between each model and its associated instances in the program library were also populated.*

The MIS Benefit

As the system became part of the accounts-payable process, requests for enhancements surfaced. The original analyst had now moved onto a major decision support project, and a new employee, unfamiliar with the original application history, evaluated each application enhancement request as follows:

- *A request to the repository listed all of the logical processes that exist in the accounts-payable production system, as well as their relationships to each other and their associations with other systems, namely the check-writing system.*
- *Another request to the repository showed the detailed specifications behind a particular process. The assigned analyst determined the best place to incorporate the new or modified functionality.*
- *The analyst downloaded the appropriate models into her workstation-based CASE tool and detailed the proposed change by updating the appropriate models. These were presented to the involved users and once the proposal was agreed upon, repository administration became involved as before.*
- *Assigned maintenance programmers requested the latest code from the repository and downloaded it to their workstations.* The code was modified, compiled, and tested at the workstation. Once the new code was ready for user testing, repository administration was notified. *Code was placed in the program library with a new release and status (testing) and related to the associated new processes as before.*
- When modifications moved into permanent production, repository administration was notified again, and *the status changes were reflected appropriately.*

We must not forget about the decision support project effort! As we discussed previously, upper management had the need to analyze much of the data that was involved in invoice payment. Those analysts assigned to the decision support project were in the process of determining where and if much of the executive-requested data was available. *The repository, having been populated and kept up to date throughout the development of the accounts-payable system, was able to immediately answer any data-specific questions about the involved invoice, vendor, and check information.* In fact, answers to these questions took seconds, whereas meetings were still underway in an effort to determine the source of other types of financial data. Upper management immediately realized the dichotomy that exists between application information which is documented and accessible and that which requires a series of meetings to develop. The repository was beginning to be regarded as a major corporate asset.

Imagine the preceding example without the repository. Some steps would have been lessened, because the objective of repository population would not have been a consideration. Other steps would obviously have taken considerably longer and might never have resulted in accurate information. Regardless, it is important to realize that this repository-based development example is not illustrative of *all* repository benefits. A brief list of additional benefits that could result with the proper investment includes:

- Integrated data dictionary/data administration support
- Readily available impact analysis capability
- Ease with which new development tools can be integrated with the repository
- Application (and application component) versioning
- Application component reusability

Consider the benefits portrayed in this chapter in terms of how they would be realized in your current development organizations. In Part Five we will discuss repository implementation—from evaluating an organization's readiness for a corporate repository to modifying organizational procedures based on the corporate repository's availability.

PART FIVE
REPOSITORY IMPLEMENTATION

23

GETTING THERE (IMPLEMENTING A REPOSITORY): STEP 1

You cannot endow even the best machine with initiative; the jolliest steamroller will not plant flowers.

Walter Lippmann, 1914

We have finally reached the part of the book that deals with the *how-tos* of repository implementation. Because a repository represents perhaps the only tool with potential capabilities that affect an entire organization (MIS and beyond), the first four parts of this book dealt with nonrepository issues that directly relate to the potential success of any repository implementation. We will briefly recap these issues here, and then conclude the chapter with actual case studies from organizations that have gone beyond the preparation stage and have actually established working repositories. Many of these case studies will be revisited throughout Part Five. As the book gets farther into implementation, so too will the cited case studies.

■ ARE YOU READY? (ASSESSING THE CURRENT ENVIRONMENT)

The greatest dilemma faced by organizations contemplating repository implementation is their ability or inability to honestly assess their current environment.

Typically, data administration organizations initiate the request for a repository. Perhaps a technologically out-of-date data dictionary needs to be replaced with a more flexible tool in order to meet expanding needs. However, the data administration organization may focus the tool's purpose too narrowly. Perhaps it is not considering the potential repository roles that could benefit maintenance programmers; perhaps end-user needs were not adequately assessed. Regardless of where the potential repository boundaries were unintentionally drawn, the issue is not that eventual benefits may not materialize, but rather that the organization may not even be aware of the need to involve the other potential benefactors. This subdepartmental (or sometimes departmental) perspective is the single-most cause of repository implementation failures. Without knowledgeable leadership at the top, it is likely to be the most insurmountable problem. In addition, it affects each repository readiness factor, as we will see in the following discussion.

The Models

A substantial portion of this book dealt with the evaluation of today's models. Because those organizations that have embraced modeling for a number of years consider the repository as a potential model resting place and "integrator," it is essential that the models meet the criteria that deem them worthy of repository population:

- *Accuracy*. If the models do not reflect reality when they are stored in standalone workstation-based CASE tools, they should not be targeted for a repository. When more people have access to inaccurate information, the impact exponentially increases.
- *Consistency*. Across applications, across projects, and across CASE tools, models that depict similar business concepts should explain them similarly.
- *Perspective*. Every model reflects a particular level of functional perspective when it is being evaluated for residence in a corporate repository: enterprise (corporate), departmental, functional, or application. Existing models should be categorized appropriately.
- *Modularity*. If model (or model component) reusability is to be realized, models should be easily modularized. That is, they should either represent a distinct aspect of a bigger picture or be developed so that they can be broken down into smaller submodels for eventual repository population.
- *Identification*. Finally, all of the previous model characteristics can only be beneficial when their identification via model and model component names is accurate and nonconflicting.

Standards Enforcement

Going beyond models, standards and consistency can and should apply to virtually all aspects of MIS development. The secret here is enforcement. As we discussed in Part One, the existence of standards does not imply their deployment. Also, their deployment does not imply consistent deployment. Repository eyes can see much more clearly when they do not need to be refocused before each glance.

Organizational Personality

It is very important to determine how stable your organization's mentality really is. Schizophrenic organizations change objectives almost weekly. That is, this week we are working on an information warehouse. At the end of the week, when a user group escalates an outstanding request to get an enhancement into its application, the information warehouse effort is placed "on hold." How successful are schizophrenic developers in the long run? Only as successful as their schizophrenic management (with some brilliant exceptions). Remember how encompassing a repository can be to an organization and decide whether or not an existing "distributed" environment of schizophrenia can become unified into a set of sane objectives.

For example, if the MIS function in your organization is truly scattered (technical services exist and function in one camp, DBAs functionally exist somewhere else, etc.), it is likely that the information transfer between these distinct segments is accomplished manually or verbally. Think about the implications of a central information source with a "neutral" controller. Can your organization handle this change in philosophy? Taking this concept even farther, do the distinct functional aspects of your organization have the capability (or desire) to willingly share *their* information with the other distinct camps? If your organization consists of secretive subcamps now, it is likely they will become even more secretive when a repository is planned. They must see a potential benefit in order to participate.

Management Commitment

Of course, repository readiness also applies to the ranks of management. Commitment to a potential repository implementation project implies more than the effort required to write a check. Specifically, as we will see throughout Part Five, many issues will come up throughout repository implementation. Some project developers may be asked to revise their models in order to make them suitable for the repository. Other developers may need to replace existing software in order to access the repository instead of the DB2 catalog, for example, for information. Database administrators may no longer be allowed to use their internally created database as a storage area for database performance statistics. And so on. True management commitment requires support of decisions that may be favorable to the overall MIS development organization, but unfavorable to distinct functional groups. It also involves the willingness to arbitrate those areas that can be solved equally well with a variety of options, each popular to a particular organizational faction.

Management supporters must also realize that a repository effort can represent a major investment of time and resources upon which the benefits accrued are directly related. The upper-management repository supporter must be able to justify the legitimate costs incurred, despite the fact that no tangible savings may have yet resulted. Repository readiness at the management level means the ability to see beyond the present, to realize the potential impact a well-implemented repository can have, and to justify the resources dedicated to its fruition.

■ CASE STUDIES

Despite the previous promise to discuss successful repository case studies, the first case study represents that of an unsuccessful organization. Because this chapter discusses repository readiness, it is important to put the term *readiness* into the appropriate light and point out the difference between a suborganization's definition of the word and how it conflicts with the overall organizational state.

CASE STUDY 1 Perceiving Repository Readiness

In the beginning of 1992, my firm was requested to assist with the repository implementation efforts of a major pharmaceutical company. Over the phone I was told that the firm was experiencing an application development crisis of major proportions. It had an out-of-date mainframe-based data dictionary tool which had not been upgraded (at least four maintenance releases had not even been installed) or maintained. I was told that the firm needed a replacement repository which would give it control of its application development environment.

During the first meeting with this client, we discussed the role the current dictionary played in application development efforts. The initial call to my firm came from the data administration manager of this pharmaceutical organization, and the first meeting took place with only the initiator present to act as company representative. The data administration representative explained that the major use of the dictionary was the tracking of production applications. When asked exactly what "tracking" and "production" referred to, her response was as follows:

> Any application that is run by operations needs to exist in our dictionary. We are finding that our existing dictionary tool is not as flexible as we would like, and we can't really use it for much else.

Continued questioning identified the following characteristics of the current dictionary-based production environment:

- There was no monitoring of the dictionary's contents by a central overseer (such as data administration). In fact, data administration personnel only became involved when the developers had trouble getting their information into the dictionary.
- Very few people (developers, managers, data administration personnel) liked the current dictionary. They found it hard to use, even harder to retrieve information from, and, in general, considered it an annoyance that was required of them.

- Data administration personnel had invoked an unsuccessful effort in the past to release themselves of the "dictionary" maintenance responsibility. They wanted it to rest entirely with the production operations function.

After this initial briefing, we decided to explore the realities of this organization's application development. The first area checked was the current dictionary. We found very little consistency in what had been populated across applications. In fact, the only reliable information that was tracked by the data dictionary was production job stream details, because applications were not allowed to move into production unless the job streams and all associated abends, restart steps, and so forth were documented in this dictionary. Some application developers documented much more in the dictionary, but this was based purely on individual initiative rather than a development standard. These developers used the dictionary for varying individual objectives. For example, some developers had been working on the same application for several years and needed to track versions of their programs as they related to actual production releases. Although the firm did have a working source code library, it was easier for some developers to keep all of their information in one place (in this case, the dictionary), and, as with most application development procedures, the use of the source code library was not a standardized requirement. Some applications did not even have their code stored in the library.

We then investigated all other information holding areas that were in use by the application development process. We discovered the following:

- No CASE tool usage. The data administration group had just purchased two copies of one major CASE tool, but had not used them.
- Inaccurate source code library contents (when compared to the actual code being used by production applications).
- Multiple copies of copybook members, many with subtle differences in physical structure despite the same name.
- Project-specific security implementations. It was impossible to extract information from two DB2 databases at once based on the security profile setup required for DB2 access.
- Little or no application documentation. Any documentation that existed was created by individual developers and typically kept at individual desks and/or workstations.
- Major data redundancy across applications, across databases, and across technical platforms. It was virtually impossible to tell which version of a set of data was correct in many cases.

Based on the preceding discoveries, we recommended the postponement of repository implementation. As we explained to data administration, its current environment was in no way ready for an immediate repository. Specifically, the big question that was never granted a consistent response was, "*What will we load into the repository, and where will we get the data?*" What we did recommend was a "repository preparation" effort. Specifically, current application development practices needed to be standardized. The to-be-implemented practices would require standard deliverables, which would be candidates for repository residence. In addition, the current application environment needed to be documented (following the same standard deliverables), with the results also targeted for repository residence.

Three months later the entire repository effort was abandoned. The pharmaceutical company had not even begun to streamline its application development efforts. Instead, they began an "information warehouse" effort, making an attempt to consolidate the multiple views of a major corporate subject area. What ended up being implemented (6 months later) was another application database. Although it was better designed than most of the existing disparate implementations, it still contained data that conflicted with other major corporate databases. In addition, it was not documented any differently than existing application databases. Its major objective was the provision of clean, accurate data in support of marketing analysis efforts. As of this writing, the "information warehouse" contents and design are still undergoing modification.

In this case study, it appears that the organization wore constant blinders when evaluating its own effectiveness. Rather than solve problems by getting to the root causes, new efforts were constantly started, which all eventually failed. It is easier to tout success than to admit failure. However, when those who tout success have reputations that reflect failure, they often change their objectives to those of defense rather than improvement. When considering repository implementation, defensiveness will not lead to success.

So much for failures. We will now talk about true repository-ready organizations. As we discussed previously, these case studies will be continually expanded throughout Part Five. For now, we will talk about how organizations decided to implement a repository and the qualities that ensured their readiness.

CASE STUDY 2 Concurrence on the Need for a Repository*

At the Canadian head office of Metropolitan Life Insurance Co., a former CEO and a senior information technology executive obtained CEO support to begin a study of the current operation of the personal insurance line of business. An information technology manager and a senior systems analyst also participated in the effort. In 1990, the study confirmed the need for a major restructuring of the personal insurance line, and the information resource management (IRM) organization was charged with the following tasks:

- The implementation of an information engineering approach to application development

*As submitted by Bill Post, Director of Data Administration, December 4, 1992. Follow-up phone call conducted January 14, 1994.

- The development of a central client information file which would assist retail distribution by providing the accessibility of accurate client information subsets to individual salespeople (approximately 1000) via laptop computers

As part of this application-specific initiative, a separate marketing information technology department was formed. It chose Ernst and Young's Navigator® Methodology along with Knowledgeware's ADW. At the onset of the project, several weeks of training in both the tool and the methodology were provided to project members, and it was decided to initially develop a "proof of concept" environment.

In support of this project, a data administration (DA) organization was formed which initially provided project-specific modeling and encyclopedia management services. This effort was categorized a "proof of concept" effort and was completed in early 1991. In addition to project support, the newly created DA organization created its own in-house data dictionary (in DB2). Because many of the existing legacy applications needed to be documented and categorized, the in-house database was necessary in order to store the application inventory. The creation of this in-house dictionary familiarized the IT organization with repository concepts, particularly those of reusability and standardization. Via clerical support, various legacy system project managers had their applications documented in this home-grown dictionary implementation. In addition, an E–R model of the existing systems was created by the DA organization.

The success of the initial "proof of concept" dictionary along with the DA's repository awareness campaign demonstrated the limited functionality of its home-grown "dictionary" to senior management. A recommendation for the acquisition of a fully functional repository tool was shortly thereafter agreed upon by both management and the involved IRM members.

CASE STUDY 3 A Unified View of the Repository's Role in Eliminating Application Development Chaos*

A U.S. government agency, created to support financial institutions, is the subject of this case study. Its applications had been developed by outside contractors in "vacuum" environments. It wasn't long before many problems resulted, particularly in the areas of data integrity and synchronization. Management was well aware of these data-specific issues and needed to respond to the U.S. government with a proposed solution. An office of corporate information was established.

Because outside contractors had been developing systems long before the office of corporate information was established, they were not guided by any

*As submitted by Bobbi Amos, computer specialist, U.S. Government Financial Agency, Arlington, VA, December 7, 1992.

data management practices. Specifically, there had been no defined standards, no defined information architecture, no dictionary, and no standard development tools. A newly created data administration unit (DAU) consisted of four members and an overwhelming objective—to identify both the areas of data redundancy and potential data synchronization problems, to establish data stewardship, and, of course, to establish data administration standards. All members agreed that this task could not be accomplished without the support of a repository tool. They had been granted the necessary budget and realized that they could provide immense benefit to the organization by beginning a program of data management. The repository was viewed as a way of controlling and managing the corporation's data as well as identifying the true problem areas.

Perhaps the major difference between this once-chaotic application development organization and the still-chaotic organization cited in the first case study is the organization's unification in terms of objective. This agency saw the repository first as a data administration aid. In addition, it had a management directive to improve the current data situation.

■ SUMMARY

Repository readiness involves several related factors. As we have seen in the preceding case studies, if one of the readiness factors is extremely out of line, the effort is likely to fail. Success stories always involve upper-management support. In both of our cited successful examples, this was the case. As we continue throughout this part of the book, we will reveal the details of repository implementation success. It is important to remember, however, that an organization's readiness is one of the first factors to consider when contemplating a corporate repository.

24

GETTING THERE: STEP 2

Assuming that you are ready to implement and that your organization is mentally prepared for a repository, the next most important aspect of repository implementation is detailed project planning. As with any software project, the scope, implementation specifics, resource allocation, and schedule must be defined at the beginning. However, repository implementation is a bit more complicated than the typical software engineering project because it involves more than just software development; it also involves the preparation, load, and/or integration of non-repository software, databases, and data. In addition, unlike traditional software engineering projects, repositories often do not have a firmly defined end-user base. Depending on the contents of the repository (and their accuracy and value to the organization), potential end-users could come out of the woodwork. For all of these reasons, the development of a firm repository implementation plan is the first step to repository implementation success. The next step is getting agreement and commitment from those organizations directly affected by the planned implementation.

■ DEFINING THE REPOSITORY'S SCOPE

Before anything else, it is important to confirm the scope of your planned repository—from the perspectives of the functions to be performed, the types and volumes of information to be stored and controlled, and its planned accessibility (how and by what types of people/platforms/tools). There are many roles a repository can perform, and each directly implies certain categories of supporting repository metamodels and associated instance data. In addition, the fulfillment of the planned repository role is dependent on a feasible and successful access plan.

When repositories cannot be used by those who need them (or are more difficult to use than desktop E-mail), they simply are not used.

The repository's defined scope should address the following components:

Repository Functionality

Identify the primary benefit desired from repository implementation. As we have already seen with the few case studies that have been presented, this initial objective can range from simple data dictionary functionality to the tracking and enforcement of standardized application development practices. Choose a realistic initial objective and then determine how the repository will meet this objective as a developer (and/or end-user) tool. The *how* needs to consider the relationships that the repository will have to any existing or planned interfacing tools as well as to current (or planned) application development practices.

For example, a crying need of MIS organizations in the 1990s is that of "getting a hold on" their current production applications. Not all organizations are necessarily about to rewrite all of them, but because a substantial amount of development time is spent maintaining these applications, the idea of having an accessible application inventory is quite appealing. In this scenario, however, the repository must function as more than a program library and more than a database catalog. It must catalog and relate each production application to a more abstract concept (such as a business function) in order for it to functoin as more than a program library. It is important to break down each application development task which would involve this application inventory in order to derive the required repository functions.

Consider the list depicted in Fig. 24.1. Application maintenance will involve the proposed repository as both an impact analysis tool and a program library. Therefore, from a functional perspective, in order for the repository to meet its planned objective and assist in the actual maintenance tasks as outlined, it must be capable

1. Determine existing application architecture: list those programs that comprise the production application
2. Relate each program listed to the application functions performed
3. Determine where existing application functionality best fits with planned modification
4. Determine impact of proposed maintenance item on any interfacing applications
5. Retrieve those programs necessary for implementation of application maintenance item
6. Once implementation and testing are complete, update application inventory with new (revised) source and asssociated business functions

Figure 24.1 Sample application maintenance task list, as affected by availability of an application inventory.

of the following services:

- Retrieval of all production source by application name
- Relatability of all production source and its associated application(s) to design level functions (e.g., update Customer record) as well as business functions (visit customer)
- Retrieval of application components (programs) by business and/or application function
- Selective update of production source and its related functions (application and business)

Repository Contents

Related to the scoped functionality, the repository must contain the information required to support the desired objectives. Following our example, the repository must contain (or appear to contain):*

- A record of all production source code by production application name
- Established business functions
- Established application functions
- Populated relationships between all of the preceding

Repository Accessibility

The initial scope of a repository must include its initial benefactors. Accessibility does not refer only to user id's when dealing with a repository; it also pertains to tools, platforms, and interfacing databases. By limiting the initial scope of a repository to one that is achievable in the near future, success and the ability to delve beyond the initial functional arena are more assured. Most repository implementers overlook the accessibility issue of their initial plan. Using our example of an application inventory, implementation success depends on the accessibility of the inventory to all application developers (regardless of their development platform). But, more important, it relies on the accuracy of the repository contents—in this case we are dealing primarily with production source code. If this source code is stored in a source code library or configuration management package, *accessibility* implies the ability of the repository to communicate (interface) with the appropriate package.

---

*As we will discuss in the next chapter, the repository does not necessarily contain the *data* to be accessed. In most circumstances the actual data is stored in an interfacing tool, yet retrievable via the repository.

Once tool-to-tool communication becomes part of the implementation plan, metadata and tool- (package-) specific metamodels must be reviewed. We will discuss this very important aspect of repository implementation in the next chapter. However, during this initial implementation phase where we are concentrating on the repository's practical and feasible scope, the issue of repository/tool interface brings reality to repository plans. The ability to represent the pertinent components of the underlying database structure (via the metamodel) of the to-be-interfaced package is a crucial capability of any potentially successful repository.

To conclude our accessibility requirements, remember to include the following as part of the initial scope definition:

- The number and types of users who will need repository access
- The types of access required (by user category)—read only vs. restricted update vs. unrestricted update; batch vs. on line
- The platforms requiring access and the types of access (as before)
- The types of repository-specific information that will need to be accessed (including metamodel access) by user category and by platform (as before)
- The repository access by interfacing tools, databases, applications, or other implemented software and the types of access (as before)

Although the preceding list may seem a bit detailed for this early phase of repository planning, it is often by overlooking these requirements that the best plans turn into implementation failures. Access requirements are a direct determinant of appropriate repository tools in many cases. Therefore, as we will see in the next section, it is important to think about (and get concurrence on) who and what will be initially accessing your repository.

■ REPOSITORY/TOOLS ARCHITECTURE

Based on the requirements identified thus far, it is important to detail the high-level architecture that will be required to support the repository's initial scope. Items that must be considered as part of the overall picture include:

- *Interfacing repository tools*: This includes the tools that will need and/or populate information from/into the repository.
- *Repository access platforms*: End-user, developer, and software-based access requirements should include the necessary technical platforms that will be transmitting and accessing repository contents.
- *Centralized or distributed repository*: Most initial repository implementations start with one physical repository. It may only contain a subset of the overall planned repository contents, and may even be intended to represent one of many related repositories. If you already know that you will be implementing

multiple repositories, your architectural requirements must be addressed from both an "enterprise" perspective (the whole picture, including all tools and repositories) and the perspective of each individual repository implementation. The details of distributed repository implementation will be discussed in a later chapter.

Figure 24.2 represents a typical planned repository/tools architecture. Although it represents a high-level view of the planned environment, it provides an easy reference point for discussing repository interface requirements.

■ TOOL SELECTION

Based on the requirements discussed thus far, it is possible to conduct a high-level tool selection process at this point. The following criteria will all be covered in detail in terms of implementation specifics in later chapters. For now, this list should be considered representative of *minimum* requirements for any candidate repository tool:

- *The ability to support application development via an "active-in-production" role*: Not as simple as it sounds (based on our earlier definitions in Part Four), this implies the ability of the repository tool to "directly connect" to any of the tools that may already constitute those application development practices that will require repository access. The "connection" could imply write access (at either the tool or repository side) depending on your requirements and may also imply certain execution platform needs.
- *The ability to support user-defined metamodels and user extensions to repository-supplied metamodels*: Related again to the active development role mentioned previously, the interfacing of the repository with in-use application development tools may require specific metamodel constructs that are not part of the base tool offering. Or, the base tool offerings may not be complete enough in that they only provide interfaces to certain components of the to-be-interfaced tool. This ability also implies the ability to relate various metamodels to each other.
- *The ability to implement various security levels*: Depending on the role(s) to be fulfilled by the repository, certain restrictions may need to be implemented in terms of access (e.g., read vs. update vs. none). Specifically, the repository tool should minimally be equipped for security based on:
    - User id
    - Metamodel (a specific application or tool view, so to speak)
    - Accessing tool
- *The ability to validate data targeted for the repository*: Because the repository is the key to an organization's information, the data within it must be accurate.

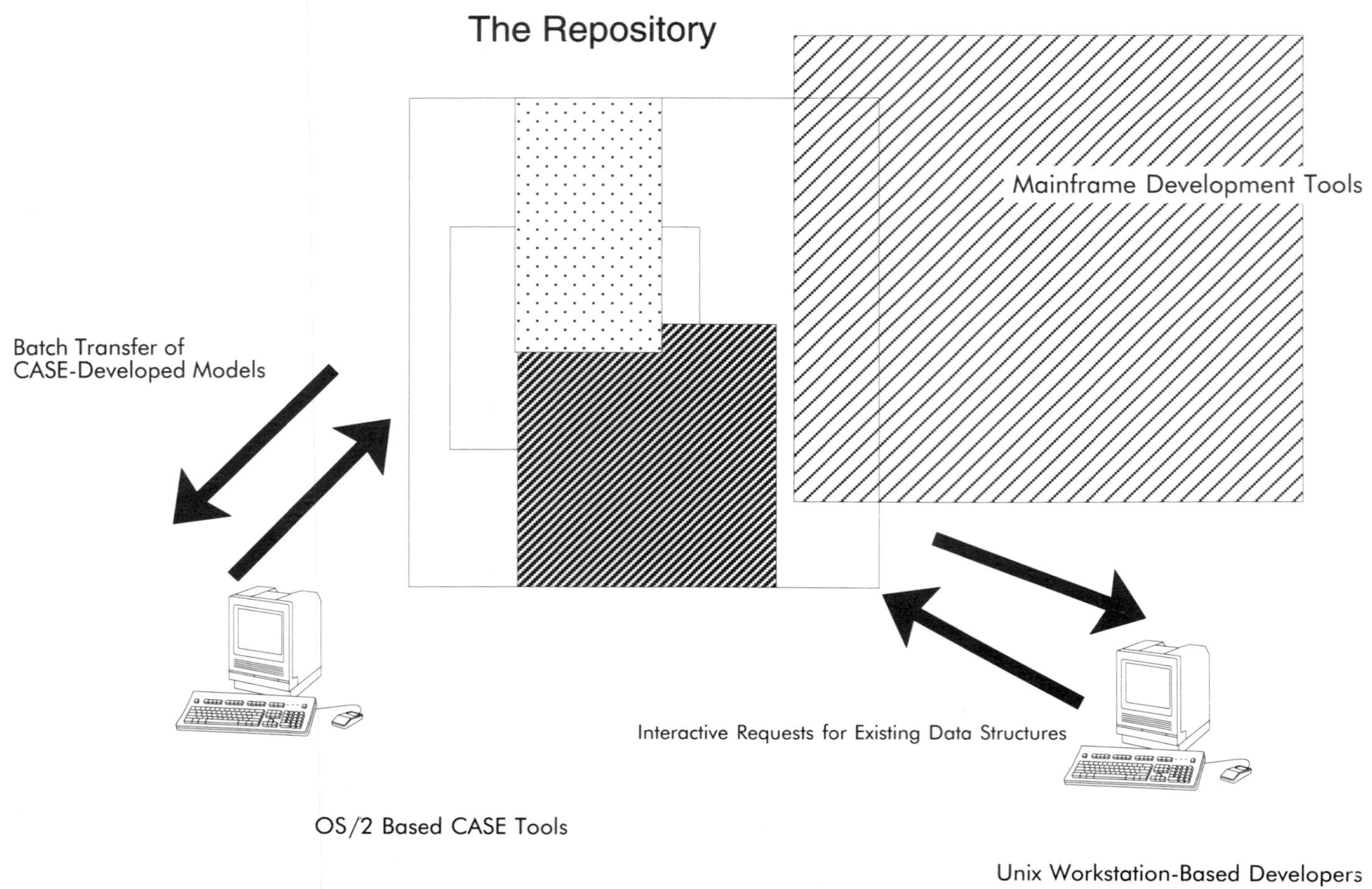

The Repository

Mainframe Development Tools

Batch Transfer of
CASE-Developed Models

Interactive Requests for Existing Data Structures

OS/2 Based CASE Tools

Unix Workstation-Based Developers

Figure 24.2 A sample repository / tools architecture

This capability must be handled by the tool either via supplied functions (policies) or the ability of the tool to support user-defined and/or written validation routines.

- *The ability to support change management*: The repository tool must be capable of storing multiple renditions or versions of its contents. Minimally, these versions must be capable of supporting various change levels (e.g., development, test, production) with the move from one level to the other being user controlled.
- *The availability of batch repository load routines*: Minimally, these routines should support easy-to-create standard file formats.
- *The availability of repository backup and recovery routines*: Aside from the obvious need to back up repository software, supplied backup and recovery routines should allow the ability to backup (and recover) repository contents. Ideally, the level of backup (and therefore recovery) should be user definable (for example, one should be allowed to backup the instance data associated with an entire metamodel (submodel) or any subordinate level of definition). Minimal backup/recovery capability must cover the instance data associated with the entire repository metamodel.
- *The ability to support custom repository queries*: There should be no restrictions on how repository contents must be requested, based on repository tool specifics. Minimally, application program interfaces (APIs) should allow custom repository access.
- *Concurrency control for multiuser repository access*: Minimally, the simultaneous update of a repository instance should be prohibited.

When evaluating candidate tools, the weights to be assigned to each of the preceding criteria should really be equal because they are all crucial requirements. However, depending on the planned usage of your to-be-implemented repository, one factor may outweigh the others. Any tool that does not provide the preceding *bare bones* functionality is most likely not a true repository offering.

From a technical perspective, the only factors that are likely to eliminate some candidate tools immediately are those that revolve around repository *accessibility*. Particularly, if the repository must be accessible from specific platforms based on your current development environment, it is essential that your list of candidate tools consist of repositories that either run on the required platform(s) or can be accessed (directly or indirectly) by them. It is important to note that the repository tool itself does not need to supply this interplatform communication capability. If the tool is "open" enough, these access requirements can often be implemented via custom interfaces or existing operating system utilities. The issue, however, is whether or not any translation is required between the repository and the target (or sending) platform. Depending on the extent of the translation that is custom-developed, the developer and/or end-user may in fact not be viewing the repository's contents, but an application's interpretation of them. As with most "hard coding" the issue becomes maintainability. If the hard-coded translation assumes a particular interfacing environment, problems are likely to ensue when an aspect of these assumptions is either eliminated or changed. Consider inherent flexibility as a requirement in any custom programming that may be required to access your to-be-implemented repository.

Continuing with the requirement of inherent access flexibility, it is important to consult with potential vendors regarding their support of customer-built interfaces. As we will discuss in more detail in Chap. 27, most "open" repository tools supply APIs (application program interfaces) and/or repository access via a standard language such as SQL. As long as these APIs are part of the base tool, they should comprise most of your implemented repository interface. Tool selection should include an evaluation of the functionality supplied by a vendor's API set in terms of whether it will meet your planned repository interface strategy. In addition, the relationship between the supplied APIs and the repository base metamodel is an additional consideration. What happens to an existing API if the vendor changes the metamodel that it relies on (in a new repository release for example)? More important, what about any user-implemented extensions to the metamodel—how can they (or their associated instance data) be accessed from outside of the repository? Are they also supported by vendor-supplied APIs?

At this early stage of the game, repository-bound organizations should concern themselves with any unique accessibility requirements that may be a prerequisite to full repository implementation. High-level tool evaluation can concentrate on whether or not it will be possible to fully meet these needs.

Related to the issue of accessibility, available vendor-supplied repository interfaces can often provide an easy way of integrating the multiple tools that may be part of your planned repository architecture. Not all interfaces are what they appear to be, however. Some vendors allege full interface to a particular vendor's CASE tool, when, in fact, only the tool's logical data models are supported, for example. As of this writing, most repository/CASE interfaces do not go beyond the analysis state anyway. That is, physical design models are not supported via the interface. It has always been my theory that many CASE vendors prefer this arrangement because it requires the repository user to do most of the application development within that vendor's CASE tool, particularly if it is being used to generate code from the tool's design models. They might see the repository as a place to only store the multiple versions of the logical, analysis-type models. Everything else stays in the CASE internal encyclopedia. During this initial tool selection process, consider what interfaces come with each candidate repository tool as well as the scope and integrity of the supplied interface. When shortcomings are noted, consider the potential "openness" of the candidate tool, as discussed previously.

▪ DETAILED IMPLEMENTATION PLAN REQUIREMENTS

After having defined the scope of the preliminary repository and its planned intertool architecture, some candidate tools were most likely eliminated. Ideally, tool selection will now center around a few (less than three) vendor offerings. At this point a detailed implementation plan must be devised. In most initial repository efforts, vendors offer their products for a limited in-house trials before contract signing. Potential repository customers then have the option of not pursuing the tool's in-house implementation.

The implementation plan should address several basic perspectives of the repository project:

- *Immediate, short-term objectives*: As discussed previously, this typically involves preparation for a short-term in-house trial of one or more of the repository product "finalists" as well as the actual trial plan itself.
- *The initial scope*: This plan should address the completion of all steps necessary to populate the repository as initially planned. The repository should then meet its initially defined objectives and be accessible to all those identified as part of the initial requirements.
- *The phased approach to complete repository-based development*: Repository implementation should not be treated as a short-term project, however. It is true that in order for success, a short-term, limited scope is recommended initially. This philosophy is based primarily upon the increased cost/benefit philosophy that is paramount in most U.S.-based MIS organizations. In the recessionary climate of the 1990s, it is very difficult to justify any effort that does not provide payback within 6 months to 1 year. In order to remain practical, therefore, I have been recommending an initial limited-scope implementation that is doable yet functional enough to provide immediate benefit (unlike "proof of concept" efforts). However, because the repository represents a tool with ultimate functional flexibility in terms of where and how it can affect virtually all aspects of application development and access, it is important to keep the global perspective in mind at all times.

  For example, assume as we have been all along, that our initial repository scope will be that of an application inventory, as discussed. Keep in mind that the eventual target (integrating current application components with CASE-based application models) affects how the initially planned repository contents are identified and related. Likewise, publicizing the target plan allows modelers to be aware of the existing repository's contents as potential physical building blocks for their under-development applications. Finally, this ultimate objective puts another requirement on repository accessibility. It will eventually be required that a CASE tool have access to repository-stored application components (or at least have access to the fact that they exist—remembering the metadata rule).

In addition to the multiple perspectives that repository implementation plans must cover, they must also address the following required phases of repository implementation:

- *Establishing the metamodel*: This is one of the most important phases, in that it sets the stage for what can and cannot be represented by the repository. The metamodel must be capable of symbolically representing any information that will be conveyed via the repository.

- *Populating the repository*: Based on the initially defined scope of the repository's contents, the instances of the defined metamodel must be loaded. this phase could involve the use of vendor-supplied interfaces, custom programming, or standard DBMS load routines. Implied in repository population is the definition and use of validation and integrity policies to ensure the accuracy of the loaded contents.
- *Integrating repository contents*: Depending on the scope of the loaded contents, it may be necessary to relate models that come from disparate sources. Manual integrity checks, manual relationship creation, and sometimes manual administration of the loaded information may all be required.
- *Establishing repository access and update rules (policies)*: In order to ensure continued repository integrity, additional policies need to be implemented. Security, validation rules, and other policies all geared toward maintaining accuracy despite openness need to be developed before the repository becomes accessible to the interested application development world.
- *Incorporating the repository into the application development environment (ADE)*: Application development practices must be revised to reflect the incorporation of an active repository. This iterative process will also improve the role and potential of the repository itself.

All of the preceding implementation phases will be discussed in detail in upcoming chapters.

It is important to note that the scope and duration of each of the preceding implementation phases is dependent on the state of an organization's current application environment. For example, if current application development practices are redundantly and inconsistently implemented from project to project, it may be essential to spend major amounts of time concentrating on a repository-based strategy instead of beginning right away with metamodel definition. Many short-sighted organizations step into new technology areas prematurely and eventually abandon the efforts when they fail to improve their still-chaotic application development practices.

A good example of this suboptimal practice is the organization that immediately delves into repository technology as a way of integrating multiple standalone CASE products. In this "implement now, improve later" scenario, CASE may never have become a standardized tool in terms of its role in the application development environment. For example, a data-modeling-oriented CASE tool may have been in use by a data administration organization as an aid to its creation of an enterprise-wide logical data model. Unrelated to this effort, one major application development project started trialing an integrated CASE tool as a way of generating some of its to-be-delivered code. The organization's management decided to implement a repository so that data administration personnel could "get their hands on" any already existing logical data models. The fact that the other CASE-based project effort involved a different CASE tool triggered the repository idea. Because the two efforts were functionally disparate, however, the "integration" objective was extremely naive. It was quite likely that the logical data models in use by the application development effort were in fact more "physical" in that they were used by the CASE tool to generate the required database definitions. Despite their becoming accessible to the data administration modelers, the models would not represent the same modeled perspective. Also, what about all of the other application development efforts in progress without the assistance of CASE tools? They should also have been reassessed in terms of their potential repository impact. Even if the immediate short-term objective of this particular organization's repository setup was based only on the needs of data administration personnel, the other functional departmental components should have been considered early on. It is quite likely that their needs could have affected tool selection requirements or fundamentally identified the need for a consistent application development methodology.

Likewise, organizations with mature and consistently deployed application development practices may already be delivering the intended repository functionality without the aid of a repository tool (they may have implemented a limited-scope internal database, or perhaps they are importing files into one particular vendor's integrated CASE platform). In these scenarios the implemented repository would provide a consistent approach to intertool integration. Based on their internal development efforts, they may already have defined tool-specific metamodels as the basis for their internal database design.

■ CASE STUDIES

Before continuing the case studies cited in Chap. 23, I would like to introduce another case study that appropriately demonstrates some of the advice delivered previously. In particular, this case study demonstrates a situation in which repository access requirements may not have been adequately scoped at an early enough phase of the implementation effort.

CASE STUDY 1 Multiple Model Consolidation at a German Bank

Mummert and Partner, a Germany based management consulting firm, was involved in a 2-year repository implementation effort with one of its customers, a major German bank.* A sizeable application development effort involved 50 analysts across 10 subprojects. Developers were using Knowledgeware's CASE tool ADW to depict both data and process models. The work was divided among the 10 subgroups by major subject area (hence the separate data models) as well as by major application function (resulting in distinct process models).

When the separate efforts needed to be combined, project developers looked for a repository solution. Because the concept of "model owner" needed to be maintained, the encyclopedia provided by the CASE tool was not sufficient. In addition, the separate encyclopedias that existed in each subproject had to be

*As submitted by Stefan Möller, consultant, Mummert and Partner, Hamburg, Germany. Follow-up phone call conducted April 22, 1993.

consolidated. The encyclopedia consolidation procedure supplied by the CASE tool was quite simple in that it required a lot of manual effort. Based on the large size of the project, after 1 month, the team decided to implement R&O's *ROCHADE* (the C version) as a PC-server-based repository. It also purchased R&O's ADW interface (ADWBUS). A repository-based solution was expected to provide immense flexibility in terms of encyclopedia consolidation options in that extensions (such as *owner*) could be added to the metamodel and used to relate and combine the individual subproject encyclopedias. In addition, the repository was expected to provide model versioning capabilities as well as be the holding area for a centralized definition of project standards.

Approximately 3 months were spent configuring the tool-provided translation of some ADW-specific constructs into their appropriate *ROCHADE* counterparts. Throughout this phase it became obvious that many common object instances existed among the diverse subproject models. These instances were not always identified consistently; yet they were in fact identical based on their inherent meanings and definitions. Repository developers learned that a common encyclopedia is much more than the sum of its parts!

The project eventually became too big to implement in a client/server environment. After 1 year, the repository was moved to the mainframe MVS version of *ROCHADE*. After almost 2 years of involvement, the existence of 20,000 object instances (across 50 developers) forced the project's termination after the analysis phase.

Perhaps the repository accessibility requirements were not given enough detailed attention during the preliminary 1-month tool selection phase. Although the limited scope of this repository implementation effort (single-tool-based model consolidation) may not have cried out for an accessibility analysis, an evaluation of the volumes of models and resident constructs that were to participate in the consolidation effort most likely would have raised the required red flag. According to Mummert and Partner, the project's cancellation was based primarily on the complexities involved in implementing the application in a client/server environment, as opposed to the actual repository usage scenario. Despite the project's cancellation, it was not without its benefits. Developers learned that the need for automatic model consolidation (as opposed to the manually controlled functions that are provided with some CASE tools) is absolute when working on large development efforts. This requirement is based on the need for consistent translation. In addition, the developers' approach to model consolidation was a good one and will be covered in more detail in Chap. 26.

CASE STUDY 2 Phased Repository Implementation at Metropolitan Life Insurance Company

Continuing our previous case studies, we will revisit the Canadian head office of Metropolitan Life. As you may recall, the initial repository efforts involved the development of an in-house data dictionary to support a new application development effort. Once approved by management (late 1991), the data administration (DA) organization set out to establish a data-driven development environment, with a centralized repository as the backbone.

The detailed implementation plan included both short- and long-term objectives as well as the strategies for reaching them. Specifically, the task objectives were scheduled as repository implementation phases in the following order:

1. *The repository-based enforcement of standard naming conventions for the DB2 environment*: In order to meet this objective, the following steps were required:
   - The acquisition of the BrownStone Data Dictionary/Solution, the BrownStone Cross Case Enabler, along with available interfaces to both the Bachman DBA and Knowledgeware's ADW.
   - The load of the BrownStone repository with naming standards stored in the homegrown dictionary as well as names from both ADW- and Bachman-resident models. Involved in this effort was the need for both identifier and random key consolidation, as well as general domain cleanup.
   - The integration and full automation of the DB2 development life cycle. Analysis occurred in the ADW Analysis Workstation. Models were then uploaded to BrownStone via their interface, and downloaded to the Bachman DBA where they were forward-engineered into their respective DB2 physical designs. These physical designs were then returned (uploaded) to the BrownStone repository where the physical DB2 subsystems are maintained. This process is currently operational.
2. *The implementation of repository-based reusability*: The DA organization has implemented its "data layer" approach to application development alongside the efforts required to support repository implementation. Currently, data layer code is generated for two platforms: DB2 and DB2/2. This approach has been accepted by the development team and is expected to use the same access and business rule modules and expects reuse to grow substantially in the next few years.
3. *The provision of multiplatform impact analysis capability and company-wide version control (for new projects)*: In order to accomplish this objective, integration of PVCS (a LAN-baesd versioning and configuration management package) with BrownStone is already underway. Efforts will also include the integration of the mainframe library management system with the BrownStone repository.
4. *The preceding impact analysis capabilities for legacy systems.**
5. *The support of repository-based code generation for both COBOL and C++.*

*As of this writing, all aspects of DB2-based application design, production, implementation, and maintenance are controlled by the Brownstone repository. Some elements of change management, configuration mangement, software distribution, and version control are already operational.

6. *The development of a central enterprise model as a way of controlling development objects for future projects.*
7. *The provisions of repository-based control for downsized client/server applications*: Via the current trial of their repository software, DA hopes to provide reusability, version control, and impact analysis capabilities for client/server-based applications.

As noted in the preceding objectives list, this insurance company's DA organization has a multiyear task ahead of itself. However, by starting with the initially practical small scope of naming standards enforcement, data administration will be constantly able to build on that which has already been accomplished as it continues its implementation of the fully functional repository. Likewise, by realizing today what its ultimate objectives are, it will not be making the confining mistake of limiting its current implementation efforts to project-specific visions.

■ SUMMARY

In this chapter we addressed the practical planning requirements necessary for repository success. As some case studies have demonstrated, the extra time spent at the beginning can often result in a repository with cross-organizational benefit. Those organizations that adhere to the philosophy of "Do it yesterday" or "There is never time to do it right, but there is always time to do it over" are already marked for potential repository failure. The best repository to be expected in a suboptimally planned implementation effort is one that meets only the needs of those who worked on its establishment.

25

ESTABLISHING AND POPULATING THE REPOSITORY

The implementation specifics of setting up a corporate repository begin here. Although the planning and organizational prerequisites discussed in the previous two chapters are certainly crucial beginning steps, the details discussed in this chapter will form the backbone which determines what your implemented repository can and cannot store, relate, and functionally manage. Specifically, this chapter will discuss the repository metamodel: its evaluation, depiction, and modification. The issue of metadata returns for the final time; this time it represents its ultimate objective—that of defining the backbone of the well-integrated information environment.

■ THE REPOSITORY METAMODEL (THE META-METAMODEL)

Imagine a resting repository. It contains all of the information necessary to provide a gateway to its described contents. In addition, it consists of the framework required to depict this gateway. This framework, known often as a tool-independent view of the tool's world, is the repository metamodel. Metamodels are often called *schemas*, and, for the purposes of logical understanding, they are often broken down into several submodels or subschemas.

For the sake of definition and consistency, consider the following clarifications of the various levels under which metamodels can exist.

The Repository Metamodel The big picture, so to speak, it is often referred to as the meta-metamodel. It represents the commonality among the various submodels within the repository, as we will see later in this chapter.

Metamodels Without the word *repository* in front, and by nature of the fact that this instance of the word is plural, we are referring here to the various *submodels* that exist in a repository. Each represents a distinct functional view of the information that is either stored or related in a repository. Most vendor repository offerings come with a set of basic metamodels, each conforming to the underlying structure of a particular type of information (CASE models, database catalog definitions, programming language constructs, etc.). Metamodels are often called subschemas.

Every vendor repository offering has a basic meta-metamodel as its underpinning. Remember, as we discussed in Chap. 20, that repositories are concerned with the intertool (or tool-independent) metadata perspective, often referred to as the "meta-meta" perspective. A repository view of the world attempts to take the specific construct and make it as generic as possible. In other words, when modeling the repository view, model instances are looked at first in terms of their similarities to already modeled constructs, and second in terms of their unique characteristics. In addition, meta-metamodel components are grouped together into various submodels, each representing a logical grouping with its own perspective. The various perspectives that are included with a particular repository tool's underlying meta-metamodel are usually indicative of the repository's desired role in the application development environment as well as the types of development tools it sees itself as integrating.

For example, consider the sample meta-metamodel depicted in Fig. 25.1. As illustrated, considering this is the uppermost level of metadata definition, the model appears simple in terms of the number of inherent constructs. In fact, the meta-metamodel consists only of the generic constructs that are prominent and pertinent to the entire repository picture. The practical reality of this meta-metamodel's implementation lies with its various underlying metamodels, each representing a distinct aspect of the repository tool's functionality and related information structure. For example, by continuing downward (from the meta-meta perspective illustrated previously) to the various submodels (metamodels) that are part of this repository tool's information architecture, we can see an emerging set of functional roles.

The metamodel illustrated in Fig. 25.2, for example, contains those constructs necessary to interface the repository with a particular CASE tool. The shaded boxes represent data-specific CASE constructs; the others represent process depiction within the CASE tool. Look back to the meta-metamodel (Fig. 25.1) and realize that practically every box in the CASE-specific metamodel is an instance of the Entity box in the meta-metamodel.

To make things clearer, remember the different metadata perspectives as discussed in Chap. 13 and revisited in Chap. 20 (in particular, see Fig. 20.3). Because the metamodel perspective represents the tool's view (perspective 3), remember that the meta-metamodel perspective integrates multiple tool views into a tool-independent view (perspective 4). By starting (from left to right) with the *repository* view (the tool-independent view) and working (to the right) to the tool-specific view (perspective 3), each view becomes progressively more specific and hence more restrictive.

What "connects" all of these various perspectives? As alluded to previously, the meta-metamodel is really the representation of the overall commonality among all

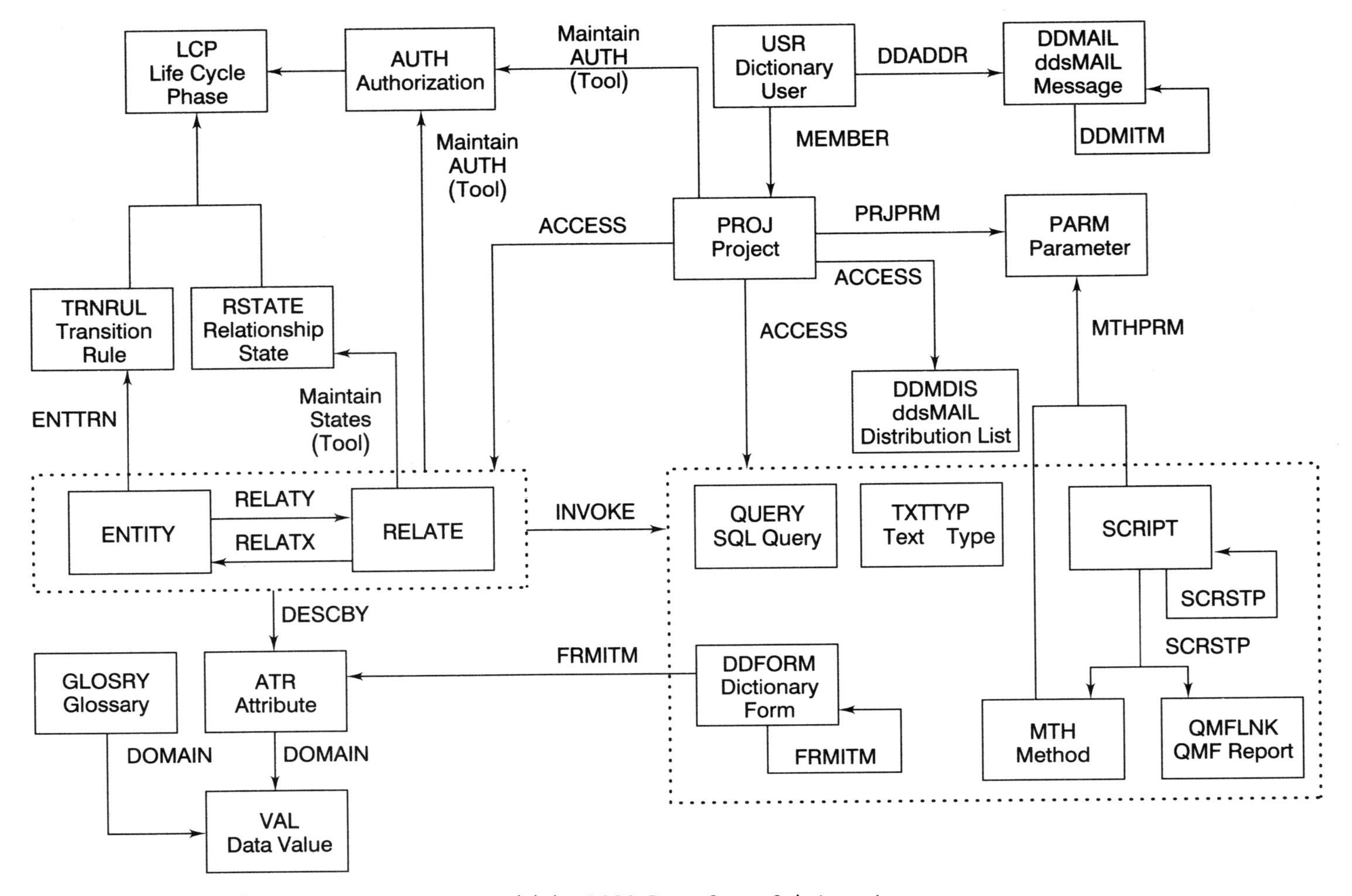

Figure 25.1 A sample repository meta-metamodel (© 1993 BrownStone Solutions, Inc., Version 5.1.0).

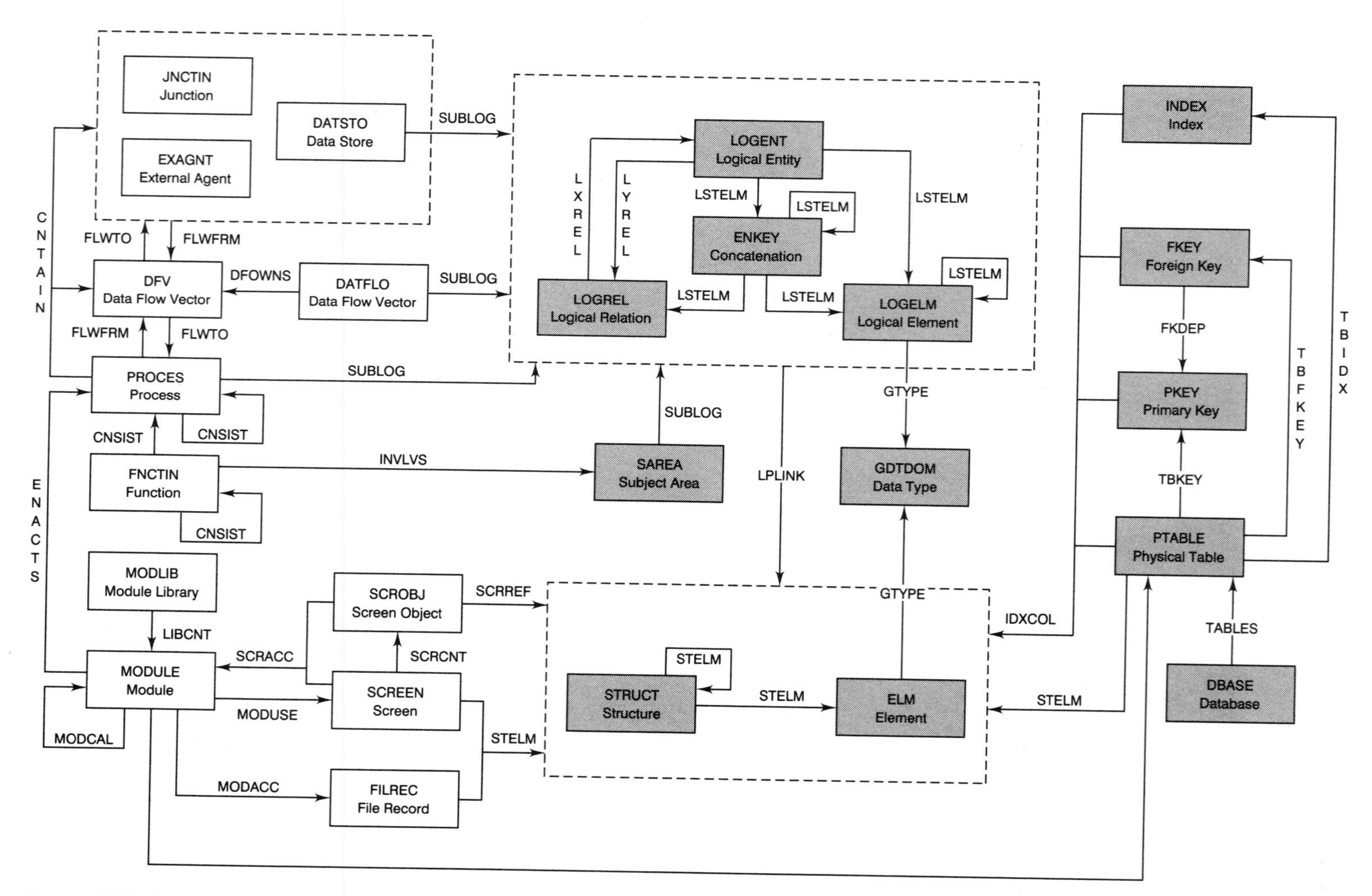

Figure 25.2 A repository's CASE tool specific metamodel (© 1993 BrownStone Solutions, Inc., Version 2.1.1).

metamodels. This is not intuitively obvious at first glance to the repository newcomer, however. Although not illustrated here, the attributes that are associated with the ENTITY entity (in Fig. 25.1) represent those attributive characteristics that are common to *all* entities, regardless of their implemented metamodel affiliation(s). Likewise, when we move to the illustrated metamodel in Fig. 25.2, the illustrated entities (LOGENT, ENTKEY, etc.) all have their own unique characteristics. Therefore, the perspectives *are* different in some respects, yet *alike* in others. The similarities are typically part of the meta-metamodel, whereas the specific differences become more defined in the respective metamodels (or submodels).

A simple illustration of the two perspectives modeled previously is the way in which the CUSTOMER entity, as defined in the interfacing CASE tool, would be stored and related in the repository. In the CASE-specific metamodel (Fig. 25.2), it would appear as an instance of the LOGENT entity. From the meta-metamodel, or repository perspective (Fig. 25.1), however, LOGENT (like all entities in all metamodels) is an instance of the ENTITY entity. If this is too theoretical for you as a reader, consider the translation of these perspectives into the relational tables shown in Fig. 25.3. As we can see from Fig. 25.3, the LOGENT instance is referenced via the value of ENTITY TYPE which relates to a row in the actual LOGENT table. In our very simplified illustration (many of the live instance data values that are required to be part of both tables are not shown), this LOGENT row describes the CUSTOMER logical entity (LOGENT instance).

To close the metamodel loop so to speak, consider the metamodel illustrated in Fig. 25.4, which depicts the same repository tool's COBOL supporting metamodel. As illustrated in Fig. 25.4, COBFDs (COBOL file definitions) relate PROG (programs) and their data (STRUCT, ELM). Therefore, when we view the meta-metamodel along with the two sample metamodels given previously, we start to get a feel for how repositories relate our world via their many components. In the simple examples depicted previously, the data (as defined in the STRUCT and ELM entities) relates the CASE world's view of information to the COBOL view of

ENTITY

ENTITY TYPE	TOOL ID	...
ATTRIBUTE	833	
LOGENT	900	

LOGENT

NAME	CREATOR	MODEL ID	...
EQUIPMENT	spspq	0332	
CUSTOMER	slg	0332	

Figure 25.3 Relationally implemented metadata perspectives.

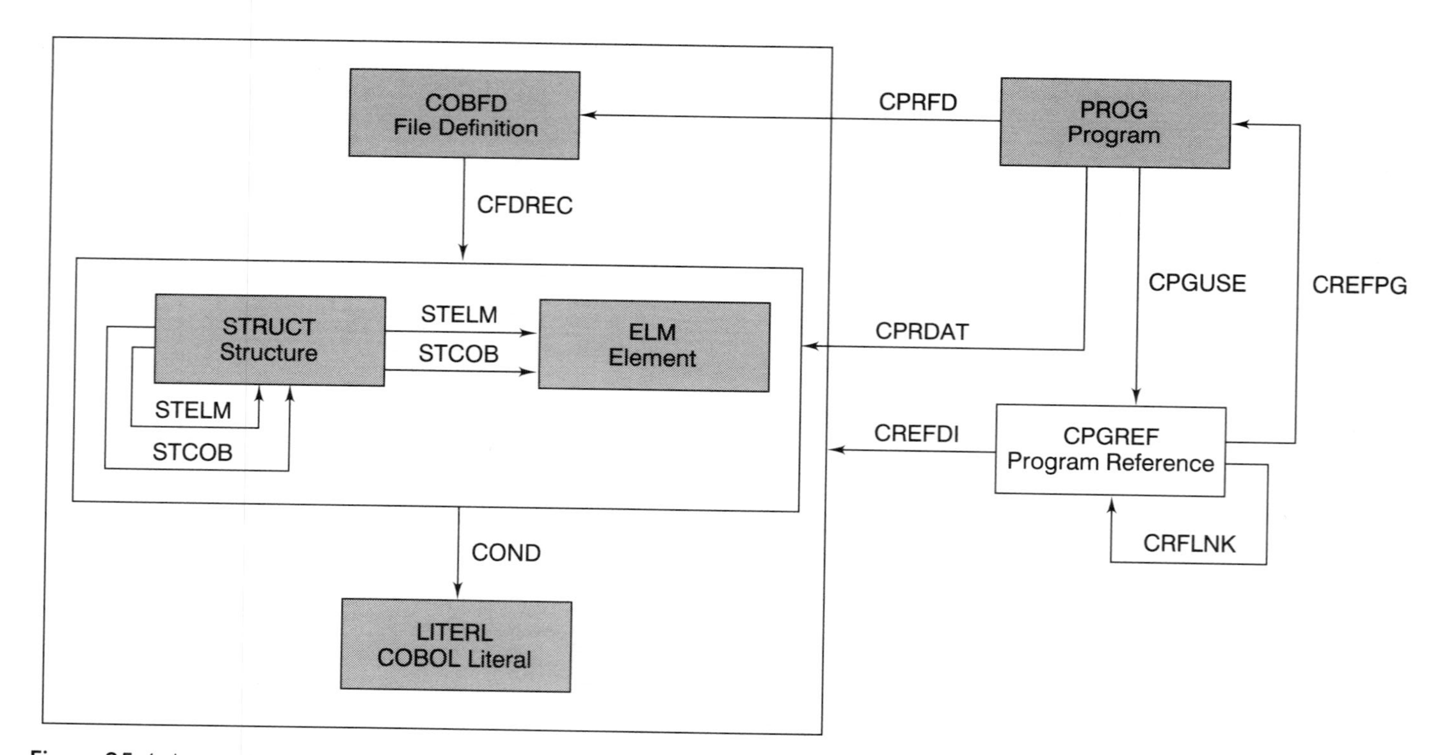

Figure 25.4 A repository's COBOL metamodel (© 1993 BrownStone Solutions, Inc., Version 1.0.2).

information. Readers should be reminded that this is just an example. Not all repositories contain the base metamodels depicted here, and even those with functionally equivalent metamodels may tie the various metamodels together via different common constructs and relationships.

For the sake of completeness, we will consider a repository metamodel from another vendor (see Fig. 25.5). As metamodels begin to depict the physical world (an SQL server database, for example, as illustrated in Fig. 25.5), they become quite similar from repository vendor to repository vendor. Because the actual physical constructs deployed are constant (and not subject to interpretation by the database designer and implementer), the supporting metamodels typically contain mirror images of the implemented database internals. In fact, the only variation that can be expected among different supporting repository metamodels rests with the way these physical constructs relate to other areas of the repository, that is, to instances of other metamodels. In the example illustrated in Fig. 25.5, this connection occurs with ELEMENT, ALIAS, and GROUP instances as well as with other relational database-specific constructs (e.g., COLUMN).

When evaluating the base metamodels that are part of your target repository, consider their potential conformance to your planned repository scope and functionality. In easy, straightforward situations, a vendor offers basic metamodels that conform to the underlying structures of one or more of your installed products: CASE tools, DBMSs, programming languages, source code libraries, for example. If you are this lucky, be wary of how these distinct metamodels connect (if at all) in the overlying repository metamodel. Will you be able to relate a logical entity, as defined in your CASE tool, to its multiple physical implementations regardless of their implemented DBMS? Will you also be able to easily retrieve the names of all programs that access these physical implementations by logical entity name? Insist on the ability to perform an evaluation of metamodel connections, commonalities, and relationships. A repository will not do much to improve your current scattered application development environment if it merely serves as a resting place for separate, unconnected, and distinct views (based on separate and distinct vendor metamodels) of your information.

■ A REAL-LIFE METAMODEL

Because of the ability to view the same information from different perspectives is an important prerequisite to the understanding of metamodels and metadata, our librarian example will return again as a way of solidifying the relationships between the various metamodel perspectives. As you may remember from Chap. 13, we used the card catalog as an example of a librarian's metamodel. When we consider this metamodel from a repository (library) perspective, it represents one of many tool views. Other metamodels are part of the library world, too. For example, one represents information conveyed via microfiche; another represents information conveyed in the *Reader's Guide to Periodical Literature*. The library metamodel can be considered the equivalent of the repository metamodel in that it relates all of these various metamodels (submodels) into one overall schema. Consider Fig. 25.6. In this simplified example each "library item" can participate in any combination of the illustrated metamodels (*card catalog*, *microfiche*, and *reference*). If we consider

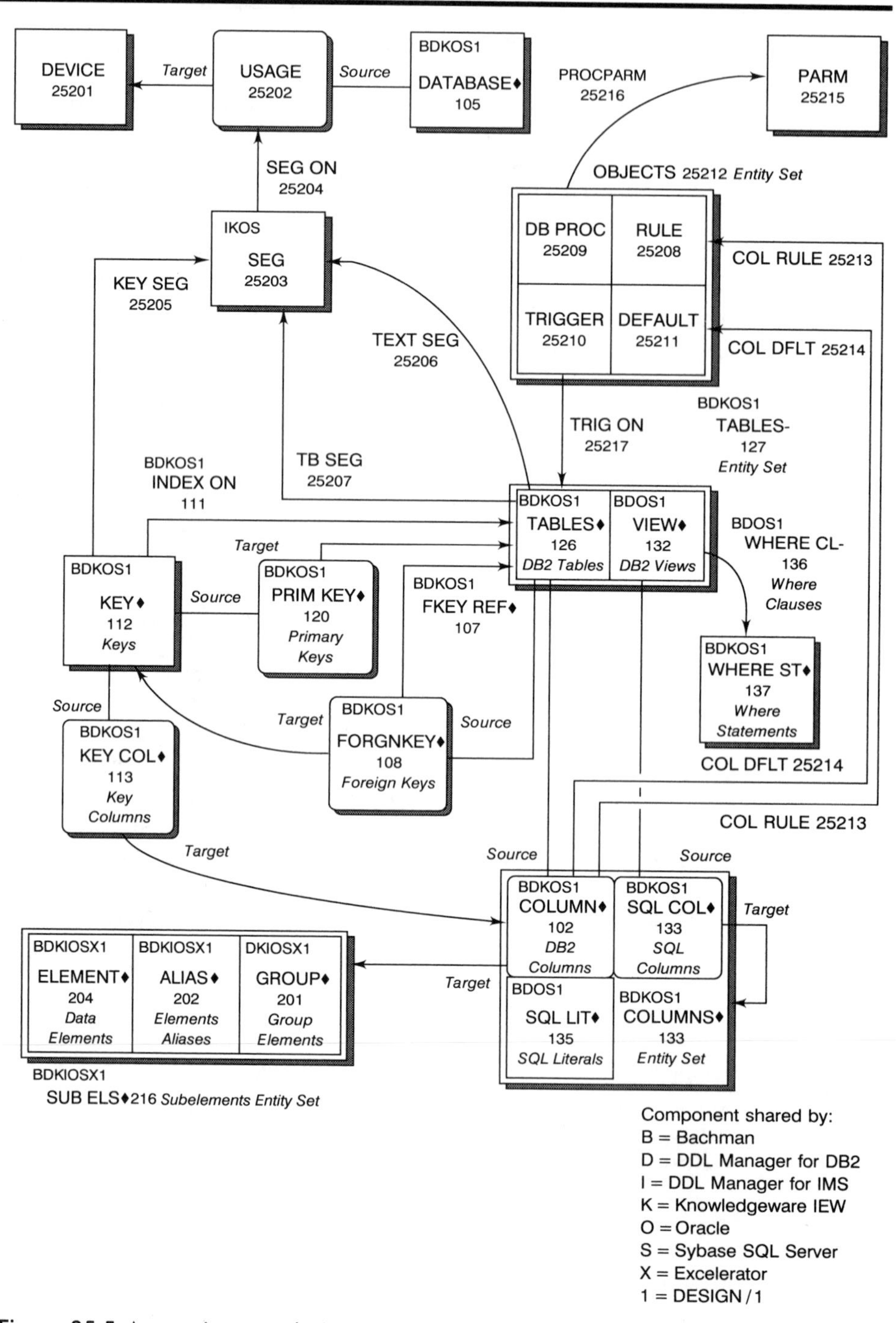

Figure 25.5 A repository vendor's supporting Sybase SQL Server metamodel (© Reltech Products, Inc.).

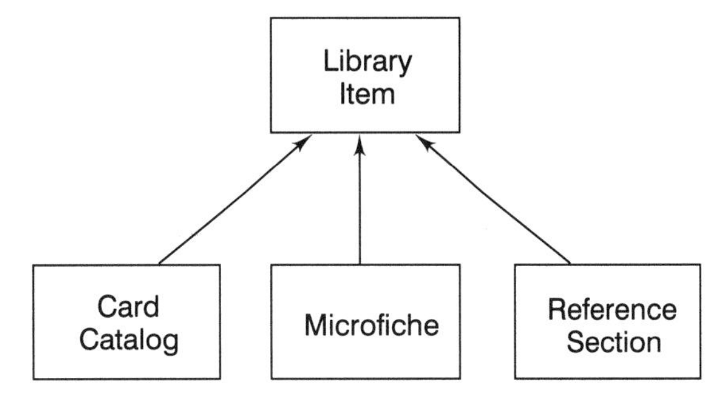

Figure 25.6 The library metamodel.

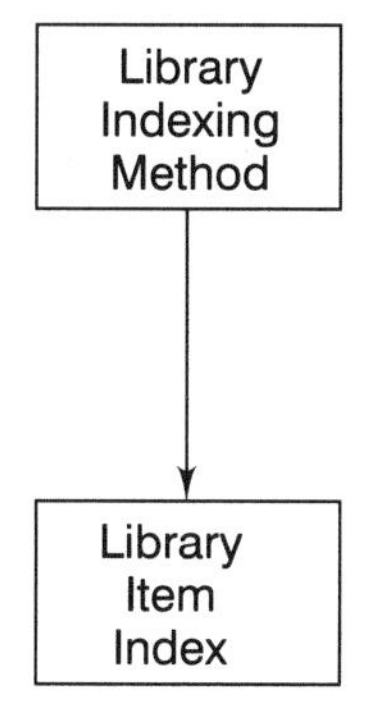

Figure 25.7 The library meta-metamodel.

the library to be the repository, it represents an integrated conglomeration of the various "indexed storage areas," that is, metamodels.

But if we want to take our analogy up one level to the meta-meta level (perspective 4, so to speak), we could potentially see the library's information from the perspective of Fig. 25.7. Hopefully, you are starting to see how each level of metadata definition represents an entirely different set of integration needs. In the library's meta-metamodel, consider that in order to provide an indexing system–independent view of the library's information, each indexing system must be looked at from a generic perspective (as illustrated in Fig. 25.7). Similarly, in the MIS arena, the repository perspective represents a tool-independent view of each tool's depicted information.

■ ESTABLISHING *YOUR* METAMODELS

With an appreciation of the role and power of the underlying repository metamodel, the definition and structure of the metamodel that will comprise your repository's information backbone is essential and demands considerable planning. Even in those situations where an off-the-shelf vendor-supplied set of metamodels is part of the implementation strategy, it is important to be aware of any limitations that may exist when relating the distinct submodels.

The evaluation of repository metamodels begins with an evaluation of the application development environment that will be supported by the target repository. Remembering the advice of the previous chapter, keep in mind the intended repository scope in terms of its affect on both initial and planned repository contents. Be sure to concentrate (at first by functional area) on the following aspects of the repository-targeted information:

- *The relationship between the actual information* (*the instance data*), *its representative metadata construct*, *and its name*. In other words, a DEPARTMENT entity may be defined in a CASE tool's encyclopedia, represented in the repository as an instance of the LOGICAL-ENTITY construct, and accessed by all interested parties by the name DEPARTMENT_ENTITY. The metamodel that supports the interfacing CASE tool must be capable of reflecting this scenario.
- *Relationships* (*if any*) *between information that may be represented in several metamodels*. Following the example given previously, consider how DEPARTMENT_ENTITY may relate to the DEPARTMENT file that contains payroll processing codes for each department. When these relationships do exist, determine whether they are truly relationships or merely redundant implementations of the same concept.
- *Relationships between the separate metamodels* (*submodels*). This is perhaps the most likely aspect of the repository metamodel to need special attention. The relationships between a CASE tool's metamodel and the metamodel that supports DB2 may not exist in today's application development environment in terms of actual instance data. That is, even though the CUSTOMER table is defined in the CASE tool, there may not exist any physical link or actual dependency between the CASE-based table definition and the definition in the actual DB2 catalog. Here, the scope of the planned repository role may need to concentrate on "what should be" rather than "what is." Having decided that this link really does exist (although it was never formally documented), evaluate the vendor-supplied metamodels for the existence of this intermodel connection.

After the preceding metamodel-specific considerations are evaluated in terms of their supporting application development practices (application maintenance, application impact analysis, CASE-based application design, CASE-based code generation, application testing, database integrity checks, etc.) they should be revisited as part of the overall application development picture. For example, if the need to access a logical entity by its defined logical entity name applies only to *CASE-based application development*, consider whether this information is valuable during *application impact analysis*. If so, how would it be accessed? By the same logical entity name, or by its physical implementation name? These types of questions will determine the need for aliases, multiple indexes, metamodel relationships, and other nonobvious paths through the repository information model.

The result of this effort should be a firm picture of the necessary repository metamodels. The next step is comparing *what needs to be* with *what is provided by the tool*.

■ MODEL METADATA MAPPING AND CONSOLIDATION

What if *what needs to be* simply is not there? Or what if *what is provided by the tool* is too much? Remember that a feature of true repositories is the ability to *extend* the metamodel! *Extensions* are changes, additions, and/or even deletions to the vendor-supplied metamodel. These revisions can imply anything from the simple addition of a relationship between aspects of two distinct metamodels to the addition of an entire submodel (either related or unrelated). The problem with extensions is that in most tools they are too easy to implement. Although this is a somewhat facetious statement, many repository implementers are too quick to extend a metamodel that may not meet their requirements when their time may be better spent determining what is unique about their requirements and why, that is, true systems analysis as opposed to the standard *patch it* syndrome. Shall we also consider this debate to be one of short-term interests vs. long-term solutions?

We should not get the idea that extensions are without merit because they are justified in many situations. However, proposed extensions should be evaluated in several lights.

- Their functional role within the base repository metamodel, when compared to those constructs that are supplied by the vendor.
- How they are or will be treated by vendor-supplied repository functions and utilities (when compared to the standard metamodel constructs).
- Their upgradability. When new repository software releases need to be installed, they often include updates to the vendor's metamodel. How will your extensions be treated by repository maintenance procedures?

When contemplating an extension to a repository submodel, it is always important to imagine its effect on the vendor's tool. Many repository implementing organizations initially saw extensions as the solution to their installation-specific needs. In one example, an organization had a unique naming standard that needed to be enforced *before* repository-targeted items were populated. It decided to implement an extension that would initiate the execution of the standards enforcement routine upon load of any new instance of the affected metadata constructs.* However, the implementation of this extension had an impact on those policies that needed to be executed as part of the generic vendor-supplied load routine. Repository administrators were finding that by executing their extension first, many new repository instances (those that failed to pass the naming standard policy) were being loaded anyway as part of the next executed procedure. Their names were taken from the user-supplied input, although they did not meet standard naming

---

*Repository policies will be discussed in detail in Chap. 27.

policies. After an evaluation of the problem, repository administrators determined that the only way to get their extension to execute in its appropriate sequence without affecting standard repository policies was to disable a relationship between the metadata construct and the standard repository-supplied policy.

The implications of disabling this standard policy were not pleasant. By not executing this policy, newly added repository instances were not verified as being unique. Some duplicates were slipping into the repository, when they were in fact updates to existing repository instances! The solution was the creation of a new policy which combined the needed functionality of the standard, repository-supplied policy with the unique naming standards enforcement of the initially implemented extension. This new policy was implemented as a replacement for the standard policy. The following extensions were required, in order:

1. Disabling of the standard policy, by eliminating the relationship between the metamodel construct and the procedure name
2. Creation of a new procedure which enforced this installation's specific naming standards first, then verified the to-be-loaded instance's uniqueness
3. Definition, via an extension, of this new procedure to the repository
4. Addition, via an extension, of a relationship between the new procedure and the desired metadata construct to ensure its execution upon load

Another, less complicated example is that of the addition (via an extension) of a new metadata construct. Perhaps an organization's data modeling methodology requires the definition of subtypes. The base repository metamodel does not have a subtype construct, so data administration needed to create one in order to support the existence of the many subtypes that had been defined to date. Easy, right? The repository administrator created the extension, and voilà!

Everything seemed fine until the first repository software maintenance upgrade arrived. Upon reviewing the accompanying documentation, the repository administrator noticed that the base metamodel was now going to support subtypes. The only difference was that the repository's definition of them was slightly different from that which had been already implemented via an extension. The repository metamodel version had three additional attributes defined and was not related to other metamodel constructs directly, only via the parent entity. Fortunately, by reviewing the documentation before implementing the repository maintenance, the repository administrator was able to revise the current implementation to take advantage of the new, standard subtype support provided by the vendor.

Notice that, as illustrated in Fig. 25.8, before the installation of the new maintenance release, the extension was not treated as part of the base repository metamodel by the repository software. In fact, subtypes were always considered "outsiders." By properly incorporating the installation-specific subtype requirements, the new maintenance release solved this dilemma. However, it should be noted that the following steps were most likely required:

1. An extraction of all instance data defined by and related to the extended subtypes

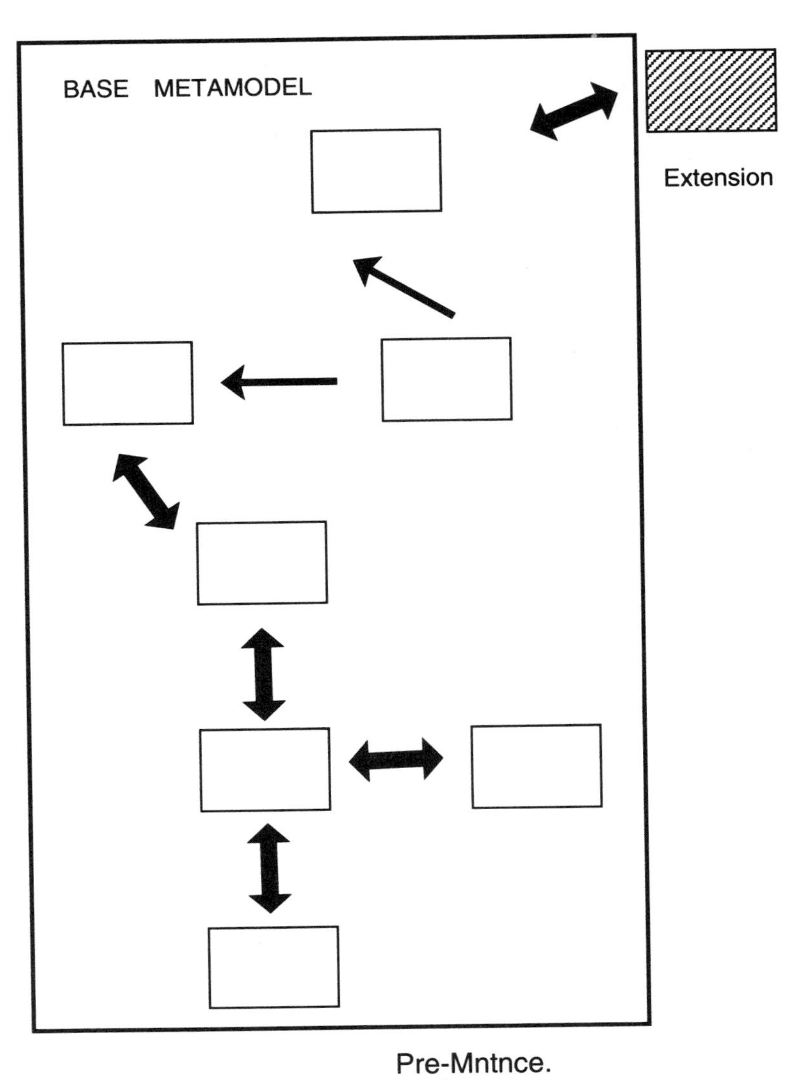

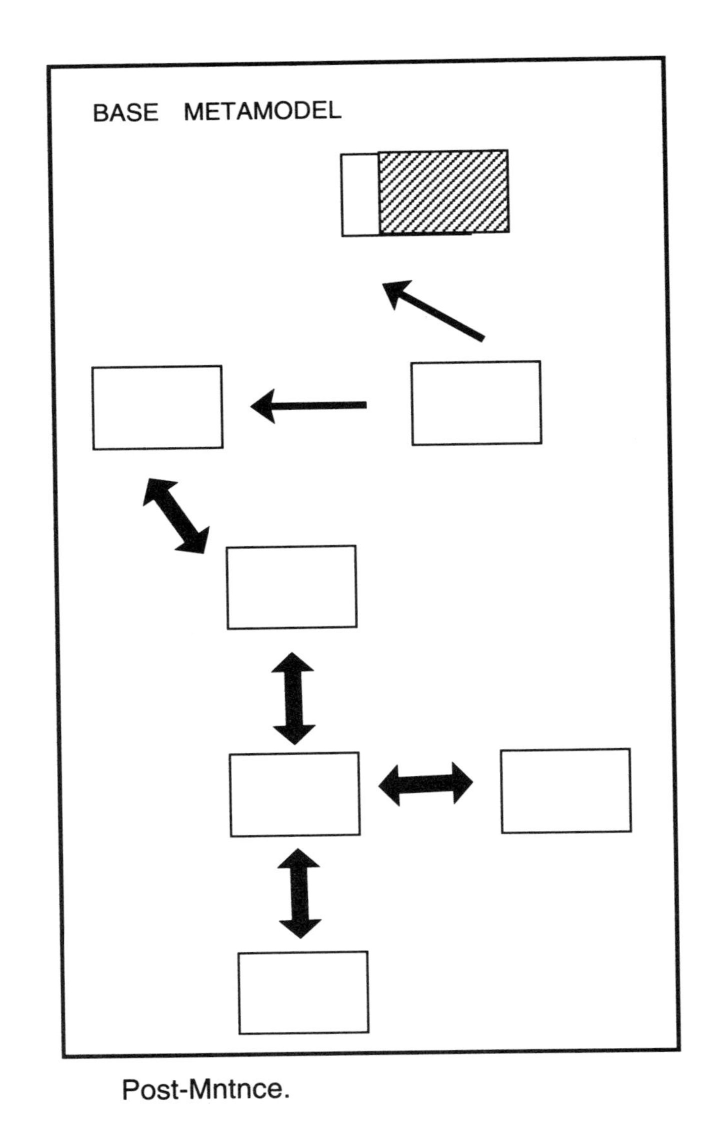

Figure 25.8 An extension before and after repository maintenance.

2. A reversal of the initially applied subtype extension
3. Installation of the new repository metamodel via the supplied maintenance procedures
4. Extension of the new metamodel to accommodate the specifics that were not covered by the new *subtype* construct
5. A reorganization of the originally extracted subtype instances (and their associations) in order to accommodate the new extensions
6. A reload of the subtype instances

The safest way to deal with the issue of extensions is to evaluate what is needed against what is supplied. The lack of a direct one-to-one match does not always imply the need for an extension. Often, a similar construct meets the same functional requirements, despite its existence in a different metamodel, for example.

■ EXAMPLES

Consider the example of a firm that has a working data dictionary and is expanding the functionality of this tool from plain database administration support to full repository functionality. The biggest issue involved in this functional expansion is the consolidation of the various different, yet logically similar, production names that exist across distinct physical DBMS implementations. In support of database administration, names were input into the dictionary within the restrictions of the target physical DBMS. For example, if the target database did not allow column names to exceed 24 characters, the dictionary names met this requirement. If the target DBMS did not allow the underscore (_) character to be a part of the column name, the dictionary name met this requirement also. Names, as input into the dictionary, were used to generate the database definition of the target database. Each database was defined within the scope of a project, which translated for the most part into a production application acronym.

Now, with the flexibility to be gained by a repository implementation, database administration support was about to become *data* administration support. Logical names, without physical DBMS-specific restrictions, would control the generation of all physical database definition. Based on the type of target DBMS, the repository software would automatically rename data elements as appropriate to conform to DBMS restrictions. In addition, the relationship between the logical (business) name and each implemented physical element would be populated and tracked by the repository software.

Repository implementers needed to address the fact that today's database environment had no connection to a logical world. In addition, today's physical names needed to become instant logical names in order for the maintenance of these production databases to remain repository controlled.

An evaluation of the options available based on the target repository's metamodel revealed the following choices:

- The addition of an extension, *Production-Name*, which would reflect the names as they exist today. This name would be used in place of the *Element-Name* for the regeneration (based on maintenance requirements) of any database definition required to support today's production databases. The actual generation of database definition would also have to be modified to reflect the use of this construct as opposed to the *Element-Name* in some circumstances. *Element-Name* would begin to be populated for new development only.

- The creation of business *Element-Names* for all existing production database elements. These names would be populated, as expected by the repository software, into the *Element-Name* construct. The support of production database maintenance would require that the existing production names be used as is. These names therefore would have to be loaded into the appropriate *Physical_Name* instance within each physical DBMS metamodel. In addition, the relationship between each physical name instance and the to-be-defined business *Element_Name* would also have to be loaded. This option requires no extensions to the underlying metamodel.
- A modification to the supplied procedure that generates database definition from the populated *Element_Name*. This extension would modify the process so that the *Physical_Name* is used when no corresponding *Element_Name* exists. As with the second option, the physical name instances would need to be populated based on today's production existence.

It is clear that the target repository architecture assumes the functionality depicted by the second option given previously. That is, it assumes the existence of a logical business name upon which all physical database element names are based. But changing the current environment to reflect this "new way of doing business" involves a lot of manual input, verification, and cross-referencing of the existing production database world and the nonexistent logical database world (hence my previous point regarding short- vs. long-term solutions.

Another example involves an organization with its own unique internal development methodology. The deployed methodology, followed by all developers, involves different standards depending on the state of a particular project. For example, all new development requests (including maintenance requests) begin with an assessment of their category. Categories include *new application development*, *new package acquisition* (for requests that are satisfied via purchased software), *legacy application enhancement*, and *one-time user reporting requests*. The assigned category determines the amount of up-front analysis that must be performed and documented as well as the extent of "sanity checking" that is required before the request is actually implemented on a production scale. It is this assigned category that was looking more and more like a needed repository extension.

Because the request category was affiliated with not only the request itself, but also a project (which could have several affiliated requests, each with a different category), repository implementers looked at the metamodel from a *project* perspective. Relationships at the project level, as defined in the tool's metamodel, involved *life cycle phases* (each with varying authorization levels) and a set of related *users*, each with a related set of defined *permissions*. Life cycle phases typically referred to application statuses (e.g., test, development, production) and were used to trigger the initiation of various repository routines based on their value. Flexible options included the definition of additional *life cycle phase* values (instance data) to cover the application categories discussed previously. In addition, by adding an iterative relationship from project to project via extension, projects become capable of consisting of other projects. Now, the needs of the repository users are met. The life cycle phase, which is related to a project, contains the values specific to the organization's category values (i.e., the development request categories discussed earlier). In addition, because projects can now consist of other projects, the individual requests can be considered projects unto themselves (as they often end up becoming), each part of the main project and each with its own assigned life cycle phases.

■ DATA VS. METADATA

After discussing the definition and consolidation of underlying metamodels, the next step is obviously the load of the repository contents. What do repositories contain anyway? With the confusion that exists today (as we discussed in Part Four), the need again arises to clarify what the metamodel is describing as well as *where* those items being described should reside.

As we have discussed many times, *metadata* resides in repositories. Repository gurus (like myself) may have a tendency to confuse repository-naive readers by interchanging the terms metadata and data. Then, when we add the fact that vendors all allege repositories as substitute words for their underlying databases, everyone gets confused. Perhaps, before leaping into a discussion of repository population, it would be beneficial to describe some types of information that would be accessible via a well-planned repository in terms of where they should reside and how the repository should represent them.

Models The primary focus of this book has been the use of the repository as a model integrator. Models, as we discussed in Part One, support application development before, during, and after the application's fruition. To a repository, these models can be considered instance data. That is, if they do reside in the repository (they do not have to), they are instances of specific metamodels (usually CASE-specific metamodels, as discussed previously). If they do not reside in the repository, they are merely represented in terms of schema via their repository existent metamodel. In this case the repository would store the metamodel, the models' location (e.g., in an interfacing tool), and *how to get there* (this is typically the name of a to-be-executed procedure or call that gets the information and brings it back).* Of course, a special type of model, the metamodel, resides in the repository as we have been discussing throughout this chapter.

Source Code We all know what this is, and it typically does not reside in a repository. It is referenced in almost an infinite variety of ways, though, via the repository. First, those models that logically depict an application's programs can be related (via metamodel connections) to models that represent a physical application design. The actual source code itself (which most likely resides in a program

---

*Repository procedures will be discussed in Chap. 27.

library) can then be related to the components of the physical models via the same *how to get there* connection described previously.

Databases This area starts to get tricky. Because repositories are themselves databases, I would like to focus this area on application databases, that is, the databases that actually contain the data being used by the end-user organizations. These databases are not part of the populated repository. However, they are most typically accessible via the repository in several ways. First, they are part of the logical and physical data models and the many application models that may or may not physically reside in the repository. The connections of these models to their physical database reality can occur similarly to the process/source code connection discussed previously. Second, their DBMS specifics are represented via associated metamodels which are stored in the repository. In many scenarios their actual creation (database definition) stemmed from associated logical data models and hence the logical/physical DBMS link. The actual database definition (typically what is populated in the DBMS-specific catalog) also does not typically reside in the repository, but is referenced via the DBMS-specific metamodel, the logical or physical data model instances, or even an application that uses the repository as a gateway to database specifics.

Etc.: What a great name for everything else! Many installations do actually store *data* in their repository. The data typically describes aspects of the application environment. For example, some installations may create and populate an attribute of a metamodel that names the implemented hardware platform of an application (VAX, IBM3090, RS6000 Server, etc.). The only justification for storing data in the repository is its nonexistence anywhere else and its direct pertinence to the information being represented within the repository. If data that comes from an application database or another software package is simply copied and loaded into a repository, the repository is apt to create some of the problems it was probably supposed to reduce (such as data redundancy, conflicting information, etc.). Be wary of the potential to make a repository into a substitute "information warehouse"!

■ POPULATING THE REPOSITORY

At this point, the repository is well defined: We know what is going to be stored, how it is going to be represented, and how it will relate to everything else (if at all). The next step is getting the information in, or, for information that will not be repository resident but repository accessible, this step involves implementing the *go get it* routines.

Every repository tool should have its own batch load routine. Typically, these routines require a predefined input format. In some situations accepted standards (such as CDIF) dictate the format of the to-be-loaded files. Regardless, the required definitions for batch load include the target metamodel name as well as the names of each target construct along with the to-be-loaded instance data. The interesting issue that arises when using the standard repository routines (such as a batch load) is how any user-defined extensions are handled in terms of target to-be-populated constructs. Some tools treat them no differently, whereas others simply cannot handle them in their standard load routines.

Another means of repository load is via vendor-supplied interfaces. Particularly pertinent in the CASE-based model arenas, again these are typically batch load routines. Because the metamodel and the batch transfer process are all packaged together, very little (other than the source and target model names) usually needs to be clarified before executing the load. However, standard interfaces should be evaluated in terms of their execution options. For example, if it is only possible to transfer entire models (as opposed to selected model components regardless of their source model), then the supplied interface may not be the best load option.

Finally, repositories are typically accessible (including for load) via custom programming. The custom programming can involve simple database update (many repositories are accessible via standard access languages such as SQL), the use of a repository-specific command language (in many cases IRDS compliant), or the execution of a series of APIs (application program interfaces). Depending on the extent of customization involved in your underlying metamodel, custom programming may represent the best way of getting your data in. Aside from the required initial investment in terms of time and resources, the developed routines will be available for any subsequent information loads.

Perhaps one of the biggest questions to consider is the issue of input verification. Because we spent a substantial portion of this book discussing what makes a model (for example) a candidate for repository population, we can only assume that the to-be-loaded data is of loadable quality at this point. However, because the repository is the gateway into the world of corporate information, it certainly could not hurt to recheck the important data quality aspects. Herein lies another reason for custom developing a load process—the execution of policies both before, during, and after the information is loaded. Many repository tools allow the definition of *validation rules* at submodel definition time. These validation rules can often be associated with particular submodels, submodel-participating constructs, or even the attributes of a particular construct. For example, if an *entity name* must begin with an alphabetic character and not exceed 40 characters, this type of validation rule would be associated with the *name* attribute of a populated entity. Depending on the repository tool's internals, the execution of this validation rule could occur at any point in the load process, or after the data has been loaded. Some tools even allow the execution priority to be defined by the repository administrator. By defining validation rules, much of the custom programming burden is removed from the repository implementer. However, serious thought should be given to the permanence of each validation rule and whether or not a backup plan is necessary in case the rules change later in the repository's development.

In most repository environments the loading of information involves a mixture of the preceding options. Information that comes from a standard, interfaced tool is often uploaded via a vendor-supplied standard interface. Other information, depending on its origination, may be loaded and validated via a custom-developed series of APIs. The best load arrangement depends on the following factors:

- *The frequency with which your repository will be loaded*. Typically, after a major initial load, many installations do regular updates (as opposed to reloads).

Some installations maintain their repository accuracy at all times through on-line, immediate access.

- *The "openness" of the selected repository tool.* If the underlying database is accessible via SQL, for example, the development of a custom load may not be very resource intensive.
- *The source(s) and format(s) of the to-be-loaded information.* The more variety, the less likely standard routines are to meet your requirements. If it takes more work to export information into the required repository import format than it would to write a program, maybe you should reconsider your plan.
- *The amount of manual validation required.* The more suited your to-be-loaded data is to its target repository relationships, the more likely a standard repository load routine will be suitable.

As with every aspect of repository implementation, repository population is a subproject in itself. Evaluate the candidate data in terms of its compatibility with repository input requirements and establish a suitable implementation plan.

■ CASE STUDIES

CASE STUDY 1 The U.S. Government Agency (Revisited)

The major tasks discussed in this chapter are critical components of repository implementation. Returning to the previously cited case study involving the U.S. government agency,* we can get a feel for the amount of effort involved in these initial tasks as well as the direct paybacks. As you may remember, this agency was faced with a chaotic application development environment. The repository was targeted as a medium for standardizing the scattered application development practices.

A substantial amount of time was spent creating a logical data model of the information targeted for repository population. The model was developed over a period of 6 weeks and involved the full-time effort of two modelers along with on-site repository vendor support. The developed metamodel consisted of six "views" (or submodels), all related to each other:

- *Information resource management.* Here, entities such as *Mission*, *Goal*, *Business Function*, *Business Process*, *Organizational Unit*, and *Employee* reside. This view is used by management to track application support of the business as well as those organizations and employees associated with this support.
- *Database.* Entities such as *Table*, *View*, *Column*, and other relational database constructs are tracked. This view is used primarily by DB2 DBAs, but it also gives application users a current report of their database structure.

*As submitted by Bobbi Amos, computer specialist, December 7, 1992.

- *Application*. This view contains programming-specific entities such as *Program*, *Screen*, *Report*, *Element*, *File*, *Record*, *Non-DB2 Table*, *Job*, *Procedure*, and so forth. Application developers use this view for impact analysis and maintenance task estimates. Likewise, project managers use this view to manage and finalize project work estimates. Data dictionary–type reports are also produced from this view (e.g., elements in a given application) for end-users.
- *Hardware/software*. *Circuit*, *DASD*, *Modem*, *Printer*, and so on are tracked here. Telecommunications and computer operations organizations use this view to maintain an inventory of hardware/software configurations within the corporation.
- *Security*. Application access is controlled via this view. Entities such as *User ID*, *Authorization ID*, *Employee*, *Application*, *Database*, *Table*, and so on are accessible as a means of implementing security.
- *Change request*. This view contains entities pertinent to the tracking of application work, such as *Change Request*, *Contract*, *Task Order*, *Program*, *Project*, and so forth.

The scope of the metamodel covered virtually all aspects of the agency's application environment. The selected tool's base metamodel did not support many of the agency's needs (including the entire hardware/software submodel) and hence many extensions were required. The extensions were implemented by the on-site repository vendor consultants in 3 weeks time.

An example of an implemented extension was the addition of an EMPLOYEE entity. This entity (actually implemented as an entity set which includes CONTRACTOR) tracks employees and contractors assigned to projects and specific requests. The repository's base metamodel did not have this capability.

Based on the high amount of implemented extensions, the repository load was also a major task. The product in use required the manual handling of all data targeted for population in user-defined extensions. That is, the standard repository load procedures could not populate "nonstandard" metamodel constructs. Once the initial repository was defined and loaded, efforts have concentrated on the accessibility and maintenance of the repository's contents, as we will see in forthcoming chapters.

The significance of this initial effort in terms of the overall repository implementation time frame is apparent when we look at the time frame of the involved tasks to date:

Defining repository requirements, *tool selection*, *preparing the current environment for a repository*: 8 months
Defining and creating the metamodel: 6 weeks
Populating the repository: 6 weeks
Validating and maintaining repository contents: ongoing (product has been in house for 10 months as of this writing)

At the time of this case study's submission, the repository implementation process had already spanned a period of 18 months, 8 of which occurred before the actual repository product was installed. Involved developers expect another full year of effort before the repository is usable throughout the entire agency. We will revisit this case study again in subsequent chapters as we address the remaining phases of repository implementation.

CASE STUDY 2 The Health Care Financing Administration's Voluminous Data Tracking Requirements

Another case study, introduced here for the first time, is that of the Health Care Financing Administration (HCFA), a U.S. government agency based in Baltimore.* Because this organization is responsible for the development of regulations for Medicaid/Medicare insurance coverage, it is known as the source of all related data including coverage, claim, and policy regulation data. The volume of data processed by this organization approaches approximately 600 million claims annually. The need to track and identify all data sources was obvious. The organization implemented a mainframe repository as the means of consolidating CASE tool (Excelerator 1.9) based models with their physical implementations, as defined in the Model 204 DBMS catalog. Their systems development approach, as a result of this effort, was targeted to become standardized and model driven.

The metamodel definition involved the breakdown of the entire systems development process into several tool-independent logical views, as follows:

- *Data modeling*. Constructs required to support the development of E–R diagrams and all of their components
- *Process modeling*. Those constructs that support the logical definition of application processes as well as their use and creation of the logical data defined in the data modeling view
- *Database design*. The support of the physical database design as well as its relationships to logical data and process model components
- *System modeling*. Supporting metadata for physical program structures and their interrelationships with physical files and databases

Figure 25.9 shows the integrated result. This schema was implemented in both Manager Software Products' (MSP) DATAMANAGER and a front-end tool (PC Dictionary by Software Solutions, Inc.). The metamodel was intended to support all known HCFA data management functions.

*As submitted by Cindy Walker, vice president information resource management, and Elaine Stricklett, program manager, Software Solutions, Inc., Alexandria, VA, April 30, 1993. Follow-up phone call conducted with John McGuire, program analysis officer, HCFA, May 11, 1993.

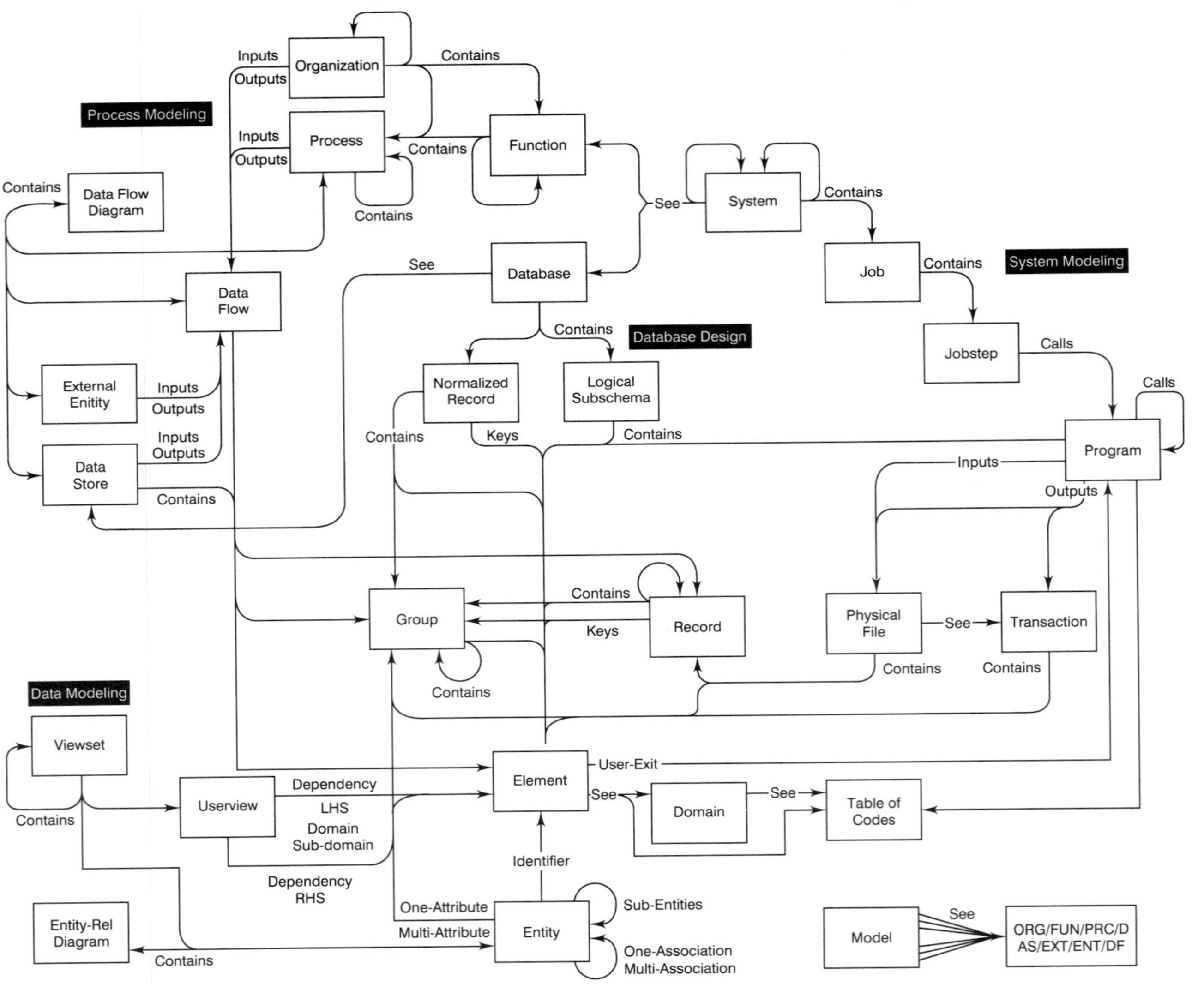

Figure 25.9 The HCFA metamodel.

The implementation of extensions was a backbone requirement of the development of the preceding metamodel. Through trial and error, many extensions were created and subsequently modified. Modifications typically resulted when the extension was viewed in terms of its overall role in HCFA's application development methodology as opposed to its isolated role within a particular tool. Upon completion of the metamodel, the full architecture became repository driven. The repository controls the metamodels of all related products. Therefore, each implemented construct needed to be viewed in terms of the entire repository architecture and the coordination of the various individual metamodels. The establishment of the original repository metamodel took approximately 12 months.

Once the metamodel was established, the remaining effort was spent establishing the full repository-driven application development environment. Specifically, custom interfaces between the repository and each tool were built. The specifics of this work will be discussed when this case study is revisited in a subsequent chapter.

■ SUMMARY

In this chapter we covered a substantial amount of implementation specifics. As the case studies have proven, the initial setup of a repository should carry the same weight as the planning and analysis phases of major application efforts. Spending substantial analysis time up front is sure to reap its rewards later on when it is dedicated to repository metamodel specifics.

26
MODEL INTEGRATION

Having defined and loaded our repository, we now face the issue of how to continually maintain the relationships defined in our repository metamodel. These relationships, defined at the metadata level, place an increased "integration" focus on instance data to be loaded and/or referenced within the repository. When we talk about *model integration*, we could potentially refer to several perspectives:

- *Metamodel integration*. As we discussed in the previous chapter, this is a required aspect of the definition of the overall metamodel. At the metadata level (perspective 2), each submodel (perspective 3)* must be compared to the others. Constructs within each submodel may be functionally shared among other submodels. Commonality implies connectivity. Other submodel connections occur when constructs within one submodel are functionally related to constructs in another submodel. Similar to relationships that exist within a particular submodel, relationships can exist across submodels.
- *Metamodel instance integration*. Going down one level (in our metadata hierarchy), we arrive at the instances of the defined metamodel, otherwise known as instance data (perspective 1). If, in fact, our instance data refers to an application model, model integration implies the consolidation of various renditions of one or more models of one or more applications. An example is the consolidation of application models that spanned many developer workstations, each (using either the same or differing CASE tools) representing a distinct functional aspect of the overall application. This is the focus of our present chapter.
- *Meta-metamodel integration*. Finally, we can refer to model integration at the uppermost level of the metadata hierarchy (perspective 4). Integration at this level implies separate physical repositories, or, in the simplest situation, separate physical areas within a single repository. In either situation the transfer or access of data from one repository (area) to the other requires this level of integration. We will discuss this type of "model integration" in Chap. 28.

---

*Refer to Chap. 20 for clarification of the various perspectives.

This chapter will therefore concentrate on integration at the metamodel instance level; that is, the relating and consolidating of the data that is represented by each metamodel—regardless of whether the data resides inside or outside of the repository.

▪ MODEL VS. PROJECT

When discussing integration at the metamodel instance level, some basic assumptions about model and project scope and definition must be consistent among the to-be-integrated pieces. Although Part One of this book discussed models in their entirety, they were discussed from a standalone project (application) perspective. Now that we are putting these models together with an eye toward the repository, the relevance of how we define *project* and *application* cannot be understated.

Models, projects, and applications can be named at the discretion of the tool user. Some organizations do deploy application naming standards, yet I have not seen too many that actually define *what* an application is. Trivial point? Maybe. But what does the organization do when it is time to integrate a set of *application* models from different *projects* from one or more local encyclopedias, when their names are as follows?

Encyclopedia 1:
- Project: *Update-Customer-Master*
  - Application models:
    - Logical data model: *Customer*
    - Process models: *Get-New-Custid*, *Delete-Customer*, *Consolidate Cust-Master*
- Project: *New-Customer-Processing*
  - Application models:
    - Logical data model: *New-Customer*
    - Process model: *Add-Customer*
    - Structure charts: *Add-Customer*, *Update-Customer-Master*

Encyclopedia 2:
- Project: *Update-Customer-Master*
  - Application models:
    - Logical data model: *New-Customer*
    - Data flow diagrams: *New-Customer Processing*, *Deleted-Customer-Flow*
- Project: *Purchase-Order System*
  - Application models:
    - Logical data model: *Inventory*
    - Data flow diagram: *Generate-PO*
    - Process models: *Add-Purchase-Order*, *Add-Line-Item*
    - Structure charts: *Create-PO*, *Update-Customer-Master*

Hopefully, this example does not look familiar to too many readers. If it does, your organization needs to standardize the definition of the following terms:

Project In most large development efforts where teams exceed five developers, all creating pieces of the overall application specifications, this is pure common sense. During initial project planning meetings, developers must agree on a universal name for their project as well as their intentions to uniformly use it in their local modeling tools. The organizational point, however, is uniformity both *across and within* projects. Typically, *project* equals *deployed application* in most implementations. Problems with this approach arise in the following situations (as can be partially gathered from the preceding example):

- Interapplication efforts (e.g., enterprise data modeling)
- Major application maintenance or enhancement efforts (sometimes these have a tendency to become defined as separate projects themselves based simply on the amount of involved developers)
- Nonapplication related efforts (application and hardware/software inventories, budgets, etc.)

It is important to uniformly address how any potential repository-targeted set of information is to be named. Most organizations look at each effort as a project, although as we have seen previously, this is not a requirement. Practicality will require some allegiance to tool-based definitions of terms such as project if they are to be the source (or location) of the repository-defined information sets. A convenient compromise is the equating of a project with an *effort* (rather than an application).

Application No arguments here, applications can and should be defined based on discrete physical implementations, as named. If an application is to be distributed, however, consider how to handle any requirements to name a single implementation differently from the overall application.

Subproject Sometimes a legitimate need exists to encompass portions of a larger effort. In our preceding example, this seems to be the case. If subprojects are used consistently they can prove to be lifesavers when it comes to the consolidation of models at the project level.

Model Originating in a tool, little flexibility exists in terms of defining what a model is. But the names of their implemented instances are very important, particularly when viewed from both a project and an enterprise perspective. Consider developing standards for model names that address the identification of the following:

- The source tool (although this can be derived from the repository-resident metamodel)
- The related project
- The related application
- The related subproject (if applicable)
- The *type* of model

Now I know what you are all thinking—hard coding? No way! True, many of the preceding can be derived via relationships models may have with particular repository counterparts. From a naming perspective, consider how much the name alone needs to convey when the model is considered as a standalone repository instance.

■ INTEGRATION WITHIN MODELS

Realizing what a model is, we can now talk about how to integrate the various renditions via a repository. First, it is important to address the integration of models that comprise instances of the same metamodel. Models must be integrated at the tool level before they can become adequate repository-referenced residents. Repositories often serve as interim integrators when large application models span several encyclopedias. For example, imagine the repository as the means of integrating multiple modeling efforts (all involving the same CASE tool) on a large project. To some extent, we can consider this to be *vertical* integration.

Most tools that are suitable for large modeling efforts supply *encyclopedia consolidation* routines. These utilities are used to combine various renditions of a particular set of models that may physically exist in separate encyclopedias. Usually, the "consolidator" can establish various option settings before the actual consolidation. For example, if the multiple renditions of models may consist of redundant names, the consolidator can set the process to flag every matching name and await user input as to whether or not the "duplicates" are truly duplicates. More sophisticated consolidation routines allow user definition of just how redundancy should be flagged (similar alternate names, matching names in the first *n* characters, etc.). However, today's encyclopedia consolidation routines are not as fully functional as a well-defined repository-based consolidation. For the most part, CASE-based model consolidations require manual intervention. In addition, most of the supplied routines assume narrow definitions of *source* and *target*. In other words, what is being consolidated has already been assumed by the tool to be either a single model, a single "project," or a single encyclopedia, and the target (what it is being consolidated *into*) most likely is a target encyclopedia/project combination.

With the intervention of a repository as the model integrator (consolidator), substantial leeway exists as to how the following required aspects of vertical model integration are defined:

- *Integration levels*. As we discussed previously, many large development efforts require effort breakdowns which include *subproject*, or maybe even *submodel* definition. In a well-implemented multiencyclopedia configuration, individual encyclopedias can be representative of distinct integration levels. For example, a very large data model may be under development by two distinct groups (perhaps the division was by subject area). Each encyclopedia consolidation, once complete, therefore represents a submodel in terms of repository level integration. These levels could either be preserved in the repository, or consolidated, or both, depending on the development needs.
- *Versioning*. Perhaps the need for integration is not always there. A repository can provide the option of versioning the various renditions of projects, models,

submodels, and so forth. Of course, a well-defined integration/versioning plan must address the impact on the various repository-based schemas that would be affected. In most large development efforts, there is always a need to know what the "official" construct instance is and to compare it to what is being considered as development continues.

- *Ownership*. With a repository one could define ownership at any level. For example, ownership of each model component instance could be maintained (assuming it exists or can be derived from within the base modeling tool), or ownership at the subproject or project level may instead be desired. The tracking of ownership is useful when implementing repository-based security, as we will see in the next chapter.
- *Integration rules and policies*. Unlike most CASE tool consolidation procedures, a repository allows the integration process to be as flexible and consistent as custom programming permits. Depending again on the capabilities supplied with the repository tool, an "integration procedure" could be developed which is executed based on user-defined triggers.

By defining the preceding aspects and then integrating them into the target metamodel and its associated relationships to other repository-resident metamodels, various policies can then operate on these integration-specific metamodel constructs as part of the overall integration process. The policies to be implemented will most likely address the relationships between the various integration levels as well as the correct processing required to integrate the multiple renditions as necessary. As we will see in the case study cited at the end of this chapter, vertical integration alone can involve several complicated issues. However, a well-designed plan which includes the metamodel, the integration process itself, and the required integrity policies can prove to be a consistent means of handling this very complicated process.

■ INTEGRATION BETWEEN MODELS

Remember that when we integrate *between* models we are concerned with intermodel relationships. For example, we want to ensure that the entities defined in a logical data model (an E–R model) are adequately related to their references in several process models. Or, because all of these referenced models may in fact be part of the same repository metamodel (e.g., if they came from the same CASE tool), another example involves the assurance that these same entities, referenced from both a data and a process perspective, relate appropriately to physical implementations that may exist in a DBMS catalog. Remember also that when a repository comes into the picture, this integration needs to be ensured regardless of the source modeling tool(s). Therefore, continuing our example, we may want the logical data models from Tool A to be integrated with aspects of the process models from Tool B.

Most intermodel integration is based on underlying relationships that have been defined in the repository metamodel. That is, if a metamodel exists that relates E–R models to process models via common use of an entity construct, the population of each of these with their associated instance models will automatically ensure the population of this relationship. Likewise, continuing our previous example, the fact that a relationship has been defined from these entity representations to occurrences in a DBMS catalog should require the automatic population of this connection via a repository-initiated procedure.

Consider Fig. 26.1. In this particular vendor's implementation, we can see the relationship between the *Data Entity* that exists as a component of both the entity–relationship and logical data models and the *Data Process* (*Process*) that exists in the data flow model and is further refined in the program design model.

Therefore, when the models to be integrated originate from and/or reside in the same tool, these intermodel relationships are often handled by the tool itself. That is, it is impossible in a truly integrated tool to reference an entity in a process model that does not exist as a defined entity in a data model belonging to the same project. But life is not always this easy, and even when the models are part of the same tool's domain, true integration is not often a requirement in the creation of models in some tools (as we discussed previously in this book). Therefore, the secret to intermodel integration (regardless of originating tool) via a repository lies in the proper implementation of the following areas:

- *A well-defined interrelated repository metamodel*. We discussed this topic in detail in the previous chapter. It is necessary to reiterate that the constant update of model instances as well as the constant addition of new models may result in the need to revisit the metamodel from time to time. Expect the metamodel to be dynamically created as your repository is rolled out.
- *Properly integrated models at the tool level*. If the models are not properly integrated in their source tool, the repository will not work magic. As part of the evaluation of today's models (as discussed in Part One), evaluate their "connections" to each other. It should be clarified, however (as discussed previously), that a repository can play a major role in the integration of multiple renditions (and variations) of project models that may exist across several single-tool encyclopedias. In this scenario models may not yet be properly integrated at the tool level, but they should be properly integrated within each local encyclopedia's rendition of the "project" level.
- *Well-defined intermodel integrity policies*. Even though the tools are supposed to enforce the integrity of intermodel relationships, we know that tool users can still input incomplete and unconnected models. In addition, why rely on tools to validate data that once accessible via a repository will have a potential impact that goes well beyond the source CASE tool user? We will be discussing repository policies in detail in the next chapter. Simply stated, policies can be invoked upon load of any model or model component, or, if desired, "integrity checks," which could consist of a set of policies, maintenance procedures, and validation rules, can be run on recently loaded repository data as an after-the-fact check. The specifics of each of these options are quite tool dependent, but they all share the same functional objective—that of validating the repository's contents before it is too late!

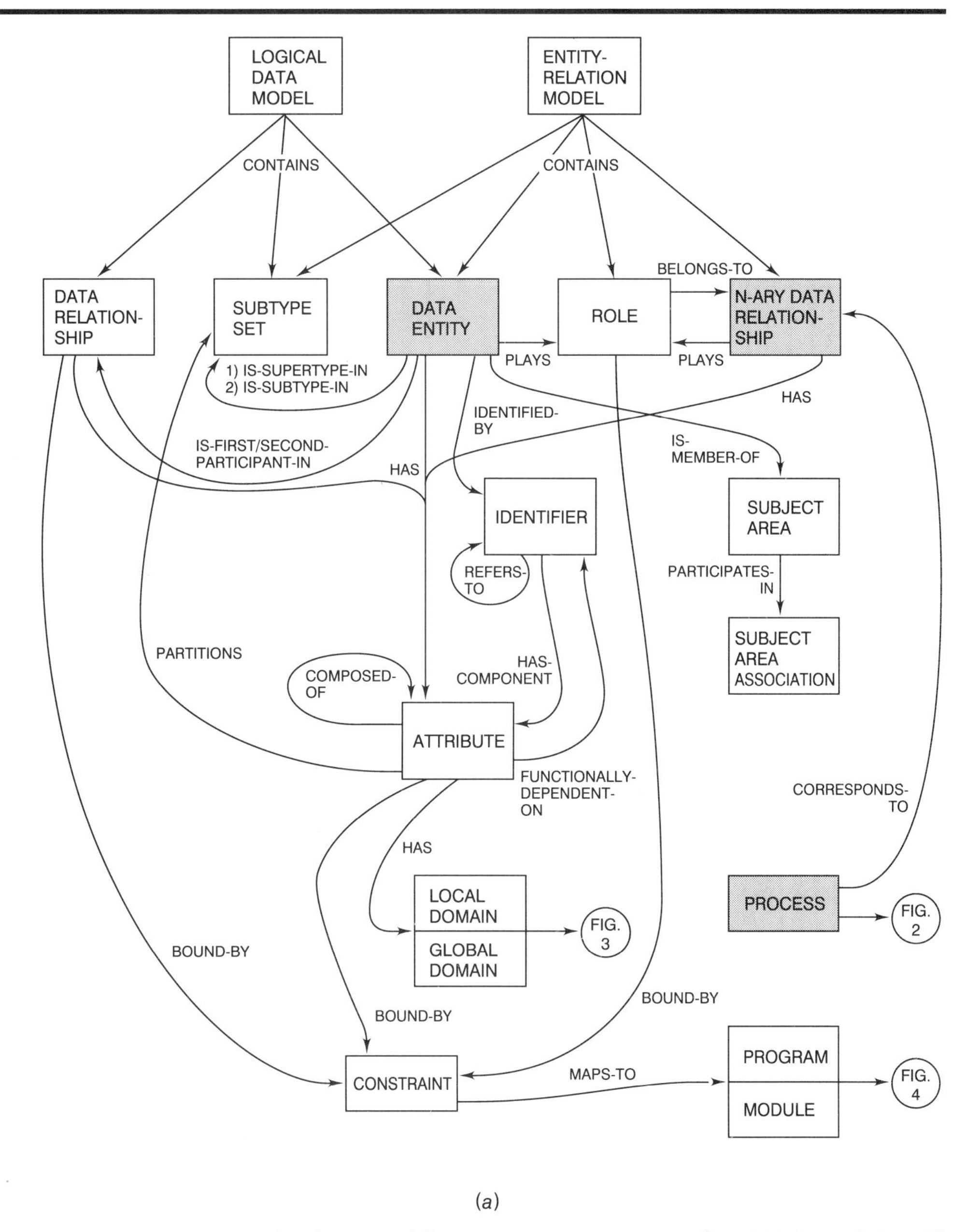

(*a*)

Figure 26.1 An example of intermodel integration in a repository (© 1992 Intersolv Inc. All rights reserved).

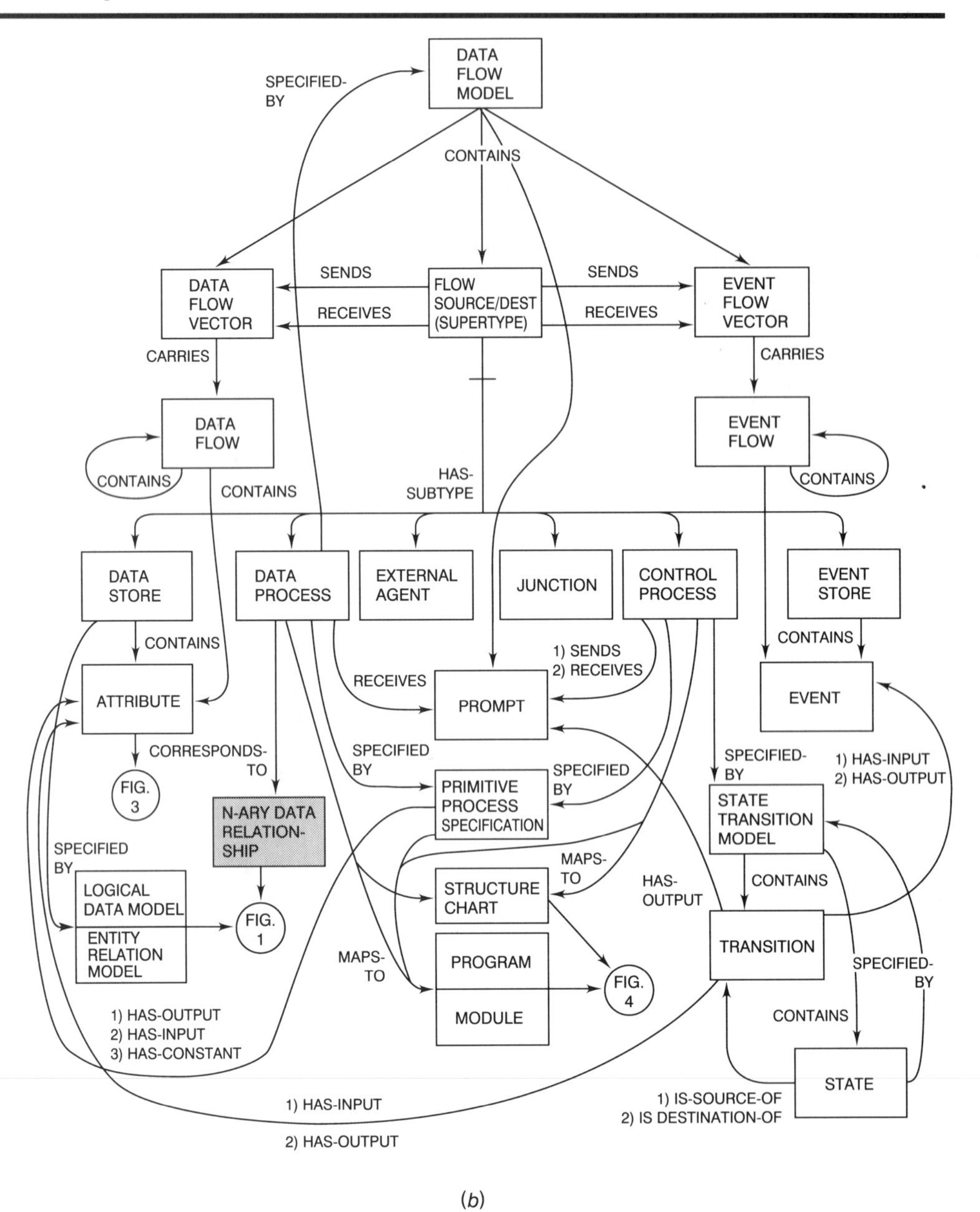

(*b*)

Figure 26.1 (*Continued*).

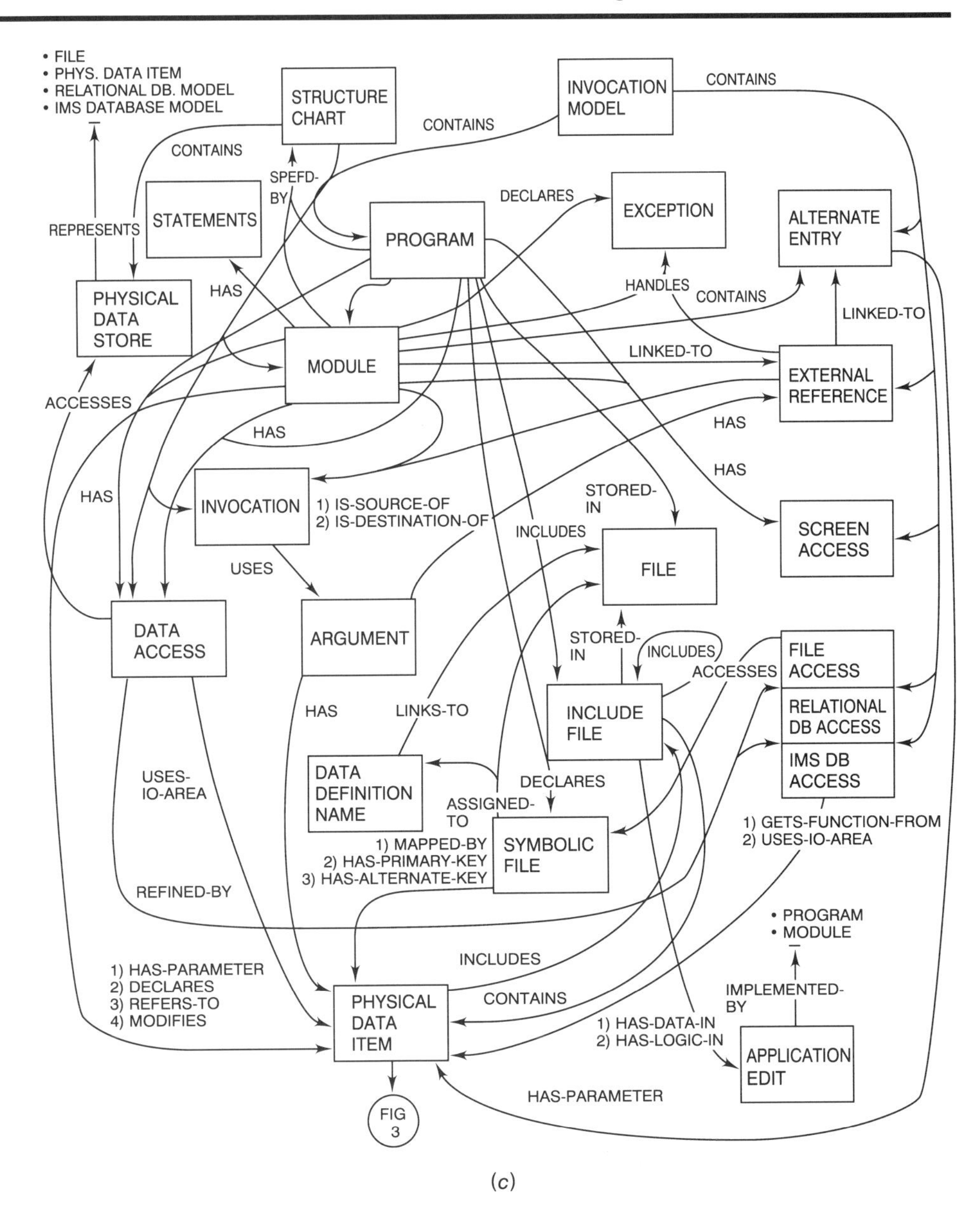

(c)

Figure 26.1 (*Continued*).

■ ELIMINATING REDUNDANCY

Integration is the consolidation of several into one. Despite how the *several* or the *one* are defined, the result should be free of duplication or conflict. One of the biggest concerns with model integration is the elimination of redundancy. Redundancy in models implies many situations:

- *The existence of duplicate construct instances.* That is, two *Customer* entities exist, each appearing in a distinct model, yet each representing an identical concept.
- *The existence of partially similar construct instances.* Two *Customer* entities exist as before, yet they do not represent identical concepts. One, for example, represents all customers, regardless of their current status (current, previous, and potential customers are all represented here). The other *Customer* entity only represents current customers. Delving under the covers depicts different lists of related attributes for each.
- *The existence of contradictory construct instances.* Two *Customer* entities exist as before, yet they represent distinctly different concepts. One represents any consumer of the company's services; the other represents any recipient of an application's output (obviously internal to the organization).
- *The existence of different construct instances with similar intentions.* Here, the distinct constructs may not even be representative of the same construct type. For example, a *Department-Name* attribute in one model may represent the name of an organizational unit. Similarly, in another model a *Department-Name* program may represent the physical implementation of a process that assigns departments to various office building locations. The similarity, we hope, rests with the fact that both distinct construct types use the same instances of *Department-Name* (in reality). A more common example involves the existence of two distinct constructs (not necessarily of the same type) with distinct names, yet similar intentions. Consider the previous example again, only this time the program's name is *Assign-Organization*.

Regardless of the type of redundancy, its handling is dependent on many factors. Perhaps the most obvious factor is that of consistency. Like any other process that is about to be mechanized, redundancy elimination can only be automated if consistent treatment of consistent situations can be mimicked. With the advent of rule-based expert systems, this situation is becoming more feasible, yet the rules still need to be defined, and every exception still needs to be documented and handled, even if the only practical handling of the exception is via manual intervention.

When encountering any of the aforementioned scenarios, the consolidation options involve only the following:

- *Translation.* If a construct of one type should really be represented as a construct of another type, the source is typically translated into the desired target. Translation implies the movement of some source attributes into different target constructs and/or attributes.

- *Elimination*. If the source construct totally contradicts the intentions of the target, it is typically eliminated in that it does not become a part of the target. This action, of course, must be evaluated in terms of any resulting "logic holes," and usually requires later manual intervention.
- *Merger*. In this scenario the source construct and the target construct are complementary. That is, each construct individually represents a partial aspect of the integrated whole. By merging the two together, redundancy is eliminated (where the aspects are common), and the validity of the resulting merged construct instance is an improvement, typically with a larger scope.

■ EXAMPLES

The practical execution of each option requires careful planning. Initially, it is essential to determine whether or not commonalities exist among redundancy occurrences in the various models. For example, if the integration process always involves the translation of a *subtype* construct that exists in one tool's metamodel into an entity/relationship combination such as *entity*, and *entity_is_a_subtype_of*, this "translation rule" is a practical example of consistent repository-based redundancy elimination. In this simple example a translation rule would be executed based on the existence of the *subtype* construct in the particular source tool.

An example of a redundancy rule that results in the elimination (or ignorance) of a source construct instance is that of the handling of obsolete instances. Consider the situation that results when one corporation buys another. Many information systems immediately become extinct. However, their models may not become extinct (so soon, anyway) if they truly represent business requirements. It is most likely necessary to evaluate these requirements under the auspices of the new regime and the new information systems. But, if the corporate merger results in an immediate takeover of one of the old corporation's functional areas, any reference to the old area in any application model is immediately contradictory, out of date, and redundant. Hence, integration of those models containing these obsolete instances should eliminate them.

Finally, the most common way to integrate is via merger. Perhaps a standard problem is the limited scope of most application models when it comes to defining their data requirements. One application's logical data model may define an entity instance of *Product* that really represents an aspect of the corporate *Product* definition. For example, the application may really be dealing with product components that are later assembled into true, consumer-ready products. These "components" may be considered products to the application, however, because they are bought and sold by wholesalers (this application's customer). An integration scenario in this case would involve the merger of some of the application entity's attributes into the corporate *Product* entity along with the translation of the application's entity instance into that of a *Product Component*.

Mechanization of these policies implies consistent treatment of all source and target constructs that meet the criteria being searched for during the integration procedure. If the truth surrounding your redundancy is that it is inconsistent and hard to identify, even the best implemented repository policies and integration rules are not going to be of assistance.

Redundancy elimination is a very difficult task. Ideally, it should be attempted as soon as the models to be compared are complete (i.e., the sooner the better). When historic models are being evaluated, the task becomes exponentially more difficult. The difficulty is attributed mainly to the fact that, as discussed previously, manual intervention is required in order to determine the true meaning of vague model construct instances. The older the model, the less likely it is that the reviewer will be able to find the appropriate person with the most accurate model knowledge.

Various tools that can assist in the identification of redundancy have been introduced over the past few years. Although the primary objective of these tools was the identification of redundant data across corporate databases (regardless of their physical implementations and designs), they could operate similarly on information targeted for a repository. The requirement, of course, is the ability to represent the model instances in a tool-accessible DBMS. Whether or not this effort is worthwhile is dependent on how scattered and prominent model instance redundancy is in your organization.

■ CASE STUDY

As promised, we will return to one of our previously cited case studies—that of Mummert and Partner.* As discussed previously, this project involved the use of a repository (R&O's *ROCHADE*) for the consolidation of multiple encyclopedias, all representing a portion of the overall application model, as depicted in Knowledgeware's ADW. The goal of this multideveloper, multimodel, multiencyclopedia project was the creation of a consistent, project-wide model.

The goal involved several requirements. First, there was a need to track ownership at the construct level. Answers to the question, "Who can process which constructs and with what authority?" needed to be handled via the repository. Related to the issue of ownership, developers needed to know the current state of a particular model construct as well as be aware of all developers who had expressed an interest in their own construct instances. In addition, their integration efforts needed to address some of the typical redundancy problems discussed previously: the existence of *synonyms* (similar constructs described repeatedly, but with different names) and *homonyms* (constructs with the same name that have different meanings).

Consolidation required the establishment of a consistent composite model. This consistent model needed to be free of redundancy. Developers learned early on that a composite model is not produced by simply joining the individual models. The consolidation effort was therefore shifted from departmental development to

---

*As submitted by Stefan Möller, April 22, 1993.

central data administration. In addition, the effort was assisted by automated tools wherever possible.

The effort began therefore with the definition of a uniform metamodel that encompassed the necessary extensions. The most important step was the addition of the "owner" concept at the construct instance level. In the Mummert and Partner implementation, owners were represented as either a person (user id) or a subproject. In this way various security levels could be implemented. Each construct had one and only one owner, and only the owner was permitted to alter or remove the associated construct. Another major extension was that of the addition of a new attribute, STATUS. This attribute, associated with every model construct instance, identified the current development status of that construct.

Project-wide reports that were based on the existence of the composite model were then defined. Because the repository version of the model was considered to be the "official" project version, developers would always be required to minimize the differences between their individual models and the repository version. These reports were to be used by the developers as a way of determining the best way to relate their local model to the project-wide version. Next, the effort concentrated on the creation of this composite model from the local encyclopedias.

The *owner* concept proved to be essential in the creation of the composite model. For example, homonyms were easily identified because each construct instance had to have a unique identifier and only one owner. Any construct that appeared with the same name but different owners was immediately considered a homonym. The composite model resulted from comparisons at several levels. Based again on the owner concept, construct instances were only changed when the owner information indicated the proper authority. All of the "differences" were stored separately, converted to update commands, and eventually executed to produce the repository version.

Mummert and Partner relied on a process they call "temporal consolidation" to maintain the composite model. Simply speaking, on a daily basis local encyclopedias were compared with the central composite model. Approved differences, as with the local encyclopedia consolidation process used to create the initial composite model, were saved and translated into repository update commands. In order to ensure the use of the latest composite model components at each ADW workstation, a download of the latest model (reflective of updates) followed each daily update. In addition, a report that listed those changes that could not be permitted in the respective local encyclopedia (based on the concept of ownership) was given to each involved developer. The report listed the developer's rejected changes as well as the "owner" of the in-conflict constructs that existed in the corporate model. Based on this report, developers were required to resolve these differences each day. When proper resolution resulted, developers received a much shorter list of "not allowed changes" the next day. This entire process occurred automatically each business day.

The automatic consolidation process also guaranteed quality control via the enforcement of consistency checks with each upload. Via the use of "encyclopedia overlap" reports, synonyms were easy to identify. Quality control was necessary because this project consisted of 55 encyclopedias. The composite model translated into 18,000 repository instance items.

The Mummert and Partner effort demonstrates the success that can be gained with well-planned vertical integration efforts. Redundancy elimination in this case was virtually automatic. By studying the reasons for each type of redundant model component instance, developers were able to determine the solution via the use of an associated owner.

■ SUMMARY

As discussed in this chapter, consistent integration can only be achieved with consistent integration policies. This is why the state of to-be-loaded repository information is so important. Hopefully, by evaluating today's models as recommended in Part One of this book, redundancy control will be a manageable part of your repository implementation process.

27

PUTTING THE REPOSITORY TO USE

Luck is what happens when preparation meets opportunity.

Darrell Royal, 1976

Our repository is populated and accurate. We have assessed its initial scope and have a well-planned implementation strategy. Before making the repository a productive part of the application development practices in your organization, it is essential to revisit repository access considerations. Now, with a live repository in existence, access is viewed from a true production requirements perspective. In this chapter we will discuss how access requirements should be addressed and controlled in your repository implementation and then portray the fully functional repository in terms of its incorporation into the organization's application development environment. As with all implementation-specific chapters, we will conclude with live case studies.

■ REPOSITORY ACCESS REASONS

As alluded to in the preliminary chapters of Part Five, the repository's accessibility must be evaluated in terms of *why* it will be accessed. An obvious factor, in that access reasons typically drive the decision to implement a repository, it should be revisited before the repository is "turned loose" on the development organization.

Reconsider which of the following areas apply to the *why's* of your implemented repository:

- *The "look-up" of application-specific metadata*. Application names, program names, program components, database names, database components, implemented application versions, installed sites, execution platforms, and so on
- *The load/download of application-specific metadata*
- *Inter-tool gateways*. The use of the repository as an intermediary between various development tools (CASE, source code library management packages, testing tools, source code analyzers, etc.)

- *The generation of applications.* The use of repository-referenced (or repository-resident) instance data to generate actual application code and database implementations
- *General inventory support.* Accessing the repository in order to determine how to get to what is really desired, as in a roadmap
- *Application development life cycle control.* The use of the repository to control the flow of an application from development to test to production, for example. The repository in this scenario verifies the readiness of an application for migration to the next development phase and/or generates many of the options necessary for migration itself (e.g., compiler options)

After determining your access reasons, each should be evaluated in terms of the following characteristic access qualities:

- Immediate (on-line) access vs. batch requests
- Consistent vs. on-demand requests (will the same types of requests be issued each time or will the syntax and contents of each request vary?)
- GUI vs. command-driven requests
- User id vs. program vs. tool access
- Read-only vs. write access
- Transaction-based vs. file-transfer response
- Distributed vs. standalone access/response

Access characteristics are an important predeterminant to the establishment of repository access policies. These policies, as we alluded to in previous chapters, can make or break the maintenance of your repository as a useful and practical source of corporate information. Specifically, the nature of repository access can be varied in terms of how the repository is accessed, what (within) the repository is being accessed, and how it is being returned and displayed. Access, of course, becomes complicated when it also implies repository update.

The next sections will discuss repository policies. Because policies alone are often not the single most factor that controls repository access, other repository "controls" (such as templates) will also be discussed as necessary component features.

■ REPOSITORY POLICIES

Repository policies are program code which are ideally implemented, controlled, and executed by the repository software to perform a wide range of services including data validation and security checks. The use of policies in any repository tool can take on several implementation flavors. In the most desirable scenario the policies themselves are defined and stored within the repository. Their relationship(s) to other populated repository constructs guarantees their invocation based on any type of event that involves these related constructs. Less desirable alternatives involve the use of *user exits* which invoke custom-developed software outside of the repository. Even with user exits, however, the mere fact that they exist is kept as repository-resident information, related to specific repository constructs in much the same manner as repository-resident policies themselves. Finally, the least desirable means of establishing a policy is totally outside of the realm of repository control. Simply speaking, in this scenario custom-developed software controls repository access with no "knowledge" or tracking of this fact within the repository.

Although we are separating our discussion of repository policies by their functional use, it is important to note that the actual implementation of policies within repository tools is not a consistently deployed characteristic. Most repository software has a so-called *firing order* when it comes to the actual execution of user-defined policies. In addition, the categorization of policies varies among repository tools. Practically speaking, the reader must realize that policies here will be discussed generically, but the specifics as to whether or not the discussed policy types exist, as well as their impact on the overall repository's functionality, will be somewhat tool dependent.

In general, repository policies can be defined to control the following aspects of repository usage:

Repository Access Typically, access is controlled via *security policies*. However, security policies alone are not usually the only way access is controlled. For example, as we will see in the next section, *repository templates* can control what a repository user sees or has access to.

Repository Update Write access to repository contents deserves a special categorization in terms of policy-based control. The issues involved in the use of policies as a means of repository update management involve many factors, most of which were introduced at the beginning of this chapter.

Repository Functionality Aside from defining the repository in terms of its contents, a need exists to define the execution of its embedded and user-defined functions. Most practically, this area pertains to repository administration in that the involved policies typically dictate what tool-specific functions can be executed by a particular repository-defined user, program, and/or tool.

The actual deployment of policies in the preceding categories involves the following generic *policy types*:

Validation (Integrity) Policies These policies are used to ensure the accuracy of populated repository contents. For example, verifying a particular range of values would constitute an integrity policy.

Assignment (Derivation) Policies Policies of this type populate repository constructs with predefined values, most typically based on the existence of a particular condition. They are often considered *derivation policies* because the populated values may be based on values that exist elsewhere.

Trigger Policies These policies invoke a particular repository function based on the existence of a particular condition or event. They are most typically used as a means of automatically invoking user-defined repository functions.

Security Policies As discussed previously, these policies control all levels of repository access, update, and execution.

Repository Access Policies

In most repository scenarios the need exists for various levels of access restriction. For example, access to repository contents can be uniformly available based on the qualities of the retrieving user id as well as the affiliations and associations of the to-be-retrieved information. When repository *access* needs to be restricted, security policies are typically involved. When the *display* of the accessed repository contents needs to be controlled or refined based on any number of factors (e.g., the actual repository construct type, its project level affiliations, and/or the user-id permissions, *repository templates* are usually also involved.

Security policies can affect virtually any aspect of a repository's role in an organization. We will consider them first as controllers of repository access. As we discussed in Part Four, the inherent architecture of a repository lends itself to various levels of security. Security at the uppermost level controls access to the entire repository, whereas the lowermost level of security involves access to repository constructs themselves, often at levels as low as the attribute level.

The implementation specifics of your organization's repository access policies are dependent on the repository access reasons which should have been laid out in detail. Simply stated, the various levels of security that can be implemented via security policies may not all be appropriate for your implemented repository architecture. In addition, higher levels of security (e.g., those that control the access to the entire repository) have less complicated policy implications. Finally, as we stated previously, the security policies discussed in this chapter are generic in that not all repository tools offer the same range of security options.

Security policies are the most common means of controlled repository access. They are most typically implemented at one or more of the following levels:

The Repository Level Here, an open-and-shut case exists. Like any installed piece of software, the repository can be installed so as to require installation-defined permissions as a prerequisite to its access. For example, it can be established as a developer tool only, leaving no access to end-users, regardless of their established user-id permissions in terms of other installed databases.

The "Tool" Level Within the repository architecture, various interfacing tools can be defined to the repository in terms of their own tool-specific security restrictions. In this scenario one could consider each tool as a user id and define the appropriate tool-specific security policies. For example, perhaps an interfacing CASE tool should only be allowed read access to the repository. The appropriate security policy would forbid any user from pursuing repository update through this tool's repository interface. As we will see in the following discussion, tool level security almost always involves the definition of an associated *template*.

The Metadata Level Within the repository metamodel, security policies can address the access of specific constructs. In most repositories various levels of granularity exist in terms of how deeply the implemented security policy affects the access to the repository's contents. All of the following variations are possible:

- *Metamodel security*. Repository access can be restricted at the metamodel level. Simply stated, a particular user id (or tool) can be prohibited from accessing the DB2-specific metamodel. When metamodel access is prohibited, it typically applies to both the metamodel constructs and the associated instance data, assuming the metamodel is the gateway to the instance data, regardless of where it is stored.

- *Metadata (i.e., metamodel construct) security.* Within one or more metamodels, security policies can control access to particular constructs. In some tools metadata security can be implemented at a level as low as the metadata attribute. For example, perhaps end-users are prohibited from viewing the project entity and all of its associated attributes. A security policy could restrict access to the entire project entity or, if needed, to a specific attribute such as its development status. As with metamodel security, the inability to access a metadata construct implies the inability to access its populated instance data.
- *Instance data security.* Although not really "metadata" security, repository access to particular sets of instance data can also be controlled. Continuing our project example, perhaps end-users should only have access to those instances of the project entity for which they have funding authorization.

When security is implemented at the metadata level, its impact often goes beyond the immediate construct for which the security policy was intended. For example, if a security policy is associated with a relationship, many tools automatically cascade the policy's effect to both the source and target entities of the relationship. Some tools offer dependent construct coverage as an option that needs to be user defined. Regardless of the situation, the establishment of metadata level security policies requires considerable evaluation.

Once security pertains only to a subset of the entire repository (a tool-, metamodel-, or metadata-specific set of security requirements), the implementation of this security almost always involves the definition and use of an associated *template*. Templates represent a logical view of repository metadata. A functional equivalent (for those readers familiar with DB2) is the *DB2 view*. Simply stated, a defined template represents a named collection of metadata that can generally be associated with a user id, a repository tool, a repository function, and/or a repository policy. Therefore, when we look at the template as a means of restricted access, it becomes obvious how most security policies that restrict access within the repository require an associated template. In fact, in many tools templates themselves can have associated security policies.

It is important to realize that templates represent logical as opposed to physical groupings of repository data. If a repository interface involves a GUI front end, this actual front end itself is not a template, but a possible physical implementation of an associated template. The defined template, however, represents the structural skeleton of the data that comes from the repository and populates this front-end panel interface. Think of a template as an intermediary between the actual repository and what the user actually sees.

Many repository tools allow the implementation of template hierarchies which allow templates to be embedded within other templates. For example, a template that defines the set of metadata accessible by the IMS database tuning group can contain another template that defines COBOL program metadata. Access to the "parent" template includes access to the "child" template, but not vice versa. In this example source code library auditors may only have access to the COBOL-specific template and may not need or be granted access to the associated IMS parent template.

Finally, when we view templates in conjunction with repository policies, it is important to return to the *firing order* concept mentioned previously. When a repository architecture consists of metadata, policies, repository functions, templates, and optional instance data, an embedded priority exists in terms of where control begins. Typically, repository level policies have the upper hand in terms of repository control. Next, the priority of templates, repository functions, and the various policies in terms of when, where, and how their control starts and stops within the repository architecture is usually somewhat user definable. The reader should realize, however, that the amount of allowed user-specified control is variable from tool to tool. As long as the repository architect is aware of the tool's internal processing priorities, the flexibility that exists among the various means of implementing repository access policies is sure to meet the organizational access requirements.

Repository Update Policies

In addition to general repository access, there is often a greater need to place security policy control on the write access of a repository and its contents. Repository update policies follow the same strategy discussed previously for repository access policies. However, because of the added complexity of determining where write access is allowed and by which repository passageways (user ids, tools, etc.), additional security-related constraints can be configured.

Because it is quite common for repository access to involve a wider range of read-only permission, within which exists a subset that the reader can also update, many tools offer the ability to establish security policies at the *template field* level. In a practical example a template could define the contents of a tool's access to the repository, and template field level security would determine which template-defined fields (if any) the tool has authority to update.

Once update of a repository's contents is authorized, other policies (in addition to security policies) are required. As with repository load, any information that goes into the repository needs to be validated. Updates, however, require several levels of validation, beginning with their validation as standalone entries and ending with their validation as part of the overall metamodel in which they will participate. Starting most probably at the template field level, *validation policies* and/or *assignment policies* can be used to confirm or generate the values targeted for repository update. The two types of policies are often combined to validate repository input at the various required levels. For example, a common validation scenario would involve the following:

1. The assignment of a *validation policy* upon a particular template field to verify the to-be-loaded value.
2. The association of an *assignment policy* with other fields on the template or with a related subordinate template. Based on the valid input of a particular

template field (which could represent the key into a set of instance data), an assignment policy could be used to generate the remainder of the template, for example. Perhaps the values that were generated resulted from a database read, using the prevalidated key value.

3. The association of a *trigger policy* with the entire prepopulated template. The trigger policy could invoke the required repository function (e.g., *repository write*) which would update the repository contents. The trigger policy's execution would be based on the condition that the template was fully populated and/or that the previous policy was successfully carried out.

Repository Execution Policies

In addition to controlling what a repository user can see and update, there is also a need to control what a repository user can do in terms of repository function execution. Specifically, remember, as discussed previously, that security policies can be implemented at the tool level. Tool-specific security policies can usually be associated with sets of repository functions. In this scenario a repository-defined tool (such as an interfacing configuration management package) would be defined with associated:

- *Templates*, which control what the configuration management package has access to from within the repository as well as what the package can supply to the repository.
- *Template-associated policies*, as discussed under repository update policies.
- *Allowable repository functions*, each with its own defined security policy(ies) and *parameter templates*. Without trying to confuse the template issue, parameter templates serve the same functional role as the *data templates* we have discussed thus far in that they represent a logical grouping of information. The reason for the distinction rests with the *type* of information that is logically represented. With data templates, as we have discussed, subsets of repository contents are defined and passed from the repository to the interfacing tool, user id, or function. *Parameter templates*, on the other hand, are associated exclusively with repository functions and typically are predefined and populated. However, many tools allow user override capability. With this flexibility execution policies can be assisted by associating a parameter template that always has certain fixed parameter values whenever a tool, for example, executes the particular repository function.

As explained, the implementation of repository policies can be almost as involved as the definition of the repository metamodel. Because the repository architecture involves a series of interrelated components, the definition or modification of any embedded repository concept is sure to have implications on other aspects of the overall repository.

The key to successful repository policy implementation is a firm understanding of your tool's underlying repository architecture. Specifically, you must be aware of

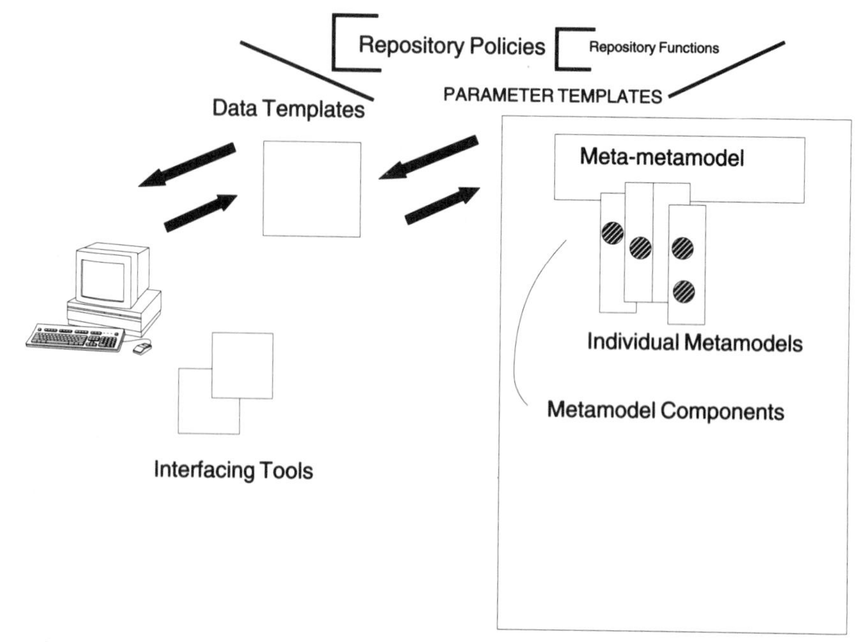

Figure 27.1 An architected repository policy example.

the interrelationships of the following architectural components:

- Repository meta-metamodel
- Individual metamodels
- Metamodel components
- Repository policies
- Repository functions
- Data and parameter templates
- Interfacing tools

As illustrated in Fig. 27.1, we can see the overall hierarchy of security execution when all repository components are viewed. Most repository tools have similar functional priorities. However, the specifics as to the actual security implementation options and how they relate to tool-supplied, unalterable security remain vendor specific.

■ REPOSITORY ADMINISTRATION

The establishment of the functional repository is not possible without repository administration. Similar to the functional role of database administration, it should be the only organizational function with the authority to establish and update the repository backbone. Remembering our metadata perspectives (Chap. 20), repository administrators work on the definition and maintenance of perspective 3, the tool's perspective, by defining and relating the various metamodels.

In addition to metamodel maintenance, repository administration is also responsible for all other aspects of the repository's underlying architecture. Repository policies, especially those that are repository-wide in impact, are the full responsibility of the administrative repository arm. Tool-specific policies are often developed, but as a minimum, authorized for repository implementation, by repository administrators. In essence, all aspects of repository security fall under the domain of repository administrators.

Repository security and the repository metamodel are commonly accepted as administrative responsibilities. There are many other aspects of repository-based development that could typically become repository administration obligations. The deciding factor when evaluating the need for administrator input rests with the determination as to whether or not the function in question deserves "centralized" treatment. Unlike database administration where the "centralized" function usually represents one step above the application in terms of responsibility (e.g., it may concern itself with the specifics of one particular DBMS, regardless of the characteristics of the associated implemented applications), the repository has the potential to cross all previously implemented functional boundaries.

Unfortunately, many organizations do not distinguish between the functional roles of repository administration and data administration. There is much more to repository administration than the maintenance of a corporate data dictionary. For example, aside from the dictionary-like responsibilities of metamodel and security maintenance, repositories allow the definition of many repository-wide features, such as:

- Global repository functions, including the ability to define new repository functions in most tools
- Global templates and template trees
- Tool enablement
- Standard application interfaces

Typically, the development of APIs (application program interfaces) is often left to individual application developers. The centralized development of these interfaces would lead to consistent and efficient use of repository resources.

When viewing the potential involvement of repository administrators in the establishment and maintenance of a functional repository, it is clear that the skill set of the average data administrator may not be sufficient. Repository administration involves much more than the maintenance and development of logical data models. Many organizations naively expect existing data administration organizations to take on the implementation of a corporate repository. Because of the repository's impact on all aspects of an organization's information environment, successful repository administration involves the skills of:

- Data administrators
- Database administrators
- Systems programmers

- Application programmers
- Application development managers
- Knowledgeable users of all to-be-interfaced tools
- Developers of the to-be-interfaced tools (which typically means outside vendors!)

Although it is not necessary to create a massive organization with representatives from each of the preceding functional areas, it is important to realize that these skills must play a part in the implementation and maintenance of your corporate repository. Expecting a continually successful implementation with the availability of two data administrators is a bit unrealistic! However, I do not mean to portray the typical repository administrator as a rare gifted individual with abilities that match all of the previous skill requirements. The important message to be delivered here is that the preceding skills will at times be necessary in order to deliver a fully functional repository.

Repository administrator skill requirements are, of course, directly dependent on the functions supplied by the repository software. For example, if the repository itself offers a set of repository administrator utilities which are easy to use and part of a friendly interface, it may not be necessary for the administrator's application programming skills to be up to par. Remember though, as stated previously, that it is very likely for custom programming to be an eventual part of most repository installations.

■ INCORPORATING THE REPOSITORY INTO YOUR APPLICATION DEVELOPMENT ENVIRONMENT

The final step involved in putting your repository to use is the transition of your current application development practices into a repository-based environment. As we have discussed throughout the book thus far, repositories should not be considered silver bullet solutions to poorly managed application development environments (ADEs). Aside from the fact that the planning, design, and introduction of a repository require major amounts of organizational discipline, the introduction of the well-designed tool into the repository developer's "outside world" will require progressively greater levels of self-control from the pro-repository faction.

The introduction of a repository into the ADE assumes a relatively stable ADE. If that is not the case in your organization, the process must be approached with extreme caution. Poorly managed application development organizations are always looking for something on which to blame their problems. A new technology such as a repository is always ripe for such a role. Put yourself in the position of the fretful application development manager, already behind schedule and working double overtime in an attempt to deliver a subfunctional first application release. A newly created repository administration organization approaches him and requests the upload of his "frozen" CASE-based models into the recently implemented corporate repository. His first answer is obviously that he does not have the time now, he is already behind. His second answer is that once the first application release is in production, he would be more than happy to oblige. One week later, when his participation in the repository load becomes "mandatory," his tight schedule is impacted even more. The model upload becomes even more time consuming when repository administration requires changes to some of the model components as a means of conforming to the newly created modeling standards. The application's first release is delivered, but with many inaccuracies. The already visibly shaken project manager is called on the carpet and asked for an explanation. Used to defensiveness, the project manager blames a substantial part of the schedule slip on the newly created repository administration function. A few more situations like this (e.g., with other applications) are sure to extinguish any potential for repository-based development.

Revisit your phased repository implementation plan, particularly the objectives and scope of your initial repository target. A well-designed implementation plan includes an assessment of the initial repository's functional contents as well as the extent of the first repository interfaces. Should we assume that this first architectural target is reflective of an immediate application development improvement need? We hope so. If not, now is the time to identify one and hope that all of your repository preparation will satisfy the defined need.

Incorporation of the repository into your ADE begins with its successful fulfillment of the defined application development need. Consider how the current task is being accomplished (if at all) and put the repository right in the heart of the current data flow. The repository should become the residence of the information involved in this current development practice.

Consider the following example. An organization's phased approach to repository implementation declares the existence of an accessible application inventory to be the repository's immediate roll-out objective. Without the availability of such an inventory, requests for this type of information are handled as follows:

- Phone calls to each application development manager are placed whenever the information requester needs answers to questions such as, "Which applications are used by the personnel department?" or "What release of DOS are your end-users using?"
- Phone calls to database administration are placed whenever information regarding the following is needed: "What release of DB2 is deployed at our field sites?" "Are there any customer invoice databases still implemented in IDMS?"
- On-line queries are executed against single, standalone application databases to determine answers to questions such as "Does this database track our product-specific revenue?"

Incorporation of the repository (fully loaded, accurate, and *ready*) as the replacement source of the necessary answers involves its availability to those requesting the information. The first step in the incorporation of the repository requires repository access to be available to the specific phone call initiators cited previously. Continued incorporation requires the consistent guarantee that the information being requested is maintained and up to date. Application developers must also have access to the repository if they are to be the source of the repository-accessible information.

Keeping the repository as the sole information vehicle will ensure its viability as a mainstream component of application development. Direct interfaces between the repository and other "information suppliers" ensure nonredundancy. Another aspect of this example's first-cut repository incorporation involves a direct link to all production DBMS catalogs. As we discussed in previous chapters, the repository should be considered the gateway to the catalogs, and, in this example, it would replace the phone calls to database administration organizations.

Based on the remaining steps in this sample repository implementation strategy, the repository's role in the ADE will expand over time. Successful incorporation requires the constant evaluation of all information requests, including those that are satisfied by repository access. It is not unusual for ease of information access to breed the need for additional types of information which may not have been initially anticipated.

Continually consider the role of the repository as your ADE embraces additional technical solutions. A successful repository-based ADE uses the repository as the gateway to all of its development tools. Developers are no longer forced to rely on import/export between tools, and they are no longer required to reinput information that was input by another developing organization or project. Despite the promises of any new to-be-embraced technology, it should always be evaluated in terms of its place in the repository architecture.

■ CASE STUDIES

Substantial ground was covered in this chapter. As before, our case studies will substantiate the presented implementation strategies. The following case studies will cover both repository access and the incorporation of a fully functional repository into an organization's application development environment.

CASE STUDY 1 Optimizing Repository Accessibility

First, we will return to the previously cited Health Care Financing Administration (HCFA) case study.* The implemented mainframe repository serves as a gateway between the CASE tool and the physical DBMS catalog. As discussed, considerable time was spent establishing the integrated metamodel in order to support and relate the multiple views of information. The successful payback of the invested resources depended on accurate and reliable accessibility of the repository and its contents.

HCFA's repository was targeted initially as a tool for systems analysts, programmers, and database developers. In order to guarantee their active participation in repository-based development, a custom front end to the repository was developed. This front end is used for all repository input, query,

*As submitted by Cindy Walker, Elaine Stricklett, and John McGuire, May 11, 1993.

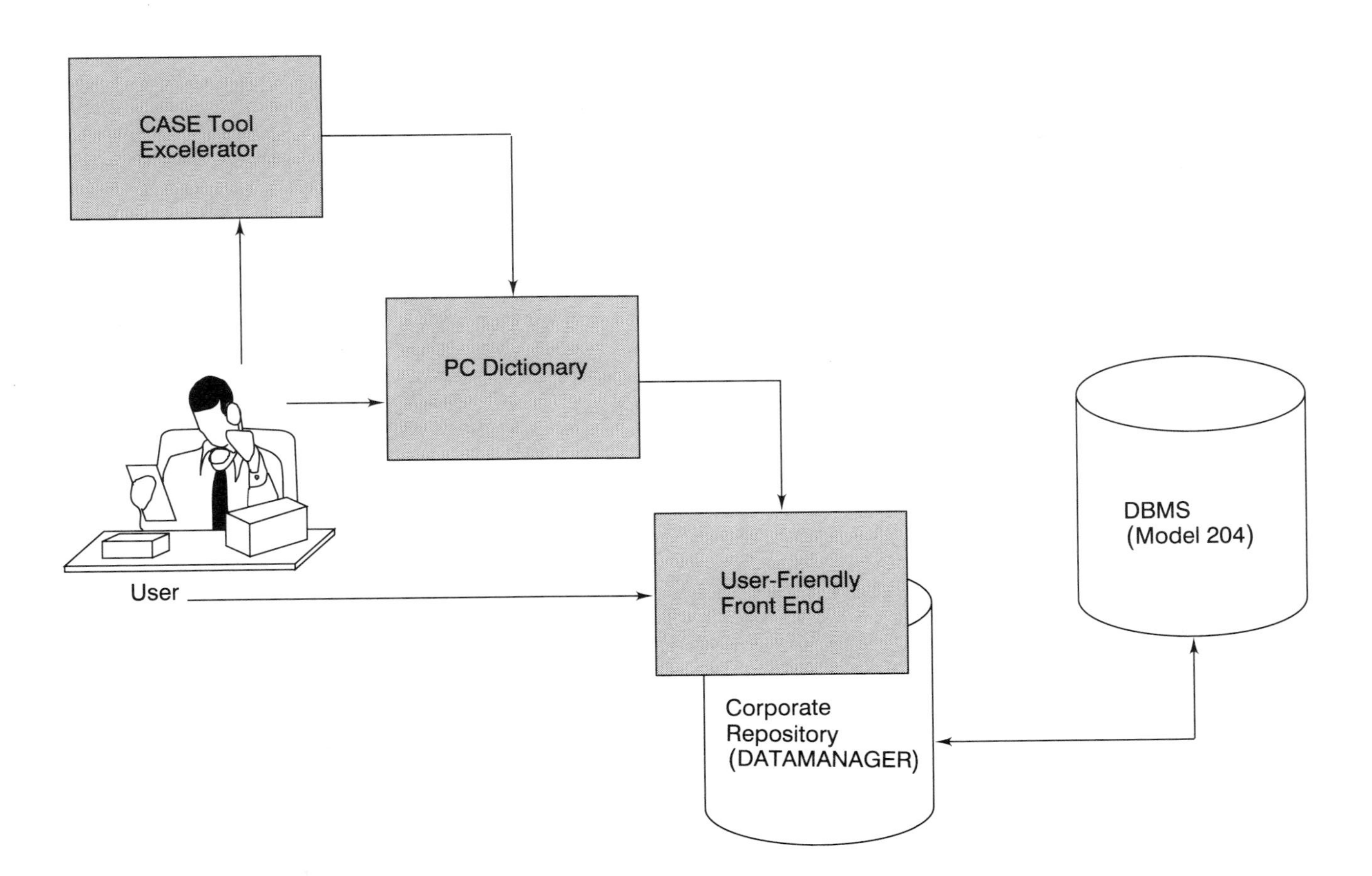

Figure 27.2 The HCFA repository architecture.

reporting, and help, and interfaces with both the mainframe (DATAMANAGER) repository and the downloaded PC Dictionary version. The resulting architecture is illustrated in Fig. 27.2.

The associated development effort spanned approximately 9 months. It is important to realize that, despite the initial effort spent in establishing the repository's metamodel, repository implementers were still aware of the importance of the continued effort required to make the repository a working part of the application development environment.

The HCFA repository is still not an integrated piece of the application development environment. Because application developers are still in the process of populating the repository with the documentation of existing systems, the current contents of the repository are not suited to the needs of all developers. The objective, however, is to use the HCFA repository as the gateway to all agency data. This gateway will be used by both developers and end-user data analysts. For developers, the repository front end will operate as follows:

1. Developers type in the names of the data elements they need (e.g., for a new development effort).
2. The repository initiates a search and returns the results.
3. After developer approval, the repository generates the code necessary to include these elements as part of the application (COBOL copybooks, DDL, etc.).

HCFA end-users will be using the repository as a gateway to a proposed data warehouse. The strategy involves the layering of the massive volumes of data into various decision support levels. Access to the data warehouse will only be via the repository, and the same "search" functionality used by the developers will be provided as part of the end-user front end. The result of the search, however, will be the location of the actual physical data.

CASE STUDY 2 Controlled Repository Access

A more detailed set of repository access policies was implemented by the Defense Logistics Agency (DLA), a U.S. government agency.* This case study is being introduced here for the first time based on its implementation concentrations in the repository access and security areas.

The DLA repository is accessed based on functional need. Specifically, the DLA data administration function involves the use of *data stewards*. These stewards are each responsible for specific functional subject areas and hence have control over only a subset of the entire corporate data picture. In order to properly address the diversity of access and security requirements, DLA's repository needed considerable policy establishment.

*As submitted by Cindy Walker, vice president information resource management, and Elaine Stricklett, program manager, Software Solutions, Inc., Alexandria, VA, May 6, 1993.

Because all DLA repository data needs to be accessible by the data stewards, every repository user id enjoys read privileges to any repository instance. However, data steward–specific panels (associated with specific user id's) control write access to repository instance data. Data stewards, via these panels, only view those constructs for which they have update authority. The DLA approach is similar to the use of templates discussed previously in the chapter. However, it is important to note that a sophisticated repository user could access the repository directly (instead of via the custom panels) via the repository software. The implemented tool's security features do not include the ability to enforce "repository-wide" security as a means of preventing unauthorized update to selected construct instances. In addition, the implemented repository architecture does not prevent access to the repository without using the custom "panels."

Although the implemented security may appear to have its shortcomings, DLA does not expect to suffer from any attempted breach of its implemented update policies. Because the custom panels are easy to use without knowledge of the underlying repository software, repository users have not delved beyond the panels' limited functional scope. The concentration on security can be seen when we evaluate its implementation time frame in terms of the entire repository implementation effort:

Development of methodology, naming standards, data stewardship procedures: 12 months

Repository metamodel definition: 2 months

Access policy evaluation and definition: 8 months

Repository usage is being incorporated into DLA application development practices in the area of data administration. Specifically, developers will be required to use repository-resident data elements (along with their standard names) in all major system redesign efforts.

CASE STUDY 3 The Repository as an ADE Tool

Our final case study returns us to a previously cited U.S. government agency determined to eliminate its application development chaos.* As part of the plan to make the repository into a mainstream component of the agency's application development practices, repository developers were aware of the need to keep the repository contents current. This objective required two major accomplishments:

- The development of automated repository update which was based on the true production environment
- Buy-in from all application developers in order to guarantee their participation as repository suppliers during new application development

*As submitted by Bobbi Amos, computer specialist, December 7, 1992.

Because maintenance programmers had not been cooperative in supplying their changes to the repository before production implementation, repository administrators needed a surefire way of keeping their repository contents accurate. The automated repository update involves a close link between the implemented repository and the production application environment. Whenever a change is made to a production system, production control triggers jobs that update the repository. The repository update procedure generates reports that itemize the updates. These reports are then verified with application users.

Developers of new applications have been much more cooperative. It was not always this way, however. In fact, during the initial repository implementation phases (when the metamodel was being created), most developers saw no personal value in their participation. Many formal presentations as well as group training sessions were conducted. In addition, a repository support person was assigned to each application development area. This one-on-one involvement eventually demonstrated repository benefits to even the most stubborn developer. These investments have paid off because today any developer with a data-specific problem or question consults the repository. Developer interest was not mandated; it evolved based on the increasing benefits gained from the repository as *the* accurate and accessible source of information. This evolution took over a year!

28

SPECIAL CONSIDERATION FOR DISTRIBUTED REPOSITORY IMPLEMENTATION

Most of our repository implementation aspects have now been discussed. However, as readers may have realized, our repository concentration seems to have assumed the existence of one, centralized repository as part of a multitool, multiuser architecture. The 1990s bring with them a trend to downsize—the size of everything from the corporate organization to the corporate budget to the corporate information system is being reduced. The corporate repository is no exception.

The downsizing of the corporate repository assumes one of two strategies:

- The repository itself is downsized (perhaps in terms of function, perhaps in terms of its contents), but there still exists only one.
- The repository is downsized, but still represents the functional equivalent of a complete corporate information gateway. In this scenario multiple "downsized" repositories exist. Together, they encompass the corporate objective.

In this chapter we will focus on the second strategy of repository downsizing. Distributed repositories were discussed in terms of their various architectural options in Part Four. Now, as part of our Part Five discussion of implementation specifics, we will discuss the practicalities of distributing your repository.

THE IMPORTANCE OF THE REPOSITORY ARCHITECTURE

When an organization considers distributing anything, there is still a need to keep track of the distribution points and their relationships to each other. Distributed repositories cry out for this need perhaps more loudly than any other "spread-out" information resource. The tracking of distribution involves several components, all of which need to be part of the overall distribution plan:

- *The distribution criteria*. How is the "bigger picture" broken down?
- *An overall directory*. What exists where? How do I get from here to there?
- *An overall architecture*. How does each implementation relate to the other (if at all)? What ties them all together (if anything)?
- *A maintenance plan*. How do the distributed contents stay distributed? How does the update of one implementation affect the contents of another? How are backups handled?
- *An access plan*. Who has access to each distributed implementation? What types of access?
- *An administration plan*. Who is responsible for administering each implementation? Is there an overall administrative responsibility for the entire distributed repository architecture?

Because of the preceding considerations, the importance of the overall repository architecture cannot be understated.

Within any distributed repository architecture, there must be a way of deriving the entire repository schema. In addition, this overall view must be relatable to each of its subviews as appropriate. The fact that the repository is distributed should not in any way affect its metadata/metamodel mapping and relationships. Distribution, however, does add the need to track additional metamodel-specific information—the location(s) (e.g., which server) of the metamodel, the location(s) of the associated instance data, and, to some degree, the security-specific qualities of all remote information suppliers and seekers. Any distributed repository tool would require the definition of these qualities as part of the repository setup.

Therefore, once a repository is implemented in a distributed fashion, the overall architecture must not only depict what tools are part of the repository-based environment, but also which "parts" of the repository the tools have access to and how each part relates to "the whole."

As illustrated in Fig. 28.1, the various components of a distributed repository configuration need the ability to access the overall perspective, despite their execution platform or accessing tool. Hence, the repository architecture serves as a functional blueprint of the various distributed access paths and their connections with each other.

When discussing the distributed implementation of a repository's architecture, distribution can theoretically apply to each component of the repository backbone. Specifically, the repository architect needs to determine which of the following will actually be distributed:

- The repository metamodel (aka the meta-metamodel)
- Individual metamodels (aka repository submodels)
- Repository instance data (aka repository contents)
- Repository processing (i.e., a functional repository breakdown)

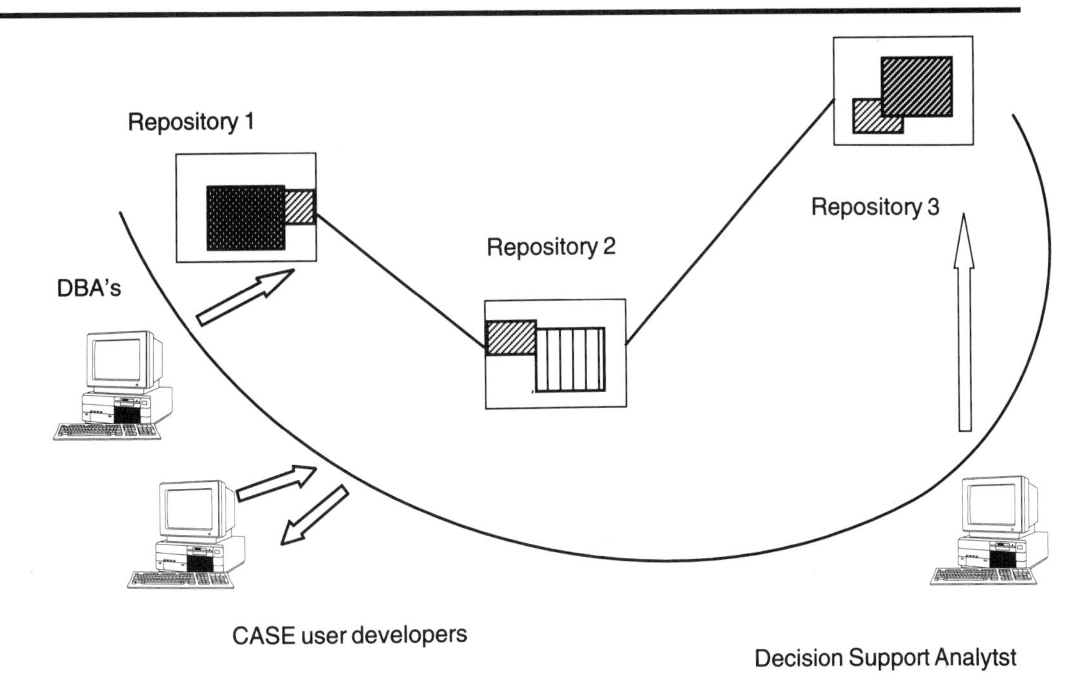

Figure 28.1 A distributed repository architecture.

▪ DISTRIBUTING THE REPOSITORY METAMODEL

The distribution of the repository metamodel is not always an administrator option. Dependent totally on the repository tool's underlying architecture, today's tool options do not support the ability to physically segment components of the meta-metamodel (perspective 4); yet vendors are vigorously working on the ability to do so because it represents a key desired feature of distributed repository functionality. With the ability to distribute at the meta-meta level, a configuration of multiple repositories is feasible. In practical scenarios, however, the appearance of equivalent functionality is achievable by distributing the perspective 3 metadata, or the various submodels. In other words, it is possible to functionally equate distinct repository servers with different submodels, all representing a part of the overall repository metamodel. One could argue that today's tools do not represent true distributed repository capability.

Alluding therefore to scenarios that were discussed in Part Four, metamodel distribution implies the distribution of the repository's functional usage. Consider the functional metamodel distribution example illustrated in Fig. 28.2. As depicted, the fact that each repository server is the heart of a distinct development area implies the need to access distinct aspects of the information described by the overall repository metamodel (the meta-metamodel). However, the need to access information that typically belongs to another functional area (and is described by a metamodel resident in another server's repository) is not beyond comprehension. Various scenarios allow this capability. For example, in a nonredundant scenario,

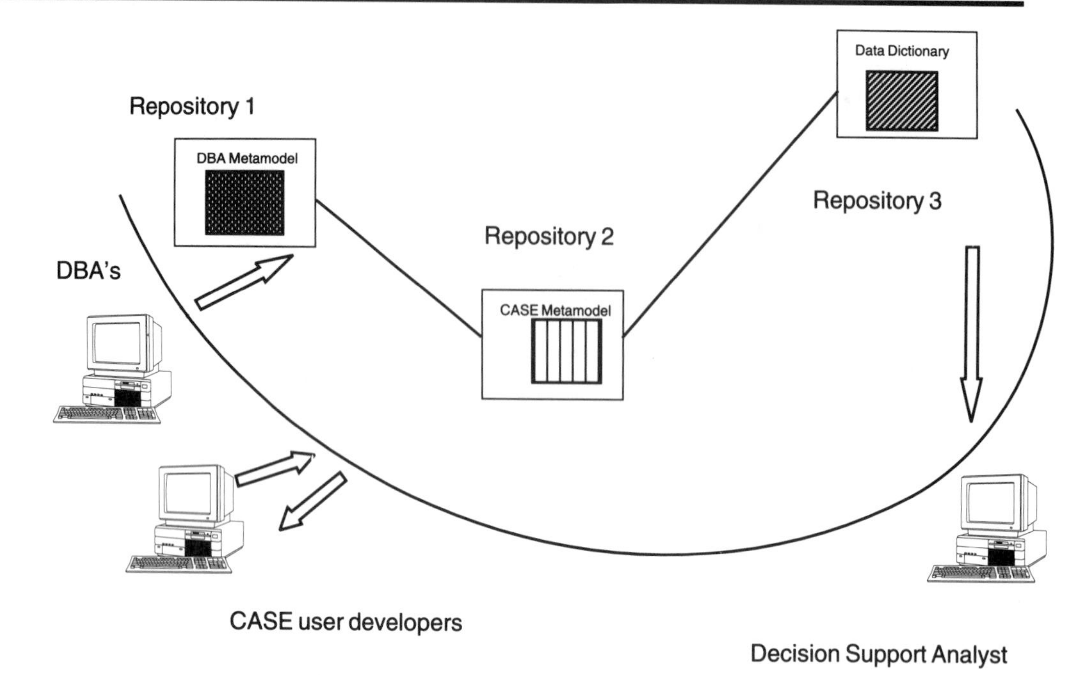

Figure 28.2 Functional metamodel distribution.

each repository contains only the metamodels for which it controls associated instance data. A request for information not "tracked" within the receiving repository's metamodel would be channeled elsewhere by the same repository server. In another scenario the metamodel is not really distributed. Instead, it redundantly exists in all repositories. However, because the associated instance data is not redundantly stored within the multiple repository servers, access of the metamodel-associated instance data varies from server to server. Specifically, some aspects of a particular repository's metamodel may not even be populated if the associated instance data represents something rarely requested from the immediate local clients. When these rare requests are received, this repository would channel them to a different repository, based on populated "repository directory" information.

The scenario that is best suited for a particular distributed repository implementation depends on the capabilities of the repository tool. Many repository vendors leave these issues to the architectures of their underlying DBMSs. For example, if their repository tool can be implemented on top of various available "distributed" DBMSs, the capabilities available to support metamodel distribution rely on the interrelatability of multiple database servers—and the interrelatability of each vendor DBMS also depends on whether or not the other database servers are implemented with the same DBMS.* Likewise, the architecture of the distributed

*For a list of readings on distributed database design and implementation, see the References at the end of the book.

repository tool is a major factor in the ability to distribute the repository metamodel. Specifically, the relationship between the various metadata levels and their implementation in the underlying DBMS plays a major role. Finally, as we discussed in a previous chapter, the ability to establish policies that can be enforced in a distributed fashion are also a consideration.

■ TYING THE ARCHITECTURE TO THE CONTENTS

Regardless of how your architecture is designed, the functionality of your "overall directory" relies on the relationship of this architecture to the populated contents of the repository. Similar to the mapping required for centralized repositories, each metamodel may relate at various levels to its actual associated instance data. As we discussed in Chap. 25, the relationship of the metadata construct to the information that it is describing involves either the population of a relationship between the metamodel construct instance *and* the actual instance data (relating the entity construct of a CASE-specific repository-based metamodel to the actual entity instance CUSTOMER that actually exists as part of a populated model in the repository) or the population of a relationship between the metamodel construct instance and the repository procedure that needs to be executed in order to access the actual instance data. When these relationships involve the existence of multiple repositories, obviously the potential exists for these relationships (and/or procedures) to involve the execution of remote or even distributed requests.

In order to relate the distributed architecture to the repository metamodel, many of the same issues involved in establishing a distributed database architecture come into play:

1. The first step depends on whether or not your repository metamodel is distributed. As we discussed previously, distribution at the meta-meta level is left to the repository tool. Assuming the capability exists, the definition of each location and its required addressing syntax are specific to the vendor's underlying distributed DBMS architecture. A theoretical example, however, is illustrated in Fig. 28.3.
2. Once the location of the overall metamodel is determined and accessible, it needs to be related, of course, to the actual information to which each construct refers. As with the repository metamodel, information locations need to be identified in terms of their physical addressing requirements, again dependent on the underlying distributed DBMS. (see Fig. 28.4)

Additional complication enters the picture when, as we discussed in Part Four, the distributed repository implementation consists of redundant architectural components. If, for example, as we discussed previously, the repository metamodel is redundantly distributed, the associated "connections" to the real information instances must be redundantly stored and maintained. Likewise, if the information instances are redundantly distributed, the issues of which instances to relate to which metamodel depictions as well as the overall maintenance of the multiple renditions still remain.

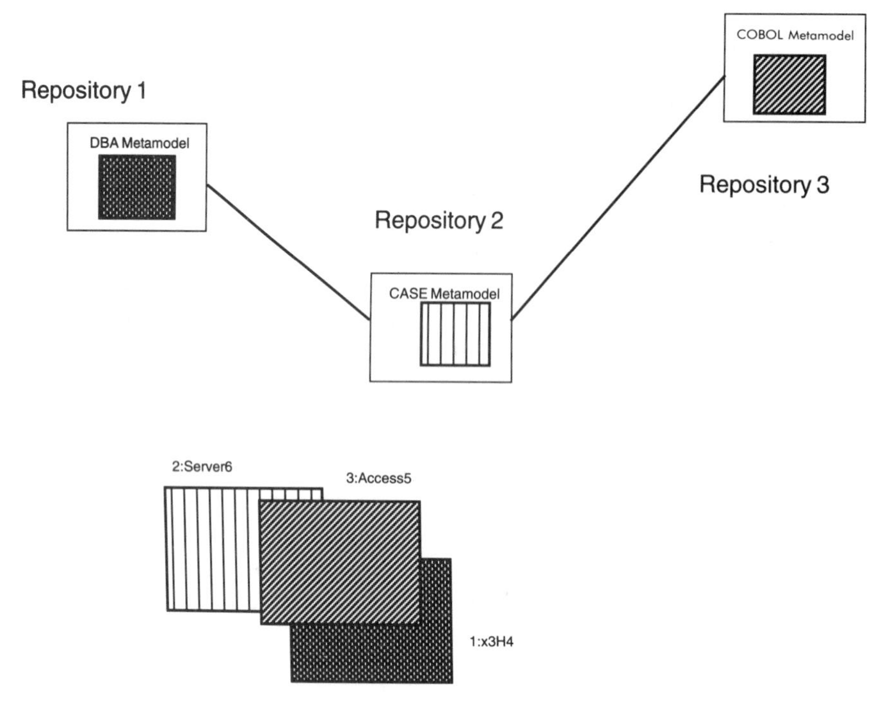

Figure 28.3 Relating the distributed metamodel to its physical server locations.

■ REDUNDANT VS. NONREDUNDANT DISTRIBUTED REPOSITORY CONTENTS

Data management is a crucial concern in distributed implementations. Regardless of whether each distinct repository server contains an isolated view of the enterprise, is related or unrelated to its companion repositories, or merely contains a redundant copy no different from any other of its connected repositories, a central point of control must be maintained in order to guarantee the overall repository's integrity. Many have referred to this central point of control as a *meta-repository* in that it represents the viewpoint that can be represented in any repository and is capable of translating one repository's view to another's. In any case this central point of control must be accessible from any client, regardless of where its most immediate repository server resides. And, of course, in true distributed repository environments, this central point of control should be accessible regardless of the client's interfacing tool, execution platform, accessing communications protocol, and underlying DBMS. In addition, in order to prevent performance bottlenecks, the central point of control should be dynamic (or perhaps redundant) in that its definition should not be dependent on any one server component of the distributed repository network.

In redundant distributed architectures, where each local repository contains a mirror image of every other populated repository, this point of control is only

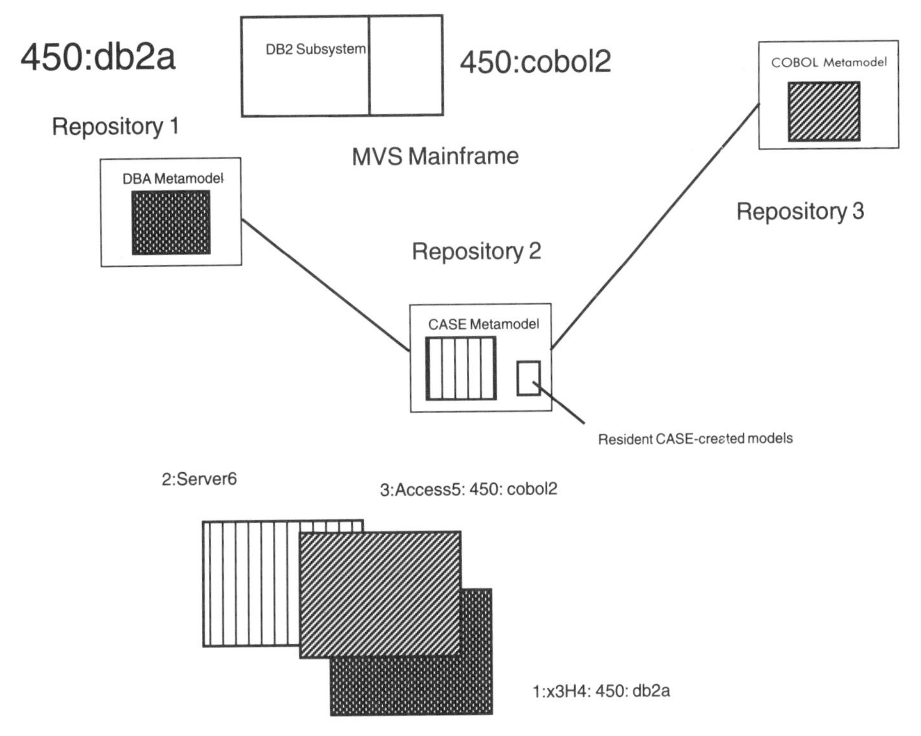

Figure 28.4 Relating the distributed metamodel to the server locations of its associated instance data.

essential if one server is down or unavailable. In this case accessing the "control point" channels the client request to the next best repository.

In nonredundant distributed architectures, the point of control is required as both the functional "directory" as well as the provider of the same channeling function in the event of the unavailability of a particular local repository. This "central" point of control does not in fact need to be physically central in terms of its location within the distributed repository architecture. It is considered central in terms of its role, however. For example, consider the distributed repository depicted in Fig. 28.5.

As illustrated in Fig. 28.5, Server A typically serves the information access needs of all of its immediate clients, the data administration group. Occasionally, data administrators need to know where to get information that pertains to other aspects of the enterprise (other than its data). Because their repository represents the most mature in terms of its design and populated contents, the other repositories cannot be relied upon to satisfy these occasional information needs. In fact, the other repositories have only been "made public" within the last year and are still undergoing increased scoping in terms of the range of their accessible information. Based on the immaturity of other local repositories, data administrators always need to determine whether the information they are seeking is even available via the repository—hence, the need for the preceding control point.

Regardless of the need to appropriately channel repository access requests (in good times, when all repositories are up and running, as well as in bad times, when some may be down), the control point is required as a means of tracking the source of all repository-accessed data. If, for example, one repository contains CASE-uploaded application models and another repository is used to access the associated physical implementations via an interface with a source code library, the two repositories need to remain in sync in terms of the relationships between model instances and their relationships to source code reality. The failure of an upload to the CASE model–populated repository creates the risk that updated applications are not reflected properly via their ties to the logical representations in the CASE-prominent repository. A properly implemented dependency would prevent the access of the newly updated source from the "not updated" application models, and, more important, this dependency would need to be reflected via the "central control point."

Therefore, in order to preserve the integrity of all distributed repository-accessible information, the implementation must pay particular attention to how the multiple repositories are populated, or, if the repositories are serving as gateways to information that exists outside of the repository, the concentration should be on the integrity of the remote information.

■ APPLICATION VS. ENTERPRISE VIEWS

Another consideration that merits special attention in a distributed repository environment is the use and reuse of metamodel components in multiple, related submodels. For example, an entity that is part of an application's logical data model may also be part of another application's logical data model, or, more important, even part of a higher-level, enterprise data model. The proper way to illustrate this multiparticipation of model instances varies with distributed implementations.

One obvious implementation is that of redundancy. Simply stated, if the models themselves reside in the repository, the entity instance alluded to in our example would be repeated as a component of each submodel in which it participates. If the models reside outside of the repository, things can get a little tricky. First, as we discussed previously, the issue of metamodel redundancy needs to be considered. In other words, if the metamodel itself is distributed, its design must accommodate the particular components that participate in more than one submodel, regardless of where the other submodel definitions physically exist. If the metamodel is not distributed (in other words, each repository has the whole picture), the existence of multiple models each with instance components that refer to the same metadata constructs (remember perspectives 3 and 4!) again requires the enforcement of data management policies.

Without redundancy, careful consideration must be given as to how the metamodel's relationships to its various submodels are maintained despite distribution. Likewise, the relationships between the metamodel components and their multiple instances must also be maintained.

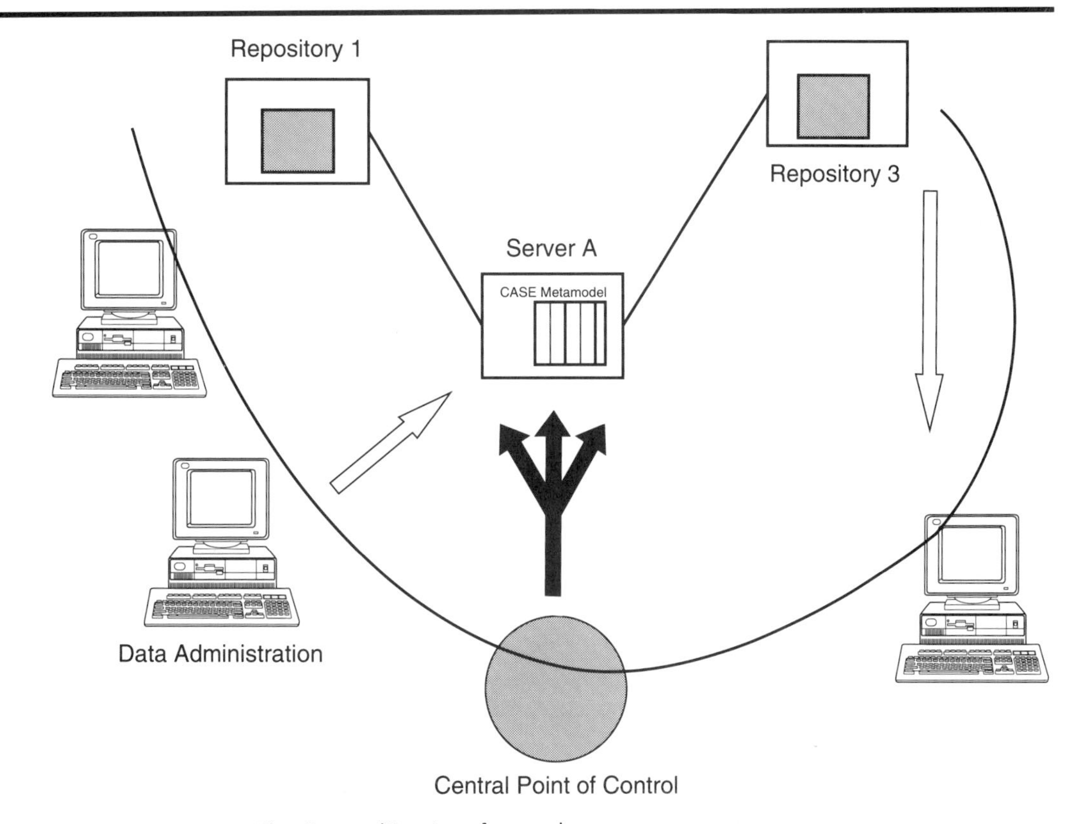

Figure 28.5 The "central" point of control.

■ DISTRIBUTED REPOSITORY FUNCTIONS

Aside from the distribution of the repository's metamodel and/or the repository contents, repository functionality also requires special consideration when evaluated from a distributed approach. As we discussed in previous chapters, repository functions can exist as part of the base repository tool or as the result of user-developed add-ons. Regardless of the origin of each repository function, the widespread usability of each function needs to be evaluated as part of repository distribution.

Getting back to our "central point of control concept," it is important to consider how the execution of a repository function could be affected. The distribution considerations that determine what is to be stored and accessed from each local repository should likewise be used to evaluate any locally distinct requirements for embedded repository functions. For example, if only one of the local repositories will receive regular updates, the availability of a repository load routine to its immediate clients is not necessarily a consideration. Likewise, prewritten queries, packaged as repository procedures, may not need to be accessible beyond one immediate local repository.

When deciding where and how repository functions need to be distributed, consider the following factors:

- *The architectural relationship of the repository function to the repository itself*. In other words, if this repository function is a vendor-supplied part of the repository tool, its distribution possibilities, like those of the meta-metamodel, may not be that flexible. In fact, vendor-supplied repository functions would typically be accessible from each distributed implementation, unless prevented via implemented security. If the function was custom-developed by your organization's repository developers, its distributed execution options should offer considerable leeway. In this situation the populated relationship between the custom-developed repository procedure, the repository metamodel, and any defined security policies will determine how distributed the executable procedure really is. Typically, the procedure will follow the shadows of its related repository components (the specific metamodel constructs, templates, and policies with which it is associated) in terms of its distribution philosophy.
- *The role fulfilled by the repository function as compared to the role fulfilled by the local repository*. If the local repository was set up based on the distinct functional needs of a particular set of repository clients, the types of repository functions required by these repository users are likely to differ from those required by the generic users of the wider repository network.
- *Locally specific repository security*. If a local repository is controlled with unique security policies, many generic repository functions may not be executable. Proper and flexible design could limit their accessibility via repository metamodel relationships. Likewise, the inability to execute mainline repository functions may generate unique requirements for less-global local functions.

As with central repositories, the development of add-on repository functions is intended to fill voids that may exist between built-in repository utilities and user requirements. But as we discussed previously, application programs that access repository contents can sometimes be considered functional equivalents. These programs should also be evaluated in terms of their appropriateness beyond a particular local repository. Those with generic appeal can be incorporated into the overall repository architecture by becoming defined in the "overall directory."

■ DISTRIBUTED REPOSITORY ACCESS CONSIDERATIONS

Finally, anything (such as distribution) that affects the location of a repository's contents in relation to its seekers requires a revisit to the repository access strategy. As we discussed in the previous chapter, the various factors that determine the types of access to a repository and its subset contents include policies, templates, and to some degree repository functions.

When we evaluate repository access within a distributed architecture, the same rules discussed in the previous chapter apply. Now, however, the rules become more complex because they may need to be enforced at both the standalone (local) repository level and the distributed (enterprise-wide) repository level. In addition, security is impacted by the distribution (if any) of the repository metamodel and its components.

A practical way of dealing with this complexity is via the use of local repository-specific templates. If a well-planned distributed repository design separates its repositories by using the functional needs of the various user factions as the primary separation criteria, the contents of each local repository can have (within its own functional world) defined "local" templates (both parameter and data) as well as access to the administrator-defined "global" templates. In fact, to avoid a performance bottleneck, both sets of templates can reside in each local repository. Global templates would be associated with requests that require remote fulfillment; local templates would handle all the "close to home" needs. The templates themselves are defined to the repository and have associated security options that determine who can use which template and with what functional capacity. The success of this approach relies on the proper maintenance of template integrity across the multiple repositories. Well-implemented distribution treats templates as equal components of the overall distributed repository metamodel in that the same data management issues discussed previously are addressed.

■ DISTRIBUTED REPOSITORIES IN THE NON-MIS WORLD

Remember our library? We should finalize the non-MIS perspective by discussing what it would be like to distribute the library's view of a repository. In some advanced areas distributed "repositories" are a reality for libraries. Simply speaking, a library user can walk into his or her local library, use a library-resident PC, and access any U.S. library's repository. For example, a high school student with a term paper assignment checks the local library shelves and sees no pertinent material. She checks the "library network" (by subject area) and discovers a wealth of information at the university library. Depending again on the implemented functionality, she may be able to actually request the university's information from the local library and see the results either immediately (if the information is part of the university's on-line "repository" contents) or the next day (either sent to the local library or directly to her home).

The librarians needed to consider all of the issues in this chapter when each library's metamodel was connected to the others. However, the library network is not representative of a centrally planned distributed repository architecture. Before the connections each library had its own standalone repository. Similarities and differences came into play when the decision to "hook up" was made. However, from an access consideration, each existing "repository" was designed to meet the needs of its immediate users (the town's library borrowers). Enterprise (national) access is not something every library borrower needs!

Regardless of what came first (the distribution plan or the local library repository), it is a sure bet that the newer libraries found it easier to become part of the national library network. Older libraries (like the one in my town) are still trying to computerize their own card catalogs. Even so, they have the option of taking the "enterprise" approach and designing their own as a local component of the larger library world. Consider the areas of concern that the local librarian, looking to become part of the national network, needs to appraise:

- *The overall architecture*. What does each library offer in terms of its role in the entire library network? How do they relate to each other? What information is redundantly distributed? What functions are redundantly executable?
- *Maintenance*. How is the local library's repository kept up to date when compared with other repositories that may contain redundant information?
- *Access*. Which borrowers have access to the entire library network (the enterprise view)? What types of access? Will access only be from library-controlled front ends?
- *Administration*. Does each librarian only administer the local repository? What about the relationship to the enterprise library network? Are there enterprise administrators? What abilities will they have to administer local repositories?

Complicated? Repositories require considerable thought when they are part of a distributed environment, regardless of whether they join as later "members" or participate as part of an initially planned enterprise.

■ SUMMARY

With today's distributed database technology, organizations *can* implement multiple repositories. The specifics of their interrelationships, however, require a substantial amount of evaluation. The evaluation requires equal emphasis on organization needs and vendor tool capabilities. Successful distribution results from a practical compromise.

29

THE TIME HAS COME

Success is more a function of consistent common sense than it is of genius.

Al Wang, 1986

We know that repository technology has progressed to the point where it can be practically deployed. We also know that in order to benefit from a functional repository, the organization must be "repository ready." Being "repository ready" implies organizational consistency in terms of both systems development as well as systems deployment.

So what is everyone waiting for? Could it be that today's MIS organizations are so far away from repository readiness that they do not even know where to start? Or could it be that repositories cannot simply be plugged in and turned on? Whatever the reason, it is no longer acceptable. The time has come.

■ CURRENT TASKS TO ENSURE AN ORGANIZATIONS'S REPOSITORY READINESS

We spent considerable time evaluating today's models. We also evaluated organizational approaches to application development and discussed the effects of management directives and support. It should be clear that a repository in and of itself does not solve an information integration dilemma.

Before pursuing repository implementation, an honest assessment of your readiness is a prerequisite. To maximize the potential of repository-based development in your organization, the following should represent noncontroversial, accepted procedures within your application development environment:

- *The deployment of a standard application development methodology* When two disparate functional areas of MIS develop a new application, the same types of deliverables should result.
- *The deployment of a standard approach to application maintenance and enhancement* Once an application moves into production, any changes made should be

designed and implemented with organizational consistency. Regardless of the type of application maintenance (enhancement, bug fix, etc.), the maintenance process itself should result in the delivery of updated deliverables (based on the standards deployed previously) as well as a permanent record of why the maintenance was requested and how the implemented result satisfied the request.

- *The use of a standard set of tools for specific application development functions* Instead of sporadic "proof of concept" tool evaluations, a confirmed suite of development tools should be in use by your developers. The tools, when used correctly, should aid at least half of the application development life cycle. That is, a typical application should have a mechanized consistency tracker as an aid throughout at least three of the major application development phases: planning, analysis, design, construction, testing, deployment, and/or maintenance. In addition, these mechanized aids should be consistent from project to project.
- *The maintenance of accurate records of your production environment* There should be no problem getting an accurate picture of deployed programs, databases, job streams, and so forth. Simply speaking, an accurate source code library, accurate production database catalogs, file definitions, and COBOL copybooks should be part of everyday production practices.

The preceding items represent the bare minimum in terms of repository readiness. If any of them are not characteristic of your current application development environment, your current tasks should concentrate on their achievement. As reiterated throughout this book, it is too easy to buy a tool today—it takes a lot more work to deploy it properly.

■ SHORT-TERM REPOSITORY OBJECTIVES

Assuming you have reached the bare readiness level, your repository objectives should be concise enough to have a short-term impact on your organization's development practices. This short-term impact should be in one of two major areas:

- *Increasing the span of standardized application development practices*: Adding more items to the preceding list, a repository could add one or more of the following features to the current application environment:
  - A centralized data administration function
  - The consistent tracking and assignment of versions to applications and application components
  - The ability to enforce the adherence to deployed methodologies by validating tool-created deliverables
  - More diverse knowledge (and application) of development standards based on the repository-based access of actual textual and diagrammatic contents
  - The incorporation of additional tools in order to extend tool usage further into the application development life cycle

- Model-driven development
- *Capturing the results of existing standardized application development into a multideveloper-accessible storage area*

By starting small, the repository effort is likely to be successful. Consider revisiting each of the preceding items until they have all been realized. Expect to spend 1 to 2 years achieving all of these objectives.

■ LONG-TERM REPOSITORY-BASED DEVELOPMENT GOALS

As the repository becomes populated with more and more aspects of your standardized application development, it becomes more valuable as a development tool unto itself. Having achieved all short-term repository objectives, it is time to permanently reap their benefits. Migration steps which begin after the achievement of a functional populated repository concentrate on its movement into production, so to speak, as the gateway to all application development–related information.

The next phase of corporate repository implementation results in the realization of the following:

- Access to the repository from every developer's workstation, via every deployed development tool
- Repository-driven generation of databases and their associated application programs
- The use of the repository to determine:
  - What impact a requested change will have on an application. What application components will be affected, that is, true impact analysis
  - The source(s) and definition of any type of corporate data, that is, traditional data dictionary usage
  - Whether or not existing application components can be reused in other planned applications
  - Application and database redundancy
  - Planned and deployed application configurations

Organizations should expect to spend from 2 to 5 years achieving the preceding repository-based development objectives.

■ BUSINESS STRATEGY/MIS COLLABORATION

In conjunction with the steps toward achieving repository-based development, steps should be taken to ensure the achievement of the ultimate repository goal: the use of the repository as the gateway to *all* corporate information. The realization of this objective involves the alignment of MIS development with corporate business strategy, both inside and outside of the repository.

In terms of the repository, the introduction of the business perspective involves the following tasks:

- *The alignment of applications (both existing and planned) with business functions.* Knowing the business functions, all repository-accessible applications need to be categorized.
- *Providing accessibility of the repository beyond MIS.*

In addition, organizational philosophy must grow to support the maintenance of the repository as a corporate information asset. The role of MIS must go beyond that of a service organization to that of a strategic business partner. Instead of implementing applications to support business objectives that are already in place, MIS should be helping to define these objectives via the information that exists in the repository.

Once an organization has reached this phase of repository implementation, it will have achieved its ultimate objectives in terms of application development.

■ THE FUTURE DIRECTION OF REPOSITORIES AND THEIR DEPLOYMENT

As stated previously, repository tools *are* practically deployable today. Organizations looking for silver bullet solutions, however, may be disappointed. As discussed throughout this book, the implemented repository's organizational benefits parallel the amount of organizational investment in terms of time and resources.

The repository marketplace has undergone substantial change since its early inception. At the beginning, the term *repository* was virtually unheard of, and many of the tools were really "data dictionaries." As CASE tools became popular, so too did the terms *integration* and *repository*. Even so, the practical integration that early repositories offered was extremely limited. Today, the term *repository* is, for the most part, being used honestly. A limited set of true repository products is available in the 1993 marketplace.

The future holds major inroad potential for the repository arena. First, the number of deployed repositories can only increase exponentially. Organizations with historical short-term focus are now realizing why their application development environments are in a constant state of chaos. In most situations the downsizing of application development into client/server environments is being approached from a carefully architected perspective based on the results of previously shortsighted implementations. Customers are demanding integration capabilities from repository tools—they need to relate the legacy systems of the past with today's development of tomorrow's architected enterprise systems.

The repository of tomorrow may alleviate much of an organizations's information preparation requirements. In a truly integrated development environment, a repository sits as the environment's backbone, validating development data as it is entered and refined by each interfacing development tool. As development processes are completed, the repository is automatically cognizant and then becomes the only source of the tool-input information. Today, this repository potential requires organization-specific custom development in order to provide this true integration. Tomorrow, vendors, working together, will make this "integration" a customer product purchase option.

As repository standards mature so too will vendor adherence. As today's users, vendors, and standards committees continue to improve their application development practices and offerings, tomorrow's application development environment becomes more cost effective, efficient, and business supportive. The repository serves first as the backbone of one organizations's application environment and later as a member of a multiorganization repository network.

We can conclude our repository implementation topic by remembering the public library. Consider the wooden card catalog and then compare it to the international library network. Can one organization start by turning its card catalog into a unified on-line information source? Start small, but never forget the potential.

REFERENCES

Data Modeling

Fleming, Candace, and Von Halle, Barbara. *Handbook of Relational Database Design*. Reading, MA: Addison-Wesley, 1987.

Inmon, W. H. *Effective Data Base Design*. Englewood Cliffs, NJ: Prentice-Hall, 1991.

Tsichritzes, D., and Lochovsky, F. *Data Models*. Englewood Cliffs, NJ: Prentice-Hall, 1982.

Distributed Database Design and Implementation

Berson, Alex. *Client/Server Architecture*. New York: McGraw-Hill, 1992.

Date, Chris. *An Introduction to Database Systems*, Vol. 1, 4th ed. Reading, MA: Addison-Wesley, 1986.

Hackathorn, Richard. *Enterprise Database Connectivity*. New York: Wiley, 1993.

Khoshafian, S. A. Chan, Wong, A., and Wong, H. *A Guide to Developing Client/Server SQL Applications*. San Mateo, CA: Morgan Kaufmann, 1992.

Manilla and Raiha. *The Design of Relational Databases*. Reading, MA: Addison-Wesley, 1992.

Object-Oriented Analysis and Design

Booch, G. *Object-Oriented Design with Applications*. Menlo Park, CA: Benjamin/Cummings, 1991.

Cattell, R. G. G. *Object Data Management*. Reading, MA: Addison-Wesley, 1991.

Coad, Peter, and Yourdon, Edward. *Object-Oriented Analysis*, 2nd ed. Englewood Cliffs, NJ: Prentice-Hall, 1991.

Coad, Peter, and Yourdon, Edward. *Object-Oriented Design*. Englewood Cliffs, NJ: Prentice-Hall, 1991.

Cox, Brad. *Object-Oriented Programming*. Reading, MA: Addison-Wesley, 1986.

Khoshafian, S., and Abnous, R. *Object Orientation: Concepts, Languages, Database, User Interfaces*. New York: Wiley, 1990.

Martin, James. *Principles of Object-Oriented Analysis and Design*. Englewood Cliffs, NJ: Prentice-Hall, 1993.

Meyer, Bertrand. *Object-Oriented Software Construction*. Englewood Cliffs, NJ: Prentice-Hall, 1988.

Rumbaugh, J., et al. *Object-Oriented Modeling and Design*. Englewood Cliffs, NJ: Prentice-Hall, 1991.

Shlaer, S., and Mellor, S. J. *Object-Oriented Systems Analysis*. Englewood Cliffs, NJ: Yourdon Press, 1988.

Shlaer, S., and Mellor, S. J. *Object Lifecycles—Modeling the World in States*. Englewood Cliffs, NJ: Yourdon Press, 1992.

Wirfs-Brock, R., Wilkerson, B., and Wiener, L. *Designing Object-Oriented Software*. Englewood Cliffs, NJ: Prentice-Hall, 1990.

Repository Standards

American National Standards Institute, Inc. *Information Resource Dictionary System (IRDS) Standard X3.138–1988*. New York: ANSI, 1989.

Electronic Industries Association. *CDIF-Framework for Modeling and Extensibility IS-81*. Washington, DC: EIA, 1991.

Electronic Industries Association. *CDIF-Standardized CASE Interchange Meta-Model IS-83*. Washington, DC: EIA, 1991.

Electronic Industries Association. *CDIF-Transfer Format Definition IS*-82. Washington, DC: EIA, 1991.

European Computer Manufacturers Association. *Portable Common Tool Environment (PCTE), Abstract Specification, Standard ECMA-149*. Geneva, 1990.

European Computer Manufacturers Association. *Portable Common Tool Environment (PCTE), ADA Programming Language Binding, Standard ECMA-162. Geneva*, 1991.

European Computer Manufacturers Association. *Portable Common Tool Environment (PCTE), C Programming Language Binding, Standard ECMA-158. Geneva*, 1991.

International Business Machines Corporation. *AD/Cycle Information Model; Reference, Volume 2: Technology and Global Submodels*, 2nd ed. San Jose, CA: IBM Corporation, 1991.

International Business Machines Corporation. *AD/Cycle Information Model; Overview*, 4th ed. San Jose, CA: IBM Corporation, 1992.

International Business Machines Corporation. *AD/Cycle Information Model; Reference, Volume 1: Enterprise Submodel*, 4th ed. San Jose, CA: IBM Corporation, 1992.

Software Development Methodologies

Brown, A. W. *Database Support for Software Engineering*. Chapman and Hall.

Buxton, J. M., Naur, P., and Randell, B. *Software Engineering, Concepts and Techniques*. New York: Petrocelli/Charter, 1976.

DeMarco, Tom. *Structured Analysis and System Specification*. Englewood Cliffs, NJ: Yourdon Press/Prentice-Hall, 1978.

Fisher, Alan S. *CASE: Using Software Development Tools*. New York: Wiley, 1988.

Gane, Chris, and Sarson, Trish. *Structured Systems Analysis: Tools and Techniques*. New York: Improved Systems Technologies, 1977.

Inmon, W. H. *Information Engineering for the Practitioner*. Englewood Cliffs, NJ: Yourdon Press/Prentice-Hall, 1987.

Martin, J. *Information Engineering: A Trilogy*, Vol. 1–3. Englewood Cliffs, NJ: Prentice-Hall, 1989.

Page-Jones, Meilir. *The Practical Guide to Structured Systems Design*, 2nd ed. Englewood Cliffs, NJ: Yourdon Press/Prentice-Hall, 1988.

Teory, Toby J. *Database Modeling and Design: The Entity–Relationship Approach*. San Mateo, CA: Morgan Kaufman, 1991.

Yourdon, Edward and Constantine. *Structured Design*. Englewood Cliffs, NJ: Prentice-Hall, 1979.

INDEX

B

C

D

L

M

N

O

P

S

T

V